ELEPHANT

ELEPHANT

THE ANIMAL AND ITS IVORY IN AFRICAN CULTURE

DORAN H. ROSS, EDITOR

FOWLER MUSEUM OF CULTURAL HISTORY
UNIVERSITY OF CALIFORNIA, LOS ANGELES

Front Cover: *Ekpo* society mask from Nigeria (Ogoni peoples). Wood, pigment, vegetable fiber. Height 85 cm. The Trustees of the British Museum, 1954, Af 23.877.

Back Cover: Elephant coffin signed "Kane Kwei, Super Coffin, Teshie," 1985. Accra, Ghana. Wood, paint, cloth. Length 105.5 cm. Collection of Ernie Wolfe III.

Page I: African elephant skin. Zig Leszczynski, Animals, Animals.

Pages II-III: Murchison Falls National Park, Uganda, 1983. Robert Caputo.

Pages IV-V: Amboseli National Park, Kenya. Betty Press, Animals, Animals.

Pages VI-VII: Botswana, 1990. Frans Lanting, Minden Pictures.

Pages VIII-IX: Botswana, 1990. Frans Lanting, Minden Pictures.

Page X: Wood mask from the northwestern Grassfields of Cameroon. Height 79 cm. Private collection.

Page XVI: Zimbabwe. G.I. Bernard, Animals, Animals.

© 1992 Regents of the University of California

Fowler Museum of Cultural History
University of California, Los Angeles
405 Hilgard Avenue
Los Angeles, California, USA 90024-1549

Printed and bound in Hong Kong by Pearl River Printing Company.

Library of Congress Cataloging-in-Publication Data

Elephant: the animal and its ivory in African culture / edited by
    Doran H. Ross.
        p. cm.
    Includes bibliographical references.
    ISBN 0-930741-25-0 (hard): $69.00.
    ISBN 0-930741-26-9 (soft): $39.00

1. Ivories – Africa, West. 2. Art and society – Africa, West.
3. Ivories – Ethiopia. 4. Art and society – Ethiopia. 5. Elephants in art.
6. Elephants – Africa, West. 7. Elephants – Africa, North.
I. Ross, Doran H. II. University of California, Los Angeles.
Fowler Museum of Cultural History.
NK5989.E44 1992
730'.096'07479494—dc20   92-73840
                                                             CIP

This catalogue and associated exhibition
were supported by funding from the following:

THE NATIONAL ENDOWMENT FOR THE HUMANITIES
THE AHMANSON FOUNDATION
THE TIMES-MIRROR FOUNDATION
THE ETHNIC ARTS COUNCIL OF LOS ANGELES
THE AL BARDWELL MEMORIAL FUND
MANUS, THE SUPPORT GROUP OF THE FOWLER MUSEUM OF CULTURAL HISTORY

LENDERS TO THE EXHIBITION

Peter Adler Collection
Ernst Anspach
Mr. and Mrs. Harold Benjamin
Staatliche Museen zu Berlin, Museum für Völkerkunde
Sandra Blair
Nancy and Richard Bloch
Maurice Bonnefoy
The Bowers Museum of Cultural Art
Mr. and Mrs. William W. Brill
Trustees of the British Museum
The Brooklyn Museum
Nancy N. Carroll
Herbert M. and Shelley L. Cole
Charles and Kent Davis
Mort Dimonstein
The Faletti Family Collection
Dr. and Mrs. Ernest Fantel
Dr. Vaughana Macy Feary
Marc Felix, Brussels
Field Museum of Natural History, Chicago
The Kenneth G. Fiske Museum of the Claremont Colleges
Jean Garret
Collection Paolo Sprovieri
Mr. and Mrs. Joseph Goldenberg
Clayre and Jay Haft
Collection of Toby and Barry Hecht
U. and W. Horstmann Collection, Zug, Switzerland
Indiana University Art Museum
Indianapolis Museum of Art
Jerome L. Joss Collection
Jill and Barry Kitnick
Helen and Dr. Robert Kuhn
The Leavitt Collection
Collection of Marilyn V.C. Liebman
Linden-Museum Stuttgart

Drs. Daniel and Marian Malcolm
The Metropolitan Museum of Art
Staatliches Museum für Völkerkunde, Munich
National Museum of African Art, Smithsonian Institution
National Commission for Museums and Monuments, Nigeria
Collection of The Newark Museum
Robert and Nancy Nooter
Numismatic Fine Arts International
Peabody Museum of Archaeology and Ethnology,
     Harvard University
Sara Penn Textiles
Collection of the Portland Art Museum
Mr. and Mrs. Gilbert Rice
Françoise Billion Richardson
Eric D. Robertson
Royal Museum of Central Africa, Tervuren (Belgium)
Collection of the Santa Barbara Historical Society
Schomburg Center for Research in Black Culture,
     Art and Artifacts Division, New York Public Library,
     Astor Lenox and Tilden Foundation
Shango Galleries, Los Angeles
The Saint Louis Art Museum
Collection of Don L. Simmons
Saul and Marsha Stanoff
Collection of Diane Steinmetz
The Paul and Ruth Tishman Collection of African Art,
     the Walt Disney Company
The University of Iowa Museum of Art, The Stanley Collection
Museum für Völkerkunde, Vienna, Austria
Fern and Leon Wallace
James Willis
Ernst Winizki
Collection of Ernie Wolfe III
M. Zarember, Tambaran Gallery, New York
Five Private Collections

CONTENTS

ACKNOWLEDGMENTS

The acknowledgments to this volume deserve to be as massive as the wildlife migrations in northern Tanzania. Major exhibitions require the loan of diverse objects from numerous disparate sources. Without the trust and generosity of the many lenders listed at the beginning of this volume, this project would have been impossible. Their willing cooperation is greatly appreciated. Similarly a cross-cultural interdisciplinary study such as this demands the participation of a variety of scholars. I would like to thank all the authors listed in the Table of Contents for their unique perspectives and considerable efforts.

The National Endowment for the Humanities, a Federal Agency, has provided funding for a number of our projects over the years. Their support, however, always extends well beyond the realm of finances. With *Elephant*, the application process was again instrumental in helping to shape both exhibition and publication. Marcia Semmel and Tom Wilson (now with the Southwest Museum) have our sincere gratitude for their many thoughtful suggestions. Further funding was provided by the Ethnic Arts Council of Los Angeles, the Ahmanson Foundation, the Al Bardwell Memorial Fund, the Times-Mirror Foundation, and Manus, the support group of the Fowler Museum of Cultural History.

A number of key objects were purchased for or given to the Fowler Museum in support of the exhibition. I am grateful to Helen and Dr. Robert Kuhn, Mr. and Mrs. Edwin Silver, Judith Timyan, Philip Ravenhill, and Ernie Wolfe III. Jerome L. Joss was particularly helpful in locating and acquiring key pieces for the exhibition and the Museum's collections.

The steadily growing reputation of the National Museum of African Art as the center for bibliographic and archival research on African Art is directly attributable to Janet Stanley, Librarian, and Christraud Geary, Curator of the Eliot Elisofon Photographic Archives. Their many courtesies during the development of this project are warmly appreciated.

For facilitating select acquisitions and loans I am extremely grateful to Claude Ardouin, Director, West African Museums Program, Dakar, to Adedze Agbenyega, and to Ibironke P. Ashaye, from the National Commission for Museums and Monuments, Lagos. Without their good offices and considerable help, several important objects would not have been available for the exhibition.

A number of colleagues in European museums shared their collections and facilitated loans. My gratitude extends to: Armand Duchâteau, Museum für Völkerkunde, Vienna; Herman Forkl, Linden-Museum, Stuttgart; Huguette van Geluwe, Royal Museum of Central Africa, Tervuren; Lorenz Homberger and Eberhard Fischer, Rietberg Museum, Zurich; Maria Kecskési and Walter Raunig, Staatliches Museum für Völkerkunde, Munich; Hans-Joachim Koloss, Museum für Völkerkunde, Berlin; Malcolm McLeod (retired) and John Mack, British Museum; and Keith Nicklin, Horniman Museum, London.

In the United States, I would like to thank the following museum directors, curators, and staff who provided support for various phases of this project. Ramona Austin, Art Institute of Chicago; Lynn Bilotta, Cincinnati Art Museum; Gerald Bolas, Portland Art Museum; David S. Bisol and Donna Senning, Santa Barbara Historical Society; Theodore Celenko, Indianapolis

Museum of Art; Kate Ezra, The Metropolitan Museum of Art, New York City; William Fagaly, New Orleans Museum of Art; Louise Lincoln, The Minneapolis Institute of Art; Pamela McClusky, Seattle Art Museum; John Nunley, St. Louis Art Museum; Diane Pelrine, Indiana University Art Museum; Albert Rice, The Kenneth G. Fiske Museum of the Claremont Colleges; Teresa Ridgeway and Tim Campbell, The Bowers Museum of Cultural Art; Enid Schildkrout, American Museum of Natural History; William Siegmann, Brooklyn Museum; Anne Spencer, Newark Museum; Van Romans, the Walt Disney Company; and Sylvia Williams and Philip Ravenhill, National Museum of African Art.

In addition to those who contributed essays to this volume, many scholars have generously shared their own research. I offer my gratitude to: Suzanne Blier, Columbia University; Herbert M. Cole, University of California, Santa Barbara; Daniel Crowley, University of California, Davis; Joanne Eicher, University of Minnesota; Gary Haynes, University of Nevada, Reno; Ivan Karp, National Museum of Natural History; Donna Klump; Cory Kratz; Frederick Lamp, Baltimore Museum of Art; Polly Nooter and Susan Vogel, The Center for African Art, New York City; Robin Poyner, University of Florida; Roy Sieber, Indiana University; and Tom Wilson, Southwest Museum, Los Angeles.

Among many special contributions to the exhibition and publication I would like to single out Steve Ogden, Mike Schrimp and A.M. Decker of Third Street Sound, Los Angeles, for their help with audio components of the exhibition; Amy Hill for her narration of the introductory slide program; Jill Ball and Sylvia Kennedy for illustrations in both book and exhibition.

Without herculean efforts on the part of the Fowler Museum staff, this exhibition could not have taken place. Early concept development owes much to brainstorming sessions with Lynn Anderson, Rachel Hoffman, Betsy Quick, and David Mayo. Fullfledged exhibition planning, started two years ago, engaged the entire staff. I would first like to thank Christine Griego, who played Park Ranger to my Rogue Elephant. As assistant to the project director for the past two years, she handled a maze of research, correspondence, filing, and other logistics with considerable energy, efficiency, and grace. Her predecessors, Lynn Anderson and Rachel Hoffman, did much of the early work and solved myriad problems that eluded my grasp. Additional research assistance was provided by Elisabeth Cameron, Rosalinde Wilcox, Paulette Parker, Adedze Agbenyega, and Roger Colten. Richard Chute handled many details of contracts and grants. To all of them I am genuinely grateful.

Henrietta Cosentino performed the monumental task of editing this volume with unreserved energy and care, and with the steadfast assistance of Mark Livengood. Carol Anne Garrison, Kristin Lang, and Mary Kay Kendall were also helpful in the process. Daniel Brauer and Anthony Kluck designed the publication with taste, imagination, and insight. Denis Nervig handled the bulk of the publication photography with a sensitive eye for the unique qualities of each work. The exhibition was designed by David Mayo who combined strong aesthetic statements with humor to produce a compelling installation. His design was beautifully executed by Gene Riggs, Don Simmons, Victor Lozano Jr. and Patrick White, with additional help from Patrick Dowdey, Greg Martin, and Susan Philips. Robin Chamberlin Milburn, assisted by Susana Zubiate, skillfully solved a number of difficult conservation problems in the preparation of objects for exhibition. The challenges of an elusive bibliography were met by Judith Herschman, Museum Librarian, who also offered her sharp proofreading skills at several stages. The complicated logistics and paper work of moving objects in and out of the Museum were dealt with by Sarah Kennington, Registrar, Owen Moore, Collections Manager, and Fran Tabbush, his assistant. Polly Svenson, Sue Kallick, and Marilyn Liebman creatively organized all merchandizing related to the exhibition. Security staffing and procedures were developed by Guillermo Cock, Bobby Whitaker, and George Kershaw.

The ambitious interpretive agenda for the exhibition was created by Betsy Quick in collaboration with the Los Angeles Unified School District, The Natural History of Museum of Los Angeles County (NHM), and the Los Angeles Zoo. School tours in the "Elephant Tracks" program included visits to both of the latter institutions in addition to the Fowler Museum in a coordinated effort to maximize our understanding of the Elephant and its relationship to the peoples of Africa. Special thank are due to Lyn Avins, Leo Lobsenz, Mary Shambra, John Shambra, Paula Benard and Esther Taira (LAUSD), Cindy Wallace and Linda Countryman (LAZ), and Joan Grasty and Isabel Rosenbaum (NHM). The Curriculum Resource Unit was designed by Chris Blum and Anthony Kluck. Mary Kay Kendall, Christina Gold, Lisa Eriksen, Marcia Melkonian, and Jane Bardwell assisted in the development of the curricular materials and teacher workshops.

Gratitude is also due to Carolyn Yoder, Enid Schildkrout and Francelle Carapetyan of *Faces* for developing a special issue dealing with the elephant in Africa for their young reader's anthropology magazine.

Special gratitude goes to Christopher Donnan, Director of the Museum, and Vice Chancellor (Emeritus) Elwin Svenson for their consistent backing of *Elephant*. This project, like all others in the Museum, would not have happened without the daily efforts of Barbara Underwood, Executive Assistant. She juggled schedules, correspondence, and numerous lead balloons to ensure that the work of others was successfully completed. Likewise, Millicent Besser walked the minefield of museum accounting with a careful attention to detail and a mischievous smile. Additional administrative support was provided by Betsy Escandor and Daniel Shen.

Finally I would like to acknowledge the friendship and warm-hearted support of Philip Ravenhill, Diane Steinmetz, Ernie Wolfe III, Diane L. Ross, and especially Marla Berns. Their consistant good humor reduced stress, sustained energy, and helped ensure that this project would not be a white elephant.

Doran H. Ross

PREFACE

This book and its accompanying exhibition had its origins during 1985 in discussions with the late Dr. Arnold Rubin of UCLA and Dr. Herbert M. Cole, University of California, Santa Barbara, concerning a potential project that would examine the relationship of animals to the material culture, art, and ritual of Africa. There had been a number of earlier exhibitions with modest catalogues that broadly dealt with the subject of "the animal in African art," but from them it was clear that, given the breadth of the topic, any serious and substantial study would have to limit its focus. Various possibilities were considered, ranging from animal representation and use across object types in a single culture, to representations of animals in a given object type (e.g. shrine sculpture or initiation masks) across cultures. Finally it was decided to limit the number of animals studied, yet cover them cross-culturally. The basic criterion was that each animal to be studied should have a significant presence in a number of African cultures, as both image and material; i.e. not only must it be represented in the art, but it must be hunted, and the parts of its body used for food, domestic utensils, and/or ceremonial functions. Its use as material was seen as critical since this added important dimensions for understanding the various roles of a specific animal in a given culture, and thus of its artistic representation.

When the political, religious, economic, and social ramifications of a broad spectrum of fauna had been considered, a final selection was limited to four creatures: the hornbill, the python, the crocodile, and the leopard. Significantly, the elephant was not included, losing out to the leopard as a representative of Mammalia. It was generally felt that while the elephant commanded great attention in many traditional African cultures, Western notions of the pachy-derm conjured up images of Jumbo, Dumbo, and Babar. The elephant was seen, ironically, as being too "cute."

Soon it became clear that even with only four animals, the scope of the project was still unmanageable. To achieve focus and depth, the topic had to be further narrowed. At this point the elephant came back into consideration. It was apparent that many of the elephant traits exploited in the West were the very ones that inspired the artistic imagination of Africa. The animal's extraordinary attributes figured prominently in the folklore and art of many African cultures.

Jonathan Swift (1733) anticipated post-modern discussions about elephants and the invention of Africa when he wrote:

> *So geographers in Afric-maps*
> *With savage-pictures fill their gaps*
> *And o'er unhabitable downs*
> *Place elephants for want of towns.*

Elephants are indeed a component of the Western world's invention of Africa. They are also, however, an end product of this same process of invention. Most of us have as little accurate information about elephants as we do about Africa. This volume attempts to counter the stereotype that Africa equals jungle and animals, not by placing the elephant in the foreground, but by highlighting the cultural dimensions and intellectual framework that surround the elephant in African communities.

The elephant also offers historical dimensions not available with most other fauna. Perhaps as much as the horse and camel, the elephant played a pivotal role in shaping the nature of contact with the rest of the world. Ivory was a major commodity in commerce with Europe, Asia, and the Americas. Moreover, the nature of the export market for ivory and its use in the West and East provided a telling contrast with indigenous patterns of consumption. We also considered the elephant's significant role in the tourist industries of several countries. Finally, of course, there was the specter of the potential extinction of the elephant through poaching and the illegal trade in ivory. All this led to the conclusion that it was the right time to examine what the elephant means and has meant to the peoples of Africa.

Having decided on the elephant, we were subsequently influenced by two exhibitions and publications that should be acknowledged here: *Elephant and Ivories in South Asia*, by

Pratapaditya Pal (1981), for the Los Angeles County Museum of Art; and *Elefanten, Elefanten...*, organized by Eberhard Fischer (1983), for the Rietberg Museum in Zurich. Likewise some influential studies of African ivory-carving traditions provided models for the present work, most notably Kate Ezra's monograph *African Ivories* (1984) for New York's Metropolitan Museum of Art.

In spite of the above precedents, this project is still something of an experiment. The basic assumption is that the elephant is as much of a cultural resource as it is a zoological resource. The question remained, how far could we take this idea? Specialists were invited to consider the role of the elephant and its ivory in the expressive cultures of their areas of interest. Contributors were asked to begin with a short introduction to the people, their social organization, subsistence patterns, and so forth. A few general comments on elephant populations and the ivory trade were also requested. They were encouraged to examine the elephant not in isolation, but in relation to the array of animal imagery that typically exists in most of these cultures. In some areas, we know unfortunately little about the symbolic role of the elephant in a culture even though impressive sculptural and other representations of the animal are found in today's private and public collections. Our general ignorance of the elephant as a cultural entity – lamented by anthropologists and art historians – is matched by our ignorance of the animal's biology. With the single exception of Shoshani, none of our contributors went to Africa specifically to study elephants or their use and representation in art and material culture. Nevertheless several of them focused on cultural phenomena where the elephant plays a leading or significant role.

The organization of the essays in this volume is loosely geographic. We have not attempted to resolve contradictions or redundancies across essays and have maintained selected spelling and orthographic conventions at the behest of several authors. The between-chapter "Interleaves" are double-page layouts that constitute visual mini-essays, meant to entertain as well as to broaden the scope of the volume. Several relate to themes mentioned in the Introduction and some include material not otherwise dealt with. Their order is relatively random and the captions were authored by myself.

The approaches here are primarily descriptive and normative. Yet there is sufficient variety in *who* is describing and in *what* is being described to represent a range of perspectives. Their efforts recall the Indian parable of three wise men describing an elephant in a dark room solely on the basis of touch. One feels the trunk and says the elephant is like a snake. Another touches its side and says the elephant is like a house. The last grabs the tail and says the elephant is like a broom. They are all accurate about their observations, of course, but then again they are all examining different parts of the whole.

This volume attempts to bridge that increasingly deep chasm that seems to separate the goals of a scholar from the goals of the general reader (or non-reader). It searches for that idealistic middle ground that will satisfy both audiences. As a university museum serving a larger community, we have a mandate to make our work approachable to the non-specialist. So while we have necessarily maintained some of the scholarly apparatus of academia, we have also maintained a strong commitment to a compelling visual presentation that will jointly serve both those primarily interested in aesthetic expressions and those mostly looking for a "picture book." While the phrase "coffee table book" is used pejoratively by academics, this volume frankly aspires to such status. We want people to look in it as much as we want people to read in it. In our wishful scheme of things it is hoped that this volume might also serve as an entry point for those otherwise not interested in the peoples and cultures of Africa. In the final analysis, this book should serve as an homage to the African elephant and as a celebration of African creativity.

Doran H. Ross

So geographers in Afric-maps

With savage-pictures fill their gaps

And o'er unhabitable downs

Place elephants for want of towns.

JONATHAN SWIFT

1733

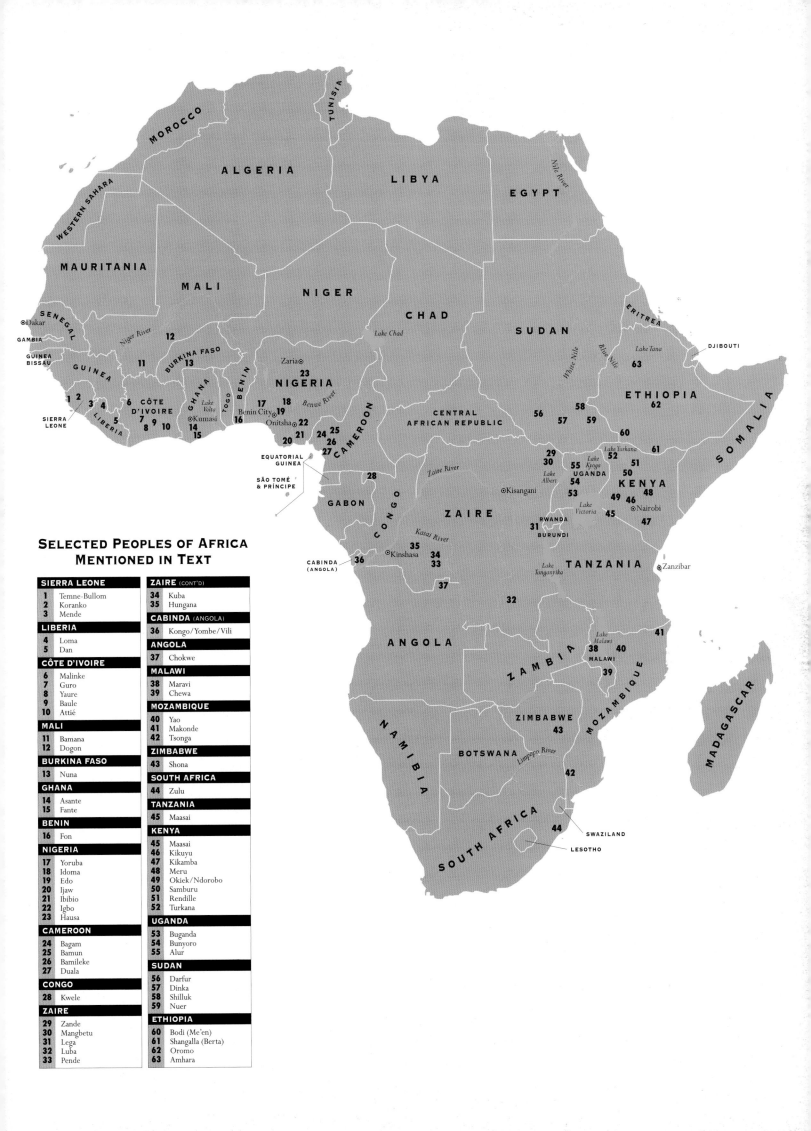

MOROCCO
TUNISIA
WESTERN SAHARA
ALGERIA
LIBYA
EGYPT
MAURITANIA
MALI
NIGER
CHAD
Nile River
SUDAN
ERITREA
SENEGAL
◉Dakar
GAMBIA
Niger River
12
Lake Chad
White Nile
Blue Nile
Lake Tana
DJIBOUTI
GUINEA
BISSAU
11
BURKINA FASO
13
Zaria◉
63
GUINEA
GHANA
BENIN
NIGERIA
23
ETHIOPIA
62
SIERRA
LEONE
1 2
3 4
6 Côte
D'IVOIRE
Lake
Volta
17
18
Benue River
CAMEROON
CENTRAL
AFRICAN REPUBLIC
56
58
57 59
60
5
7
9 10
Benin City◉ 19
16 Onitsha◉ 22
61
Lake Turkana
LIBERIA
8
◉Kumasi
14
15
20 21
24 25
26
27
28
GABON
CONGO
Zaire River
◉Kisangani
ZAIRE
29
30
31
55 *Lake*
Kyoga
54 UGANDA
53
52
51
50
49 46
45
SOMALIA
KENYA
48
47
◉Nairobi
EQUATORIAL
GUINEA
SÃO TOMÉ
& PRÍNCIPE
Lake
Albert
Lake
Victoria
RWANDA
BURUNDI
TANZANIA
◉Zanzibar
CABINDA
(ANGOLA)
36
◉Kinshasa
35
34
33
Kasai River
37
32
Lake
Tanganyika
ANGOLA
Lake
Malawi
41
NAMIBIA
ZAMBIA
38 40
MALAWI
39
MOZAMBIQUE
MADAGASCAR
ZIMBABWE
43
42
BOTSWANA
Limpopo River
44
SOUTH AFRICA
SWAZILAND
LESOTHO

SELECTED PEOPLES OF AFRICA
MENTIONED IN TEXT

SIERRA LEONE
1	Temne-Bullom
2	Koranko
3	Mende

LIBERIA
| 4 | Loma |
| 5 | Dan |

CÔTE D'IVOIRE
6	Malinke
7	Guro
8	Yaure
9	Baule
10	Attié

MALI
| 11 | Bamana |
| 12 | Dogon |

BURKINA FASO
| 13 | Nuna |

GHANA
| 14 | Asante |
| 15 | Fante |

BENIN
| 16 | Fon |

NIGERIA
17	Yoruba
18	Idoma
19	Edo
20	Ijaw
21	Ibibio
22	Igbo
23	Hausa

CAMEROON
24	Bagam
25	Bamun
26	Bamileke
27	Duala

CONGO
| 28 | Kwele |

ZAIRE
29	Zande
30	Mangbetu
31	Lega
32	Luba
33	Pende

ZAIRE (CONT'D)
| 34 | Kuba |
| 35 | Hungana |

CABINDA (ANGOLA)
| 36 | Kongo/Yombe/Vili |

ANGOLA
| 37 | Chokwe |

MALAWI
| 38 | Maravi |
| 39 | Chewa |

MOZAMBIQUE
40	Yao
41	Makonde
42	Tsonga

ZIMBABWE
| 43 | Shona |

SOUTH AFRICA
| 44 | Zulu |

TANZANIA
| 45 | Maasai |

KENYA
45	Maasai
46	Kikuyu
47	Kikamba
48	Meru
49	Okiek/Ndorobo
50	Samburu
51	Rendille
52	Turkana

UGANDA
53	Buganda
54	Bunyoro
55	Alur

SUDAN
56	Darfur
57	Dinka
58	Shilluk
59	Nuer

ETHIOPIA
60	Bodi (Me'en)
61	Shangalla (Berta)
62	Oromo
63	Amhara

IMAGINING ELEPHANTS

AN OVERVIEW

DORAN H. ROSS

As the largest land animal on the planet, the elephant is a potent symbol of the animal kingdom, distinguished by its size, prehensile trunk, ivory tusks, and enormous ears (Fig. 1-2). In the West, where the elephant is an exotic creature known only from books, movies, circuses, and zoos, its image suffers distortion and even exploitation. Whether romanticized or trivialized, the elephant is rarely presented in its complex reality. But in Africa, where humans and elephants – or their respective ancestors – have coexisted for a million years or more, the elephant is known in fuller dimensions. It has been a source of food, material, and riches; a fearsome rival for resources; and a highly visible, provocative neighbor. Inevitably it has had an impact on the artistic imagination. Even in areas where the elephant has now vanished, it persists as a symbol in expressive culture. As interpreted in African sculpture, masquerade, dance, and song, its image undergoes a startling range of transformations. But no matter how it is represented, its size and power are the features most likely to be dramatized, for they not only inspire respect, but stand, for better or worse, as emblems for human values.

The elephant is of course only one creature within the vast drama of intricate relationships that link the animal world with the human one. It should not be isolated from the hierarchy of fauna that give it context not just in actuality but also in its symbolic life. In its symbolic functions, it is at times interchangeable with other creatures, depending on culture and circumstance: qualities ascribed in one instance to the elephant may be given in another to the leopard or duiker. Even within a single culture the meanings ascribed to it can shift. Or it may be just one of an array of animals treated more or less equally, much like those of the Biblical Noah's ark – a theme that has been explored in glass paintings from Senegal (Fig. 1-3), thorn carvings from Nigeria, and popular paintings from Ethiopia (Fig. 16-15).

For the purpose of this anthology, the elephant serves as a microcosm – a large one, to be sure. By virtue of its sheer size and prominence, the roles it plays in art and historical processes are magnified. In the broader terms of the macrocosm, this book is about how humans relate to their environment and the fauna they share it with; and above all, how they interpret that relationship. In Africa as elsewhere, people represent their relationship to animals in multiple ways, and their complex experience of it can be read in the symbolic language of their respective cultures. Although elephant imagery may have its origins in actual observation, it is just as often a product of the imagination, and African depictions of the elephant have as much to say about human society as about the animal itself. Ultimately, historical events, social responsibilities, religious

1-1. Kinabo II, King of Kom, Cameroon, with two of his wives. He is using two elephant tusk trumpets as footrests in front of his palace at Laikom. Photograph, Hans-Joachim Koloss, 10 January 1976.

1-2. Bull elephant, Botswana. Photograph, Frans Lanting, Minden Pictures, 1990.

1-3 (OPPOSITE). Noah's Ark, by Mor-Gueye, 1992. Glass painting from Dakar, Senegal. 48 x 32 cm. Private collection.

beliefs, and political relationships are the primary subjects of elephant imagery.

For some, this may appear problematic. Within the scientific community, finding *human* traits in *animals* is often seen as sentimental anthropomorphizing even though it is, according to Lévi-Strauss (1968), a fundamental activity of the human mind. On the other hand, finding *animal* traits in *humans* tends to be seen outside the scientific community as pernicious and degrading. Mary Midgley puts it quite succinctly (1988:43):

Unquestionably there does remain a non-scientific but powerful tendency to resent and fear all close comparison between our own species and any other. Unquestionably we often tend to feel – at times extremely strongly – that the gap between our own species and all others is enormous and unbridgeable.

Yet in African cultures, the perception of this "unbridgeable gap" provokes much thoughtful and creative response. Of all creatures, the elephant, so huge, so remote, and yet so apparently human, most dramatizes the gap between the species. Donald Cosentino, surveying the elephant in oral traditions, sees it as the Gray Planet, whose sightings are full of mystery and portent. But the phenomenon is by no means confined to oral literature; indeed, many visual representations are driven by the impulse to mediate the breach between worlds.

The typical model for interpreting animal imagery is described by Mary Douglas in "The Pangolin Revisited" (1990:26):

Most of the analyses of the symbolism of animals show the animal kingdom as a projection or metaphor of social life; the analysis depends implicitly on resemblance or picturing. It may be directly, as when the

animal is said to depict particular human feelings, such as compassion or cruelty. Or more indirectly, as when by their industry or unruliness, for instance, they are taken to represent certain kinds of human behavior. All metaphorical identifications depend on making a match. The exercise is to identify some sameness in both fields. However, there is no limit to the power of the imagination for seeing patterns and finding resemblances. So there is no limit to the scope for finding similarity between any sets of object.

To minimize problems with the above model, Douglas cautions that any analysis of metaphor must be based on "local testimony," have "some evidence for the wider use of the metaphor," and be "institutionalized as a part of the regular habits of the people, a resemblance picked out by *their* theories of the world and *their* hypothesis" (1988:27, my emphasis).[1] From a producer's – in this case, African – perspective, one might add that there is no limit to the power of the imagination to create patterns and resemblances.

Hilda Kuper's analysis of Swazi leadership metaphors, which meets the above criteria, provides considerable insight into animal symbolism in that society (1973:613):

At the head of the polity is the king, titled Ngwenyama (lit. Lion), who rules with his 'mother', real or surrogate, titled Nolovukati (lit. She Elephant). They are metaphorically described as 'twins' (*emapahla*); their powers however are complementary, not identical, and at times overlap.

Complementary qualities are stressed in Kuper's analysis, which is based on the testimony of seven informants: The lion eats only meat, for example, and the elephant only vegetation, and "no one has ever seen lion and an elephant fight" (p. 621). Gender issues are not ignored (p. 621): "Sex differences within and between animal species appear to provide a fundamental paradigm for human behavior and at one level the lion epitomizes masculinity and the she-elephant female qualities." Kuper cites a Swazi colleague (p. 622):

According to my thinking, you could not have a lion and a lioness rule together, or an elephant and a she-elephant: it is necessary that they are different...but equal...and...government is best shown through a lion going together with the she-elephant.

Nevertheless, during the annual kingship ritual called Ncwala, the king does assume some attributes of the elephant: "The elephant is conspicuous in the Ncwala costume when, at dawn of the main day, the king walks naked before the women and warriors with only a glowing white penis covering made from the tusk of an elephant" (p. 622). Here he is praised as "You of the elephant" and "Elephant of the Swazi." The symbolic paradigm that embraces lion and elephant has extensive ramifications, for it is a defining force in such crucial arenas as political hierarchy, gender relationships, body decoration , and conventionalized oral literature. Here as in so many African paradigms, the world of symbol mediates the chasm between species. In contrast, the actual physical relationship of humans to elephants has until most recent times been largely adversarial.

ELEPHANT HUNTING

The interaction of humans and elephants on the African continent was undoubtedly preceded by interaction between their respective ancestors, as John Van Couvering explains in Chapter 3. At a butchery site in Olduvai Gorge in northeast Tanzania, a large number of stone tools have been found in conjunction with the bones of an extinct "elephant" (*Elphus reckii*) believed to be more than 500,000 years old. Whether such creatures were actually hunted at that time is not clear, but they were nevertheless exploited as a source of food since many of the bones were smashed to gain access to the marrow (Clark 1971:71).

Elephant hunting was a prized occupation in many African cultures, as many of the essays in this volume make clear (notably, Ezra and Arnoldi, Drewal, Geary, Wilcox, Binkley, Cameron, and Fisseha). Successful hunters were often celebrated in story and song. In some societies, the single-handed killing of an elephant was a test of manhood. Sometimes this was achieved with nothing but a poisoned spear, which generally required tracking the prey, sometimes for days, until it fell. More common was hamstringing, which required the hunter to approach from the rear and sever the elephant's tendons with either a heavy sword or axe. Thus immobilized, the elephant then became easier prey for the spear. Hunting in groups,

1-4. Twa elephant hunters, Ruasa, Ruzizi Plain, Rwanda. Photographer unknown, 1909. White Father's Collection, Eliot Elisofon Photographic Archives, Smithsonian Institution.

however, was the more widespread practice throughout Africa (Fig. 1-4). Typically several hunters would surround the animal. While one or two tried to distract it, the others would attempt to strike a serious or killing blow with a long, heavy spear. This process would continue until the animal dropped. Hunters also employed a variety of traps. The most common were dead falls with a weighted spear, foot snares generally attached to logs, and pit traps. In some areas, bush fires were also used to prevent the animal's escape.

As a source of meat, the elephant has offered the potential for greater bounty than any other animal in Africa. Since the elephant is more difficult to kill than most game, its meat was rarely a staple, but rather a prized dietary supplement. The killing of an elephant was momentous and often occasioned feasting for several days. The Mbuti of the Ituri Forest, in Zaire, would move their whole campsite to the vicinity of the kill (Turnbull 1961:138). In more sedentary cultures, the elephant is often butchered in formally prescribed ways; specific parts of the animal go to designated individuals based on their status in society, with hunters responsible for the kill generally receiving a favored portion (e.g., Smith and Dale 1968, I:384-85).

In many cultures the spirit of the dead elephant must be ritually placated (Smith and Dale 1968, I:168; Schwab 1947:85-86).

Ironically, while the elephant may be a source of food, it is also a threat to crops. In agrarian cultures it is often hunted as much to protect the fields as for the meat. Monica Wilson, for example, noted that in Nyakyusa country (Tanzania), "elephants were purposely shot out before 1935 because they were so destructive of crops" (1951:59). The problem is even greater in contemporary Africa, where expanding human populations and increased cultivation have encroached upon elephant homelands (see Chapter 19).

As long as hunting was restricted to spears, arrows, axes, or various trap devices, man was not a serious threat to the survival of the elephant in Africa (see Chapter 3). The introduction of firearms changed all that. European firearms, coupled with the Asian, American, and European desire for ivory, transformed subsistence hunting into what ultimately became a species-endangering massacre (Fig. 1-5). This began in the seventeenth century with muzzle-loaders and is now enabled by the high-powered hunting rifles and Uzis of the late twentieth century.

Scenes of hunting and trapping, regardless of prey, are surprisingly rare in African art. Still, important examples do exist, as in the rock art of the Sahara and southern Africa and the paintings of Ethiopia (Fisseha, Chapter 16). Spear hunting and hamstringing are illustrated much more frequently than trapping. Perhaps the latter removes in large part the element of courage and distances the hunter from the crucial initial part of the kill, the immobilizing blow.

African rock art aside, most examples of elephant hunting seem to occur in highly acculturated genres such as the decorated gourds (Fig. 1-6 and Interleaf II) made for export by

1-5. Painting of hunters with rifles, by an unknown artist. Ethiopia. Tempera on canvas. Width 186 cm. The Leavitt Collection.

1-6. Gourd with hunting scenes. Kongo peoples of Zaire. Height 35.5 cm. FMCH X65.8505. Gift of the Wellcome Trust. (See also Interleaf II.)

1-7. Elephant engraving, Gonoa, Tibesti, Algeria. Photograph, Merrick Posnansky 1966.

1-8. Elephant engraving, Gonoa, Tibesti, Algeria. Photograph, Emil Schulthess.

several groups in Zaire and Kenya, and the engravings on Zande ivories influenced by the European presence early in this century. These hunting scenes and others like them are more a reflection of Euro-American values than African ones. The massive ivory hunts of the nineteenth century created a commercial context for the hunt that carried over into art forms that represent it. Many of these pieces were either commissioned by Europeans or made specifically for sale to them.

THE IMAGE OF THE ELEPHANT

Some of the earliest artistic representations of the animal occur in the rock art of the central Sahara in the Hoggar, Fezzan, and Tibesti regions of southern Algeria and Libya (Figs. 1-7, 1-8). The sites around Tassili n'Ajjer are the best known, and though dating remains problematic, arguments have been offered that place the earliest variously at 8000, 6000, or 4000 B.C. Equally problematic is the function of these works. Initial interpretations generally argued that they constitute some form of sympathetic magic associated with the hunt; however, some scholars have suggested that they simply commemorate a successful hunt. These alternatives, of course, are not mutually exclusive, but they are based entirely on conjecture (Lhote 1973:213-14).

Our understanding of African rock art is expanded by the research of J. David Lewis-Williams and his colleagues on the San of South Africa.[2] Using nineteenth-century ethnographic

accounts, Lewis-Williams demonstrated (1981, 1983) that the prominence of the eland (a large antelope) could be explained by its role in the spiritual life of the San and rituals related to female puberty, boys' "first kills," marriage ceremonies, and especially in trance dances related to curing. T. M. O'C. Maggs and J. Sealy followed this line of reasoning to explain the relative prominence of the elephant in the Olifants River Basin of Western Cape, South Africa. They interpreted the representations of elephants surrounded by concentric or zigzag lines and images of elephant men as:

> ... a stage of San trance performance in which the elephant, a culturally controlled and highly emotive symbol of trance power, was superimposed upon physiologically controlled hallucinatory forms. Then at 'peak hallucinatory periods,' as Siegal puts it, the San trancer seems to have 'seen' himself as part of the imagery, participating in therianthropic form with the symbol of the elephant power he was exploiting in trance. (Maggs and Sealy 1983:48)

Other representations of "elephant men" have been interpreted as "rain animals" intended to help regulate precipitation (Pager 1975:49). A hoofed elephant man in the midst of a swarm of bees (Interleaf V) has been interpreted with more emphasis on bees and honey than on the elephant traits. Honey is represented as a medicinal liquid in San myths and is seen as

1-9. Rock art depicting a speared elephant and antelope, Rodedede Cave, Mtoko, Zimbabwe. Drawing, Jill Ball, after Summers (1959:26).

1-10. Drawing of an Asian elephant brought as an item of tribute by a Syrian to Thutmose III, an 18th-dynasty Egyptian ruler. From a wall painting from the tomb of Rekmere, Thebes, c. 1500 B.C. Drawing, Sylvia Kennedy, after Sillar and Meylar (1968:43).

the food of gods and spirits (p. 74). The identity or role of the elephant man is left to speculation.

By about 3200 B.C., First Dynasty Egyptians had developed a symbol for the wild elephant and another for the trained elephant, the latter showing a man riding on the animal's neck — evidence that, contrary to popular thought, the African elephant could be tamed. Archaeological evidence reveals, moreover, that ivory was worked in pre-Dynastic Egypt as well as throughout later periods (Fig. 1-10; see also Alpers, Chapter 17, and Shayt, Chapter 18). Since the Egyptians apparently did not encounter the Asian elephant until about 1500 B.C., in wars with Syria, their experience prior to this time would have been entirely with the African genus.

The most famous domesticated African elephants were those kept at Carthage. By 225 B.C., the city had stabling for 300 elephants, and coinage of the period depicts the sway-backed, large-eared African varieties (Fig. 1-11). In 218 B.C., Hannibal crossed the Alps into Italy with an army that included thirty-seven elephants, a few of which were probably of Syrian origin.

Roman records document the lavish use of ivory in the classical era. It was this appetite for ivory that ultimately led to the extinction of the elephant in North Africa by late Roman times. Thus with the exception of small quantities traded from Ethiopia, southern Sudan, and parts of Somalia, ivory was relatively unavailable in Europe for a period of roughly a thousand years, until the Portuguese explorations down the west coast of Africa.

1-11. Silver half shekel, Carthage, Tunisia, c. 213-210 B.C. Numismatic Fine Arts International.

1-12. Elephant head of unknown function, Nok culture, Nigeria, c. 500 B.C. to A.D. 200. Terracotta. Height 19 cm. National Commission for Museums and Monuments, Nigeria, N291.1. Photograph, Dirk Bakker.

1-13. Bronze elephant of unknown date found at Tada, Nigeria. Height 63 cm. National Commission for Museums and Monuments, Nigeria, 90.R.1756.

Most of the early sculptural record of elephants in sub-Saharan Africa comes from Nigerian sources. One of the most famous terracotta sculptures from the Nok culture (500 B.C. to A.D. 200) in northeast Nigeria is an elephant head about eighteen centimeters or a little over seven inches high (Fig. 1-12). Since most Nok remains have been recovered in alluvial tin mining operations, no information is available on the function of this or related objects. At Igbo Ukwu in southern Nigeria, as Herbert Cole notes in Chapter 10, four cast bronze elephant head pendants were obtained from a site dated to the ninth or tenth century A.D. (Fig. 10-1). From the same site, elephant tusks were found to comprise a prominent part of the elaborate burial of a priest/chief excavated by Thurstan Shaw. One tusk served as a footrest for the deceased leader. The corpus of art from Ife (twelfth to fifteenth centuries A.D.), discussed by Henry Drewal in Chapter 9, includes a magnificent terracotta elephant head which was used as a pot lid in a presumed royal burial excavated by Ekpo Eyo (Fig. 9-1). Cole and Drewal show that the high-status contexts of the Igbo Ukwu and Ife finds are consistent with those of elephant imagery used by present-day cultures in the same areas.

An elephant (Fig. 1-13) and two ostriches are the lesser-known bronze castings from the famous corpus of nine Tsoede bronzes found on the island of Jebba and in the village of Tada in an area now occupied by the Nupe. This group includes the largest bronze castings of any antiquity in sub-Saharan Africa. Frank Willett traces the origins of the six human figures to the Yoruba and cites thermoluminescence dates of around the fourteenth century for the two largest figures (1980:47). While there are few points of stylistic comparison between the animal and human figures, it is not implausible to suggest a Yoruba origin for the animal figures as well.

A rich array of bells, some representing elephant heads (Fig. 1-14), has been classified under the catch-all heading Lower Niger Bronze Industry. The age, function, and origin of these bells have yet to be determined although the Igbo are most frequently identified as the possible casters (Neaher 1976:127-56, fig. 21; Jacob 1974:13; Lorenz 1982). The example shown here, however, holds a leaf in its trunk recalling imagery more typical of Benin (see Chapter 8). Many of these bells were obviously buried at some time in the past, although none have been recovered in archaeological contexts. As archaeology in Africa matures, similar finds will undoubtedly shed more light on the use and meaning of elephants in older African cultures. With few exceptions most representations of the elephant documented in this volume date from the late nineteenth and twentieth centuries.

Elephant Contexts

Images of the elephant span a wide variety of contexts from spiritual to secular and from serious to playful. The use of elephant imagery in ritual contexts has been extensively documented in the chapters of this volume. Ritual containers, royal staffs and scepters, masks, altar pieces, and body ornaments are

1-14. Bronze bell possibly from the Igbo peoples of Nigeria. Height 10.5 cm. Collection of Toby and Barry Hecht.

1-15 (ABOVE). Divination instrument from the Kuba peoples of Zaire Wood. Length 23.5 cm. Jerome L. Joss Collection.

1-16 (BELOW). Divination instrument from the Kuba peoples of Zaire. Wood. Length 34.6 cm. The Stanley Collection, The University of Iowa Museum of Art, CMS 264.

1-17 (ABOVE). Divination object from the Senufo peoples of Ivory Coast. Iron. Length 19.5 cm. Collection of Maurice Bonnefoy.

1-18 (BELOW). Detail of lid on an Afro-Portuguese saltcellar (full view seen in Interleaf M). From Sierra Leone. Ivory. Museum für Völkerkunde, Vienna (Inv. Nr. 118.609b). Photograph, Fritz Mandl.

some of the object types widely used for ceremonial or spiritual purposes. Interesting examples of elephant imagery not mentioned elsewhere here include a friction oracle (*itombwa*), used by the Kuba of Zaire for divination and sometimes carved in the shape of an elephant (Figs. 1-15, 1-16). The diviner interrogates the oracle while rubbing a small wood knob against its back, and interprets the answer as affirmative when the knob sticks to the oracle. Used to diagnose causes of illness and to single out miscreants, the oracle is said to be especially effective in identifying thieves; the clairvoyant powers of the elephant give it meaning in such a context (Thomas 1960:78-83). The Senufo also occasionally employ an elephant image (Fig. 1-17) in their divination ensembles, along with carved wooden male, female, and equestrian images, an array of cast brass forms, and bits and pieces from the natural environment (Holas 1969a: 230). To invoke the ancestors and ensure success in the hunt, chiefs and medicinal specialists among the Kongo and related peoples of western Zaire use small antelope horn whistles. Sometimes these are topped by carved images of an elephant, probably serving as a charm to attract the prey (Cornet 1975:16).

Images of elephant riders are found in many African cultures – for example, Mende, Baule, Asante, Temne/Bullom (Fig. 1-18) and Luba (Fig. 1-22).[3] Contrary to appearances,

most do not represent literal riding, but rather symbolize political or spiritual domination; broader control over nature in general is probably also implied. Actual riders on elephants trained by Indian *mahouts* appear in a photograph from the 1920s (Fig. 1-19) documenting the forestry project established by King Leopold of Belgium in 1899 at Kiravunga, in what is now Zaire, and later moved to Api in 1925 (Sikes 1971:296).

A conceptual variant of elephant riding is found in the variety of stools carved in the shape of the animal; these are especially common among the Akan of Ghana (Chapter 7), the grassland kingdoms of Cameroon (Chapter 11), and the Luba of Zaire (Interleaf XIV). In these instances the chief or other prominent individual actually sits on the back of an elephant, inanimate though it may be. Tangential to this idea are the footrests and headrests (Figs. 1-20, 1-22) that represent elephants, and the ivory tusks used as footrests (Fig. 1-1) found in different parts of Africa. Perhaps the ultimate statement in elephant riding is seen in the image of an elephant carrying a

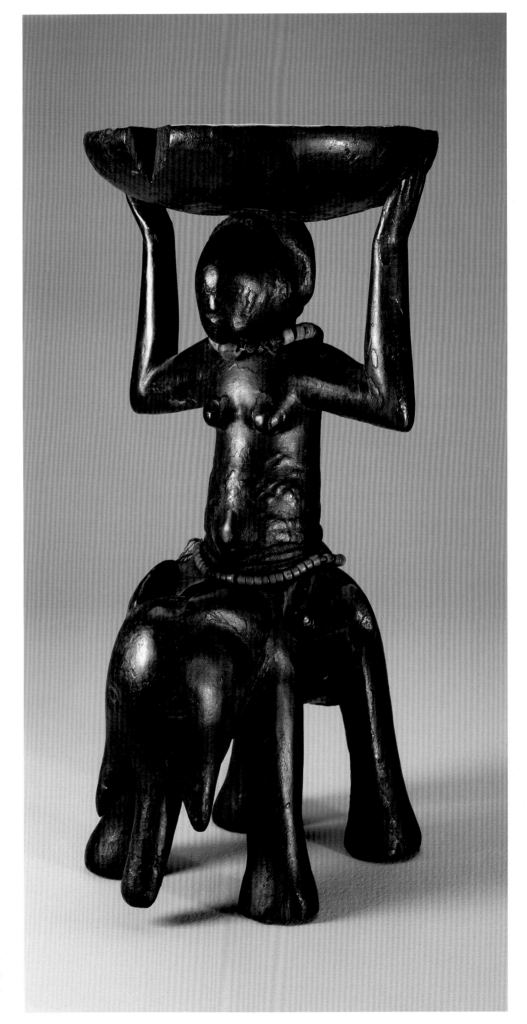

1-19 (OPPOSITE). Domestic elephants, Buta Mission, Central Africa (Elephants domestiques de la Mission de Buta, Central Africa). Photographer unknown. Eliot Elisofon Photographic Archives, Postcard Collection: Mission des Prémontres de Tongerloo. NELS Ern. Thill, Édition Bruxelles. National Museum of African Art, Smithsonian Institution.

1-20 (OPPOSITE). Headrest from Tsonga peoples of South Africa. Wood. Length 54.6 cm. National Museum of African Art, Washington, D.C., 91.14.1 A.

1-21 (RIGHT). Stool from the Luba peoples of Zaire with a woman riding an elephant as a support. Wood, glass, fiber. Height 56 cm. Collection of Dr. Vaughana Macy Feary.

1-22. Headrest from the Tsonga peoples of South Africa. Wood. Height 13 cm. U. and W. Horstmann Collection, Zug, Switzerland.

1-23. Drawing of a carving on a wood Akan drum showing a steamship on the back of an elephant. Collection of Dr. Vaughana Macy Feary. Drawing, Jill Ball.

European steamship on its back (Fig. 1-23). Here the accomplishment would seem to be on the side of the elephant rather than the rider.

Not all elephant images in African art carry profound meaning, however. On some utilitarian forms they are employed simply as pleasing embellishments selected from many possible animal motifs. Guro heddle pulleys, Rotse food bowls (Fig. 1-24), and Akan goldweights fall into this category. While it is tempting to speculate, for example, that the elephant appears on the pulley to strengthen this hardworking loom part symbolically (if not spiritually), it is more likely that it appears in this context for "fancy's sake" as is often heard of similar decorative accents in English-speaking Africa.

Elephant imagery in Africa is not, of course, limited to categories of objects typically called "traditional." The glass paintings of Senegal (Interleaf III), the popular paintings of Ethiopia (Chapter 16), and the kinetic toys from Zimbabwe (Fig. 1-25), all created for an expatriate/tourist/export market, are just a few of the more interesting examples. These exist in the midst of herds of brass, ebony, soapstone, and synthetic ivory elephants that populate the souvenir stands of Africa's major cities and the curio shops of much of the Western world. Many of these same objects also appear in the parlors of middle-class Africans.

For the very reasons that elephants are potent symbols for traditional leaders, elephants are increasingly common as commercial logos on such products as chocolate, tea, detergent, cigarettes, and postage stamps (Interleaf VI). Cigarettes named "Tusker" are undoubtedly punning on the visual appearance of the white cigarette that projects from the side of the smoker's mouth. A Kenyan malt lager also called Tusker was "named in memory of the Breweries' founder, Charles Hurst, who was killed while on safari by a rogue bull elephant," or so it says on the cardboard six-pack imported into the United States! Nevertheless, the advertisers seem to think that it is more important to identify the strength of the beer with that of the elephant than to honor the memory of the founder. Invoking or appropriating the elephant when "power" is the desired message has proved a successful marketing device throughout much of Africa.

A number of artistic traditions, especially in Nigeria, appear to be connected with elephants only in name. The largest of the Dakakari terracotta grave monuments are called "elephants" presumably based on their size and on small projections at the very top of the sculptures that are "said to symbolize tusks and/or trunk" (Bassing 1973:36,39). That there were once six of these small points on the top of the two examples illustrated in Bassing would seem to deny a tusk/trunk identification.

1-24. Food bowl from the Rotse peoples of Zambia. Wood. Length 51 cm. FMCH X91.421A,B. Gift of Helen and Robert Kuhn.

1-25. Articulated push-toy from Zimbabwe made primarily for export. Wood, wire, paint. Length of elephant 36 cm. Private collection.

1-26. Cap purchased in Zaria, Nigeria, 1991. Cotton. Height 14.5 cm. FMCH X92.54. Anonymous gift.

Urhobo *ivwri*, Isoko *ivri*, and western Ijo *ejiri* have also been commonly identified as elephants (e.g., Willett 1971:149). Lacking trunks and consistently featuring open mouths with bared teeth and two upward and two downward projecting tusks, there is little in these objects to suggest elephants visually. Similarly, the Yoruba *egungun* mask from Abeokutu called *erin* (elephant), discussed by Henry Drewal in Chapter 9, and the northern Igbo *ijele* called the "elephant among masks," mentioned by Herbert Cole in Chapter 10, have little if any visual correspondence with the elephant. Still, as Drewal argues for his Yoruba example, these references may be based on other perceived qualities of the elephant quite apart from its physical attributes. On the other hand relative size or importance of a given tradition may be sufficient in itself to merit the descriptor *elephant*.

This seems to be the case with the Hausa of northern Nigeria where the elephant is called *giwa*; a huge boat, *giwan jirgi;* and a large motorcar, *giwar mota* (Abraham 1962:327). As might be expected, high-ranking authorities in the emirates are also called *giwa,* and the familiar embroidered robe worn by a man of status is known as *rigan giwa* or "robe of the elephant" (Kriger 1988:52,55). This should also help explain the name *'Alhaji Elephant'* stitched on a Muslim cap which would have been worn with one of these robes (Fig. 1-26). Since *Alhaji* is the honorific designating a man who has made the pilgrimage (*hadj*) to Mecca, the hat proclaims its wearer's status on at least two levels.

Masquerades

Identification with the elephant may be manifested by something as simple as the wearing of ivory bangles, as seen in the Nigerian Igbo women's elephant society (discussed by Cole in Chapter 10); or by something as complex as a belief in the actual physical changing into an elephant (mentioned by Cosentino regarding the Koranko of Sierra Leone in Chapter 4, and by Rosalinde Wilcox in relation to the Bakwiri of Cameroon in Chapter 12). Transformations into an elephant, however, take place most often in the rich masking traditions of Africa.

At least forty African peoples have been documented as possessing elephant masquerades. The contexts for these performances are as varied as African masking in general. Initiations, funerals, agrarian rites, ancestor veneration, and kingship ceremonies may all prompt the appearance of an elephant masker. The character of the elephant mask ranges widely. It may be a minor performer in the midst of fifty or sixty other masks, or it may be the central figure of a secret society that has taken its name. In one case it may serve as entertainment in a lighter secular masquerade. In another it may have judicial, even executioner roles in political and religious masquerade societies.

Elephant masks vary in appearance from abstract to naturalistic. In some instances, only one or two attributes are recognizable — trunk, tusks, and large ears being the most

1-27. Mask for *Glewa* or "great masquerade" carved by Son, from the Dan village of Nuopie, Liberia. Collection of Museum für Völkerkunde, Hamburg.

common referents seen (Interleaf VIII). In others, most of the salient features of the animal are included. Likewise, performance behavior ranges from highly stylized gestures to motions that closely mimic the animal's ways. Masquerades are the focus of several of the articles in this volume; what follows here are brief discussions of selected traditions not otherwise dealt with in other chapters.[4]

War and law are two key areas of concern for the Dan of Liberia and Côte d'Ivoire. The use of an elephant masquerade in these contexts reflects the elephant's power and strength. Dan masks have often been interpreted as agents of social control. Recent research shows that the roles they play are actually quite fluid, able to change over time (Steiner 1986; McNaughton 1991). A mask may be promoted as it gains power and respect through repeated performances, and so the *glewa* or "great masquerade" may feature a variety of mask forms. An elephant mask filmed by Eberhard Fischer, and now in the Hamburg Museum für Völkerkunde (Fig. 1-27), began its life as a war masquerade but was subsequently elevated to the status of *glewa*. This "great masquerade" is also called the "law-giving masquerade" since one of its most important roles is announcing justice (Fischer and Himmelheber 1984: 89-90). A mask with a related function (Interleaf VIII) was documented for the nearby Mano peoples. According to

1-28. Elephant mask used in Jolly Society, Freetown, Sierra Leone. Wood, wire, fabric, plastic. Depth 68.6 cm. FMCH X86.2971. Anonymous gift.

George Harley (1941:19), "this mask was kept in the sacred house and used when any person was spoiling the town laws, or refused to pay his debts. The matter had to be settled at once or the 'elephant' would break down his house."

An elephant masquerade of a more entertaining variety is one of many so-called Jolly masks played in Freetown, Sierra Leone, around Christmas and New Year and during weddings. Jolly, performed by young men's societies, has nothing to do with law or war; it is purely for fun. Its headpiece consists of a wooden face mask in a style typical of Ikot Ekpene in Nigeria, and a wire superstructure bent into representative shapes covered with cloth, rickrack, sequins, synthetic furs, and beads. The Jolly elephant (Fig. 1-28), called by the Yoruba name *erin*, performs with other masks that include images of unicorns, airplanes, Mami Wata, Al Buraq, tigers, and mosques. According to John Nunley (forthcoming), both the Indian-style face painting on the mask and the tigers on the cloth forming the elephant's body suggest that this Jolly mask was strongly influenced by Indian chromolithographs – common in Freetown markets – of the Indian god of fortune, Ganesh. An elephant associated most directly with "good fortune" seems especially appropriate at New Year and wedding festivities.

A much more somber representation of elephant was among the seventy-some Dogon mask types documented by Marcel Griaule in Mali during the early 1930s (Fig. 1-29). Rare even then, the masquerade was performed at a funerary rite (*dama*) for the dispatch of the spirit of the deceased and the purification of the surviving kin (1935:344). Griaule described the mask as having a conical armature covered with the stems of dried plants. The wooden component covering the face, which resembles several Dogon masks, does not seem to bear any traits peculiar to the elephant, unless one interprets as tusks the small projections at either side of the bottom of the mask. According to Griaule, the masker did not dance, but contented himself to walk around for the duration of the ceremonies, encouraged by the audience with the following (pp. 468-70):

Greetings! Elephant
of the good body
Stuffed with large trees
Stuffed with small trees
Coming to the village [and doing] damage
All the bush is your bush
All are the eyes on you
Good bush!

Of a comparable nature, perhaps, was a large wooden helmet mask over six feet long, now in Nigeria's Jos Museum, which is identified as an Idoma elephant from Asa (Fig. 1-30). Museum records indicate that it appeared "at funerals of members and at important events, for example the visits of governors."[5] A similar Idoma mask named *Utro Eku* ("Chief of Masks") was illustrated by Roy Sieber (1961:10-11), who also mentioned a harvest-time performance. Sidney Kasfir refines

the name to *Itrokwu* and sees it as a composite elephant-crocodile mask that is a "metaphor of destructive power." Its costume is an indigo burial cloth worn like a cloak and the masquerader is accompanied by a stool-bearing attendant, a reference to its chiefly attributes. According to Kasfir (forthcoming), "Its dance is 'hot,' bursting into the compound aggressively, knocking over food-drying platforms, scattering cooking pots and audience, who remain at a respectful distance. The footwork is very rapid, unlike that of other chiefly masquerades who move in stately fashion, and the masker is fanned by attendants with boughs of green leaves in an effort to cool its power and alert danger."[6] Another mask also identified as Idoma may fit into this same tradition (Fig. 1-31).

Ancestors are associated with an intriguing elephant masquerade performed at night in Malawi. In 1900, Edouard Foa published a provocative drawing of such a masquerade, featuring an elephant character from the Mang'anja or southern Maravi people (Fig. 1-32).[7] This tradition still existed in the early 1970s as part of the men's organization called Nyau, which according to Blackmun and Schoffeleers "functions both as an expression of reverence for and communication with the ancestors" (1972:36). The example they document is a wooden armature covered with leaves and cloth; it has erect, circular ears and sticks for trunk and tusks (Fig. 1-34). Of several masks danced in Nyau masquerades, the elephant is considered to be the most important. Made in a restricted work area by senior

1-29 (OPPOSITE). Elephant mask from the Dogon peoples of Mali. Illustrated by Marcel Griaule in *Les Masques Dogons* (1935:469).

1-30 (RIGHT). Mask called *Itrokwu* from the Idoma peoples of Nigeria. Carved by Ogbudu about 1948. Wood, mirrors, paint. National Commission for Museums and Monuments, Nigeria. Photograph, Doran H. Ross.

1-31 (BELOW). Elephant mask from the Idoma (?) peoples of Nigeria. Wood, paint. Length 169 cm. Jerome L. Joss Collection.

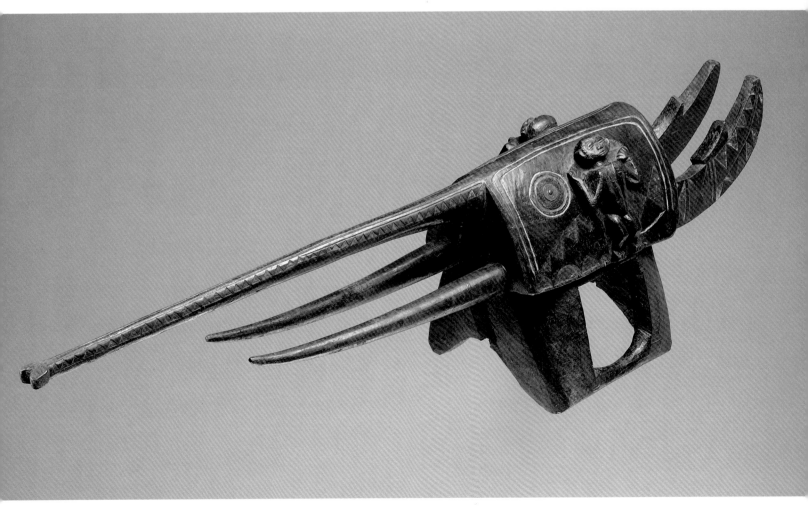

1-32 (ABOVE). Drawing of night masquerade featuring elephant, bush cow and cape buffalo characters performed by the southern Maravi peoples of Malawi and published in Foa (1900).

1-33 (BELOW). Mask from the Luba peoples of Zaire. Trunk has reed tube for inhaling or expelling water. Wood, reed. Length 77 cm. Section of Ethnography, Royal Museum of Central Africa, Tervuren, Belgium, 3722.

1-34. Elephant masquerade construction from the southern Maravi peoples of Malawi. Photograph, Matthew Schoffeleers.

Nyau members, it can be seen only by initiates, at night. In performance it is accompanied by old men representing elephant hunters. After being performed, the mask is burned (p. 69). Among the Chewa or northern Maravi people, a sisal basketry mask ensemble with a carved wooden face piece represents the Nyau elephant. According to Laurel Faulkner, the mask appears "only for the funerals of chiefs and esteemed village leaders. Because the elephant is a symbol of strength and respectability, only well-regarded members of the society are permitted to perform this dance" (1988:31).

Elephant masks are also found among the Luba of Zaire, whose art features a number of intriguing but poorly understood elephant images (Interleaf XIV). One remarkable example collected in 1898 and now in the Royal Museum of Central Africa, Tervuren, has a hollow reed running the length of the trunk, which allows the masker to ingest water or other liquid (Fig. 1-33). As photographed by its collector, Charles Lemaire, the masker was clad in a leopard skin and carried a spear. Lemaire called it a war mask. Joseph Maes speculated it might even be worn into battle (1924:42). William Burton thought this unlikely and wrote (1961:177):

> The mask was simply one used by the members of the elephant society. They would put their hands and feet into old dancing drums, cover their bodies with dry banana leaves, and wear the mask representing an elephant. These disguised men were accompanied by a group of retainers, who were actually in league with them, but pretended to be coerced by them. With the help of such retainers they would capture solitary passers-by, holding them to ransom. A number of elephant men would work a whole neighborhood, terrifying the populace, and claiming slaves and goods. Then when opposition became too strong, they would move to another part of the country.

The serious tone of this description is at odds with material in the Tervuren archives, attributed to Burton, asserting that these masks "are not magical/supernatural in character but are strictly for entertainment purposes, with some practice of petty swindling."[8]

Amidst a profusion of python, hippopotamus, crocodile, shark, and sawfish images, the elephant also occasionally occurs in the water spirit masquerades of the Ijaw people of the Cross River region of Nigeria. Water spirits are dedicated to placating and controlling environmental forces — especially those related to the rivers on which the Ijaw depend for food and trade. That the elephant's role is minor can perhaps be attributed to the fact that it doesn't actually live in water. Water spirit masks, reflecting the multivalent powers of the environment, rarely depict a single animal in isolation; thus composite animal masks are widespread. One remarkable variant represents a dramatic visual pun with the elephant tusks terminating in human hands on either side of a rigidly straight trunk (Fig. 1-35). The motif of a trunk-hand is prevalent in the court arts of Benin (see Chapter 8) as well as in other southern Nigerian cultures. Yet the Ijaw seem to be playing with this image by reversing the physical capabilities of two important features of the elephant (Horton 1965:5, 34-35). Consistent with the composite imagery of water spirit masks, the rear section terminates in the tail of a manatee with shark fins projecting from the top.

1-35. Mask from the Ijaw peoples of Nigeria. Wood. Length 75 cm. FMCH X85.326. Anonymous gift.

Several of the elephant masks discussed above and elsewhere in this volume include material or visual references to other animals as well. The Kuba *Mukenga* mask (Fig. 13-13) often incorporates a ruff of hair from the colobus monkey as a beard and the inset face of the mask is frequently made from leopard skin. In Cameroon, masks used in the highest grade of the elephant society include a beaded headdress representing a leopard and a leopard-skin cape (Fig. 11-24). The nose of the Igbo *Ogbodo Enyi* mask terminates in a serpent's head, a visual pun that exploits the similarities of trunk and snake (Fig. 10-11). In each case, the elephant is the dominant image, and the other animal referents are seen as supplementary attributes that reinforce the power of the elephant.

From a survey of elephant masquerades found in Africa, it is difficult to find any consistent trends aside from traits related to the animal's size, strength, and potentially destructive power. That a majority of elephant masks perform in funerary events says very little, since this is probably *the* most

common context for masquerades in Africa regardless of the character represented in the masquerade. Nevertheless, the considerable body of folklore relating ancestor transformations into elephants, and vice versa (e.g., Chapter 4) suggests that there is much more to learn about elephant masquerades and funerals.

A number of African harvest-time performances also include an elephant masquerade. It is easy to imagine how the elephant, with its huge appetite, might be viewed as the ultimate harvester, or alternatively as the greatest threat to the harvest – a beast that must be placated. On the other hand, in some African cultures the elephant's part in harvest masquerading is only minor. In masking genres as elsewhere, the representations of elephants are so varied that it is difficult to generalize.

ELEPHANT AS MATERIAL

Organic parts of the elephant often carry many of the same symbolic messages as actual representations of the animal. The role of ivory is most obvious, but other materials can be equally important. Hide, bone, hair, and callus from the sole of the foot connote status and power and are usually employed in restricted contexts by the elite of a society. Hair and callus bracelets (Fig. 1-36), anklets, and necklaces are found in many cultures, as are shields, bags, and drum-heads made from hide. Elephant hide, however, does not consistently have prestige associations, perhaps because practical and utilitarian considerations often obscure more symbolic ones.

The thick coarse hairs of the elephant's tail have leadership associations in several areas (Fig. 1-37). Among the Lega of Zaire an elephant tail projection from the top of a man's hat is the exclusive prerogative of membership in the highest level of the highest grade in the Bwami secret society, as Elisabeth Cameron explains in Chapter 14. According to Daniel Biebuyck, "high initiates identify strongly with the elephant because of the animal's calm appearance: if disturbed, however, the elephant explodes in ferocious destruction" (1984:84). The contrasting qualities of calmness and ferocity are both considered essential to leadership among the Lega.

In Ghana, the association of the elephant tail flywhisk with Akan royalty is based in part on observations of the way the animal uses its tail (see Chapter 7). The symbolic role of this item of regalia is metaphorically elucidated by a proverb: *Though the elephant's tail is short, it can nevertheless keep flies off the elephant.* When applied to a chieftaincy context, the aphorism suggests that despite any apparent shortcomings, the chief is prepared to solve all problems.

Ivory Usage in Africa

Ivory, admired for its hardness, color, and luster, and for its obvious identification with the elephant, has been the prerogative of chieftaincy or leadership in many parts of Africa. Typically, one tusk from each elephant kill was reserved for the local ruler, and often this was prescribed as the tusk resting on the ground after the animal fell under the belief that it was the largest and heaviest. Large unworked tusks were often displayed with a ruler as he sat in state at public events, and in some places they still are — for example among the Igbo of Nigeria and the Bamileke of Cameroon. In the Lakes Region of Africa, David Livingstone noted, "they reverence the tombs of their ancestors, and plant the largest elephants' tusks, as monuments at the head of the grave, or entirely enclose it with the choicest ivory (1865:231). In Bunyoro, William Burton reported cattle pens made of tusks (1961, II:198), and Henry Stanley mentions a small shrine with thirty-three tusks serving as columns supporting the roof (1878, II:272). Such ostentatious (and generally rare) uses of unworked ivory were abandoned by the late nineteenth century as its value increased and as the ivory and slave traders ravaged the country. One

1-36. Wristlets from the Loma peoples in village of Zolowo, Liberia, collected in 1968. Elephant callus, aluminum (top three), elephant tail hair (bottom). Diameter of largest wristlet 8.255 cm. Collection of Barry Kitnick.

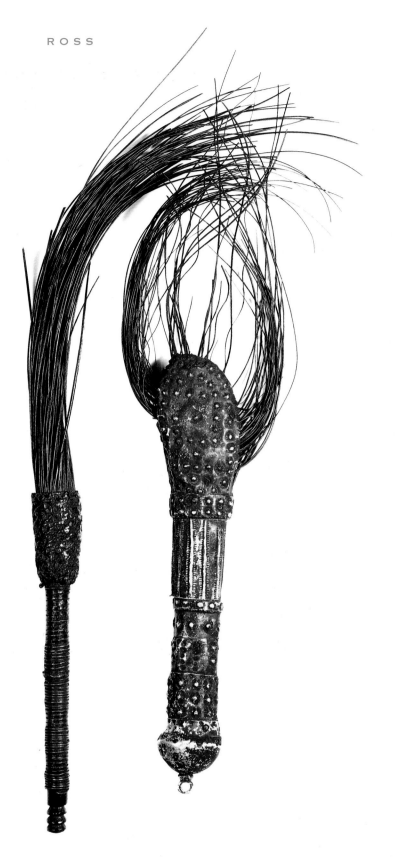

1-37. Elephant tail flywhisks: Left, Kuba peoples of Zaire, Length 169 cm. FMCH x91.235. Museum purchase. Right, Toma peoples of Sierra Leone, Length 48 cm. FMCH x91.236. Museum purchase.

explanation of the Western myth of "elephant graveyards" is that it was created by ivory traders during the nineteenth century to conceal their sources and to disguise their activities.

Among the most widespread worked ivory objects in Africa are side-blown trumpets. Most examples retain the shape of an intact elephant tusk; the blow hole is typically carved on the concave side of the tusk near the tip, and the tone hole placed at the tip, where it can be manipulated by the thumb. Horns range from small, shrill ones, six to twelve inches (fifteen to thirty cm) long (Fig. 1-38), to the enormous *siwa* trumpets of the Swahili coast (e.g., Chapter 15), which may be made

from tusks as long as eight feet (245 cm). In many areas several horns of different sizes are played in concert; such ensembles are especially common in royal contexts (Fig. 1-39).

The sound produced by a medium-sized ivory trumpet is remarkably similar to the actual trumpeting of an elephant. In some cultures with tonal languages, for example the Akan of Ghana, trumpet blowers replicate the sounds of the language by opening and closing the tone hole. This technique is used to produce conventionalized praise names and other verbal forms. The net effect is of having the praises of the chief or elder sung through the "voice" of the elephant in an

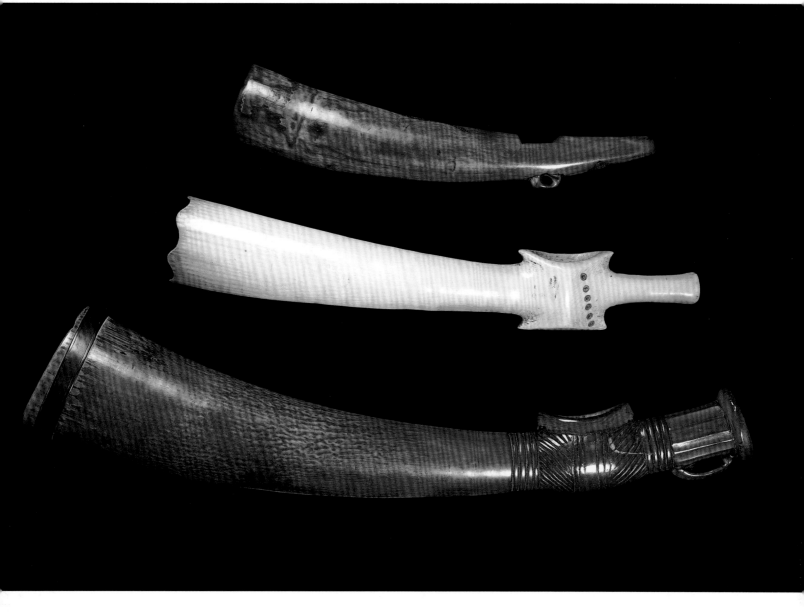

1-38 (ABOVE). Ivory side-blown trumpets. Top to bottom: Kuba peoples of Zaire. Collected by Reverend Lachlin C. Vass III, missionary of the Presbyterian Congo Mission 1898-1909. Length 25.4 cm. FMCH x82.973. Lega peoples of Zaire. Length 31.5 cm. FMCH x378.305. Museum purchase. Mende peoples of Sierra Leone. Length 43.2 cm. FMCH x86.1915. Gift of Helen and Dr. Robert Kuhn.

1-39. Royal trumpeters from the court of the king of Benin, Nigeria. Photograph, Joseph Nevadomsky, 1978.

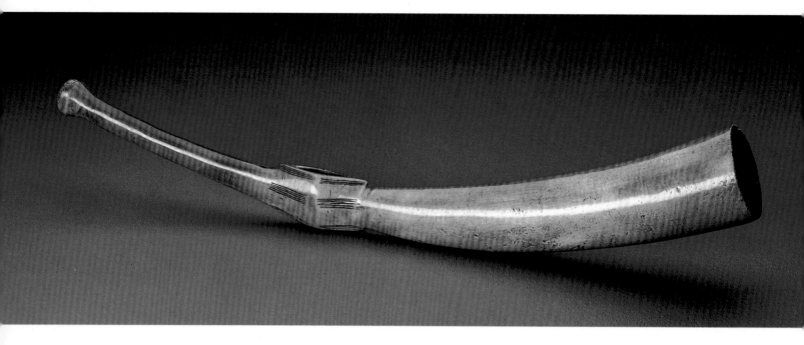

1-40. Side-blown trumpet from central Zaire. Ivory. Length 61 cm. FMCH X86.1874. Gift of Helen and Dr. Robert Kuhn.

1-41 A-C (OPPOSITE). Three ivory trumpets from the Mende peoples of Sierra Leone. Top to bottom: 87.309497, Length 73 cm; 87.309514, Length 76 cm; 87.309511, Length 61 cm. Staatliches Museum für Völkerkunde, Munich.

instrument made from the animal – perhaps the ultimate form of accolade.

Praise singing is only one of the many functions served by ivory side-blown trumpets. They accompanied court dances among the Mangbetu (Schildkrout and Keim 1990:203), funerals and investiture ceremonies among the Kongo ruling elite (Thompson 1989:41), Swahili weddings on Lamu and the royal circumcision ceremony on the island of Pate (Sassoon 1975). In various parts of Liberia ivory horns were used "to call people to work, and to wrestling matches, and to give directions to people lost in the forest" (Schwab 1947:154). They also had roles in men's and women's initiation societies (ibid.). In the Cameroon grasslands ivory horns were owned by men's judiciary societies where they were played in public to settle disputes (Koloss 1983:26a). In Ghana, they were "used in the opening ceremonies of parliament and as part of the pageantry in welcoming diplomatic envoys to the capital at Accra" (Carter 1984:257). Elsewhere ivory trumpets play secondary roles – for example, as footrests in the Cameroon grasslands (Fig. 1-1) and as title insignia among the Igbo of Nigeria (Fig. 10-1).

In view of the symbolic and musical complexity of the ivory trumpet, it is not surprising that the instrument receives considerable artistic attention (Fig. 1-41). Surface engravings and relief carvings embellish the instruments of many cultures. In several, the tips of the horn are sculpted into human and animal shapes (Interleaf I). In other cultures the simple elegance of the natural shape is subtly modified to incorporate a swelling of the mouth hole (Fig. 1-40). This is possible because the thick walls of the tusk are reduced by carving in most societies to produce a lighter, more portable instrument with greater resonance.

Ivory is also selectively used on other items of regalia. Ivory finials top the staffs of chiefs among the Kongo peoples of Zaire (Interleaf J). Both Kongo and Kuba chiefs often hold

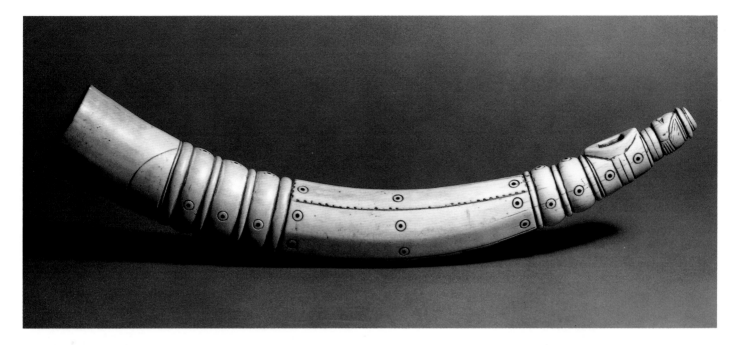

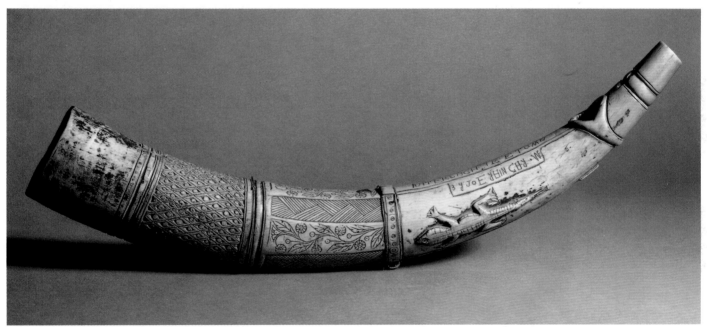

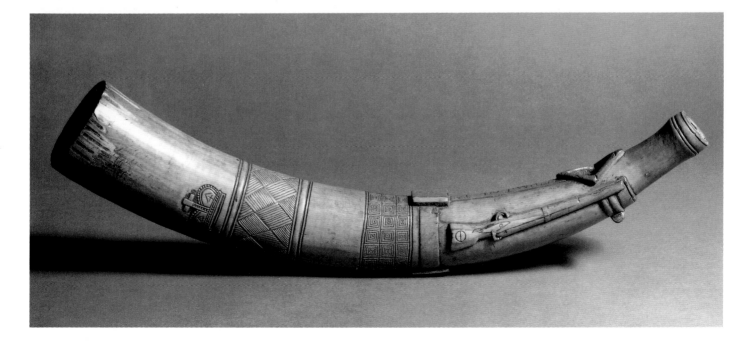

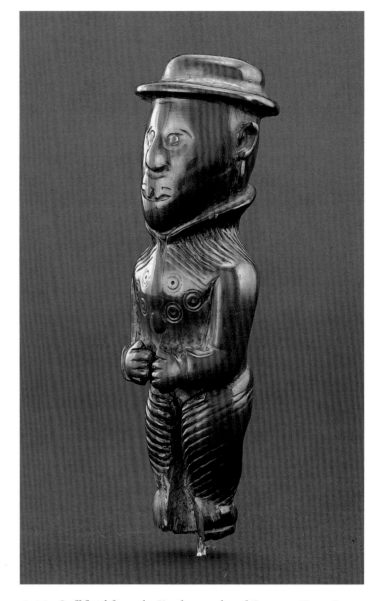

1-43. Staff finial from the Yombe peoples of Congo or Zaire. Ivory. Height 16.5 cm. National Museum of African Art, Smithsonian Institution. Museum purchase, 85-15-4. Photograph, Jeffrey Ploskonka.

1-42 A,B (DETAIL, RIGHT). Ivory scepter from the Kongo peoples of Zaire. Ivory. Height 38.7 cm. The Paul and Ruth Tishman Collection of African Art, the Walt Disney Company. Photograph, Richard Todd.

1-44. Staff finial, Owo-Portuguese from southwest Nigeria. Ivory. Height 17.8 cm. Collection of Jay Haft. Photograph, Ken Cohen.

1-45. Staff finial from the Akye peoples of the Côte d'Ivoire. Height 12.7 cm. The Paul and Ruth Tishman Collection of African Art, the Walt Disney Company.

ivory-handled flywhisks (e.g., Chapter 13). A recurring motif on a Kongo ivory sceptor (Fig. 1-42) depicts an elephant with a bird on its back, a reference to a Kongo myth "in which the elephant is said to have carried the sons of the great father, Ne Kongo, across rivers when they dispersed within Kongoland" (Volavka 1981:206).

Ivory staff or cane finials representing men in European dress – nineteenth century or earlier – are known from several areas of Africa (Figs. 1-43 to 1-45). Some clearly represent Africans and some, Europeans; others are more difficult to distinguish. Undoubtedly they represent elite members of societies on or near the coast. While we cannot rule out the possibility that some represent local rulers, it also seems likely that certain figures represent a growing merchant class. Indeed

some may have even been ivory traders. The possession of ivory coupled with the depiction of European dress certainly suggests affluence.

Ivory is a highly favored item of body adornment in many African societies. Hair, ears, lips, arms, wrists, fingers, necks, legs, and ankles may variously receive ivory ornaments of differing sizes and shapes (Interleaf IV, XVI), depending on the culture. Ivory may also adorn clothing like the famous belt masks from Benin, the ram's heads discussed by Drewal (Chapter 9), or the not-so-modest buttons from the Ovahimba of Namibia.

Ivory armlets and leglets are probably the single most common genre of ivory object used in Africa (Interleaf IV). They range from simple, unadorned rings of ivory to the

1-46. Kasena woman from northern Ghana wearing a large ivory on her upper arm. Photograph, Angela Fisher, early 1980s.

massive foot-long cylinders worn by women in the Igbo elephant society discussed by Cole in Chapter 10. The most virtuosic examples are the openwork double-cylinder wristlets with complex iconography discussed by Blackmun and Drewal. Other areas feature highly sculptured abstract shapes (Figs. 1-49, 1-50) or examples with incised decoration. In northern Ghana, lateral sections of the tusk are even pierced to form an armlet (Fig. 1-46). In most of these societies the ornaments convey status and wealth.

Ivory necklaces and pendants cover an equally wide array of forms from large, rough-hewn, four-inch ivory beads to the elegant human heads worn by the Pende of Zaire (Interleaf XVI). Figurative pendants are relatively common among several Zairean groups including the Chokwe, Pende, and Hungana (Fig. 1-47). Some pendants serve additional functions, doubling, for example, as whistles (Figs. 1-48, 1-51), knife sheaths (Fig. 1-52), or snuff containers (Fig. 1-53), and thereby adding social or ritual dimensions to their ornamental roles. The Rendille and a few other East African groups even use ivory pendants around the necks of animals (Interleaf XVI).

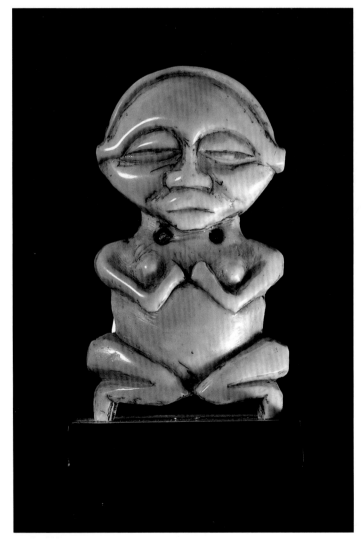

1-47. Pendant from the Hungana peoples of Zaire. Ivory. Height 4.5 cm. U. and W. Horstmann Collection, Zug, Switzerland.

1-48. Whistle/pendant from the Pende peoples of Zaire. Ivory. Height 10.6 cm. Collection of Mr. and Mrs. William W. Brill.

1-49. Armlet from the Chaga peoples of Kenya. Ivory. Diameter 15.3 cm. Collected by Dr. W. L. Abbott. National Museum of Natural History, Smithsonian Institution. Cat. No. 151,554.

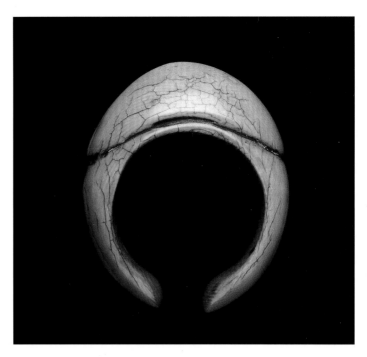

1-50. Bracelet from the Bamum (?) peoples of Cameroon. Ivory. Height 8.5 cm. U. and W. Horstmann Collection, Zug, Switzerland.

1-51. Whistle/pendant from the Chokwe peoples of Angola and Zaire. Ivory. Height 11.7 cm. Private collection.

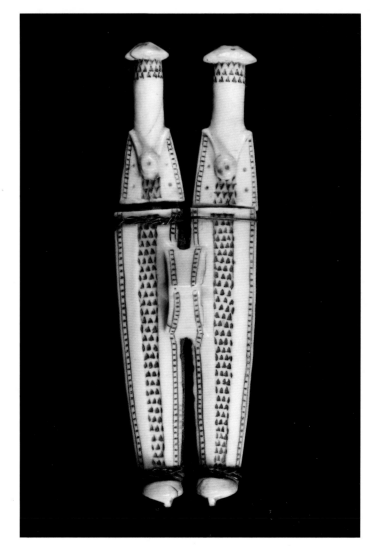

1-52. Two ivory-handled knives with ivory sheath from the Shona peoples of Zimbabwe. Ivory and steel. Height 11.4 cm. Collection of The Newark Museum, Gift of Miss Helen Dougherty, 1938.

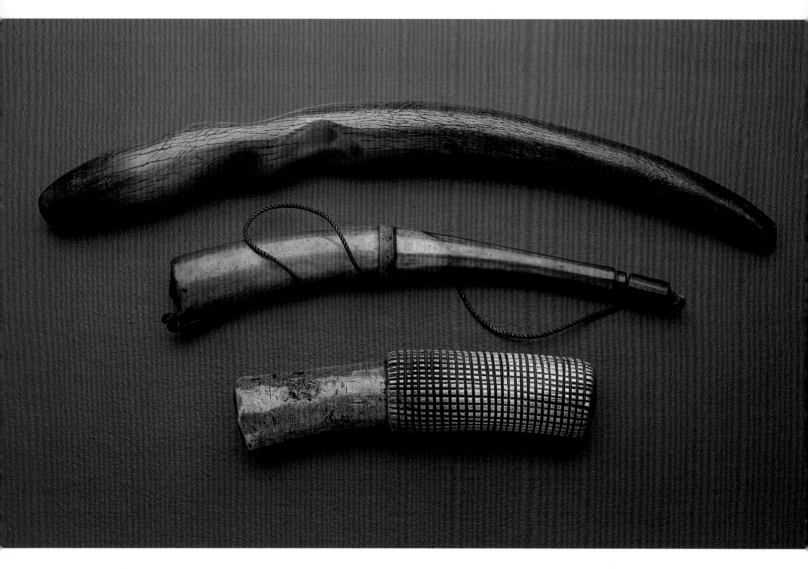

Given the hardness and durability of ivory, it is not surprising that it was often used for utensils and tools (Figs. 1-53 to 1-55). In central and eastern Zaire, ivory pestles were relatively common; and ivory barkcloth beaters, powder horns, and snuff containers have also been documented in some of the same areas. In others, ivory needles or awls were used for mending fishing nets or for working hide. Also mentioned in the literature are wedges made of ivory used in log splitting. While these relatively mundane, utilitarian uses of ivory probably do not involve any complex symbolism, it is likely that associations with the strength of the elephant were not lost on the users of these tools.

Carved Ivories for Export

Most of the *earliest* extant ivory carvings from sub-Saharan Africa were not made for African consumers. The so-called Afro-Portuguese ivories came from two centers of production — the Temne-Bullom of Sierra Leone and the Kingdom of Benin in Nigeria (Interleaf XIII). Dating primarily to the sixteenth century, they were produced in a limited number of object types generally alien to African cultures (Curnow 1983; Bassani and Fagg 1988). Saltcellars, end-blown hunting horns, forks, and spoons constitute most of the corpus (Figs. 1-56 to 1-60).

1-53. Ivory utensils. Top to bottom: Pestle from the Kuba-related peoples of Zaire. Length 60 cm. FMCH x90.373. Museum purchase with Manus funds. Powder horn, central Zaire. Length 42 cm. FMCH x65.9143A,B. Gift of the Wellcome Trust. Bark cloth pounder, Central Zaire. Length 28 cm. FMCH x65.8586. Gift of the Wellcome Trust.

1-54 (OPPOSITE). Snuff container from the Shona peoples of Zimbabwe. Ivory. Length 19 cm. U. and W. Horstmann Collection, Zug, Switzerland.

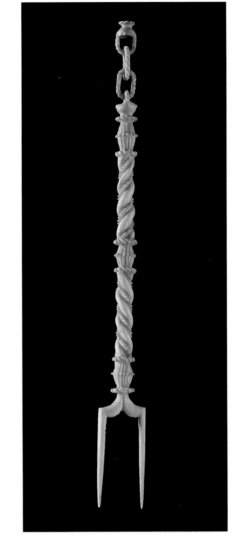

1-55. Spoon from the Nuna peoples of Burkina Faso. Ivory. Length 20 cm. U. and W. Horstmann Collection, Zug, Switzerland.

1-56. Fork from Temne-Bullom peoples of Sierra Leone. 15th or 16th century. Ivory. Length 14.4 cm. Museum für Völkerkunde, Vienna (Inv. Nr. 91908).

1-57. Spoon from Temne-Bullom peoples of Sierra Leone. 15th or 16th century. Ivory. Length 24 cm. Staatliches Museum für Völkerkunde, Munich (26 N 129).

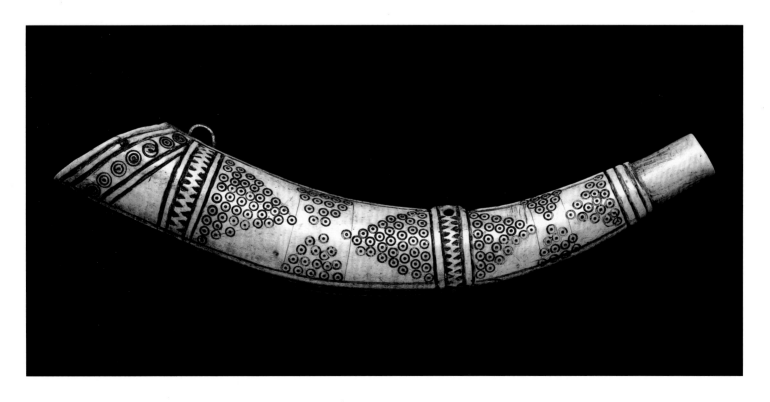

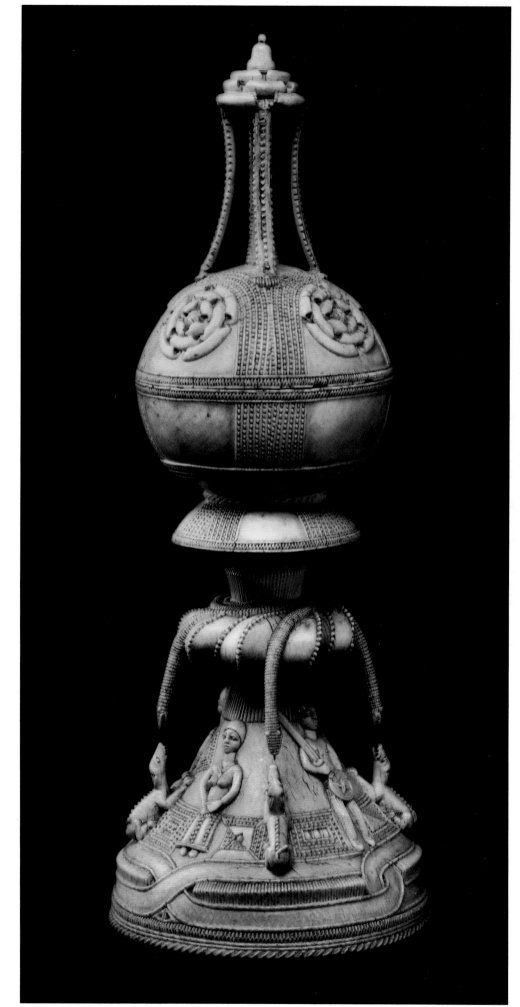

1-58. Saltcellar from Temne-Bullom peoples of Sierra Leone. 15th or 16th century. Ivory. Height 29.8 cm. Metropolitan Museum of Art, New York. Gift of Paul and Ruth Tishman. Photograph, Richard Todd.

1-59. Saltcellar from Temne-Bullom peoples of Sierra Leone. 15th or 16th century. Ivory. Height 30.4 cm. Seattle Art Museum, Gift of Katherine White, 81.17.189A,B. Photograph, Bryce P. Holcombe.

Portuguese soldiers and traders are common motifs on the saltcellars, as are Christian motifs – e.g. Europeans wearing crosses and, on one piece, angels (Fig. 6-4). One example features a sailing ship; another, mermaids (Interleaf XIV). The hunting horns usually display the Portuguese royal arms and on one example, the arms of Castile and Aragon are also represented (Fagg 1981:64-67). These ivories are frequently called Africa's first "tourist arts," but the designation trivializes the immaculate artistry characteristic of most examples.

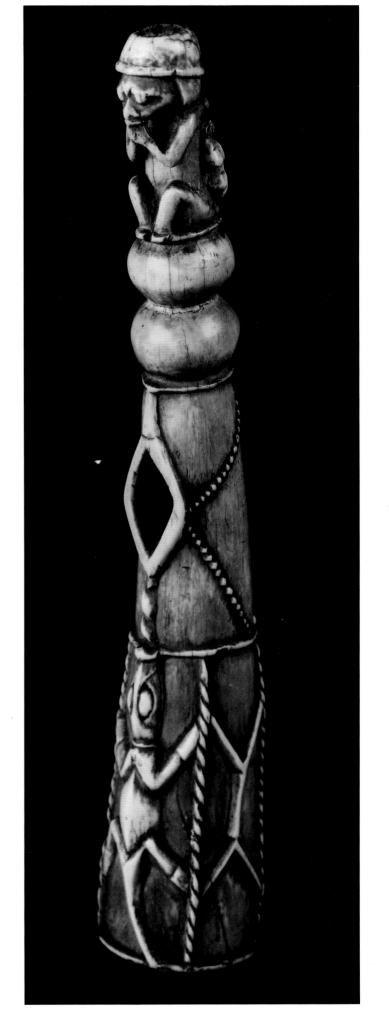

1-60. Side-blown trumpet from Temne-Bullom peoples of Sierra Leone, 15-16th century (?). Ivory. Length 32 cm. Collection of Ernst Anspach.

1-61. Carved ivory tusk from the Loango coast of Angola and Zaire, Kongo peoples. Ring on base reads: "Paymaster Geo., Kennedy U.S. Navy to Dudley Kavanagh 1863. Procured on West Coast of Africa in 1861." Height 34.3 cm (w/base). Gift of Edward I. Elisofon, 74-20-002. National Museum of African Art, Eliot Elisofon Photographic Archives, Smithsonian Institution. Photograph, Franko Khoury.

Post-dating the Afro-Portuguese ivories by three centuries, another major export tradition flourished on the Loango coast of Zaire and Angola from about 1830 to 1900 (Figs. 1-61 to 1-64 and Interleaf VII). These ivories, intended to be displayed vertically, are adorned with carvings in relief that climb the tusk in spirals from the bottom up. They feature commonplace scenes of contemporary life, especially commercial transactions between whites and blacks — for example, a line of porters carrying headloads of ivory for export or boxes of goods destined for the interior. Period dress is carefully detailed on both the Africans and the Europeans.

1-62. Carved ivory tusk from the Loango coast of Angola and Zaire, Kongo peoples. Length 99 cm. The Brooklyn Museum, A. Augustus Healy Fund (35.679).

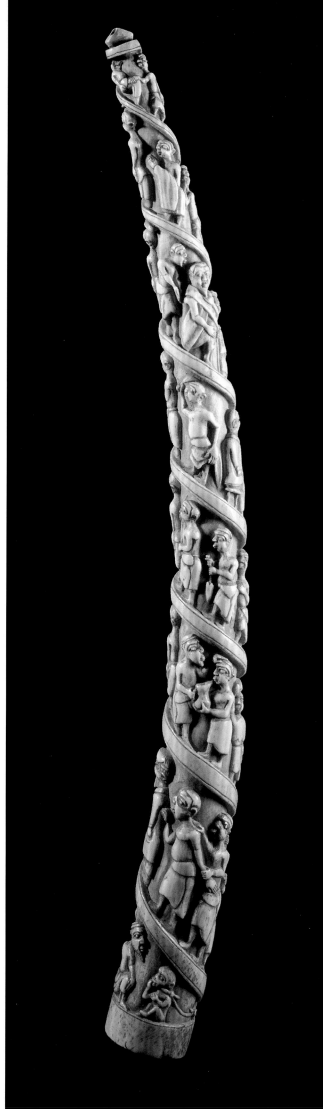

The Ivory Trade

More ivory was exported from the continent than was ever used by Africans themselves. This simple fact is critical to understanding the subsequent decimation of the elephant in the late nineteenth and twentieth centuries. The North African elephant was the earliest victim of ivory for export, as has already been mentioned. A thousand years later, beginning with the Age of Discovery, first the Portuguese and then other European powers began trading for ivory along the accessible parts of West, Central, and Southern Africa. They also sought gold and slaves. Within this highly competitive commercial atmosphere, it was prohibitive to pay porters to carry ivory from the interior. The standard practice was to use slaves that could also be sold upon reaching the coast.

The depletion of the elephant in West and Southern Africa was a relatively gradual process spread over about four hundred years. In East Africa the initial process of attrition was largely concentrated in the second half of the nineteenth century, when ivory and slave raiding reached their peak. A vigorous trade in both continued around the Indian Ocean long after slavery had been outlawed by European powers. Significantly, the price of the average tusk was about two or three times that of the average slave. The trade was thus driven in part by the quest for

1-63 (OPPOSITE, LEFT). Carved ivory tusk from the Loango coast of Angola and Zaire, Kongo peoples. Length 46 cm. FMCH X87.560. Gift of Peter Kuhn.

1-64 (OPPOSITE, RIGHT). Carved ivory tusk from the Loango coast of Angola and Zaire, Kongo peoples. Length 66 cm. Collection of Joseph and Barbara Goldenberg.

ivory and the slaves were a profitable by-product of the trade. Edward Alpers argues in Chapter 17 that the relationship of the ivory and slave trade was exaggerated by "propaganda" from the second half of the nineteenth century. It is clear, nevertheless, that as Zanzibari Arabs pushed firearms further to the interior, substantial violence was wrought on both people and animals. This was reported in quite inflammatory language by Livingstone, Stanley, Burton, and others. Several accounts relate that for every tusk brought to the coast, one human life was lost. Both A.J. Swann and David Livingstone recorded instances where a female slave with a child on her back and carrying a tusk on her head could not sustain the dual burden, whereupon the infant was killed by the traders so that the woman could continue to carry the ivory. In some areas whole villages were reported destroyed and their inhabitants enslaved. The decimation of both elephant and human populations in the nineteenth cen-tury set the stage for the European colonial presence in East Africa during the twentieth century.

The ivory trade is a leitmotif that runs throughout this volume. To a greater or lesser degree it is mentioned by virtually all the contributors, and its effects are reflected in myriad images illustrated here. The trade itself is the focus of Alpers's essay (Chapter 17), and its by-products — piano keys, billiard balls, chess pieces, etc. — are examined by David Shayt in Chapter 18. Elephant *in* Africa is the primary subject of this book. But ivory *out* of Africa is the foremost threat to that subject. The concluding chapter, therefore, surveys the current status of the African elephant — both the real creature and the imagined one.

NOTES

1. Qualifying this methodology, Douglas is careful to cite Goodman's (1972) "seven strictures against treating similarity as explanation" (1990:26) to avoid some of the pitfalls of her earlier work. I recommend other articles in Willis (1990) and indeed other volumes in this series ("One World Archaeology") for a variety of perspectives that relate to problems addressed by essays in the present anthology (see especially Ingold 1988; Hodder 1989; Davis and Reeves 1990).

2. Following the lead of Lewis-Williams and other contemporary scholars, San is used in lieu of the more widespread but pejorative "Bushmen" (Marshall 1981:v).

3. Significantly, women riding elephants appear with some frequency in African art; undoubtedly such images emphasize the roles they play as rulers, priestesses, and so forth.

4. There are numerous elephant masquerades not included in this volume. They appear, for example, among the Pende of Zaire (Gangambi 1974;

Munamuhega 1975), select Jukun-related groups of northeastern Nigeria (Rubin forthcoming), and the Kuyu of the Republic of Congo (Nicklin 1983:fig. 14; Kerchache, Paudrat, and Stéphan 1988:figs. 636,637). The elephant is also represented in the *Dodo* masquerades of Ouagadougou (Mongory 1980; Hinckley 1986).

5. Jos Museum records state that this mask was carved by Ogbudu and owned by Oba. Sieber (1961:20) says that this mask was carved by Oba of Otobi village. Kasfir (forthcoming) speculates that the mask was carved by Ochai.

6. I would like to thank Sidney Kasfir for allowing this data to be published in advance of the Berns and Rubin anthology, *Sculpture of the Benue River Valley.*

7. I would like to thank Barbara Blackmun for bringing this illustration to my attention.

8. I would like to thank Polly Nooter for bringing the Luba reference to my attention and for sharing her translations of Tervuren archival materials.

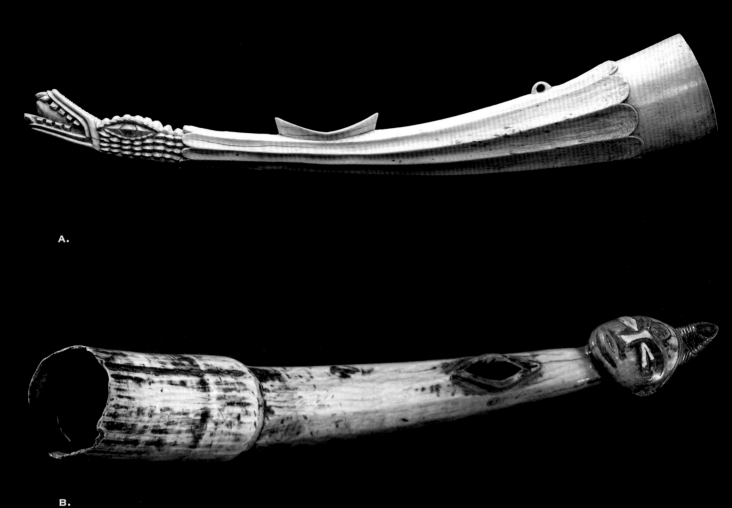

A.

B.

IVORY SIDE-BLOWN TRUMPETS have typically served the prerogatives of leadership. In many areas they were used to announce the arrival of the chief, sometimes actually replicating the local tonal language to "sing" his praises. Often they were used in a military context to encourage success in battle or to celebrate victory. Other documented contexts of use include weddings, funerals, investiture ceremonies, court dances, and royal circumcisions; initiation and judiciary society rituals; calls to work, announcements of visitation, and warning calls. In some areas they are also used for visual effect, as title insignia or as footrests.

A. 16th-century Afro-Portuguese side-blown trumpet with crocodile head. Length 57.15 cm. Collection of Drs. Daniel and Marian Malcolm.

B. Side-blown trumpet from the Ogoue River area of Gabon. Length 41.9 cm. The St. Louis Art Museum: Museum Purchase, 203:1942.

C. Side-blown trumpet (*kithenda*) from the People's Republic of the Congo (Vili peoples). Ivory and metal. Length 44.4 cm. The University of Iowa Museum of Art, The Stanley Collection, CMS 526.

D. Side-blown trumpet from Zaire (Pende peoples). Length 50.2 cm. The Brooklyn Museum, Gift of the Ernest Erickson Foundation, 86.244.145.

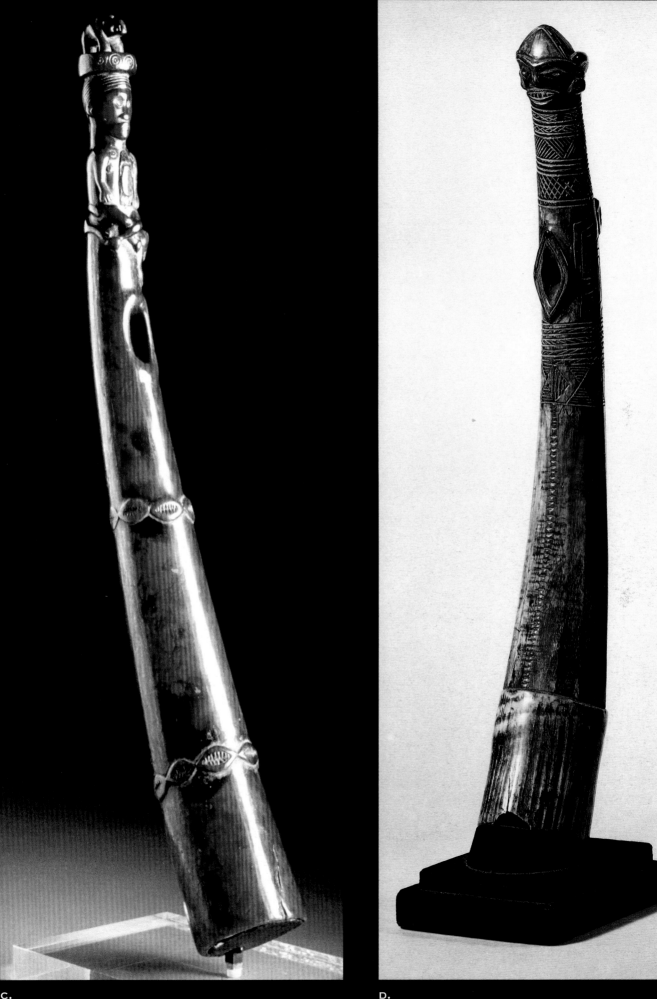

C.

D.

TWO

THE AFRICAN ELEPHANT AND ITS ENVIRONMENT

JEHESKEL SHOSHANI

Elephants are classified in the order Proboscidea, after their most distinguishing feature – the proboscis or trunk. Henry F. Osborn identified 352 proboscidean species and subspecies of which 350 were extinct (1936, 1942). Today, only about half of his species and subspecies are recognized as valid. The two living species, assigned to two distinct genera, are the Asian elephant, *Elephas maximus* (genus *Elephas*), and the African elephant, *Loxodonta africana* (genus *Loxodonta*), the latter consisting of two subspecies.[1] Some 60-50 million years ago, ancestors of the modern elephants are believed to have inhabited the shores of the ancient Tethys Sea (see Map, p. 66); they occupied extreme environments, from desert to tropical rain forest and from below sea level to high altitudes. With the exception of Antarctica and Australia, the proboscideans have, at some time, inhabited every continent on this planet.

The word "elephant" and the scientific name for the genus *Elephas* have possible origins in Greek, Latin, or a combination of the two. In Greek, *elaphos* means a stag or an antlered beast.[2] In Latin, *eboreus* or *ebur* means "ivory" or "of ivory" (Partridge 1963).[3] Alternatively, "elephant" may be derived from the Greek *ele*, meaning arch, and from the Latin *phant,* meaning huge; thus elephant would mean "huge arch." The genus name *Loxodonta* means "lozenge-shaped teeth" after the diamond pattern on the occlusal or chewing surfaces (Fig. 2-2). The species names *maximus* and *africana* are self-explanatory.

ANATOMY AND PHYSIOLOGY: AFRICAN AND ASIAN ELEPHANTS

There are a number of contrasts between the two living elephant species, African and Asian. African elephants are generally heavier and taller; a bull African may weigh seven metric tons (7,000 kg, or about 15,500 lb.) and can reach four meters, or over thirteen feet, in height. The most obvious difference is their ears: those of the African are larger. Tusks are usually present in the African elephant of either sex; in the Asian, tusks are confined mostly to the males. Their trunks differ, as well. The African's has more visible skin folds ("rings" or annulations), and at its tip there are two finger-like projections instead of one, as in the Asian. It appears to be slightly floppier than that of the Asian (Fig. 2-3). Anatomical differences are usually manifested in corresponding, observable behaviors. With a series of elegant observations, Racine (1980)

2-1 (OPPOSITE). Play behavior is seen most often in elephants under the age of ten. Photograph, Frans Lanting, Minden Pictures.

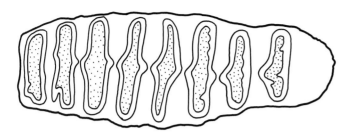

2-2. Lozenge-shaped teeth, characteristic of African elephants, define the species: *loxo* = lozenge, *dont* = tooth. Drawing, Jill Ball.

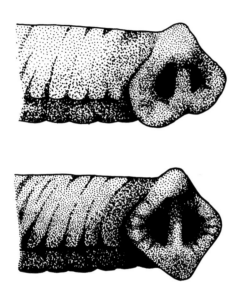

2-3. Finger-like projections at the trunk's tip aid in dexterity. The Asian elephant's trunk has one; the African's has two. Drawing, Jill Ball, after Racine (1980:58).

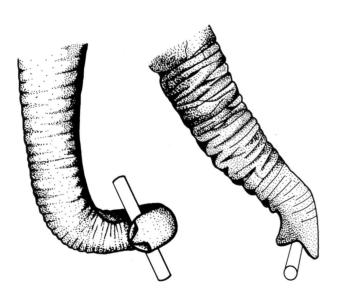

2-4. The Asian elephant tends to 'grasp' objects, the African to 'pinch' them. Drawing, Jill Ball, somewhat after Racine (1980:60).

demonstrated how captive African elephants would pick up objects with their trunks using a "pinch" method, while the Asians relied mostly on the "grasp" (Fig. 2-4).

Some of the major differences between the African and Asian species can be observed in their skeletons, the shape of the skull and the back. In profile, the back of the African elephant is concave, while that of the Asian is convex. In both species, the vertebral column between the fore and hind limbs is convex, and only the outline of the tips of the spinous processes are visibly different. In a side view of both species, one notes that the legs are in an almost vertical position under the body, similar to the legs of a table. This arrangement provides a strong support for the vertebral column, thoracic and abdominal contents, and, of course, the great weight of the animal. By contrast, in other mammals – dogs or cats, for instance – the legs are in an angular position.

Differences between the African subspecies, the Bush African elephant *(Loxodonta africana africana)* and the Forest African elephant *(Loxodonta africana cyclotis),* include these features: *L. a. cyclotis* occupies a habitat with generally more canopy forest than that of *L. a. africana*; its ears are shorter and more rounded (hence *cyclotis,* meaning "round ear"); and its tusks are straighter and thinner than those of the Bush elephant. There are other less obvious and apparently inconsistent differences as well. For example, *cyclotis* is said to have darker skin, more hair especially on the trunk and around the mouth, and more toenails (5 in the forefoot and 4-5 in the rear foot versus 4-5 and 3-5) than *africana*. The so-called pygmy elephants attracted much attention for centuries[4]; it is possible, however, that all the "pygmy" and/or "water" elephants were varieties of the Forest and/or the Bush African elephant subspecies (Morrison-Scott 1947; Laursen and Bekoff 1978; Western 1986).

The similarities and differences between the two living African and the Asian species become clearer when one examines the entire "Elephant Family Tree" (Fig. 2-5), not just two of its twigs. This wholistic approach provides us not only with empirical comparisons, but also with a data-base for determining which of the two living species is more primitive (generalist) or derived (specialist) than the other, a statement which cannot be made when comparing the two species alone. This distinction, as it applies to African and Asian elephants, is the foundation for our understanding of the differences in elephant anatomy, behavior, and ecology.

Scientists believe that 60-50 million years ago, pig-sized mammals comprised the basic stock from which elephant-like creatures, proboscideans, evolved. Based on morphological and biochemical evidence, the prevailing consensus among students of mammalian evolution is that manatees and dugongs (dolphin-sized and strictly aquatic – order Sirenia) and hyraxes or conies (rabbit-sized, terrestrial – order Hyracoidea) are the present-day relatives of elephants, even though all three orders have sharply contrasting external appearances and occupy extremely different habitats (Romer 1966; Shoshani 1986;

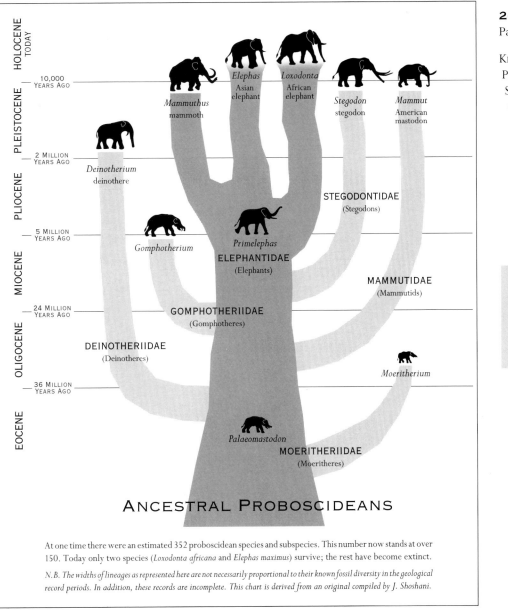

2-5. The Elephant Family Tree (left) with Partial Classification of Proboscidea (below).

KINGDOM: Animalia
PHYLUM: Chordata
SUBPHYLUM: Vertebrata
CLASS: Mammalia
ORDER: Proboscidea

FAMILY: *Mammutidae*
  GENUS: *Mammut*
    SPECIES: *Mammut americanum*
    (American mastodon)

*FAMILY: Elephantidae

  *GENUS & SPECIES: *Loxodonta africana*
  (African elephant)
    *SUBSPECIES: *Loxodonta africana africana*
    (Bush or Savannah African elephant)
    *SUBSPECIES: *Loxodonta africana cyclotis*
    (Forest African elephant)

  *GENUS & SPECIES: *Elephas maximus*
  (Asian elephant)
    *SUBSPECIES: *Elephas maximus maximus*
    (Sri Lankan elephant)
    *SUBSPECIES: *Elephas maximus indicus*
    (Indian or mainland Asian elephant)
    *SUBSPECIES: *Elephas maximus sumatranus*
    (Sumatran elephant)

  GENUS & SPECIES: *Mammuthus primigenius*
  (Woolly mammoth)
    SPECIES: *Mammuthus imperator*
    (Imperial mammoth)

*Not yet extinct.

At one time there were an estimated 352 proboscidean species and subspecies. This number now stands at over 150. Today only two species (*Loxodonta africana* and *Elephas maximus*) survive; the rest have become extinct.

N.B. The widths of lineages as represented here are not necessarily proportional to their known fossil diversity in the geological record periods. In addition, these records are incomplete. This chart is derived from an original compiled by J. Shoshani.

Novacek and Wyss 1986). Fischer (1989), however, noted that hyraxes are related to horses, tapirs, and rhinoceroses (order Perissodactyla).

Looking at the evolutionary tree of the Proboscidea, one may note that the family branch called Mammutidae, which includes the American mastodon (*Mammut americanum*), reaches a dead end; thus, mastodons were not the predecessors of the family Elephantidae. The partial classification of the Proboscidea seen in Figure 2-5 illustrates that elephants of both genera (*Elephas* and *Loxodonta*) have been placed within the family Elephantidae,[5] whereas mastodons (genus *Mammut*) are in the family Mammutidae; their placement highlights the difference between them. This chart also shows that mammoths (genus *Mammuthus*) were more closely related to the living Asian elephants (genus *Elephas*) than to the living African elephants (genus *Loxodonta*).[6]

It is generally accepted that among the four proboscidean taxa mentioned above, in terms of evolutionary developments, *Mammut* is the least specialized, or most primitive, followed successively by *Loxodonta*, *Elephas*, and *Mammuthus*; the last being the most specialized (Maglio 1973; Coppens et al. 1978; Tassy and Shoshani 1988). Why, then, are *Loxodonta africana* and *Elephas maximus* the only two to survive out of the 352 proboscideans identified? One possible explanation involves the inability of a lineage (one genus or species) to adapt to environmental changes fast enough to avoid catastrophes. Both *Loxodonta* and *Elephas* exhibit mosaic attributes that enable them to adapt to widely varied environmental conditions, ranging from mild to extreme. This adaptability was apparently not as successful in the dead-end proboscideans.[7] In terms of the evolutionary advantage of a species, the generalized features are probably more significant for survival than the specialized ones. One must keep in mind that each of the four genera mentioned above is to be treated independently. For example, *Mammut*, although least specialized when compared to the other three genera, may have been subjected to a combination of factors such as climatic change, competition for food by other large herbivores, and targeting by Paleoindian hunters.

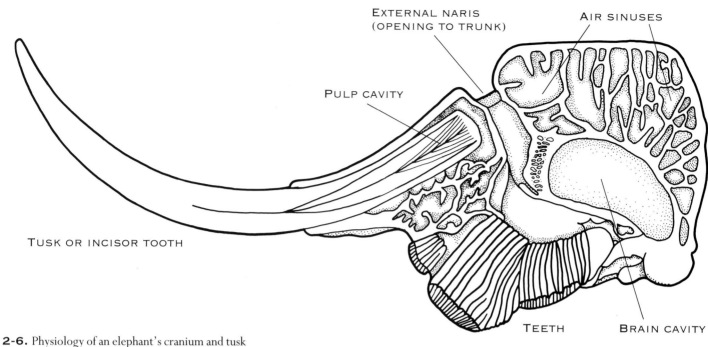

EXTERNAL NARIS
(OPENING TO TRUNK)

AIR SINUSES

PULP CAVITY

TUSK OR INCISOR TOOTH

TEETH

BRAIN CAVITY

2-6. Physiology of an elephant's cranium and tusk as revealed in cross section. Drawing, Jill Ball.

SPECIALIZED FEATURES: THE TRUNK, TUSKS, AND MUSTH GLANDS

The attributes peculiar to proboscideans, and those we first associate with them, are found mainly in the head and include the trunk, teeth, and temporal glands. The trunk, or *proboscis* (of Greek origin, meaning "before the mouth"), is the single most important feature of an elephant and its most indispensable tool. Functions attributed to the trunk include feeding, watering, dusting, smelling, touching, producing sounds, communicating, and lifting. It can also serve as a weapon of defense and offense.

Anatomically, the trunk is a union of the nose and the upper lip. Photographs of elephant fetuses (Fischer and Trautmann 1987) show how the upper lip and elongated embryonic nose combine to form the adult proboscis. Cartilage found at the base of the trunk helps divide the nostrils near the single external bone opening on the cranium. The nostrils continue as separate openings from the base of the trunk to its tip, and each is lined with a membrane; the septum is composed of tiny muscle fasciculi, actual muscles stretched horizontally between the nostrils. The trunk itself has no bones or cartilage; it is composed of muscles, blood and lymph vessels, nerves, some fat, connective tissues, skin, and hair and bristles. Its dexterity and its ability to perform various functions have probably contributed to humankind's fascination with elephants.

Artists and writers from the sixteenth to nineteenth centuries ascribed special qualities to the elephant's trunk. Petri von Hartenfels (c. 1723), for example, depicted it as a series of spiral rings similar to the "horn of plenty." In the mid-ninteenth century, Harrison, contemplating the number of muscles in the trunk, ventured that some people "have attempted to count these muscles, but such an attempt is totally useless" (1847:394). Nevertheless, the famous French anatomist Cuvier (1849) and his colleagues examined the trunk of an elephant and estimated the number of muscles to be about 40,000. Not much later, Nott was inspired to write this appreciation (1886:256):

> This trunk is composed of a mass of interlacing muscles, marvellously arranged, numbering, Cuvier estimates, nearly forty thousand. Some running longitudinally and others radiating from the center to the circumference, all so beautifully combined and adjusted to give it flexibility and strength, enabling it to be expanded or contracted, or wielded with that diversity of motion, and used in these manifold ways that must excite amazement when first seen, and from time immemorial have made the elephant's trunk an object of wonder and admiration. Some have described it as 'the elephant's hand,' others as 'the snake hand.'

Preliminary results of our own recent investigation show that there are eight pairs of muscles, four of which contain about 150,000 units, or muscle fasciculi, making the trunk precisely dextrous (Shoshani et al. 1990). The finger-like projections at the tip of the trunk are fleshy, mobile, and extremely sensitive. The projection on the dorsal side is a continuation of the *Maxillo-labialis (Levator proboscidis)* muscle which arises from the frontal bone and stretches through the entire length of the trunk to its tip. The ventral projection is a continuation of the

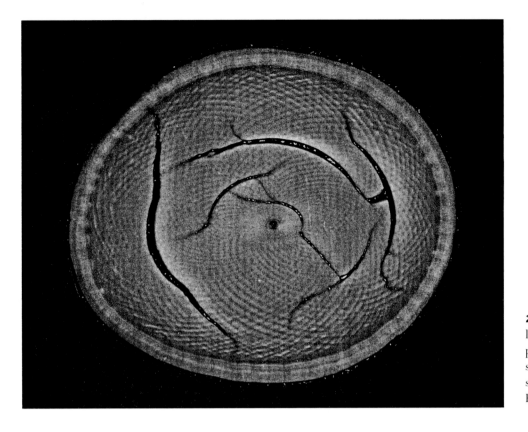

2-7. Elephant ivory is extremely hard and lasting, yet highly carvable. This is due in part to the phenomenon of "engine turning," shown here in cross section as diamond-shaped patterns. Width approximately 15 cm. Photograph, Jeheskel Shoshani.

Pars rimana muscle. The extraordinary flexibility of the elephant's trunk, as seen in the wild and in captivity, corroborates the underlying complexity of the anatomy and physiology enabling the animal to conduct such a variety of functions and antics.

The tusks are highly specialized teeth – incisors to be precise (Fig. 2-6). African and Asian elephants both have the same number of teeth in the course of a lifetime, a total of twenty-eight, including two upper milk incisors (tusks), two permanent tusks, no canines, twelve deciduous premolars, and twelve molars. Cheek teeth (molars and premolars) are not replaced vertically with a new tooth developing and replacing the old one from above or below, as in other mammals. Rather, elephant teeth are replaced in a horizontal progression. A newborn elephant has two or three cheek teeth in one jaw quadrant and as it grows, new teeth develop from behind and slowly move forward. Simultaneously, the previous teeth progress forward, are worn away, and fragment. Pieces of teeth can be found in the field or enclosure, or in the feces if the elephant has swallowed the teeth. As in a very slow conveyor belt system, new and bigger teeth replace the old ones a total of six times in an elephant's life.

In living elephants, milk (deciduous) incisors or tusks are replaced by permanent second incisors within six to twelve months after birth (Deraniyagala 1955). Permanent tusks grow continuously at the rate of 17 cm (6.8 in.) per year (Colyer and Miles 1957) and are composed mostly of dentin. In cross section, a tusk exhibits a pattern of lines that intersect each other to form small diamond-shaped areas visible with the naked eye (Sikes 1971) (Fig. 2-7). This pattern has been called "engine turning" and is unique to Proboscidea. The tusks of pigs, hippopotami, and walruses are pairs of canine teeth; the

single tusk of the narwhal is an incisor. Although all these tusks are termed "ivory" in common parlance, none exhibits "engine turning." Therefore, strictly speaking, the term ivory should be applied only to elephant tusks.

Ivory carvers are familiar with this unique "engine turning" and other unusual properties of their material. In mineralogical terms, tusks are relatively soft — equivalent in hardness to calcite minerals. It has been noted that hardness and, therefore, carvability of ivory differs according to country of origin, habitat, and sexual dimorphism. For example, the ivory from western and central Africa, where *Loxodonta a. cyclotis* is more prevalent, is considered the best of all ivories because it is the hardest yet very elastic, and thus more suitable for carving than that of the Bush African (*Loxodonta a. africana*) or the Asian (*Elephas maximus*). Some also claim that a cow's ivory is better than that of a bull as it has a closer grain (Sikes 1971:15,323; Eltringham 1982:206; Carrington 1958:163). It is possible ivory carvers developed a "feel" for the ivory of female *L. a. africana* and therefore prefer it over that of *L. a. cyclotis* and *Elephas maximus*.

Anatomically, ivory is a non-cellular matrix, secreted by the odontoblasts located in the pulp cavity but reaching into the body of the tooth via microscopic tubes called *dentinal tubules* or *canaliculi*; the secretion constitutes the biological substance called dentin.[8] Early in development, the tusk bears a conical cap of smooth enamel which wears off at a later stage. Like all mammalian teeth, elephant incisors have pulp cavities containing highly vascularized tissues innervated by fine nerve branches; tusks are thus sensitive to external pressure. On average, three-quarters to two-thirds of a tusk is visible externally; the rest is embedded in the socket or alveolus within

2-8. *Loxodonta africana* eats a variety of trees, including thorn trees (genus *Acacia*) and baobabs (genus *Adansonia*). Here elephants are debarking trees in East Africa. Photograph, Frans Lanting, Minden Pictures.

the cranium. Although two tusks are the norm, three, four, five and even seven tusks have been observed (Carrington 1958; Murray 1976). Supernumerary tusks may result from abnormal bifurcation to the permanent tusks (e.g., due to a bullet, a spear, or a splinter) during calfhood.

Annual growth rings on tusks resemble those seen on the external surfaces of other animal's horns – sheep, for example – but differ from annual growth rings on trees. The cross section of a tusk exhibits not only the "engine turning" criss-cross lines mentioned above, but also concentric circles. These are the edges of multiple cone-shaped structures whose annual growth layers were visible on the external surface of the tusk at one time during tusk development (Simpson 1942). Microscopic examinations of tusks show not only annual but also a regular seasonal growth pattern (Fisher 1987). Once removed from an elephant's body, however, ivory soon dries and begins to split along the concentric circles. Hot, humid conditions will also cause deterioration. To retain its original beauty and quality, it is best kept in a cool, moist environment.

Tusks are indispensable instruments. Elephants may use their tusks for a variety of purposes: to dig for water, salt, and roots; to debark trees (Fig. 2-8); as levers for maneuvering felled trees and branches; for work (in domestic animals); for marking trees; as weapons of defense and offense; as trunk-rests; as protection for the trunk (comparable to a bumper on a car); and even for display, possibly as status symbols. It has

been said that old elephants which have longer and larger tusks, such as Ahmed (Fig. 2-9), the famous elephant from Marsabit, Kenya, command greater respect and have more personal bodyguards than those with shorter tusks.

Just as humans are left- or right-handed, so elephants are left- or right-tusked. The tusk used most often is called the master tusk. Master tusks can easily be distinguished since they are shorter and more rounded at the tip due to wear. In addition, they usually have grooves near their tips, where the constant action of the trunk pressing grass against the tusk wears a transverse furrow in the ivory (Sikes 1971).

Bull elephants usually have longer and heavier tusks than cows. In the African elephant, both sexes may have tusks of equal length, but those of males are thicker. The longest recorded tusks of an African elephant measured 326.4 cm (10 ft. and 8.5 in.), and the heaviest weighed 102.7 kg. (226.5 lb.).[9] Ahmed had tusks measuring just under three meters, or about three yards, and weighing 67 kg, or about 150 lb. (Shoshani et al. 1987). Recent data indicates that the average tusk weight for the African elephant has decreased at an alarming rate, a direct result of poaching. Data from Parker and Amin (1983:152), Buss (1990:4-5), and Western (1991:88) indicate that the average tusk weight for certain elephant populations dropped during the last sixty years by about five-fold, from fourteen kg in the 1930s to ten kg in the 1960s and three kg in the late 1980s.[10]

2-9. Ian Redmond poses with Ahmed, the legendary long-tusked Kenyan elephant, looking rather stuffy. Photograph, Jeheskel Shoshani.

Musth, almost a household word among elephant handlers in the Far East, means "intoxicated" in Hindi. It is a puzzling phenomenon of periodic physiological and behavioral changes, associated with secretion from the subcutaneous musth glands, also known as the temporal glands because of their location midway between the eye and the ear on each side of the elephant's head. A web of intricate blood vessels, more evident in the male than the female, is present between these glands and the deep muscles of the head.[11]

While musth occurs in both Asian[12] and African elephants (Poole and Moss 1981), it is perhaps more marked among the former, where it occurs only in adult males, than among the latter, where it occurs in both sexes.[13] Nevertheless, the behavior of African musth elephants is also remarkable. Male elephants in musth are known to be especially difficult to control and may attack and kill their keepers.

The exact function of the musth glands is not known. They might be associated with sexual activity and/or communication. Musth is not exactly the same as rut, however, and does not always imply mating drive. Deer stags in rut have a heightened mating drive and female deer are receptive. Most males in a herd of deer exhibit simultaneous rutting behavior, called *flehmen*: they raise their heads, sniff, open their mouths to evaluate the female's urine and her readiness to mate, and are generally aggressive. Among elephant populations it appears that this is not always the case: males may or

may not exhibit rutting behavior, and females may or may not be receptive. Wild African musth males in Amboseli National Park, Kenya, however, have been observed walking with their heads high, exhibiting *flehmen*-like behavior, and mating during this period (Moss 1988).[14] The exact nature of musth remains a mystery.

OTHER BODY ORGANS AND THEIR FUNCTIONS

Generally speaking, the elephant's eyesight is poor, except in dim light, hearing is excellent, smell is acute, touch is very good, and taste seems to be selective; acuteness of the senses of elephants appears to change with age. The old name of the order Proboscidea, "Pachydermata," refers to elephants' thick skin (Fig. 2-11). Despite its thickness, it is a sensitive organ system due to the sparse hair and bristles distributed unevenly on the body; these in turn are in contact with nerve endings. Most noticeable hair concentrations are around the eyes, ear openings, chin, genitalia, and the end of the tail. Young elephants are covered with brownish-red hair, especially noticeable on the back and head profile. The amount of hair decreases with age; its color also darkens. The bodies of both African and Asian elephants are gray; but African elephants often appear brown or even reddish, a condition that results from wallowing in mudholes of colored soil, which gets plastered on their skins.

Generally speaking, ear size, like tail size, is directly related to the amount of heat dissipated through them. On a global scale, those species that live close to the equator have, on the average, bigger ears and tails than those species of about the same body sizes which live closer to the poles (Smith 1974). The differences in the sizes of ears among *Loxodonta africana, Elephas maximus,* and *Mammuthus primigenius* can be explained based on their geographical distribution: *Loxodonta,* being closest to the equator, has the largest ears, and the extinct *Mammuthus,* which lived closest to the north pole, had the smallest. Poole suggests that bull elephants in the wild also use their ears to spread the odor released from their temporal glands during the period of musth. The smell informs other males and possibly females of their presence (Moss 1988:113).

But the ears also serve, of course, to receive sound, and large ears trap more sound waves than smaller ones. The "secret" language of elephants has been demonstrated recently by K.B. Payne and her colleagues. This infrasonic communication, a vocalization not audible to the human ear, appears to carry long distances. Elephants at a distance of 1.6 to 2.4 km (1-1.5 mi.) from the source of the voice seem to recognize signals emitted by other elephants and respond accordingly. Males, for example, move in the direction of a sound produced by a female in estrus (ovulation); other elephants at different locations seem to synchronize their behavior and appear to respond to stress signals (Payne 1989; Payne et al. 1986; Poole et al. 1988).

2-11. An elephant's skin may be as thick as 2.5 cm along the back and in some places on the head. Photograph, Bruce Davidson, Animals, Animals.

The brain of an adult elephant weighs 4.5-5.5 kg, or about 10-12 lb. Its cerebrum (controlling motor coordination) and its cerebellum (controlling muscle coordination) are highly convoluted. The temporal lobes, known to function as memory centers in humans, are relatively large in elephants. Elephants have good memories; they can be taught to recognize 60-100 spoken words or phrases. Under certain experimental conditions elephants are said to perform better than horses.

The heart of an elephant, in absolute terms, is huge and very heavy: it weighs 12-21 kg, or about 26-46 lb. In relative terms, however, that is only about 0.5% of the elephant's total body weight. Compared to other mammalian hearts, its shape, with its double-pointed (bifid) apex, is atypical.

An elephant's digestive system is of the simple type among mammals. The combined length of the small and large intestines may reach 35 meters (about 100 ft.). It takes an elephant about 24 hours to digest a meal. The animals digest only about 44% of their food intake; the rest is excreted undigested. The reason for this is not entirely clear, but it may be related to several factors: the simplicity of the stomach, which is non-

ruminant; the low metabolic rate; the small surface area of skin relative to body size (elephants lose less heat per body volume than do small mammals); and, finally, coevolution with the type of plants they eat.

The elements of the male reproductive system are typical of those found in other mammals. Unlike many mammals, however, the elephant's testes are permanently located inside the body, near the kidneys. The penis, in a fully grown male, is long and muscular (controlled by voluntary muscles, *Levator penis*). Its length can reach 100 cm (over 3 ft.) and its diameter is 16 cm (over 6 in.) at the base. When fully erect, it assumes an S-shape with the tip pointing upwards; its orifice is Y-shaped.

The female reproductive system is also typical of most mammals. The cervix, however, may not be a distinct structure. The clitoris is a well developed organ; it can reach 40 cm long and it is manipulated by the *Levator clitoris* muscle. The urogenital canal is very long (about 70-90 cm), and the vulval opening is located between the female's hind legs, not under the tail as, for example, in bovines and equines. Its unusual position, being similar to the male's, has confused many elephant handlers.

Female mammary glands are located between the forelegs, a condition which enables the mother to be in touch with her calf while it nurses. When not pregnant or nursing, the mammary glands are shrunk and the nipples are shriveled and pointing downwards. During the later stages of pregnancy, the glands swell and the nipples distend diagonally downwards and sideways, enabling the newborn to reach them easily. Each nipple may have 10-12 lactiferous ducts.

2-10 (PREVIOUS PAGES). Wallowing in mud protects elephants from ultraviolet radiation, insect bites, and moisture loss. Photograph, Anthony Bannister, Animals, Animals.

2-12. Elephants reach sexual maturity between the ages of eight and thirteen. Adult females are in estrus and receptive to mating approximately every 16 weeks. The bull pursues the female until she is ready; after a brief interval of trunk and body contact he mounts her, and copulation – lasting only about a minute – takes place. Photograph, Don McClelland.

REPRODUCTION, CHILDBEARING, AND SOCIALIZATION

Elephants do not confine mating to any specific time of the year, except when severe environmental conditions – namely, drought – cause them to defer it.[15] Copulation may take place at any time of day; it is usually performed on land, but elephants have been observed to mate in water. The bull pursues the cow until she is ready, at which time a short interaction period of trunk and body contact may take place, followed by the act of mounting (Figure 2-12).[16]

The animals attain sexual maturity between the ages of eight and thirteen. The interval between estrous periods in non-pregnant females is about sixteen weeks, estrus lasts a few days, and the egg is viable only about twelve hours (Hess et al. 1983; Eisenberg et al. 1971). The gestation period may last eighteen to twenty-two months – the longest pregnancy of any known living mammal. The number of offspring per birth is usually one, rarely twins, and more rarely triplets (Douglas-Hamilton and Douglas-Hamilton 1975; Macfie 1916). In her lifetime, which may be sixty to seventy years, a female elephant has the potential of giving birth to about seven offspring.[17]

"The elephant, the slowest breeder of all animals, will in a few thousand years stock the whole world," wrote Darwin (1859:430). He was speaking of a hypothetical situation in which there are no natural disasters and all offspring survive. In actuality, field studies show that environmental conditions apparently play a role in the reproductive cycle of elephants (Hanks 1979; Laws et al. 1975). Like all animals,

elephants are exposed to natural selection, and their numbers, size, and strength are no match for disease, drought, and predation, especially when it comes to the young, the aged, and the sick.

Elephants are highly social mammals that rear their young in a matriarchal society of related individuals. The matriarch is the oldest and usually the most experienced female in the herd (Douglas-Hamilton and Douglas-Hamilton 1975; Moss 1988). During a drought, for example, the matriarch will often lead her family and relatives to the best possible foraging habitats. The rest of the herd, being in close relationships, learn and accumulate knowledge to be used when needed.

As in most mammalian societies, the most fascinating period in elephant family life is early childhood. Newborn elephants weigh 77-113 kg (170-250 lb.) and are 91 cm (3 ft.) tall at the shoulder, and they may consume 11.4 liters (2.5 gal.) of milk a day. Calves are tended not only by their mothers but also by other females in the herd. Young females in the immediate family of the newborn show the greatest interest and interact with the calf as much as they can. These tight kinship relations appear to be mutually beneficial to the newborn and the young mothers-to-be. Weaning is a very gradual process beginning during the first year of life and may continue until the seventh or sometimes the tenth year of the animal. Long infant dependency appears to be a mechanism for extended social contact and an imperative educational period. The capacity for learning appears to increase with age and this may be corroborated by anatomical observation that the brain of an elephant grows simultaneously. The brain

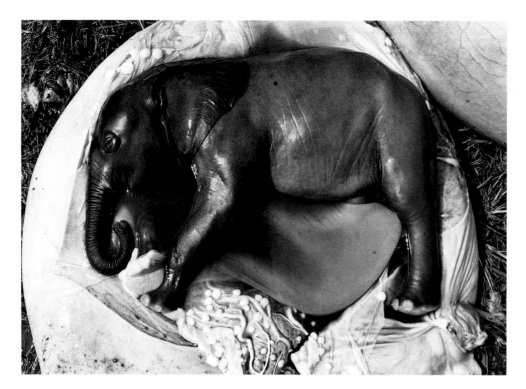

2-13 (LEFT). A nearly mature fetus. The gestation period in elephants lasts anywhere from 18 to 22 months. At birth, babies are fully developed, but their elephantine features can be seen clearly in fetuses of three months, which are the length of a man's index finger. Photograph, Peter Beard, Visions.

2-14 (OPPOSITE). Elephants are highly social mammals that rear their young in a matriarchal society. Young elephants are attended not only by their mothers but also by other females in the herd. Photograph, Anthony Bannister, Animals, Animals.

of a newborn elephant is about 30-40% of the size of that of an adult.

Infant dependency among elephants is intensified by the fact that the "baby" may weigh over 100 kg (220 lb.) and does not know what to do with its trunk. It may suck on it, bite it, swing it from side to side, and step on it, by accident, of course. It soon discovers that with its extra hand it can pick up food items and bring them to its mouth. Also, this hose-like extension is very useful to reach water on the ground, suck it up, and bring it to its mouth. Suckling from its mother's nipples is an instinctive phenomenon. Because the mother's breasts are between the front legs she can caress her calf and be in direct contact with it during the nursing period, a very important reassurance for both. The infant's dependence upon the mother continues for several years and it may continue to nurse until a sibling is born, in which case the mother may reject the older one if there is not sufficient milk to nurse both. Alternatively, a baby elephant may stop nursing when its tusks grow so long that they poke the mother's chest (Douglas-Hamilton and Douglas-Hamilton 1975; Laws 1970; Moss 1988; Moss 1990).

Maturity brings change most dramatically to the male youngster. While female offspring are likely to remain with their families until death, males leave the herd at maturity, about thirteen years of age. Sometimes they join other males to form bachelor herds. These adult bulls join cow herds when a female is in estrus. There is no evidence for territoriality; home range varies from 15 to 50 sq. km (approx. 6-20 sq. mi.) for females and from 500-1,500 sq. km (195-600 sq. mi.) for males, depending on the size of the herd and season of the year (Shoshani 1991:195).

The search for food and water sends elephants on long migrations. During the dry season, they gather in large concentrations near wetlands, where members of different families and herds intermingle. At the start of the rains, the elephants leave the damp basins where they have congregated and return to the savannahs and grasslands where they will pass most of the wet season. An aerial view would show long gray lines of animals moving outwards from the center in all directions. In earlier times, before migration routes were cut off by human settlement, a herd may have travelled 5-10,000 km (about 3-6,000 mi.) a year in the course of a cycle of seasonal migration. Even now, the huge elephants of Namibian desert trek 100 km or more a day through the barren landscape in search of nourishment.

THE DAILY LIFE OF ELEPHANTS

Elephants are crepuscular animals; that is, they are active mostly during early morning and twilight hours. When the sun is at its zenith and until early afternoon, elephants take their siestas. Feeding constitutes about eighty percent of total behavior and other activities such as bathing, playing, sleeping, and reproduction constitute the balance (Douglas-Hamilton and Douglas-Hamilton 1975; Eisenberg 1980:41; Moss 1988).

Eighteen to twenty hours a day are devoted to feeding or moving towards a food or water source. The elephant diet is strictly herbivorous; adults consume 75-150 kg (160-320 lb.) of food and 75-150 liters (20-40 gal.) of water per day. Broadly speaking, the African elephant feeds more on branches, twigs and leaves than the Asian elephant, which feeds on grassy materials.[18] A glance at a distribution map of elephants of either species confirms that both elephants and humans prefer areas with high rainfall suited for plant growth, thus both compete for the same resources. In many places, humans win,

but recently there has been a tendency to help elephants "recuperate" from the killing because they have proven valuable assets for tourism.

Wallowing appears to be an important activity in elephant daily life. As they wallow, elephants may be observed playing. Such behavior takes place mostly at a watering hole or by a river bank (Fig 2-10); there the elephant is cool and has just had a good drink, and the water provides buoyancy. Young males probably engage in such behavior more often than females, and eventually the "winners" may position themselves higher in the adult hierarchy than the "losers." Play between young and adult animals, and even between adults, has also been observed. In the course of wallowing, the young elephant may try to climb over a sister or mother, who is slippery. The young one may fall over, cover itself with mud, step on its trunk, and generally look silly but appealing.

Of course, elephants also sleep. My observations in a circus barn revealed that, like humans, elephants sleep in different positions, and that they snore heavily. To "sleep" while standing, the animals may partially close their eyes and let their trunks hang down, sometimes to the ground, in a behavior reminiscent of dozing. Elephant anatomy is such that the upper leg bones are positioned vertically above the lower leg bones; upper and lower legs almost seem to lock together, enabling them to remain standing in one position for long periods. They do not, however, sleep in the true sense of the term while standing up. Based on observations of field workers and elephant keepers, elephants lie down mostly during the latter part of the night, and sleep anywhere from one to four hours at a time. In the field, one may encounter elephant "beds" where the animals have lain down and flattened the grass. It has been said that if they can find them, elephants rest their heads on natural cushions, such as inactive termite mounds, bushes, or bunches of grass.

ELEPHANT INTELLIGENCE

Elephants are intelligent. They have been observed using a tree branch to scratch their backs and legs, places where their trunks and tails would not reach. This behavior has been interpreted as tool-using. On one occasion, an Asian elephant, tied so that he could not reach dry ground, was observed to break branches from a tree and place them under his feet which were sinking into mud. The branches supported him until his owner returned – so it was told.

Several anecdotes of elephant behavior suggest the degree of cognition and/or intelligence in elephants. The first, concerning elephants in Burma (Myanmar), is reported by J.H. Williams (1950:86):

Many young elephants develop the naughty habit of plugging up the wooden bell (kalouk) they wear hung

round their necks with good stodgy mud or clay, so that the clappers cannot ring, in order to steal silently into a grove of cultivated bananas at night. There they will have a whale of a time, quietly stuffing, eating not only the bunches of bananas, but the leaves and, indeed, the whole tree as well, and they will do this just beside the hut occupied by the owner of the grove, without waking him or any of his family.

Pillai (1941) tells of a large Indian bull elephant named Chandrasekharan that was pulling logs out of a truck and placing them into pre-dug holes. The elephant followed his master's commands until they reached a certain hole where it refused to lower the log. The mahout, upon investigating, found a dog sleeping at the bottom of the pit; only when the dog was chased away would the elephant lower the log into the hole. A third report comes from South Africa (Gordon 1966). An elephant was observed digging a hole and drinking water. Afterward he stripped bark from a nearby tree, chewed it into a large ball, plugged the hole, and covered it with sand. Later he removed the sand, unplugged the hole, and had water to drink. This story illustrates what might be interpreted as cognizance, and shows that the elephant probably can be viewed not only as

a tool-user but also as a tool-maker. I have witnessed two elephants using their trunks ingeniously, with the highest degree of muscle and neural coordination. A 25-year-old female Asian elephant, Miss Billie, owned by the Hawthorn Corporation, cracked peanuts with the back of her trunk, blowing the shells away and eating the kernels in one smooth motion. Belle, a female Asian at Metro Washington Park Zoo in Portland, Oregon, used her trunk in an equally clever way. She would tap the tip of her trunk against its side and produce the sound of someone knocking on a door; this regularly deceived her handlers, who would open the door and find no one there.

Elephants seem to exhibit several human-like attributes. They are known to use leaves and grass to bury elephants' ears and feet and to cover dead elephants and humans, and have been seen shattering tusks of dead elephants against trees or rocks. They are also capable of exhibiting sympathetic behavior towards other living creatures.

Sagacity is usually associated with a long life, and because it was thought that elephants could live hundred of years, it was also believed that they were extremely wise and experienced. The oldest recorded age in captivity is that of Jessie, an Asian elephant in Taronga Zoological Park, Sydney, Australia; her

2-15 (LEFT). Close bonding of families and herds has contributed to the survival of the elephant. Photograph, Frans Lanting, Minden Pictures.

2-16 (RIGHT). An elephant cools off in Addo Elephant National Park, South Africa. Photograph, Anthony Bannister, Animals, Animals .

estimated age was 69 or older (Patten 1940). According to unconfirmed reports, a Sri Lankan elephant named Raja, renowned for leading the annual Perahera procession from 1930 to 1988, died at the age of 62. Given the lack of accurate data it is more difficult to determine longevity in the wild.[19]

Elephants and humans have some of the longest lifespans among mammals (elephants over 70 years, humans over 90 years), and they also share many ecological similarities. Like humans, elephants have relatively unspecialized food requirements and survive in a wide range of habitats. Furthermore, they are able to modify their habitats. Like humans, they maintain a strong extended family system characterized by longterm attachments which enable a prolonged childhood associated with learning tool use and manufacture and deferred sexual maturity. As in human society, females experience a long post-reproductive phase (similar to human menopause) as well. The natural mortality pattern and birth interval of elephants is like that of humans (elephant mean calving intervals are 3-9 years). Their speed of movement is not unlike ours: the walking gait of an elephant is 6.5 km/hr. (4 mph), and a charge may be 48 km/hr. (30 mph). Even their diseases seem to parallel those of humans: elephants are prone to cardio-vascular diseases and arthritis (see Laws 1978),[20] and

may serve as models for treating those diseases, both of which are known to be age-dependent.

ELEPHANT: A SUPER-KEYSTONE SPECIES

Elephants play a pivotal role in their ecosystem. Foremost, they modify their habitats by converting savannah and woodlands to grasslands and thereby provide new macro- and micro-habitats for other species. The best example of this occurs on Mount Elgon, Kenya, where caves excavated by elephants are used by ungulates, hyraxes, monkeys, bats, birds, and other animals either to get salt or as shelters.[21] Elephants also provide water for other species by digging waterholes in dry riverbeds. The depressions made by their footprints and bodies trap rainfall, as do the enlargements they make in existing waterholes as they plaster mud on their bodies when bathing and wallowing. Their paths, which usually lead to waterholes, act as fire breaks and conduits for the rain water, and their journeys through high grass provide food for birds by disturbing insects and small reptiles or amphibians. Seeds (e.g., of acacia trees) are dispersed via their fecal material, which is carried below the ground by termites and dung

2-17. Elephants are fiercely protective of their young. This elephant mother, distraught by the approach of a safari truck, does her best to chase it away from the vicinity of her children. Photograph, Gregory Ahlijian.

beetles, thereby aerating the soil and distributing nutrients. Elephants also help protect other species as they are tall and can see and alert the smaller animals to approaching predators. Thus by preserving elephant lands, we protect plant and smaller animal species within the same ecosystem. The reverse is not true: protecting smaller species does not help preserve larger ones. Given these attributes, the elephant can be considered a *super-keystone species.*

The accumulated knowledge of elephant natural history leads one to believe that the elephant is indeed what early naturalists called "an evolutionary oddity." This is, of course, only a superficial observation, for if one takes into consideration all the data on elephant biology, one may conclude that an elephant incorporates a mosaic of generalized (or primitive)

and specialized (or derived) attributes.[22] It appears that the generalized nature of the elephant overides the specialized features, for it needs them to adapt to changing environmental conditions. This is only one possible explanation for the survival of two elephant species out of 352 that were believed to have existed in the past.

It is said that when a person observes elephants in the wild, the time spent that particular day, week, month or year is not counted in the person's years to live. Adding all the days that I have observed wild elephants in Africa and Asia, I have therefore extended my lifespan by about five months. I hope that this article will encourage further conservation, if not for the sake of the elephants, then for the sake of those individuals who want to live longer by seeing elephants in the wild.

NOTES

Acknowledgments: Eleanor Marsac, Jules Pierce, Sandra Shoshani, Jan Weiss, and Susan Wolak made constructive comments and/or helped type this essay. Gary Marchant and Jann Grimes helped with the line drawings.

1. The Asian elephant, *Elephas maximus*, includes three extant subspecies. Classifications are based mostly on external characters, and present subspecies represent a synthesis of the many more subspecies classified in the past.

2. The scientific names *Cervus elaphus,* for the red deer, and *Elaphurus davidianus,* for the Pere David's deer, are apparently from the same origin.

3. A variant of *eboreus, ab* or *abu,* as used in Dynastic Egyptian (3,200-330 B.C.) meant elephant or ivory. Ivan T. Sanderson, author of *The Dynasty of Abu* (1962:6-8), wrote that the Hebrew word *elaph,* meaning "ox," may have been derived from *ebur,* which in turn gave rise to the Greek *elephas.*

4. See the correspondence between Shoshani and Arthur Horn, as recorded in the publication of the Elephant Interest Group, *Elephant* (1982, 2/1:168-71). Sikes (1971:7) referred to the pygmy elephant as the "'pygmy elephant' myth."

5. Theoretically, the African and the Asian elephants, being of two distinct genera, would not be able to interbreed. And given their current geographical distribution on different continents, inbreeding in the

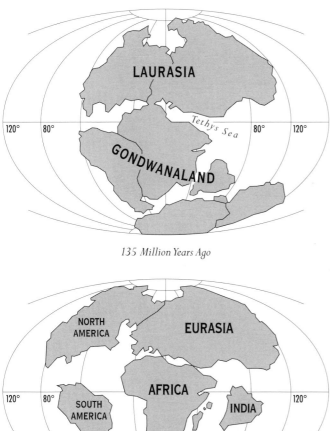

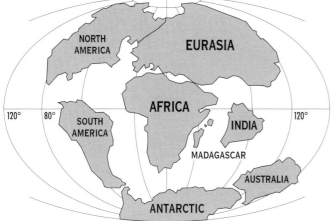

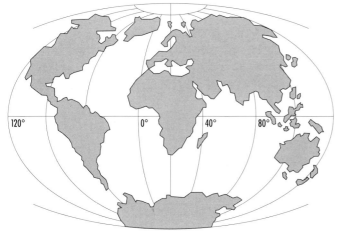

135 Million Years Ago

65 Million Years Ago

The Present

3-2A,B,C. Until 18 million years ago, Afroarabia was an island continent on the southern flank of Eurasia, a drifting fragment of Gondwanaland like Australia, Antarctica, and South America.

in Pasadena. He noted that the Afroasian territory occupied by the surviving proboscidean species was essentially the same as the area inhabited by humans up until their sudden expansion during the last ice age, and that the wave of extinction among the other proboscideans was synchronous with the earliest well-documented records of humans in the newly inhabited lands. To account for these coincidences, he speculated that the still-living proboscidean species, which apparently co-evolved with humans, had millions of years to adapt to the growing skills of human hunters, while their cousins in more distant lands were altogether unprepared for the challenge and were rapidly exterminated. While this hypothesis requires much elaboration to account for the circumstances in detail, the results of research since then have only made it seem more likely.

SWEEPING REVELATIONS: THE FAYÛM OF EGYPT

Afroarabia was, until a geologically recent date (18 million years ago), an island continent on the southern flank of Eurasia, a drifting fragment of Gondwanaland (Fig. 3-2) like Australia, Antarctica or South America. It is a commonplace of biogeographic theory that when ecosystems which were formerly isolated from one another come into contact, the animals of the smaller region usually become extinct or are reduced to marginal specialists. The exceptions seem to be species that happened to possess some unique adaptation, like the South American armadillo, which is free from competition in the new, combined ecosystem. It would be difficult to think of two land mammal lineages that are more unusually specialized than the proboscideans and the hominids, and it should not be surprising that when these extraordinary (not to say weird) products of almost 50 million years of largely isolated evolution in Africa rejoined "ordinary" mammals, first one and then the other conquered the world.

An unforgettable picture always comes to mind when I think of the antiquity of the elephant and human lineages in Africa. In 1981, I was visiting the Duke University paleontological field camp in the Fayûm Depression south of Cairo (Fig. 3-3). The Fayûm is a great polished bowl forty miles wide and over a thousand feet deep which Saharan winds have scoured out of fossil-bearing sandstone at the edge of the Nile valley. The fossils found in the sandstone formation are thought to be about 38 to 36 million years old – the end of the Eocene, a time when the Cenozoic "age of mammals" had only fairly begun.[4]

It was barely dawn when I stepped out of my tent. Behind me the truncated edge of the Sahara Desert plain hung in the sky, 500 feet above the camp. Except for a whisper of wind the long slopes were totally silent, with only a glint far down to the east from the salty seep of the Birket Qarun, 200 feet below sea level. The air was cold and icy clear, and from one horizon to the other there was no living thing to be seen, animal or plant. Nothing, that is, except a row of Egyptian workers a quarter of a mile away, on the flats below the camp. Shoulder to shoulder,

THREE

PROBOSCIDEANS, HOMINIDS, AND PREHISTORY

JOHN A. VAN COUVERING

When the "Recent"[1] epoch opened 12,500 years ago, with a sharp change from Pleistocene ice age to modern climate patterns, humans and elephants occupied more or less the same unequal territories as they do now. *Homo sapiens* was distributed worldwide, *Loxodonta africana* (Fig. 3-1) inhabited most of Africa, and *Elephas maximus* roamed the forests of southern Asia and Indonesia. When we look back to 40,000 years ago, however, just before the final advance of the last Pleistocene glacial age, the picture was astonishingly different.

This was the period of transition from middle to late Paleolithic technology in the temperate zone of Eurasia (Thomas 1988), as well as the transition from "archaic modern" to "fully modern" *Homo sapiens* in the same region.[2] Tools and ornaments were becoming steadily more complex and better made, presaging the "microlithic" technology of the upper Paleolithic, but the evidence from campsites indicates that at this time humans were still spread thinly in family bands of hunters and gatherers in Africa, southern Eurasia and Indonesia, with a population density and geographic range not significantly different from that of primitive humans over the previous half million years.

In contrast with the scatter of humans in the warmer lands of the Old World, some twenty species of proboscideans – not only the two modern elephants and their close kin but also mammoths, gomphotheres, mammutids, and stegodonts – were living in uncountable numbers in every major land area of the world except Antarctica and Australasia. Compared to the scanty fossil remains of contemporaneous humans, the fossils of late Pleistocene proboscideans are extraordinarily numerous, and they were unquestionably the dominant large mammals[3] in all well-vegetated habitats, from tropics to tundra, in both eastern and western hemispheres.

There are reasons to believe that the virtual destruction of the great nation of proboscideans was part of the global massacre of large animals for which prehistoric humankind stands accused, if not yet convicted (Martin and Klein 1984). If humans were at fault, it may be a major irony worthy of a novelist's pen. In this chapter, I will review paleontological and archaeological evidence which suggests that of all the other mammals on earth, the proboscideans were the most deeply involved in human evolution. The final steps towards modern humanity, with all its dire consequences for proboscideans, may in fact have been shaped in very large part by the proboscideans themselves. The clues are circumstantial, and are found mainly in attempts to answer a simple question: what caused so many kinds of elephants to become extinct virtually at once, and why did *Elephas maximus* and *Loxodonta africana* alone survive?

I first heard this question posed by L.S.B. Leakey during a discussion of human aggression in one of his famously overcrowded public lectures at California Institute of Technology

3-1 (OPPOSITE). Photograph, Jim Brandenburg, Minden Pictures.

D.

E.

A.

A. Line drawing of a rock art scene depicting an elephant that is thought to be falling into a trap. From Pahi, Tanzania. Length of elephant, 68 cm. After Leaky (1983:72). Drawing, Sylvia Kennedy.

B. Fon appliqué from Benin. Herskovits Collection, ca. 1930. 176.5 cm x 105.4 cm. The Schomburg Center for Research in Black Culture, The New York Public Library.

C. Image on a gourd from the late 19th-century with hunting scene. Probably from Kongo peoples of Zaire. Height 35.5 cm. FMCH X65.8505. Gift of the Wellcome Trust. (See also Fig. 1-6). Drawing, Jill Ball.

D. Line drawing of Azande/Mangbetu ivory. AMNH cat. no 90.1/2728. Collected by Herbert Lang in Akenge Village, Zaire, 1913. American Museum of Natural History Congo Expedition.

E. Line drawing of a rock art scene in which a Zulu hunter uses an iron axe to hamstring an elephant. From the Elephant Shelter in Ndedema Gorge, South Africa. After Pager (1975:20). Drawing, Jill Ball.

B.

IN SUB-SAHARAN AFRICA, elephants were traditionally hunted primarily for subsistence purposes; ivory was a useful by-product but not a necessary one. Elephant hunting was typically a group effort; but one of the group would inevitably deliver the immobilizing blow. In most cultures the spirit of the dead elephant was appeased with song and ritual offerings. Traditional African hunting practices were never a threat to the elephant as a species.

C.

wild is practically impossible. In captivity, however, conditions are artificial and inbreeding among species and genera may take place. An unusual mating occurred in Chester Zoo, England, in 1979, between a female Asian named Sheba and a male African named Jumbolino. The resultant hybrid, named Motty, died ten days after birth (Howard 1979). This is the only known case of interbreeding between *Loxodonta africana* and *Elephas maximus*.

6. The two proboscidean species found in the Rancho La Brea tar pits in California are *Mammuthus imperator* and *Mammut americanum* (see Stock 1956; Harris and Jefferson 1985; Shaw and Quinn 1986); they are believed to have arrived here via the Bering Land Bridge (see Van Couvering in this publication).

7. Proboscideans have been ecologically versatile and adaptable to extreme environmental conditions from below sea level to high mountains, and from deserts to lush habitats (Osborn 1936, 1942). Field observations of *Loxodonta africana* and *Elephas maximus* population corroborate these statements (Sikes 1971; Douglas-Hamilton and Douglas-Hamilton 1975; Olivier 1978; Sukumar 1989; Eltringham 1982; Moss 1988). Among these mosaic characters are the primitive or generalized low metabolic rate, the presence of paired anterior venae cavae in the heart, and plantigrade posture and presence of five digits of the feet.

8. Dentin is a bonelike tissue found in teeth of many animals and consists of about 80% inorganic materials and 20% water and organic matter. The inorganic matter consists of deposits similar to the mineral hydroxiapatite (calcium, phosphate, oxygen, and hydrogen), and the organic components are mostly collagen (a fibrous protein). The dentinal tubules mentioned above are present along the radial section of a tusk; their openings are microscopically visible in the pulpal section. A cross section of a tusk which passes along the tubules, depicts the checker-board appearance or "engine turning" mentioned earlier. Theoretically, the greater the density of these dentinal tubules, the more flexible, and subsequently the softer the tusk is. On a larger scale, generally the earlier the geological record, the harder the ivory.

9. Comparable figures for the Asian elephants are: 302 cm (10 ft.) and 39.0 kg (86 lb.) (Shoshani and Eisenberg 1982).

10. According to Leakey (1992), the price of ivory dropped from US $100 in 1989 to US $2-$3 per kg in 1991, because of the success of the worldwide ban on ivory import and export.

11. From an evolutionary point of view, the temporal or musth glands are a specialized subcutaneous derivative, not found in other mammals. Among herbivorous mammals (order Artiodactyla) which evolved from ungulate stock closely related to the order Proboscidea, there are glands on the sides of the face but not in the temporal region. It is possible that the temporal glands of elephants and the facial glands in artiodactyl species (e.g., a deer) developed from a similar subcutaneous structure. Those in elephants became extremely specialized.

12. For details on musth in Asian elephants, see details in Shoshani and Eisenberg (1982). The phenomenon of musth has been known for hundreds of years. "The Mad Elephant" in the medallion Jataka – a story carved on a stone railing in Amaravati, India – dates to about A.D. 150-300 (Late Andra Period); it is one of the most fascinating stories carved in stone. The carving depicts an elephant, apparently in musth, bowing in submission before Buddha (Rowland 1970:210).

13. The temporal gland of *Elephas maximus* seems to be more specialized than that of *Loxodonta africana*. This latter statement is based on the generalized nature of the temporin (temporal gland secretion) in the African elephants – both sexes of all ages secrete it, while in the Asian species, it is mostly confined to adult males. In addition, in both species at early stages of musth (or in the case of females and young Africans) the temporin secretion is clear, and in the Asian elephant, it becomes dark and sticky with increased aggression. This may partly explain why the African and the Asian elephants are said to behave differently when

in musth. I believe that the differences in musth structures, physiologically and behaviorally, are related to the evolutionary position of the African and the Asian elephants in their "family tree;" the African exhibits the more generalized conditions and therefore displays some sexual response to musth. Tisdale (1989) has raised some interesting questions as a result of interviews with Michael Schmidt, veterinarian at Metro Washington Park Zoo, Oregon (USA) and Lois E. Rasmussen (a biochemist). Both Schmidt and Rassmusen reportedly agreed that musth in African and Asian elephants is not the same phenomenon. Furthermore they stressed that musth is not the same as rut – at least not as it is known in the deer family.

14. The Asian elephant cows of the Metro Washington Park Zoo in Oregon may or may not mate with bulls in musth (Tisdale 1989:82)

15. Hanks (1979) and others have noted that African elephants defer mating in such a way that their offspring can be born when foraging conditions optimal. A successful mating during rainy season results in a calf born when the grass is green and food is plentiful. Considering that gestation lasts between 18 and 22 months, it is interesting that the gestation period can be synchronized with optimal seasonality.

16. During mounting, the female squats and may spread her legs a little, her head may be held straight with the trunk down. The male's forelegs are at about the middle of the cow's back, his head down with the trunk in contact with her body, while his erect penis searches for the opening of the vulva which is between the female's legs, not under the tail. Because of the vulva's low position, finding it is not an easy task; the long, muscular penis is strong and appears to guide itself up and down and sideways with relative ease. All movements are penile, i.e., there are no pelvic thrusts, or if there are, they appear to be insignificant. Once the tip of the penis is inserted into the vulva, upward and forward movements are required to reach the vagina which is about 80 cm (30.5 in.) from the orifice. The length of the penis of an adult bull (which may reach 100 cm or 39.5 in.) plays an important role in the fertilization process; a young bull with a short penis may be able to mate with a cow in estrus, but most likely he would not fertilize her, and thus would not fulfill the function of "survival of the species."

17. This estimate is based on a mean calving interval of four to six years and on optimal environmental conditions. Field conditions are often skewed from the optimum and only a few individuals attain their maximum potential.

18. According to Shoshani and Eisenberg (1982:5), Asian elephants "favor an ecotone with an interdigitation of grass, low woody plants, and forests." No clear ecotone – or transition zone between forest and grassland – preference was reported for the African elephant, though Redmond and Shoshani (1987) noted that the elephants in Mount Elgon National Park, Kenya, appear to favor the variety of plants found in ecotones during the wet season.

19. Methods of age estimation include: condition and number of crosslophs (lamellae) on the cheek teeth, posthumous dry weights of the eye lenses, and condition of the ears (Laws 1966; Laws et al. 1975; Sikes 1971; Eltringham 1992).

20. In addition to the pivotal role of elephants in their ecosystems, much basic and applied knowledge has been gained by studying elephants (e.g., in the fields of mammalian comparative anatomy and evolution, diseases common to elephants and humans, due to longevity).

21. The hypothesis that elephants were the original "excavators" was proposed by I. Redmond and supported by J. Shoshani in *Elephant* (1987).

22. Between 1977 and 1987 there have been at least 2,446 articles published, with an average of 222 per year (data from the journal *Elephant*). In addition, there have been about 30 books on elephants published in the years 1988 through 1991, and at least 10 more are in press, scheduled for 1992. For General Reference, see the "References Cited" section of of this volume.

3-3. The Fayûm basin fifty miles south of Cairo has been sandblasted by Saharan winds into a huge bowl with its bottom over 100 feet below sea level. The winds have eaten down into hundreds of square miles of fossil-bearing Tertiary strata which were deposited at the edge of the Tethys seaway between 50 and 35 million years ago. Photograph, Elwyn Simons.

their shadows stretching far out before them, the distant figures were working enormous pushbrooms along a swath thirty feet wide. Gritty dust billowed up as the workmen struggled to push ridges of pebbles aside, their loose clothes flapping in the cold morning breeze.

For one long, wonderful moment it seemed that this spectral crew was merely passing by, having swept thirty miles across the desert from Cairo during the night. All I could think was that it was some demented government scheme to tidy up the Sahara for tourists. Then, what I was seeing clicked with shop talk of the night before, and I realized that the sweepers were actually fossil preparators of a rough kind, working for the expedition. Later in the day, when the wind increased, it would whip savagely abrasive sheets of low-flying sand at any exposed surface, carrying the loosened grit and dust away. Millennia of such daily windstorms grinding away at the landscape had left behind a solidly packed residue of pebbles and larger stones which were too heavy to fly. These "pavements," impervious to the wind, are rarely disturbed in nature, so that centuries pass without any further erosion of the beds beneath. Paleontologists, however, love erosion, so the workers were hired to clear away likely spots where fossils might be hidden in the sandstone. After a few weeks of wind erosion the "bone patches" are ready to harvest, and in the quiet of the early morning and dusk the paleontologists crawl around on hands and knees looking for emerging fossils. The low sun emphasizes the bumps of half-buried specimens, and in the relative calm one can peer closely at the ground without being blinded by a face full of driven sand.

Excitement was running high in the camp because the new technique of area-sweeping was bringing forth hundreds of well-preserved specimens. These included some which were previously unknown – marsupials, which had never been found or even suspected in Africa before, and the earliest pangolin –

and even more importantly, many new specimens of Fayûm mammals which had been studied previously only from incomplete and often heavily weathered or sandblasted material.

I shared the excitement; to all students of African prehistory, the Fayûm is a legend. Discovered in 1878, not only was this the first site of fossil mammals in Africa, but as a double first the Fayûm fossils are still the oldest comprehensive sample of mammals known from the continent. Discoveries recently made in the Atlas Mountains go back considerably earlier in geological time, to not many millions of years after the worldwide extinction of dinosaurs, but these specimens are relatively quite rare and fragmentary. Even in the oldest of these sites, however, we find proboscideans and primates, as well as other mammal groups, developing along their own lines. For the first half of the Cenozoic age of mammals, the fossil evidence shows that Africa was an island continent, with a largely independent history of mammalian evolution.

The Fayûm being exhumed by a team of fellaheen with push-brooms was a strange, almost australian land. Most of the fossils were of the ancient and eccentric group known as subungulates (dugongs, hyraxes, aardvarks, and elephants plus some even more peculiar extinct lineages: see Savage and Long 1986) which seem to have originated at the beginning of the Cenozoic "age of mammals" in the island continents south of the ancient Tethys Sea (Fig. 3-4).[5] The most abundant animals in the Fayûm were all kinds of primitive hyraxes, in great variety from rat-size to pony-size, and the largest and most bizarre was the extinct subungulate "rhino," *Arsinoitherium*. Most of the larger mammals, however, were stout, long-snouted primitive proboscideans (Fig. 3-5), identifiable to two kinds of moeritheres, plus early elephantoids *Phiomia* and *Palaeomastodon*. There were also strays from Eurasia such as the pangolin, the marsupial, and a pig-like beast that was the ancestor of the hippopotamus; and there were other kinds of

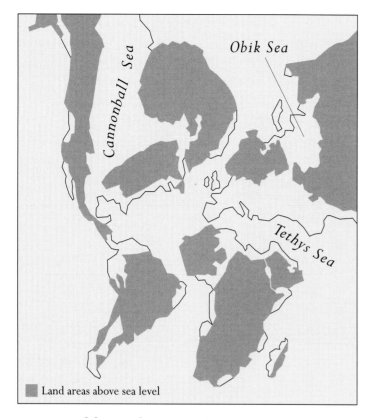

3-4. Most of the animals represented by fossils excavated from the Fayum seem to have originated at the beginning of the Cenozoic "age of mammals" in the island continents south of the Tethys Sea.

3-5. Most larger mammals recovered from the Fayûm were stout, long-snouted proboscideans. This creature is *Phiomia*, the ancestral gomphothere (see Figs. 3-7 and 3-8). Photograph, John Van Couvering.

ancient African mammals, such as elephant-shrews and "southern rodents" related to porcupines, capybaras, and guinea pigs of South America.

The greatest amount of scientific attention, however, was devoted to the primates. At this time, in the later part of the Eocene epoch at 40-35 Ma (millions of years before present), primates were common everywhere except Australia, Antarctica, and South America. The perfect little skulls, teeth, and limbs being uncovered in the Fayûm, however, were confirming a startling hypothesis about the species from Africa. With better fossils it was becoming clear that some were ancestral prosimians – lemurs, lorises, and galagos – and the rest were primitive anthropoids – the suborder of monkeys, apes, and men. Taken as a whole, these fossils were more closely related to one another than to the hordes of Eocene primates in the northern hemisphere, and this appeared to prove that all living primates – not just humans and great apes – originated in Africa.

We naturally tend to see the seeds of greatness in the proto-anthropoids of the Fayûm, but in fact there is no way of knowing whether they were in any way superior to their northern relatives. One or two million years later at the end of the balmy, equable Eocene, world climate took the first major step towards modern cold-winter, dry-summer weather patterns. All of the primates of the northern continents were soon extinguished, and since there were as yet none in South America, only the lucky ones in the tropics of Africa happened to survive.

ELEPHANTS BEFORE HUMANS: SETTING THE STAGE

After the Eocene, the fossil record of Africa is virtually blank for the next fifteen million years until the Miocene. Behind this curtain, primitive proboscideans and anthropoids underwent dramatic transformations in response to the continuing changes in global climate (Fig. 3-7). Although conditions under the equator may not have been greatly affected, world climate change helped breach the ocean barriers that had formerly protected African animals from competitors and predators to which they were not adapted. During this transitional period, ocean circulation was being steadily rearranged towards the modern pattern by the drift of Australia, South America and Africa away from Antarctica and against the continents to the north (Fig. 3-2). Isolated from equatorial warmth by the progressively widening south-polar seas and the strengthening circum-Antarctic winds and currents, the Antarctic ice cap grew much larger, and its frosty touch began to chill the world ocean towards its present-day temperature, two degrees above freezing (we sail, fish, and swim in a thin, sun-warmed film above the thermocline). With the oceans turning cold, the periodic variations in the amount of solar radiation reaching the earth's surface had an increasingly strong effect. The size of the Antarctic ice shield began to oscillate more and more widely and sea level began to fall and rise by significant amounts as the ice fields grew and melted.

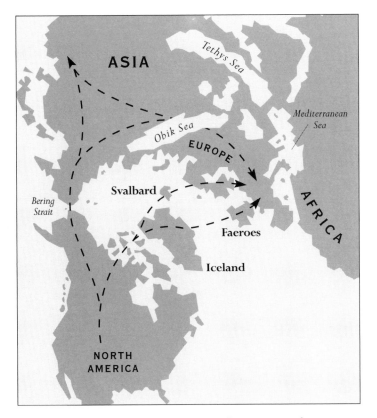

3-6. Starting about 35 million years ago, fluctuations in the Antarctic ice cap caused sharp rises and falls in sea level. Mammals invaded from the north across low-water land bridges between Afroarabia and Eurasia. In the face of new competition, proboscideans and primates flourished.

Taking advantage of temporary land bridges exposed during the drawdowns, the ancestors of most of the mammal groups which we now associate with Africa entered from the Eurasian-North American world between 35 and 30 million years ago (Fig. 3-6). As these invaders flourished – especially the true carnivores (cats, weasels, otters, skunks, dogs, and hyaenas), as well as the rhinos, pigs, ruminants, rabbits, squirrels, rats, and gerbils – the pressure on the pre-existing fauna was severe, and many formerly diverse Fayûm lineages such as the hyraxes and southern rodents were pushed into their present narrow niches. By Miocene time, however, when the fossil record resumes, remains of proboscideans and anthropoid primates are if anything more abundant and varied than in the Eocene, indicating that the special adaptations of these two groups continued to be successful.

In areas of central Kenya that were forested highlands in the Miocene, remains have been found of a wide variety of proconsuls. These were arboreal and semi-arboreal anthropoids that occupied many of the niches later taken by monkeys. The forest proboscideans, now almost the size of modern elephants, included mammutids, shovel-tusk and straight-tusk mastodons, and the earliest known deinotheres (Coppens et al. 1978; Tassy 1986).

In the temperate northern lowlands and the coastal plains of Afroarabia, the new global climate had a greater effect and open, grassy woodlands and low bush had replaced closed-canopy evergreen forest over wide areas. Because this type of environment was more like today, the fossil mammals of this region were also relatively more like today's than those of the forested highlands. Instead of ordinary proconsuls, the anthropoids in the coastal sites included the first monkeys and also several recently-discovered kinds of "kenyapithecines," the specialized proconsul group from which the great apes and humans probably derived (Andrews 1988). The proboscideans in the coastal sites were also more modern than their forest relatives (Coppens et al. 1978; Tassy 1986), and their teeth show a trend towards the complex enamel folds needed to deal with grasses and thickly cuticled, drought-resistant leaves.

The most significant event in the early Miocene was the final closing of the Tethys between Afroarabia and Eurasia, in the Persian Gulf-Zagros Mountains suture.[6] This event had as its immediate consequence the sudden and dramatic invasion of proboscideans into Eurasia about 18 million years ago. A short time later (about 17 Ma), they spread into North America. In fossil beds of this age all across this vast area, from Portugal to Japan and on to Nebraska and Florida, virtually identical species of proboscideans[7] are found in the earliest occurrence. This fossil evidence makes it clear that elephantoids were astonishingly successful in adapting to the conditions of the temperate region, and their spread was virtually uninhibited. Other African groups such as deinotheres, bovids, and giraffids also spread rapidly into southern Eurasia at this time, but of these African pioneers only a few of their most advanced descendants among the bovids (sheep, goats, musk-ox and bison, but no true antelopes) were ever to join the adventurous elephantoids in the New World, millions of years later.

Compared with the more aggressive African emigrants, let alone the world-conquering proboscideans, the anthropoids were slow and tentative in spreading beyond the tropics. While various species of small, relatively hardy anthropoids entered Europe directly via a Balearic land bridge at about 16 Ma,[8] it was not until the unusually warm and equable middle Miocene climate maximum between 14 and 10 Ma that monkeys and tropical hominoids appear to have ventured outside of Afroarabia. Using the "southern route" via the Strait of Hormuz, primitive monkeys reached Austria, China, and Mongolia at about 11 Ma, and the proconsul *Oreopithecus* found its way to Italy. A lineage of primitive great apes – precursors to orangutans – ventured from the Indopakistan beachhead at least as far as Turkey, Greece, and Hungary in the west and southern China and Vietnam in the east, a route which must also have been followed by the proto-gibbons.

In the late Miocene, the global trend towards modern seasonal climates took another downward step, with winters becoming cooler and summers drier than at any time previously in the Cenozoic. Proconsuls, dryopithecines and pliopithecines became extinct, and the northern range of the remaining primates in temperate Eurasia contracted markedly. Fossil evidence indicates that from about 8 Ma until the emergence of modern humans, the only primates that were

EVOLUTION OF ELEPHANTS AND THE ORDER PROBOSCIDEA*

FIGURES 3-7 AND 3-8

The lineage of elephants traces back some 50 million years. Early proboscideans originated in Africa and southwest Asia and migrated via land bridges to every continent except Antarctica and Australia (see Fig 3-6).

One of the earliest known proboscideans was *Moeritherium* (1), of the suborder Moeritheroidea. These hippo-shaped creatures had relatively small tusks in both jaws, and represent the group out of which, some 45 million years ago, evolved two distinct lineages of giant long-trunked proboscideans: deinotheres and elephantoids. The deinotheres, exemplified by *Deinotherium* (2), were majestic animals, differing from elephantoids in that their heavy tusks were back-swept like the claws of a hammer and grew only from their lower jaws. Deinotheres became extinct in recent geological times, surviving until only a half a million years ago in Africa.

Palaeomastodon (3), which lived about 40 million years ago, was one of the earliest of the Elephantoidea. Parallel trends can be seen in all elephantoid groups during the last 15 million years. These include the tendency to lose lower tusks, to increase the size of cheek teeth and the number of enamel cross-ridges, and to space out molar eruption so that, as the old ones wear out, new chewing teeth take their places in the jaw.

Mammutids (family Mammutidae) (4) originated at least 30 million years ago in Africa, but by the later Pleistocene were found only in North America. Their tusks were short and stout, the cheek teeth had three to five large cross-ridges, the skull was relatively wide, and the body was very short and broad.

Gomphotheres (family Gomphotheriidae) (5), commonly but incorrectly known as "mastodons," were known from the Eocene of Africa to the latest Pleistocene in the Western Hemisphere. Most species had four tusks, with some having broad flattened lower tusks used as scoops or shovels.

Stegodonts (family Stegodontidae) (6) evolved from African gomphotheres in the Miocene, but in the Pleistocene were restricted mainly to southeast Asia. Their cheek teeth displayed numerous transverse crests, grinding fore-and-aft as in elephants.

Elephants and mammoths (family Elephantidae) (7, 8, 9, 10) also evolved from gomphotheres in Africa. The trend, among all proboscideans, toward great body size and large, complex cheek teeth reaches its extreme in this group. Numerous parallel cross-folds make cheek teeth highly effective fore-and-aft "grinders" to process abrasive vegetation (e.g., grass, bamboo, and roots). The most advanced elephantid was *Mammuthus* (8), to which *Elephas* (9) is closely related and *Loxodonta* (10) less so. Dwarfed species of elephantids and stegodontids, ½ to ⅔ normal size, lived on islands from the Mediterranean and Indonesia to California, as well as in some mainland sites.

*This summary draws from Maglio (1973), Coppens et al. (1978), and *The National Geographic*, vol. 179, no. 5, p. 21. I am also grateful to J. Shoshani for valuable advice.

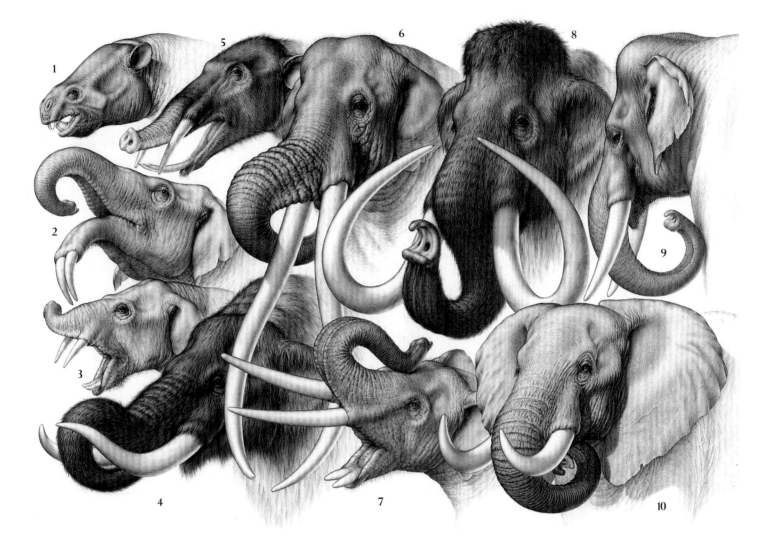

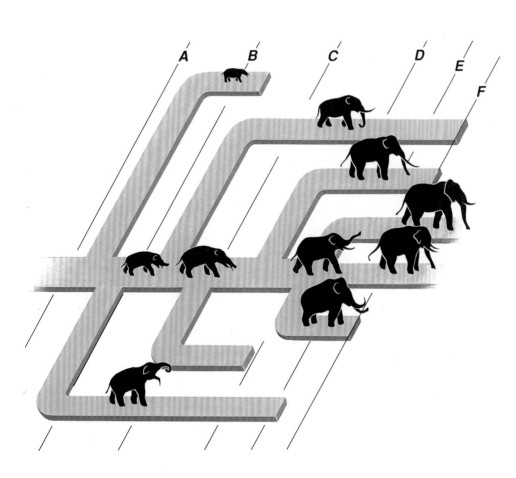

3-7 (ABOVE). The proboscidean model was enormously successful, with many different lineages proliferating throughout Africa, Eurasia, and the Americas during the past 17 million years. See boxed "Evolution of Elephants and the Order Proboscidea" (opposite). Illustration by Karel Hevlicek, courtesy of National Geographic Society.

3-8. All proboscidean lineages originated in Africa. Deinotheres and mammutids were early offshoots, while gomphotheres gave rise to the more advanced families. Diagram by Mark Seidler, after a chart by Jeheskel Shoshani, courtesy of National Geographic Society.

Key:

A. EOCENE: 55 million years ago.
B. OLIGOCENE: 40 million years ago.
C. MIOCENE: 25 million years ago.
D. PLIOCENE: 5 million years ago.
E. PLEISTOCENE: 2 million years ago.
F. HOLOCENE: 10 thousand years ago.

able to live outside of the tropics were macaques and the aberrant hominid *Gigantopithecus*, which together with a northern species of *Stegodon* shared the range of the giant panda until quite recently. Other than this, the Asian hominid lineages survived only in the Indomalaysian tropics, henceforth forever sepa-rated from the kenyapithecines and their descendants, which had remained in Africa.

In the Pliocene, from about 4.5 million to 1.5 million years ago, the final pieces were set into place. The ages-long isolation of South America ended when the first "cold snaps" in the half-million year cycles of the ice ages were felt at about 2.5 and 2.0 million years ago (Marshall 1985). Rapid if temporary reductions in sea level due to polar ice expansion made it possible for mammals to walk across the isthmus lowlands of Nicaragua and northern Colombia for the first time. In the ensuing Great Exchange (Webb 1985) the North American proboscidean *Cuvieronius*, a gomphothere characterized by a set of large corkscrew tusks, entered South America (Marshall 1985) and spread rapidly through the tropical savannah. Unauthenticated fossil scraps suggest that mammoths may also have crossed the isthmus, but no conclusively identified remains are known. Later genera, *Haplomastodon* and *Notiomastodon*, occur abundantly in fossil beds of Brazil and Argentina (Simpson and Paula Couto 1957) up until the latest Pleistocene.

In Africa, the earliest fossil remains of *Mammuthus*, *Elephas* and *Loxodonta* appear in the Pliocene, together with a few scraps of bone assigned to the genus *Australopithecus*, the first trace of the lineage leading on to modern man (Fig. 3-7).

ON THE ELEPHANT'S TRAIL

Despite their common heritage in Africa, there is no reason to suppose that anthropoids and proboscideans had a significant functional relationship until the appearance of the australopithecines. At this early stage, there is little likelihood that interaction was predatory, although it is fairly certain that australopithecines included meat in their diet. While the archaeological evidence for hunting in earliest *Homo* is inconclusive (Isaac and Crader 1981), we know that they used stone tools for butchering large animals and were obviously meat-eaters (Hill 1982; Stringer 1988). Furthermore, studies of our closest genetic relatives, the chimpanzees, find that they gang up to capture and eat animal prey (usually colobus monkeys) as often as every other day, with a success rate equal to that of full-time carnivores (Boesch and Boesch 1989). We may thus assume that a predilection for fresh meat (not carrion, for which neither humans nor apes have any physiological tolerance) was not something recently acquired in human evolution.

There is nothing to indicate, however, that australopithecines could have been more dangerous to a grown elephant than a gang of chimpanzees – perhaps less so, being considerably lighter for the same height and presumably inferior in strength. Furthermore, the evidence from the minutely analyzed fossil sites indicates that australopithecines did not make or use any kind of edged tool (Howell 1978; Isaac and Crader 1981). Even if their abilities were adequate to trap or stampede elephants, or to dispatch them with pointed sticks, rocks, and clubs, the fact remains that without anything with which to cut up the prize except their teeth (very like our own) they could not in the end have eaten it.

According to current guesses as to the habitat preferred by australopithecines in the Pliocene (Richard Klein 1983; Robert Klein 1984; Vrba 1985), the first significant interaction of the elephant and human lineages may have been the role played by loxodonts and other proboscideans in creating an environment in which the initial trends towards human characteristics were advantageous. Ecological studies identify the living loxodonts as prime architects of the open woodlands of Africa (Wing and Buss 1970; see also Stevens 1989). In their daily foraging these great beasts create and maintain broad paths through impenetrable bamboo and elephant grass belts, and in forested areas they keep extensive glades in a permanent state of "early succession" (Wilkie 1989), not only breaking down large trees but also tearing up acres of saplings for their roots (Maugham 1906). They also excavate and weed out water holes, and "garden" the tangled bush and forest-edge vegetation into interconnected glades and clearings. In all of these activities, elephants open up for other ground-dwelling mammals a habitat zone which is more productive, by reason of access to both sun and water, and more ecologically diverse than either the deep forest or the open grasslands. During the Pliocene, australopithecines were living in relatively well-watered and naturally forested habitats (Vrba 1985), and the role of loxodonts as an environmental mediator may have been crucial.

Humans differ from their fellow hominids, the forest-dwelling great apes, in a constellation of behavioral and physical characteristics which have been attributed to survival in relatively more dry, open habitats. All of these features were present in *Australopithecus*, well before the development of the enlarged forebrain, enlarged and repositioned larynx (Laitman 1984), and finger-thumb coordination for a small-tool grip (Marzke and Shackley 1986) that physically distinguish manufacturing, speaking, and reasoning *Homo*. While the adaptations of *Australopithecus* opened the way for the evolution of humans, they were obviously developed for the survival of australopithecines. For instance, Hatley and Kappelman (1980) hypothesized that the non-ape-like features of human dentition which were already well developed in australopithecines – reduced canines, vertically meeting incisors, broadened tooth arcade, retention of thickened enamel – can be explained as an adaptation to a diet of raw tubers,[9] a last resource in those times of hardship when natural selection comes into full force. Tuberous plants are characteristic of seasonally dry habitats and while this food supply would be out of reach for other animals even the most primitive hominine could probably operate a digging stick (Marzke and Shackley 1986).

As for social characteristics which distinguish hominids, Lovejoy (1981) pointed to obligate food sharing and two-parent responsibility (if not complete monogamy) as a probable reflection of life in open country, either because of greater range or of a greater dependence on hunting as a steady source of food.[10] Life in open country is also indicated by the selection for increased emphasis on sight relative to smell or hearing and the much greater range and endurance (compared to the semi-upright apes, and even to most true quadrupeds) conferred by upright striding gait and hands free to carry trail rations.

None of these characteristics, it should be noted, have anything to do with the sharp increases in reasoning ability or dexterity which distinguished *Homo* from *Australopithecus*. As far as the fossil record is known the skeletal features associated with these basic hominid specializations were already present in the earliest known australopithecines, dated to about 4.5 Ma. Accordingly, it is widely if not universally held that adaptation to open country is basic to human evolution. Today we use heavy equipment and chain saws to expand the clearings we need, but it seems possible, even probable, that it was the effect of numerous and ubiquitous proboscideans on the prehistoric landscape that provided the original opportunity for some forest-dwelling proto-hominid to move out into the open air.

The question remains: what about pre-australopithecines allowed them to first begin to take advantage of proboscidean activity? How did weaponless, slow-running, four-feet-tall hominids defend themselves in the open, where all other hominids, even gorillas, fear to tread? Barbara Isaac has noted that because of the combination of thumb-grip, shoulder structure, balanced stance, accurate stereoscopic visual peception, and a "versatile ballistic sense…which must be founded on an intricate neurophysiological basis…"(1987:4), humans are alone among all animals, living or extinct, in the ability to throw a stone (or other projectile) accurately and with lethal force at a moving target from a distance of at least ten meters. All the physical requirements for this unusual capability appear to be developed in *Australopithecus*; *Homo* is arguably an improvement in terms of greater stature (thus longer limbs and a better line of sight), more balanced posture, and perhaps an improved neurological integration. Higher levels of intelligence, speech, or finger-thumb dexterity, however, were probably not essential for bouncing a rock off a target.

All hominids throw things, and all hominids have the basic prerequisites of stereoscopic vision, ability to stand however awkwardly, and long arms with prehensile fingers. In the other hominids (and sometimes in humans, to be sure) throwing is undirected agitated flinging as an agonistic display, or as a calculated disturbance. It requires only throwing a little harder and more accurately, as humans do, to open an entirely new strategy of purposeful behavior (Fig. 3-9). Morphological change appropriate for this behavior seems to satisfy some difficult questions about the origin of australopithecine characters – i.e., what advantage was furthered when one group of

3-9. The first step in the differentiation of the human lineage may have been selection for an 'ape with a fastball'. The unique ability of humans to throw hard and accurately, which preceded the development of intelligence or verbal ability, would have been an advantage in landscape opened up by elephant activity. A Philadelphia Athletics player c. 1925. National Baseball Library, Cooperstown, New York.

hominids began to develop more erect and balanced stance, an improved grip, broader shoulders, and longer legs? Furthermore, the advantage gained by throwing would be strongly reinforced in open terrain, where this group evidently found success in contrast to all their forest and woodland-living relatives. If this is how the specifically human lineage was born, then proboscideans should be given credit for the role of nursemaid.

HUMANS AS HUNTERS

The development of modern hunting capability and the spread of the late Paleolithic hunting cultures is now well documented. In Africa, southern Europe, and southern Asia this is seen as the *in situ* adoption[11] of diversified, specialized, and technically accomplished tools and utensils. This transition, even more dramatic than earlier ones,[12] was a "quantum leap" in cultural development (Richard Klein 1983; Brooks 1988) that culminated about 35,000 years ago.

In its location and timing, the technological transition appears to be closely coincident with the appearance of completely modern humans in place of the "archaic moderns" and the Neanderthals. To summarize the present state of knowledge in a vast literature, the newer tools ("Mode IV toolkits") were first seen sporadically in Africa and the Near East at about 90 Ka (thousand years before present), and in Europe and temperate Asia between about 35 to 30 Ka (Robert Klein 1984; Stringer 1988; Sofer 1988). At the same time, late Paleolithic humans made their way by seagoing canoes across deep ocean straits to New Guinea, Australia, Tasmania, and the New Hebrides, and across glacially exposed land bridges to the Philippines, Taiwan, and Japan – routes which were evidently out of reach to their immediate ancestors, who had essentially the same physique, but not (it seems) a comparable level of culture.

The late Paleolithic improvement in technical and social skills was also coincident with the spread of humans into the untapped hunting grounds of Siberia (Sofer 1988). Abundant archaeological remains show that in this new land, a large population was quickly established which depended almost entirely on mammoths and steppe elephants for food and building materials. Within a relatively few generations, however, the "walking meat lockers" vanished from the continent; and the hunters' lives, and their technology, became more complex.

When did humans reach the Americas? Assuming that they walked there across the plains of Beringia (that land exposed by the drawdown of the Bering Straits), it followed after the spread of modern humans into new hunting grounds of Siberia. Archaeological sites indicate that this expansion also came about 35,000 years ago, coincident with the waning of the next-to-last advance of the continental ice sheets in the Pleniglacial period, the last and coldest pulse of the last ice age. The first part of the Pleniglacial, which began about 75 Ka, was characterized by "polar desert" climate, with intensely cold and dry conditions in both arctic and austral high latitudes and "hyper-aridity" exceeding today's in the low-latitude regions; due to low precipitation rates the ice sheets of the north were thin, and sea level may not have been drawn down low enough to completely expose the Bering plains. The 30-23 Ka interval known as the Denekamp or Farmdale interstadial was relatively mild and Beringia was more likely to have been inundated. Even so, glacial ice sheets still extended across the North American continent from the Gulf of Alaska to Long Island Sound (Denton and Hughes 1981). Between 20 to 15 Ka, stormy conditions and intensely cold winters fattened the continental glaciers, exposing the ice-free corridor across Beringia for the last time. The highroad to the Americas went no further than Alaska, however; ice flowing out from the Hudson Bay centers and the fjords of the coast ranges coalesced in iceberg shelves extending for thousands of kilometers along the Atlantic, Arctic, and Pacific coasts. These vast ice plains must have been barren of all life and impassable even to a modern Inuit until about 13 Ka, when they began to stagnate and a clear path opened to the south.

This geological evidence indicates that the Siberian hunters had two periods – before 30 Ka and at about 18 Ka, roughly –

when lowered sea levels favored land passage into the Alaskan anteroom of the New World. The archaeological evidence seems to suggest, however, that the North American ice barrier held until the end of the Pleistocene. All evidence which has been presented for the presence of humans in North America before this time is controversial (Thomas 1988). The earliest reliably documented signs of habitation date to no more than 14 Ka, and almost every one of these is a mammoth butchery site (Kreutzer 1988; Thomas 1988).

OVERKILL OR OVER-REACTION?

The clear evidence for a wave of extinction in many groups of large mammals at the end of the Pleistocene has engendered a spirited debate (see Martin and Klein 1984). In many regions, the New World in particular, the extinctions were markedly sudden and across the board, removing every species in entire families or orders of mammals no matter what their adaptive specialty; furthermore the extinctions came not at the height of the final glacial advance, but during the first millennium of the interglacial climate that we call Recent.

A number of researchers view this wave of extinctions as the result of human predation, but others have objected to drawing such conclusions from the available, mainly circumstantial, evidence, and appeal to climate change or other factors (Horton 1984). Many in the second camp also cite the fact that in numerous well-known cultures whose meat comes exclusively or largely from large wild animals, such as the Inuit (Eskimo), Aleut, Northwest Coast native Americans, !Kung (Bushmen), and native Australians (Horton 1984), there is a functional equilibrium between the human hunters and large prey species. Leakey's thesis, simply put, was that this equilibrium is not a matter of choice on the part of the "noble savage," but is forced on him due to his inability to do any better.

Taking recent offenses into account, the case against unsophisticated humankind armed with nothing more than the neolithic hunting kit appears to be irrefutable. The three best documented examples of trespass and murder are Madagascar, New Zealand, and Hawaii, none of which were inhabited until after A.D. 500 (Diamond 1984). In each case the remains of a wide variety of extinct animals are associated with the earliest evidence of human activity, and the few surviving edible species live in refugia characterized principally by the past scarcity of people. In some instances, the depredations of humankind are documented in oral histories, as in descriptions of moa hunting in Maori legend. Many other examples are known from other islands, particularly in the Caribbean, where the last remains of extinct large mammals come from the ancient kitchen middens of human settlers.

If humans are so destructive, why are there any large mammals left on the major continents? Of the four living giants, proboscideans and rhinos live in Africa and southern Asia, while hippos and giraffes are restricted to Africa. Furthermore, these are the regions with the greatest diversity of

3-10. The imperial mammoth (left) was primarily a grazer; fossil finds indicate its preference for open country. In contrast, the American mastodon (right) occupied forests and open woodlands. Courtesy of George C. Page Museum, Los Angeles. Artist, John Dawson.

other large mammals in historic times, and also the "Old Regions" (Spuhler 1988) of *Homo erectus* and pre-modern human occupation, as Leakey noted. The geographical coincidence suggests that an explanation for survival in proboscideans applies to the other giants, and by extension to other large mammals as well. Looking at this another way, we may consider the rather remarkable variation in the pattern of extinction in the various major land masses during the latest Pleistocene and earliest Holocene, and the relationship of this pattern to the presence of human hunters.

PATTERNS OF EXTINCTION

Studies of late Pleistocene extinction in large mammals (summarized in Martin 1984) from donkey size on up indicate that in Africa and southern Asia perhaps one out of ten species died out in the 35,000 years prior to historic times. In temperate Eurasia during the same interval this figure was closer to three or four species out of ten. In Australia and the Americas, however, approximately eight out of ten large mammal species disappeared in this same brief period. By and large, proboscideans and other giant mammals suffered the most.

Large mammal species in North America had already declined from seventy-nine at the beginning of the Pleniglacial to twenty-two by the time Europeans arrived (Martin 1984). The turnover rate of all the latest Pleistocene mammals, large and small, is 71%, or three times higher than in any

comparable interval in North American fossil history (Savage and Russell 1983:402), including many earlier glacial maxima.

Furthermore, the extinct large mammals included more than fourteen species of giants or near-giants (Figs. 3-10, 3-11). At a minimum, there were six proboscidean species – the imperial mammoth (*Mammuthus columbi*), Jefferson's mammoth (*Mammuthus jeffersonii*, the pygmy island mammoth *Mammuthus exilis*), the woolly mammoth (*Mammuthus primigenius*), the American mastodon (*Mammut americanum*), and Cuvier's gomphothere (*Cuvieronius*). Other lost giants included five species of giant edentates (ground sloths, glyptodons, armadillos) and three species of longhorn bison. In addition, there were some extremely large species among the nine equids, five camels, seven pronghorns and three tapirs that disappeared from North America and the world at this same time (Savage and Russell 1983). A similar fate befell the half-dozen *Notiomastodon* and *Haplomastodon* gomphothere species of South America, together with eight species of giant sloths, a variety of pampas-dwelling camelids, three kinds of horse, and all but one of several tapirs. All that remained of the New World large mammal fauna were various cervids (caribou, moose, deer) two bovids (muskox, bison), and the mountain goats and

3-11. Proboscideans of the Americas may have been easy prey for humans armed with little more than rocks and spears. Courtesy of George C. Page Museum, Los Angeles. Artist, John Dawson.

mountain sheep, all shared with Eurasia, and one pronghorn, one guanaco, one tapir, and the high-mountain llamas. Extinction among the large carnivores affected mainly those which appear to have specialized in the slower and larger prey species, such as the saber-toothed and dagger-toothed cats, the dire wolf, and the short-faced bear.

In the case of Australia, until recently it was possible to hold a view of aboriginal hunters in tune with nature, but surprising discoveries, such as the Kow Swamp bone bed, gave evidence of the demise of a remarkable late Pleistocene fauna of much greater diversity than the present. This fauna was dominated not by the lean and speedy kangaroo but by various giant, slow-moving marsupial herbivores and a "komodo dragon" top predator, all of which vanished in the past 20,000 years (Horton 1984).

The woolly mammoth (*M. primigenius*), steppe elephant (*Elephas namadicus*), Mediterranean island elephant (*Elephas falconeri*), and northern woolly rhinoceros, and Irish elk were among the giant mammals that vanished from the islands and northern plains of Eurasia as soon as they came within the range of humans in the upper Paleolithic. In the north the only large herbivores that survived to historic times were one species each of horse, ass, aurochs, and yak, together with the same bison, muskox, cervids, and mountain ovines that

persisted in North America. Giant cave bears and the European hippopotamus may also have been exterminated in southern Europe during the later Pleistocene, but the northern race of lions and the ancient cattle survived until historic times.

While the large mammals of previously uninhabited regions were disappearing, what of the "Old Regions" (Spuhler 1988) in which "archaic" humans had lived for hundreds of thousands of years before the upper Paleolithic transformation? In the far east, *Stegodon* of "Sundaland"[13] and several species of island elephants, from Celebes, Timor, and the Philippines, became extinct at the beginning of the Holocene, but the range of *Elephas maximus* did not greatly change; the Javanese and Indian rhinoceroses, the carabao ("water-buffalo"), giant panda, and a great many kinds of large lowland antelopes also survived.

In Africa, the "grasslands elephant" (*Elephas reckii*), the huge short-necked giraffe *Samotherium*, and the great *Deinotherium* disappeared in the middle Pleistocene during the early days of archaic *Homo*, about 500,000 years ago, together with giant species of antelope, baboon, and bushpig (Stringer 1988). Mortality profiles of herd animals from archaeological sites of this age indicate some catastrophic kills, probably cliff drives (Richard Klein 1983), and some opportunistic individual kills, some of which may have been scavenged. With the advent of the "fully modern" humans about 35,000 years ago, only five or six more large mammals disappeared (e.g., giant zebra, giant hartebeest, giant buffalo) from the great variety of African game. This "restraint" compared to what was happening in the New World is even more remarkable in view of evidence that the human population greatly increased and hunting pressures intensified at this time (Richard Klein 1983; Robert Klein 1984). Analysis of middens shows that by this time large mammals were all being captured individually, the average size of limpets and tortoises in the middens was smaller, and birds and fish became an important part of the diet for the first time.

One interpretation is that in Africa the remaining prey species had become wise to humankind's ways, and the selection for fully modern humans gave little additional advantage in hunting in this region. It is one of the seeming paradoxes in natural selection that such apparently small rewards are the sign of active selection in the core areas of an evolving lineage. The variation in proboscidean (and other giant mammal) extinction rates from continent to continent after the appearance of "anatomically modern man" is thus directly in proportion to the length of time that pre-modern humans inhabited these regions, and is not readily explained on a global basis by such impartial factors as climate change. On the other hand the marked difference in timing of these extinction peaks from region to region is clearly synchronous with the timing of modern human occupation (Martin 1984).

Subsequently, the rise of Neolithic farming and pastoralist cultures began to preempt and destroy big game habitats, and domestication of dogs, horses, and (in Indopakistan) the elephant itself helped hunters to increase their effectiveness, so it is also true that the low density of pre-Neolithic human populations and the low agricultural fertility of tropical forests and grasslands made it impossible to dominate and exterminate the wildlife there as completely as in, for example, Mesopotamia. However, the extent of irrigated or intensively settled land in Siberia, the New World, and Australasia was minimal, and neither habitat destruction nor horsemanship can account for the wholesale extinction of so many large mammals when humans first arrived in these vast areas.

MEAT ON THE TABLE

It is an urban, and even subtly racist myth based on the concept of "natural" humans to credit indigenous peoples with an intuitive dedication to ecological balance when they are found living in the midst of large numbers of animals, undisturbed stands of trees, and clear streams full of fish. The observed equilibrium is not always to the liking of the people who must participate in it, as witness the alacrity with which they abandon their wholesome way of life as soon as they can obtain more certain and effective methods of dominating the environment.

Martin (1984) has noted that "overkill" may be associated with the abundance and innocence of prey species and the absence of real or cultural limits on human population in the first phase of exploitation. The "harmony" seen in existing hunting cultures comes later, rather like the newly discovered

ecological conscience of industrial societies, as the remaining prey becomes more difficult to secure. As of today, of course, all big game animals (by elimination, so to speak) are in the difficult to kill category, and we have no clear idea of what an "easy" elephant, such as the woolly mammoth, may have been like. A long-nosed dodo, perhaps.

One of the difficult elephants is the loxodont, but its survival is not due to a lack of trying on the part of African hunters. Of the tactics used by modern hunters which were available to the archaics (Fig. 3-10), mob attacks with spears can be successful (Long 1871). Pitfalls are also used, but loxodonts are very wary of these (Andersson 1861; Roberts 1951) even when driven by beaters or fires. Hamstringing can be devastatingly effective, since elephants are too heavy to walk on three legs (Roberts 1951), but this entails a high risk on the part of a hunter equipped only with a stone axe or knife. Above all, loxodonts are reported to stampede in a frenzied rage directly at an attacker, according to many eyewitness accounts (see in particular Andersson 1861:102-27). Whether this was true of the ancestral *Loxodonta adaurora* of the middle Pleistocene we cannot say, but this lineage survived and evolved after the advent of archaic *sapiens* while the extremely abundant and widespread African grasslands elephant (*Elephas recki*), became extinct.

Modern hunters in Africa have other techniques, probably of later origin, which are useful against the loxodonts. Among these are deadfalls along elephant trails fixed with huge spears (Livingstone cited in Waller 1875), and an even more effective technique of preparing a fire-ring in an area of elephant grass and setting it alight on all sides when a large herd is inside (Long 1871). Although bows and arrows are a late Paleolithic invention (Kuhn 1989), their use against elephants may have been limited; Wilkie (1989) notes that Efe pygmies do not use their poison arrows against elephants, but bring them down with spears (or guns) instead, and late Paleolithic hunters employed heavy lances in the great majority of documented elephant kills.

It is necessary to remember that the problem faced by late Paleolithic hunters in dealing with the innocent herds of Siberia and the New World, not to mention New Guinea and Australia, was not how to kill them, but how to get at them. Access to the northern hunting grounds and eventually the Beringia plains required an advance in survival skills (i.e., social support, shelter, clothing, and food storage) more than improved hunting techniques. After all, the hunting strategies developed to cope with co-evolved tropical proboscideans should have been more than adequate against "easy elephants" in the new lands. The characteristic projectile points of the early Paleoindian hunters (Fig. 3-12) — the Clovis points of North America and similar fish-tail points in South America — were too large for arrow-heads and must have been hafted on spears or javelins (Thomas 1988). Their principal association is with proboscidean kills, and their production ceased after the New World proboscideans became extinct.

3-12. Projectile points found at Fisher site in Southern Ontario. Points similar to these are found in association with the geologically youngest mastodon and mammoth remains. Courtesy of the Royal Ontario Museum.

Historical records show that subsistence hunters are very fond of proboscidean flesh, and go to great efforts to kill the animals at every opportunity. Even during the great ivory massacres few carcasses went to waste (Andersson 1861; Long 1871). Nevertheless, the most diligent and cunning Neolithic techniques were no more than an even match for the loxodonts, which were so abundant as to be a nuisance at the beginning of European and Arab exploitation.[14] Almost as soon as muskets were put into the hands of West African native hunters, however, the loxodont herds in the coastal regions and interior agricultural districts were quickly reduced to a few stragglers. The crucial role of firearms is even more clearly seen in East Africa where Arab traders did not equip client tribes with guns, but sent out their own bands of heavily armed plunderers to bring back slaves and ivory. The diaries of Livingstone (Waller 1875) document how abundant the animals were in "new grounds" where they had been hunted only by traditional methods prior to the arrival of the Arab-led gangs, and the rapidity with which all ivory-bearing adults could be wiped out by organized teams of a dozen or so men with muzzle-loading matchlocks.

SUMMARY

In the beginning, modest physical variation in the "kenyapithecine" hominids, perhaps selected for throwing ability, was the basis for a shift to an entirely new niche, that of the open-terrain gatherers and scavengers called australopithecines. This niche was made available in large part by elephant activity. In the new environment, greater manual dexterity and intellect, as well as food-sharing and pair-bonding, were advantageous to some australopithecines and were progressively enhanced in one gracile lineage. By great chance, such features turned out to be the vital pre-adaptations for another strategy: that of the hunting hominine, genus *Homo*, which could make and use edged tools for killing and butchering large animals. With this shift, humans were able to change from scavenger to top predator in the tropics and warm temperate region of the Old World, and the economy of scale seems to have made elephants the preferred prey almost from the beginning.

In the late Paleolithic, modern humans appeared. By their ability to overcome problems which were beyond the capability of their immediate ancestors, *Homo sapiens sapiens* spread swiftly across the globe. Bridles, baskets, cities, chimneys, diapers, dowries, irrigation systems, and a host of other innovations followed in due course, but this fantastic acceleration in human cultural evolution occurred *after* all physical evolution had ceased (Howell 1978; Stringer 1988). The last small step, which appeared in a local African population about ninety thousand years ago, must have included the full development of the speech association centers of the brain and a correlative expansion of understanding, in order to explain the sudden quickening of human culture.

Darwinian logic says that the mental and physical capabilities of modern humans must be explained exclusively in terms of the marginal advantage they originally conferred on members of the evolving population in times of high mortality and calamitous stress: in this case, late Paleolithic humans. In Leakey's hypothesis, many of the African and south Asian prey species had time to adapt under the selective pressure of early human hunters, and thereby survived to modern times. The corollary follows: as the prey either became extinct or harder to kill, hunting became more difficult, and the humans were likewise constantly under pressure to evolve into better hunters and gatherers. Not only hunters but also the hunted evolve in a never-ending duel of adaptations. In Africa, the prey species, including *Loxodonta*, are time-tested veterans of an escalating contest going back three million years, and the selective pressure on hunters was therefore consistently highest in this region. The growing aggressiveness and cunning of the elephant, in other words, may have been a major contributing factor in the evolution of first "archaic" and then "fully modern" humans in Africa.

Self-awareness would seem to be advantageous in improving hunting skills, but it would be crucial in the social skills — empathy, recognition of responsibility, projection, innovation. The development of society meant radically augmented powers of survival, mobility, and destruction compared to merely opportunistic bands of less reflective individuals.

Loxodonta and *Elephas* even then held their own, but when people who had descended from the survivors of millions of attacks on these "difficult" elephants entered northern Eurasia they found vast numbers of "easy" proboscideans and other large mammals which were no match for their skills. The resulting elephant rush carried humankind first into Siberia and then across the Bering Strait. The ancient world of the mammals in which proboscideans had reigned for seventeen million years melted away before their spears; thousands of years later, the current wildlife crisis hardly amounts to a postscript at the end of the last terrible chapter in the story of humans and elephants.

Physical evolution in humans has come to an end, at least temporarily. Culture is now the dominant factor in reproduc-tive success of weak and strong alike, and genetic variation is no longer being selected under any systematic longterm pressure. It bears repeating that the last increment in evolution, which liberated humans among all biological species from the inexorable statistics of natural selection, was the result of ruthless culling among African Paleolithic families some 90,000 years ago. Those who tended to survive were, by definition, more human than the others, and the most human among them may have survived when others died because they were better than the rest at finding and killing loxodonts. If without such tragic pressure our basic nature cannot change, then we must hope that human civilization – the gift, in large part, of our fellow African mammals – may yet be able to meet the challenge of our late Paleolithic selves.

NOTES

It is a pleasure to dedicate this essay to the memory of Louis Seymour Bazett Leakey.

1. In every way except human activity the "Recent" epoch appears to be a normal interglacial phase of the Pleistocene Ice Age.

2. Anatomically modern humans may be classed in the subspecies *Homo sapiens sapiens*; most workers now distinguish between "archaic" and "fully modern" subspecies on physiological evidence. The earliest remains of *sapiens sapiens* date from Africa and the Near East about 90,000 years ago, succeeding the pre-modern subspecies, *Homo sapiens heidelbergensis*, which first appeared about 500,000 years ago. Neanderthals were a separate European offshoot of the *heidelbergensis* subspecies who survived up to about 30,000 years ago.

3. A mammal's size is the major factor in the kind of food it needs, and thus its life strategies. Due to the scaling effect, smaller mammals lose heat more rapidly and must constantly eat high-quality food (seeds, buds, nectar/honey, meat, eggs). A larger herbivore, with less surface area compared to its mass, is more efficient at conserving heat and can subsist on rougher food like roots, grass, twigs, and mature foliage; (likewise, larger carnivores need to eat less often). Giant herbivores, i.e. those in which average adult weight exceeds 1,000 kg, are in a class by themselves in the ability to thrive on low-nutrient forage. Only four giant herbivores (giant in terms of body weight) exist today: the elephant, the hippo, the rhino, and the giraffe. To improve efficiency in gathering low-grade food, cranelike structures – trunk and neck respectively – were developed by proboscideans and giraffes to reach forage with a minimum of body movement. Proboscideans also added the bulldozer and the forklift to concentrate foliage for easier processing, in a combination that is the ultimate in giant mammal design.

4. The Cenozoic era encompasses Paleocene, Eocene, Miocene, Pliocene, and Pleistocene epochs.

5. The Tethys extended from Gibraltar to to the South China Sea before Fayum time (Dercourt et al. 1986). The Taurides, Elburz, Hindu Kush, and Himalayan mountain chains mark where different sections of the Tethys were squeezed shut about 50 million years ago by continental masses such as Anatolia, Iran-Afghanistan, and Indo-malaysia drifting up from the south. The Pontian-Zagros chain marks where the Mesopotamian shoulder of Afroarabia followed behind some 20 million years ago.

6. With infrequent exceptions the only dry-land connections between Africa and the outside world in the Miocene were isthmuses at the shallow south end of the Red Sea and at the Straits of Hormuz at the present mouth of the Persian Gulf.

7. The earliest emigrants were species of the four-tusker *Gomphotherium*, the shovel-jaw *Serbelodon*, and the primitive mammut *Zygolophodon* (C.T. Madden, pers. com. 1989).

8. Remains of these immigrants, including the primitive pliopithecid monkeys and the hominoid *Dryopithecus*, have been found throughout southern and central Europe. Between the first discovery in 1840 until Dubois found *Homo erectus* in Java in 1891 the European specimens were the only extinct hominoids known to science.

9. Hatley and Kappelman (1980) noted that the configuration of human molars, if not the canines and incisors, strikingly resemble those of bush-pigs and bears, and that these two groups also rely on deeply buried tubers when other food is scarce.

10. Interestingly, when normally selfish male chimpanzees come into possession of a piece of meat, they will share the food with begging females and juveniles, showing a marked preference for current or recent sexual partners and their offspring (Boesch and Boesch 1989).

11. Specifically, the transition from technologies classified as J. D. Clark's Mode III (Richard Klein 1983), with prepared-core and flake technology (Mousterian, Levalloisian, Aterian, most African Middle Stone Age sites) to those of Mode IV (e.g., the typical Upper Paleolithic of Eurasia, and some precocious Middle Stone Age sites in Africa and the Near East), together with Mode V (microlithic industries).

12. E.g., the shift from Mode I Acheulean hand-axe cultures to Mode II Mousterian re-touch (Volman 1984).

13. During Pleistocene glacial periods, the ocean level was lowered by approximately 100 meters, exposing the floor of shallow coastal seas all around the world. During these intervals the western Indonesian islands and Malaysia were transformed into a single enormous peninsula known to paleographers as Sundaland, and the Chukchi Sea became Beringia, a plain almost 2,000 km wide between Siberia and Alaska.

14. See Willem Bosman's account of conditions in the aptly named Ivory Coast in 1698, and the experiences of Mungo Park a century later, both quoted by Sanderson (1962).

A.

B.

A. Scene by Ndioba Sall, copied from "Tin Tin au Congo," depicting an exploit of the Belgian comic-strip character Tin Tin, 1990. 32.5 cm x 48.2 cm. Private collection.

B. Elephants drinking at a river, by Serigne-Gueye, 1990. 33 cm x 48.2 cm. FMCH X91.1611. Museum purchase.

C. Kenyan landscape, by unknown artist, 1991. 33 x 48 cm. FMCH X91.1609. Museum purchase.

D. Animal scene, by Mor-Gueye, 1991. 33 cm x 48.2 cm. FMCH X91.1610. Museum purchase.

PAINTINGS ON GLASS were apparently introduced into Dakar from North Africa around the turn of the 20th century. The first images were Muslim subjects for local consumption. Lately this focus has shifted, and artists make views of Africa directed primarily at tourists (Vogel 191:117). Despite its virtual disappearance from Senegal, the elephant figures prominently in these paintings. The medium lends itself to repetition, since figures are easily traced through a pane of glass. Some compositions are inspired by idealized Kenyan landscapes, others imitate the inventions of earlier artists. One artist, Ndioba Sall, specializes in copies of scenes from the Belgian comic strip character Tin Tin. The example seen here is from "Tin Tin au Congo."

FOUR

THE TALKING (GRAY) HEADS

ELEPHANT AS METAPHOR IN AFRICAN MYTH AND FOLKLORE

DONALD J. COSENTINO

I first glimpsed the African elephant from the verandah of a compound in the Mende village of Mattru in central Sierra Leone on a dry season night in 1974. I am speaking of an image, not of the species *Loxodonta africana* which I had seen as a child in a cage at the zoo, and knew in caricature from reading *Babar* to my own kids. My acquaintance with elephants wasn't great, but the others who were gathered on the compound to hear the storytelling that night could hardly claim better. Around Mattru wild animals were rare, other than the monkeys, duikers, and smaller bush mammals who survived the hunters' expeditions to the low forests surrounding the village.

This Mende separation from physical elephant, *helei*, had not always been the case. Oral histories record that many villages were founded by a hunter and his party at the site of an elephant kill. As Kenneth Little describes it, "whilst skinning the animal and consuming its flesh, they would erect a few temporary huts and clear enough, perhaps, of the surrounding virgin forest to grow a few grains of supplementary food. The reputation of the kill would attract outsiders, more huts would be set up, and the settlement grew into a large village under the leadership of the original pioneer and his kin" (1967:26-27). Within oral tradition there is even the suggestion that the land

itself may have been given to the Mende by the elephants, who were its first owners. Thus the foundation myth of Serabu, in Bumpe chiefdom, relates how a Mandingo hunter met a Banta (the name Mende give to the original inhabitants of their country) in the forest. The Banta became friends with the Mandingo, and gave him charge of the forest. Later, it turned out that this Banta was an elephant, "because in those days, elephants had the power of changing themselves into human beings" (Little 1967:26 n.).

A stone *nomoli* (Fig. 4-2) carved near the coast centuries ago recalls that original encounter between Mende and elephants. Splendid ivory carvings testify to Portuguese interactions with the Bullom Shore in the sixteenth century (Interleaf 13). And elephants are still seen in eastern Mendeland, near Liberia, as they are in the Kuranko lands to the north. But in Mattru, in 1973, the only physical remnant of the elephant was an ivory side-blown trumpet belonging to the section

4-1 (OPPOSITE). "...a herd of Elephant travelling through dense Native forest, where the sunlight is strewn down between the thick creepers in small spots and patches, pacing along as if they had an appointment at the end of the world" (Isak Dinesen, *Out of Africa*, p. 15). Photograph, Frans Lanting, Minden Pictures, 1990.

chief (Fig. 4-3); similar ones were prized as regalia throughout Mendeland (Interleaf 9). No one in Mattru, however, was likely to have seen an actual elephant ... least of all the middle-aged woman named Boi who was preparing to tell the next tale.

After the formulaic *Domei o domeisia!* (Story, stories!), which opens every Mende narrative performance, Boi began developing a familiar plot: the story of the young birds in search of their mother. The tale begins with a bird-mother who lays her eggs on a beach, waits until she despairs of their hatching, and finally wanders off. The babies hatch, of course, and the body of the narrative then consists of repeated encounters between the orphaned fledglings and a series of female birds, each the cause for a choral re-singing of the fledglings' call, until the bird-mother is discovered through the matching call of the narrator. When the two songs merge, the bird family wheels off into the sky to live happily every after.

4-2 (RIGHT). Stone carving of a person riding an elephant, made by people living on the Bullom coast of Sierra Leone probably in the 15th or 16th century. Works such as these, frequently unearthed in Mendeland, are called *nomoli* and believed by the Mende to be connected with an earlier race of small people. The elephant rider is a bit unusual; more often such carvings depict a single figure, seated or crouching. Steatite. 22.5 cm. The Trustees of the British Museum, 1953 Af.19.1.

4-3 (BELOW). Pa S.K. Weaver, Mattru Section Chief, Tikonko Chiefdom, demonstrates his method for blowing his ivory trumpet, one of several pieces of prized regalia. Mattru Kolainima near Bo, Sierra Leone, 1974. Photograph, H. Cosentino.

But not in Boi's version.[1] It was apparent from the start that she had a more perverse dénouement in mind. *It is a time of war*, she began, jerking her story out of mythic time and into an unhopeful present. Boi's bird-mother lays her eggs, waits, despairs, and wanders off, as usual. But Boi makes the terms of her desertion even more profound, and the hiatus between mother and fledglings more extreme: the mother is transformed from a bird to a human being. The transformation is unjustified and unexplained; Boi shares Somerset Maugham's insight on good storytelling, "Do not explain over much." The disjunction she creates is no longer just geographical. The young birds must move through space, but they must also cross from the animal world of the bush to the human world of the village in order to regain their mother. That dividing line is the most decisive in Mende narrative and social reality.

So the birds do not visit other birds in search of their mother. Instead, they move from one human group to another, in an ascending scale of prestige from young girl to chief. Finally they confront their mother manqué in the most banal of circumstances — having her hair plaited by a friend on a verandah. When she hears the choral sound of the young birds' song, she excuses herself saying she wishes to urinate in back of the house. Once out of sight, she undergoes a second metamorphosis. The mother bird becomes an elephant!

PLANETARY SIGHTINGS

The audience on the verandah that night appreciated and yet was not startled by what seemed to me an extraordinary twist of the plot. As Mende people, they knew that metamorphosis occurs, especially among those who operate at the periphery of the human sphere. Sometimes in their stories the significance of the transformation is ambiguous, but Boi's meaning was apparently quite plain. From other stories, and from what the Mende say of the world, it is apparent that the change from human to elephant is also the move from life to death.[2] Elephants are the physical form assumed by the spirits of the dead. By evoking the image of this second metamorphosis, Boi made the hiatus between mother and children complete. She has escaped them forever by becoming the ineffable "other," the shadow of the dead whose unapproachable presence the Mende have sensed in the solemn gray hulk of the elephant.

That Mende understanding of the elephant metaphor was made clearer a few days after Boi's performance, when I heard our neighbor Kini Sam perform a variant of another familiar story — one I have entitled "A Defiant Maid Marries a Stranger."[3] In this tale, the defiant heroine is smitten by a handsome stranger so she follows him into the bush against the advice of friends, family, and the handsome stranger himself. As they are about to cross the threshold to the stranger's place, his comely features drop away one by one and he stands revealed as a monster. In Mende narrative, the exact proportions of the monstrosity are rarely made explicit. Rather such creatures are

referred to as Big Things (*Ha'i Waisia*), a vague metonymy suggesting an Other as tremendous and unnamable as the Semitic God. This Other is made all the more frightening by the narrator's nasalized chortle as the Big Thing menaces the heroine. But in Sam's version the defiant heroine accepts her lover's metamorphosis, changes herself into an elephant, and tramps after him into the forbidden bush.

Kini Sam was playing with a range of metaphoric meaning in allowing this final transformation to the heroine. As elephant she has become an ancestor, yes, but more profoundly, she has become the most absolute of the Other: the ultimate Big Thing. Elephant is dominant in the bush; Human is master of the village. Village and bush are the ultimate entities in the Mende cosmos. They are separate planets made of disparate stuff, but bound by gravitational pulls. An elephant-sighting in a Mende narrative is Voyager transmitting a picture of Neptune back to Pasadena — an awesome view of another world — vastly different from our own, but bound by physical laws of ineffable attraction. In Mende cosmology, the elephant is the gray planet (Fig. 4-4). This same association of the elephant with the astral and the ineffable reverberates from Africa to Europe, from oral traditions to the written word.

Comparison of the august status of elephant in Mende art and thought with its position in other African oral traditions begs some scholarly questions of elephantine proportions. As Lévi-Strauss discerned, "The truth of a myth [or the symbols it contains] does not lie in any special content. It consists in logical relations which are devoid of content…" (1969:240). Thus we can't gauge the comparative significance of the elephant in African folklore merely by cataloguing her/his narrative intrusions in some hypothetical pan-African folktale anthology or *Bibliographa Elephanta*. We can only know elephant as s/he operates within particular narrative contexts.

But field experience, library research, and existing (inadequate) motif indices do suggest that there are symbolic universals, tempered by ecological and historical factors, at work in African oral narrative traditions, and the art derived from it. The most important of these universals is sacred geography. Every African narrative tradition I know divides the cosmos into human and non-human sectors, the Village/Bush split described for Mende. And that division is marked by sanctions which will differ from society to society. Elephant contra other forest creatures, Wo/Man contra forest creatures, Woman contra Man: all will take their symbolic atomic weight from the content of those sanctions. Within that common division of sacred geography, then, the relative position of elephant as queen/king of the forest and wo/man as master of the village can be compared in traditions across the continent. It must be understood, however, that the comparisons are purely platonic. They remain unknown to the artists who employ the image of the elephant. Comparative symbolic analysis may suggest a dazzling holistic dimension to oral traditions, but it is well to remember the cautionary note sounded by Octavio Paz in his critique of *The Raw and the Cooked*:

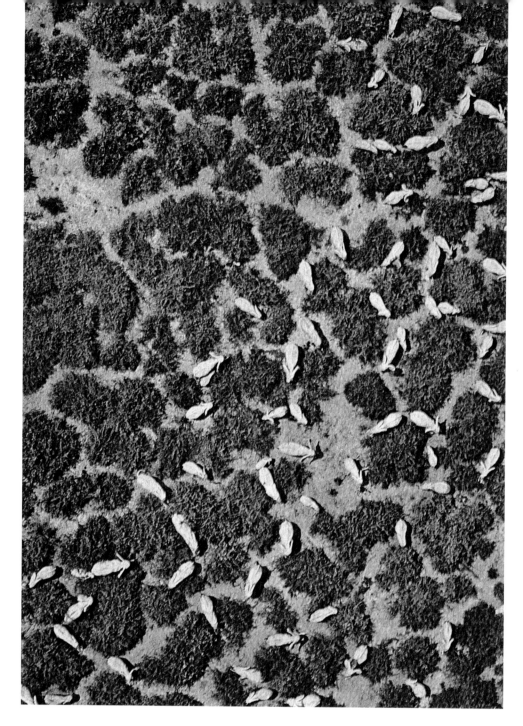

4-4. An elephant-sighting in a Mende narrative is Voyager transmitting a picture of Neptune back to Pasadena – an awesome view of another world – vastly different from our own, but bound by physical laws of ineffable attraction. In Mende cosmology, the elephant is the gray planet. Photograph, I. Douglas Hamilton.

The situation ... is analogous to that of musicians performing a symphony while being kept incommunicado and separated from each other in time and space: each would play his fragment as if it were the complete work. No one among them would be able to hear the concert because in order to hear it one must be outside the circle, far from the orchestra. (Paz 1970:40)

One such fragment, exquisitely counterpointing the Mende elephant transformations, is found in the Chadian tale of "The Woman Elephant" (Edicef 1975:29-35). In that tale a hunter spies a number of young women playing in a river. After their bath, they come out of the water and slip into the rough gray skins which they had left on shore. They are elephant-women. The next day the hunter hides the skin of the most beautiful so she cannot return with the herd to the forest. By this trick he takes her home and she becomes his human wife. He hides her real skin at the bottom of his millet granary. Years later their son spies the hidden skin and tells his mother. And so on that day elephant-woman prepares her revenge:

> That day she was so excited that she worked quickly, quickly. This surprised many people who asked her if she was going somewhere. She just laughed .... Then she just plaited her hair, took her bath and oiled her body with vegetable oil. Next she bathed her children. After doing this, she took her skin and put it on. She took a pestle and threw it: peenre! and the pestle became her trunk. She let fall the mortar: dii, she took another and let it fall: dii, and her four feet appeared. The children ran in all directions crying: "Our mother has become an elephant! Our mother has become an elephant!"
>
> She broke the straw fence, and started running with heavy steps and disappeared into the bush. She breathed in the forest air with furor and found her husband. She caught him, tore him and threw him away.[4]

How many messages flash from the furor of the traduced elephant-wife? With the perfect economy of image, the narrator has dramatically revealed the unbridgeable dichotomy that must separate the worlds of bush and village. Between human and elephant there is no sympathetic correspondence. There is only respect for the chasm. And by extension, the images suggest that something of the same chasm separates human husbands and wives. The price for a false conjunction is death.

Powerful metaphors indeed, but the ethnographic data suggest that these transformational concepts are more than metaphors. They are existential realities. In two extraordinary dialogues, anthropologist and poet Michael Jackson recorded the shape shifting experiences of Mohammed Fofona, diamond prospector and *Yelamafentiginu* (1990:59-78). In his Kuranko language, the term means "change thing master," and denotes a man who has the ability to change himself into a predatory or dangerous animal. Jackson discovered Fofona's special gift in October, 1979. While they were staying together as guests of a Kuranko M.P. in Freetown, Sierra Leone, the anthropologist queried the prospector about his clan totem (p. 62):

Kamei, the elephant! [Mohammed] said; *to eat elephant meat would make one's skin disfigured.* Then he told me, *Some Fofona men can change into elephants,* and added that he *himself possessed that gift.*

Given Mohammed's rather elephantine build, his claim amused as much as intrigued me. I asked him to tell me more. Would it be possible for me to accompany him to an isolated place in the bush and observe him undergo the change? When he changed, did he feel enlarged and powerful like an elephant – a change in the way he experienced his body rather than an actual physical metamorphosis? His replies were disheartening. The change would not be possible in my presence, but yes he did actually undergo a physical metamorphosis. The power was something he had been born with; he had possessed it even as a child. It was, he said, an inner faculty – *bu ro koe* ('belly in thing') – a private matter – *morgo konta koe* ('person inner understanding') – and could only be discussed among and comprehended by others having the same bent.

In 1985, both men met again in the diamond town of Koindu, and continued their dialogue (p. 68):

Did he change by first conjuring up an image of an elephant in his mind? *No,* he said, *that was not necessary. But you must have a purpose, such as destroying someone's crop. If someone offends you and you cannot take your revenge by any ordinary means you'll walk ahead of that person in the bush, change, then fall on him as he passes on his way back to his village.*

Do people change into animals to get a sense of power? I asked.

Yes.
How long does the metamorphosis last?
That depends – but usually no more than 12 hours.
Is it difficult to remain an elephant all that time?
No.

I then asked Mohammed if he retained full consciousness during metamorphosis. *Yes,* he said, *because you must know to change back to human form.* He reflected a moment. *But you must be alone in the bush to do it.*

Regarding this extraordinary testimony, Jackson observes, "It may be because Kuranko so often interpret changes in experience as evidence of changes in the external world that many informants, Mohammed among them, were so dismissive of my questions as to whether shape shifters *really* changed or only *thought* they did. Perhaps the Kuranko are more pragmatic than most anthropologists: if illusions have real and useful consequences, then they are truths" (p. 73).

CODING THE TRUNK: IS ELEPHANT AN OLD WOMAN?

For the pastoral Samburu of northern Kenya elephants are often referred to as "old women." When anthropologist Elliot Fratkin asked why, Samburu informants remarked that their anatomical similarity was perfectly obvious: *The elephant has breasts the same as an old woman, and her vagina is in the same place – no difference.* When Fratkin retorted that the elephant's trunk reminded him of a male feature conspicuously missing from the female, the Samburu seemed genuinely shocked, insisting that there was no relation between a man and an elephant (1974:3-5). These beliefs are ratified in food taboos. A Samburu may never eat elephant meat. If he dared to bring elephant meat into the *manyata*, all the cattle would die from the smell. Questioning further, Fratkin was told the story of "How Elephants Came to Eat Trees," which illuminated these Samburu beliefs and customs (see page 86).

In this myth Elephant is the undisputed master – or matriarch – of the bush, the apotheosis of the natural world. But she is pitted against God, who is master of the supra-natural. In the terminology of structural anthropology the opposition is ultimately Nature vs. Culture, imaged in the myth as Elephant vs. God, and understood in Samburu society as Woman vs. Man. So from this tale the following relationships can be postulated:

WOMAN : MAN :: ELEPHANT : GOD :: NATURE : CULTURE

And indeed in Samburu society we find all the familiar hallmarks of this formula: sexual segregation of boys from mothers, their rebirth into culture through genital mutilation by other males, ritual categorization of women as unclean – all the baggage of male separation and domination ingeniously boxed on the back of old woman elephant.

HOW ELEPHANTS CAME TO EAT TREES

Long ago, Elephant said to God, "I am bigger than you, and I will eat animals." God replied, "No. You will eat trees," to which Elephant refused.

So God said, "Can you beat me?" and Elephant replied, "Yes, if you rain, I can rain."

And God said, "Let me see you rain. I want to see the water run."

So Elephant made a small hole into which he urinated. When he finished, God asked, "Have you rained?" to which Elephant replied, "Yes."

Then God said, "Make a light as a signal," and Elephant wagged his head so that his tusks moved back and forth, and God asked, "Have you made a signal?" to which Elephant replied, "Yes."

And God said to Elephant, "Can you shout?" and Elephant made a mighty sound.

Then God said, "Let me hear you shake in your stomach," and Elephant made a rumbling noise in his stomach.

Finally God said, "Wait for me!" And He brought forth a wind and rain and lightning, and He shouted and blew until Elephant could take no more and said, "Leave me alone. I will eat trees!"

ELEPHANTS AND ORISAS

The Yoruba/Fon cultures of Nigeria and the République du Bénin (formerly Dahomey) also conceive of the elephant operating within complex supernatural hierarchies, ineffably distanced from the human world like the gray planets of the Mende, but intimately connected with the *orisas* (divinities) Sango of Lightning, Ogun of Iron, and Orunmila, master of Ifa divination. The complexity of this taxonomy is immediately apparent in the baroque verse-praises of "Salute to the Elephant" *(Oriki Erin)* recorded by S.A. Babalola (see page 88).

These praises *(oriki)* constitute an *ijala* (hunter's poem), a genre of Yoruba verse similar to the ode in its enthusiasms, and random articulations. The randomness of form serves to articulate the many-sidedness of the elephant in Yoruba thought: its stature and strength only the physical manifestation of vast spiritual power *(ase)*; its enormity at once a source of amazement and dread. This Yoruba elephant is not at all unlike William Blake's Tiger: …"What immortal hand or eye/Could frame thy fearful symmetry?/ In what distant deeps or skies/ Burnt the fire of thine eyes/ On what wings dare he aspire?/ What the hand dare seize the fire?/ And what shoulder, and what art,/ Could twist the sinews of thy

heart?/ And when thy heart began to beat,/ What dread hand? and what dread feet?"

But unlike Blake, the unnamed composer of the Yoruba *ijala* was not constructing simply from the fire of his imagination. Oral poets create their metaphors from concrete observations, as the elegant descriptions of elephant's eyes and ears and trunk reveal.

It is easy to move from reverence to apotheosis. Thus another Yoruba oral poet finds no incongruity in linking the forest and sky thunderers in his *oriki*:

If the elephant trumpets in the forest, fright seizes the hunter.

If Sango thunders, woods and forests tremble. [5]

To the Yoruba, the metaphor may become the god. Thus Erinle, whose name means "elephant of the earth," is regarded as the *orisa* of the bush. Like Ogun, he is a hunter deity who according to R. G. Armstrong disappeared into the earth after turning himself into an elephant. He became one of a coterie of elephant-related hunters associated with Ogun, including

Timoyin, the culture hero of Oshogbo. A priest of Ogun, Timoyin one day killed a female elephant who was in the act of giving birth. To atone for this crime, Timoyin established a shrine for the elephant calf, and in time became himself an avatar of the *orisa* Ogun. Susanne Wenger, impresaria of the neo-Yoruba art revival known as the Oshogbo School, celebrated this myth by creating a huge batik in which the unfortunate elephant mother in parturition is the central figure (Barnes 1989:30).

Nor are the Yoruba themselves loath to bring heaven down to earth. The divinatory verses, *odu*, state quite specifically the practical uses that Orunmila, the patron of Ifa, may make of the elephant:

> *After Orunmila had performed sacrifice,*
> *The elephant died without even falling sick at all.*
> *Orunmila then commanded that its tusks should be removed;*
> *And with it he carved iróké....*
> *"When the elephant died,*
> *We used its tusks to carve delicate objects."* [6]

Ifa is fate, and Orunmila, like the Norns in Germanic myths, holds the power of secrets greater than the Gods, or the spirits of dead elephants (see Drewal in this volume).

Much the same conclusions may be drawn from the myths of the enterprising Fon who live to the west of the Yoruba. Over the last three hundred years the Fon have borrowed extensively from their neighbors' mythology, incorporating some of the *orisas,* as well as Ifa divination, into their religious systems. In the Fon divination myth, "The Boxing Contest: Bird Outwits Elephant," recorded by Frances and Melville Herskovits (1958:197-98), Elephant is humiliated and ultimately killed through the agency of Legba, patron of the dark side of the divination process. But while subservient to fate, Elephant still remains clearly superior to humans in those same myths. When Dada Segbo, the culture hero of the Kingdom of Dahomey, seeks to sacrifice Elephant to the dead, his plans are forever undone by a pious old woman who insists that Elephant must never be tied (pp. 319-20). And when Amifunhè tries to sell his friend Hetablè, the bird, an elephant as a riding horse, they both learn a sorry lesson (p. 415):

> *Amifunhè said, "This is a horse from Gbo-odè." Hetablè said he had never seen a horse like that before. The elephant, Ajinaku, now told Amifunhè and his friends who brought him here, to play the drum for him that he might dance. While he danced, Ajinaku uprooted trees and threw them everywhere. He broke down walls, broke down everything. Hetablè said, "I don't want the money and I don't want the horse. Take him back to his master."*
>
> *And to this very day, the bird, Hetablè says, "Take him away. Take him away. I don't want him here.*

The Fon Elephant (Interleaf XI), like the ones who have

marched in the previous myths, cannot be contained within merely human arrangements. His obligations are cosmic, not social.

CHARTERING ELEPHANTS: *IN THE BEGINNING...*

Since Malinowski's time, we have understood that myth may function as charter, sanctifying origins and legitimizing institutions. Elephant myths have functioned as such in traditional African societies, and continue to legitimize contemporary social and economic arrangements, and exalt particular political heroes (or tyrants).

There is a Kongo myth in which elephant plays all the key genesis roles: the conditions of life are created out of his great gray flesh, and the ur-Bantu Adam out of a suspiciously familiar fruit discovered by the ur-Bantu Eve. According to that myth, long ago elephant came down to earth from heaven where he was born. One day he met Lightning, who had also come down from heaven. They agreed to hold a competition in noise making (according to the pattern of the God/Elephant contest established in the Samburu myth). Elephant trumpeted grandly, but Lightning let forth such a blast that Elephant dropped dead of fright on the spot. *His body just lay there, and his bowels started fermenting. His stomach began to swell up until it burst, and out of it came all the seeds of all the good plants that Elephant had been eating in Heaven. That is how vegetables came to the Earth.* (Knappert 1971:166).

One day a young girl finds a *tondo* fruit (used to cure yaws) nicely ripe and red. She brings it home and puts it in a box. Later she opens the box and finds a complete man inside. He says his name is Tondo-lindo. They fall in love and marry. One day Tondo-lindo goes to the forest place where the ur-elephant burst, and there he finds many seeds and vegetables. He too collects them, brings them home, and puts them in a box which no one is able to open. One day an old woman (an elephant avatar à la Samburu?) comes along and opens it, and *Lo, innumerable little children emerged, who flew away in different directions, like young ants in the rainy season* (Knappert 1971: 166). Presumably from these little flying Cains and Abels of the Kongo Genesis myth the world was populated – our world, born out of and sustained by elephant's putrefying, fecund flesh.

The Kongo myth takes place *in illo tempore,* that shadowy time before history when the outlines of the present world were created. A decidedly more historical account of genesis, and elephant's place in the creation of the modern world, is told by other Bantu speakers living on the shores of Corisco Bay in Gabon. In that myth, collected at the beginning of this century by R. H. Nassau (1912:82-84), many of the terms of the Kongo Genesis are reversed, and the message accordingly darkened.

In the beginning are three human brothers Uhadwe, Bokume, and Njaku, born of one mother. Uhadwe insists that the brothers separate, he to the Great Sea and his brothers to the

ORIKI ERIN (SALUTE TO THE ELEPHANT) [7]

O elephant, possessor of a savings-basket full of money.

O elephant, huge as a hill, even in a crouching posture.

O elephant, enfolded by honor; demon flapping fans of war. *

Demon who snaps tree branches into many pieces and moves on to the forest farm.

O elephant, who ignores 'I have fled to my father for refuge',

Let alone 'to my mother'.

Mountainous Animal, Huge Beast who tears a man like a garment.

    And hangs him up on a tree.

The sight of whom causes people to stampede towards a hill of safety.

My chant is a salute to the elephant.

Ajanaku who walks with a heavy tread. †

Demon who swallows palm-fruit bunches whole, even with the spiky pistil-cells.

O elephant, praisenamed Laaye, massive animal blackish-gray in complexion.

O elephant, who single-handed causes a tremor in a dense tropical forest.

O elephant, who stands sturdy and alert, who walks slowly as if reluctantly.

O elephant, whom one sees and points towards with all one's fingers.

The hunter's boast at home is not repeated when he really meets the elephant.

Ajanaku looks back with difficulty like a person suffering from a sprained neck.

The elephant has a porter's knot without having any load on his head.

The elephant's head is his burden which he balances.

O elephant praisenamed Laaye, 'O death, please stop following me'

This is part and parcel of the elephant's appellation.

If you wish to know the elephant, the elephant who is a veritable ferry-man,

The elephant whom honour matches, the elephant who continually swings his trunk,

    His upper fly-switch,

It's the elephant whose eyes are veritable water-jars.

O Elephant, the vagrant par excellence

    Whose molar teeth are as wide as palm-oil pits in Ijesaland. **

O elephant, lord of the forest, respectfully called Oriiribobo.

O elephant, whose teeth are like shafts.

One tooth of his is a porter's load, O elephant fondly called Otiko

Who has a beast-of-burden's proper neck.

O elephant whom the hunter sometimes sees face-to-face.

    O elephant whom the hunter at other times sees from the rear.

Beast who carries mortars and yet walks with a swaggering gait.

Primeval leper, animal treading ponderously.

forest. Bokume goes to the forest and becomes the Mahogany Tree. But Njaku is angry with the division (Nassau 1912:83):

> Njaku departed; but he went in anger, saying, "I will not remain in the forest. I am going to build with the townspeople." He came striding back to the town. As he emerged there from the forest, his feet swelled, and swelled, and became elephant feet. His ear extended way down. His teeth spreading, this one grew to a tusk, and that one grew to a tusk. The townspeople began to hoot at him. And he turned back to the forest. But, as he went, he said to them, "In my going now to the Forest, I and whatever plants you shall plant in the forest shall journey together," [i.e., that their plantations should be destroyed by him]. So Njaku went; and their food went.

Uhadwe himself went down to the sea and created a sand bank which brought him to the land of the whites. There he prepared a ship full of white man's cargo, and a crew to bring it back to Africa. The ship went back to Africa and put down anchor, but the natives had no way to reach it since they were destitute of canoes. Finally, Uhadwe appears to the townspeople in a dream, and tells them to cut down Mahogany, dig it into a canoe, and paddle out to the cargo ship. The whites and Africans eventually create a pidgin language which allows one white sailor to explain (p. 84):

4-5. Instead of the lush Kongo association of Elephant with seeds and fecundity, there is the exchange of rifles for tusks, and Europe's charge to kill the herds. These instructions come from the cargo ship anchored offshore like a Death Star, offering Java prints, tobacco, red caps ... the detritus of 19th-century industrial Europe, for the teeth or feet of the elephant. Photograph, Private collection.

> "I have come to buy the tusks of the beast which is here in the forest with big feet and tusks and great ears, that is called Njaku." They said, "Yes! a good thing!" When they were about leaving, the white man advancing to them, deposited with them four bunches of tobacco, four bales of prints, four caps, and other things.
>
> When they reached the shore, they told the others, "The white men want Njaku's tusks; and also have things by which to kill his tribe."
>
> The next morning, they went to the white men; they were trusted with guns and bullets and powder; they went to the forest, and fought with the elephants. In two days the ship was loaded, and it departed. This continues to happen so until this day, in the Ivory-Trade.

History is pushing hard at the surface of this myth, the evil eye of Joseph Conrad's world beaming through the crust of

4-6. Ivory bric-a-brac for sale in the tourist art market in Dakar, Senegal. Photograph, Raymond Silverman, 1982.

4-7. Guro mask depicting Houphouet Boigny, president of Côte d'Ivoire, with his hands on two elephants. Jeremiah Cole Collection. Photograph, John Nunley, 1989.

Bantu allegory. The elephant, source of life in the Kongo myth, here is the commodity of colonial imposition. Instead of the lush Kongo association of Elephant with seeds and fecundity, there is the exchange of rifles for tusks, and Europe's charge to kill the herds. These instructions come from the cargo ship anchored offshore like a Death Star, offering Java prints, tobacco, red caps … the detritus of nineteenth-century industrial Europe, for the teeth – or feet – of the elephant (Fig. 4-5). It is the responsibility of myth to rationalize social reality, to create a logical narrative order out of the caprice of history. So the myth projects onto Elephant – angry, anti-social, crop-destroying Njaku – responsibility for the fate he has suffered since piano keys, cue balls, and bric-a-brac became things of value to white people (Fig. 4-6). This is not cosmology, it is an allegory of the ivory trade, and the world of imperial economies and colonial rule which it generated.

Killing African elephants did not of course begin with instructions from the cargo ship. Maasai youths kill elephants and lions as part of their rite of passsage into the warrior class, *moran*. But, maintains Cynthia Moss, their hunting is part of elephant ecology. Both elephants and warriors have adapted their life styles to that ritual combat (1988:272-74). And elsewhere in African cosmologies, the death of the elephant is circumscribed by ritual and taboo. Cardinall reports that in Togo one must take care to have nothing to do with a dead elephant. That will surely bring bad luck, especially if one takes his tusks away. The discoverer of the dead elephant is in the same category as its slayer. He must give it a funeral which usually ends in the hunters' dance, "…a practice common to every tribe from the sea to the desert" (1931:122).

A very different kind of relationship between man and elephant is established in the Corisco Bay myth. This myth marks the moment when Europe joins Africa in the transformation of elephant from being to commodity. And that transformation becomes reflected in the narrative imagery of Euro-America as well. There is a line of historical and literary descent from Uhadwe's cargo ships trading arms for ivory, to Kurtz piling up tusks amid unspeakable horrors in the *Heart of Darkness*, to Ernest Hemingway shooting everything in sight in *The Green Hills of Africa* (1935). By Hemingway's time, there is no ritual left in the hunt. The White Hunter he describes (e.g. the narrator in *The Short Happy Life of Francis Macomber*, Harry in *The Snows of Kilimanjaro*), desperate to find his manhood, seems unable to step outside his tent without killing something.

But the world of the White Hunter inspires a contrary reaction in Romain Gary's novel, *The Roots of Heaven* (1958). Writing in the years after World War II, Gary describes a bomber crew of idealists willing to die to save the Sahelian elephant from the poachers. For this very peculiar foreign legion, the elephant is the antidote to Hitler and Stalin, Auschwitz and Hiroshima. The destruction of the enormous, clumsy, free-tramping elephants can only prelude the destruction of man. In his review of this novel, V. S. Pritchett drew this lesson from Gary, "If the elephant vanished the loss to human laughter,

wonder and tenderness would be a calamity" (cited in Moss 1988:14). The ineffable image of the elephant, so powerfully expressed in Kongo, Mende, and Yoruba myths, comes full circle to re-expression in this brilliant, neglected novel.

RUNNING WITH THE ELEPHANTS

It has been the fate of myth to become politicized in the twentieth century. Our heroes are now our political leaders who become the protagonists of our folklore, and the subjects of our sentimental and often kitschy industrial arts: for a while, Lenin (and for a shorter time, Stalin), the Kennedys (JFK, Bobby, and Jackie), Dr. King, Mao Tse-Tung – or, in an African context: Houphouet Boigny (Fig. 4-7), Jomo Kenyatta, Patrice Lumumba, Samora Machel, the Mandelas (Nelson and Winnie), Steve Biko. These modern African heroes certify their statures by association with venerable icons of power, including the image of the elephant.

For the Yoruba, coupling man's fate with the elephant is an honor reserved for heroes, as expressed in this elegy from the kingdom of Ede:

> I say rise, and you will not rise.
> If Olu is told to rise, Olu will rise.
> If Awo is told to rise, he will rise.
> The newly wedded bride gets up at a bidding,
> Although she dares not call her husband by name.
> The elephant on waking gets up,
> The buffalo on waking gets up,
> The elephant lies down like a hill.
> Alas! The elephant has fallen,
> And can never get up again! [8]

This same imagery is used to garland the elegy for an imposing contemporary hero, the late Nigerian General Murtala Ramat Muhammed who was killed in a coup attempt in 1976:

> What are we to do about this?
> The elephant has fallen, the elephant cannot get up
> See how the elephant lies down like a mountain
> Where is Murtala, the Head of the Armed Forces
> of our nation?
> They say he is dead
> And battle has killed him
> The leader of the Armed Forces has fallen,
> He cannot get up
> And you plotters have brought death on Muhammed. [9]

A more dramatic example of the expropriation of Elephant lore for modern political purposes occurred during the Biafran War (1967-70). Igbo soldiers fighting against the federal armies of General Murtala (inter alia) sang and pushed their bodies to the pounding, mantric rhythm of a well-known chant [10] whose lyric goes:

Nzogbu, nzogbu	Trample, trample
Enyi mba, enyi	Elephant herd, elephant
Nzogbu, enyi mba	Trample, elephant herd[11]

This chant is not confined to times of war; in southern Igboland, at least, it is more commonly used in communal work parties: men raise and lower their hoes in unison voicing these words as they prepare yam ridges for planting; chanting the same phrase, school boys at their afternoon chores have wielded machetes to clear the playing fields of grass. The great looping swing of arms from torso mimics the sway of the elephant's trunk and bodily evokes that animal's power to mow down all before it.

That elephants are so vigorously remembered in song and in body, as well as in mask and sculpture, attests to the enduring power of elephant as concept in Igbo culture. Or perhaps it is the other way around. Perhaps it is the power of song that sustains the image of the elephant. The simple chant, sung frequently, with complementary dance gestures, in a quotidian context, would act as a powerful mimesis, drawing men together in traditional communal activity that is energized and even sacralized by the elephant model. Thus the elephant as metaphor keeps living in the minds and bodies of the Igbo people.[12]

These observations on the curious persistence of the elephant as trope – long after the animal itself has physically retreated or even disappeared – have equal relevance for other genres of African myth and folklore. The herds remain in the minds and repertoires of the artists.

DUPING THE CHIEF: ELEPHANT AND TRICKSTER

From the diverse African folklore so far discussed a certain figure of the elephant consistently emerges: an enormous creature distant from humans but linked closely to the supernatural in the chain of being. But there is an entire subset of oral narrative where none of this is true. In the trickster tales, quantitatively the major part of most oral narrative traditions, the elephant is merely big. And arrogant. And dumb. To understand this precipitous decline in elephant's reputation, one must understand the function of trickster tales – particularly their relationship to social structure – and the use of animal imagery to objectify social relations.

Everything about a trickster tale is paradoxical. All the characters in these tales are animals, but all their characteristics are human. The tales are set in mythic time, but they are intensely relevant to the current scene. The protagonist is always the littlest and the least: a creature like Spider, Hare, Tortoise, Mouse, or household animals like Cock or Goat, all of whom are physically weak and taxonomically ambiguous. Pitted against the trickster is the biggest and most powerful: Lion or Leopard, Bre'r Fox or Bre'r Bear, Coyote, Elmer Fudd – or Elephant. Trickster the eternal child, motivated only by his perpetual quest for self-gratification, challenges the biggest guy in town. And through the tactics of his tricks, almost always manages to undo him.

It is no wonder then that trickster tales are so popular, especially among children for whom the plight of the powerless is an existential reality. But trickster tales are also told by and to adults, for unequal distribution of power is also a social reality. And within the powerful/powerless paradigm established by these tales it is possible to see another set of integers: the rulers and the ruled. From village to village, or state to state, the definition of those categories change. But the categories themselves remain. And when Elephant appears, he is always the chief. The Bamileke have a simple tale which explains the natural kingship of Elephant, and provides a precedent for tempering the royal will:

The Hare and the Elephant

In fact, impressed by the size of the elephant, the hare went to ask him for his secrets. But by the law of the elders, such secrets are not revealed for nothing. The elephant gave hare three riddles to solve in order to become as big as he.

At the appointed day, the elephant realized that the three riddles were perfectly solved. He therefore called an extraordinary assembly of all the animals in the forest. On the appointed day, every one was present, and the elephant standing before his throne started to speak, "People of the forest, my citizens, the hare had asked me to teach him the secret to become as big as your majesty. To challenge his ambition, I proposed to him three difficult riddles – but, let me tell you the truth, all the truth. Thus, to make you or anyone as big as myself, I regret that I cannot do it. Only God can do that. We are all born according to the creator of the world. Nevertheless, because you deserve it, I can do one thing for you. By these words, I swear today that I will never do anything or henceforth take any decision concerning the kingdom without discussing with you or listening to your opinion."[13]

Like many trickster tales, this Bamileke narrative ends with an etiology: the establishment of checks on the rule of the powerful. It is primary material for a grasslands Magna Carta. But in very few tales do the duper or the duped act so reasonably. More typical are the many variants of "The Cord of Competition," where Trickster (Hare, Tortoise, etc.) taunts Elephant into a tug of war (Bikoi and Soundjok 1978:59-61). Eager to pay back the insults, Elephant grabs one end of the rope while Trickster surreptitiously ties the other end to (inter alia) another elephant, a tree, or a hippotamus. Exhausted, Elephant finally gives up, learning that size is no match against wit. There may be other lessons to be drawn from this contest, such as the Yoruba adage, "Where two elephants engage in a fight, the grass will never thrive again" (Areje 1985:13).

A more profound etiology emerges from the many versions of "The Battle between the Cock and the Elephant." A Sahelian

version begins *in illo tempore*, when all the animals lived together without categories, and the species intermarried. Cock is fighting Elephant to marry the farmer's daughter. Elephant is furious at the presumption, stamping his foot so hard that a water hole appears. Cock in turn pulls out his tail feather, trying to frighten Elephant by saying it's a hair from his nose. The two set a duel and each arrives with his supporters: all the quadrupeds with Elephant, all the birds with Cock. When Elephant sends Monkey up the tree to reconnoiter, Cock dispatches Buse and Calao to fly over him dropping a calabash full of millet and a calabash of shea butter on his head. Monkey cries out in pain. Elephant, seeing the white and red liquids flowing down Monkey's face, is hoisted on Cock's petard:

The elephant, who raised his head as the monkey screamed, cried: "We are in trouble! Cock is not joking. He just broke the head of monkey. Look at his brains and the blood flowing!" At this sight fear spread among the four legged troupe. The bees, who belong to the group of cock, upon seeing that decided to take advantage of the situation and went on the attack. They approached the elephant and all of a sudden penetrated his ears, his trunk, his mouth and went about stinging him here and there.

The elephant, in great pain and not able to defend himself against the insects which occupy the interior of his body, ran very far into the forest, breaking all that was in his way.

The animals on four legs did not resist but also ran away leaving the arena for the animals with wings. Cock was declared

4-8. *Who dares say Mr. Elephant blows a fart?* (Baule proverb). Photograph, Rick Weyerhauser, World Wildlife Fund – U.S.

the winner and was warmly congratulated by the spectators. He could now marry the girl.

That is the reason why since then the elephant has remained in the bush and the cock in the village, even if they no longer give him beautiful girls for marriage.[14]

Seminal changes occur beneath the busy surface of this tale. Animal categories are established, and places assigned to them within Sahelian cosmology. The farthest removed, deep in the forest, is Elephant. This narrative account for his distancing may be slight, but so is the narrative which accounts for the distancing of the supreme god Mawu-Lisa in Fon Mythology. At one time, says the myth, the androgynous deity hovered a few feet above earth, but being constantly annoyed by an old woman who threw dirty dishwater up at him/her, Mawu-Lisa drifted to the farthest reaches of the sky (Herskovits and Herskovits 1958:150). Theologians term this far-removed god, who presides over nearly all African pantheons, *deus otiose*. May this trickster tale not, in much the same way, be speaking of the conception of *elephantus otiose*?

On the most popular level trickster tales constitute a kind of Jacobin tradition, where the wounds of social inequality are fantastically revenged by the wretched of the bush and the barnyard. Yet it must be remembered that all this elephant

4-9. Like African storytellers, Jean de Brunhoff is busy "belling" the elephant. Babar is the ideal chief for the indirect rule France never achieved, king of the the magic kingdom of colonialism. Height, about a thumb's length. Collection of Daniel Brauer.

4-10. Space Elephant. Sculpture by Salvator Dali. Courtesy of Serena Fine Art, Geneva, Switzerland.

talk is only in code. The laughter of *lèse majesté* can be heard in the Baule proverb, *Who dares say Mr. Elephant blows a fart?* (Arbelbide 1974:22). It is not the gray head of the elephant these Jacobin-tricksters seek, it is the gray head of the chief. But beneath the farcical plots and etiologies, the trickster tales ironically affirm that even in motley, Elephant rules.

CONVERGENT ELEPHANT

The farcical elephant king from the African trickster tradition is mirrored in *Babar*, elephant king of an endless series of childrens' books by Jean and Laurent Brunhoff. The *Babar* books are staples of the Euro-American children's library, and have generated a never-ending stream of Babar kitsch (Fig. 4-9), and even an animated movie (1989). Unlike his cartoon rival, Walt Disney's *Dumbo*, Babar is indisputably a "native." He is a bush creature saved from the cruelty of the hunters who shot his mother, and civilized in Paris by the (evolutionary) grace of the little old (French) lady. He now wears a suit of bottle green and bathes in a tub. He has been crowned king of the elephants at his drip castle capital of Celesteville where the little old lady whispers in his great big ear.

All of this charming plot – the record of Babar's reign, his marriage to Celeste, their children, his travels – is narrated with intriguing parallels to the elephant-dupe of the African trickster traditions. In both cases, the satire is obviously political. African storytellers and the Brunhoffs are busy "belling" the elephant. Babar is the ideal chief for the indirect rule France never quite achieved in West Africa. Life in Celesteville was the devout wish of all the little old lady colonial administrators who presided over Afrique de l'Ouest. And

indeed, in the City Park in Niamey, Niger, Celesteville has been built. That park is to *Babar* what the town plan of Constantinople is to St. Augustine's *City of God*. The animals are in whimsical white cages with spires and curls, like Gaudí drip castles. The hippo splashes in a large bathtub next to a cluster of picture pretty Tuareg huts. And at the nearby museum there is an evolutionary tree painted on the wall with a Frenchman (son of the old lady?) perched at the top. It is the magic kingdom of colonialism, where Elephant reigns and Old Lady rules.

———— ❧ ————

Whether considered in wonder, fear, or derision, it is the immensity and sheer otherness of the animal which unites all the elephant tropes devised by African artists, and their Euro-American imitators. Remembering that first narrative glimpse on the verandah in Sierra Leone, I still see elephant as the gray planet moving in its own orbit through all these African oral traditions: a celestial presence for all its terrestial weight. And that African trope, like so much African art and culture, has now become international currency. So it came as no surprise when I encountered Salvador Dali's "Space Elephant" (Fig. 4-10) in a 1989 show of his late pieces at the Scuola San Teodoro in Venice. Of his surrealist bronze sculpture Dali wrote, "Moving through Space, towards heaven, legs stretched out and more delicate in the weightless atmosphere, the Space Elephant carries an obelisk, symbol of the progress of technology." Dali's image in bronze, and his words of explication, seem anomalous in Western art traditions. But together they constitute a visionary perception of Elephant, threatened to extinction in the African forest, as now he enters the global village.

NOTES

1. See Cosentino (1982:62-66).

2. For a discussion of Mende belief concerning this transformation see Julian Winch (1971:26). See also my analysis of the following narrative, "A Defiant Maid Marries a Stranger" (Cosentino 1982).

3. See Cosentino (1982:144-92). The story is told from Senegal to Zaire, and has achieved literary fame as the "Compleat Gentleman" section of Amos Tutuola's amazing novel, *The Palm Wine Drinkard* (1953).

4. For this and all the following translations from French texts into English, I wish to thank Mr. Adedze Agbenyega, who served as Research Assistant for this project.

5. Olatunji (1984:156).

6. Abimbola (1977:113).

7. As translated by S.A. Babalola (1966:92-95). Babalola's notes are reproduced here.

  * *abèbè ìjà*: 'fans of war.' The reference is to the elephant's large, flapping ears."

  † Àjànàkú: an attributive name for the elephant; it means 'Pa-Àjànà-kú (Killer of Ajana). According to a legend, there was a certain hunter named Ajana whose hobby was capturing live animals. He succeeded in capturing a sample of every animal, but one day his captured

elephant trampled him to death. Thenceforth the elephant was know by the attributive name 'Killer of Ajana.'

  ** [...] The Ijesha method of producing oil from palmfruits is different from the Oyo method. The distinctive feature of the Ijesha method is the use of a number of rectangular pits side by side with a circular area marked out as a unit. The elephant's molar teeth are likened to these rectangular pits, in surface area each about four feet by three feet!

8. Finnegan (1970:149-50).

9. Olatunji (1982:109).

10. The chant can be heard in an album entitled *War Songs of Fighting Biafra*, issued in 1967 (and by now of course long out of print).

11. I am indebted to Caroline Nkeonye Nwankwo for providing the first line of this chant and confirming its translation.

12. I owe observations on the non-wartime use of the elephant chant to Henrietta Cosentino, who witnessed it often during two years in southeastern Nigeria and thought about it recently.

13. Nkamgang (1970:90-93).

14. Edicef (1975:16-23).

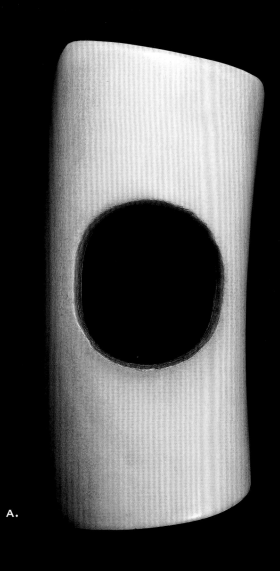

A.

B.

C.

A. Kasena armlet worn above the elbow. Collected in Navrango, Ghana, 1976. FMCH X86.1488. Anonymous gift.

B. Bracelets (left to right): Congo. Diameter 9.5 cm. FMCH X65.8099. Gift of Mrs. Herbert Bradley; Angola. Length 8.4 cm. FMCH X80.361. Gift of Louise Round; Africa. Diameter 11.5 cm. FMCH X67.2081. Gift of George G. Freylinghuysen.

C. Bangles around a plant-fiber base with a sewn skin sheath. Bamileke peoples, Cameroon. Height 25.4 cm. Collection of Nancy and Richard Bloch.

D. Bangles. Mijikenda (top left) and Igbo peoples. Largest diameter 11.5 cm. Collection of Herbert M. and Shelley L. Cole.

E. Bangles. Largest width 14.2 cm. Collection of James Willis.

CROSS-SECTIONS of an elephant tusk are carved with a minimum of effort to adorn the arm, wrist, leg, or ankle. The natural taper of the tusk conveniently allows a wide spectrum of bangle sizes. In parts of West Africa, lateral sections are used as an ornament for the upper arm. The ivory color ranges from an intense white, often maintained by means of sand or bleach, to a deep red resulting from repeated applications of palm oil or camwood and oil. Prolonged contact with skin naturally darkens the ivory, producing yellows, oranges, and browns, and the inherent grain of the material adds additional pattern to its surface. Western-style bracelets of plastic, glass, and metal have largely replaced their ivory predecessors in most of Africa.

D.

E.

FIVE

SAMA BA

THE ELEPHANT IN BAMANA ART

MARY JO ARNOLDI and KATE EZRA

You have made wogo, the mother of elephants, become rare,

You have made keleku, the mother of nyamu the giraffe, become rare,

You have made the son of nasu barama, nasu of the voluminous navel, the massive bull turakuru,
the buffalo who is difficult to combat unless with bow and arrow, you have made him become rare.[1]

This praise song for great Mande hunters poignantly conveys the decline during the last century in the numbers of big game which once proliferated in the savannah grasslands of Mali, West Africa. The Bamana are the most populous Mande-speaking group in this area. Although they are primarily farmers, many Bamana men are also prolific hunters who place a high value on knowledge of the forest and its denizens. Animals which once abounded here still frequently appear in Bamana verbal and visual arts. Antelopes, monkeys, lions, and buffalo are the subjects of hunters' songs and proverbs; they are the subject of a large body of folktales; and they are represented in masks and puppets for youth association theater and in objects for initiation societies. The largest animal of the forest – the elephant, *sama* – also plays a significant role in Bamana art and thought.[2]

As early as the eleventh century, medieval Arab authors remarked on the presence of great herds of elephants in what they called *bilad al-Sudan,* "the land of the blacks," as this part of West Africa was known. In 1068 al-Bakri wrote that the region near ancient Ghana known as Gharantal was a land in which "elephants and giraffes propagate their species" (Levtzion and Hopkins 1981:81). Writing in 1275, al-Qazwini was also struck

by the exotic flora and fauna of the region. He recounted the story of a traveler to the area along the Senegal River, west of where the Bamana live today, who had seen "an enormous host...countless elephants [who] had come to drink at the water near Takrur" (Levtzion and Hopkins 1981:179). His anecdote suggests the size of the elephant population at that time.

Descriptions of the rich fauna inhabiting the area from the coasts of Senegal and Guinea inland continue throughout the ensuing centuries. In 1695, for example, Dancourt noted the havoc wreaked by elephants in the villages, overturning houses and crushing them "like nutshells" (Jeannin 1947:170). A century later, Mungo Park, traveling inland on an expedition to chart the course of the Niger River, observed that elephants were more numerous away from the coast, "in the plains of Bambarra and Kaarta, and the extensive wilds of Jallonkadoo" (1983:256,300,306). During the dry season particularly, herds of elephants would descend towards the Niger in search of food and water, staying until the beginning of the rainy season in June or July. Bamana hunters pursued the elephants during the dry

5-1 (OPPOSITE). Bamana elephant puppet-mask, *sama kun*. Length 95 cm. FMCH X90.193. Museum purchase with Manus funds.

5-2. Elephants in one of the few remaining herds, seen in 1989 near the Niger Bend, Gourma Region, Mali. Photograph, Robert Pringle.

season, although with difficulty, Park noted, due to the scarcity of firearms in that area (1983:236).

References to the abundance of elephants in the Western Sudan continue throughout the nineteenth century. On his voyage to Timbuktu in 1824, René Caillié noted the presence of herds of elephants between Lake Debo and Diré (1968, II:36). In southern Mali, near the Bagoé River, Gustave Binger remarked upon the destruction caused by elephants, including uprooted trees and broken branches. Although the damage was extensive, Binger concluded that the elephants must not be very large, because of their relatively small tracks and the fact that only the lowest branches of the trees were affected (1892, I:170).

In the contemporary period, elephants have not been a common sight in the Bamana area. Even in the early part of the twentieth century Maurice Delafosse noted that elephants were rare in the Western Sudan except in the extreme southern parts of the region (Delafosse 1912, II:81). There have been isolated accounts of elephants, either single individuals or small herds of no more than seventeen in the regions of Nioro, Dioïla, and Gao and in the Baoule National Park near Kita (Vézia 1957; Vacquié 1950; Edmond-Blanc 1954, II:117; Seliquer 1943). Jeannin estimated that by 1947 there remained only 500 to 700 elephants in the area (1947:176). More recent estimates for Mali are not very different, varying from 780 (in 1981) and 600 (in 1987), according to an unpublished report of the African Elephant Conservation Coordinating Group in Nairobi (Steve Johnson, pers. com.). Meester and Setzer indicate that while in the recent past elephants were known across the Western

Sudan to a latitude north of the Niger Bend, the present limit of their habitat extends approximately only as far north as Bamako, with an isolated population in the Niger Bend (Fig. 5-2). Two sub-species of the African elephant, *Loxodonta africana*, are represented in Mali: the smaller *Loxodonta cyclotis*, often called the "forest" elephant, and the larger *Loxodonta africana africana* or "bush" elephant.[3]

There are many complex reasons for this decline in the number of elephants in Mali. The commercial trade in ivory, the increasingly dry climate in the region, and the expansion of the human population all contributed to the drastic reduction in elephant herds. Most devastating to the elephants has been the increased availability of firearms in the late nineteenth century, which made elephant hunting much more efficient.

Elephants in the Western Sudan have been killed for their ivory at least since the ninth century, in spite of Muslim laws discouraging the use and trade of parts of animals that had not been ritually slaughtered (Levtzion and Hopkins 1981:55,61). According to al-Zuhri, writing in the mid-twelfth century, the people of "Kawkaw," probably Gao, "take many elephants by hunting and eat their flesh, then export the tusks to Egypt and Syria" (ibid., p. 97). By the late eighteenth century the ivory trade was directed along the Senegal and Gambia Rivers towards the Atlantic coast rather than across the Sahara. The Bamana sold the tusks to itinerant merchants who carried them to the coast (Park 1983:8,236-37).

In the last two decades of the nineteenth century, the elephant population in southwest Mali was decimated largely as a result of Samory Toure's military operations. He engaged Mande hunters to kill great numbers of elephants in order to trade their tusks to the British in Sierra Leone for muzzle loaders, breechloaders, and later, repeater rifles (Person 1968, I:35; II:905-12).

This ivory trade never reached the proportions it did elsewhere in Africa in the eighteenth and nineteenth centuries, perhaps because the elephant population had already been depleted due to centuries of killings for the trans-Saharan trade. Exports of ivory from the French Sudan to Europe rose from about two and a half tons in 1896 to about five tons in 1898 but declined to about four tons in 1899 (Exposition Universelle de 1900:79). Despite their rapid decline, elephants continue to be killed for their ivory. As recently as 1978, a wave of elephant killings in the Baoule National Park in western Mali is believed to have been organized and financed by a group of merchants in Bamako who provided local hunters with high-power rifles and ammunition (Cashion 1984, I:113, n. 52).

Although there are few published accounts of elephant hunting in Mali, the sources all agree that it is an activity requiring powerful weapons, extraordinary skill, and mastery of spiritual forces. Before the widespread use of firearms, elephants were hunted with bows and arrows and harpoons. An important event among Bozo fishermen in the Niger Bend in the nineteenth century was an annual communal elephant hunt. Hunters would encircle the elephant and raise an alarm to frighten the animal, a diversionary tactic allowing one of the hunters to approach the elephant and thrust a poisoned harpoon into its shoulder while others sang the praises of the weapon, probably to ensure its efficacy. In recounting these hunts, the Bozo emphasized the dangers, noting that before it expired the elephant almost always killed one of the hunters (Ligers 1960:95-99).

In the late eighteenth century, Mungo Park described the technique used for hunting elephants with guns (1983:237), stressing the expertise of the Bamana hunters as well as the danger they faced in their encounter with the elephant:

> The elephant-hunters seldom go out singly; a party of four or five join together; and having each furnished himself with powder and ball, and a quantity of corn-meal in a leather bag, sufficient for five or six days' provision, they enter the most unfrequented parts of the wood, and examine with great care everything that can lead to the discovery of the elephants…many of the hunters have, by long experience and attentive observation, become so expert in their search, that as soon as they observe the footmarks of an elephant, they will tell almost to a certainty at what time it passed, and at what distance it will be found…. When they discover a herd of elephants, they follow them at a distance, until they perceive some one stray *[sic]*

> from the rest, and come into such a situation as to be fired at with advantage. The hunters then approach with great caution…. They then discharge all their pieces at once and throw themselves on their faces among the grass. The wounded elephant immediately applies his trunk to the different wounds, but being unable to extract the balls, and seeing nobody near him, becomes quite furious, and runs about amongst the bushes, until by fatigue and loss of blood he has exhausted himself, and affords the hunters an opportunity of firing a second time at him, by which he is generally brought to the ground.

For the Bamana, weapons are necessary but not wholly sufficient to ensure a successful hunt. Physical prowess is less important than the hunters' ability to control the animal's *nyama*, or life force, which is released at death (Bird et al. 1974, I:viii). The importance of supernatural means in hunting elephants was noted as early as 1337-38 by the the Arab writer al-Umari, who noted that "in the territory of the infidels adjacent to their country [Mali], the elephant is hunted by magic" (Levtzion and Hopkins 1981:265).

Bamana hunters categorize the creatures of the bush by the intensity of their life force or *nyama*, and according to Cissé, elephants are among those animals with the most *nyama* (1964:205). Men who have succussfully hunted elephants, lions, hyenas, bush buffalo, hippos, and other *nyama*-laden creatures are accorded the highest status within the hunter's society. A hunter who has killed an elephant is given the praise name *sama faga donso*, "elephant-killing hunter" (Cashion 1984, I:104) or *sagana muru*, "the elephant-skinning knife" (Bird et al. 1974, I, II:lines 75-78).

As a public statement of their accomplishments, Bamana hunters bring back trophies from their kills. The hunter who slaughters an elephant keeps the tail, shoulder hair, and ears (Zahan 1963:9 n. 2; Cashion 1984, I:147-48; Ligers 1960:95-99). He also keeps one of the tusks. The other tusk must be given to the chief of the land or the head of the province or canton (Delafosse 1912, III:10; Travélé 1923:30). Although ivory was not used as frequently by the Bamana as it was elsewhere in Africa, tusks were made into side-blown trumpets in the royal court of Segou in the 1860s, when Mage referred to them as the Bamana "national instrument" (Mage 1869: 581-82). The *nyin tege foli*, "tooth-cutting praise," is sung for elephant hunters and refers to the extraction of the tusks (Cashion 1984, I:220).

Despite the near eradication of elephants and the consequent decline of elephant-hunting in Bamana regions, both the animal and its hunters continue to play a significant role in Bamana expressive arts. Images of elephants appear less frequently than certain other animals such as buffalo, lions, monkeys, and antelopes. Nevertheless they are particularly important in youth association puppet masquerades and in the initiation rituals of the Komo and Jo men's associations.

THE ELEPHANT IN YOUTH ASSOCIATION PUPPET MASQUERADES

The youth association in the Segou area of central Mali, known as Kamalen Ton, incorporates young men from the ages of fourteen to about thirty-five and young women from the age of fourteen until their marriages. Elephants, along with other prominent bush animals, are frequently depicted in their puppet masquerades. Puppet theater of a similar nature is performed by the Bozo, Somono, Maraka, and Malinke people living in the Segou area as well.[4]

Prior to the 1930s, puppet theater in most villages was performed only during the period of the first harvest in September/October, the period which ushered in the dry season and the beginning of hunting season for the village. Nowadays the youth associations stage their dramas twice annually within the larger contexts of calendrical festivals associated with critical phases in the agricultural and fishing cycles. One performance in October coincides with the first harvest. Another, in late May, takes place directly prior to the rainy season which marks the beginning of the planting season for the farmers and signals the rise of the rivers and the recommencement of fishing for Bozo and Somono groups (Arnoldi 1983).

A puppet drama typically comprises ten or more discrete masquerade sequences which are punctuated by musical

5-3. The large ears, trunk, and tusks of this puppet head identify it as elephant. During performance, its size and bulk, its slow ponderous, swaying dance, and the praise song sung by the women's chorus reinforce this identity for the audience. Photograph, Lynn Forsdale-Denny, 1979.

song and dance interludes. Each sequence represents a specific puppet-mask character who is danced in mime and accompanied by a chorus and drummers. The character is escorted into the arena by a group of young men who sing its signature song; as they enter the plaza, the women (lead singer and chorus) take up the song. The puppet moves counter-clockwise around the plaza, stopping periodically to twirl and move its head from side to side in an acrobatic display that generally brings the audience to its feet, inspiring some to enter the ring and dance in praise of the performance. This pattern is repeated for each character although troupes may vary the length of each character's performance and the order of its appearance from year to year (Arnoldi 1988b:79). During a single evening's performance the troupe may perform well over fifteen different characters.

Rod puppet heads give the Segou theater an immediate and unique visual identity and distinguish it from other masked and non-masked youth dramas performed in adjacent regions. Ranging in length from just a few feet up to six or more, the majority are fashioned to represent various animals. The

5-4. This Bamana youth association elephant masquerade, *sama ba*, sports a costume constructed of cloths borrowed from the mothers, wives, or sisters of troupe members. The striped handwoven cloth covering the elephant's neck is a type made throughout the Segou region. The handwoven tapestry with geometric design that covers the animal's back was most probably imported from around the town of Gao, some distance north of the Segou region. The representational velour tapestry covering the front of the elephant's chest is commercially produced and regularly imported. All these cloths are today a standard part of most young women's wedding dowries. Photograph, Lynn Forsdale-Denny, November 1979.

puppet head extends from the front end of a costumed bamboo construction which serves as the body of the animal. The puppeteer, hidden beneath this costumed stage, operates the head by manipulating a rod which is attached to the underside of the sculpture.

People say that sculpture in the youth drama should be the "namesake" (*togoma*) of the animal it represents. The character's features must correspond to those of the animal in nature, and should be immediately identifiable to the audience (Arnoldi 1986:138). In the case of the elephant puppet, critical features include the size and shape of the head, which is most frequently a large half-sphere, as well as a trunk and tusks (Figs. 5-3 through 5-9).

From the oral histories of the theater which are preserved in many communities, it appears that the elephant was one of the earliest characters in the drama's repertoire. Along with the hyena, lion, and bush buffalo, its importance in the early theater is linked to its definition as a black or dark animal, *sogofin*, meaning a creature that is dangerous, powerful, and difficult to hunt because of the intensity of its life force or *nyama*. In the early colonial period and before, there was a close correlation between animals deemed important to the hunt and those that constituted the subjects of the youth drama's repertoire. That wild animals such as the elephant are still represented in puppet theater is a statement about the nature of power in

the bush. The songs accompanying puppet performances praise not only the animal but the hunter triumphant, who is a man of action, a hero in his community. His celebration in youth drama dramatizes the importance of this aspect of male identity in Bamana society (Arnoldi 1989 Ms.).

Contemporary performances of these powerful bush animals also contain several overlapping levels of meaning. For example during the first half of the elephants' sequence, the male, female, and young of the species arrive together at the dance arena. The bull elephant leads the way, followed by his mate with her young flitting about her. People interviewed in 1978-80 interpreted this part of the elephant's performance as a celebration of ideal social relationships. They stated that the relationships within the world of animals mirror the ideal

5-5 (ABOVE). Bamana elephant puppet-mask, *sama kun*. Length 4.5 cm. FMCH X88.916A-E. Gift of Rachel Hoffman.

5-6. This particular puppet masquerade represents a baby elephant and was performed along with the mother elephant (see Figure 5-3) in a 1979 performance in the Segou region. It is not uncommon in the youth theatre for masquerades to represent male and female or mother and child animal pairs, alluding to valued social relationships in the human community. Photograph, Lynn Forsdale-Denny, November 1979.

5-7 (ABOVE). Bamana elephant puppet-mask, *sama kun*. James A. Mounger Collection, New Orleans.

5-8. Hunting scenes are popular in contemporary youth theater among both farmer's and fishermen's troupes. In this Bamana performance a master hunter stalks a lone male lion, dramatically enacting a successful hunt. Lions, hippos, and bush buffalo as well as elephants were considered to be among the most dangerous animals once regularly encountered by hunters in this region. Photograph, Lynn Forsdale-Denny, 1979.

within the human community. Later in the same sequence, the female and the young exit, and the bull elephant takes center stage. The interpretation shifts away from the celebration of familial relationships towards one where the bull is seen as a powerful *sogofin,* dark animal, and as an elder. Cissé notes that an old solitary male animal, whether lion, elephant or bush buffalo, is characterized by virulent *nyama,* life force (1964:205). According to hunters, the age of the animal determines its capacity and its power in much the same way that elder men and women in the community are seen to be more powerful than their juniors.

Within the contemporary puppet masquerade theater, skits directly related to hunting are sometimes also introduced in an evening's performance. In one village's 1979 drama (Fig. 5-8), the hunter's manipulation of various power objects was a key to his triumph, underscoring the belief that a master hunter's ability in the bush is dependent upon both physical prowess and control of spiritual forces. The scene was not intended to instruct the audience in the use of specific power objects, but rather to present to the community a scenario about the idiom of power operative in the bush (Arnoldi 1988a:94). Puppet sculptures themselves are not considered agents of power; on the contrary they are defined as *tlonkefenw,* playthings. But the masquerades, though not intrinsically powerful, are interpreted as a discourse about power relationships between men and animals (Arnoldi 1983).

THE ELEPHANT IN BAMANA MALE INITIATION RITUALS

Another dimension of animal, and particularly elephant, imagery is evident in the initiation of young men into the "power associations" or *jow* (sing., *jo*) which have traditionally been the focus of Bamana religious life. Bamana men are initiated into one of these associations after they are circumcised. In the past this was done during their teens or early twenties, although now circumcision is performed on younger boys. Following induction into a *jo,* they may be initiated into higher levels of knowledge, responsibility, and authority within that society, and they may also enter other associations. The most well known of the Bamana *jow* are Komo, Kono, Korè, Nama, Chi Wara, and Jo, each found in a different part of the Bamana area (although there is some overlap and a few of the associations, such as Komo, are found over a very wide area). Each has its own body of esoteric knowledge, its own hierarchy of officials, its own rituals, and its own distinctive objects (McNaughton 1979; Zahan 1974).

Allusions to the elephant occur most particularly within the Komo and Jo society initiations. Within the Komo society, allusions to the elephant do not appear, however, in the context of the well-known Komo zoomorphic helmet masks. Instead, the idea of the elephant is used very specifically to contrive the special effects surrounding the induction experience. Descriptions of Komo initiations vary somewhat from author to

author, most probably because the rituals themselves vary from one society branch or lodge to the next. The Komo described by Henri Labouret provides the most insight into the significance of the elephant in Komo art and ritual (1934:83-84).

According to Labouret, the boys who are to be initiated first encounter the elephant soon after their circumcision, while they are in the forest, recovering from the operation. One night, they are made to lie down outdoors with their heads covered. It is then that they are visited by the Komo elephant *(komo sama),* "a mysterious being, invisible, a monstrous kind of elephant, a colossal force" (p. 83). The *komo sama* approaches the boys with heavy rhythmic footsteps, overturning trees, breaking off branches, and throwing them at the youths. It visits the young men in this manner almost every night during their healing retreat, each time provoking terror. The elders use this emotion in order to extract promises from the would-be initiates, before finally reassuring them by forcing the beast away.

The boys never actually see the *komo sama,* nor are they aware of the techniques used by the elders to create the effect of the colossal creature. Some of the older Komo members set up a system of cords with which to pull down previously cut and prepared trees and branches. Others are given heavy wooden pounders, sometimes called *sama senw,* "elephant feet," with which they strike the earth in imitation of the elephant's footsteps (Dieterlen and Cissé 1972:33, 44, 52-55). The *komo sama* is actually a series of carefully staged sound effects and props and is more an idea or an experience than an actual object.

The idea of a great and terrifying animal appears again at the final stage of induction into Komo (Labouret 1934:85). The young men are told that in order to be initiated they must be swallowed by the *komo ba,* "great Komo." If they are lucky, the beast will not chew them, and they will not be caught in its stomach, but they will come out whole when the animal defecates. If they are not so fortunate, they will be chewed to a pulp by the beast, or get stuck on the nettles in its stomach and will be torn to pieces. In this sequence of Komo initiation, as in many descriptions of initiation throughout Africa, the uninitiated children are swallowed by a mysterious being from which they emerge as newly formed initiated adults after being delivered, vomited, or excreted by the beast. Although Labouret did not record the name *komo sama* as being used in this specific context, one can easily see how the "great Komo" might be interpreted as an elephant. The already terrified boys would think that it could accomodate them in its enormous belly, and because of the elephant's well-known strength and destructiveness, it lends itself to the atmosphere of danger, fear, and uncertainty that characterize the initiation ritual.

The idea of entering the belly of an elephant as a non-initiated child and emerging as an initiated adult is seen again in the rituals of the Jo society (Ezra 1983, 1986), an initiation association found primarily in the southern part of the Bamana area. The rituals and objects associated with Jo vary and it is in the areas of Banan (southeast of Bamako) and

Baninko (south of Dioïla) that the image of the elephant appears most prominently.

In Jo initiation, as with the Komo society, the first step is circumcision; actual initiation, called *jofaga*, "Jo killing," takes place six years later. In each of the intervening six years the initiates-to-be undergo a series of emotionally and physically demanding rituals referred to as *nye yele*, "opening their eyes," during which they are allowed to see objects, places, and persons that are significant to the Jo society.

In Banan and Baninko villages the most crucial of these visual experiences occurs immediately before *jofaga* and involves the

5-9. Bamana elephant puppet-masks, *sama kun*, are often painted in bold triangular and striped patterns. Added human and bird figures act to energize the basic form. Such embellishments are intended solely to heighten the visual appeal of the sculpture and to provoke a positive aesthetic response from the audience. Length 73 cm. FMCH x89.59. Promised gift of Jerome L. Joss.

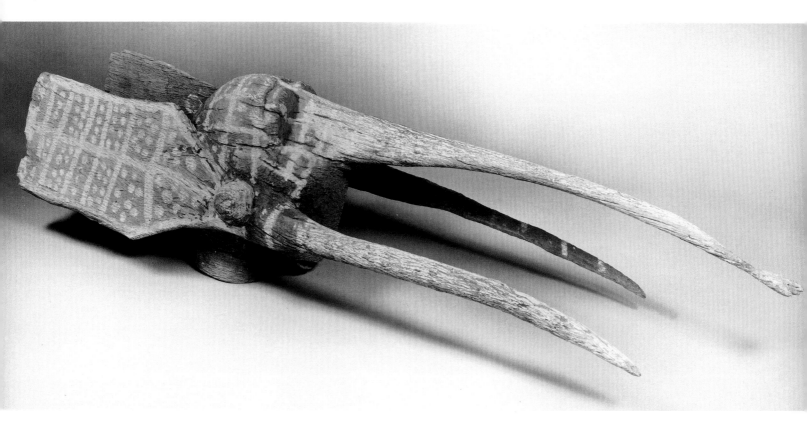

5-10. Bamana Jo society elephant head, *sama kun*, created as part of an initiation house that simulates the elephant body. Oval eyes bulge on the upper surface; below the base of the trunk, where the head drops off sharply, a deep gouge indicates the mouth. The heavy, hard wood is a light greyish tan, with grid-like designs in a cream-colored, clay-based pigment. 142.8 cm. The Metropolitan Museum of Art, 1979.206.209. The Michael C. Rockfeller Memorial Collection, Bequest of Nelson A. Rockfeller, 1979.

image of an elephant in the form of an "elephant house" called variously *sama bon*, *sama so*, *sama bugu*, or simply *sama*. It is a tent-like construction made of wooden poles bent to form an armature on which cloth and straw are tied to make the elephant's sides and back. The surface is plastered with earth and then decorated with designs made with black charcoal, white chalk, and a red pigment made from red stone. Holes are cut in the elephant's chest and rear to serve as entrance and exit. When the body is complete, a carved wooden elephant head, *sama kun*, is attached to the front. The elephant house is constructed by the previous group of initiates, whose own *jofaga* took place seven years earlier.

One such elephant house was recently created for a Jo initiation that took place in a village in the *cercle* of Dioïla in May, 1989.[5] Measuring 12 meters in length and 1.6 meters in height, it consisted of two sloping walls that met at the top, forming a structure triangular in cross-section. The walls were made of thick, sometimes forked, branches covered with plaited millet-straw screens that were plastered with grey banco. Openings at the front and back provided access to the interior, the floor of which was quite muddy. Affixed horizontally to the front of the structure was a wooden elephant head painted with red ochre, black, and white pigments in linear and geometric patterns.

A Jo elephant house, considered very beautiful, is called "a thing to look at" (*laje fen*), words also applied to human figure sculpture (Ezra 1986:10). Many people, men and women alike, go to see it. In one village it was located just on the outskirts of the village, open to the view of anyone entering or leaving the village or simply going out to the fields to farm. People who have seen these elephant houses compare them to a *nyenaje*, the general Bamana word for a theatrical performance, a masquerade, or the puppet theater.

Yet for all the visual enjoyment and entertainment it provides, the elephant house represents a serious aspect of Jo. As soon as it is announced that the Jo candidates will be introduced to the elephant, all except Jo members are forbidden to approach or look at the house. Thus the context of its definition shifts, from one reminiscent of performance, where spiritual power is only the subject of allusion, to a ritual one in which the spiritual powers are actually in force.

On the day initiation is to take place, at the beginning of the rainy season, the candidates are brought to the elephant house. They circle the elephant three times as a senior Jo official, the *nanfiri*, inspects them. Finally they enter through the hole in its chest, passing first through the outspread legs of older, fully initiated men. Once inside they encounter a large hole dug in the ground, the sight of which is forbidden to anyone not associ-ated with Jo, and they are anointed with medicines that have the power to harm anyone not connected with the society. Finally, they exit through the hole in the elephant's hindquarters, again passing through the legs of their elders. Their actual initiation or "Jo killing" takes place later the same day.

5-11. This Bamana Jo society elephant head, *sama kun*, and the one in Figure 5-12 both start with a basic form to which elephant's features are applied; the trunk, projecting strangely from the top of the forehead, is sharply bifurcated at the tip; tusks extend directly from the ears. Wood. 119.4 cm. The Newark Museum, 83.445. Gift of Mr. and Mrs. Arthur A. Cohen, 1983. Photograph, Sarah Wells.

The new initiates spend the following week isolated in a clearing in the forest, while the powerful medicines applied during their initiation wear off. During this period, hunting is one of their major preoccupations and they are said to have remarkable powers in this regard: the mere sound of their voices, for example, is considered capable of killing a lion. In addition, they are provided with specially endowed sticks or wooden swords that allow them to capture alive any animal in the bush, and protect themselves from any of the dangers that may be found there.

The importance of hunting at this stage of Jo initiation, and particularly the emphasis on spiritual means in dominating the creatures of the bush, suggests the associations in Bamana thought between hunting, occult knowledge, and adult male identity. In the rituals of both Jo and Komo, the boys' ability to overcome their fear of the forest's largest inhabitant, the elephant, clears the way for them to achieve full status as adult men. Being an adult means being able to pass unscathed through the belly of the giant beast, and this ability is inextricably linked with the knowledge and powers they acquire through initiation. Although it has been almost a century since elephants actually posed a threat, a Bamana farmer's capacity to master the animal is still crucial to his self-image.

Although the Jo society elephant houses and the carved wooden heads attached to them have never been photographed in the field, examples in collections correspond very closely to the descriptions provided by Jo society elders. They were not made to be worn as helmet masks, since the cylindrical openings at the bases are too narrow and shallow to fit over the head. These openings are similar to the sockets at the base of some Segou area rod puppets.

Unlike the moveable stages of the puppet masquerades, however, the elephant houses are stationary, and the heads in collections do not have nail holes to indicate they were ever attached to rods (Figs. 5-10 through 5-14).[6] The heads display a variety of approaches to the animal's distinctive form, from shapes that are massive and dome-like (Fig. 5-10) to blocky, geometric forms (Figs. 5-13 and 5-14), to long horsehead shapes (Figs. 5-11 and 5-12) like those used by both the Korè and Jo societies (Ezra 1983:104-6, figs. 34,35). The wooden head of the elephant house described earlier, seen in the *cercle* of Dioïla, had long, flat, paddle-shaped ears, and it completely lacked one of the elephant's most distinguishing features, the trunk. Like the example in Figure 5-12, it resembled Korè and Jo society horseheads, with the addition of tusks. These were carved parallel to the side of the head, with barely any space between the tusks and the head, and did not project at all in front of the head.

Bamana elephant images — whether the brightly painted puppets in youth theater, the auditory experiences created for Komo initiation, or the massive heads for Jo society elephant houses — all make manifest an animal which few Bamana today have ever seen outside the Bamako zoo. Even earlier in this century, elephants were a rarity, especially in the Segou region where the puppet theater is performed. Although the form of

5-12 (ABOVE). Like the preceding figure, this elephant head, *sama kun*, features a long snout similar to those found on Bamana horse or hyena heads. It is carved at the tip to indicate the open jaws and tongue. Here again the unusually short trunk projects from the top of the forehead. Wood. The Metropolitan Museum of Art. 1989.347.2. Gift of Renée and Chaim Gross, 1989.

5-13. Bamana Jo society elephant head, *sama kun*. The front of this head drops off sharply and extends to form a short, shelf-like mouth at the very bottom. The two very short parallel tusks are curved inward in the manner of wart hog tusks. Wood. 137.5 cm. The Paul and Ruth Tishman Collection of African Art, the Walt Disney Company.

some of the Segou region elephant puppets and Jo society elephant heads might suggest that their carvers had never actually seen an elephant, the animal's unique features — its large ears, enormous trunk and menacing tusks — make it immediately recognizeable no matter how much the anatomy is misunderstood. If a carver has never seen the animal he is commissioned to sculpt, he relies on existing models or verbal descriptions from hunters. This may account for the imaginative renderings of the elephant's features in the sculptures.

Yet the elephant's enormous size and strength, notorious destructiveness, and distinctive features make it a particularly useful symbol. Dominique Zahan has suggested that for the Bamana, elephants represent both the enormity of all knowledge and — because they are believed to embody parts of all other animals — the universality of knowledge (1960:228; 1963:122). The elephant's size is certainly a factor in its choice as the ultimate test which Komo and Jo initiates must pass, and literally pass through. Its destructive behavior and powerful *nyama* contribute to the fear it is meant to provoke in those contexts. The dangers and difficulties posed by elephants are summed up succinctly in the Bamana hunter's song,[7] which states:

The big-eared ones are not fought unless you suffer!

Even in the context of Segou youth association theater, the elephant's status as a *sogofin* — a dark, dangerous animal — determines its continuing role in the drama. Despite a drastic decline in its numbers, the once-plentiful elephant remains an animal that, for the Bamana, is still "good to think" (Lévi-Strauss 1962).

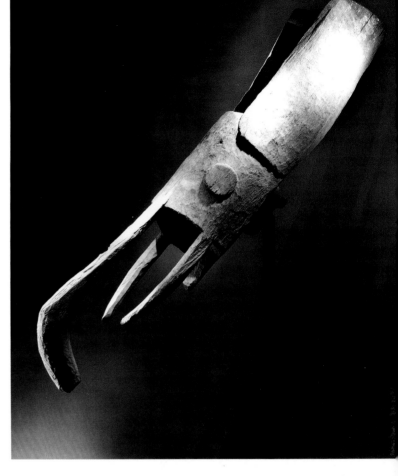

5-14. Bamana Jo society elephant head, *sama kun*, with a curiously carved trunk and rather short tusks; a projection from the base of the head may indicate a mouth. Wood, traces of pigment. 165 cm. Collection of René Garcia, Paris. Photograph, Philippe Guerin.

NOTES

1. Cissé (1964:222).
2. Fieldwork on Segou puppet theatre was conducted by Arnoldi from 1978-1980 and 1987. Fieldwork on the Jo initiation society was conducted by Ezra in 1978 and 1985. We would also like to thank Steve Johnson, New York Zoological Society Library, Ross Day of the Metropolitan Museum's Robert Goldwater Library and Mary Kay Davies and Janet Stanley of the Smithsonian libraries for their help in obtaining materials for this article.
3. Meester and Setzer (1971:pt. 2, maps 1 & 2); Dorst and Dandelot (1970:155).
4. The puppet masquerade theatre is known by three different Bamana terms within the Segou region: *sogobò*, *dobò*, and *ceko*. *Sogobò*, "the animals are revealed," is the term most frequently used by farmers in the western portion of the Segou region. *Dobò*, "the secrets are revealed," is the preferred term for the theatre among Bozo and Somono fishermen throughout the region. *Ceko*, "the affairs of men," is the most common term for the youth association.
5. This house was observed by Georges Meurillon of the Musée National du Mali, who is involved in an extensive, ongoing research project to document the Jo society. The authors thank M. Meurillon for graciously providing the description of the elephant house and its carved wooden head.
6. Descriptions of the elephant house with its carved wooden head also invite comparison with the *nosolo* masquerade performed for initiation into the Poro society of the neighboring Senufo people (Glaze 1981:147,258; Darbois 1962:82-83; Huet 1978:figs. 140-44). *Nosolo* is a tent-like structure covered with mats or cloths with a carved wooden antelope mask mounted in front. According to Glaze, the name *nosolo* refers to the masquerade's large size, and is based on the Senufo root *so*, or elephant, suggesting its relationship to the Bamana elephant house. Unlike the Bamana elephant construction, but like the Bamana puppets, *nosolo* moves through the village manipulated by a man hidden inside. The historical relationship between the Bamana puppets, elephant house and the Senufo *nosolo* warrant further investigation.
7. Cashion (1984, II:94).

A.

B.   C.

A. Hoofed elephant-man surrounded by a swarm of bees from Ebusingata, Royal Natal National Park, Republic of South Africa. Reproduced with permission from Pager 1975:75.

B. Elephant with calf, apparently in a protective posture at the approach of a leopard. Redrawn from Wilcox 1984: Figure 6:3.B. Drawing, Sylvia Kennedy.

C. Engraved elephant. Redrawn from R. Mauny 1954: Photo 3. Drawing, Sylvia Kennedy.

EARLY INTERPRETATIONS OF ROCK ART in Africa inevitably centered on themes related to "hunting magic." As our understanding of these arts expanded, it became increasingly clear that the functions and meanings of animal imagery in African rock art are as varied and complex as any other category of African expressive culture. The images on these two pages were selected to suggest the range of invention found in the painted, pecked, and engraved elephant images scattered around many parts of the continent.

D.

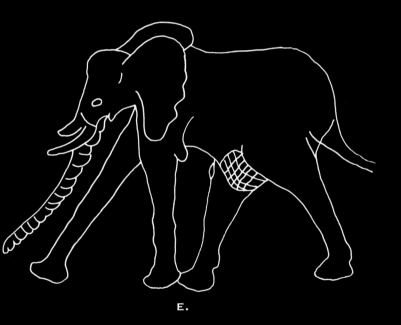

E.

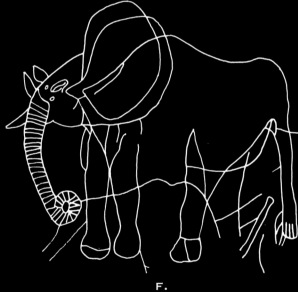

F.

D. Three painted elephants from the Sahara. Redrawn from Mission Henri Lhote, photographed at Musée de l'Homme, Paris (Erich Lessing from Magnum). Drawing, Sylvia Kennedy.

E. Elephant from Tassili-n-Ajjer. Redrawn from Lhote 1973: Figure 756. Drawing, Sylvia Kennedy.

F. Elephant from Tassili-n-Ajjer. Redrawn from Lhote 1973: Figure 683. Drawing, Sylvia Kennedy.

G. Elephants possibly in a trap from Fenga Hill, Tanzania. Redrawn from Wilcox 1984: Plate 9.3. Drawing, Jill Ball.

G.

OF PACHYDERMS AND POWER

IVORY AND THE ELEPHANT IN THE ART OF CENTRAL CÔTE D'IVOIRE

PHILIP L. RAVENHILL

He who follows the elephant is not touched by the dew [1]

This Baule proverb tellingly encapsulates a cultural attitude towards the elephant held by various peoples in the central region of Côte d'Ivoire. There is a recognition of the elephant's overwhelming mass and girth, and his physical preeminence in relation to other animals and to humans. Like most proverbs, this one presents an accepted "given" from which is derived a corollary. In its use, the proverb allows a metaphorical equivalence to be made between the preeminence and power of the elephant and the preeminence and power of, for example, a chief or a family elder, thus setting up an argument for a necessary corollary in terms of behavior and acts.

The immediacy, however, of the experience of the elephant, whether invoked by proverbs or depicted in art, is increasingly attenuated in central Côte d'Ivoire. As the ecology continues to change under the pressure of an expanding population and intensified agriculture, the increasing lack of forest cover has made it more and more unlikely for people to have any direct experience of elephants. At present in the central region, it appears that elephants are only to be found in and near the Marahoué game reserve to the west of the town of Bouaflé. Earlier in this century, however, elephants were not only present in the forest and the forest-savannah contact zone, but also in the grassy savannah to the north.

THE ELEPHANT AND NATIONAL IDENTITY

The predominance of ivory as a trade commodity gave this part of the West African coast its descriptive names in different European languages: Ivory Coast, Côte d'Ivoire, Costa de Marfim, Costa d'Avorio, Elfenbeinküste, Ivoorkust, etc. Before guns made their appearance on the Ivory Coast,

6-1 (OPPOSITE). Detail of a gold-leafed flywhisk shown in Figure 6-4. ca. 20 cm. FMCH X92.310. Gift of Judith Timyan.

6-2. Elephant symbol shown on an enameled bowl issued for the 29th Anniversary of Côte d'Ivoire. Private collection.

elephants could only be hunted with pit-traps or weight-traps and they posed a very real danger to human settlements and agriculture: in the southeastern part of the country, there are still to be found traces of the protective earthworks that surrounded villages like moats (Polet and Saison 1981; Garrard 1980:49). The overseas trade in ivory – both of raw ivory and manufactured goods – reached record proportions during the period from the 1860s to the 1930s, with the result today that with the exception of the elephants found in national parks – Comoé in the south of Côte d'Ivoire, Marahoué in the center, and Bouna in the north – there are only a few herds scattered in the forests of the southeastern and southwestern regions.

The identification of the elephant and the country was formalized with the French creation of the Ivory Coast Colony (Colonie de la Côte d'Ivoire) on the 10th of March 1893 (Duprey 1962:77). It was further consolidated during the late colonial era when Félix Houphouet-Boigny and the other founders of the Rassemblement Démocratique Africain (R.D.A.) chose the elephant as their party symbol (Figs. 6-2, 6-3). The R.D.A. as a regional political party no longer exists, but the R.D.A.-P.D.C.I. (Parti Démocratique de Côte d'Ivoire), the formerly unique political party in Côte d'Ivoire, still continues to use the elephant symbol, and it is found on virtually all party publications. The elephant is also the pervasive national symbol: it is the central symbol on the national coat of arms; the national football team is called "Les Éléphants"; the leading Abidjan hotel is called the "Ivoire"; and "Éléphant" is a common brand name for manufactured or processed goods, such as soap and coffee.

The appropriation of the elephant as a symbol of political and nationalist identity and power is built directly on widespread traditional concepts of chieftaincy and kingship. The extensive use of the preserved elephant tail as a symbol of chiefly power and *the* sign of a summons to report to the chief or the king has been a virtual constancy in most of the societies of central Côte d'Ivoire. Handed the elephant tail, one cannot avoid the meeting (Niangoran-Bouah 1987:162). The fashioning of tusks into oliphants used as heralding instruments in political ceremonies is also widespread, and reinforces once again notions of leadership and preeminence. In the use of both the elephant tail and the tusk/oliphant, one can argue that, to a certain degree, the power of the symbol is due to its retention of its natural state.

6-3 (ABOVE). Elephant symbol of the Rassemblement Démocratique Africain (RDA) on the cover of *Actes du Colloque International sur l'Histoire du RDA*. Abidjan, 1987.

6-4 (RIGHT). Gold-leafed flywhisk of Baule manufacture, part of a chief's regalia. Length 92 cm. FMCH X92.310. Gift of Judith Timyan.

The tail *is* the tail, not a representation; the oliphant retains both the form and smooth surface of the tusk. The power of the elephant is thus invoked directly by the physicality and original naturalness of two parts of its body. A literal synecdoche occurs – the part represents the whole animal – and a metaphor is invoked: the elephant represents the chief (or king). The chief's presence is at times heralded by an elephantine blast of the ivory trumpet. The tail, which also functions as a leader's flywhisk (*nandua blaliwa*) (Figs. 6-1, 6-4), perhaps evokes not only images of power – elephant crushing man, man crushing fly – but also images of contempt, derision, or ignominy, the "tail end" of power (see Ross on Akan imagery, Chapter 7).

117

IVORY FOR PERSONAL ADORNMENT

Ivory has long been used as a prestige material for personal adornment in the central region of Côte d'Ivoire, where it was traditionally fashioned into smooth, rounded bracelets as much as three inches in height. Among the Baule, it was a sign of wealth for a man to be able to offer such a bracelet (called *nzɛkloa*) to his "senior wife" (*bla kpɛngbɛn*) when he married a second woman. It was not uncommon for a senior wife to wear a set of two or even three of these bracelets (Fig. 6-5), the rule apparently being that the husband could not give an ivory bracelet to any one of his other wives without first offering an additional one to his senior wife. Worn constantly, the bracelets would rub and bang together until the connecting surfaces fit perfectly against each other; each downward stroke of the pestle pounding the yams in the mortar would be accompanied by the rhythmic clack of the bracelets. In Baule figurative sculpture, governed by the canons of human aesthetics and depicting Baule ideals of beauty (Ravenhill 1980; Vogel 1980), one finds such bracelets depicted on both female and male statues (Figs. 6-6, 6-7).

Ivory was also carved into hair picks and combs (Fig. 6-5). Most common was the elegant and simple pick, whose point led to a circular, rounded head. With its point pushed into a coiffure, only the head was visible as a round plug of ivory. At times these picks – common throughout the entire central

6-5. Personal objects in ivory made in the past by Baule artists (clockwise from upper left): women's bracelets, hair ornaments, an ivory baby pacifier, decorative combs, ranging from 3.8 cm (pacifier) to 11 cm (larger bracelet). Collection of Judith Timyan.

region and beyond – were carved with barbs that helped them stay put. Other picks in ivory were longer and flatter, culminating in a simple triangular or forked form. Combs in ivory can be referred to more accurately as hair jewelry in comb shape, since the comb teeth functioned *not* as a tool for combing or plaiting the hair but rather as a means of securing the ornament in the hair. Forms could be relatively simple or decorative as well as figural (Figs. 6-8a,b); but whatever their form, they functioned as tonsorial highlights. Another use of ivory, somewhat unexpected, was the "mushroom" (*ndrɛ*) pacifier in ivory used by the Baule (Fig. 6-5); it was attached to a cord bracelet around the wrist of a teething infant. Ivory was also carved into forms resembling leopard teeth (Fig. 6-9) which were strung on necklaces; at times one sees such a necklace, with "teeth" carved of wood, around the neck of a Baule statue (Holas 1968:pl. 21 and 1969b:cover). In southeastern Côte d'Ivoire, beyond the central region which is the focus of this essay, ivory was also carved into pendants and finials of chiefly staffs (Fig. 6-10) (Visonà 1985:47-50).

6-7 (ABOVE). Baule wood carving of a male figure wearing an ivory bracelet, 30.5 cm. Private collection.

6-6 (LEFT). Baule wood carvings of "other-world" people often depict costume elements such as ivory bracelets. Male figure, ca. 65 cm. The Seattle Art Museum, Gift of Katherine White and the Boeing Company. Katherine White Collection. 81.17.233. Photograph, Paul Macapia.

6-8 A, B (TWO VIEWS). Ivory comb photographed in Bouake, Côte d'Ivoire, 1975. Photographs, Philip Ravenhill.

6-9. Ivory "leopard" teeth for a collar. Length 5.2 cm. FMCH X92.361. Anonymous gift.

6-10. Among the Akye (Attié) and other Lagoon peoples of Côte d'Ivoire, staff finials were often carved from ivory. The depiction of prestige European dress elements on these finials does not necessarily indicate that a foreigner is represented. 13.5 cm. FMCH X91.2241. Anonymous gift.

6-11. Guro heddle pulley.
Height 14.8 cm. Collection of
Jean Garrett.

6-11, 6-12, 6-13. In central Côte d'Ivoire, artists often created heddle pulleys that, being publicly visible, would call attention to their carving skills and ingenuity. Both anthropomorphic and zoomorphic forms were common; often they imitated the shapes of masks.

6-12 (LEFT). Baule heddle pulley, 19th-20th century. Height 15.3 cm. The Metropolitan Museum of Art 1978.412.289. The Michael C. Rockefeller Memorial Collection, Gift of Margaret Plass, 1955.

6-13 (ABOVE). Baule heddle pulley. Height 11.4 cm. Eliot Elisofon Photographic Archives. National Museum of African Art, Smithsonian Institution. Gift of Mrs. Evelyn A.J. Hall. 86-09-002.

ELEPHANT REPRESENTATION

The importance of the elephant in central Côte d'Ivoire has not been limited to the use of its tusks and tail as chiefly symbols, or its ivory as material for personal adornment. The elephant has also provided a fertile source of representational imagery for masks, linguist staffs, doors, heddle pulleys (Figs. 6-11, 6-12, 6-13), spoons (Figs. 6-14, 6-15), jewelry, and recently even pottery (Etienne-Nugue 1985:103) and statuary for tombs (Bouchart and Beautheac 1988). In these art forms, the elephant may be depicted in whole or in part, such as by the head alone, or alternately its attributes may be invoked by the selective representation of its tusks, trunk, or ears.

Elephant as Metaphor for the Status Quo

Looking comparatively at those art forms of central Côte d'Ivoire which in any way depict elephants, one is struck by the fact that the (more or less) naturalistic representation of the *entire* elephant is almost always limited to that art which McLeod calls "statement art," in other words, "art concerned with copying or reiterating an existing social order. It summarizes and stresses basic propositions about rule or human relations" (1976:101).

In such art the elephant is invoked as a metaphor from the "real" world. Just as the elephant is the dominant animal in the life of the wild, so, too, the chief is the "naturally" preeminent leader of social life; both epitomize power in their respective realms. Among the Baule, goldweights, gold-covered regalia, and linguist staffs make frequent recourse to elephant symbolism in their reiterative statements about power. An interesting illustration of this use of elephant symbolism to describe the world "as it is" is found in an anecdote related in reference to the Côte d'Ivoire President Félix Houphouet-Boigny. Standing in front of a gold-covered carving of an elephant riding on a tortoise, the president said, *Power should never go faster than wisdom permits* (Kirtley and Kirtley 1982:114) – clearly an appeal to a presumed universal principle and a statement he was making about his own rule.

Gold-covered, low-relief wood plaques depicting elephants are often found with other power symbols on the

6-14 (LEFT), **6-15** (RIGHT). Carved wooden spoons of Guro make. Left, 13.9 cm. Right, 26.6 cm. Collection of Ernst Winizki.

6-16 (OPPOSITE, TOP). Tomb with concrete statuary, including an elephant. Kékréni. Côte d'Ivoire. Photograph, F.X. Bouchart.

6-17 (OPPOSITE, BOTTOM). The linguist staff in itself speaks of chiefly power and prerogative, and the depiction of an elephant further evokes his social pre-eminence. Chiefs and elephant linguist staff. Eliot Elisofon Photographic Archives. National Museum of African Art, Smithsonian Institution.

crowns of Baule chiefs (Fischer and Himmelheber 1975: 12, ill.8; 34, ill. 15). Other items of Baule regalia in the Baule genre of "gold-covered objects" (*sika blawa*) that also make use of the elephant are the flywhisk and the linguist staff (*kpɔman*) (Fig. 6-17). Although Himmelheber has stated that he never "found a Baule who could elucidate any of these animal figures" (1972:200), it is quite reasonable to assume that even in the absence of an explicit proverb, one is dealing with art that makes a statement about power. In fact, Himmelheber illustrates a linguist staff finial (p. 200, ill.11.37) which depicts the same combination commented on above by President Boigny: a static elephant – with marvelously wrinkled skin – on the back of a tortoise. The depiction of an elephant standing on a springtrap is common to a large area of the Akan region of Côte d'Ivoire and of Ghana.[2] Holas illustrates a large drum whose base is an elephant standing on a trap (1969a:202-3); it belongs to the king of the Abron, and he asserts that it

represents an adage to the effect that "no real chief allows himself to be taken in a trap," instead crushing his enemies under his feet.

For Baule chiefly regalia, it is unclear whether the curled and tucked-in trunk has a different meaning from that of the extended and upraised trunk, in spite of Niangoran-Bouah's assertions that "an upraised trunk signifies that the animal is happy" and that through it "the chief is pro-claiming his economic strength, his power and his happiness" (1987:91). Cast gold pendants in the form of an elephant are also worn by kings and chiefs, or by their atten-dants (Fischer and Himmelheber 1975:10). It should also be noted that in recent years, elephants, with raised or curled trunks and prominent tusks, have become common as ornamental statuary on chief's tombs (Fig. 6-16) in the central and eastern regions of Côte d'Ivoire (Bouchart and Beautheac 1988).

Elephant as Metaphor for Change

The static representation of the elephant as seen in items of regalia or display sculpture contrasts with the dynamic use of elephant symbolism in a variety of masking traditions in central Côte d'Ivoire. In regalia, the elephant is invoked in order to affirm an immutable, "natural" order of power. In masking, elephant imagery is used to evoke other aspects of power: the power to transform and change, and the power, also, to respond to and deal with change. The elephant is thus invoked not merely because of what he *is*, but also because of what he *does*. The elephant is no longer reduced to depictions in fixed, inanimate images; instead his attributes – both of body and of character – are expanded upon in the artistic procreation of living cultural beings: masks. The representational elephant model, predictable and immutable, yields to the phantasmagoric, created being – an unpredictable living entity whose form asserts that this is an elephant of a totally different order. Its name may be "elephant," but there is no confusion with the animal of the same name.

The realm of nature is often called upon as a fertile source of analogy for the realm of culture, or as Lévi-Strauss would have it, nature is "good to think." But selected elements of nature can also be appropriated and combined with the creations of culture to form a new realm that exists betwixt-and-between them as a mediating and creative force. It is these culturally constructed forces that a society may utilize in grappling with the ultimate futility and reality of nature: the fact that from the genesis of life a path leads inexorably to the final destination of death.

SHARED IMAGES: ELEPHANTS IN REGIONAL CULTURE

Neighboring cultures may draw upon a shared stock of images due to a shared environment and shared components of history. That is the case in central Côte d'Ivoire, where the cultures that straddle or live on either side of the forest-savannah contact zone deal with quite similar ecologies and have coexisted for centuries. The whole region of central Côte d'Ivoire, which we now divide by ethnolinguistic criteria and label as Baule, Yaure, Wan, Guro, Malinke, and Senufo, is characterized historically by a tremendous flux among its component populations. For example, Malinke created the historic town of Boron near the present Wan village of Kounairi; Senufo groups were once as far south as the present Baule town of Tiébissou (Salverte-Marmier and Salverte-Marmier 1962-64); and the Baule region around Béoumi was formerly inhabited by Wan (Ravenhill 1976:42-53).

Even an informed historical view of cultural movement due to population migration, however, needs to take into account the subtleties of cultural assimilation and adoption. By "cultural assimilation" I refer to those processes whereby a dominant group continuously subsumes and incorporates not only "alien" cultural practices but also the "aliens" themselves. By "cultural adoption," I refer to the fact that minority groups may change their ethnic identity while still maintaining to a certain degree a separate social identity. Within a shared culture, ideas of "groupness" may be created and maintained in diverse ways: shared prohibitions on certain types of food; shared linguistic codes – i.e., dialects; shared specialization in craft production; shared history of origin; shared allegiance to a political or religious leader, and so forth. Another means of maintaining group identity is through the creation and use of art forms which become *inter alia* emblems of that identity (Arnoldi 1989).

In the southeastern Malinke region known as the Worodugu, or the "country of kola" that lies immediately to the north of the forest-savannah contact zone which is a southern terminus of the long-distance kola trade, are to be found masquerade traditions that provide a fertile field of inquiry into the relationships between art and social identity. At the present time, these masquerades – known collectively by the Mande term *Do* (Ravenhill 1984) – are principally performed on the occasion of Tabaski, as the Muslim festival of *id-al-qabir* is often called. The various mask types make use of animal, and other, imagery that creates powerfully affective emblems of group identity. Groups – whether entire villages, village wards, or other socially constituted groups – are represented and perceived by the forms of their masquerade headdresses. Most of the masquerade headdresses in use in the Worodugu are three-part horizontal helmet masks of the type that is widely distributed in West Africa (Adams 1963). One mask type, with flat, wide, circular horns, is inspired by and named after the African savannah buffalo, *Sigi*. Another, whose horns are long, slight, and tapered, is modeled and named after the waterbuck, *Senze*. Yet another type of helmet mask is inspired by and named after the elephant, *Sama* (Fig. 6-18).

Although similar to the Buffalo and Waterbuck masks, the Elephant mask is much larger, having a total length of some 150 centimeters, as befitting the largest land animal in Africa. The main elements of the mask are the elegantly long, inward-curving tusks, the trunk which is extended above and parallel to the tusks until its tip curves sharply between them, and the large oval ears which extend beyond the back of the head.[3] One might not think to classify this helmet mask as a three-part horizontal mask due to the absence of the typical feature of projecting horns. I would argue, however, that it fits into the three-part horizontal mask category quite well, due first of all to the ears which, when seen from the front, project outward from the top of the head and thereby echo the horn structure of the other masks, and secondly to the agressiveness of the projecting tusks which are functionally and affectively comparable to horns.

The *Do* masks in the Worodugu appear collectively but perform individually and compete for performance primacy. Each has its own entourage of acolytes and musicians led by a ritual specialist *gnambla* (Dosso 1988:4) and griot. The words and chants of the griot, like the mask itself, evoke a particular historical identity. Claims to origins and boasts about the ownership of occult powers are put into play in an

6-18. Elephant, *Sama*, is one of the largest helmet masks found among the Malinke of the Worodugu region of Côte d'Ivoire. It surpasses in size the related masks known as Buffalo and Waterbuck. 150 cm. Musée National, Abidjan, Côte d'Ivoire (B 900).

ongoing social negotiation of group identity from which individual personal identities are ultimately derived. The identification of one group with the buffalo, another with the waterbuck, and another with the elephant – as well as other forms used by yet other groups – is more subtle, however, than a mere generic equivalence. The name buffalo is used to denote the general form, but as is common to many African masquerade traditions, each mask has its own highly specific individual name, *individual* identity, and specifically individualized form.[4] Thus *Dagne* refers to an over-sized buffalo mask who overcomes all enemies, and *Gbosso* is the "ingrate" whose

uncontrollable powers are capable of harming even his own masters (Dosso 1988:5).

Do-like masquerades are also practiced to the south of the Malinke by the Southern-Mande groups of the Wan and Guro. Among the Wan, *Do* refers to a masquerade performed by those people characterized as "vassals" (*kro*) – i.e., descendants of ancestors incorporated into "noble" lineages through pawning (Ravenhill 1976:206-7; 1988) – who thereby maintain a ritual unity which stands in marked contrast to their lack of residential or corporate unity. Among the Wan, each clan of the village has its own pantheon of *Goli* masks (Ravenhill 1989),

6-19. This helmet mask, although attributed to the Baule due to the faces carved on the surface of the ears, also shares stylistic features with masks of the Guro and the Malinke. Length c. 65 cm. The Brooklyn Museum. 22.1771. Museum Expedition 1922, purchased with funds given by Frederick Pratt.

but vassals have only one *Do* per village, with the result that the *Do* stands in marked contrast to the *Goli*. The *Do* of the Wan is seen to be directly linked to the *Do* of the Worodugu, and thus of the same northern origin as the ancestors of those who still today bear the stigmatized status of vassal. *Do* masks among the Wan do not have a single prescribed form – an interesting reflection of their owners' lack of unity. Generally, however, the masks are three-part horizontal masks that are

comparable to both the *Do* masks of the Worodugu and the *Gye*[5] helmet masks of the northern Guro region, although they are not modeled quite so distinctly on the forms of specific wild animals.

In the central region of Côte d'Ivoire it is quite clear that there are fascinating connections between the peoples whose cultural identities we have tended to pigeonhole with the ethnic appellations Senufo, Malinke, Wan, Guro, and Baule.

6-20. The *klolo* mask of the Baule demonstrate great artistic inventiveness, with horns and tusks often being doubled. Musée National, Abidjan, Côte d'Ivoire.

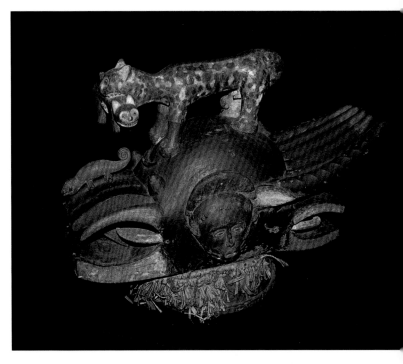

6-21. Baule *klolo* mask with both elephant and warthog tusks. 64.3 cm. Musée National, Abidjan, Côte d'Ivoire.

The helmet masks in all these cultures have composite "wild-animal" forms, and the comparisons are too striking to be accidental: domed crowns, flaring mouths, multiple horns and/or tusks – whether of warthog or elephantine form, and raffia and bark-fiber costumes.[6] As Glaze has said of Senufo forms, the expressive power of these masks is based on "the combination of natural forms in unnatural ways, and the addition of accumulative materials to the assembled masquerade unit" (1981:137). In both the *Do* masquerade of the Wan and in certain Senufo helmet mask masquerades, masks are at times worn backwards during performances.[7] Among the Wan, this is explained by the *Do* mask's power to "see" in all directions; the mask has a field of power that expands outward in increasing circles. One is tempted to hypothesize that it is this regional characteristic of reversability or bi-directionality that led historically to the creation of double-ended Janus helmet masks whose twin jaws and horn configurations may be almost identical. Such masks are found among both the Senufo and the Baule. It is the latter group, however, which interests us here, because of the fact that some of these Baule helmet masks incorporate elephant symbolism.

Among the Baule, there are a number of helmet masks called *glao* or *klolo* (Vogel 1977:84-88; Holas 1969a:310-11; Ravenhill 1986:7) – seemingly of relatively recent origin – which have motifs and compositional elements drawn from a wide variety of sources, including other masks such as the disc-shaped *kplɛkplɛ*, which are often depicted on them in miniature (Fig. 6-20). The principal sources of inspiration, however, are the aggressive denizens of the natural world (Figs. 6-19, 6-20).[8] These *glao/klolo* masks are classified by the

Baule, along with the *Do*, *Dye*, and *Goli*, as *bonu-amuin* ("gods of the forest-grove"), masks which are danced "to protect the village against various threats, to discipline women, and for the funerals of [their] former dancers and important men. Their performances feature violent behavior and powerful feats" (Vogel 1977:71).

Horns on *glao/klolo* masks may present a visual equivalence to those of various antelopes or the buffalo. They may be in pairs – as in nature – or they may be carved as doubled pairs or even as multiple parallel horns (Fig. 6-19). They may project backward from the head, forward from the mouth, or backward from the mouth and over the crowned dome, and on Janus helmet masks these configurations can also be doubled from the vertical axis. At times one is hard pressed to differentiate between horns and tusks, and among the latter between elephant tusks and warthog tusks.

Horns and tusks, naturally and inherently aggressive, are ready-made elements of nature that the artist puts into play by working within a culturally defined canon. The visual ambiguities of forms intermediate between the tusks of the elephant and the warthog (Fig. 6-21) – or hippopotamus (Fig. 6-20) – paradoxically create an immediacy of imagery that conveys an unambiguous message of power. In this creative cultural *bricolage,* the artist re-combines and re-articulates components of nature into a cobbled-together ensemble of visual images, purposefully seeking to create visual redundancies that reverberate with the essential message of power. When the Baule artist doubles up or juxtaposes both elephant and warthog tusks (Fig. 6-21), he creates a repetitive visual punch. When he invents canine tusks that function – on a

6-22. Guro elephant masquerade in Dabuzria, Côte d'Ivoire. Photograph, Eberhard Fischer, 1975.

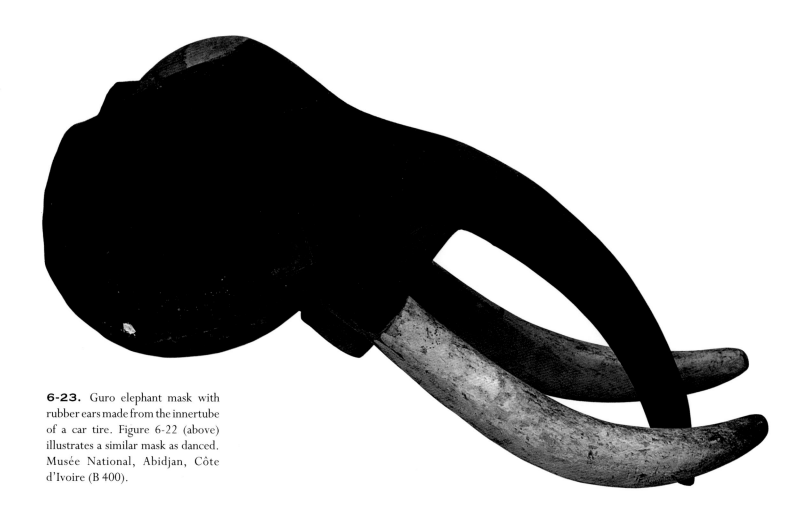

6-23. Guro elephant mask with rubber ears made from the innertube of a car tire. Figure 6-22 (above) illustrates a similar mask as danced. Musée National, Abidjan, Côte d'Ivoire (B 400).

6-24. An artist has imaginatively combined elephant traits and human physiognomy in this mask from central Côte d'Ivoire. The extension of the elephant trunk from the chin evokes the beard that is often depicted on face masks from this region. Height 33 cm. Collection of Nancy N. Carroll.

Janus-faced mask — as both tusks and horns (Fig. 6-20), he thereby produces doubly aggressive forms.

Elephant and warthog tusks, as depicted on central Côte d'Ivoire helmet masks, are clear emblems of aggressiveness and of potentially destructive power. While to the Westerner's vision of the natural world, the elephant and the warthog are considered to belong to two different orders (Proboscidea and Artiodactyla, respectively), to the Baule the warthog, known as the bush-pig (*blo kokoti*), has clear relations to the elephant. Both animals are greyish in color, rough-skinned, and small-eyed, and both have snouts and aggressive tusks. In this regard, Himmelheber relates an interesting Baule folktale which explains that the pig got his snout thanks to "medicine" supplied by the elephant whose form he so emulated (1951:57-58). Clearly there is a conceptual overlap that links the two animals together in Baule thought, just as in the English language they can be linked together by the term *pachyderm* — "any of various, nonruminant hoofed mammals that mostly have a thick skin and include the elephant, rhinoceros, and pig" (*Webster's Collegiate Dictionary*).

The use of the elephant in the art of central Côte d'Ivoire draws upon culturally channeled perceptions of the natural world: its cultural ecology and cultural 'ethology,' as it were. The natural world, as it is experienced in society, is very much a created world. Responses to nature and the animal kingdom are conditioned by cultural notions that have great historic depth. I have argued that in central Côte d'Ivoire there is a certain degree of commonality in cultural perceptions of the elephant and consequently to the use of his whole or partial depiction in art, and that this is due to shared history and shared environment. Unfortunately, the tendency of researchers to investigate art, or material culture, in *ethnic* rather than *regional and historical* terms, often results in serious gaps in cross-cultural data. Looking at the type of elephant face mask (Figs. 6-24, 6-25) attributed to the Yaure (Holas n.d.:ill. 6; 1969b:143) and apparently belonging to their category of *Dié* masks (Holas 1969b:134-35), one can raise the question of how this form of mask might relate to the *Dye* masks of the neighboring Guro (Fischer and Homberger 1986:35) with whom they share a linguistic affinity.[9] Both Guro and Yaure versions of this type of face mask incorporate elements of human physiognomy and animal morphology into animate creations which bridge the discontinuity that otherwise keeps apart the worlds of society and nature. As culturally created beings they partake of both.

There would appear to be intriguing connections between the elephant helmet mask of the Worodugu Malinke (Fig. 6-18), the *Dye* elephant mask of the Guro (Figs. 6-22, 6-23), and that of the Yaure (Fig. 6-24). In examining these masks, one is confronted by the inadequacy of the commonly used descriptive terms "face mask" and "helmet mask," with their respective assumptions of verticality and horizontality. All of these masks are worn and perceived on vertical, horizontal, and diagonal planes. When one expands further the

6-25. Elephant mask with repoussé plaques. This mask might have originated anywhere along the artistic continuum that links "Guro," "Yaure," and "Baule" styles in the region between Bouaflé and Yamoussoukro in central Côte d'Ivoire. Museum für Völkerkunde, Frankfurt am Main. NS 29322. Photograph, Maria Obermaier.

field of investigation, and includes the double-ended helmet masks of the Baule (Figs. 6-20, 6-21), one is further struck by how from the common source of elephant imagery there flows a creative river whose energy is channeled in different ways.

The art forms discussed here do not mirror nature; rather they make use of artfully selected components drawn from nature that are carefully modified, transformed, and juxtaposed, so as to refract — and thereby concentrate — stimuli and energy into powerful cultural forms. It is these forms, works of ART, that actively serve to create meaning for the life lived in society. Nature is not imitated, it is re-invented for cultural ends.

NOTES

I would like to express my appreciation for the fellowships, employment, and friendships that made field research possible. Initial fieldwork among the Wan was financed by a fellowship and grant from the National Institutes of Mental Health. Subsequent work among the Wan and Baule was facilitated by a post-doctoral grant from the Wenner Gren Foundation for Anthropological Research. Research among the Worodugu Malinke was undertaken while I was employed by the government of Côte d'Ivoire as a researcher in the Institut d'Histoire, d'Art, et d'Archéologie Africains (I.H.A.A.A.) of the Université d'Abidjan. I would also like to ackowledge the assistance of Dr. Victor Diabaté, Adou Koffi, and Yaya Savané, successive directors of the Musée National d'Abidjan, with whom I had the privilege of sharing ideas and working on the museum's collections. During two years of residence among the Wan I was privileged to work with Jean-Baptiste Degao Todjou who not only helped me in the translation of the Wan language but also in the translation of Wan culture. I owe a tremendous debt to Félix Léto Zibo who first brought to my attention the *Do* masquerade in the Worodugu. I would also like to thank Heidi Overing for the bibliographic research she so skillfully undertook for this article. Finally, I acknowledge with gratitude the ongoing collaboration with Judith Timyan who undertook fieldwork with me and whose profound knowledge and understanding of Baule culture has been shared with me for twenty years.

1. *Sran nga ɔ sui su, nyansue ɔ bo mɛn.*

2. Re images of the elephant standing on a springtrap see Niangoran-Bouah (1987:176) and Fischer and Himmelheber (1975:10,13, ill. 12); the latter is probably an Asante carving by Osu Bonsu. See also Ross (1982b:ill. 9) and Augé et al. (1989:236).

3. To the best of my knowledge, only three masks of this type have ever been published. The one seen in Figure 6-18 belongs to the Musée National of Côte d'Ivoire in Abidjan (no. B 900), and was published by Holas (1966:pl. 86), with his usual imprecision of attribution, as "Guro." Another was formerly owned by the dealer Harry Franklin (Kuchta 1973:ill. 13), and a third, misidentified as being "from Cameroon," is illustrated in an article in *Architectural Digest* that features a river barge transformed into elegant living quarters on the Seine in Neuilly, France (Styles-McLeod 1986:152).

4. In the existing literature on African masks more attention has been paid to the description of categorical types than to the specificity of individual form. A relatively untouched area for field research on African masking traditions is that of the indicators of individuation, i.e, those aspects of the visual forms of a mask that convey its individual identity. Two significant exceptions are the work of Cole and Aniakor on Okoroshi masquerades (1984:186-204) and the work of Ruth Phillips, on Sande *Sowei* mask traditions (forthcoming in a Fowler Museum publication). I agree wholeheartedly with Freedberg's assertion that "...each individual and each group that makes an image strives precisely to avoid the schematic — however poorly ideogrammatic it may seem to us. *The image is particularized in strategic ways...*" (1989:276, emphasis added).

5. In the literature on the arts of the Guro, Yaure, and Baule, one finds references to various mask types identified by the names *Gye, Dye, Dié.* Given that these languages have but one voiced palatal stop, it would seem that the *gy/dy/di* orthographic differentiations have no basis in linguistic fact. The vowel transcribed as *e*, or *é*, may, however, represent either of two vowels: the so-called "open" (ɛ) and "closed" (e) vowels. This orthographic confusion contributes to the larger confusion over names and mask types in the region.

The one *Do* mask that I was able to photograph among the Wan in the early 1970s was very close to the Guro *Gye* style, although it did not depict warthog tusks (Fischer and Homberger 1986:26). The horns were generic, rather than being specifically derived from the either the waterbuck or the buffalo. Another *Do* mask I saw — but was unable to photograph — was a helmet mask quite similar in general form to the Senufo fire-spitter mask, and it, too, had the ability to spit fire.

6. There are also fascinating and interesting connections that link some horizontal mask types both to vertical face masks and to other masks which are intermediate in size and orientation to the two forms. These latter masks, worn obliquely, cover the face and the front part of the head. The *Zauli* and *Zamble* masks of the Guro, for example, bear such striking resemblances to the *Goli glen* helmet mask of the Wan that there must exist clear historical links: they all have horns modeled on the Waterbuck, pronounced eye orbits or cavities, "bridges" as part of the nose, and similarly gaping maws. The *Goli* and the *Zamble*, furthermore, often feature a row of seven marks over the mouth. The *Zauli* has another feature, "warty cheeks" (Fischer and Homberger 1986:20), drawn from the warthog. "Warts" are also found below the eyes of some Baule *Dye* masks (Vogel 1977:ill. III-5).

7. The change of direction in how the mask is worn can be seen on a number of occasions in the Stephan Kurc film *Les chasseurs des esprits maléfiques: les masques wabélé des sénoufo* produced by Les Films du Sabre (Paris) in 1982.

8. The confusion in the literature that surrounds Baule masking traditions, and named types of masks, is due in part to the use of an implicit paradigm in which it is assumed that there is but *one* taxonomy of Baule masks and that the salient characteristics of each ideal type can be fully delineated. In fact, the real unit of analysis should not be pan-Baule "culture" — which is, after all, a chimera — but the individual Baule village in which specific mask forms are created and perceived in terms of both opposition and complementarity to other forms that exist in *that* village. Between forms there can be purposeful, marked contrast, but there can also be purposeful gradations of conceptual overlap. Compare, for example, the seven striped "noses" of the *Goli glen* (Ravenhill 1989), the accented nose ridge and "crest" of the *Botiwa* (Holas 1969d:106-7), the "rainbow" bridge on some *Dye* (Vogel 1977: III-2) or other helmet masks, and the crest line in the form of a snake on other masks (Holas 1969a:314-15).

9. Both groups speak languages belonging to the Southern Mande family (Prost 1953).

A.

B.

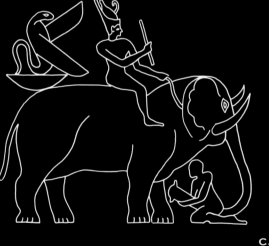

C.

A. Saltcellar, Temne-Bullom peoples, Sierra Leone. Height 24.3 cm. Museum für Völkerkunde, Vienna, 118.609 a,b.

B. "I Now Believe in You" by Bruce Onobrakpeya, 1980. Deep etching, #5/75. 40 cm x 52.8 cm x (26.4 cm). Nigeria. Gift of Warren Robbins, 1991-11-009. National Museum of African Art, Smithsonian Institution. Photograph, Franko Khoury.

C. Drawing from column 6 at the Temple of Apedemak, Musawwarat es-Sofra, Egypt: a crowned man riding an elephant. The double crown may identify him as a king, but his nudity may indicate he is a god-like being. He holds a rope and a short stick with which to lead the animal – tools like those employed by Indian mahouts. The trunk of the elephant is held by a kneeling slave while behind the rider floats the cobra-goddess Uatchit. Drawing, Sylvia Kennedy.

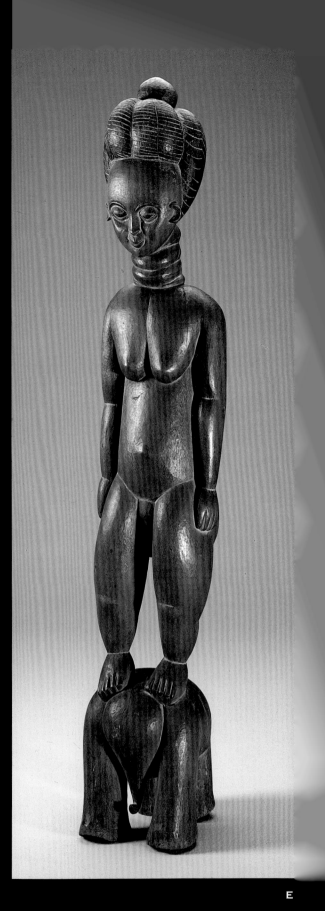

D.

E

OST IMAGES OF ELEPHANT RIDING in African art are not ended to portray actual elephant riding, but rather to symbolize the ver of the human figure. Some pay homage to historic figures, for mple Onobrakpeya's tribute to Stephen Biko. The elephant riding ge in Twin Seven Seven's painting is drawn from mythology. In hy instances, the riders are women, which demonstrates that this

D. "King Elephant Comes to Town" *(A O MU ÉRIN JE OBA EWEKU EWELE)*, by Twin Seven Seven, 1989. 121.9 cm x 60.6 cm. Shango Galleries, Los Angeles.

E. Female elephant rider from Sierra Leone (Mende peoples). Wood. Height 67.5 cm. Collection of Mr. and Mrs. Harold Benjamin.

SEVEN

MORE THAN MEETS THE EYE

ELEPHANT MEMORIES AMONG THE AKAN

DORAN H. ROSS

The Akan say, *No one knows what the elephant ate to make it so big* (Christaller 1990:24). In fact there is a great deal "no one knows" about the animal that the Akan call *ɛsono*, since most Akan have not seen living, breathing elephants for over two hundred years. Nevertheless, today *ɛsono* thrives in the folklore and art of the Akan where words and objects sustain the idea of the elephant (Figs. 7-1 to 7-4). And that idea is as big and multi-faceted as the animal itself.[1]

The Akan live in the forest and coastal areas of southwestern Ghana, the former Gold Coast of West Africa. Principal subgroups include the Asante, Fante, Brong, Wassa, Aowin, and Akuapem. All Akan were and still are organized into a series of states each headed by a paramount chief who rules with the aid of a council of elders and a hierarchy of divisional, town, and village chiefs.

The Asante (Ashanti) are the largest and best known of these states and are concentrated in the forests areas around their capital of Kumase. This powerful kingdom was founded at the end of the seventeenth century when several independent chiefdoms were consolidated under the rule of Osei Tutu, the first king or Asantehene of the dynasty that continues to the present. Throughout the eighteenth century the empire expanded through military conquest, eventually

bringing many of its Akan neighbors under Asante hegemony. The Asante economy was traditionally based on the cultivation of food crops, especially yams, plantains and maize, and an export trade that sent gold and kola to the Islamic peoples in the north and gold and ivory to Europeans in the coastal forts to the south. These were exchanged for metalware and cloth from both areas and for European firearms from the coast.

The Eurocentric view of the elephant in the Gold Coast from the late fifteenth through the nineteenth centuries is largely represented in terms of the ivory trade, even though in reality that trade appears to have been of only modest importance and one that clearly diminished in time from the beginning to the end of this period, despite the proximity of the Gold Coast to the Côte d'Ivoire. The European quest for ivory is evident from some of the earliest accounts. The records of ivory exports from the Gold Coast are often misleading, however, as Daaku points out, since they frequently represented consolidated shipments of ivory brought to the coastal

7-1 (OPPOSITE). A Fante chief's counselor with gold-leafed staff representing the proverb, *Only the elephant can uproot the palm tree.* Carved by Osei Bonsu, c. 1950. From the state treasury of the paramount chief of Mankesim. Photograph, Doran H. Ross, 19 August 1976.

forts from elsewhere. Citing a 1706 letter from the Royal Africa Company archives, Daaku notes, "The biggest single haul of ivory from the Gold Coast [for the period 1600-1720] was in 1706, when the English shipped 339 teeth of twenty-seven pounds each, which was described as something never seen 'before from the Gold Coast'" (1970:28). Summarizing the situation for the nineteenth century in the Asante kingdom and citing two British envoys to Kumase, Wilks writes (1975:435):

> Little is known of the ivory industry, which was not of major importance in Asante. Bowdich noted that a tax was imposed upon private elephant hunters, but Dupuis' passing reference to 'hunters of elephants in the king's name, and on his account...' may indicate that there was a level of state involvement in the enterprise.

The Akan view of the elephant, however, is best represented by their rich and diverse oral literature. A number of Asante proverbs collected and published by Christaller in 1879 emphasize their fundamental view of the pachyderm as a substantial source of food:

> It is from the elephant that big lumps of meat are cut.
>
> When an elephant is thin, that is not to say its meat will not fill a hundred baskets.
>
> It is one man who kills an elephant, but many people who eat its flesh.[2]

The theme of the elephant as a food source also recurs in several of the folktales collected and published by Rattray (1930: 147,183,269).

Significantly very little Akan folklore focuses on elephant ivory as a commodity. Two telling exceptions are:

> The poor man's elephant tusk is the wart-hog's tooth.
>
> The vulture has not a gun, but he sells elephant tusks.[3]

The first of these emphasizes the association of ivory with the wealthy. In the second, it is tempting to associate the vulture metaphorically with the European traders occupying the coastal forts, since they, like the scavengers, did not actually kill the elephants but nevertheless profited from their death.

The arming of the central Akan kingdoms with European muzzle-loaders in the late seventeenth century undoubtedly hastened the demise of the elephant in the southern forests and their northern fringes. By the early nineteenth century the Asante had several thousand men with flintlocks. A wonderful folktale collected by Rattray (1930:147-51) makes a strong connection between the presence of hunters with guns and the disappearance of the elephant from the forests (pages 147-48). Titled by Rattray "How the elephants

7-3. Cast brass ritual vessel *(kuduo)* used as a container for offerings or for gold dust. Height 28 cm. The Trustees of the British Museum, 1956. Af 27.42.

7-2 (OPPOSITE). The principal drum of an Akan popular band is typically female and viewed by band members as "the mother of the group." The elephant with the drum riding on its back represents the "strength of the group." Carved by Osei Bonsu c. 1935 for the Asante *ntan* group at Abofo. Wood, hide, paint. Height 111.7 cm. FMCH X78.136. Gift of Dr. Donald Suggs.

7-4. In some situations the elephant is given no more weight than any other animal in the Akan environment. The proverb for this Fante Flag is, *Before the lion, the leopard ruled the forest.* Cotton and rayon trade cloth. Length 170.1 cm. FMCH X81.1665. Gift of Beth and Richard Rogers.

came to go off to the long-grass-country," the story begins with a head-butting contest between Ananse the spider (the trickster in Asante folklore) and the elephant. Through a series of deceptions the spider wins the contest and kills the elephant. When the elephant's family insists that Ananse bury their relative in a massive rock, the spider carves a wooden man with a gun, which frightens the elephants to flee to the long-grass country. The spider then eats the dead elephant. Aside from celebrating Ananse's wisdom and cleverness, the tale clearly casts the musket-armed hunter as the precipitating force in the disappearance of elephants from the forest.

Elephant hunting in Asante required certain ritual prescriptions. Rattray documented an obligatory hunter's dance called "the elephant's funeral" which was performed to appease the spirit of an elephant killed in the hunt. The dance reenacts the stages of the hunt from the initial stalking of the quarry to the final carrying away of the meat. Celebratory songs accompanied this ritual theater (1923:184-85; see also discussion about *atumpan* drums, below). It is important to note that meat and not ivory is seen as the final product both here and in the folktale cited above.

Even though elephants had become scarce in most Akan regions by the nineteenth century, the animal has endured in the arts and material culture of the Akan, and especially in their court arts. The regalia of the Asantehene is the most varied and symbolically complex of all Akan paramount chiefs and indeed the historic regalia of this kingdom provided the model for many other paramountcies. From A.A.Y. Kyerematen's careful documentation of this Asante "panoply" (1964), it is clear that the elephant plays a most prominent role – not only as image, but as actual material.

THE ELEPHANT AS MATERIAL

Elephant hide is an especially critical component in several items of Asante royal regalia. Most significantly, it is associated with the principal symbol of the Asante Kingdom, the Golden Stool (Sika Dwa). According to oral tradition, a powerful priest named Okomfo Anokye brought the stool down from the heavens, amidst thunder and lightning, to land gently on the knees of Osei Tutu, the first Asantehene. In part because of its miraculous origins the Golden Stool became the religious and political catalyst of the Asante kingdom, which it remains to the present.

Stools in Akan culture are the focus of ancestral veneration. When a revered elder dies, one of his stools is blackened and stored in perpetuity in a room specifically reserved for such use where it receives periodic offerings and libations. During Adae ceremonies, the principal occasion for honoring ancestors (Rattray 1929:fig.139), elephant hide sometimes serves as a ground cover for blackened stools. In a unique situation, the Golden Stool is considered the blackened stool of Osei Tutu, the first Asantehene.

No one ever sits on the Golden Stool except the Asantehene upon his installation or "enstoolment," as the Asante refer to it in English. On other occasions the Asantehene uses either a chair or stool as a seat. When the Golden Stool is displayed in public it rests on its own chair, called the Hwedomtea, which in turn stands on an elephant skin called Banwoma.[4] This hierarchy of stool, chair, and skin is a metaphor of Asante hegemony. Although the chair is Asante made, it is modeled on European prototypes (Cole and Ross 1977:142). While a stool functions as the official "throne" for Akan chiefs, a chair serves this function for European monarchs. Non-Akan rulers to the north sit upon an animal skin (usually lion, leopard, or elephant) which acts as their symbol of office (Kyerematen 1964:11-12). The stool/chair/skin ensemble thus represents the Asante view of the political order of the region with the Asante, of course, on top.

Elephant hide is also the material of the treasury bags called Sanaa and Fotoɔ.[5] The first of these held the cast brass weights used for measuring gold dust (see below) while the second contained the dust itself. On public occasions these were displayed as part of gift-giving rituals (Kyerematen 1977:8). Thus the bags were symbolic of both the Asantehene's wealth and his generosity, two appropriate themes for containers made from the skin of an elephant. In a very real sense these bags were an answer to the Asante proverbial query, *You may make a bag out of elephant hide, but what are you going to put in it?* (Christaller 1990:65).

In addition, elephant hide was used to make an historically important shield (Apimasanta) and parts of some royal headdresses. According to Kyerematen, "The shield was used by Kings Oti Akenten (1631) and Obiri Yeboa (1663) together with swords, bows and arrows, the fighting weapons of the Ashanti before King Osei Tutu who introduced the use of guns" (1961:8-9). The skullcaps of some of the Asantehene's bodyguard (Atumfufoɔ) are made of the skin of an elephant as is the headdress of the bearer of one of the principal swords of state (Bosumuru). This headdress is worn by the Asantehene during the most solemn part of his installation, when he takes his oath of office while holding the Bosumuru sword in his right hand and the elephant hide shield in his left (Kyerematen 1961:13 and 1970:25). It is also worn "when there is a grave national crisis, such as the declaration of war" (1961:13). The gravity of these contexts is symbolically emphasized by the presence of the elephant as ornament and protector of the Asantehene. The skin of the headdress and that of the ground cover for the Golden Stool share the same origin. According to Kyerematen, "the elephant had been slain by King Osei Tutu on his march back to Ashanti from Akwamu to succeed his uncle King

7-5. Master drummer Kwasi Asare with a pair of *atumpan* "talking" drums which typically have elephant hide drum heads. When played, the drums sing the praises of the chief or recite oral histories. From Kranka, Brong Ahafo. Photograph, Raymond A. Silverman, 9 April 1980.

Obiri Yeboa" (1961:13). Through this explicit connection, both items evoke the bravery of the hunter, the conquests of the warrior, and more generally the history of the state and the ruler's family.

Skin, and more specifically the skin of the elephant's ear, plays a recurring role in Asante ceremonial and ritual life. Kyerematen, writing of the Banwoma, refers to "a broad piece of the skin of an elephant ear" (1970:26). According to an Asante proverb, *The ears of a chief are as big as those of an elephant* (Christaller 1990:109), suggesting that the chief is a good listener and hears the voices of his subjects. Listening well and speaking well are two social and political skills highly valued by the Akan.

Thus it is perhaps not surprising that the drum heads of the *atumpan* are also fashioned from elephant ears. The *atumpan*, an important component of the court drum orchestra, actually comprises a pair of drums each producing a different tone (Fig. 7-5). According to Rattray, the heads of the so-called "talking drums" of Asante (*atumpan*) are "invariably made out of the skin of an elephant's ear, preferably female, the hairy side being outermost" (1923:259). Played by a single drummer, they can reproduce the tonal language of the Asante;

7-6. Elephant tail flywhisk from the treasury of Asantehene Kwaku Dua Panin, dating before 1874. Elephant tail, gold plate, glass beads. Length 54 cm. FMCH X65.8521. Gift of the Wellcome Trust. Photograph, Richard Todd.

thus to a certain extent the drums can talk. Drum language is largely confined to conventional praise songs and to recounting state histories. The *atumpan's* elephants ears that can talk represent a marvelous Akan conceit wedding two skills in a highly expressive object type. The elephant is not just a lifeless component of this drum ensemble. Rattray considers the drum "the home for the spirit of the elephant whose ears form its tense membrane" (1927:6). This spirit of the elephant is frequently invoked with drum language on state occasions:

You of mighty bulk, Gyaanadu, the red one
The swamps swallow thee up oh elephant,
Elephant that breaks the axe,
(Spirit of) the Elephant, the divine drummer declares that
He has started up from sleep,
He has made himself to arise....[6]

And in another version:

There are swamps, swamps, swamps,
Which can swallow up the elephant.
A river may lie small in the valley
Between great hills.
But it flows on forever and ever.
If you (spirit of the elephant) have gone elsewhere
and I call upon you, Come.[7]

The idea of invoking the spirit of the elephant by beating its ear can hardly be more explicit. Although the elephant is celebrated and given respect in the above passages, it is significant that one of the praise names of the Asantehene is *Swallower of Elephants* (Quarcoo 1975:21).[8] In drum passages such as the above, the "swamp" metaphorically represents the Asantehene (and other paramount chiefs) as the conqueror of elephants.

Elephant ears also play a role outside of the realm of royal regalia, in female puberty rites. Describing part of the ceremony, Rattray notes (1927:73):

> Three roasted pieces of an elephant's ear were now produced, and her mouth touched with each in turn, the pieces being allowed to fall to the ground. As this was done the following words were addressed to her, being repeated three times: *May the elephant give you her womb that you may bear ten children.*

Here the elephant is clearly associated with fecundity, rather than with listening or speaking. Paradoxically, however, it is interesting to note that the Asante call their eunuchs *ɛsono*. Since they are both castrated and deprived of their penises, the name may exist principally in the realm of irony (Rattray 1927:119 n.).

The elephant is capable of whisking off flies with his tail, short as it is.[9]

A warning not to underestimate someone on the basis of appearance, this proverb is also a reminder that despite its apparently humble function, the elephant tail is no mere domestic implement. Indeed, the elephant tail is prominent in court regalia as a flywhisk (*mena*). Only the Asantehene is allowed to possess the Gold-handled Whisk, Sika Mena (Fig. 7-6), which is the preeminent symbol of the empire's wealth. Moreover, the use of an elephant tail whisk without a gold hilt must be authorized by the Asantehene; it is an honor bestowed only upon those most accomplished in the accumulation of wealth, and have earned the title *ɔbirɛmpɔn* (Wilks 1975:430,695,696).[10] In addition to gift-giving and other displays of wealth, part of the installation rites for this title included a mock hunt of a slave wearing an elephant tail on his backside. When the "elephant" was "killed" its tail was ceremonially cut off by the newly installed *ɔbirɛmpɔn* (pp. 13-15). Wilks discusses the Golden Stool and the Golden Elephant Tail as the twin pillars of the Asantehene's power (pp. 17-18):[11]

> The Golden Stool and the Golden Elephant Tail are the grundnorms of the political and fiscal systems respectively. That is, the hierarchies of superordinate and subordinate political authorities are constituted into one closed system by the institution of the Golden Stool — than which no higher level of authority can exist in Asante. Similarly, the relations of appropriation (of surplus, through taxes, tributes, fees, fines, etc.) are constituted into one closed system by the institution of the Golden Elephant Tail — than which no higher level of appropriation can exist in Asante. The Golden Stool and the Golden Elephant Tail thus define two crucial

aspects of Asante sovereignty. The nature of the intimate relationship between the two is expressed metaphysically by the Asante who say that the Sika Mena "enfolds" or "wraps" (*nnuraho*) the Sika Dwa.

Speculating on the symbolic relationship between the elephant tail and wealth, Wilks notes the dominance of the pachyderm in the animal kingdom and cites the previously quoted proverb in a slightly different translation: *The elephant's tail is short, but it is able to sweep flies away.* His analysis continues (p. 16):

> The sense is that the elephant did not allow the handicap of a short tail to prevent him from achieving preeminence… thus should the citizen sweep away all obstacles in his or her pursuit of riches. The elephant tail or *mena* is the symbol in other words, not so much of wealth as such, but rather of the accomplishment and achievement which characterize the acquisitive process. The incumbent of – if the phrase may be used – an elephant tailship was subject to acute social disapprobation if he dissipated his wealth; few more severe strictures could be levelled at the wealthy citizen than that he "boiled and ate the elephant tail…." Not even the Asantehene, however, could revoke the grant of an elephant tail, however dramatic the decline in the fortunes of the grantee.

An interpretation of meaning within an entirely different conceptual realm is offered by McCaskie (1983:31):

> Why a Golden Elephant Tail? It must be confessed at the outset that, from the perspective of twentieth-century Asante informants, the symbolism of the elephant (*ɛsono*) is opaque in the present context. However, from other areas of discourse we might adduce evident considerations of size, of weight, of bulk, of density, of substance. But I think that we can take conjectural interpretation a stage beyond these general observations. As indicated, we are dealing with a single and very precise anatomical feature – the tail. And to anyone who has observed the process it will be readily apparent that in the structural sense the elephant's tail 'presides' over the discharge or production of excrement. We might also note that within the Asante cognitive universe this was – volumetrically – the largest such 'transaction.' Let me reiterate my conjecture about the association in the Asante mind between excrement and wealth. Both 'substances' are mediated, uncertain or ambiguous by nature; they possess clearly parallel associations – through evident processes of convertibility – with ranges of other substances (that is, different constituents of reality). It might be added (although it is something well known to anthropologists), that the volatility of

7-7. Goldweight representing elephant tail flywhisk. Brass. Length 11.5 cm. Collection of Maurice Bonnefoy.

7-8. Goldweight representing a wickerwork shield with four elephant tail flywhisks displayed on its surface. Brass. Length 10.2 cm. Collection of Maurice Bonnefoy.

both wealth and excrement – their capacity to transgress and to rupture categorical boundaries by conversion – exists cognitively in cultures other than Asante.

If Wilks is too literal, and McCaskie a bit obtuse, there are undoubtedly elements of truth in both of their analyses. Nevertheless it is probably useful to remember that Akan folklore repeatedly emphasizes a view of the elephant as a bountiful source of food. The connection between sustenance and wealth does not require any great leap of faith. Although we only have indirect evidence from the Asante that the elephant tail was the prerogative of the hunter who killed it (Wilks 1979:13-14), this is a common practice in much of Africa. If the tail is specifically identified with the hunter, who is the ultimate provider, then its symbolic extension to other realms of accumulation including wealth is more understandable.

The institution of *ɔbirɛmpɔn* apparently declined in importance toward the end of the nineteenth century and according to McCaskie "the Asantehene Kwaku Dua Panin [r. 1834-67]

was the last ruler of the nineteenth century to create his own Golden Elephant Tail…"(1983:39). In addition to the Sika Mena shown in Figure 6, there is at least one other Golden Flywhisk extant from the late nineteenth century, now in the British Museum (McLeod 1981:84). Identifying either one with a specific Asantehene is problematic. Both seem to date from the 1874 British "punitive expedition" against the Asante in Kumase. Both are virtually identical in workmanship, except for the configuration of rivets that hold the tail hairs to the handle. Wilks and McCaskie constantly refer to the Sika Mena in the singular but Kyerematen continually uses the plural.[12] For the regalia of Prempeh I, Rattray makes the point that the bearers of the Asantehene's whisks are twins, suggesting that there were two whisks, unless they alternated in the carrying of a single whisk (1923:99). While we can only speculate, it is possible that the two extant gold-hilted flywhisks are both from the regalia of Kwaku Dua Panin.

Like other regalia, the elephant tail also appears among the enormous corpus of motifs represented in Akan goldweights

(Fig. 7-7). Since virtually all court arts are reproduced in brass miniatures used as counterbalances in the weighing of gold, the appearance of the flywhisk in this genre is not surprising. That it is a symbol of wealth simply adds resonance to its occurrence here. Its presence is puzzling, however, on the outside of goldweights in the form of wickerwork shields (Fig. 7-8). Examples with one, two, and four whisks have been documented. To my knowledge, whisks have not been recorded as being attached to actual shields, nor have I been able to obtain any explanation from Akan elders who were shown photographs of the goldweight versions. Perhaps this juxtaposition indicates that the shield (either in miniature or full scale examples) is that of an *ɔbirɛmpɔn*. In conquest states like the Asante, the conjunction of war and wealth is taken for granted. It is also possible that the physical linkage of shield and whisk on the side facing the enemy is a metaphorical statement that indicates that the adversaries' weapons can be deflected by the shield in much the same fashion that flies can be deflected by a whisk. Militant insults such as this are common in Akan political arts. The tail as the presider over the discharge of excrement (McCaskie's view) may also play a role here.

The density of meaning previously suggested for the *atumpan* drums with heads of elephant ears is paralleled by the elephant ivory horns that produce much of the same effect as the paired drums. A tone hole at the tip of the side-blown trumpets provides the player with the opportunity to reproduce the Asante language, which in this context is confined to conventionalized praise songs and histories. The Asantehene's regalia contains a number of ivory horns, many of them named and having specific roles (Kyerematen 1961:4,14). Following a fairly common Akan practice, some of these horns are adorned with human jawbones taken from defeated enemies of the state (Fig. 7-9). George Preston has suggested that the symbolic effect here is one of the enemy singing the praises of his conqueror (1972:58). This can be taken one step further. Since the trumpeting of a medium-sized ivory horn is remarkably similar in tone quality and range to the trumpeting of an elephant, it can be argued that the chief's praises are also being sung by the elephant through its own teeth. Having both enemy and elephant as praise singers is perhaps the ultimate honor.

As suggested above, the Asantehene's ivory trumpets are frequently associated with war. One horn (*ntahera*) was purportedly captured by Asantehene Osei Tutu from a conquered state (Kyerematen 1961:4) and another (*tatwia*) was used "to give a warning to the enemy that total annihilation awaited them if they did not surrender" (p. 14). More generally, Akan proverbs also make this connection:

If you don't have a horn and you go to war, nobody hears.

When an army suffers defeat a horn is not blown.[13]

In addition, the war horn (*akoben*) is one of the most common

7-9. Fante royal trumpeter blowing ivory horn adorned with human jawbones from defeated enemies. The playing of such horns produces the symbolic effect of having the chiefs' praises sung from the mouths of both elephant and enemy. State treasury of Mankesim. Photograph, Doran H. Ross, 25 August 1974.

7-10. Goldweight depicting ivory trumpet with human jawbones on end. Brass. Length 7.7 cm. FMCH x65.9257. Gift of the Wellcome Trust.

7-12 (ABOVE). Elephant jawbone serving as seat for Sumampim (lit. "One thousand medicines") in shrine compound of a Tano deity. Tanoso, Brong Ahafo region. Photograph, Raymond A. Silverman, 21 May 1980.

7-11 (LEFT). Goldweight representing man playing ivory trumpet. Brass. Height 9 cm. Collection of Ernst Anspach.

motifs on royal umbrella finials in many Akan states. In the context of war, the elephant is an especially convincing metaphor for the power and strength of a warrior.

As with elephant tail flywhisks, representations of ivory trumpets complete with jawbones are also common in the goldweight corpus (Figs. 7-10, 7-11). Menzel associates the images with the following saying: *If a horn deserves a jawbone, they attach one to it* (1968:220). Here the jawbone is depicted as a tangible measure of achievement.

A number of disparate references to elephant hide and bone from other Akan areas outside of Asante suggest that there once was a variety of practices where the elephant served as a seat. As early as 1602, de Marees wrote that coastal peoples made chairs from the skin of elephants (1602 [1987]:129). In

1909, Moore and Guggisberg recorded in Abetife that "...it was a common sight to see big [elephant] skulls being used as seats outside the houses" (p. 288). More recently Raymond Silverman documented and photographed an overmodeled elephant jawbone used as a support for a "thousand medicines" outside a Tano shrine in Brong Ahafo (Fig. 7-12). Silverman makes the telling point that the arrangement of deities in Tano shrines and their associated regalia mirrors similar practices of Akan royalty (1986b:4,5). Likewise imitating royal practice, Meyerowitz recorded a praise name for Taa Kora, a Tano deity, *The great spirit...that is everywhere, it is he we call elephant* (1951: 138, see also Rattray 1923:196). Oral literature aside, seats or altars made of elephant bone are variant forms of the "elephant rider" motif discussed in the introduction to this volume.

How the Elephants Came to Go Off to the Long-Grass-Country

We do not really mean, we do not really mean,
(that what we are going to say is true)

There once was an Elephant, and he said he wanted some one with whom to play the game called 'butting heads.' All the animals said they were unable (to play this game with the Elephant). Now there was Kwaku Ananse (the Spider), and he said, 'As for me, I shall be able, but the condition I stipulate upon with you is that, if you should happen to kill me, then you must bury me anywhere else but in a rock.' The Elephant said, 'I have heard, and I shall come and strike you for seven days, and you, too, will come and strike me for seven days.'

Kwaku Ananse went and dug up yams, and he placed them in the fire, to roast them, and he went and made a latrine near a path. Now, whenever Ananse rose up, he took a yam in his hand, and went and squatted down over the latrine. He saw the little Adowa antelope passing. Now words with their left-behinds (i.e. I forgot to mention something), a great famine had come (at that time). As he (the Adowa antelope) passed, the Spider threw down the yam on the path. Immediately the Adowa took it. He said, 'Father Spider, a great famine like this has come, and is this what you use when you go to ease yourself?' Ananse replied, 'There is no difficulty at all about food at my home.' The Adowa said, 'I and you shall go and get some.'

Ananse and he reached the house; he told the Adowa, saying, 'There is a certain man, and it is he who brings me food at night; so go and sleep there at the doorway, and when he comes he will say, 'Asikoto!' (and you will bend you head) and reply, 'I take my head to receive it,' and as soon as you have said so, he will take some of the food and place it there, for you to take.' The Adowa said, 'I thank you, Aku; as for you, Father Ananse, really I have never seen a man like you.' The Adowa went and lay down in the entrance to the courtyard. Not long after, the Elephant came. He said, 'Asikoto.' The Adowa antelope replied, 'I take my head to receive it,' and the Elephant hit him, pan! and the Adowa antelope has died. The Elephant went off.

Early next morning, when things became visible, the Spider took Adowa and gave it to Aso (his wife) to make a soup-stew for him. Ananse now went off to the Elephant to give him morning greetings. The Elephant said, 'Are you quite well?' Ananse replied, 'I am well.' Ananse set off and came to his home. He took another of the yams, and went off again to the latrine. He saw Otwe, the Duyker, passing, and he threw the yam away. The Duyker said, 'Oh, Father Ananse, a famine like this has come, and this is what you take with you when going to the latrine?' Ananse replied, 'If you want some, come, let us go to my home, that I may go and give you some.' The Duyker and Ananse went off. Ananse said, 'Lie down here at the entrance to the yard, and this evening my slave will come with food, and when he reaches here, he says, 'Asikoto'; you also say, 'I take my head to receive it.' The Duyker said, 'I thank you, Aku, you (alone) are capable of arranging such things.' The Duyker went there to lie down. In the evening the Elephant came. He said, 'Asikoto.' The Duyker said, 'I take my head to receive it.' And he hit the Duyker, and he fell down, (and the sound of his falling was) kum! Then the Elephant went off.

Early next morning, when things became visible, then Ananse took the Duyker and gave it to Aso, and set out for the Elephant's house to bid him good morning. The Elephant said, 'Here is Okuamoa, are you quite well?' Okuamoa replied, 'Perfectly well.' Then they conversed for a while, and Ananse begged leave to go, and returned to his home. And now Ananse did the same thing with Oyuo, the black duyker; Wansane, the Bush-buck; Kokotee-Asamoa, the Bush-pig; Otromo, the Bongo; and Oko, the Roan.

Now, it was Ananse's turn to go and strike the Elephant. Then he went off to a blacksmith's forge to fashion an iron wedge; and he made an iron hammer to go with it. In the evening, he went to the Elephant's home. Ananse said, 'Asikoto.' The Elephant said, 'I take my head to receive it.' The Spider took the iron wedge and placed it on the crown of the Elephant's head, and took the iron hammer and hit it, pan! pan! pan! and it (the wedge) disappeared (into the Elephant's head). Ananse then came home.

Early next morning, when things become visible, the Elephant said to his wife, 'I have a splitting headache,' and his wife said, 'Don't talk like that, you ought to be ashamed about it; even Ananse, whom you hit for seven days, did not get a headache, nor has he died, and you talk like this; now be off and give Ananse good morning as he used to do.' The Elephant pressed his eyes (i.e. made a great effort), and went off; he got to where Ananse lived. The Spider said, 'Powerful hero, are you quite well?' The Elephant replied, 'Oh, I am all right.' The Spider said, 'Really.' Ananse went and forged another wedge.

When night fell cool, he set out to go to the Elephant there. 'Asikoto,' he said. The Elephant replied, 'I take my head to receive it.' Ananse took the wedge, placed it there, and hit it with the iron hammer, pan! pan! pan! Ananse come back to his home.

Now there he was, when a messenger arrived and said, 'Ananse, the grandfather of all the Elephants says that I must come and inform you that your friend, the Elephant, when he lay down, did not rise up again; so come and open a rock and take him and put him inside.' Ananse said, 'Not at all, that was not the arrangement we made. We said that if one died, the other should boil him to chew.' The messenger went off to give the message to the blood-relations of the (dead) Elephant. They said, 'Go and take him and fetch him (here) at once.' The messenger came there to the Spider and said, 'They say you are to come at once.' Ananse said, 'You must wait for me.' The Spider went to the bush and cut a tree, and carved it into a wooden-man, and he carved out a gun, and put it in its hand, and he gave it to Aso, saying, 'Take it, go in front, put it down at the place where they say I must split the rock, and you will also stand there, and when I come, you will call to me.' Aso picked up (the wooden figure) and went off The Spider, too, set off with the messengers.

Ananse arrived in front of the Elephants, and they took a hoe, and a crow-bar, and an axe and a knife, and placed them in his hands. They said, 'Get on.' Then they took the Spider to where there was a certain great rock. They said, 'Split it open, dig a hole, and place the (dead) Elephant inside.' Spider went to it, pe! pe! pe! (sounded his tools). There Ananse was, when he (suddenly called out) 'Yes.' He said, 'Elephants, do you hear, (it is) as if some one calls me?' The Elephants said, 'Get out, you seek a way to escape.' Ananse said, 'I have heard.' And he went on with his work, pe! pe! pe! Then again he shouted, 'Yes.' He said, 'Some one calls me.' The people said, 'We will not allow you to go.' (It was) thus, thus, seven times. At length they said, 'Go and listen (who it is) and return at once, and if you run away, we shall get you.' Ananse went off to where Akua's child was.

Now Ananse ran (back), kiri! kiri! kiri! (was the sound of his feet). The Elephants said, 'Ananse, what is it?' He said, 'Oh, you must be off, for surely there is some hunter standing there, and he says I must draw myself a little to one side to allow him to fire his gun and hit you. That is why he has called me, and called me, saying I must stand aside.' When the Elephants were about to make search there in the bush, of a truth they saw that some one was standing there, and they fled. Ananse said, 'Father hunter, kill them for me.' The Elephants fled; it was into the Tall-grass-country, and they left the dead Elephant behind there, and Ananse took it and went and chewed it. That is how Elephants came to go to the Tall-grass-country, for once upon a time Elephants (only) lived in the forest.

This, my story, which I have related, if it be sweet, (or) if it be not sweet, some you may take as true, and the rest you may praise me (for telling of it).

From R.S. Rattray, *Akan-Ashanti Folk-Tales*, Oxford, Clarendon Press, 1930, pp.147-51.

7-13A,B. Akan goldweights of elephants. Brass. Lengths 7 cm, 13.5 cm. Collection of Maurice Bonnefoy.

THE ELEPHANT AS IMAGE

Although the elephant is a prevalent image in the arts of the Akan, it still occupies only a small niche in the total corpus of artistic representations. The subject matter of Akan art is among the richest and most varied of all sub-Saharan African peoples. It represents in different contexts virtually the entire realm of the zoological and botanical environment; domestic, religious and political scenes from Akan society; and a wealth of objects drawn from Akan material culture, both indigenous and imported. Meaning in Akan art, however, is rooted in oral literature. Most images are typically paired with verbal expressions that can be metaphorically applied to a variety of contexts in Akan life. One of the most pervasive and fundamental principles of Akan art is this consistent tendency to take as an iconographic focus the representation of traditional oral literature including folktales, proverbs, praise names, jokes, riddles, boasts and insults. This verbal-visual nexus is at the root of understanding all Akan representations, including elephants.

Many of these visual images and their verbal counterparts are highly conventionalized and are displayed on a wide range of art objects often regardless of their functional context. Although elephant imagery may have its origins in actual behavioral observations, it just as often is a product of the creative mind that produced the wealth of Akan folklore. Simple images of a single elephant may represent any one of the large inventory of sayings related to the elephant (Christaller 1879 includes at least thirty-nine maxims).

The best known and without question most numerous of all Akan arts are the cast brass goldweights. These are often called "proverb weights" in the literature since they are the quintessential expression of the verbal-visual nexus. Isolated images of an elephant (Figs. 7-13, 7-14) may depict a variety of expressions. In addition to those mentioned previously a few of the most frequently cited include:

There is no other animal as big and as strong as an elephant.

The person who walks behind the elephant doesn't get wet from the dew on the grass.

One does not stop pursuing an elephant to go and throw stones at a small bird.[14]

More involved scenes elicit a narrower range of proverbs. Perhaps surprisingly, one of the rarer images in Akan art is that of an elephant hunter, although it is still an important theme in the oral literature:

The hunter's name is always connected to the meat of the elephant.

A wax bullet is not used to shoot an elephant.

After the elephant there is a still greater animal, the hunter![15]

One or more elephants with no other associated images have been documented on a range of court arts, including chief's rings (Fig. 7-15), sword bearer's hats, cast brass ritual vessels called *kuduo* (Fig. 7-3) and wood stools (Fig. 7-16). At one time in the Asante confederacy, stools with elephant supports were strictly the prerogative of the Asantehene (Rattray 1927:273) although today they are in general usage. Among the Asante's neighbors, the paramountcy of Akuapem has a state stool of a gold-leafed elephant said to symbolize the strength and power of the state (Fig. 7-17). Its gold covering was effected in defiance of the Asante kingdom and its Golden Stool and as a statement of Akuapem's independence.

It is curious that the elephant is absent from the documented corpus of cast gold images ornamenting the state swords of the Akan which after stools are the most important of the court regalia (Ross 1977). A sword ornament of a tusk tied into a knot from the Agonahene's treasury is as close as we get to an elephant (Fig. 7-18). This unusual ornament represents another miracle of the famous priest Okomfo Anokye, who as

mentioned earlier brought the Golden Stool down from the sky. Anokye was a former chief of Agona; in a rivalry with another famous priest from the enemy state of Denkira (according to tradition), Anokye tied an ivory elephant tusk into a knot and challenged his nemesis to untie it.[16] The sword ornament commemorates Anokye's victory.

The greatest variety of more complex scenes with the elephant are found in two object types: linguist staffs (*ɔkyeame poma*) and warrior's flags (*asafo franka*). The former have a two-part shaft and a figurated finial carved from wood and covered with gold leaf. They are carried by the chief's principal counselors and typically feature motifs celebrating the powers of the chief and defining his responsibilities. These staffs are found throughout the Akan area and important chiefs may have six or more (the Asantehene had sixteen in 1980, see Ross 1982b). Asafo flags are typically appliquéd from commercial millwoven cloth in bright colors. They are danced, paraded through the streets, and flown from warrior shrines by many southern Akan peoples, but especially the Fante. Fante warrior

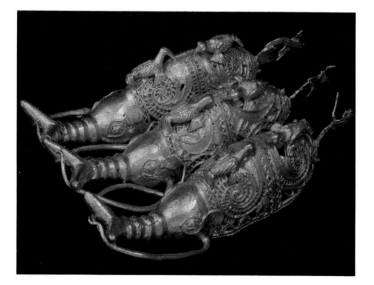

7-15. Three elephants from an Asante chief's ring. Before 1874. Gold. Length 7 cm. The Trustees of the British Museum, 1900. 4-27.44.

7-16. Child's stool or shrine stool. Wood, brass. Length 44.7 cm. Collection of Diane Steinmetz.

7-14A-D (OPPOSITE AND ABOVE). Akan goldweights of elephants. Brass. Lengths 8.8 cm, 9.2 cm, 5.5 cm. Collection of Maurice Bonnefoy.

7-17. Gold-leafed state stool of Akuapem at Odwira festival in Akropong. Photograph, Herbert M. Cole, 1972.

7-18. Cast gold sword ornament depicting a miracle of Okomfo Anokye when he tied an ivory tusk into a knot. State treasury of Agona. Photograph, Doran H. Ross, 2 September 1980.

7-19. Counselor's staff illustrating the proverb, *When an elephant steps on a trap, it does not spring.* State treasury or the Asantehene. Photograph, Doran H. Ross, 21 August 1980.

7-20. Chief's counselor's staff depicting the adage, *If the elephant were not in the forest, the buffalo would claim to be a large animal.* Wood, goldleaf. 163 cm. Musée Barbier-Mueller, Geneva. Photograph, P.A. Ferrazzini.

groups are organized into highly competitive "companies" that, within a given state, maintain exclusive prerogatives for selected colors, patterns of cloth, and motifs. Violation of these prerogatives by a rival company is considered an act of aggression. The more successful companies may have thirty or forty flags displaying their principal emblems, generally animals with which they identify (Ross 1979).

Both staffs and flags depict many of the same images. One of the most straightforward is of an elephant standing on a metal animal trap (Figs. 7-19, 7-21) illustrating variants of the idea,

When an elephant steps on a trap, it does not spring.[17]

When elephant steps on trap, no more trap.[18]

Either way, the elephant is seen as invincible and all-powerful and the expressions are apt metaphors for either chief or warrior.

A number of motifs juxtapose the elephant with another animal. The buffalo is generally seen as a near rival to the elephant in size and strength and the two are depicted together on a number of object types (Fig. 7-20) to illustrate the saying:

If the elephant were not in the forest, the buffalo would claim to be a large animal.[19]

This commonplace saying acknowledges that everyone has a superior. In the paramountcy of Kokofu where I recorded this image/proverb, the chief said the motif recognized the leadership of the Asantehene.

A related theme depicts a female elephant with her offspring next to a man holding a bush pig (Fig. 7-22). Many Fante consider the wild pig to be the "little brother" of the elephant because of its exposed tusks. With this image the owners of

7-21. Fante warrior's flag depicting maxim, *When elephant steps on trap, no more trap.* Sewn by Nana Manso for Lowtown No. 2 Company c. 1940. Cotton cloth. Length 147 cm. FMCH X86.2056. Anonymous gift.

7-22. Fante warrior's flag illustrating a boast by the flag's owners that they can help both the elephant and the bush pig deliver their children. Sewn by Kweku Kakanu for No. 2 Company, Lowtown c. 1940. Cotton cloth. Length 163 cm. FMCH X86.2050. Anonymous gift.

7-23. Asante chief's counselor's staff depicting the proverb, *Although the elephant is the strongest animal, it is the wise duiker that rules the forest.* Wood. State treasury of the Agonahene. Photograph, Doran H. Ross, 4 September 1980.

7-24. Drawing of detail on a carved drum showing updated version of Figures 7-23 and 7-25. National Museum of African Art 68-36-297. Drawing, Jill Ball.

the flag are asserting their ability to do the impossible while emphasizing the dominance of the elephant. The black figure represents a rival company telling the kneeling figure, who represents the flag's owner, that he is not brave enough to help the bush pig give birth. The kneeling figure responds by saying:

> *If I can deliver the child of an elephant, what is there to fear from the bush pig?* [20]

Even though the elephant is universally recognized as preeminent in terms of size and strength, in the Akan world view it is not necessarily superior to all animals in all characteristics. In the folktale cited earlier, for example, Ananse the spider conquers the elephant. A small antelope called a duiker is also seen as wise and clever like Ananse and is often put in a position of leadership over the elephant:

> *Although the elephant is the strongest animal, it is the wise duiker that rules the forest.* [21]

On a linguist staff from Agona this relationship is expressed by placing the antelope directly on top of the elephant (Fig. 7-23). On an *asafo* flag from Kormantine the antelope's leadership is determined by placing the duiker on a stool facing the elephant (Fig. 7-25). Yet another version on a drum with elaborate relief carving shows an antelope driving a truck with the elephant as cargo (Fig. 7-24).

Despite the highly conventionalized and fixed interpretations of the preceding four motifs, there are a number of Akan images that elicit contradictory expressions. A vulture standing next to an upside down elephant on one Asafo flag (Fig. 7-26) produced the expression:

> *Even though the vulture eats carrion, it is still afraid of the dead elephant.* [22]

Here the owners of the flag identify with the elephant which though dead is still greater than the living vulture. A virtually identical flag by the same artist but for a different Asafo company depicts the saying cited earlier:

> *Although the vulture does not have a gun, he still sells elephant tusks.* [23]

Here the vulture is an emblem of the flag's owner. Such paradoxes are not uncommon in Akan art, and indeed are part of their rich multivalent imagery (Ross 1988:118-19).

It can be argued that the Akan image of the elephant was heavily influenced by European heraldry and commercial imagery, as has been shown for the lion (Ross 1982a). Although the elephant does not play any significant role in European heraldry, it did appear in two important and widely seen British emblems. The first was authorized by an Act of

7-25. Fante warrior's flag illustrating same proverb as Figure 7-22. Sewn by Kɔbina Badowah in 1978 for an unidentified Asafo company. Cotton cloth. Length 162 cm. FMCH X86.1979. Anonymous gift.

7-26. Fante warrior's flag depicting the saying, *Even though the vulture eats carrion, it is still afraid of the dead elephant.* Sewn by Kwamina Amoaku for Yamoransa No. 1 Company in 1979. Cotton cloth. Length 163 cm. FMCH X86.2009. Anonymous gift.

Parliament and was granted to the African Company of Merchants in 1750. Featured on their crest was an armed elephant with a tower and castle (Crooks 1923:12). This image was spread widely as British trade goods penetrated Africa throughout the second half of that century.

Near the end of the nineteenth century an image of an elephant standing in front of a coconut palm tree was struck on the reverse of a medal given to selected chiefs who were British allies during the Anglo-Asante war of 1895-96 (Fig. 7-27). With the annexation of the Asante kingdom and the formal declaration of the Gold Coast Colony in 1902, this image was adopted as the official emblem of the colony. It then circulated widely, embossed on the globular heads of British-made linguist staffs. Given to chiefs officially recognized as local rulers by the British, these staffs were called by the Akan "government sticks" (*aban poma*). From the British perspective the coconut palm stood for the coastal areas and the elephant for the hinterland.[24]

An elephant and a palm tree constitute one of the most common images in the Akan motif pool. In Akan examples the palm is frequently identified as the oil palm (rather than the coconut) and the composition typically features the elephant with its trunk wrapped around the erect tree (Fig. 7-28) although versions with the palm behind the elephant, springing out of its back (Fig. 7-1), or uprooted and held in its trunk are also known. Whether the Akan juxtaposition of elephant and palm came before or after the European version is unclear. Nevertheless, the British use of the image undoubtedly helped spread the motif among those seeking the favor of colonial officials.

Historical precedence aside, the image of the elephant with its trunk around the palm appears to be distinctly Akan. I have recorded three different expressions associated with this image and with versions more consistent with the British design. Unquestionably the most frequently cited is:

Only the elephant can uproot the palm tree.[25]

The palm is seen as the strongest tree in the plant kingdom ("it bends but it does not break") and the elephant the strongest creature in the animal kingdom. On one level this motif asserts the superiority of the animal world over that of the plant, and on another, the superiority of one chief or company over its respective rivals. At one time elephants apparently subsisted in part on the oil palms of the south (Sutherland 1954:17).

The ambiguous nature of this image is emphasized by the other two expressions recorded for it:

Even the elephant is unable to pull down the palm tree.[26]

Since the elephant could not defeat the palm tree, he made friends with it.[27]

7-27. Medal made for presentation to chiefs allied with the British during the Anglo Asante war of 1895-96. State treasury of the Kokofuhene. Photograph, Doran H. Ross, 29 August 1976.

7-28. Fante warrior's flag representing the maxim, *Only the elephant can uproot the palm tree*. The man with the scales is weighing the strength of the two contestants. Cotton cloth. Sewn by Kweku Kakanu c. 1940. Length 163 cm. Collection of Sara Penn Textiles. Photograph courtesy of Eric D. Robertson.

7-29. Detail of commercially printed textile honoring "Dr. Kwame Nkrumah First Prime Minister Gold Coast." The cloth features images of the elephant and palm (*Only the elephant can pull down the palm tree*) and the elephant and duiker (*Although the elephant is the strongest animal, it is the wise duiker that rules the forest*). Cotton. Height of detail 71.1 cm. Michigan State University Museum, Gift of Mr. Val Berryman. Photograph, Peter Glendinning.

Like the two expressions associated with the vulture, these three interpretations do not coexist in the same place. As such they demonstrate that the Akan understanding of the elephant can be manipulated to serve local situations and systems of symbols. These sayings also provide evidence of the Akan practice of developing alternative meanings for British colonial emblems – in a sense usurping some of their power and making it Akan. This would seem to be the case with the commemorative cloth dedicated to Kwame Nkrumah which uses the motif both isolated and as part of the hilt of the state swords (Fig. 7-29).

Although the elephant is generally dominant in most situations, we have seen that the spider (Ananse), vulture, duiker, hunter, and palm tree can gain the upper hand in some circumstances. In each case the elephant serves as a foil for the abilities of its adversary. The latter's accomplishments are manifest only in relation to the elephant's strength and power.

From the foregoing, it should be clear that elephant imagery ranges widely in meaning, depending on form and context. Ideas related to leadership, hierarchy, trade, wealth, excrement, sustenance, fecundity, speaking, listening, strength, power, and war are variously invoked in the oral literature associated with these images. Undoubtedly there were many more meanings that have not survived any better than the elephant in the Akan forests. Nevertheless, the elephant today still clearly flourishes in the intellectual life of the Akan, for as it is said: *Even if the elephant is thin, its meat will fill a hundred baskets.*

NOTES

1. I would like to thank Professor J. H. K. Nketia and Dr. A. K. Quarcoo, both formerly at the Institute of African Studies, University of Ghana, for making this research possible. B.A. Firempong, Dr. Yaw Boateng, and Elijah Kannagey-Asibu transcribed and taped interviews on which part of this paper is based with additional assistance from Nii O. Quarcoopome and Frederick Dennis. Other colleagues who made significant contributions include Emmanuel Kofi Agorsah, Charles Obo, Asi Sutherland, Kwamina Amoaku, Kɔbina Badowah, Kweku Kakanu, Mansa Ahoner, and R.M.P. Baiden. I would also like to express my continuing appreciation of Herbert M. Cole, who stimulated my interest in Ghana and with whom I shared some of this research.

2. Rattray (1916:59,60). Christaller (1879) is a compilation of 3,670 proverbs published in Twi. Rattray (1916) is a translation and explication of 830 proverbs from Christaller. Lange (1990) is a new translation of the 1879 volume in its entirety by Lange. The decision to use either the Rattray or the Lange translation is largely a matter of the author's personal preference.

3. Rattray (1916:161,83).

4. In *Regalia for an Ashanti Durbar*, Kyerematen refers to the Banwoma as "elephant skin" at least three times (1961:5,7,13).

5. There are several inconsistencies and contradictions both within and between Kyerematen's various publications. On the one hand, he states that both Sanaa and Fotɔɔ are made of elephant hide (1961:5 and 1977:8); in another publication, however, he says that the Fotɔɔ is made from civet cat or monkey (1964:43).

6. Rattray (1923:278-79).

7. Rattray (1923:101).

8. One of the Asantehene's linguist staffs is called the "bog that swallows the elephant" and depicts an abstract elephant's skull (Ross 1982b:60, fig. 7).

9. Kyerematen (1964:48).

10. Asantehene Osei Bonsu gave a golden flywhisk to Joseph Dupuis for presentation as a gift to King George III of England in 1820 (Dupuis 1824:174).

11. Wilks's view of the "unity of the systems of authority and finance" is

convincing and merits further attention, especially as it is reflected in Asante expressive culture.

12. See Wilks (1975:430,696; 1979:17,18); McCaskie (1983:29,31,33); Kyerematen (1961:9, 1970:9, and 1977:10).

13. Christaller (1990:76,81).

14. Christaller (1990:250,22,16); Rattray (1930:269-71).

15. Christaller (1990:51,91,250).

16. Rattray (1929:278).

17. Recorded at an interview with Akyeamehene Nana Nsuase Poku and Ɔkyeame Baffour Osei Akoto at Kumase, 21 September, 1980.

18. Recorded at an interview with the flag-maker Kɔbina Badowah at Lowtown, 30 September, 1980.

19. Recorded at an interview with Kokofuhene Nana Osei Assibey III and his elders in Kokofu, 29 August, 1976.

20. Recorded with an interview with flag dancer Kwesi Amonɔɔ and the elders of No. 2 Company, Lowtown, 27 August, 1980.

21. Recorded at an interview with Kɔbina Badowah, the flag's artist, at Kormantine, 10 August, 1978. Alternative versions of this proverb may end: ...*that is elder,* or ...*that receives the stool.*

22. Recorded at an interview with Kwamina Amoaku, the flag's artist, at Anomabu, 29 September, 1979.

23. Recorded at an interview with Kwamina Amoaku, the flag's artist, at Anomabu, 29 September, 1979.

24. See Quarcoopome (n.d.:20,21,25). Sutherland (1954) illustrates and discusses "state emblems" based on European logos and heraldic models. The elephant figures prominently in several of them. At Akuapem it is "emphatically told" that the image of the elephant and palm was their invention, and was appropriated by Governor Griffiths during the reign of Nana Kwame Fori (p. 17).

25. Recorded at an interview with Kɔbina Badowah at Kormantine, 5 December, 1976.

26. Recorded for a flag belonging to Cape Coast No. 4 Company (Ewusi 1971:64).

27. Recorded for a flag currently in the British Museum, London, in an interview with Kwamina Amoaku, at Anomabo, 26 September, 1981.

A.

B.

C.

D.

FROM ABOUT 1830-1900, Kongo artists around the mouth of the Zaire River along the Loango coast carved numerous ivory products for foreign consumption. Most impressive are ivory tusks, relief-carved in a spiral band climbing from base to tip. These range in length from eight inches to three feet; a few thousand may still be extant.

Some 116 human figures (African and European), six birds, two monkeys, and two dogs adorn the densely carved tusk opposite, center. Images of chained Africans juxtaposed with scenes of indigenous fishing, hunting, and trading create a poignant view of 19th-century coastal African society. Far right, assorted Roman gods and goddesses (including Jupiter, Minerva, Diana, and Apollo) are copied from a European book. Opposite left, two Europeans drink at a table, a man tries to hit another with a pan, and a rifleman shoots a monkey. The little well-dressed gentleman, above, appears on a wax seal from the same workshops that produced the carved tusks.

A. (DETAIL OF G). The Roman goddess Diana.

B. (DETAIL OF F). Man with an umbrella.

C. (DETAIL OF E). An African porter carries an ivory tusk.

D. Stamp. Height 7.5 cm. FMCH x65.11605. Gift of the Wellcome Trust.

E. Carved tusk. Height 78.74 cm. Collection of Drs. Daniel and Marian Malcolm.

F. Carved tusk. Height 83 cm. Collection of Peter Adler.

G. Carved tusk with Roman gods. Height 66.7 cm. Collection of Drs. Daniel and Marian Malcolm.

161

The Elephant and Its Ivory in Benin

BARBARA WINSTON BLACKMUN

Benin City, the capital of the 800-year-old Edo Kingdom of Benin, is located in the dense rain forests of southern Nigeria. About eighty miles to the north, near the Yorubaland border, these thick forests become open woodland where the elephant, *eni*, once roamed in herds. To the east, the Niger River forms the traditional boundary of the kingdom. Between the capital and the southern seacoast the forests are cut through by a network of wide rivers and swampy, overgrown streams. Some of these empty into the sea, while others form inland waterways from the Niger Delta westward to the Lagos River and its lagoons.

When the Portuguese arrived on the "Slave Coast" about 1472 (Blake 1942:6,8), Benin was an established, centralized state, well placed to influence African traders on the delta and to organize supplies and merchandise for European ships. By that time, the elephant (*Loxodonta cyclotis*) and its ivory were already playing major roles in the economic, political, and conceptual life of the people of Benin.

According to Edo oral history, the Oba (hereditary king) at the time of Portuguese arrival was Ewuare the Great,[1] the first of Benin's great warrior kings, who reigned from about 1440 to 1473.[2] By 1472, Ewuare had reorganized the kingdom and was expanding its borders northward into Owo and Ekiti Yoruba territories (Egharevba 1968:15,16; Poynor 1976: 40). Yoruba traditions record that this conquest brought elephant hunters from Benin in search of new sources of ivory (Law 1973:35), and Portuguese traders immediately began to purchase elephant tusks from the Oba (Pereira 1505:127). Ivory carving was an established art at the court, and Ewuare was a generous patron of the hereditary royal ivory carvers' guild, *Igbesanmwan*. He is especially remembered for sponsoring Eghoghomaghan II, a master artist whom the Edo credit with the introduction of ivory designs which remained in use for generations (Egharevba 1968:17). Nevertheless, no extant ivory carving from this kingdom can be traced to the fifteenth century (See chart, p. 182).

In Benin at the time of European contact, ivory and copper were more important than gold. Both materials had long been traded overland for considerable distances (Shaw 1978:120) and were highly valued. The ivory carvers' guild competed for prestige and royal patronage with a second major guild belonging to those who worked with brass, an alloy of copper and zinc; the brass casters' guild was called *Iguneronmwon*. The elders of the ivory carvers' guild illustrate the antiquity of their hereditary carving tradition by claiming that the *Igbesanmwan* was founded in mythical times by the first ruler of Benin, long before the brass casters' guild was established.[3] By the fifteenth century, however, brass pendants and other objects were probably being cast very skillfully in Benin (Ben-Amos 1980:24). Both guilds worked primarily

8-1. The Oba's royal trumpeters, Ikpakohen, at the 1978-79 ceremonies marking the accession of the 38th Oba of Benin, Omo N'Oba N'Edo, Uku Akpolokpolo, Erediauwa. Photograph, Joseph Nevadomsky.

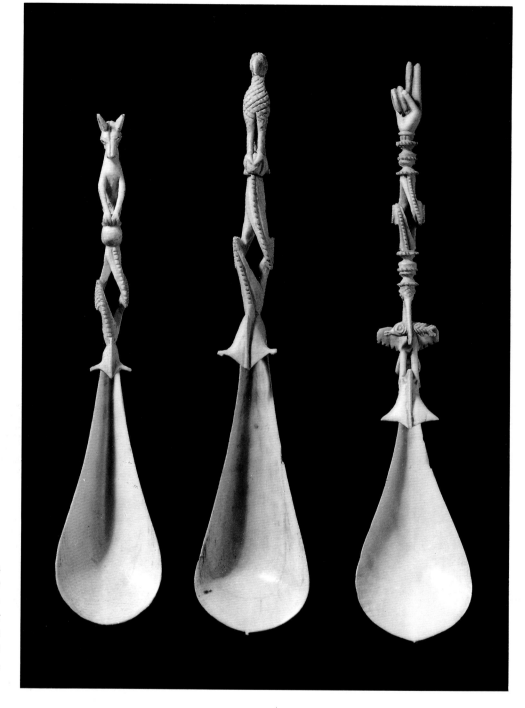

8-2. Ivory spoons carved by Benin's *Igbesanmwan* craftsmen in the 16th century for export to Europe. Such items, commissioned by the Portuguese, English, and other traders on the southern Guinea coast, were being produced as early as 1530. Museum für Völkerkunde, Vienna 91-914, 91-913, 91-912. Photograph, Fritz Mandl.

for the Oba, and the display of large brass sculpture was a royal prerogative. Nevertheless, Benin's wealthy upper classes could commission ivory carvings and heavy brass jewelry and insignia.

Although these two royal guilds were in competition, they also complemented each other, much like the materials with which they worked. To this day copper and ivory coexist as opposites in a satisfying conceptual balance. Copper has a lustrous surface which in Benin belief offers glimpses into the dangerous world of the gods and spirits, *erinmwin*. Its shining red evokes the magnificent power of Olokun, god of wealth and of the sea, with whom the Oba is closely associated. Like red coral beads (*ivie*), scarlet cloth (*ododo*), and the kingly leopard (*ekpe*), copper is "hot" with creative energy and the threat of death (See Ben-Amos 1980:64). Through mysterious fiery

processes, copper must be wrested from stone and shaped or cast into objects that endure for generations.

In contrast, the smooth whiteness of ivory is considered "cool," like *orhue*, the white kaolin clay that is fundamental to Benin life and thought. *Orhue*, the essence of purity, abundance, and happiness, is particularly valued in offerings to Olokun (Omijeh 1975:122-25) and suggests Olokun's ability to create luxury and harmonious relations. Ivory bears similar associations and its coolness and richness outlast a person's lifespan.

Even when it was abundant, ivory was as difficult to obtain as copper. Before the introduction of firearms, it required cunning and extraordinary courage for the hunter to overcome the *Loxodonta cyclotis*, the most massive of the animals known in Benin. Under the authority of the Oba's court, professional hunting specialists stalked and killed these beasts using traditional methods, which included poison (Roth 1903:144,145). One tusk of every dead elephant was claimed as tribute by the Oba, who had the option to buy the other.

SIXTEENTH-CENTURY BENIN-PORTUGUESE IVORIES

Portuguese sea captains, arriving on Benin's coast in the fifteenth and sixteenth centuries, offered new and desirable resources to the warrior Obas, supplying luxury materials such as red coral beads, scarlet cloth, and quantities of copper and brass (Ryder 1969:40). In return for these imported goods the Portuguese received indigo-dyed cotton cloth, blue beads, and Benin's prisoners of war, whom they bought as slaves. The slaves and export commodities were taken by ship to the coast of Ghana, where they were traded for gold from the Akan kings (Ryder 1969:24,26,37).

For the European market, the Portuguese wanted hot pepper to send to Lisbon and ivory from elephants in Benin's forests and northern woodlands (Pereira 1505:127). Perhaps because of heavy local demand during the sixteenth century, the Portuguese were not always able to get as much ivory as they desired from Benin (Ryder 1969:64). They did, however, patronize the ivory carvers' guild, and commissioned some remarkable pieces which were collected by European nobility.

At the present stage of research, it appears that the earliest Benin ivories documented in Europe were five delicate spoons registered as the property of Cosimo I de Medici of Florence in 1560 (Bassani and Fagg 1988:150). By that time Benin's royal Igbesanwam had exported similar carvings (Figs. 8-2, 8-3) for at least thirty years (Curnow 1983:218,239), reaching the peak of its achievement about 1550 (Fagg 1963:33). In 1588 an English navigator referred directly to Benin "spoons of elephants' teeth, very curiously wrought, with divers proportions of foules and beasts made upon them" (Welsh 1903:297). Other documents mention twelve Benin spoons acquired in 1590 in Leipzig by the Grand Duke of Saxony, and six more were recorded in an inventory of the estate of the Grand Duke of Tyrol, Ferdinand of Habsburg, in 1596 (Bassani and Fagg 1988:150).

Benin ivories carved for export often depict the Portuguese themselves and also reflect influences from European objects that traders may have introduced as models. For example, one of the *Igbesanmwan's* earliest[4] extant saltcellars (Fig. 8-4a,b) portrays Portuguese swordsmen and small half-figures that were probably derived from observation of Benin's foreign visitors. In addition to these, however, there are adult male nude winged figures grasping branches. Curnow has suggested that this motif, as unusual in Europe as in Africa, may have been inspired by fifteenth century northern Italian Embriachi boxes with relief-carved bone panels (1983:221,360). Such boxes, popular and widely circulated, could have been carried by the Portuguese for their own use or for presentation to the Oba.

8-3. Ivory spoon portraying Portuguese visitor to Benin, carved by *Igbesanmwan* craftsmen in the 16th century for export to Europe. Although this figure appears to have been based upon observation of a particular individual, similar early 16th-century clothing and shoulder-length hair became conventions used by ivory carvers to represent any European for the next three hundred years. The Trustees of the British Museum, 9194.

8-4 A,B (TWO VIEWS). The middle portion of an early 16th-century ivory salt-cellar commissioned for export reflects European imagery such as Portuguese swordsmen in early 16th-century clothing and winged male nudes grasping branches. The latter motif may have originated in 15th-century northern Italian portable boxes that circulated throughout Europe and could have been carried by the Portuguese for their own use or for presentation to the Oba (Curnow 1983:221,360). Height 8.3 cm. The Paul and Ruth Tishman Collection of African Art, the Walt Disney Company. Photographs, Richard Todd.

ELEPHANTS AND IVORY IN INDIGENOUS SIXTEENTH-CENTURY ART

On Benin ivories carved for indigenous use, images related to the elephant are of great importance. Elephant iconography is significant within the political structure of Benin on many levels. To appreciate these, it helps to understand the basic structure of Benin's government, and the traditional struggle for dominance between kingship and chiefship which has shaped the nation's history.

Every Oba is believed to have supernatural powers based upon his close relationship with the god Olokun. His powers are annually venerated in a fundamental national ceremony known as Igue, when the Edo gather in support of the Oba as he makes sacrifices to enhance the wisdom and judgment of his own head. Subordinate to the Oba are a number of very influential chieftaincies. On the practical level, state affairs are conducted by means of a ruling council in which power is balanced between three palace associations,[5] headed by chiefs who serve the needs of the palace and the Oba, and four independent town chiefs[6] who are considered principal defenders of the state. The leader of the town chiefs, and spokesman for the general population of the kingdom, is known as the Iyase. At the time of European contact, the Iyase was considered a very great lord and he was also the military leader of the Oba's forces (Egharevba 1956:7,17; Bradbury 1968:17).

In addition to the palace associations and the independent chiefs, there are seven hereditary nobles, collectively known as the Uzama, led by a titled chief called the Ezomo. These nobles traditionally have ruled certain areas peripheral to Benin City and their power is based upon privileges bestowed upon their ancestors (Bradbury 1973:55-60). The pattern of organization was established by successive early Obas, who enhanced their supremacy through skillful manipulation and firm control of the chiefs until the seventeenth century.

In Benin, and in the kingdom of Owo with which it has shared specific historic relationships, the elephant is considered a great chief among the animals, and conversely, a high-ranking chief is often conceptualized as an elephant (Ben-Amos 1976:247; Poynor 1978:169). Chiefs who are descendants of the Ogiso, the indigenous Edo ruling line, are particularly identified in this way (Meyerowitz 1943:250). In Figure 8-5, for example, an ivory oliphant of uncertain date suggests the relationship between the Oba and the chiefs under his control by portraying the Oba mounted upon an elephant. This is not a literal reflection of actual practice in Benin. Nothing from Benin history or oral tradition suggests that the Oba ever actually rode an elephant. Rather, the image is a metaphorical assertion of royal power (cf. Vogel 1979:87-100; Ben-Amos 1984:70,71), in particular the power of the Oba over the indigenous chiefs.

On another level, the relationship symbolized by this icon refers to an early linkage between the Benin and Yoruba dynasties of kings. It signifies not merely that chiefs are under the control of the Oba, but that the autochthonous line of rulers was superseded by a foreign Yoruba lineage which continues to assert its dominance. This interpretation is reinforced by the presence on the oliphant of a bat or birdlike form with outstretched wings, an ancient emblem that belongs to broader-based Yoruba traditions in southwestern Nigeria (Willett 1988:121-27).

Oral histories relate that the present dynasty of Obas was founded by a Yoruba prince named Oranmiyan, son of Ododuwa, the deified king of the ancient city state of Ile Ife. Ododuwa, who commanded his sons to establish kingdoms of their own, sent Oranmiyan to Benin at the request of the Edo people, who were in rebellion against the last of their Ogiso rulers (Egharevba 1968:6,7).[7]

While the descendants of the Ogiso are conceptualized as elephants, the Oba himself, a descendant of Oranmiyan, is conceptually a leopard. Ewuare the Great emphasized this symbolism long ago by decreeing that every Oba must decapitate a live leopard at least once in his lifetime, during the national Igue ceremony. This act is believed to strengthen the mystical power of the kingship (Egharevba 1968:16). Praise names associate the Oba with the leopard (Ben-Amos 1983:51); and a pouncing leopard (*ekpelobo*) symbolizes the monarchy in court art. Leopard images are interpreted as manifestations of the Oba's regal qualities. Conceptually, the royal leopard

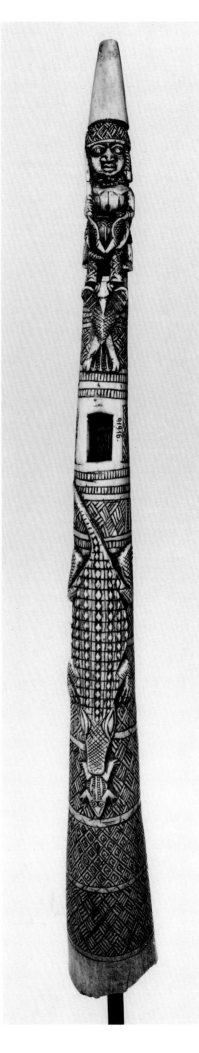

8-5. This ivory oliphant metaphorically asserts royal power and may also refer to a linkage between the Benin and Yoruba dynasties of kings. The bat or bird form with outstretched wings is an emblem shared with broader-based Yoruba traditions in southwestern Nigeria (Willett 1988:121-27). Height 54.5 cm. Museum für Völkerkunde, Vienna, 91-916. Photograph, Fritz Mandl.

contends forever with the great chief of the forest, the elephant (Ben-Amos 1984:70).

Thus the motif of the elephant as a symbol of opposition to Benin's Yoruba kingship reaches back to the original imposition of Oranmiyan's rule over the autocthonous Ogiso dynasty. When the Oba is represented astride the elephant, he personifies the Oranmiyan line asserting royal control over the Ogiso, over the chiefs, and over any other challenge to his authority.

The birdlike form with outstretched wings that appears below the mounted Oba on the oliphant in Figure 8-5 is one of a vocabulary of images shared by Benin and ancient Yorubaland. Many versions of this motif and of the ram's head pendant, the fishlegged figure, and other symbols of power have been in use for centuries (Fraser 1975:34,35). The constant revival of ancient emblems has been encouraged in Benin, as in Yorubaland, because a living ruler often identifies himself with a legendary predecessor who brought wealth and glory to his people. These emblems, some of which are cognates, proclaim an eminence that is sacred as well as political, and allude to profound social sanctions that are controlled through legitimate inheritance of divine authority (Williams 1974:128,129). They are also cautionary in that they warn of catastrophic cosmic aberrations if the sanctions that they represent are ignored (Fraser 1972:263-65; Ben-Amos 1984:77).

THE TRUNK-HAND MOTIF IN THE SIXTEENTH CENTURY

One early symbol of power is the trunk-hand. If present-day associations can be extrapolated into the past, the elephant was a reference to the original Ogiso rulers and symbolized indigenous leadership among the Edo. Yet an elephant's head with its trunk ending in a human hand appears on a brass pendant (Fig. 8-6) and brass aegis plaques (Figs. 8-7, 8-8)[8] of probable sixteenth-century date, a time associated with the most powerful Obas of the Oranmiyan dynasty that usurped the Ogisos' rule. The age of a similar pendant with more human features (Fig. 8-9) is harder to determine.[9] Because manipulation of iconography is characteristic of Benin's art history, one or more of these great warrior kings may have appropriated the elephant image to create the trunk-hand. The emblem does not occur on any of the archaeological finds from Owo or from Ile Ife, most of which predate the sixteenth century.[10] Neither does it appear on any of the thousand or more rectangular plaques from the Benin palace believed to date from the mid-1500s to the early 1600s (Dark 1975:58,59). If these temporal parameters are correct, the original use of the trunk-hand emblem, the precise significance of which is unknown, may be confined to the early part of the sixteenth century, a period associated

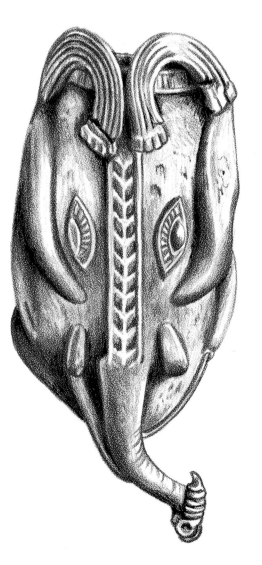

8-6 (LEFT). The trunk-hand motif in this pendant is similar to the images on the aegis plaques. In the early version of this motif, the trunk is slender and the small human hand holds a netted spherical object with a cone-shaped handle. Brass, probably 16th century. Height c. 17 cm. Hamburgisches Museum für Völkerkunde (C3823). Drawing, S.A. Green, after Luschan (1919:fig. 572).

8-7 (OPPOSITE, TOP). Fragment of aegis plaque, with a trunk-hand similar to that in Figure 8-5. The central fishlegged figure appears in many variations throughout southern Nigeria as an ancient reference to divine authority. Fagg suggests this work dates "from the transition between the early and middle periods" of Benin art, or near 1550 (1963:pl.16). Brass, probably 16th century. Width 28 cm. Museum für Völkerkunde, Berlin, No. IIIC 19276. Drawing, S.A. Green, after Fagg (1963:pl. 16).

8-8 (OPPOSITE, BOTTOM). Aegis plaque that may date to the reign of Oba Esigie, one of Benin's great warrior kings. Two elephants' heads, each ending in a human hand holding a small netted object, flank a single ram's head, a motif associated with classical Ile Ife, the copper-alloy figures at Tada, and the earliest Benin art (Ben-Amos 1983:176,177). The human face is striated in the style of ancient Ife. Two serpents suggest the looping outstretched wings of the Yoruba bat or birdlike motif (Willett 1988). This plaque was in the collection of the Liverpool Museum until that museum was severely damaged during the Second World War. Brass, probably 16th century. Width 40 cm. Drawing, S.A. Green, after Roth (1903:230, fig. 268).

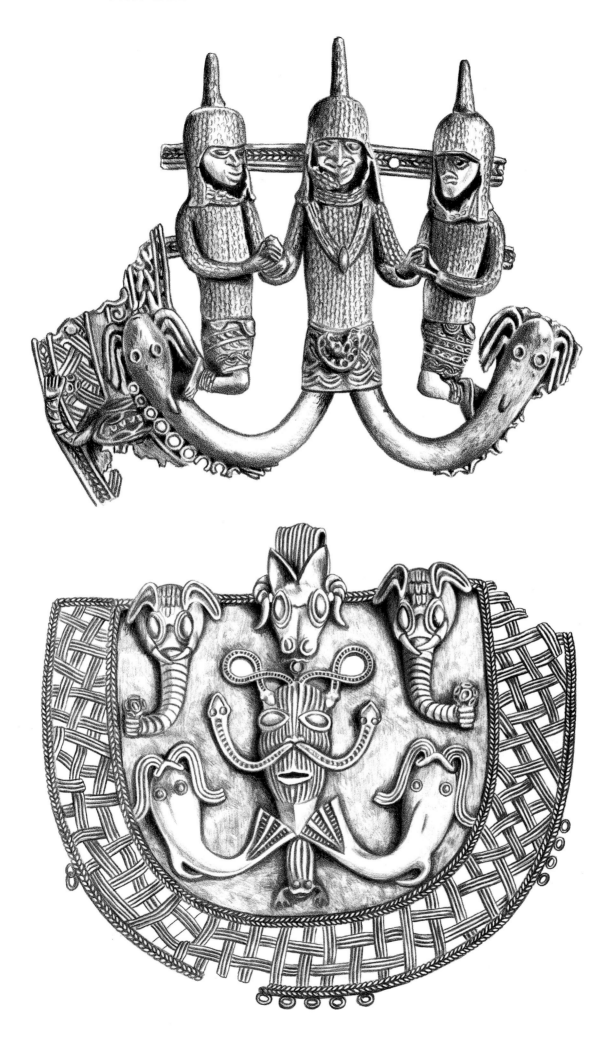

8-9. In this composite trunk-hand pendant of uncertain age, the elephant's head is depicted as human, complete with a stylized cap of hair, and the trunk-hand extends from beneath the bridge of the nose. Although Fagg has suggested a probable 16th-century date (1963:pl. 28b), this version of the trunk-hand differs from those illustrated in Figures 8-6 to 8-8 in that the trunk is thicker and the large hand grasps a branch. Brass. Height 16.5 cm. Hamburgisches Museum für Völkerkunde. Drawing, J. Ricks, after Fagg (1963:pl. 28b).

with Oba Esigie (c.1517-1550), one of the most admired of Benin's warrior kings (Egharevba 1968:26-29).

In the first few decades of the seventeenth century, however, the age of warrior kings came to an end. As the century progressed the various councils of chiefs exerted increasing influence, and Benin abandoned direct inheritance of the kingship in favor of a rotating succession among eligible branches of Oranmiyan's descendants (Egharevba 1968:34-37). The kingdom was at the height of its expansion, and a stable, well-organized society by Dutch accounts (Ruiters 1602:354-56; Dapper 1668:486). Nevertheless, Europeans rarely dealt directly with the Oba, who was kept secluded and could not make independent political decisions (Ryder 1969:102-8).

By 1651, when the Spanish Capuchins sent a mission to Benin, they reported that the Oba seemed a prisoner of the chiefs (Ryder 1969:307-15). It was during this period of government by various councils of officials that the domestic use of ivory became increasingly visible to European visitors. The

expansion of the kingdom further into Yorubaland had given professional hunters access to new herds of elephants, and a Capuchin was the first to mention that ivory tusks were displayed on the ancestral altars of ordinary citizens of Benin (Ryder 1969:314). The Portuguese had moved their principal trading activities westward along the coast, focusing on Allada rather than on the Niger Delta. Benin had also extended its authority westward at least as far as Lagos, where the kingdom had established a military post and trading center. Benin held considerable political power: Ijebu paid tribute, and by the 1680s Lagos was the biggest town on the coast, with the best laws and policies (Law 1983:331).

In the early eighteenth century, the Dutch replaced the Portuguese as the most active European traders on Benin's delta rivers. Their demand for elephant tusks was the source of unparalleled wealth for whoever could supply them, and the struggle for control of this ivory trade contributed to two disruptive periods of civil war in Benin. First Oba Ewuakpe (c.1690-1709) and then his son Akenzua I (c.1713-1735) fought to reestablish the Oba's former dominance over the chiefs.[11] So important was the elephant, conceptually, that an entire succession struggle was defined in terms of elephants and elephant hunting.

The most formidable opponent that these two kings faced was the Iyase n'Ode, leader of the town chiefs and Benin's great Captain of War. This powerful chief led a civil rebellion against Ewuakpe and then fought again to keep Ewuakpe's son Akenzua from inheriting the throne (Egharevba 1968:39). The bitterness of the contest between Akenzua I and this Iyase is vividly recalled in folklore (Egharevba 1969:8-10), in which challenges to royal authority by ambitious chiefs are a constant theme. Indeed, the office of any Iyase implies that he speaks for the opposition to the Oba (Bradbury 1973:68,69); but in Benin tradition the Iyase n'Ode's role was far more hostile: his name personifies open defiance.

Any Benin chief who can marshall impressive political forces is customarily conceptualized as an elephant, gigantic among his contemporaries. In a magnification of the usual symbolism, legend relates that the Iyase n'Ode could literally transform himself into this powerful animal (Egharevba 1969:8). The forested land between Benin and the Yoruba kingdom of Owo was a major source of ivory, as was Ishan to the northeast. The Iyase, who was influential in these areas, settled about twenty miles north of Benin City (Bradbury 1973:255) at Ore Oghbene. This village is still considered the home of the elephant hunters' guild.[12]

In 1715, the Oba signed an exclusive trading contract in ivory with the Dutch (Ryder 1969:140). Akenzua's conflict with the Iyase may have been over control of this ivory trade, as Benin soon launched a major offensive northeast into Ishan (Ryder 1969:163,164). All accounts agree, however, that Akenzua nearly lost the kingship in this campaign (Ryder 1969: 150; Bradbury 1973:28,29). He was rescued by Ehenua, an illegitimate son of Akenzua's father Ewuakpe.[13] In a traditional pattern often repeated in Benin folklore, Ehenua had been educated by the Iyase n'Ode. He had become an elephant hunter in Ishan and he knew the secrets of the Iyase's power (Bradbury 1973:254,255).

In the legendary conflict between Ehenua and the Iyase, the Iyase is believed to have changed himself into elephant form so that he would be impervious to attacks by the Oba's warriors (Egharevba 1969:8). Ehenua, in turn, used skills learned as a professional hunter of elephants. Preparing poison (*uti*) from leaves and bark,[14] he outwitted the Iyase and finally killed him. Ehenua thus won for himself and for his successors the praise name *Uti gb'eni* (poison kills the elephant). As the result of this victory, which Akenzua I announced to the Dutch in 1721 (Ryder 1969:168,169), the Oba increased his control over the ivory traded in the Niger delta area and thereby became the wealthiest ruler in Benin history (Egharevba 1968:39).

The royal brass rattle staff (*ukhurhe*) illustrated in Figure 8-10a,b celebrates the Iyase's defeat and may well have been commissioned by Akenzua himself. The figure of Akenzua I dominates an elephant (the Iyase) that is hedged in on either side by royal leopards. In Oba Akenzua's right hand is a short, thick pestle staff (*ukhurhe ovbiodo*) signifying the resolution of conflict. While any *ukhurhe* represents a link with one's ancestors, this *ukhurhe ovbiodo* is an emblem of Akenzua's father, Oba Ewuakpe (Ben-Amos 1983:166-68), whose early challenge of the Iyase n'Ode's power asserted his right to establish a strong monarchy. Akenzua's left hand grasps a thunder celt (*ughanmwanavan*). In Benin belief, neolithic stone axes are hurled from the sky by Ogiuwu, Benin's angry deity of death, and the celt symbolizes and strengthens the royal sanction to take human life. On the lower portion of this brass rattle staff the war chief responsible for Akenzua's victory, Ezomo Ehenua, is represented by a second elephant empowered by leaves grasped in his trunk-hand. This iconography, which has been discussed in detail by Vogel (1979:87-100) and Ben-Amos (1984:70-71), is typical of Benin court art during the first half of the eighteenth century. Images that depict varying relationships between the royal leopard, the enlarged human hand, and the elephant were introduced by Akenzua I some time after 1721 and remained central themes throughout the reign of his son Eresonyen (c. 1735-1750).

8-10A. This brass rattle staff proclaims the defeat of the Iyase n'Ode. The figure of Akenzua I dominates an elephant (representing the Iyase) which is hedged in on either side by royal leopards. Any rattle staff represents a link with one's ancestors. The short pestle staff in Akenzua's right hand is an emblem of his father, Oba Ewuakpe, who ruled from the late 17th century until about 1709. The thunder celt in Akenzua's left hand, alluding to those hurled by Ogiuwu, angry deity of death, enhances the Oba's divine right to take human life. A second elephant on the lower portion of the shaft represents Ezomo Ehenua, the war chief responsible for Akenzua's victory. Commissioned by Akenzua I between the Iyase's defeat in 1721 and the end of Akenzua's reign about 1750. Height 161.3 cm. Metropolitan Museum of Art, Purchase, Anne and George Blumenthal Fund, 1974.5.

8-10B. Detail of the rattle staff shown in Figure 8-10a. Width 4.7 cm. Metropolitan Museum of Art, Purchase, Anne and George Blumenthal Fund, 1974.5.

Some time after the defeat of the Iyase n'Ode, Akenzua I made a significant innovation to the national Igue ceremony. In addition to the traditional leopard sacrifice decreed by Oba Ewuare the Great, he added the sacrifice of a live elephant, thereby strengthening the wisdom of his own head (Ben-Amos 1984:70).[15] During this same period he apparently put new emphasis on Benin's cult of the Hand.

THE CULT OF THE HAND

Although its age and origin are uncertain, the cult of the Hand is considered an ancient tradition in Benin. Wherever old customs are followed, any man who has achieved respect in his community maintains a domestic altar called *ikengobo* to honor the strength of his right hand (Bradbury 1973:261-66). From time to time, in a private ceremony called Ihiekhun, he offers a sacrifice to his hand as a celebration of his accomplishments.

Just as a man's head is considered the locus of his good judgement, the efforts of a strong right hand are necessary to achieve success in any important endeavor. As Bradbury notes,

> For…warriors, the cult of the Hand has a particular significance. For the rest it is generally worshipped only by people who believe themselves to have got somewhere in life through their own efforts. The ritual of thanking the Hand is in one sense an expression of self-esteem. (1973:272)

The traditional method of sacrifice is decapitation: the head of an animal sacrificed to the Hand is then displayed near the *ikengobo* as a record of the offering. The Edo assume that when a head is severed and offered at an altar, its attributes are at the service of the one who makes the sacrifice. In contrast to ordinary forest animals, whose heads can be cut off and placed in a shrine, the head of an elephant, like that of a leopard, is bound by severe restrictions. Benin's professional elephant hunters could remove the jaw and tusks but had to leave the head in the place where death occurred. No elephant's head could enter an ordinary town (Bradbury 1957-67:379). Therefore the Oba's display of this powerful creature's sacrificed head was a significant emblem of domination. When Akenzua I decapitated a live elephant at *Igue*, he not only appropriated the sagacity of the elephant's head for his own use, but also proclaimed his triumph over the Iyase.

At this point it appears that the trunk-hand motif characteristic of the age of the sixteenth-century warrior kings was reintroduced (Fig. 8-11). Ceremonial specialists in present-day Benin no longer associate the trunk-hand with any specific Oba, but rather take it as a generalized proclamation of physical and political prowess. Nevertheless, the circumstances of Akenzua's reign suggest that this motif was revived as Akenzua's personal dynastic emblem. Referring to the power of Akenzua's head as manifest in his elephant sacrifice at Igue, it also implies the Oba's firm grasp on kingship through Chief Ehenua's triumph over the Iyase. It speaks to the enormous accomplishments of Akenzua's hand in establishing a period of unprecedented wealth and royal leadership.

The trunk-hand has come to be considered a primary characteristic of eighteenth-century Benin court art commissioned by Akenzua's son Eresonyen (Dark et al. 1960:40), and by Akenzua himself (Vogel 1979:96-98). Because of the traditional emphasis on the Iyase's defeat, the lavish brass rattle staff seen in Figures 8-10a and 8-10b, which portrays an elephant defeated by royal forces at the top of the shaft, and another grasping victorious leaves on the bottom portion of the shaft, is particularly appropriate as an emblem of Akenzua's success.

The sumptuousness and triumphant heraldry of this period of Benin art, and the importance of the elephant and its ivory, are also suggested in intricate and baroque ivory carvings. An elaborate tusk carved as a container for herbs and other mystically efficacious substances (Fig. 8-12) is replete with

8-11. A detail of the trunk-hand emblem, revived by Akenzua I as his personal dynastic emblem, appears on an ancestral altar tusk. It represents the king's right hand grasping victory with an elephant's strength. On ivory carvings the configuration of the leaf or branch held in the trunk-hand varies, and in some versions there are three leaves. These may allude to the secret forest herbs that killed the Oba's rival, Iyase n'Ode, and may also recall the ancient Yoruba custom of bestowing royal authority on a ruler by presenting him with *akoko* leaves (Willett and Eyo 1980:pls. 70,71), implying a firm grasp on the kingship itself. Emblem height about 16 cm. The Paul and Ruth Tishman Collection of African Art, the Walt Disney Company. Photograph, Richard Todd.

8-12. This 18th-century ceremonial lidded container, probably intended for ritual substances, is carved from an elephant's tusk. On its lid, the leopard of Akenzua's centralized monarchy reigns supreme. The top third of the horn represents the Oba's foot, pressed firmly on the back of the elephant, which holds a leaf or branch in its trunk-hand. At either side is a serpent-wrapped armlike form that terminates in a clenched fist with a prominent thumb, a symbol of the cult of the Hand. Mudfish signify peaceful prosperity as well as, conversely, the occult powers unleashed by the Oba's royal imprecations (see Blackmun 1983:66). Height 72 cm. Field Museum of Natural History, No. 210310, Chicago.

8-13 A, B. A pair of double cylinder armlets with trunk-hand motif, each fashioned from a single piece of ivory into two free-standing inner and outer cylinders. On the lower portion of the surface, the trunk-hand is presented holding a U-shaped branch with three leaves at each end, and the entire motif is duplicated above, upside down. These two mirror images form a single design unit, which protrudes in high relief from the delicate inner cylinder of the armlet through the perforated outer cylinder, locking them together. The elephant trunks are conceived as references to royal domination over Benin's chiefs. An extraordinarily intricate pair of armlets (Fig. 8-13), inlaid with accents of copper, which Fagg has tentatively assigned to an earlier period,[16] were probably also carved during the reign of either Akenzua or Eresonyen. These delicate armlets, a tour de force of carving, bear strong stylistic similarities to the ivory container in Figure 8-12, and employ similar iconography. Both display spirally wrapped forms, clenched fist designs, netlike patterns, delicate incised crosshatching, and similarly conceptualized mudfish.[17] Although the constant revival of old emblems makes the chronological placement of Benin motifs a perilous exercise, the ivories in Figures 8-12 and 8-13a,b were probably produced during the same period, at a time when Akenzua's iconography was paramount.

spirally wrapped forms leading to the clenched fist of the cult of the Hand. These spirals, the stylized conceptualization of the hand and the mudfish, the netlike patterns with diamond-shaped units, the finely crosshatched surfaces, and the inlaid copper accents (see note 17) suggest that these armlets were produced during the same period as the ivory container in Figure 8-12. Ivory, 18th century. Height 13 cm. British Museum, London. Photographs, (left) British Museum, (right) Barbara W. Blackmun.

During the eighteenth century the kingdoms of Benin and Owo, which had been linked for an indeterminate period after Ewuare's early conquests (Egharevba 1968:32; Poynor 1976:40-45), were involved in close interaction through the ivory trade. Although the tusks of extremely large elephants (*Loxodonta africana*) from distant savannah areas reached Benin in the 1700s, the Oba's closest source of indigenous ivory bordered on Owo territory. Much of the war between Akenzua and the Iyase n'Ode took place in the region between Owo, Ishan, and Benin. Although large herds of elephants inhabited woodlands within the Owo Kingdom, the Dutch were bound by their exclusive agreement with Benin to deal with the Oba for any ivory that Owo's ruler wished to sell. Therefore, the two kingdoms were in constant contact and it is reasonable to

8-14. The trunk-hand emblem on an ivory armlet from Owo. If Benin's trunk-hand was revived to honor Akenzua's and Ehenua's triumph, and if this group of ivories originated in Owo, one would expect the trunk-hand motif on Owo carvings found in Benin to carry a similar interpretation. It is probable that ivories featuring Owo's trunk-hand date from the 18th century and also refer to Akenzua, Ehenua, and the Iyase n'Ode. Museum für Völkerkunde, Berlin, No. IIIC 4882. Drawing, J. Ricks, after Luschan (1919, pl. C, fig. 614).

8-15 A,B (DETAIL). Elephant imagery on an *ikengobo* (altar to the Hand) probably commissioned by an Ezomo. Each elephant lays its trunk, terminating in a clenched fist, across the back of a royal leopard in a gesture that could be interpreted as hostile or protective. This message was intended for any Oba who might be inclined to question the Ezomo's considerable prerogatives. Cast brass, 18th century. Cylinder height 34 cm. National Commission for Museums and Monuments, Nigeria. Photographs, Barbara W. Blackmun.

assume that Owo ivories bearing variations of the trunk-hand emblem (Fig. 8-14) date from the eighteenth or early nineteenth century, and refer to Akenzua I, Ehenua, and the Iyase n'Ode.[18]

Ehenua, the Ezomo whose defeat of the Iyase is firmly celebrated in Benin traditions, enjoyed an extraordinary position during Akenzua's reign, so much so that Dutch reports indicate that the Ezomo's power rivalled that of the Oba himself (Ryder 1969:169,177). Akenzua I agreed to make this title hereditary, granting Ehenua's heirs perpetual membership in the *Uzama*, Benin's traditional nobility. He also allowed Ehenua to wear a coral beaded crown and regalia second only to his own. Tradition records that Ehenua lived longer than Akenzua I, and that this Ezomo's enormous wealth and

prestige began to annoy the following Oba, Eresonyen (c. 1735-1750) (Egharevba 1969:10). According to members of Ehenua's lineage, he claimed the royal right to display copper-alloy sculpture, and commissioned an impressive two-piece brass *ikengobo* or personal altar to his Hand (see Bradbury 1973:251-70). This cylindrical *ikengobo* is still in the possession of the present Ezomo's family, and although the upper portion is a larger and more elaborate nineteenth-century replacement, the original version (Figs. 8-15a,b)[19] is replete with elephant symbolism. In much of Akenzua's and Eresonyen's imagery, the leopard, or the figure of the Oba himself, clearly dominates the elephant. On this *ikengobo*, however, a more ambiguous relationship recalls Ehenua's crucial role in the great victory that preserved the kingship.

8-16A (RIGHT), **B** (OPPOSITE). Ancestral altars in the palace of the late Oba Akenzua II (1933-1978). Photograph, E.H. Duckworth, July 19, 1935. Courtesy of the Pitt Rivers Museum, Oxford University.

In a paradox typical of Benin's multivalent iconography, the elephant can represent the victorious chief Ehenua as well as the defeated chief, Iyase n'Ode.

ANCESTRAL ALTAR TUSKS AND ELEPHANT ICONOGRAPHY

Elephant referents appear not only on ceremonial ivories and shrines to the Hand, but also in the ancestral shrines maintained by male patrilineage heads to honor their forefathers — a custom of great antiquity in Benin that is still practiced today (Figs. 8-16a,b). At least since the middle of the 1600s, ancestral altars have been customarily furnished with many types of objects including brass bells, relics, carved wooden rattle staffs, small sculptures, and sometimes, elephants' tusks (Ryder 1969:314; Nyendael 1705:454,464). In the 1700s, extremely large stockpiles of tusks accumulated with the burgeoning of long-distance ivory trade under Akenzua I and Eresonyen. One account records 16,300 pounds of ivory taken in a single Dutch ship (Ryder 1969:142), and later in the century three thousand tusks were seen lying in a palace courtyard (Landolphe 1823, I:120). Even if exaggerated, these numbers indicate that elephant hunters in the widespread areas supplying the Oba had newly acquired access to firearms from the Dutch, which enabled them to conduct an unprecedented slaughter of Nigeria's elephants. The proliferation of ivory at the Benin court lasted into the nineteenth century and included a variety of objects (Figs. 8-17, 8-18, 8-22),[20]

8-17. Lidded box for the ceremonial presentation of kola nuts. The proliferation of ivory in the 18th and 19th centuries allowed domestic objects such as this, usually carved of wood, to be realized in ivory. Height 8-9 cm. Collection of Drs. Daniel and Marian Malcolm.

8-18. Figure of a young woman in service at the court of the Iye Oba. Although the function of the female figure standing on a royal pedestal is unknown, her crested hair style, abdominal scarification, and waist beads identify her as an *ibieka Iye Oba*, a young girl whom the Oba's mother, the Iye Oba, brings up and educates at her court in Uselu, near Benin City. Traditionally these girls serve as the Iye Oba's ladies in waiting until she arranges marriages for them. In the past they wore little clothing during their service at the court, except for elaborate sets of coral beads. Ivory, 19th century. Height 32.7 cm. The Paul and Ruth Tishman Collection of African Art, the Walt Disney Company. Photograph, Richard Todd.

many of which would have been carved in wood or cast in brass at an earlier period.

The most lavish use of elephant ivory during the eighteenth and nineteenth centuries, however, accompanied the ancestral altars of the Oba, the Ezomo, and other powerful individuals in the kingdom. Sixty tusks were noted in the ancestral shrine of one former king (Landolphe 1823, II:59), and from the middle of the 1700s onward, many of these large altar ivories were elaborately carved with motifs that completely covered the surface of each tusk (Landolphe 1823, II:53).

The motifs on Benin altar tusks are organized into rows typically read from the bottom moving upward (Blackmun 1983, 1984a, 1984b, 1988), as in Figures 8-19 and 8-20.[21] The images reinforce core values relating to social and religious obligations, and praise both the patron who commissioned the carving and the person whom the tusk commemorates. They also allude to legends and to historical traditions like that of Akenzua and Ehenua.[22] Every Oba is expected by the third year of his reign to commission tusks that will furnish an altar honoring his father (Akpata 1937:1). Each generation of heredi-tary *Igbesanmwan* carvers has used its own combinations of motifs, some traditional and some unique. The tusks shown here were carved within a short time of one another, yet they differ strongly in style and motif.[23] This suggests that the later of the two, Figure 8-20, was produced by a new group of carvers, who were probably brought to the palace in the aftermath of the civil war that wracked Benin about 1816.

8-19. This carved tusk is one of a matched set of six that have been identified at this point in an ongoing study. It is from an ancestral altar in the Oba's palace, probably commissioned by Oba Obanosa. The style, condition, motif choice, and arrangement on this set of ivories indicate that these tusks were carved to honor a deceased Iye Oba very early in the 19th century (Blackmun 1991a). Akenzua's trunk-hand is carved on the concave side of the tusk, in the third row of figures from the bottom. Early 19th century. Height of tusk alone without pedestal head about 118 cm. The Paul and Ruth Tishman Collection of African Art, the Walt Disney Company. Photograph, Richard Todd.

In the palace ancestral shrines, the royal altar tusks were supported by heavy crowned heads made of cast brass that commemorated in a generalized way past kings in the Oba's lineage (Fig. 8-19). Akenzua's trunk-hand and the royal leopard are prominent among images cast on the flanges of many commemorative heads (Fig. 8-21), and are often repeated in the carved motifs on the tusks. Virtually all the Oba's ancestral altar tusks include Akenzua's dynastic trunk-hand emblem.

The handsome carved tusks described by eighteenth-century European observers were found not only in the royal palace, but also at the courts of the Ezomo and of other chiefs (Blackmun 1987:89-94; 1991a:57,58). Tusks that were commissioned by the Ezomo's heirs also acknowledge Akenzua with the royal trunk-hand emblem, but in addition, many display the double trunk-hand of *uti gb'eni* (Fig. 8-23). Just as the Ezomo or his heirs commissioned a brass *ikengobo* rivaling that of the Oba (Bradbury 1973:251-70), Ehenua's double trunk-hand is a doubling of Akenzua's symbol (Blackmun 1987:89,111). The double trunk-hand honors the Ezomo who saved the kingship by killing the "elephant," Iyase n'Ode.

The slaughter of Nigeria's elephant herds for the European export trade caused their near extinction in Benin and greatly reduced their numbers in Owo and Ishan.[24] Nevertheless, the elephant and its ivory remain central to Benin iconography and to Benin history. As a symbol, ivory evokes associations of permanence and fulfillment; as an economic commodity ivory once brought unprecedented eminence to the kingdom. The desire to control the supply of ivory also stirred events which have been commemorated through allusions to the elephant. The early trunk-hand, a sixteenth-century emblem, re-emerged as the dynastic insignia of Akenzua, the richest Oba of them all. The double trunk-hand was then adopted as the proud assertion of the Ezomo's lineage that the Oba's affluence should be credited to the man who killed the Iyase n'Ode.

8-20. This ancestral altar tusk, probably commissioned by Oba Osemwende, was carved only a few years later than the tusk depicted in Figure 8-19. The two tusks strongly differ in motif choice and carving style, suggesting that a new group of carvers was brought into the palace by Osemwende after he overthrew his brother, Oba Ogbebo, in the civil war of 1816. The carvers' distinct style is evident in a range of ivory works commissioned during the first half of the 19th century. Because ancestral tusks honor outstanding rulers in the Oba's lineage, almost all of the 19th-century tusks bear Akenzua's trunk-hand. Height of tusk alone without pedestal head about 89 cm. FMCH X65.9129. Gift of the Wellcome Trust. Photograph, Richard Todd.

8-21 (ABOVE). In many cases, a flange at the base of the brass pedestal head bears small images that repeat the carved motifs on the tusks, most significantly the royal leopard and Akenzua's trunk-hand which usually grasps a three-lobed leaf. This image is extremely common on late 18th- and early 19th-century royal brasswork. Such royal altars were commissioned by Obas who were direct descendants of Akenzua. Cast brass, 19th century. Height 40.6 cm. FMCH X65.9083, Gift of the Wellcome Trust. Photograph, Richard Todd.

8-22. Ivory armlet in typical 19th-century style and design, with motifs and symbols that evoke the 16th-century warrior Oba Esigie. Height c. 13 cm. Collection of Sandra Blair. Photograph, Richard Todd.

8-23. Ezomo's double trunk-hand emblem on a tusk from an ancestral altar in the Ezomo's palace. Mid-18th century. Height c. 17 cm. Minneapolis Institute of Arts 56.33. Photograph, Petronella Itsma.

181

AN APPROXIMATE CHRONOLOGY OF SOME OBJECTS LISTED

Approximate Dates	Obas	Figure/Object
1500	Esigie	2, 3 - spoons
		4 - saltcellar
		6 - Liverpool aegis plaque
		7 - Berlin aegis plaque
	Orhogbua	8 - Trunk-hand pendant
1600	Ehengbuda	
	Ohuan	
	(Interregnum; Benin ruled by Councils of Chiefs)	
	Ewuakpe	
1700	Akenzua I	10 - Brass rattle staff
		12 - Lidded ivory container
		13 - Double cylinder armlets
	Eresonyen	14 - Owo armlets with trunk-hand motifs
		15 - Ezomo's brass ikengobo
	Akengbuda	23 - Ezomo's tusk 124 (Set E-I)
1800	Obanosa	11, 19 - Oba's tusk 135 (Set IV)
	Ogbebo Osemwende Adolo	20 - Oba's tusk 80 (Set V)
	Ovoranmwen	22 - Armlet with Esigie motifs
1900	Eweka II	
	Akenzua II	16 - Palace ancestral altars

NOTES

In the continuing study of Nigerian art history and iconography I have been assisted by many institutions and individuals. In 1980 a Dickson History of Art Travel Grant from UCLA facilitated the examination, measurement, and photography of Nigerian antiquities in British and European museums, and in 1987 an NEH Summer Stipend supported archival study of Portuguese-West African interactions in the 15th and 16th centuries at the Centro de Estudos de Historia e Cartografia Antiga in Lisbon. In 1991 an NEH Travel to Collections Grant made further documentary research possible in several archival collections in Britain and an NEH Fellowship for College Teachers and Independent Scholars in 1992 has facilitated the ongoing analysis of these materials. I am grateful to many curators, librarians, and other staff members for their willing help. I have also profited from the kindness and perceptions of William Fagg, Frank Willett, Philip Dark, Paula Ben-Amos, Luis Albuquerque, and Maria Emilia Madeira Santos, whose informed opinions have been very much appreciated.

Fieldwork in Benin City and Yorubaland during 1981-82 was financed by a Fulbright Dissertation Research Grant, and I am grateful to Ekpo Eyo for the sponsorship of the Department of Antiquities in Nigeria, to the University of Benin for the use of facilities, and to the chiefs of the Igbesanmwan and Iguneronmwon and other ritual specialists who assisted me in Benin City. I particularly wish to thank His Highness Oba Erediauwa, Oba of Benin, for his interest and generosity. I would also like to thank my husband, Rupert Blackmun, for his patience and active participation during every phase of my work. Finally, I acknowledge an enormous debt to the late Arnold Rubin, who supervised the doctoral studies that led to this essay. His never-failing encouragement was accompanied by rare insight, close analysis of my conclusions, and absolute integrity.

1. Egharevba (1968:17). Jacob Egharevba's compilations of oral traditions have been widely accepted by the Edo.

2. Benin's 15th- and 16th-century warrior Obas were Ewuare (c.1440-1473), Ozolua (c.1480-1517), Esigie (c.1517-1550), Orhogbua (c.1550-1578) and Ehengbuda (c.1578-1608). Bradbury discussed the probable dates of each reign in "Chronological Problems in Benin History" (1959), reprinted in *Benin Studies* (17-43) and they have been further discussed in Ryder's *Benin and the Europeans* (1969). The dates given here are approximations based upon Egharevba, Bradbury, and Ryder.

3. Personal communication from the late Ohanbanmu Ineh and Egbe Obawaye of the *Igbesanmwan*, April 1982.

4. Although only the middle portion remains (the lid to the upper bowl and the entire lower bowl with its base are missing), Curnow suggests that this highly original carving was probably the prototype for six other saltcellars with similar iconography (1983:198,199, Cat. 85,87-91).

5. The three palace associations, *Iweguae*, *Iwebo*, and *Ibiwe*, are open to every freeborn man in the kingdom (Bradbury 1973:60-67). Each of the associations is made up of a hierarchy of members and chiefs who rise in rank and responsibility through their personal loyalty and service to the Oba. These chiefs supervise the daily functioning of the palace and administer other affairs of the kingdom.

6. These chiefs are known as Eghaevbo n'Ene, each of whom is appointed by the Oba on the basis of his personal political following (Bradbury 1973:67,68). These four participate in ruling councils with the palace chiefs.

7. After leaving an heir in Benin, Oranmiyan founded a second line of kings who ruled the Yoruba kingdom of Oyo. Benin is therefore considered senior to Oyo and junior to Ile Ife. Nevertheless, since a ruler's rank among his royal peers is determined by the fraternal position of each royal line descending from Ododuwa, putative dynastic inheritances may have been subtly adjusted for countless generations to reflect the actual economic and political power at each ruler's disposal.

8. In addition to those shown here, portions of three other large brass aegis plaques with similar characteristics are in the Benin City Museum (Meyerowitz 1940:fig. 1; Willett 1973:figs. 17,19,20). Thinly cast with openwork borders, these three apparently date from the age of the warrior Obas. One of them is fragmentary, but the other two have been tested by thermoluminescence, yielding late 16th- to early 17th-century dates (Willett and Fleming 1976:140,141). All three include images of a frontal ram's head, which Ben-Amos has discussed in pendant form as a very early emblem common to Ile Ife as well as Benin (1983:178,179). A large fragment of an aegis plaque that was evidently identical to that in Figure 8-8, from the A.W.F. Fuller collection, is in the Field Museum of Chicago. In his collection notes, recorded sometime between 1902 and 1948, Captain Fuller described it as "Half of an aegis of large size and rare type. It came from Benin, but the face suggests Ife" (Dark 1962:no.294). Whether this fragment is the remaining portion of the damaged plaque from Liverpool has not been established.

9. Two additional versions of this composite trunk-hand pendant have been located: one in Leiden (Dark 1982:fig. 50a) and the other in the University Museum in Philadelphia (Hall 1922:fig. 49).

10. Willett places the "classical" phase of the Ife culture from the 12th to the 14th centuries (pers. com. Dec. 1991), and the terracottas recovered archaeologically in Ekpo Eyo's excavation at Igbo 'Laja in Owo yielded mid-15th-century dates (Willett and Eyo 1980:16).

11. Beginning about 1689, the kingdom was torn with civil war for seven years (Nyendael 1705:466; Ryder 1969:114). In Benin tradition these troubled years marked the rule of Oba Ewuakpe, who fought the Iyase n'Ode and other chiefs to re-establish a strong monarchy (Egharevba 1968:37-39, Ben Amos 1983:163). Ewuakpe negotiated a truce with these chiefs so adroitly that in effect he began a new dynasty. He initiated a rule of royal succession through strict primogeniture (Egharevba 1968:39), and Ben Amos has discussed the iconography adopted in Benin to commemorate his accomplishments (1983:165-80). Never-theless, at Ewuakpe's death in the early 1700s, the succession of his son was challenged (Bradbury 1973:28,29). The Iyase n'Ode backed a rival contender for the throne (Egharevba 1968:39; Ryder 1969:150) and another period of civil war wracked the kingdom.

12. Since elephants are now rare in southern Nigeria, ivory for traditional uses is often obtained through long distance trade, primarily with the Cameroons.

13. Egharevba (1969:10) has challenged the claim of Ehenua's descendants that he was of royal parentage.

14. Personal communication from Rev. S.I. Usuanlele, March 1982.

15. The late Oba Akenzua II, who ruled from 1933 to 1978, honored the Oba whose name he shared by the sacrifice of an elephant at Igue, and a brass plaque was cast by the *Iguneronmwon* to celebrate this event.

16. William Fagg, who mistakenly identified the double trunk-hand unit as "symbolic double elephant skulls" described the carving with admiration: "These are perhaps the finest of all Benin ivory armlets and may be of the sixteenth century, though the dating of ivories is less firm than that of bronzes" (1963:pl. 32).

17. Ling Roth has published sketches of a nearly identical ivory con-tainer tusk which is accented with inlaid metal in the same manner as the pair of armlets in Figure 8-12 (1903:figs. 209-12). The armlets and the containers bear strong stylistic similarities and employ analogous iconography.

18. Forty years ago, William Fagg (1951:74,75) claimed an Owo provenance for ivories found in Benin City but carved in a distinctive non-Edo style. Bassani and Fagg (1988:191-96) have suggested dates prior to 1800 for some of these ivories, and Bassani has written that one 16th-century date should be considered (1984:62). Recently it has been established that an ivory female figure which fits into this corpus arrived in Holland prior to 1700 (Bedaux and Smits 1992:76,77). My suggestion of an eighteenth-century date does not extend to an entire group of Owo ivories, but to four of those illuminated in von Luschan (1919: fig. 613 on pl. B, fig. 614 on pl. C, fig. 825 on pl. V, and fig. 827 on pl. W).

19. Vogel (1979:100) has plausibly identified the cylindrical brass altarpiece in Figure 8-15a,b as the original upper portion of this 18th-century *ikengobo*.

20. Information about the female figure in Figure 8-18 came from a personal communication with Aigbe Eson, December 1981.

21. The set of six tusks to which Figure 8-19 belongs has been discussed as Type Q in Blackmun (1984a:88-98) and as Set IV, the Queen Mother tusks, in Blackmun (1991a). The iconography of the tusk in Figure 8-20 has been interpreted in Blackmun (1983).

22. See Blackmun (1984b:10-25 and 1988:130-36) for detailed interpretation of tusk motifs in specific contexts.

23. The chronological problems posed by disparities in style and motif choice between these two sets are addressed in Blackmun (1991a: 63-65).

24. Among the first directives issued by the new British administration after the Punitive Expedition was a series of dispatches prohibiting elephant hunting. There are six of these dispatches in the archives in Benin City, issued in 1897 (Oct. 2,3,4,10) from the Resident administrator to the traveling commissioners responsible for each of these areas and for Akure to the northwest of Benin city. Two of them concern Owo.

A.

B.

C.

D.

ELEPHANT MASKS are created in a startling range of shapes. Some have a trunk and no tusks, others have tusks and no trunk. Several are basically human masks with elephant attributes. Others seem to be identified as "elephant" solely on the basis of their size. Elephant masks may be performed in diverse situations ranging from initiations and funerals to harvest festivals and rites of investiture. Sometimes they perform solo; sometimes they appear with other animal masks.

F.

A. Mask from the Ivory Coast (Guro peoples). Wood, pigment. Height 55 cm. Private collection.

B. *Ekpo* society mask from Nigeria (Ogoni peoples). Wood, pigment, vegetable fiber. The Trustees of the British Museum, 1954, Af 23.877.

C. Mask from Liberia (Mano peoples). Wood, aluminum, glass beads, monkey fur, clay pigment, vegetable fiber. Length 51.2 cm. Peabody Museum of Archaeology and Ethnology, Harvard University, 37-77-50/2744.

D. Mask from Nigeria (Ijaw peoples). Wood, encrustation. Length 53.5 cm. FMCH x89.139. Promised gift of Jerome L. Joss.

E. Mask from Nigeria (Ijaw peoples). Wood, wickerwork, pigment, plant fibers, fabric. Depth 94 cm. Private collection, Germany.

F. Mask from the Congo (Kwele peoples). 19th-20th century. Wood, paint. Height 76.5 cm. The Metropolitan Museum of Art, The Michael C. Rockefeller Memorial Collection, Gift of Nelson A. Rockefeller, 1964. Cat. no. 1978.412,292.

E.

Elephant,
Lafiaku,
spirit of the bush,
skin full of money,
one-armed spirit,
spirit that shatters the forest,
render of trees,
child of the forest destroyer,
offspring of the coconut-breaker,
elephant who kneels in a huge mass,
you with indestructible tusks,
you whose mouth utters a laugh that enjoins respect.
Big footprint opening up the thicket into a patch,
elephant who renders the thorny brake into
   an open place,
who forces his way along!
Ogoku with a back like the gbedu drum,
elephant who makes a bell-like sound like the smith
when he salutes you with the sound of his oowu hammer!
Elephant the illustrious . . . Elephant who looks back
reluctantly like a person with a stiff neck!
Elephant with a head pad, but without a load!
Elephant who balances the load on his huge head!
Elephant whom the hunter sees and says
   "I won't hunt any more today. . . ."
Elephant whom the hunter sees and throws his arrows
   into the marsh . . . .
Elephant whom we see and point to with all ten fingers
outstretched in consternation while shouting
   yaba n yaba!
Kudu, large as two hundred hills . . . .
Elephant for whom we built a pit-trap,
but who was too wise to pass that way! . . .
If an elephant passes but once through a place,
it becomes a road and if his mother later passes through,
it becomes an extensive plain! . . .
His eye socket is like a big, wide pot,
his throat is like the dye pot.
But if nobody molests you, you molest nobody.
The elephant has only one arm but he can push
   down a palmtree.
If he had two, he would tear down the sky like a rag!
Coverer who covers his child like darkness![1]

IMAGE AND INDETERMINACY

ELEPHANTS AND IVORY
AMONG THE YORUBA

HENRY JOHN DREWAL

The form of this Yoruba hunter's greeting to elephant is largely discontinuous and non-narrative, consisting of discrete, autonomous units. It jumps from aspect to aspect — from sight to sound to size to weight to movement to texture to interior state of mind to... — as it creates images of elephant-ness. It has no unified wholeness, rather its autonomous parts create a certain fluidity, flexibility, and indeterminacy. This form of *seriate* composition, which highlights the distinctness of parts, characterizes aspects of Yoruba social life as well as the form of various verbal and visual arts.[2] Seriate composition works to allow different voices to be heard, different senses to come into play, different images to come into focus or to fade. This format acknowledges the unique contributions of various entities in the arts and in society and permits them to come forth and contribute.

Such seriate composition mirrors a world of structurally equal and autonomous elements that seems to express Yoruba concepts of being and existence, especially that of generative force, *ase*, possessed by all things and spoken words (H.J. Drewal and M.T. Drewal 1983:5-7). In a sense, *ase* is the power to accomplish things. In the arts, it is the power of evocation, the power to open up thought.

The work art performs in culture depends upon its evocative power — its capacity to generate ideas, feelings, and significances that *move* audiences. This is certainly the case for Yoruba art, a complex concept that includes such ideas as skillful manipulation of media, the decoration, design, or embellishment of form (*ona*), innovation/creativity (*ara*), visual playfulness or improvisation (*ere*), completeness (*pipe*), appropriateness (*yiye*), insight (*oju inu*), design consciousness (*oju ona*), aliveness (*idahun*), and durability (*tito*) among others (H.J. Drewal 1980; Abiodun 1983; Abiodun, Drewal, Pemberton 1991). Yoruba art might thus be defined summarily as "evocative form." Such art is generative and transformative, both for artists and audiences. This idea is embedded in a Yoruba metaphor about a verbal artform, the proverb: *A proverb is the horse of speech,*[3] that is, its artfulness lifts and carries forward conversation, transforming communication into evocation that opens up and intensifies thinking.

In order to comprehend the import of the elephant in Yoruba art and thought, whether in orature, in ivory which

9-1 (OPPOSITE). The conical end of an Ifa tapper has been transformed into a hornbill bird, *agbigbo*, an infamous character in Ifa divination orature who serves as a reminder that only proper rituals and offerings can avert disaster. Below the hornbill the image of a kneeling woman with fan evokes a number of themes; childbirth, coolness, composure, endurance, and a willingness to make sacrifices (*ebo*) in order to receive blessings. Height 19 cm. Collection of Françoise Billion Richardson.

9-2 (LEFT). A terracotta elephant head pot lid from a site at Lafogido, Ife, dated c. 1300, is bedecked with an elaborate beaded headdress and globular beaded necklace resembling those depicted in terracottas of humans who were probably prominent persons in Ife society. Such beaded regalia, associated with the installations of rulers/ leaders, suggests that, since early times, the elephant has been linked with momentous matters and powerful persons. Height 15.2 cm. National Commission for Museums and Monuments, Nigeria, 63.24a. Photograph, Dirk Bakker.

9-3 (RIGHT). An Agemo masker among the Ijebu-Yoruba performs during a funeral commemoration. The thick layers of raffia are meant to evoke the enormous leg and foot of the elephant and the dance is supposed to emulate the slow, ponderous, and dignified gait of the elephant. Photograph, H.J. Drewal, 1982.

9-4 (FAR RIGHT). An *erin* or "elephant" ancestral masker processes in its magnificent ensemble of cloth, mirrors, beads, sequins, and feathers. Photograph, H.J. Drewal, 1978.

stands for elephant, or other objects with elephant referents, I first explore the art and economic history of the elephant and ivory in Yorubaland, considering their earliest-known representations and commodification. In part two, I consider a series of autonomous and evocative images and ideas generated by the notion of ELEPHANT (*erin*, Ajanaku) in the minds of Yoruba people as revealed in their orature. Finally, informed by these words, as well as the thoughts and actions shared with me by various Yoruba individuals during my stays in Yorubaland, I engage in serious play about the possible meanings occasioned by these objects, ideas shaped by medium and imagery, and in some cases the sounds and actions associated with them.

HISTORY

The significance of elephants and ivory for Yoruba people before contact with Europeans (late fifteenth/early sixteenth centuries) is highly conjectural. The only figurative image of an elephant I am aware of is a terracotta pot lid from a site at Lafogido, Ife dated c. 1300 (Fig. 9-2). Its head is bedecked with an elaborate beaded headdress and a globular beaded necklace resembling those depicted in terracottas of humans whom we presume to be prominent persons in Ife society (Willett 1967:58, pl. 49). Another possible elephant reference may be contained in the looped handles of stools (in stone, wood, terracotta, and brass) from the same era. These handles may represent

elephants' trunks. Both the beaded regalia and the stools are associated with the installations of rulers/leaders (H.J. Drewal 1989a:58-61, figs. 44,51,52,54). These images and contexts suggest that since early times, the elephant has been linked with momentous matters, having symbolic value as a metaphor for the actions and attributes of powerful persons.

The earliest written reference to elephants and ivory in Yorubaland was published in 1506 when the Portuguese explorer Duarte Pacheco Pereira described the Ijebu kingdom in the following words: "a great city, called Geebu. [...] The trade which can be done here is in slaves, who are sold for brass bracelets (manillas) at 12 or 13 bracelets each, and some elephants' teeth" (quoted in Law 1986:246).

From the first encounters between Africans and Europeans, commodities of exchange were a primary concern. Before long, Europeans named areas of Africa for what they could supply to the growing markets in Europe and the rest of the world: the "Slave Coast," the "Gold Coast," and the "Ivory Coast." Besides captives, ivory was the most important commodity exported from the Yoruba and Benin areas. The Yoruba kingdom of Owo was renowned for its supply of elephants. Ijebu was another. Starting in the early sixteenth century, tons of ivory were exported from these kingdoms – the same ones from which most Yoruba ivories come. Yet the number of such ivories is very small when compared with the abundance of the material over such a long time. What might account for this?

Elephants do not seem to have been a major source for food and very few Yoruba objects seem to have been made from elephant parts. It seems likely that, during this period of international trade, Yorubas valued the elephant and its ivory for reasons quite different from those of Europeans. For the Yoruba, ivory was not valued primarily for itself as a medium for art or other kinds of objects, but rather for its exchange value, its usefulness in obtaining other rare media – brass, beads, coral, and cloth – for prestige regalia, since rarity usually creates value. Elephants were plentiful in the southern Yoruba kingdoms of Ijebu, Ondo, and Owo and in the kingdom of Benin. Brass, coral, and beads were not. According to Rowland Abiodun (pers. com. 1991), whenever an elephant was killed, both tusks were brought to the palace and presented to the ruler, who usually gave one to the hunter. Rulers amassed large quantities of ivory which they used primarily in trade, and secondarily for gifts and for works of art. At Owo, some rulers grew wealthy and powerful because of their monoply of ivory, a situation that sometimes led to competition, rivalries, and open conflicts.

The importance of elephants and ivory in trade and political competition can be documented among the Ijebu-Yoruba in a masking tradition known as Agemo. The chiefs/priests who control Agemo are associated with ancient markets and trade routes scattered across Ijebuland. Their insignia of office are ivory bracelets. Like sacred kings and queens, they vied for control of this trade which was primarily in slaves and ivory (Smith 1969:80) and a long and ongoing tradition of rivalry emerges as a central theme during the annual Agemo festival (M.T. Drewal 1992:ch. 7). Elephant references are also explicit in Agemo masking (Fig. 9-3). Layers of raffia create large leg coverings meant to evoke the enormous leg and foot of the elephant and the dance is supposed to emulate the slow, ponderous, and dignified gait of the elephant (Alagemo elders, pers. com. 1982, 1986).

Elephants are evoked in Egungun, another ancient masking tradition that honors ancestors and may date to the early rise of the Oyo-Yoruba realm in the eleventh/twelfth centuries (H.J. Drewal 1978 and 1989a:71,239 n. 77). Ancestors for Yoruba are departed, not dead. They are *ara orun*, literally "beings from beyond." They dwell at another plane of existence, and in our memories, from where they guide their progeny in the world. Such beings possess the power to help us accomplish things, the power of *ase*. The living honor their memory and their power in moving masked spectacles.

One particular type of Egungun popular among the Egba and Egbado of Abeokuta is called *erin* or elephant (Figs. 9-4, 9-5). Its elephant name derives not so much from any literal representation of an elephant (although the large ears of the headdress may have some reference to those of an elephant), but because it is an ensemble meant to evoke elephant qualities, especially magnificence. Many of these masks are also associated with

9-5. An Egungun headdress popular among the Egba-Yoruba of Abeokuta called "elephant" (*erin*) is probably from the Adugbologe workshop. Its name derives not so much from any literal representation of an elephant (although the large ears of the headdress refer to those of an elephant), but because its full ensemble is meant to evoke elephant qualities, especially majesty and magnificence. Height 47 cm. FMCH X81.1570. Gift of William Lloyd Davis and Mrs. W. Thomas Davis.

hunter/warrior lineages – those who would have had a special relation to and interaction with elephants, as exemplified in the hunters' greeting cited. In another Egungun ensemble type (Fig. 9-7), most often found among the Yoruba of the southern Republic of Benin, graphic elephant images decorate the panels. Giants among the living become elephants from beyond.

During the colonial period, the elephant seems to have acquired other meanings. Europeans and their trading companies used it in their own heraldry to proclaim their mercantile accomplishments and imperialist ambitions. Such imagery was often included in gifts to African rulers (Ross 1979:14). In Nigeria, Yoruba traditional rulers who reigned only with the assent and support of the British authorities adapted this heraldic image to their own purposes, acknowledging the power of the colonial regime while at the same time asserting an ancient, pre-colonial symbol of power and authority. This seems to explain the prevalence of the elephant in royal beaded regalia throughout this period (Fig. 9-6).

ELEPHANT IMAGES AND IDEAS IN ORATURE

In Yoruba orature, as evident in the hunters' greeting to the elephant, words spawn clusters and fields of meanings through figures of thought and speech such as metaphors, metonyms, synesthesia, synecdoches, similes, or puns. The range and play of significances in texts seems especially relevant to studies of the visual arts and of society where meanings are unstable, fluid, and often indeterminate. Such a situation highlights the complex interactions of cultural and historical circumstances and the roles of artists, audiences, and scholars in the creation, perception, and interpretation of art's import.

Kudu, large as two hundred hills.... Size is a marker of importance and power and bigness signals greatness. More than anything, elephants loom large as in the saying: *An elephant is huge. When an elephant crosses your path, you don't need to inquire, 'Oh, did something just pass by?'*[4] Or another: *The skull of an elephant is not a load for a child's head.*[5]

The Yoruba word for "big," *nla*, means mighty (Abraham 1958:444) and connotes power both physical and spiritual. The Yoruba terms for forefathers (*baba-nla*) and foremothers (*iya-nla*) convey the extra-ordinary potentials of ancestors. Too, the most powerful crown of rulers, the one prepared with numerous efficacious medicines, is called *ade-nla*, the great crown (H.J. Drewal 1977b:12). Rulers themselves are likened to enormous, and ultimately undefinable, presences. As Rowland Abiodun has told me, the Olowo of Owo is praised in song as *oke rere*, "the great mountain that we see from afar" (pers. com. 1991).

9-6. A Yoruba royal beaded cap of the colonial era displays an elephant, a European heraldic image adapted to Yoruba purposes. Diameter 19 cm. FMCH X88.253. Museum purchase with Manus funds.

9-7. An Egungun masking ensemble, probably from the colonial era and found among the southwestern Yoruba in the Republic of Benin, displays appliqued images of elephants. During the colonial period, Yorubas adapted this European heraldic image to acknowledge the authority of their colonial rulers while still asserting an ancient, pre-colonial symbol of power and authority. Height 150 cm. Eric D. Robertson Collection.

Size as a signifier of importance and power is nowhere more evident than in the work of Yoruba artists who use *conceptual* rather than naturalistic proportion. In sculpture, large eyes dominate faces due in part to ideas about the "inner-eye" or insight (*oju-inu*); heads, because of their great philosophical importance in Yoruba thought as the site of the spiritual essence of persons, dominate torsos; rulers, priests, and chiefs loom large over their supporters; and human riders dominate their diminutive mounts (H.J. Drewal 1988:3-4). In Yoruba fashions, layers of heavy, stiff cloth enhance persons by making them bulk large. Big is beautiful because bigness connotes power and prestige. In this attribute, elephant has no equal.

You whose mouth utters a laugh that enjoins respect . . . . Fear and respect are other ideas associated with elephant as evident in the proverb: *In the presence of a dead elephant many clubs are pulled out; but how many swords appear in the face of a live elephant?*[6] It is no wonder that of the many *orile* names (totems meant to convey the power and prestige of a group), the two most important are elephant — the totem of the original line of rulers of the Oyo-Yoruba — and the ram (Abraham 1958:482-83). *Elephant who looks back reluctantly like a person with a stiff neck! . . . if nobody molests you, you molest nobody . . . .* Such images suggest the ideas of age, wisdom, and composure. The tough, wrinkled hide and slow gait of elephants evoke old age, a long life of accumulated experience and thus wisdom. The power and authority of elephant's position is expressed in its cool, detached attitude – a composure of mind associated with wise elders. Longlastingness, evidence of one's ability to persevere and survive the trials and challenges of life, is also implied here. It is significant that this quality is specifically associated with ivory as in the greeting: *. . . you with indestructible tusks.*

In sum, the elephant images a set of superlatives. It is without equal and beyond measure, as shown in several sayings: *If an elephant eats and is not satisfied, the fault is that of the forest, not the elephant;*[7] *The only thing more vast than elephant is the earth;*[8] and, *A single elephant can make the forest shake to its very roots.*[9]

Ivory, in standing for elephant, provokes these ideas. It is not surprising, then, that all the following objects are associated with "big," peerless women and men – privileged persons concerned with momentous matters – diviners, leaders, and elders – who assert their powerful positions with evocative forms in ivory.

9-8. Chief Fagbemi Ajanaku, Araba of Lagos dances and sings during his annual Ifa festival while holding an ivory tapper (*iroke*) in his right hand. "Ajanaku," an honorific name for elephant, and "Araba," the most senior title in Ifa, convey the idea of huge or beyond comparison, making Chief Fagbemi the mightiest of the mighty. Photograph, M.T. Drewal, 1977.

9-9. At the outset of a divination session, diviner Kolawole Ositola strikes the conical end of the tapper at the center of the tray where the metaphorical crossroads (*orita*) of life and the afterlife has been marked in wood dust. Photograph, M.T. Drewal, 1986.

DIVINATION OBJECTS

One of these persons is the Ifa diviner, Chief Fagbemi Ajanaku, the Araba of Lagos (Fig. 9-8). Araba is the most senior title in the Ifa community. According to Ifa lore, Araba conveys the idea of HUGE, beyond comparison (diviner Kolawole Ositola, pers. com. 1982). Ajanaku is also another name for elephant. Thus Chief Fagbemi is doubly HUGE: he is the mightiest of the mighty. In his right hand he holds a tusk carved into a divination tapper/bell known as *iroke* Ifa.

At the outset of a divination session, the diviner strikes the conical end of the tapper at the center of the tray where the metaphorical crossroads (*orita*) of life and the afterlife has been marked in wooddust (Fig. 9-9). The cone is a pervasive and deeply resonant form in Yoruba art and thought. It is an ideogram for life force or performative power, *ase*, that animates everything in the cosmos. It also visualizes the link between forces in the world (*aye*) and those in the otherworld (*orun*) (M.T. Drewal 1977). The cone shape occurs in forms symbolic of the spiritual essence of individuals; the conical crowns of rulers (*adenla*); the sites of major ritual offerings associated with treaties, boundaries, ancestors, markets and towns; the verandah roofs (*kobi*) under which rulers sit; and coiffures (*osu*) marking the spot where medicines spiritually unite persons and divine forces, to mention only a few.[10] It is no wonder then that the naturally conical form of the elephant's tusk should appear in the object used by Ifa diviners to invoke and celebrate all the forces in the cosmos during the opening invocation called the *ijuba agbelumolu* (Kolawole Ositola, pers. com. 1982). The spot where the tapper strikes is called *erilade opon*, "the-center-of-the-tray-wears-a-crown." Cone strikes cone.

9-10 (ABOVE). Miniature ivory heads such as this are sometimes kept with a diviner's set of sacred palm nuts, *ikin*. The heads are called *olorin ikin*, "head/leader of the palm nuts." Height 8.9 cm. FMCH x70.695. Gift of the Ralph B. Lloyd Foundation.

9-11 (LEFT). An *iroke* Ifa in which the conical, horn-like form emerges from the head of a kneeling mother, evoking ideas about power-laden substances, the inner, spiritual head (*ori inu*), outer, physical one (*ori ode*), and the interaction of otherworldy and worldly forces in persons' lives. Height 34 cm. Private collection.

Both hearing and sight contribute to the comprehension of the tapper's significance. Like the elephant *who makes a bell-like sound like the smith when he salutes you with the sound of his oowu hammer,* the tapper, too, sounds and greets. Underneath the center of the tray a hollowed out area creates a sound chamber. The tray's and tapper's "voices" reverberate, reaching across time and space to marshall worldly and cosmic forces. The sound created is said to be the forces responding to the greetings of the diviner (Kolawole Ositola, pers. com. 1982). Many tappers also have clappers in their hollow interiors, for they serve as bells during musical and other performances.

Hollow conical tappers may also play upon the form of horns. Since ancient times, horns have been markers of powerful persons as shown in two Ife bronzes dating from circa A.D. 1000-1200 (Eyo and Willett 1980:pls. 44,45). Horns serve as containers of efficacious substances that make words

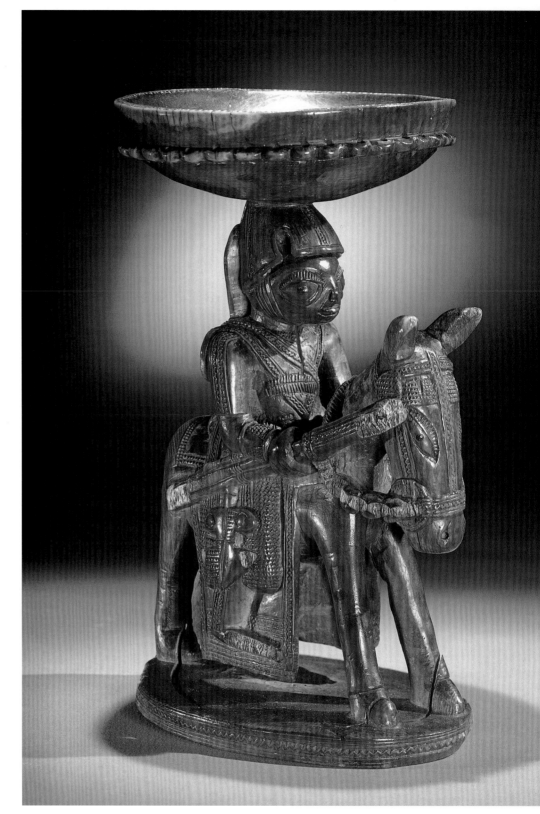

9-12. The use of ivory for an *agere* Ifa may have several explanations: It possesses the same attributes as *iroko* wood, that is, majesty, strength, and durability; it has high prestige value; and, through divination, it may have been selected as the medium to hold a person's palm nuts. The image of a male equestrian may have resulted from the owner's divination sign, some of which refer explicitly to horsemanship. Alternatively, the equestrian may be a visual metaphor for the gods and their devotees, for Yoruba describe a person possessed by the spirit of a deity as a "horse of the god" (*esin orisa*). Deity rides devotee. Height 22.2 cm. Collection of Adriana and Robert Mnuchin.

and deeds come true. In one *iroke* Ifa (Fig. 9-11) the horn form emerges from the head of the kneeling mother. Like other projections from the head in Yoruba art, it evokes ideas about the inner, spiritual head (*ori inu*) and outer, physical one (*ori ode*) and the interaction of otherworldy and worldly forces in persons' lives (M.T. Drewal 1977). The mother holds her breasts in a gesture of greeting, nurturance, devotion and love — a sacred act of giving in order to achieve good fortune and avert loss.

The conical end of a second tapper (Fig. 9-1) has been transformed into a hornbill bird, *agbigbo*. The "voice" of the tapper and that of the hornbill emanate from the same spot. The hornbill appears frequently in Ifa divination verses, usually as an infamous character, to remind us that only proper rituals and offerings can avert disaster (Abimbola 1976:211-13; H.J. Drewal and M.T. Drewal 1983:209). In one Ifa story, hornbill was cursed for killing people. As punishment, a coffin (symbol of Death) stuck to his head and became the "load" or protrusion on hornbill's beak as seen in this tapper. The load symbolizes a ritual obligation, a sacrifice. Properly performed, it can ensure long life and good fortune. Ignored, it can result in suffering and death.

Below is a kneeling woman. Her representation plays on a number of themes. For one, she herself carries a load on her head, the hornbill. Offering loaded on offering. She may also carry one within, for she assumes the childbirthing position (*ikunle abiyamo*) (Abiodun 1989:111). Her hands hold a beaded fan, suggesting coolness and composure, and visually draw attention to her womb. Her posture and gesture evoke the themes of sacrifice and the willingness to bear loads, that is, responsibilities in life. This image plays upon another often shown in sculpture – gift-giving. Whether the gift is a child in the womb or kolanuts in a bowl, both are offerings – giving in order to receive – a central tenet in Yoruba belief and religious practice.

Color, as well as imagery evocative of childbirth, combine to enrich the object's meaningfulness. Whiteness (*funfun*) is the color with which we begin life – we arrive in the world in the caul which Yoruba define as a white covering (Kolawole Ositola, pers. com. 1982). It connotes newness, freshness, coolness, and ritual purity. The conjunction of color, sound, movement, and image thus contribute to the impact of this important initial moment of divination.

Once the tapper's sights and sounds have honored and invoked the cosmic forces, the diviner begins to manipulate sixteen sacred palm nuts (*ikin/iken*), obtaining certain number signatures in order to reveal the forces operating in a particular situation that will then speak through the divination verses. The *ikin/iken* symbolize Orunmila, deified founder of Ifa divination. Miniature ivory heads (Fig. 9-10), often with conical headdresses, may be kept with a diviner's set of sacred palm nuts and are known as *olori ikin*, "head/leader of the palm nuts" (Abiodun 1975:434). Full ivory figures of women or men (Figs. 9-13, 9-14) may be somehow related to the *olori ikin* form, but the precise nature of their relationship is unknown to this author. A kneeling female (Fig. 9-13) recalls many of the same ideas seen in the tappers discussed above.

The theme of sacrifice occurs in a sculpture of a standing figure (Fig. 9-14). A male holds a staff in his right hand and an offering – an *agbigbo* or hornbill – in his left. Notice how the protuberance on hornbill's large beak is rendered as a serrated crest in both the tapper (Fig. 9-1) and this piece, visually emphasizing the mythic curse on those who fail to perform proper sacrifices. Attire also evokes appropriate ritual behavior. The male figure's upper torso is bare except for a necklace from which pendants are suspended in both front and back. His elaborately textured wrapper is suggestive of an elder's cloth known as *aso olona* or *aso ologbon*, the "cloth of many designs" or "cloth of a wise person," symbolic of a long life filled with countless experiences and challenges (M.T. Drewal 1992:40). Covering the head is a remarkable cap from the back of which hangs a monkey eating a corncob.

9-13. This ivory kneeling female, recalling themes seen in divination tappers, may be related to the miniature ivory heads with conical headdresses, *olori ikin*, sometimes kept with a diviner's set of sacred palm nuts. Height 9 cm. Collection of Robert and Nancy Nooter.

9-14 A,B (TWO VIEWS). The themes of sacrifice and proper ritual behavior are expressed in this ivory figure with its solemn offering of a hornbill and its attire suggestive of an elder. Like Figure 9-13 this ivory sculpture may be related to the miniature ivory heads kept by a diviner, although the hole in the neck suggests it may have served as a pendant. At the back of the cap is the inverted image of a seated monkey eating a corncob—possibly a reference from Ifa orature to one who uses wit and wisdom to survive. Height 19 cm. Collection of Charles and Kent Davis.

9-15. The Ojomo of Ijebu-Owo in his *orufanran* ensemble with a variety of ivory attachments (*omama*). The ensemble, thought to have been introduced into Owo by the 16th ruler, Oshogboye, from the court of Benin, was worn on occasions honoring high chiefs who had distinguished themselves in military exploits, which helps to explain references (in imagery, color, or medium) to animals possessing courage and protective and physical powers such as the crocodile, ram, pangolin, and elephant. Photograph, R. Abiodun, 1978.

This motif, widespread in Yoruba sculpture, has many possible readings, including reference to a story from the Ifa corpus in which the monkey turns a failed theft into triumph through audacious self-defense (see H.J. Drewal 1977:88 and forthcoming).

Agere Ifa are containers that hold the sixteen sacred palm nuts (*ikin/iken*) used in divination. The palm nuts symbolize Orunmila, the deified founder of Ifa divination (Fig. 9-12). According to Ifa lore, Agere was a favorite wife of Orunmila. Once, when Orunmila was threatened by his enemies, Agere saved him by hiding him in her stomach (M.T. Drewal and H.J. Drewal 1983:67). Thus the container came to be called *agere*. The *agere* is considered a female form and should be carved of female wood (*abogi*) such as *osan* wood because it produces the *agbalumon* fruit with countless seeds symbolizing plentiful progeny. But sometimes *iroko* wood is used because it is regarded as the "ruler of trees" due to its size and durability (Kolawole Ositola, pers. com. 1982). Why then would some be carved in ivory? One explanation might be that the attributes of *iroko* wood are also those of elephants and their tusks, that is, majesty, strength, and durability. The prestige value of ivory might be another. Then too, divination determines what kind of a container should hold a person's palm nuts. A variety of media such as porcelain, clay, wood, brass, or ivory may be specified during the course of divination.

Ideally, *agere*, because of its mythic origins, should depict female subjects, according to diviner Kolawole Ositola, although patrons and artists have latitude in the images they choose (M.T. Drewal and H.J. Drewal 1983:66-67). The presence of a male equestrian may be the result of the divination sign of its former owner. One of these signs, Obara Meji, includes frequent references to warriors and horsemanship (M.T. Drewal 1992:148). Alternatively, the reference may be to the gods and their devotees, for the Yoruba describe a person possessed by the spirit of a deity as a "horse of the god" (*esin orisa*). Deity rides devotee.

ART AND LEADERS

Elephants and rulers share the same conceptual space in Yoruba thought. Both are mighty, essentially undefinable, beyond circumscription. Just as it is forbidden to point with one's finger at a ruler (Abiodun, pers. com. 1991), so too the hunters' greeting to elephant refers to *Elephant whom we see and point to with all ten fingers stretched out in consternation....* Verbal references to rulers are always indirect allusions. One refers to titles, never to the personal names of those who occupy the office. The same occurs in relation to elephant, who is rarely referred to as *erin*, but rather by its praisename of Ajanaku.

The ivory-laden *orufanran* ensemble (Fig. 9-15) is said to have been introduced into Owo by the sixteenth ruler, Oshogboye, from the court of Benin in the early seventeenth century (Poynor 1976). *Orufanran* was worn on occasions

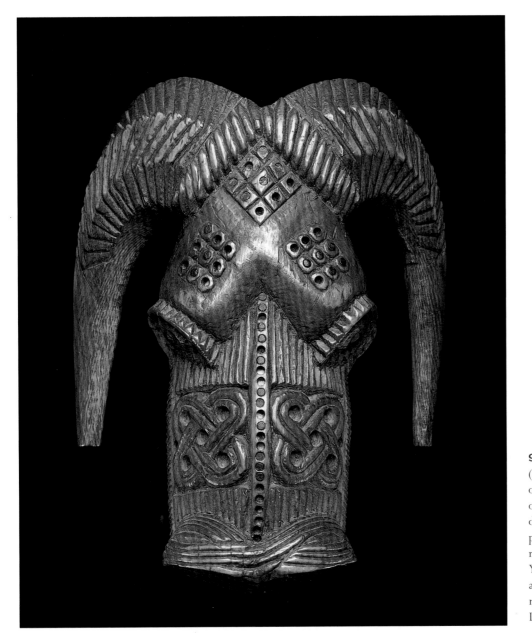

9-16. An ivory ram's head attachment (*omama*) worn by the rulers of Owo as part of a ceremonial costume (*orufanran*) on occasions honoring high chiefs who had distinguished themselves in military exploits. Together with the elephant, the ram is the most important totem among the Yoruba. It is a sign of the preeminent power and aggressiveness of one who tolerates no rival. Height 15.2 cm. Collection of Eric D. Robertson.

honoring high chiefs who had distinguished themselves in military exploits (Abiodun 1989:105,108-9). Such a ceremonial context helps to explain the themes of aggression, defense, courage, and physical power in the construction and imagery of the *orufanran* ensemble. The cloth jacket has layers of red-dyed wool cut into serrated strips in imitation of the scales of the spiney anteater or pangolin. The pangolin epitomizes one whose defense is impervious to enemy attacks: when threatened, it rolls into a tight ball, its hard scaley skin protecting its soft underbelly from attack. Because of this, pangolin is a precious ingredient in protective medicines. Its skin has become the symbol for self-preservation in the face of deadly challenges. Pangolins thus communicate ideas of spiritual as well as physical armor.[11]

Many of these same notions are embedded in the medium and imagery of the ivories attached to the *orufanran* garment. Ivory itself is seen as indestructible. It announces the presence of the mightiest warrior of all—the elephant. The array of ivory attachments (*omama*) image powerful beings — crocodiles,

fish-legged figures, kings, queens, courtiers, and, prominently positioned at the pectorals, rams (Fig. 9-16).

Together with elephant, the ram is the most important totem among the Yoruba. It is a sign of preeminent power. The saying '*two rams cannot drink from the same deep gourd*'[12] conveys the aggressiveness of the ram who tolerates no rival (Abraham 1958:29). Rams are especially important in Owo-Yoruba art and thought. The central image on ancestral altars is a ram's head or human head surmounted by one or two sets of ram's horns. At the time of the New Yam festival among the Owo, the head of a household stands in front of the ram image and offers a long prayer that includes the following:

The children (fingers) of the hand cannot die while the hand
  is watching.
The children (toes) of the foot cannot die while the foot is alert.
It is only a dead ram that cannot fight.
Please, stay awake, be vigilant.
Let no evil thing come near your children.[13]

The ram is a metaphor for alertness, aggressiveness: he is a fighter. And when we see ram, we also hear him, especially the staccato rap of horn against horn when rams clash in battle. Thus a fusion of senses – sight and hearing – contribute to the evocative power of this image.

Another object associated with the *orufanran* ensemble is the *udamalore*, a ceremonial sword made of ivory or a variety and combination of media – brass, iron, wood covered in beads – and worn by Owo rulers and their highest ranking chiefs (Fig. 9-17) (Abiodun 1989:109). Worn on the left hip above the distinctive skirt known as *ibolukun*, the sword announces its owner as a person of high status, famous and respected, with power and influence in the affairs of the community – a person of substance, like the animal from which the ivory comes. When worn by someone from a hunter/warrior family, it might also signify the special, elevated category of hunters, *ode-aperin*, those permitted to kill an elephant (Abiodun 1989:104).

In this fragment the hilt of the *udamalore* sword is still visible on his left hip. His body striations are probably signs of initiation and high status. Brandished in his right hand is the representation of an *uda*, sword of authority. Thus this fragment contains within it representations of representations – the sword of authority and its symbolic representation in the ceremonial *udamalore* sword.

On the figure's head is a coral open-work cap, like that worn by rulers in Owo (see Fig. 9-15) (Abiodun 1989:103). The bird that would have been at the side of the coral headdress evokes the gathering of birds at the tops of Yoruba crowns, sign of the spiritual powers of women and crucial to the success and longevity of rulers in Yorubaland (H.J. Drewal 1977b:12-13). Sounds were also a part of this ivory object. Crotals were attached to the perimeter, for powerful ones distinguish themselves not only by their regalia, but also by their sounds. Elephants' teeth are thus transformed into forms that create sounds of and for the powerful – tappers, bells, trumpets, and flutes – sounds that praise rulers and gods.

Ornate and delicately-carved bracelets (Fig. 9-19), probably carved by an Owo-Yoruba artist, were worn by a ruler, high-ranking chief, or priest – persons mediating extraordinary forces, whether of this world (*aye*) or the otherworld (*orun*). Imagery evokes these forces in a variety of ways. Creatures – perhaps a crocodile and a chameleon – issue from the nostrils of a disembodied head, a motif in works from Ife that may date to the Pavement Period, A.D. 1000-1400 (Drewal 1989a:46). Both crocodile and chameleon are understood as powerful, liminal beings, the former in its ability to survive in both water and on land, the latter in its ability to transform its outer appearance in order to protect itself, and to move its eyes independently, to be all-seeing.

The theme of issuing forth is a dramatic visualization of how Yorubas conceive of otherworldly presences in one's inner or spiritual head. When priests possessed by the spirit of their deity are coming out of trance, their attendants rub the backs of their necks and the tops of their heads, blow in their

9-17A (ABOVE). The *udamalore* is a ceremonial sword made of ivory or a variety and combination of media – brass, iron, wood covered in beads – and worn by Owo rulers and their highest-ranking chiefs. The sword announces its owner as a person of high status, famous and respected, with power and influence in the affairs of the community – a person of substance, like the animal from which the ivory comes. When worn by someone from a hunter/warrior family, it might also signify the special, elevated category of hunters, *ode-aperin*, those permitted to kill an elephant. Height 21.9 cm. The Paul and Ruth Tishman Collection of African Art, the Walt Disney Company. **9-17B** (BELOW). The *udamalore* as it would have appeared intact. Drawing, Robin Poynor.

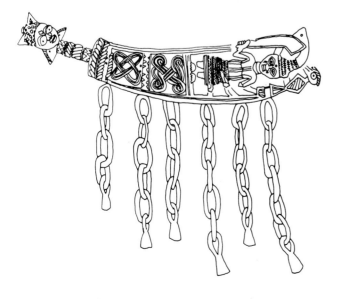

9-18 A, B. Ivory-carving virtuosity is the hallmark of an exquisite armlet, probably from the hand of an Owo-Yoruba master. The humans depicted are extraordinary – kneeling hunchbacks holding tethered monkeys. Hunchbacks are regarded as touched by the hand of the divine sculptor, Obatala, who shapes the human form in the womb. White, the color symbolic of Obatala, suggests one reason why ivory might have been used for this bracelet. Height 12.7 cm, 12.1 cm. The Paul and Ruth Tishman Collection of African Art, the Walt Disney Company.

ears, strike their foreheads and pull their legs and arms – all actions designed to remove the spirit that has temporarily inhabited the person's inner head.

Similar ideas may be present in a second motif, the fish-legged figure, a liminal being transcending the realms of land and water and symbolizing Olokun, deity of the sea. The combination of these motifs (and a corpus of others) probably symbolizes divine sanction and rulership (Fraser 1981). They may also be associated with other sanctioned mediators like

chiefs, priests, and diviners. While these bracelets may date from the sixteenth-eighteenth centuries, the age of such unusual icons appears to be much older. The fish-legged figure appears in sixteenth-century Benin works (see Blackmun, this volume) and in the Jebba bowman figure which may date to between the early fourteenth and early fifteenth centuries according to thermoluminescence dating (Eyo and Willett 1980:148). Douglas Fraser hypothesized that this motif and others in present-day Nigeria may ultimately stem from the

9-19. Ornate and delicately-carved ivory bracelets were probably worn by one mediating extraordinary forces, whether of this world (*aye*) or the otherworld (*orun*) – a ruler, high-ranking chief, or priest. This pair was probably carved by an Owo-Yoruba artist between the 16th and 18th centuries. Height 14 cm. The Paul and Ruth Tishman Collection of African Art, the Walt Disney Company.

Eastern Empire of the Roman world in the first half of the first millennium (Fraser 1972 and 1981:128).

Ivory-carving virtuosity is the hallmark of an exquisite armlet, probably from the hand of an Owo-Yoruba master (Fig. 9-18a,b). The two thin cylinders of ivory were carved from the same tusk, the inner cylinder made with loops within which the outer one (with almost three-dimensional figures) moves. Such movement facilitates the sounding of the ivory crotals suspended from ivory links.

The icons on this outer interlocking piece include a fascinating and enigmatic array of beings. The humans are *extraordinary* – kneeling hunchbacks holding tethered monkeys. Hunch-backs are regarded as touched by the hand of the divine sculptor Obatala who shapes the human form in the womb. Divination often determines that they must live lives of service to the gods and humans – both as officiants and also as offerings (H.J. Drewal 1989a:64, n. 80). White is the symbolic color of Obatala and his creations, which suggests one reason why ivory might have been used for this bracelet. The theme of ritual offerings is suggested by the disembodied heads within interlocking circles of crocodiles biting the heads and tails of mudfish, and by the tethered monkeys. In many Ifa verses, monkeys are thieves and tricksters who sometimes pay for their crimes, and at other times escape by outwitting their adversaries (Abimbola 1976:200-204).[14]

ART OF OSUGBO ELDERS

The society known as Osugbo (among the Ijebu-Yoruba where it probably originated) or Ogboni (in other parts of Yorubaland) consists of the elders, who, because of their age and experience, are regarded as the wisest female and male elders in a community. It is the judicial authority presiding over important disputes, supervising capital punishment for those found guilty of the most serious offenses, and controlling the selection, installation, abdication, and funeral of rulers. As such, the Osugbo serves to balance and complement the powers of rulers (H.J. Drewal 1989a:136-43).

One of the primary symbols of membership in Osugbo is the *edan*, a pair of relatively small brass castings on iron spikes joined at the top by a chain. The term is used in the singular, since the pair (understood as a female and a male, whether explicitly depicted or not) is viewed as one object – a concept that is central to Osugbo. The female/male couple stands for the membership of Osugbo, all the men and women in the community, and their original progenitors (H.J. Drewal 1989b). *Edan* is cast for an Osugbo member usually at the time of initiation into the society. Being portable, it is carried in public by the Osugbo member, both as an insignia of office, as a message, and as a protective amulet. When worn, it is draped around the neck and suspended downward on the chest (Fig. 9-20), just as it is shown in an ivory sculpture (Fig. 9-21) depicting an Osugbo member seated on a stool. Within the Osugbo society, usually only one titled elder may sit on a stool – the representative of the palace, known as the Olurin. This piece may have belonged to such an official. The hole piercing the conical headdress indicates that the piece was probably suspended from a cord, i.e., that it was worn as well as displayed.

9-20 (ABOVE). When worn, the *edan* is draped around the neck and suspended downward on the chest of an elder Osugbo member. Photograph, H.J. Drewal, 1977.

9-21 (LEFT). An ivory sculpture depicts an Osugbo member seated on a stool, wearing *edan* around the neck. Within the Osugbo society, usually only one titled elder may sit on a stool – the representative of the palace, known as the Olurin. This piece may have belonged to such an official. The hole piercing the conical headdress indicates that the piece was probably suspended from a cord, worn as well as displayed. Height 26.6 cm. Collection of Charles and Kent Davis.

The eyes are strongly pronounced, both by their size and their metal overlay, now partially lost. Their size may have something to do with the theme of the "inner-eye" or insight (*oju-inu*) and wisdom (*ogbon*) – the most important attributes of elders who must adjudicate matters of life and death with composure and confidence. The names "Osugbo" and "Ogboni" play on the word for elderhood (*ogbo*) and, by implication, wisdom.

The mixing of media, widespread in Yoruba sculpture generally, is strikingly emphasized in Osugbo arts where brass is fused with iron, iron is embedded in terracotta, and metal is attached to ivory. Media are gendered: clay and brass are linked with women; iron, wood, and ivory with men. Thus in Osugbo, where the themes of female and male duality, unity, complementarity, and cooperation are central, mixed media conveys the message. So too does the asexuality of the seated figure

9-23 (RIGHT). Ivory representations of *edan* are unusual. This pair may have served as a portable emblem of Osugbo membership. Alternatively it might have been owned by a ruler or *oba*, who at the time of enthronement was given a closed gourd containing various ritual objects, some in ivory. Such objects were symbolic of the various societies, like Osugbo, within the community, with which the ruler shared power and authority. The Faletti Family Collection.

9-22 (LEFT). A male figure carved in ivory, probably representing an Osugbo official, devours the feet of a second figure held upside down – an image that suggests the themes of death and execution. A wood sculpture with identical imagery was collected at Oyo before 1958 by Peter Morton-Williams (cf. Fig. 9-22). Height 19 cm. Collection of Françoise Billion Richardson.

9-24. A wood sculpture depicts a standing male figure in a wrapper devouring the feet of a second figure held upside down. Catalog information for this piece, now in the Nigerian Museum-Lagos (#58.15.4), describes it as "Eru Ogboni, from Oyo. Representing the Ogboni Society messenger who kills those who betray Ogboni secrets. Purchased from Peter Morton-Williams." Photograph, H.J. Drewal.

(Fig. 9-21), or the androgyny of many Osugbo figurative objects (Drewal 1989b:164-65).

Ivories in the form of *edan* are unusual (Fig. 9-23). They replicate objects that must actually be made of brass and iron. This translation into ivory may have served as a portable emblem of Osugbo membership. Alternatively it might have been owned by a ruler or *oba*. At the time of enthronement, a ruler is given a closed gourd containing various ritual objects, some in ivory, symbolic of the various societies in the community with which he/she shares power and authority, like Osugbo, Oro, and others. This ivory replica of *edan* may have come from such a context; however such symbolic objects were usually miniatures and this piece is not.

An unusual Osugbo ivory piece depicts intriguing images of inversion and devouring (Fig. 9-22). The image of figures held upside down, as well as other themes of inversion, occur in a variety of Osugbo/Ogboni contexts. Thompson discussed this and illustrated two (1970:ch. 6, figs. 2,3), one on a post from an Ogboni lodge, and the other on an Ogboni drum at Ilesa. Both depict female figures holding smaller figures upside down with their left hands. These were interpreted as images of

salutation to earth (ibid., ch. 6/2). Such a greeting occurs in other contexts as well. For example, during Ifa ceremonies participants must at various moments touch their foreheads to earth, a most appropriate gesture since earth is regarded as the abode of ancestral and earth spirits (diviner Kolawole Ositola, pers. com. 1986).

This Osugbo ivory with an image of inversion, but also of devouring, may have quite a different message. Here, the feet of the inverted figure are being devoured by the male figure that holds it with both hands. A very similar image in wood was collected before 1958 by Peter Morton-Williams, who has published on the Ogboni Society in Oyo (1960). This figure, now in the Nigerian Museum, is described as "Eru Ogboni,

9-25 A,B (TWO VIEWS). An enigmatic ivory sculpture of two figures with a bowl between them, probably from the Owo-Yoruba. The theme of a female/male pair, interacting, interlocking, and visually balanced, is most evocative of Osugbo ritual art. Height 15.2 cm. The John R. Van Derlip Fund. The Minneapolis Institute of Art.

from Oyo. Representing the Ogboni Society messenger who kills those who betray Ogboni secrets" (Nigerian Museum Archives, Lagos).

Such an interpretation seems plausible. The dress and coiffure of the standing figure are appropriate for a "messenger," and the image of devouring suggests death by execution, one of the primary judicial functions of the Ogboni/Osugbo whose judgements are carried out by the Oro society.

Osugbo ritual may also be implied in a highly enigmatic ivory sculpture of two figures with a bowl between them (Fig. 9-25). The female figure grasps the arms of the male. She seems suspended above the base as the male holds the spherical bowl between them. One might think this is a unique piece in the vast corpus of Yoruba art; however I came across another with some remarkable similarities. A sculpture in wood photographed by William Fagg in the Olowo's palace in 1958 depicts two figures (one standing male, one kneeling female) holding a double-necked spherical vessel between them. The theme of a female/male pair, interacting, interlocking, and visually balanced, is most evocative of Osugbo ritual art. Yet it calls to mind another image as well—that of a "royal?" couple, cast in brass, whose legs and arms (and the fingers of one) interlock (see Willett 1967:pl. 10, color pl. III).

In Figure 9-25, the artist has played with ideas of balance and symmetry/asymmetry. The female is as large as or larger than the male, except for her legs and feet, which are greatly reduced – in order to raise her above the base? Or was the piece broken and re-carved? Male and female face in opposite directions, conveying a sense of autonomy, yet also complementarity. Like much Yoruba art, it puzzles and provokes ideas that reverberate in multiple spheres of thought and action to create evocative, and to this viewer, confounding imagery.

———————

For Yoruba, the elephant stands for all those things that stretch and test the limits of imagination, like the fathomless depth of wisdom in Ifa, or the uncountable gods who are said to number "400+1, +1…" *ad infinitum*, or the adage that "it is not only seven that follows six," or the liminal status of rulers as "seconds of the gods," or ancestors as "beings from beyond" who can be reborn. Perhaps elephant's metaphorical might is due in part precisely to the way it embodies the unimaginable. If so, and if we were to play with images, ideas, and metaphors as Yorubas do, then we might say that art is an elephant!

NOTES

I acknowledge with gratitude grants from the National Endowment for the Humanities in 1981 (RO-20072-81-2184) and 1985 (RO-21030-85) (shared with Margaret Thompson Drewal and John Pemberton III) for the support of fieldwork that produced much of the data upon which this essay is based. I especially thank all my colleagues, in particular Rowland Abiodun and Margaret Thompson Drewal, for teaching me to play seriously with images, words, and ideas. This essay is dedicated to the memory of my parents, whose presence looms large, like spirit elephants.

1. Hunters' greeting for elephant excerpted and re-translated by the author from Abraham (1958:162-64).
2. For further on this, see H.J. and M.T. Drewal (1983), M.T. and H.J. Drewal (1987). More recently, Karin Barber (1991) has discussed this same compositional mode in the Yoruba verbal artform of *oriki*.
3. *Owe l'esin oro.*
4. Balogun M.O. Sote (pers. com. 1986).
5. *Atari ajanaku ki i se eru omode* (Abraham 1958:74).

6. *Oku ajanaku la a yo ogbo si; ta ni je yo agada loju erin* (Abraham 1958:467). See also Adepegba (1986:52) for a further discussion of the ideas of respect, dignity, and honor associated with elephant.
7. *Bi ajanaku ko yo, igbe ni oju yioo ti* (Abraham 1958:37; Abiodun, pers. com. 1991).
8. Abraham (1958:40).
9. Abraham (1958:37).
10. M.T. Drewal (1977); Drewal, Pemberton, Abiodun (1989:27-33, 236 n.35).
11. Similar meanings and regalia can be found in Benin, from where Owo may have adopted and adapted this ceremonial garment. See Ben-Amos (1980:pl. 76-78).
12. *Agbo meji ki i mu omi ninu koto.*
13. Abiodun (1989:113).
14. On the other hand, some monkeys are regarded as sacred among the Owo-Yoruba, where they serve as a metaphor for the courage and strength to defend one's home and property (Abiodun 1989:109, 241 n. 42). Ideas about monkeys vary greatly.

A.

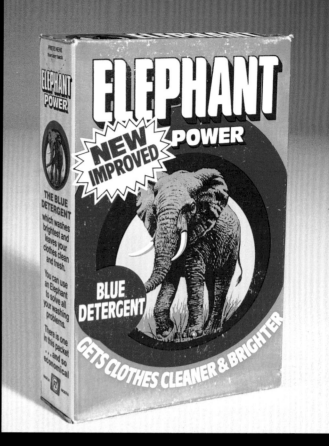

D.

Kinshasa, Zaïre

B.

C.

BEER, AIRPLANES, PUSH-TOYS, postage stamps, briefcases, and laundry detergent are some of the late twentieth-century African commercial products enhanced by elephant imagery. A coffin in the form of an elephant may be the last resting place for an important man in Accra, Ghana. Elephants or ivory tusks are found on the flags or state arms of eight countries. A big tusker symbolizes President Houphouet-Boigny's RDA political party in the Ivory Coast. A stuffed bull elephant stands outside the offices of President Omar Bongo, of Libreville, Gabon. Paper, wood, and cloth elephants are alive and well in the cities of Africa, and stuffed elephants abound. And, of course, there are also zoos . . . .

E.

A. Tusker beer carton. Cardboard, print. Height 21 cm. Private collection.

B. Hand painted stationery. Kinshasa, Zaire, 1991. 14.5 cm.

C. Baule elephant with airplane. Kongonou, Côte d'Ivoire, 1981. Wood. Height 18 cm. Private collection.

D. Elephant Power Blue Detergent. Cardboard, print. Height 17.9 cm. Private collection.

E. Tanzanian briefcase, painted by "Elizabeth," 1978. Wood, metal, leather, paint. Width 47.8 cm. Private collection.

F. Assortment of stamps. Collection of David Shayt.

G. Elephant coffin signed "Kane Kwei, Super Coffin, Teshie," 1985. Accra, Ghana. Wood, paint, cloth. Length 105.5 cm. Collection of Ernie Wolfe III.

TEN

THE IGBO

PRESTIGE IVORY
AND ELEPHANT SPIRIT POWER

HERBERT M. COLE

Live elephants are now gone from the Igbo landscape, yet they continue to stand at the forefront of Igbo consciousness and still populate the visual arts. The Igbo of southeastern Nigeria have long been subsistence agriculturists and traders[1] who live north of the Niger River delta on a gradually inclining plain bounded to the west by the Niger and to the east by the Cross River. Southern parts of Igboland were once heavily forested, giving way in northern sectors to hilly savanna country and river valleys that supported significant numbers of elephants.[2]

What may be called Igboland is characterized by marked regionalism in culture and art, the Igbo people being pragmatic, progressive, egalitarian individualists who have always resisted centralized authority. In most areas, until the advent of British colonial power, political authority was in the hands of councils of titled men and elders, and/or in masquerades deputized by such leaders, although chiefs (or kings) were traditional in a few small city-states.[3] Before the Pax Britannica there was no sense of pan-Igbo identity. In fact, numerous dialects of Igbo were spoken, some mutually unintelligible, and culture patterns showed marked variation from one region to another.

Nevertheless, Igbos from all areas, though today actually or nominally Christians, traditionally revered nature spirits – especially the land – as well as ancestral authority, often made visible in the form of spirit masquerades. Throughout Igbo territory, elephants have been valued in actuality, in thought, and in art, and while their roles have undoubtedly changed over the last millennium, these animals were first memorialized by the ancestors of contemporary Igbo at tenth-century Igbo Ukwu sites.

IGBO UKWU

Archaeological finds of Igbo Ukwu, in the northern Igbo heartland, reveal that the Igbo have occupied at least the central parts of their homeland for a very long time, and that elephants were significantly represented in the iconography of that ancient Igbo settlement. Three closely-spaced Igbo Ukwu excavated sites have yielded quantities of spectacular cast bronze objects, beads, textiles, ivory fragments, and pottery associated (by excavator Thurstan Shaw 1970, and others) with the still extant Nri clan and its semi-divine leader or *eze*, who is known as the Ezenri ("king [of the] Nri"). Elaborate regalia and sumptuous ceremonial objects unearthed at Igbo Ukwu are widely acknowledged to have been associated with ancient rites conducted by the Ezenri and his kinsmen. The king of Nri still carries out important ritual functions (for example he confers titles upon wealthy leaders and purifies the sacred

10-1 (OPPOSITE). The meeting room, obi, of the Prime Minister of Oguta city state, as it appeared in 1983. Wearing a leopard-tooth necklace and an eagle feather hat, the Prime Minister is surrounded and framed by referents to power: elephant tusks, gongs, skulls, and other ritual objects. Photograph, Herbert M. Cole.

10-2 (LEFT). Leaded bronze pendant in the shape of an elephant head from the 10th century, one of four unearthed at the site of Igbo Ukwu in the Igbo heartland. The earliest copper alloy sculptures known from tropical Africa, these and other finds, such as tusk remains, provide the earliest proof of the widespread metaphorical association between leaders and elephants, and the importance of the latter in ancient ceremonial life. Leaded bronze. Height 7.4 cm. National Commission for Museums and Monuments, Nigeria, 39.1.20. Photograph, Dirk Bakker.

10-3 (RIGHT). Ivory display in stall of Oba market near Nsukka, 1983. To this day, tusk ivory remains an important status symbol for titled men and women. Encircling bracelets, armlets, and leglets are popular though elite jewelry items traded in the marketplace. Photograph, Herbert M. Cole.

land by removing abominations) but when the British arrived in the nineteenth century, he did not have and probably never had widespread political authority (Shaw 1970, 1978; Afigbo 1981; Cole and Aniakor 1984).

Symbolic artifacts and the remains of tusks signal the importance of elephants in the ceremonial life and probably the economy of ancient Igbo Ukwu. The finds are dated to the tenth century A.D., when elephants were most likely still plentiful in the area. Elephant ivory was doubtless a valued trade item, along with slaves, and both may well have made their way from Igboland across the Sahara to the Mediterranean and beyond at this early time. Not only did the Arab world itself use quantities of ivory, it also traded sub-Saharan elephant tusks to India, where the demand for African ivory was great[4] (Shaw 1970:284-85). Artifacts from Igbo Ukwu attest to the ancient importance of elephants and ivory in title regalia, as they remain today. Three tusks, probably modified into trumpets and perhaps decorated,[5] were interred with an important deceased Igbo Ukwu dignitary (possibly an Ezenri); one tusk served as a footrest for the seated man, a practice still observed by some Igbo leaders. Among the twelve small bronze pendants of five designs, four are hollow cast elephant heads (Fig. 10-2). The delicate refinement of surface decoration in these pendants, as well as in many other lost wax (or latex) castings from the same archaeological sites, is the special mark of Igbo Ukwu style, the origins of which remain puzzling. The small elephant heads, whose precise usage and significance are not known, may be miniature versions of hunting trophies of the sort displayed in

prominent men's meeting houses in the early years of this century and doubtless earlier (Basden 1921:145). The castings are conventionalized and not quite anatomically correct, but they and the buried tusks are convincing evidence of ancient symbolic ties between elephants and Igbo leaders.

Notably, the four miniature elephant heads (and other Igbo Ukwu finds) are both the earliest copper alloy sculptures known from tropical Africa and the earliest proof of the widespread metaphorical associations of West African leaders — and undoubtedly Igbo title holders — with these venerable animals.

TITLE ATTRIBUTES

Extensive modern evidence linking elephants to titled men and women reinforces the clear but largely implicit data from Igbo Ukwu. Documentation on Igboland, however, is discontinuous from tenth-century Igbo Ukwu until written records begin about 1850, although the Igbo unquestionably continued to trade ivory, to deplete local elephant populations, and to employ an elaborate elephant symbolism. An Igbo clan called Alaenyi, Land of Elephants, may be either a literal or figurative name, that is, either a group living in an area once heavily populated by these creatures, or an aggrandizing label analogous to those adopted by individual title-holders. Elephant (and leopard) hunters were revered among the Igbo; Basden reports meeting an old hunter in 1900 who always carried an elephant ear as a trophy of his prowess, and who was thereby accorded great honor and respect (1921:145). This man used the ear "as

a fan or seat cover," so perhaps elephant ears were early versions – thus prototypes – of large round leather fans used today as title attributes. These are frequently decorated with cutouts of tusks or small elephants, among other power symbols, and serve to further cool leaders already meant to be cool of temperament.[6]

We can be sure, however, that both the lucrative export trade in ivory and local demand for it led to increasingly sparse elephant populations reported in nineteenth and early twentieth century accounts. Captain Hugh Crow, who mentioned an elephant carcass sent in 1801 from the Igbo hinterland to Bonny near the coast for the second burial feast of King Pepple's father, for example, also reported on the scarcity of elephants and the consequent depressed state of the ivory market (1830:242,259).

Today Igbo metaphors of animal powers place greater emphasis on leopards and vulturine fish eagles than on elephants but the latter are nevertheless distinctive within this complex. Two principle contexts feature elephant symbolism: title systems and masquerades. The former have long made use of elephant ivory jewelry, tail hair to string beads, and full tusks modified into trumpets, along with praise names. Masquerades are more concerned with elephants as ideas that play upon themes of power, dignity, and grandeur associated with the same titled leaders, as well as with strong spirits. These ideas find varied sculptural solutions in masks that may or may not deal with elephant prototypes visually in a literal manner.

Younger, untitled people of both sexes sometimes wear ivory jewelry – it is temporarily borrowed, for example, by young women to wear in their premarital "coming out"

ceremonies – but such uses are greatly eclipsed by the tens of thousands of pounds of tusk ivory worn or carried by wealthy men and women of high title. Encircling bracelets, armlets, and leglets – often called bangles – remain to this day highly sought after and expensive title regalia actively traded in Igbo markets (Fig. 10-3). Titled men in most Igbo regions have long been major consumers of ivory, particularly large tusks. "Taking the horn [tusk]" is a way of referring to taking titles (Henderson 1972:262 n.). Some title systems, moreover, require that a man purchase first a small, then a large trumpet for intermediate and high grades, respectively. The continuing high demand for full tusk trumpets, which have long been in finite and declining supply, has recently created a market for cleverly manufactured plastic horns convincingly colored and textured, and sold as ivory.[7]

Heirloom and display values of all sorts of ivory are demonstrated in the photograph of a high ranking Oguta chief, who wears a leopard-tooth necklace and holds a tusk, and whose public meeting room shows off the several tusk trumpets of his predecessors in the office of Prime Minister (Fig. 10-1). Other Oguta chiefs and those in Aboh and Onitsha use flanking tusks as framing devices both on thrones and in processions, as if to say that leaders so placed are both protected and dignified by the figurative and tangible powers of the mighty animals. The elephant metaphor is carried further by the sound of the tusk trumpets, which when blown have a somewhat eerie, deep-throated tone that of course recalls the elephant's voice. Ten or twenty simultaneous trumpet blasts, sounded periodically at title society meetings, are truly awesome. Attendants or other titled men may also chant the praise names of respected leaders in various contexts, at title-assumption rites, at meetings, and at funerals.

Initiates of the Ozo society, the best known of the title societies,[8] undergo a ritual death and resurrection that involves painting their bodies with white chalk to symbolize their morally pure and holy state, their closeness to the spirit world. Ascent through the title system (often comprising seven grades) is more expensive at each step and represents a process of increasing purification, as recalled in the proverb, "The eagle kills very white" (*ugo gbuzie ochakee*), a reference to popular wisdom about the seven killings by an eagle before its feathers become radiantly white. This in turn refers to the fact that as an eagle molts successively, its feathers, gray or brown in young birds, become whiter.[9] The pristine whiteness of ivory also signifies the purity, sanctity, and coolness ascribed to Ozo and other titled men, who often wear white gowns as well as white eagle feathers and sometimes ivory bracelets to signify these revered states.

A relatively small number of tusk trumpets (*odu okike, okike,*[10] *ozara,* and *mkpala*) bear carved decoration.[11] Nri men of the Agbandana lineage are said to be (and long to have been) ivory carvers (Onwuejeogwu 1981:59), although since most Igbo tusks known from hundreds of historical photographs, as well as personal observation, are not embellished, this "carving" for the most part simply may have involved cutting tusks into sections for jewelry and drilling them for use as side-blown wind instruments (see Jones 1984:111). Onwuejeogwu also indicates that the tusks of any elephant killed by an Nri man belonged to the Nri king (1981:53).

Praise names adopted by titled men include "slayer of elephants" (*ogbatuluenyi*), and "I am one whose father is elephant, whose father gave eagle feathers…" (Egudu and Nwoga 1971:87). One of the Onitsha king's praise names is, "Arm of the elephant more mighty than its thigh," a reference to the king's powerful military leadership as embodied in his personal *ikenga*, a figural shrine to the strength of his right arm – equated with the versatile elephant trunk – and therefore his success in life (Henderson 1972:277). In this regard it is notable that *ikenga* images belonging to men of highest title often show the figure holding a tusk trumpet in place of a knife. As Bentor has observed, tusks signify the moral purity and wise leadership of such elders more appropriately than do knives; the latter tend accompany those *ikenga* figures owned by younger men who were the more active warriors (Bentor 1988:70-71).

Women in the city-state of Onitsha have an elite organization actually called the Elephant Society, Iyom[12] or Otu Enyi (also called the Ivory Association, Otu Ødu – Henderson, pers. com. 1991), which is parallel to men's title societies and chieftaincies, and even more explicitly elephant-oriented. Older, wealthy women, as members, oversee much of the trade in market-dominated Onitsha; they are also known as prophets and are responsible for making sacrifices that drive evil from

10-4. An Igbo woman in Onitsha, member of the Elephant Society, Iyom, on a ceremonial occasion in (?)1962. She wears the tusk leglets and white wrapper that are prerogatives of her titled status, and signify purity. Such women oversee much of the market trade; reputed to have prophetic power, they are responsible for making sacrifices to drive evil from the community. Photograph, Richard N. Henderson.

the community. These female elephants "put on ivories" to become active members of the group (Henderson 1972:312); their ceremonial dress – of pure white except for huge, rich red coral[13] bead necklaces – includes perhaps twenty-eight pounds of white ivory (Fig. 10-4).[14] These ornaments, being heavy and cumbersome, cause considerable discomfort; yet it has long been recognized that the degree of physical comfort is sometimes inverse to the level of status in African personal decoration.[15] Tusk cross-sections measure as much as four inches for armlets and twelve for leglets.

Today the induction ceremony lasts two days, although formerly, according to Nzekwu, one day sufficed. When family members have assembled, the spiritual head of the husband's family shares kola nut, then breaks an egg and drips the blood of a sacrificed cock over the ivory ornaments, to the accompaniment of prayers. This ritual purifies the ivory and acknowledges the "blessings showered on the woman by the Creator" (Nzekwu 1963:107). Next, the woman is given a title or praise name. In the past, favored praise names included *ezenwanyi*, "queen"; *omenyi*, "one who excels"; or *odoziaku*, "one who amasses wealth." Names given more recently reflect

financial help provided by other family members: *amanlen-waeze*, "they know your father is king," *di bu eze*, "husband is king," *nwa bu nie*, "son lifted [her] up."

The ritualist then assists the woman in donning her new ivory ornaments – a difficult process because the hole in the leglet is often not large enough for it to slip over the ankle easily. To reduce chafe somewhat, pads are worn under leg ivories; but the pain of donning and doffing this heavy jewelry was often great enough to cause a woman to wear them until she died (Basden 1938:207; Nzekwu 1963:107). Nzekwu reports that white clothing may be worn only by women who have acquired both arm bangles and leglets; those with only arm bangles must wear colored cloth (p. 108). Implicit in this distinction is both a graded aspect to the society and identification of white (ivory, eagle feathers, chalk, etc.) with the most elevated status, analogous to the highest rank of Ozo. This display of white alludes to the kind of rarefied dignity resulting from ritual purity, (normally) advanced ages, and proximity to beneficent spirits and ancestors.

In the afternoon or the next day, invited guests arrive: members of the woman's age grade, more relatives, and friends, including members of any voluntary associations such as dance groups to which the woman belongs. The main attraction is a procession of Otu Enyi members in white or rich colors, wearing their ivories. The new member greets each woman in turn, an attendant carrying a basin in which they wash their hands. The hostess then pays her entrance fee, which was about ten pounds (US$30) in the early 1960s, according to Nzekwu (1963:111), but may amount to as much as 20-30,000 Nigerian Naira (US$1,200-1,800) in the 1990s.

These days, a relatively young woman's father or husband can purchase the title for her, thereby showing off his own status and wealth, as well as hers. Early in this century, however, it was incumbent upon women to raise the considerable sums necessary for purchasing their ivory by themselves, without help from a husband or family members; this was less difficult than it might seem because most women who aspired to Otu Enyi were wealthy traders in their own right, as they are today. Some amass considerable fortunes by their own

trading acumen and perseverance. Elephant women of Onitsha greet one another by touching their arm bangles: as Nzekwu observes, "ivory kisses ivory as wealth greets wealth" (1963:111).

MASQUERADES

In contrast to some quite mimetic elephant head masks from Cameroon, mid-twentieth-century Igbo elephant masks, known from five distinct style regions, are usually radical departures from literalism. Some would not be connected with elephants at all were it not for data associated with them. Thus apart from names identifying some as "elephant spirits," the masks themselves bear no, few, or misplaced elephant traits. The makers and users of these masks are clearly referring to attributes loosely and interpretively derived from a corpus of ideas about elephants and other tough, dangerous, threatening animals. These ideas are then associated with men and spirits, while the elephant itself seems to recede into a haze of distant recollection.

Thus in Bende and Abakaliki versions, tusks are respectively miniaturized and schematized nearly to the point of unrecognizability (Figs. 10-5 through 10-8). Elephant masks from the Ekpeya area look more like elephants than most (Fig. 10-9), but they, too, are rather free interpretations. North-central regions (from Udi north to Nsukka, and including Onitsha and Awka) have several varied elephant-associated

10-5. Elephant mask, *Ogbodo Enyi*,
from the Abakaliki area. Length 48.3 cm.
Jerome L. Joss Collection. Photograph, Richard Todd.

10-7 (ABOVE). Mask portraying "Elephant" collected at Umuegulungu Asa (Bende Area) where it was used for the *Ekpe* dance and paired with a "Maiden" mask considered its wife. Pairing of contrastive spirit types – one dark, masculine, often grotesque, and the other light-faced, feminine, is characteristic of Igbo masquerades. Mid-20th-century Igbo elephant headdresses are rarely naturalistic, but rather abstract, schematized, and often barely recognizable except for the names associating them with elephant spirits. Wood and pigment. Height of elephant mask, 45 cm. National Commission for Museums and Monuments, Nigeria. Photograph, Richard Todd.

10-6A,B (OPPOSITE, TWO VIEWS). Elephant mask, *Ogbodo Enyi*, from the Abakaliki area (probably Izi or Ezza). Masks from this area tend to omit the ears and transpose the trunk onto the forehead – a projection that sometimes terminates in a snake head. Wood, pigment, metal. 56 cm. Private collection. Photograph, Richard Todd.

10-8 (LEFT). Bende Igbo elephant headdress combining humanoid and highly selective elephant referents: large ears, miniaturized striped tusk-horns, and no trunk. Courtesy, G.I. Jones.

masks that use their traits creatively and broadly, though few if any of them are actually called elephant masks.

These north-central mask types can be classified generically as *Mgbedike* ("Time of the Brave"), and many actually are so named (Cole and Aniakor 1984:131-33). As a group they are characterized by hugeness, dark coloration, and oversized composite features of humans and particularly, feared bush animals: buffalo, leopard, crocodile, hippo, and elephant. But deliberately they do not look like anything in nature; they feature huge, aggressive maws with menacing teeth and especially an assortment of sharp straight or twisting horns (Fig. 10-10). One version has a trunk-like snout but overall only dimly recalls an elephant. Several have a variety of rather non-specific horns, some derived from tusks, but not much else that recalls elephants.

The functions and meanings of these masquerades are also composite: aggressive, threatening, wild, and ferocious; many must be restrained with ropes by their attendants. The spirits are humanoid but both artists and wearers draw freely from the real and imagined world of bush animals. Some maskers are "heavy" with charms and medicines incorporated into their bulky, rough costumes. They are (or at least were, when masks were feared agents of social control) powerful spirit forces, even though they sometimes danced publicly. A still more instrumental group of masks in this area, called "Bad Spirits," *Ajo Mmuo*, had even more critical executive and judicial roles. Like *Mgbedike*, these spirits drew upon terrifying bush creatures and propaganda about them to create auras of fear and intimidation. The name of one such "bad spirit" is "lineage with large teeth," *Agbo Oke Eze*, a double reference, to its devouring threat and to the might of titled elders. These men, with their collections of elephant tooth trumpets, were responsible for activating and directing strong masked spirits. Elephant references may be remote in the forms and meanings of both these mask types, and such references are certainly mixed in with the traits of other animals, but they exist firmly in the lore and background, helping to project awe, grandeur, and physical threat.

Similar ideas are associated with *Okoroshi* masks in the Owerri region that also bear few if any physical elephant traits. This masking cult honors water spirits (*owu*) which are intrusive from Delta areas to the south, yet were nevertheless very powerful in this region thirty years ago. *Okoroshi* masks divide into two general classes, one with small-scale feminine features and white faces, considered *oma* ("good" and/or "pretty") and the other with dark, often twisted male faces, considered *ojo* ("ugly" and/or "bad"). The latter, which includes literally hundreds of different characters, is also a hierarchy. Most are only mildly threatening despite their often nasty and fear-inspiring names (e.g., vampire bat, rat, pot of evil medicine, leopard poison, stinging beetle), but some few had genuine power in the old days, sanctioned by the water spirits and by elders who were the cult leaders. Such heavy masked spirits come out only at the climactic end of the six week *Okoroshi*

10-9. Elephant mask from Ekpeya, used in masquerades for the cult of water spirits (*owu*). Photograph, John Picton.

10-10. Elephant mask belonging to the Umuefi family in Umuazu Nise, used for *Mgbedike* ("Time of the Brave") masquerade. Characteristically huge and dark, these north-central mask types are a composite of human and fearsome bush animal features. Elephantine qualities are not explicit, but suggested in individual mask names such as "Head [so large it] cannot enter bush" (*Isi Aba Ofia*). Photograph, Herbert M. Cole, 1966.

season, when they are buttressed by hundreds of armed followers who march behind the masquerader and chant threatening, challenging songs. These men look for confrontations and even fights with similar groups from other villages. Each village in Agwa,[16] where I have studied *Okoroshi*, has only six or eight of these most powerful dark masks among a hundred or more male characters, and it is among these that elephant ideas come in, along with spirit names such as "Wild elephant," *Enyiohia*, "Dead Elephant," *Onwu Enyi*, and simply "Elephant," *Enyi*. But the masks themselves draw upon elephant traits only rarely and minimally apart from size.[17] Several have much-enlarged incisors, and occasional ones have horns, but none even remotely resemble the beast. The master mask carver from Agwa, Anozie, was never literal, nor did he need to be, since after all his creations are spirit embodiments, not elephants, bats or leopards.

Virtually all Igbo masking deals with — among other things — the two contrasting character types noted above for *Okoroshi*, light-faced feminine spirits explicitly or implicitly opposed to dark, often large and grotesque masculine ones. This is true in

the North-central area, with its "Maiden Spirits," *Agbogho Mmuo*, that contrast with the *Mgbedike* masks just discussed. In this region, as in *Okoroshi* near Owerri, other characters supplement the balanced pair, whereas in the Bende area, even though field data are thin, it seems that the *Ekpe* play in question dances but two characters, the Maiden and the Elephant, considered wife and husband (Fig. 10-7).

In Abakaliki, however, the male "Spirit Elephant," *Ogbodo Enyi*, has no female counterpart. Rather, a hierarchy of these imaginatively reinterpreted elephants exist. The physically smallest of these are danced by boys' age-grades, the largest ones by elders or on their behalf, with two intermediate sizes representing the two middle age-grades. The masquerades appear at festivals with their supporters to clean up and purify villages, as well as at the funerals of age-grade members (Fig. 10-11a,b). Mask displays are public indications of a grade's ability to cooperate in further "... socially and communally productive goals. This is emphasized during the dry season when a masker visits community shrines and cere-

moniously leads its age-mates in assigned tasks such as cleaning paths, the marketplace, and the dance ground."[18] Masks are heavy and difficult (especially for the boys) to carry for extended periods; the senior masker is said to visit all compounds in the village, running most of the way for several hours.

Despite the word elephant in its name, Weston was told that *Ogbodo Enyi* is not specifically an elephant spirit, but that the name is fitting because the elephant's "... singular power and endurance also characterize the volatile spirit." One of its praise names, "Strong Leopard," *Oke Agu*, reinforces this information (1984:155). Since the word *enyi* also means "friend" (depending on tone pronunciation), the name may well be a pun: elephant spirits are also friends of the village. Even the most awesome masquerades serve community needs. This interpretation is reinforced by the small heads and figures carved integrally on the backs and sides of the larger masks; some informants said these were the children of the next generation (or children of the spirit).

10-11A,B. The male "Spirit Elephant" *Ogbodo Enyi* dances for an appreciative crowd in Enyigba Izzi, 1983. This masquerade may appear at age-grade funerals and at village cleansing and purification festivals. Photographs, Herbert M. Cole.

Ogbodo Enyi masks, despite their increasingly secular, entertaining roles in recent decades, were once apparently violent and powerful agents of social regulation, a role supported by the facts that sacrifices are made to wake up and placate the "hot" spirit before it dances, that it carries and wears young palm fronds (*omu*) signaling spirit danger, and that further sacrifices are offered at the end of the dancing season to calm and keep the spirit happy for its dormant period (Weston 1984:157).

Northern Igbo communities dance one spectacular mask, *Ijele*, which is certainly not an elephant but that elicits the praise name, "elephant among masks," for the obvious reason of its gigantic size. It can be as tall as eighteen feet, as wide as seven, and weigh more than 200 pounds. An *Ijele* is also monumentally expensive to commission and dance, and normally calls upon the resources of a whole community for its construction, then an elaborate festival setting for performance. These remarkable structures, probably the largest dance masks from tropical Africa, are constructed of a cloth-covered light wood armature built on a wooden disc from which hang twelve appliquéd cloth panels. In the "branches" (*Ijele* are also referred to as trees) and spaces of this architectonic structure are sewn as many as thirty to forty small cloth-covered grass sculptures, usually including a few elephants as well as leopards, sometimes eagles or other birds, lesser masquerade characters, flowers, genre scenes, white men, and other figures – the whole topped by an equestrian sculpture. *Ijele* are symbols of cosmic renewal; they are also likened to the towering shade trees under which elders gather to govern the community, and they feature multiple "eyes" that are those of ancestors looking out from spirit anthills also incorporated into *Ijele* symbolism (Henderson and Umunna 1988). They may only dance at the funerary festivals of exceedingly prominent elders,[19] and indeed the mask is considered the incarnation of such a person, who might well have been referred to as "an elephant among men" while still living. Ijele dances are stately and dignified, in keeping with elephant allusions, and the entire performance has to do with grandeur, extraordinary wealth, great productivity, and powerful leadership.

10-12. Elephant sculpture from early 20th century seen in an *mbari* house dedicated c. 1964 to the deity Afo. *Mbari* artists knew that elephants were huge and had "horns," but did not know that these horns are actually teeth coming out of the elephant's jaw rather than from the top of the head. Not having seen an elephant or had one accurately described, they could well have omitted the salient trunk and big ears, interpreting the elephant as a bush beast with horns. Owerri Igbo, Umuahiagu village group. Photograph, Herbert M. Cole, 1966.

CONCLUSION

Another Igbo interpretation of the elephant occurs in *mbari* houses, elaborate structures filled with clay sculptures and paintings, made until about 1970 as major sacrifices to major deities in the Owerri region (see Cole 1982). These elephants – or hippos, *enyimiri*, "elephants of the water"; informants use both words for creatures that resemble neither animal – are clearly playful and may be deliberately distorted, inaccurate renderings (Fig. 10-12). Such artistic license, if that is what it is, can be partly explained by intentions that an *mbari* be entertaining, as well as reportorial, fancy, didactic, and "traditional," which is to say that it recalls traditions and the past. Images of elephants can be seen to fall under any or all of those categories. Their fancy and entertaining qualities are manifest in playful, exuberant patterns, derived from body and wall painting, that have decorated all such beasts in *mbari* that I know of. They are didactic to the extent that anything little known or powerful or traditional might be important for a parent to speak about or show to children.

But questions remain: just how and in what way are elephants "traditional" to Owerri people and to twentieth-century *mbari* artists? What is the nature and the history of this elephant tradition? I believe that rather fanciful *mbari* elephants may be departures – only partially deliberate – from elephantine reality because of the very remoteness of real elephants in time and perhaps space. The earliest documented *mbari* elephant was made in 1902 or 1903 (Whitehouse 1904). We have seen above how sparse the elephant population is likely to have been for several centuries before that time. How many twentieth-century *mbari* (or other) artists ever saw an actual elephant or a picture of one? The question cannot be answered except to say that photographs and other two-dimensional pictures have only quite recently and then only occasionally served as sources for *mbari* imagery. Pictorial sources for art were not prevalent in the earlier five or six decades of this century. While it is true that African artists can execute realistic sculpture of things they see, if they want to, how can they do so if they have never seen their subject?[20] Along with the creative license *mbari* artists have delighted in, the possibility exists that models simply were not available to "copy" – not that they would have literally copied – so artists simply did their best. The same hypothesis might apply as well to some mask distortions, when we accept the fact, too, that almost always the programmatic intention was to create a ferocious, large, and deliberately composite spirit beast.

It may be that elephants have persisted in the Igbo mind as ideas much better than they have been retained as images, which are notoriously hard to pass along verbally. The presence of elephants in chants and other oral forms (see Cosentino in this volume) does nothing to perpetuate the visual model. Tusks have been around to see, but their anatomical placement has been a problem. Ears and less frequently trunks occur in the arts, but never very accurately since tenth-century Igbo

Ukwu, when elephants were still presumably fairly common in Igboland.

A few physical traits survive in sculpture, but what has apparently been more compelling to Igbo patrons and artists is a corpus of ideas that still flourish and therefore help to keep the elephant alive. It seems to be enough for the Igbo, during most of the twentieth century, that full tusks and status-enhancing jewelry made from them remain present and available, albeit as heirlooms reverently passed down from the ancestral past. And it is enough that the elephant remains lively in Igbo consciousness, however fanciful or distorted its visual image, as an awesome, heavy, huge, dignified, mysterious—and distant—power. These characteristics are applicable equally to important men and to the instrumental spirits they deputize (or at least once did) as regulators of community behavior.

POSTSCRIPT

Some months after this paper was finished and submitted I returned to Igboland for a brief research trip.[21] Somewhat to my surprise, the elephant is both more visible and more explicit in this area than it has been, probably, for a very long period.

10-13. Recent elephant masquerades appearing at regional festivals in the Awka area appear much more highly naturalist than those from mid-century, reflecting among other things the greater availability of visual resources. This *Enyi* masquerade, animated by two dancers, is from Umudioka, Awka Local Government Area (L.G.A.)—one of over a thousand masquerades performed at the regional 1988 Mmanwu Festival in Enugu. Photograph, M.E. Nwachukwu, Ministry of Information, Anambra State.

This is true of both elephant-symbolizing institutions discussed above, masquerades and complexes of attributes that show off wealth and/or titled status.

Since 1986, for example, Anambra State has celebrated five Mmanwu [masquerade] festivals "in order to project Mmanwu institutions and to boost the rich cultural heritage of the people of Anambra in particular and the Igbo race in general." The official published program of the 1990 festival indicates that the 1986 festival even featured "over 1,080 masquerades," while in 1989 the number had increased to "more than 3,000," the figure apparently referring to individual masked performers.[22] At least two of these festivals included two rather realistic elephants (Figs. 10-13, 10-14). While the smaller one (Fig. 10-13) is a more convincing elephant, the scale and size of

10-14. Each of the elephant's four legs is animated by a dancer in this *Enyi* masquerade from Nibo, Awka L.G.A. – one of over 3,000 masquerades performed at the 1988 Mmanwu Festival. Contemporary materials – hose-pipe trunk, molded upper face, corduroy body – create realistic effects and suggest a new aesthetic. Photograph, M.E. Nwachukwu, Ministry of Information, Anambra State.

the larger is impressive. In contrast to the apparently misunderstood (or deliberately skewed) anatomy of elephant spirits of earlier date in this century, both tusked heads, with their flexible trunks and large ears, show correct understanding of the animal's physical attributes.

The same is true of the several wrought-iron elephants, sculptured in relief, on the huge double portals being made today in Onitsha (and presumably elsewhere) for the compounds of wealthy men. While title-taking thrives in Igboland in 1992, no longer are elaborate hand-wrought gate sculptures confined to titled individuals as carved doors and handles

once were; anyone who can afford these ostentatiously modern, overscaled portals can have them installed. In addition to the anatomical accuracy of the simplified show elephants, their poses are often active – with raised trunks and legs suggesting movement – as if to project a larger-than-life, animated, even threatening image for their (often new) rich owners. Such iron gates illustrate a variety of subjects, including lions, fish, "chiefs," or titled men and women, biblical scenes, and even dollar or Naira signs. Among sculptured artifacts depicted, such as cars, title fans, stools, and staffs, two large symmetrically flanking or framing elephant tusks are fairly frequent themes in those gates seen in Onitsha. Perhaps their presence betrays the continuing and even increasingly prominent or visible role of the Onitsha women's Elephant Society discussed above as an indicator of elevated social, political, and financial status. Whatever the motivations, elephants are alive and well in Igbo thought and art.

NOTES

1. In recent decades Igbo people are also doctors, teachers, lawyers, government officials and do virtually any other sort of work. The agriculturalist and trader occupations, however, remain important and were probably overwhelmingly dominant until the 1960s or '70s.

My research (1966-7, 1982, 1983, 1992) has been conducted mainly among Igbo people living east of the Niger, yet roughly fifteen percent of the Igbo-speaking population lives west of the the river.

2. Statistics for elephant populations at various dates in this or any part of Nigeria have never to my knowledge been compiled, and due to a total lack of written sources for Igboland – never in direct contact with Europeans prior to the 19th century – such tabulations for early times would be at best guesswork.

3. The city-states are Onitsha, Ogua, and Ossamiri to the east of the Niger, and Aboh on the west bank. Normally a village group, usually tracing descent to a common ancestor, was the largest political unit, although in times of war neighboring groups banded together to repel attacks, some of which came from other Igbo-speaking peoples.

4. As Shaw points out (1970:284), ivory from Indian elephants was much harder than that of Africa, so much of the raw material for "Indian" ivory carvings has in fact very long been of African origin.

5. Shaw says (1970:240), "there is one hint that these tusks may originally have been carved…" – namely, a small piece of carved ivory found in the burial but not certain to have come from one of the three tusks.

6. Older fans are leather, some perhaps elephant ears or hide, while modern versions are often vinyl, a contemporary usage parallel to elephant tusk trumpets made of ivory-colored plastic. Regrettably I do not know where or how plastic horns are manufactured, although fans are certainly crafted locally.

7. See note 5. I am uncertain whether or not the consumers of these modern "tusks" are aware of their non-traditional character. Very large display "tusks" are sometimes also carved of wood; see for example Cole and Aniakor (1984:fig. 69).

8. Not all title societies among the Igbo are called Ozo, although this is the best known title system, and the one overseen in the past by representatives of the Ezenri in most areas where it is known.

9. Conventional Igbo wisdom connects two proverbs, "eagle kills very white" and "world today, world seven," *uwa taa, uwa asa*, to arrive at the idea that the eagle kills seven times. This implies both aggressive behavior (of eagle and titled man) and symbolic death that results from a leader taking successively higher titles.

10. *Okike* is a word that means creation, and it is linked with the creator god, Chukwu. Onwuejeogwu (1981:31-33) personifies Chukwu's *okike* aspect as the creator of "…laws that govern the visible and invisible," and he sees Ozo men's tusk trumpets, at least the short one acquired at an intermediate title rather than the highest one (he is unclear about exactly when an *okike* is gotten in Nri), as symbols of their creativity.

11. One I collected in the Nsukka area for the Nigerian Museum has several geometric motifs (of unknown or no deeply significant meaning), plus a simple bird image (perhaps an eagle) and a conventionalized lizard-like creature illustrated in Cole (1972:88). Some few other tusks are decorated with geometric incising, usually on their large, open ends.

12. The title "Iyom" is not altogether clear in origin or meaning. Formerly these titled women were greeted with that word, which has for some years been supplanted by "Enyi." Some people questioned about the word felt it was an onomatopoetic reference to the graceful, dignified walk of a woman wearing ivory, as well as to the heavy gait of

the elephant. The expression "She walks like a graceful women" (*ona aga ka iyom*), high praise for the cited woman, compares her to a member of the Elephant Society.

13. Much of this so-called coral is actually red glass, probably manufactured in Europe.

14. Nzekwu (1963:105) speaks of "average weight: bangles 8 lb.; anklets 20 lb."– that is, 3.6 and 9 kilograms, respectively. From this it is probable but not certain that both the ivories, worn respectively on arms and legs, add up to the cited weights. It would seem, from photographs, that special efforts, perhaps including bleaching, are used to maintain the clean white color of this ivory.

15. See, for example, Sieber (1972:16), "Usually, a sense of propriety, prestige, or prerogative has little to do with comfort."

16. Agwa is a village group with nine villages. I estimate that, over the past thirty or so years, there have been over one thousand different *Okoroshi Ojo* masks out in the community at one time or another. The heavy, important ones tend to persist in time, while the lighter ones, danced by younger men, may dance for a few years, then disappear, with new ones materializing each year. *Okoroshi* was still active in the early 1980s.

17. Although I have photographic documentation of about fifty named masks, my field research contains names of far more masks. Among the roughly 120 *Okoroshi* masks from Agwa of which I have photographs (many without accompanying data), not one has easily identified elephant traits. There is every possibility, of course, that masks with more obvious traits have existed or still exist, and that I have not seen them.

18. Weston (1984:154-55). Much of *Ogbodo Enyi* data is from Weston 1984, supplemented by the author's own research in the area.

It is important to point out that other groups to the east and northeast of the Igbo, such as the Mbembe and Ekajuk, also dance this type of mask; so without field documentation, an exact provenance for a given mask is problematic.

19. This practice has been breaking down in recent years when *Ijele* appearances have been commissioned by politicians so as to marshal large crowds for rallies. *Ijele* also appear at the modern regional arts festivals, where they continue to be popular by virtue of their astonishing size. For more detail on Ijele, see Henderson and Umunna (1988); Cole and Aniakor (1984:138-40, 223-24); and Aniakor (1978).

20. One of Whitehouse's photographs from the turn of the century shows an elephant or hippo without a trunk, but with horns – tusks – coming from the lower jaw. See Cole and Aniakor (1984:7).

21. In January/February 1992 I spent a month studying popular urban art in Onitsha.

22. From the festival program, *Mmanwu Festival '90* (pp. 21-22). These contemporary, essentially secular festivals – held for example in the Nnamdi Azikiwe Stadium – seek to bring performers from virtually all communities in the state. They are reflexive, revivalist, and good examples of what Richard Schechner and Willa Appel (1990) call "restored behavior." The events feature speechmaking, amplified sound, fixed bleacher seats for the large audiences, and a voice-over commentary accompanying each successive performance group. In some cases a videotape has been produced that highlights many groups and that is marketed as a record of the festival. In several ways these festivals are analogous to the "restorations" created in the Museum of Traditional Nigerian Architecture in Jos as an extension of the National Museum. The buildings in Jos are actually newly created, and vary more or less from their "authentic" prototypes.

A.

B.

IVORY CANES, STAFFS, SCEPTERS, and fly-whisks are hand-held regalia adding to the visual presence of the person holding them – typically, a chief or his court officials. As an extension of the arm they intensify the gestural language of the moment. When these staffs are made of ivory, they are symbols of wealth and leadership and can invoke the power of the elephant. At the same time they serve as reminders of the animal's tusks, which are themselves are seen as display pieces, whether on or off the elephant.

A. Ivory flywhisk from Zaire (Kongo people) with metal, resin, wood, and hair. Height 27.7 cm. Collection of Drs. Daniel and Marian Malcolm.

B. Ivory scepter with medicine bundle from Zaire (Kongo people) and shell embellishment. Height 32.8 cm. Private collection.

C. Cane finial from Zaire (Yombe people). Height 19 cm. The Paul and Ruth Tishman Collection of African Art, the Walt Disney Company. Photograph, Richard Todd.

D. Chief's staff from Zaire (Kongo people) with wood, metal. Height 78.7 cm. The Paul and Ruth Tishman Collection of African Art, the Walt Disney Company. Photograph, Richard Todd.

E. Title holder staff (?) from Nigeria (Ijaw people). Collection of Kent and Charles Davis.

C.

D.

E.

227

ELEVEN

ELEPHANTS, IVORY, AND CHIEFS

THE ELEPHANT AND THE ARTS OF THE CAMEROON GRASSFIELDS

CHRISTRAUD M. GEARY

The artists of the Cameroon Grassfields have created a universe of great imagination; snakes, leopards, elephants, buffaloes, chameleons, lizards, frogs, crocodiles, and birds abound in their sculpture and two-dimensional design. These artists live in the mountainous western highlands of Cameroon, in politically diverse settings that range from independent villages (decentralized until the establishment of colonial administration) to large chiefdoms and substantial kingdoms. While each political unit maintains a distinct identity, the inhabitants have had centuries of regional interaction such as trade and intermarriage.[1]

Although their specific configurations differ, all polities in the Grassfields share common structures. All are based on the alliance of groups of filiation – patri- or matrilineages[2] – whose representatives form councils of nobles, secret societies, and associations, and thereby maintain the balance of power vis à vis the *fon* (king, ruler, leader, or chief).[3] The *fon* embodies the alliance between groups and mediates between the living and the ancestors and spirits. In some units his political power has been very limited, while in others, due to historical devel-

opment, the *fon* has acquired political power and authority (Warnier 1985:5).[4] The main protagonists in the chiefdoms are the lineage heads who aspire to high rank and titles, and who are known in Pidgin English as "Big Men" (a term that captures their role in a prestige economy).

In addition to shared socio-political structures, the peoples of the Grassfields hold similar conceptions of the world, expressed partly through a material discourse in which basic principles are constructed as well as visualized through artistic means. I want to explore the role that animals have played in this discourse by focusing on one particular beast, the elephant, and its ivory.

Any study of animal symbolism in Grassfields art encounters serious limitations because the worldview of Grassfields

11-1 (OPPOSITE). A gigantic, beautifully patinated pair of tusks to this day frames the richly beaded two-figure throne of Sultan Seidou Njimoluh Njoya of Bamum. Here he displays his throne and regalia during the filming of a television movie on Bamum history. Photograph, Christraud M. Geary, February 1984.

11-2. Carver with newly carved masks for tourists in a workshop in Big Babanki. Photograph, Christraud M. Geary, September 1970.

11-3. King Achirimbi of Bafut giving a speech during the ten-year funerary celebration for his father, who died in 1968. He wears a headdress made from the quill-like hairs of an elephant tail. According to Engard, a men's regulatory society, Kwifon, awarded these quills to the deceased rulers in recognition of their accomplishments; they were worn by the current *fon* (1986:460-61). Photograph, Christraud M. Geary, April 1978.

people has undergone many transformations since the beginning of the colonial period around 1900. Islam and Christianity made their inroads, and civil unrest in the 1950s destroyed the once splendid palaces and their treasures in the southern parts of the Grassfields. The artists who create animal representations used to produce them for rulers and big men, but now cater mainly to a foreign clientele (Fig. 11-2). Many rituals and festivals such as those in which zoomorphic masks performed have been discontinued, making direct observation difficult[5]; moreover few experts can be consulted about the meaning of animals. Any investigation of animal symbolism and animal iconography is therefore bound to be partly a historical reconstruction.

In the panoply of animals depicted by Grassfield artists, certain ones are directly associated with rulers – most notably the leopard, the python, and the elephant. They are considered the familiars of rulers, and therefore constitutive of leadership. Traditionally, when caught or killed, these animals had to be brought to the ruler, who then claimed particular parts of the animal and redistributed others to privileged members in the community.[6] The process of allocation rendered political alliances visible. Thus both the receiving of game and its distribution were prerogatives of leadership.

Many historical narratives and political origin myths demonstrate the importance of these prerogatives. Some tell of renegade sons or brothers of chiefs who appropriate the game reserved for the chief, thus declaring their independence, and of subsequent wars that either lead to their subjugation or to their rise as rulers.[7] The rights to leopard, elephant, and python thus can be interpreted as signs of political independence, power, and influence. While the leopard and python are often mentioned in the literature as animals associated with leadership (Dillon 1973; Engard 1987; Shanklin 1990b), the elephant has received less attention, in spite of the fact that elephant imagery abounds in Grassfields art, and ivory and the tailhair of elephants are prestige items par excellence (Fig. 11-3).

The relationship between leaders and royal animals, however, is more intricate than so far suggested. In the eyes of the Grassfields peoples, the leopard, python, and elephant display enormous strength and reasoning. But they also inhabit the wilderness which, as in most African systems of thought, is seen as dangerous – the antithesis to the civilized and ordered world of the human settlement. Leaders have the capability to enter this dangerous domain without being threatened or destroyed by its wild forces. They are able to manipulate the forces of the wild and assume a mediating position between both realms: the manmade settlement and the surrounding wilderness. This capacity to domesticate the wild, which is often perceived as an innate gift, marks those who are meant to lead.

Myths of origin and myths on the founders of most Bamileke chiefdoms abound with references to hunting and warfare, because the founders were hunters who, with the support of loyal heads of founding lineages, subdued neighboring chiefs and established a new polity. Hunting and warfare are thus closely aligned concepts, for both expressed supremacy and mastery of the foreign and dangerous – in one case the wild beast, in the other the alien enemy. Both were linked with the production of wealth. The elephant relates to all three conceptual spheres and thus becomes an apt metaphor: it refers to hunting because it was a sought-after game; to power and force as demonstrated in warfare, because of its own impressive force; and to economic prosperity, because of the value of its ivory.

In centuries past, the elephant was by far the most physically prevalent of the three royal animals. In the first part of the nineteenth century, elephant herds roved the Grassfields, the Katsina Ala valley, the plains of the Tikar region to the east, and the coastal rain forest. In some instances, especially in the forest, their large numbers threatened the farms of the agriculturalists and forced them to relocate their fields (Hutter 1902:465). Elephants were persistently hunted for their meat and ivory.

The inhabitants of the Grassfields practiced several modes of elephant hunting. Most commonly they dug large pits, twelve to fifteen feet deep, and drove sticks into the bottom. These were then camouflaged by means of a thin lattice-work covered with dirt and leaves, so that the elephant would fall through and be speared and trapped. Another form was the communal hunt. The participants either set fires to block the escape of the game or hundreds of men created long curving lines, driving the animals in front of their spears. Yet another method was the small group hunt. Hunters would stalk an elephant, shoot it with guns and spears, and follow it around until it bled to death. Peoples on the northeastern periphery of the Grassfields practiced a technique which they had learned from the Hausa. They would shoot poisoned arrows into the animal's feet and wait until it died (Thorbecke 1914:25). A wounded elephant was a highly dangerous creature; thus elephant hunters who faced this threat enjoyed much admiration (Hutter 1902:471-72). Men, women, and children butchered the dead elephant on location and carried home the meat, innards, and tusks, leaving nothing but the bones (Zintgraff 1895:110-11).

Ivory Trade

Throughout the nineteenth century, elephant tusks were a highly valued commodity. The Grassfields were located at the intersection of the two major flows of this ivory trade. Part of the ivory from the Grassfields went north and northeast to such trading entrepôts as Yola and Kano, while another part also flowed south to Calabar and other coastal towns.[8]

After the 1880s, when Cameroon became a German colony,[9] German explorers and traders in relentless pursuit of wealth were lured inland by tales of big ivory troves and large elephant herds. Accounts of successful elephant hunts became a conventional part of the explorers' narratives (Zintgraff 1895: 104-14; Hutter 1902:467-71). In the last decade of the nineteenth century, German military men and explorers were observing herds of up to thirty elephants in some areas of the Grassfields (Hutter 1902:466). But only ten years later, the elephant population had declined dramatically because of the heavy demand for ivory in the long-distance trade (Warnier 1985:114-15).

In fact, this trade provided a lucrative source of highly valued European imports for many Grassfields chiefs. In 1902, a German officer who was stationed in Banyo, a major ivory market east of the Grassfields, reported on the exchange value of ivory and elephant tails – information he had collected from Hausa traders instrumental in this long-distance trade (Sandrock 1902). According to his findings, the main source for ivory was the kingdom of "Bahum," later identified as Bamum, and the Tikar region. Hausa traders would purchase a large tusk in Bamum for seven lengths (each 7.5 meters) of coarse striped linen, imported from Europe and valued at around 140 Mark in Bamum; this was considered the equivalent of ten slaves. The ivory was then transported to Ibi, in Nigeria, where British merchants paid the traders in the form of five packages of the striped linen containing fifty standard-size pieces, thus valued at about 500 Mark – the equivalent of twenty-five slaves. Sandrock did not know how much the European merchants actually paid for the linen nor how high their profit was.[10] The Germans tried to divert this profitable ivory trade, which gave the British all the profit, from the British territory to the German ports on the Cameroon coast, and eventually succeeded in redirecting the flow. However, when the first Hausa ivory caravans reached the ports on the Cameroon coast shortly after the turn of the century, ivory trade was already declining because elephants were becoming scarce.

11-5 (ABOVE). In the throne chamber of the Bali-Nyonga palace, used by King Fo-Nyonga in 1908, small tusks inlaid into the floor surround the throne and form an intricate curvo-linear pattern that complements the richness of the beaded wall coverings. The stone throne dates back to the rule of Garega I, the founder of the chiefdom (c. 1860-1901). Photograph, Bernhard Ankermann, 1908. Museum für Völkerkunde Berlin, Germany, no. VIII A 5320.

11-4 (LEFT). *Foyn* Nsom Gwah of Kom sits for a formal photographic portrait, around 1970. By placing his feet on the tusk, he alludes visually to the constitutionality of his leadership, his power over the civilized spaces and the wilderness, and his economic might. His rule lasted from 1966 to 1974. Postcard, Kom photographer unknown.

THE ELEPHANT AND ITS IVORY AS CHIEFLY REGALIA

Grassfields rulers had the prerogative to possess and trade elephant tusks, whether carved or in natural form. Yet considerable amounts of ivory were kept, rather than traded. On commission of the chiefs, ivory carvers of well-known workshops produced bracelets, handles for flywhisks, dancing staffs, openwork stems for tobacco pipes, little figures with medicinal qualities, oliphants of varying sizes, and carved tusks (Harter 1986:98-103). The largest and finest tusks were used with thrones, sometimes to frame or encircle the throne, as in Bali-Nyonga and Bamum (Figs. 11-1,11-5), and often to serve as footrests for the ruler, as could be seen recently in the kingdom of Kom (Fig. 11-4).

Carved Tusks

Carved tusks resembled the uncarved specimens in functional terms; however, their relief pattern gave them multiple meanings. Babanki-Tungo was the most important center for ivory carving in the northwestern part of the Grassfields, although there were other centers as well. While most carved tusks in European and American collections have no provenance (Fig. 1-7), four collected in 1912 and currently in the Field Museum in Chicago are designated as "Bamum" (Northern 1984:133). It is likely, however, that they were actually carved in Babanki-Tungo.[11]

Several tusks in the Gebauer Collection in Portland, Oregon, can be traced to the hand of two Babanki-Tungo carvers: Bobe Ngincho, who worked in the second half of the last century (Fig. 11-8), and Tita[12] Yuefainyi, who died in 1973 (Fig. 11-6). Paul Gebauer, a Baptist missionary who spent many years in the Grassfields, recounted Yuefainyi's life history (1979:116-21). Yuefainyi had apprenticed with Babanki-Tungo Chief Fontshue Ase (Fig. 11-15), who ruled from about 1908-1918.[13] Chief Fontshue, in turn, had apprenticed with his father, Chief Ase Yuefainyi, who ruled from about 1888 to

11-6 (ABOVE). Tita Yuefainyi (1892-1973) of Babanki-Tungo carving an elephant tusk in 1956 for Queen Elizabeth II of England. According to Paul Gebauer, who observed the process and took this picture, "He divided the tusk into sections by tying grasses around it and moving them back and forth until he had the tusk separated into pleasing proportions that allowed for large motifs and restful border designs. Since he was a true temperamental artist, he worked only when the spirit moved him – and the spirit needed occasional prodding. But the piece was finished in two and one half months to meet the deadline" (1979:118). Metropolitan Museum of Art, New York, The Photograph Study Collection; Department of the Arts of Africa, Oceania, and the the Americas, Paul Gebauer Collection, no. Q 102.

11-7 (BELOW). Fragment of carved ivory tusk, likely of Babanki-Tungo manufacture. The motifs are commonly found on Babanki-Tungo tusks. From top to bottom: the bird icon, male and female human figures with drinking horn, the spider icon, and again the bird icon followed by human figures (see also Fig. 11-6). 63 cm. Collection of Fern and Leon Wallace.

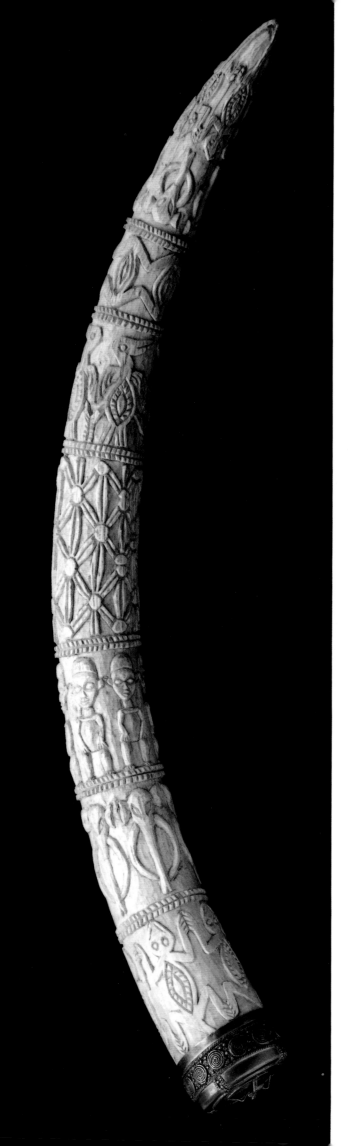

11-8 (LEFT). This tusk was carved by Bobe Ngincho, who worked in the second half of the nineteenth century in Banbanki-Tungo, the most important center for ivory carving in northwestern Grassfields. Motif bands create the design structure. Lizard and elephant motifs allude to royal power. Frog motifs may refer to propagation and increase; the stylized spider motif, to peace and protection; and the human icon, to the king's retainers. Ivory, bronze. Height 91.44 cm. Portland Art Museum, Portland, Oregon, no. 72.12.41 (Paul Gebauer Collection).

1908. Besides being an accomplished carver of elaborate stools and masks, Chief Fontshue Ase also excelled in ivory tusks. According to Emonts (1922:174), his tusks displayed artistic arrangements of men hunting, children playing, women farming, chiefs on their thrones, lizards, elephants, chameleons, and geometric designs; and he had African and German customers all over the region.

In design, these tusks closely resemble ivory carvings from Benin because the motifs are arranged in rows (Blackmun 1983). But rather than representing a narrative scene as in Benin pieces, each band repeats icons common in the Grassfields repertoire. According to Gebauer's interpretation (1979:375), the outer bands of rainbow lizard and elephant allude to royal power (the rainbow lizard dwells in palace foundations and alludes to peace). Inner bands include the frog motif (a reference to propagation and increase); birds (identified as black crow); the spider motif (an allusion to the web-weaving spider in the domestic setting); and the human icon (an allusion to the retainers supporting the kingship). It should be born in mind that these symbolic interpretations were offered by Gebauer's informants who included Chief Vugah II of Big Babanki, the carver Tita Yuefainyi, and Pastor Yohanne Nkaesei. The same icons might carry different meanings in other parts of the Grassfields.

Ivory carvers also worked in other chiefdoms. In the 1920s, the Batougong carver Umbe Massangong provided the chiefs of Batougong, Fotouni, and Banyangam with side-blown oliphants and other ivory objects. A cup made for the chief of Batougong is notable for its bold execution of human faces and figures, rendered in stylized geometric forms protruding from the deeply recessed background (Harter 1986:101; Lecoq 1953:163-64). In Bamum, nineteenth-century ivory carvers created several large oliphants with one or two zoomorphic relief carvings on the body and figurative finials. A particularly fine piece, preserved in the Bamum Palace Museum (Fig. 11-9), resembles similar oliphants found in some of the neighboring Bamileke chiefdoms, but is clearly distinct in style and composition from the carved ivory tusks in the northwestern parts of the Grassfields.

Chiefs surrounded themselves not only with ivory but also with elephant imagery carved on a variety of regalia, all bespeaking the close relationship between chief and elephant, and rendering the animal in an ingenious variety of ways. Small elephant-shaped objects included flywhisk handles, fine beaded gourd stoppers (Fig. 11-10)[14] and tobacco pipe bowls (Figs. 11-11 through 11-13).

11-9 (OPPOSITE). Ivory and leather oliphant in Bamum Palace Museum, Foumban, Cameroon. According to old Bamum princes, it was made in the first half of the 19th century during the reign of the legendary King Mbuembue, possibly as a war trumpet, or (as most asserted) a musical instrument used during numerous dances and festivals. Adorning the trumpet's end is the delicate figure of a seated man with headdress and loincloth – typical 19th-century Bamum attire. His pose, hands on spread legs, is that of a high-status male. His face displays the typical features of the conventional Bamum court style of carving: rounded forehead, circular protruding eyes under arched eyebrows, nose with a flat ridge and flaring nostrils, and a pronounced slightly open mouth. The carved motifs on the body of the lower part are obscured by protective leather. Height 111.76 cm. Photograph, Christraud M. Geary, 1977.

11-10A (RIGHT). Detail of elephant stopper from palm wine calabash shown on the next page. Height 50.8 cm. Field Museum of Natural History, Chicago, no. 174367.

11-10B. Calabash for palm wine with elephant stopper, collected around 1912 in Bagam, one of the northernmost Bamileke chiefdoms (Umlauff 1914:36, no.1074). This rendering of the elephant, at once stylized and natural in its crouching, emphasizes ears, trunk, and massive tusks — adorned here with white beads. Gourd, cloth, beads. Height 50.8 cm. Field Museum of Natural History, Chicago, no. 174367.

11-11 (ABOVE). This brass pipe of either Bamum or Bagam manufacture (see Geary 1982) combines two icons of power: the head of the German military man and the highly stylized elephant head (upside down). The power of the Germans was only too evident when they defeated, plundered, and destroyed polities hostile to their rule. To this day Germans are referred to in Pidgin English as "strong," meaning powerful in a physical and political sense. Some Grassfields rulers would enter into uneasy and often ill-fated alliances with the new powers to enhance their standing in the region. The combination of new and old icons, the white soldier's head and the elephant, emblem of the chief, can thus be read as an apt metaphor of the rulers' appropriation and integration of new and old power. In addition, such pipes, which were not uncommon, catered to the tastes of German collectors and patrons, who would buy "curious and exotic" things while in Cameroon. Length 29.85 cm. Indiana University Art Museum. Gift of Ernst Anspach.

11-12 (ABOVE, RIGHT). Bronze pipe bowl collected in Bagam Bronze pipes were widely traded in the region, and this particular elephant head design was very popular with chiefs. The presence of four tusks is said to signify the importance of ivory in commercial trade. Height 6.35 cm. Staatliches Museum für Völkerkunde Dresden, Germany, no. 47240.

11-13 (RIGHT). In the 1920s, Bamum and Bagam brass casters produced large pipes with ornate bowls for foreign clientele, such as this elephant head with the superstructure of a male figure in high-status attire and holding a drinking horn. Height 55.88 cm. FMCH X63.459a,b. Museum purchase.

11-14. Chief Kana I of Bafu-Fondong in full regalia, sitting on a beaded stool with an elephant caryatid. The photograph was taken by professional photographer Joseph Eberhard in 1909, when he accompanied Theodor Seitz, the German governor of Kamerun, on a visit to the Grassfields. Rautenstrauch-Joest Museum, Köln, Germany, glass slide no. 3995.

Stools

Notable among the larger items were elephant stools ranging from representational to stylized and abstract forms. These were reserved for the rulers' use, mostly as state thrones for public occasions (Fig. 11-14). Two different styles of elephant stools roughly correspond to the northwestern and southern regions of the Grassfields. The carvers in Babanki-Tungo produced openwork stools with representational elephant heads (Figs. 11-15, 11-16), as well as stools supported by elephant caryatids. Like the ivory tusks, these prestige objects were traded widely and could be found all over the northwestern Grassfields. Of course, Babanki-Tungo's primacy as a carving center did not exclude other workshops in the area from producing elephant imagery.

Some of the finest elephant representations in the form of stools come from the Bamileke realm to the south. In contrast to the stools of the northwestern Grassfields, these works are covered with tin foil or brass overlay or elaborated with bead-covered cloth, and ranging from highly stylized to naturalistic (Figs. 11-17, 11-19, and 11-20).[15] A number of pieces bring more than one icon together in a powerful way. An exquisite caryatid combines the two most pervasive metaphors of chiefship, one half of the caryatid representing the elephant, the other the leopard (Fig. 11-18),[16] making this stool a particularly powerful metaphor of leadership. The tendency to accumulate and fuse icons is of course typical for Grassfields art and has been discussed in detail by Northern (1984:54).

11-15. This stool, inspired by European chair design, appears to be by the hand of Chief Fontshue Ase of Babanki-Tungo and carvers of his workshop, although its provenance is not documented. Height 80 cm. See Figure 11-16, below. FMCH X65.1624. Gift of the Wellcome Trust.

11-16. Chief Fontshue Ase of Babanki-Tungo is seen here carving a royal throne in 1912. Ase and his carvers used the elephant motif in many of their works. In the typical manner of Babanki carving, parts of the stools, such as the head of the animal and the rim, are blackened with a hot iron to create an intriguing interplay between light and dark. Photographer unknown. Museum für Völkerkunde Berlin, Germany, no. VIII A 1236.

11-17A (OPPOSITE), **B** (LEFT). This beaded stool combines a square base, more commonly found in the northwestern parts of the Grassfields, with an elephant caryatid typical of Bamileke carving. Although the actual provenance of this stool is unknown, it clearly originated in the Bamileke realm Height 30 cm. Diameter 25.5 cm. FMCH x89.73. Promised gift of Jerome L. Joss Collection.

11-18. A caryatid stool collected in 1905 by Captain Hans Glauning in Banssa (not far from Bafoussam), combines the two most pervasive metaphors of chieftainship: elephant and leopard. The elephant crouches, standing on sturdy legs ending in smooth round feet, as it does in nature. Tiny eyes, big ears and big tusks (which are joined together) allude to elephant characteristics. The row of teeth and the lack of a trunk, however, are departures from the model. The rim of the stool, covered with thin tinfoil overlay, is adorned with other Grassfields icons as well, such as the stylized frog/toad motif and the representation of cowries. Height 44.45 cm. Museum für Völkerkunde Berlin, Germany, no. III C 23814.

11-19 (OPPOSITE). A double-headed elephant caryatid supports this stool, collected in Bagam in around 1912 (Umlauff 1914: 44m no. 1066). The highly stylized elephant seems to be composed of triangles, from its bent legs to the surface design created by lavish beadwork, dominated by red tubular beads, the most valued in Bamileke society. In spite of intense blue trim, and the white beads highlighting tusks and eyes, the color scheme is unusually restrained: Bamileke artists and patrons delight in bright, polychrome creations. Wood, glass beads, cloth. Height 40.64 cm. Field Museum of Natural History, Chicago, no. 175558b.

11-20 (RIGHT). This human figure that merges with the elephant caryatid spreads its arms, an unusual posture in Grassfields iconography. Beaded thrones with single figures attached to their backs are known from the Kom kingdom, among others (Shanklin 1990a) and from Bamum (Geary 1983:156, pl. 25). Their interpretation differs. In Kom they clearly represent portraits of royals; in Bamum they may have represented retainers. Thus the meaning of the figure remains enigmatic. Collected by von Knobloch in Bafoussam in 1905. Wood, cloth, glass beads. Height 134.62 cm. Linden-Museum Stuttgart, Germany, no. 43018.

11-21. Slit gongs photographed in the Dshang region, c. 1912. Though stylized, the gong on the left shows details such as the tip of the trunk, curved tusks, smallish elephant eyes, flappy ears, and straight legs with large round feet supporting its bulk. The slit gong on the right is more abstract: tusks and trunk assume a circular configuration; round ears are moved forward and there appear to be no eyes. The gong seems to rest on its heavy body, its squarish legs barely touching the ground. An elephant effigy of smaller scale is attached to its end. The thatched house, rear, contains another, undecorated wooden slit gong. Photograph, Schröder. Field Museum of Natural History, Chicago, temporary no. 33801.

11-22. Elephant slit gong photographed in the Dshang region, c. 1910, by V. Sommerfeld, who supplied the Museum für Völkerkunde Berlin with ethnographica from the Grassfields. This gong shows a tendency towards geometric design. Museum für Völkerkunde Berlin, Germany, no. VIII A 1495.

Slit Gongs

Of all elephant representations, slit gongs, which occur in Bamum and many Bamileke chiefdoms, are by far the largest in scale. They are intimately tied to leadership (Geary 1989; Harter 1986:82-90; Lecoq 1953:147-49). Their bold configuration and enormous size have drawn the attention of the earliest travelers to the Grassfields (e.g. Hutter 1907:28-29). Most commonly, the gongs display large anthropomorphic and zoomorphic figures at one of their ends; some are fully transformed into an animal. In the Bamileke region, such slit gongs often took the shape of the elephant, ranging from fairly naturalistic to highly stylized representations. This tendency to reduce animal characteristics to their basic forms has given rise to speculations about the process of Grassfields design in general, which several scholars see as having evolved over time from the representational to the more schematized or even cubist (Harter 1986:345-49; Northern 1984:50-53).

Three slit gongs, documented only in historical photographs, exemplify the different artistic solutions. Two elephant gongs — one very naturalistic, the other more stylized, appear in a photograph taken in 1912 in the region of Dshang (Fig. 11-21); a third one (Fig. 11-22), photographed circa 1910 in the same region, exemplifies this tendency towards geometrization.

11-23. The elephant society in Bafut displays this gigantic masquerade structure of cloth, fiber, and raffia sticks. Typically, two men carry and manipulate the structure from within. Such structures are documented only in Bafut, Bangwa-Fontem, and Djottin. Photograph, J.N. Akosah, Bamenda, 1968.

These slit gongs belong in the leadership context for they are closely associated with leadership and warfare (Geary 1989). Such a gong was commissioned at the installation of a new chief; it would have been placed in a gong house (like that seen in Figure 11-21) in front of the chief's palace. The gongs' voices called together the inhabitants of the chiefdom for celebrations, in times of trouble, and when a military campaign got underway. In fact, there are indications that once the chief died, they were no longer used, but rather left to the elements, thus paralleling the chief's lifespan. Considering the slit gongs' close connection with chiefship, it is appropriate that they take the form of the elephant – the familiar of chiefs.

ELEPHANT MASKS

Of all the elephant imagery produced in the Grassfields, elephant masks are perhaps the best-known genre. According to their formal characteristics they can be divided into three major groups, each of which (with few exceptions) occurs in a distinct area of the Grassfields (see also Harter 1986:46-48). Huge elephant structures of cloth, fiber, and raffia sticks, which are carried around and manipulated by two men on the inside, have been documented or observed by foreign scholars only in Bafut, Bangwa-Fontem, and Djottin. Highly abstract mask figures with fiber and beaded cloth headpieces occur primarily throughout the Bamileke region. Finally, wooden elephant crests are most commonly found in the northwest, in Babanki, Oku, Kom, and neighboring polities.

Huge Elephant Structures

Father Emonts, a catholic missionary in the kingdom of Nso from 1912 to 1915, witnessed a dance of an elephant structure in the nearby chiefdom of Djottin and noted the entertainment character of the masquerade (1922:158). The structure consisted of a large elephant mask with huge ears, big tusks, and a trunk of about one meter in length. Two men inside the mat-and-cloth-covered body of the animal imitated the elephant's movements while the crowd stood silently in a circle around them. The spectators watched, but did not participate in the dance. Emonts remarked that this dance had once been extremely popular but was disappearing as elephants became extinct. Brain describes an "elephant machine" which performed during the funeral of an important Bangwa subchief in 1967 (1971:102). It came from another chiefdom on invitation of one of the neighboring chiefs and friends of the deceased and may have well been the elephant structure which to this day performs in Bafut (Fig. 11-23). Its name is *nse*, which means "elephant," and the men's society that owns it comes from Bawum, a Bafut subchiefdom, where it has existed for at least two generations. For a fee, the members attend funerals of important men. The society thus brings prestige to its members and entertains the crowd.[17]

Beaded Cloth Masks

The elementary force, brilliant color, and movement of Bamileke elephant masqueraders have often been captured in photographs and on film (Fig. 11-24).[18] But even though they are well known, we still lack good in-depth studies of their form and context, and Northern's statement that there are only rare references in published literature holds true to this day. Northern (1975:17-23) and Hunn (1985) essentially present compilations of a few rather cryptic primary and secondary sources on these masquerades, such as Brain and Pollock (1971), Lecoq (1953), and Littlewood (1954). Neither Harter (1986: 126-27) nor Savary (1980:26-27), who have both done art historical or ethnological fieldwork in the region, add much to our knowledge.

Based on these accounts, a sketchy picture emerges of elephant masks being associated with men's societies found in most Bamileke chiefdoms: the Kuosi, Nekang, and Kem-ndze.[19] These societies were initially warrior societies with regulatory character, which might explain the use of the elephant as a fitting metaphor. Over time they changed into prestige societies, assembling wealthy, titled men who pay for the privilege of being inducted, and pay further to advance within the group. Little is known about the inner structure and workings of these particular societies; however, they were most likely comparable to those of the Bangwa Aka society, one of whose

11-24 (ABOVE). Elephant masqueraders in Bandjoun, 1985. Photograph, C. Pavard, Hoa Qui Agency.

11-25 (OPPOSITE, TOP). Prestige paraphernalia, hoods, and headpieces of elephant masquerades from the region around Dshang and Bamum are displayed for the collector's camera in 1912. Long front and back "trunk" panels were made from bark cloth, raffia or hibiscus fiber and covered with local indigo cloth and trimmed with red trade cloth. Disc-like protrusions on either side of the head allude to the elephant's ears. The face is anthropomorphized, with nose and mouth made from cloth bulges. Fabric or bead-trimmed eye holes allow the wearer of the mask to see. Intricate disc-like or conical hats accompany the hoods. Note the geometric effects of bead design on hood and head pieces. A pipe with the elephant head bowl is held by the man at far left. Photograph, Schröder. Field Museum of Natural History, Chicago, no. 51177.

11-26 (OPPOSITE, BOTTOM). Elephant masqueraders from Babessi attending the funeral of Queenmother Njapundunke in Foumban, Bamum, in 1913. Typical of Bamileke elephant society costumes, these are of precious indigo resist-dyed cloth, embellished with prestige materials such as Colobus monkey fur, beaded vests and belts, and beaded horsetail flywhisks. The members of an elephant society added a contemporary touch: German-style military jackets! Photograph, Anna Wuhrmann. Archives of the Basel Mission, Switzerland, no. E-30.29.5,8 (K 2223).

11-27. Bamileke elephant mask. Length 148.5 cm. FMCH x82.569. Anonymous gift.

11-28. Beaded elephant helmet mask. Collection of the May Weber Museum of Cultural Arts, Chicago, Illinois.

11-29. Elephant masquerade with beaded wooden elephant helmet mask. Region of Dshang, c. 1930. Photograph, Chapoulie, Collection Viollet.

performances Brain and Pollock observed in Bangwa-Fontem. In its visual aspects, such as the costume of the masqueraders, Aka resembled Kuosi and Nekang, and the Bangwa had indeed borrowed this society from Bamileke neighbors to the east. It had three grades, and members could gain access to each grade through payments (Brain and Pollock 1971:100).

The complete mask costume of elephant masqueraders consists of prestige elements, such as a tunic of resist-dyed indigo-blue and white cotton cloth (*ndop*), trimmed with the fur of the rare Colobus monkey; ample *ndop* skirts, beaded vests, beaded wide belts, and horsetail fly whisks with beaded figurative handles. In Bafoussam, Bandjoun, and other Bamileke chiefdoms, the dancers wore leopard pelts on their backs (Lecoq 1953:56-58; Huet 1978:figs. 93,94), and sometimes, as in Foumban on the occasion of a Queen Mother's funeral in 1913, contemporary symbols of prestige were added (Fig. 11-26). The Bangwa designation of the elephant masquerader's costume as a "thing of money" aptly captures the prestige aspects, "money" referring to the imported

beads which were traded for slaves (Brain and Pollock 1971:100).

The fiber and cloth hoods (Figs. 11-25, 11-27), which fit over the head of the wearer, are characterized by a long front and back panel representing the trunk of the elephant. In some instances, both panels were joined together, forming a real "trunk" (Fig. 11-27). The cloth-covered and bead-embroidered panels were made from bark cloth, raffia or hibiscus fiber and covered with indigo-dyed, locally produced cotton fabric (Harter 1986:126). They were trimmed with red trade cloth (called *pet* in Bamum). Disc-like protrusions on either side of the head represent the elephant's ears. The face is anthropomorphized, with nose and mouth made from cloth bulges. Fabric or bead-trimmed eye holes allow the wearer of the mask to see (Cole 1985:Cover). Intricate disc-like or conical hats accompany the hoods. Other headpieces incorporate leopard or elephant figures (Northern 1975:37, 48-54) or are huge superstructures with zoomorphic and anthropomorphic configurations (Figs. 11-30 through 11-32).

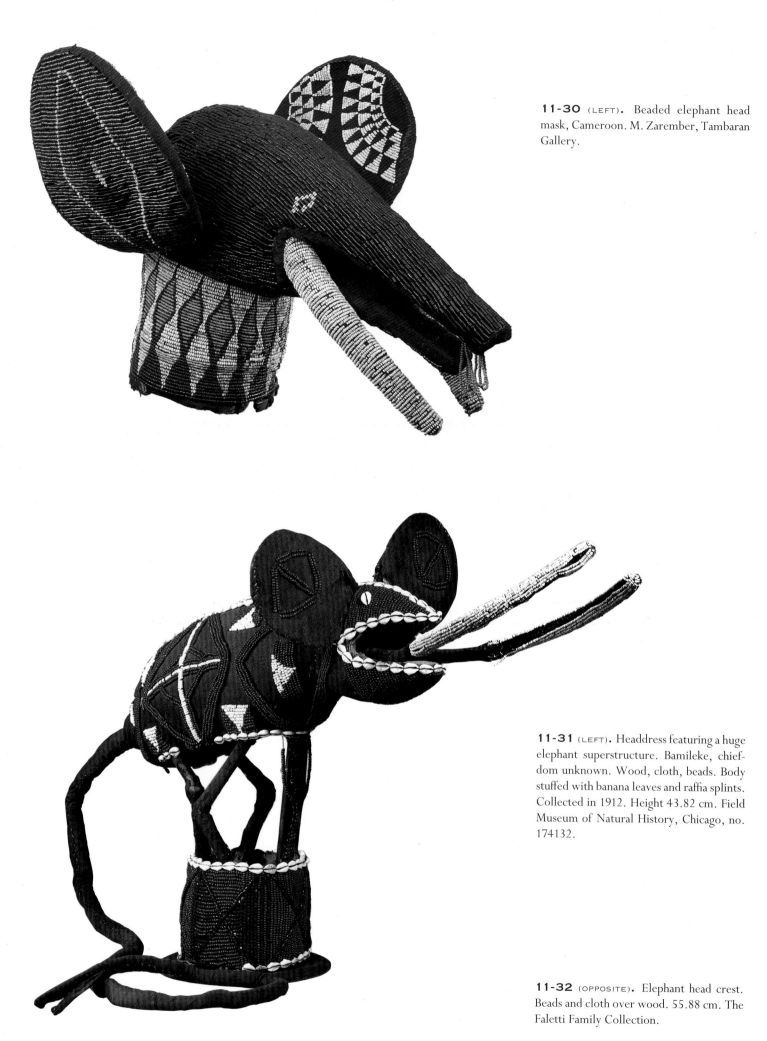

11-30 (LEFT). Beaded elephant head mask, Cameroon. M. Zarember, Tambaran Gallery.

11-31 (LEFT). Headdress featuring a huge elephant superstructure. Bamileke, chiefdom unknown. Wood, cloth, beads. Body stuffed with banana leaves and raffia splints. Collected in 1912. Height 43.82 cm. Field Museum of Natural History, Chicago, no. 174132.

11-32 (OPPOSITE). Elephant head crest. Beads and cloth over wood. 55.88 cm. The Faletti Family Collection.

11-33. Kana I of Bafu-Fondong poses with mask dancers in 1909. Historic photographs such as this and Figure 11-34 suggest that the elephant masks belonged to the masquerades of chiefs. Photograph, J. Eberhard. Rautenstrauch-Joest Museum, Cologne, no. 3870.

In some of these elephant masquerade performances, masqueraders wore huge wooden beaded elephant helmet masks. One of the most stunning examples is represented by a photograph taken in the Dshang area around 1930 (Fig. 11-29). Judging by this image, one could easily conclude that this mask took a leading role in the performance. It is nearly identical in form to a much smaller beaded wooden helmet mask of undocumented provenance in the Fowler Museum (Fig. 11-28). There are at least two other examples of this type of mask in collections, both of them without beadcover, however. One was collected by Franz Thorbecke in Fongdonera near Dshang in 1908 and belongs to collections of the Museum für Völkerkunde Berlin (Krieger and Kutscher 1960:61, no. III C 28874). It is 111 cm wide and 50 cm high. The other is in a private collection (see Harter 1986:pl. XXVII). In the caption, Harter describes this as a "royal elephant mask" from Bafu Fondong, a chiefdom not far from Dshang, and a center of elephant imagery (See also Figs. 11-14, 11-33). All these elephant helmet masks come from the same region and show similar stylistic characteristics: enormous size, a large mouth extending into a trunk, and pronounced tusks, as well as big, circular or oval ears.

There is to date no systematic study of the design of these masks. Information on the artists who produced them is equally lacking: whether for instance, there were several artists, such as tailors and bead embroiderers, whether there existed spe-cialized workshops in particular chiefdoms where members of the societies could commission the head pieces. Other questions which cannot be answered at this point pertain to the exact range of materials from which the masks were made. Was there any color symbolism associated with the bead design? Which type of imported beads were preferred? Can one see changes in these masks that could be attributed to changing economic and historical circumstances?

The lack of good documentation equally hinders an analysis of the temporal, spatial, and musical aspects of their performances. Members of the elephant society met regularly on a particular day of the eight-day week, similar to many other societies in the Bamileke region and in Bamum.[20] Such gatherings served to carry out the society's mission, namely to practice music and dance for celebrations, to create cohesion between the members, and to socialize. Performances took place during annual festivals, at funerals of chiefs and, one may assume, members of the society. Brain and Pollock (1971:100-101), who describe such an appearance in Bangwa-Fontem during the funeral of a chief, found that most elephant societies in the Bangwa chiefdoms had lapsed and been replaced by new

exotic societies for men which combined novelty with an equally effective display of wealth. According to their observations, the elephant society dancers presented themselves to the audience in slow procession around the dancing field. They carried spears and horsetails and waved poles. Their movements were deliberate and their whistling mysterious. Only a drum and an iron gong accompanied them, as if not to upstage the dancers with a large imposing orchestra. Judging by this account, it was a solemn and deliberate display, rather than the sort of complex and vigorous dance performances marking other masquerades in the Grassfields, that drew attention to these masked incarnations of high rank and prestige in Bangwa-Fontem.

The connection between chiefs and elephant masking societies still needs exploration. Clearly, the masqueraders have access to materials and icons reserved for the ruler, such as leopard pelts and imagery, horsetails, beaded human figures on flywhisk handles, valuable beads, and of course the elephant icon itself, all of which express their closeness to the chief. It would be interesting to examine the mechanisms by which such privileged materials were acquired. Indeed, the movement of these "things" in society relates a complex picture of checks and balances to Bamileke chiefship. Whether elephant masks were solely part of masquerades of these men's societies needs to be researched. I suspect that upon closer examination one would find that elephant masks also belonged to the masquerades of chiefs, as historical photographs suggest; in one, the chief himself wears the most spectacular elephant mask of all (Figs. 11-33, 11-34).

Bamileke elephant masks thus remain enigmatic. An attempt to interpret their meaning relies on several general observations. The Kuosi/Nekang/Aka and Kem-ndze societies obviously embodied prestige and wealth, although they assumed slightly different tasks. Kuosi emphasized bellicosity, and Kem-ndze safeguarded the law of the land. Their elephant masks articulated the multiple functions of these societies in form and media, for they embodied the major ideological premises on which the chiefdoms – and with it the two types of societies – were founded. One was the constancy of warfare, that is, the exertion of power and authority over an ever increasing number of people brought into the chiefdoms by force; the second was the accumulation of wealth to advance in rank (Geary 1988).

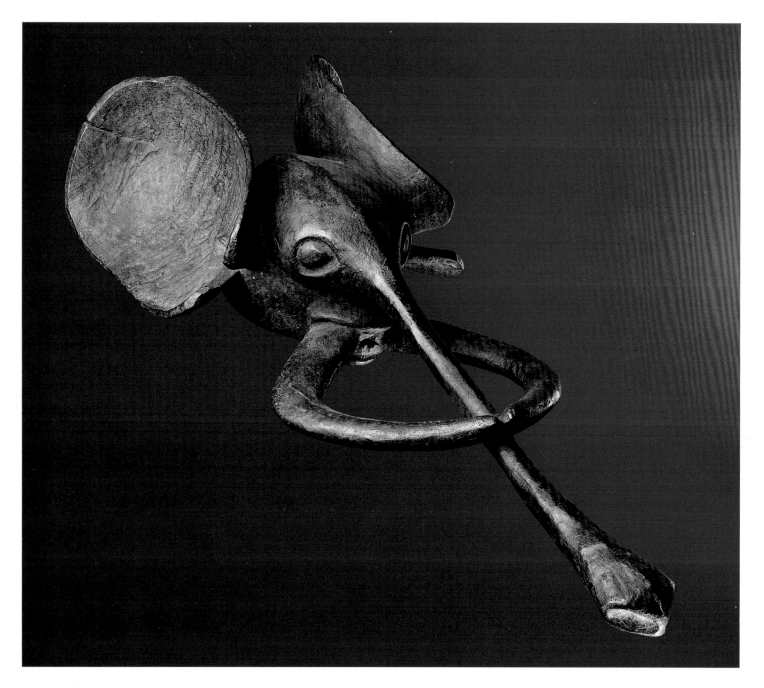

Wooden Crest Masks

Peoples in the northwestern Grassfields, having chosen an entirely different mask configuration, represent the elephant in the form of wooden crests which are produced to this day (Fig. 11-2).[21] The most common type originates from the carving centers of Oku, Babanki, and other workshops in this general area. It is a highly conventionalized crest with large convex ears, a rounded head which merges with a straight trunk, a gaping mouth with exposed teeth under the trunk, gently curved tusks on either side, and typically almond-shaped, incised eyes (Fig. 11-35, 11-36). The earliest examples of this type came into German collections shortly after the turn of this century (Germann 1910:pl. 3, no. 27).

The context of these crests remained unexplored until recent fieldwork revealed that they belonged to larger mask ensembles owned by important lineage heads and chiefs (Koloss 1977; Northern 1984; Shanklin 1982). These groups of masks,

comprising from five or six to over twenty masks, are widely known as kum[22] (or in Pidgin English, juju) and performed mainly during funerals and annual festivals. As both Koloss and Shanklin have shown, Oku and Kom masquerade ensembles include obligatory male and female protagonists, the male leader-mask kam, and the female mask ngoin.[23] Kam controls the performance and fends off adversaries and dangers. Besides these, other human characters may appear, such as Warrior, Old man, Widow, and even masks portraying particular members of the lineage (Koloss 1977:51-54). Animal masks include Buffalo, Ram, Chameleon, Flying Dog or Bat, and finally Elephant, which, if at all present in the mask ensemble, assumes the position of the final mask, protecting the others from enemies and from the bad medicines that envious people might have put in its way. As the final protagonist in the procession, the elephant mask is in effect the counterpart to the male leading mask and thus elevated above all other animal masks.

The privilege of owning such an elephant mask may or may not be vested in the chiefs or kings. In Oku, elephant masks can only be owned by the chiefly lineage, which once more manifests the close relationship of chief and elephant.[24] By contrast, in Weh, a village chiefdom with weak chiefship and influential patrilineages, elephant masks were not restricted to the chiefly lineage. For a small fee in kind, wealthy compound owners would acquire the right to create their own masquerade (*kumm*) from other masquerade owners in the village or in neighboring communities. They would then commission the necessary mask types – first the *kamm* leader mask and then the female *ngow*. Various animal masks were added until the ensemble was completed and looked impressive.

When I did research in Weh in 1984, most lineage masquerades had not been performed in years because their masks had been sold or had decayed. Some elderly carvers still knew how to carve masks, but they received no commissions. A man, then in his seventies, was one of the last men to create a lineage masquerade. In the 1940s, when he was a young man and had just returned from working in the coastal plantations, he had the inspiration for a masquerade he called *bafutori*.[25] He asked several other owners of *kumm* in the village for permission to create his own masquerade and gave each of them two chickens and raffia palmwine.[26] He then commissioned two carvers to make the masks for him. They included *kamm* and *ngow*, as well as masks representing Buffalo, Ram, Bushpig, and Elephant. Subsequently, his masquerade was performed at funerals, during *dzitisem* (the period when young men underwent rites of passages), and in later years when important government officials visited Weh.[27]

In the polities of this northern region of the Grassfields, these masking groups were clear expressions of a prestige economy accentuating wealth and the achievement of lineages, or more recently of individuals who had made good, as in the case of the man in Weh. Only a wealthy lineage head would have the means to acquire the rights to a masquerade, to commission the masks, and to recruit enough followers to perform splendidly. The masquerades thus represent symbolic capital in visual form, resembling the Bamileke elephant societies which also alluded to similar concepts of wealth and influence.

Yet from these examples in the northwestern Grassfields other interpretations of the masquerades emerge. In their masked dance, the *kumm* masking ensembles replicate social structure and history of the political unit, a meaning shared with a royal masquerade which used to be performed in the kingdom of Bamum as part of the annual *nja* festival (Geary 1983: 130-34 and 1990; Tardits 1980:790-93). The highlight of the day-long festival was a procession of up to one hundred human and animal masks, which articulated the Bamum universe. Human masks consisted of a huge leader mask which could well be interpreted as representing the king, and male and

Elephant masks (*nkum nsüo*) from the northwestern Grassfields.

11-35 (OPPOSITE). Length 115 cm. Collection of Dr. and Mrs. Ernest Fantel.

11-36 (ABOVE). Height 79 cm. Private collection.

female helmet masks, alluding to the palace organization. The predominant animal masks were buffalo crests metaphorically alluding to the royal servants who were equated with the buffalo in strength and determination when they had to protect the king. Crocodile, birds, rams, and elephant masqueraders followed in the long single-file procession, all wearing tunics and rattles around their ankles.

Since *nja* has not been performed since the 1920s, many of the *nja* masks have been destroyed or sold, but one of the elephant masks is still part of the Bamum Palace Museum collection (Fig. 11-37). With its small elephant eyes, large ears, and somewhat shortened trunk it exemplifies nineteenth-century Bamum carving which was characterized by high degree of naturalism. It is covered with local indigo-dyed

11-37. Elephant mask. Wood, cloth, glass beads, cowries. Height 65 cm. Bamum Palace Museum, Foumban. Photograph, Christraud M. Geary, 1977.

cotton cloth and embroidered with cowries and trade beads. The cloth and bead covering of carvings exemplifies the Bamum accumulation of prestige media reserved for royalty, and reflects the different sources of inspiration for Bamum artists. Located at major trade routes, Bamum maintained close connection with the peoples in the Northwestern Grassfields and as well as with its Bamileke neighbors. Thus Bamum masks seem to combine the wooden mask tradition of the Northwest and the cloth mask tradition of the Bamileke peoples.

Festivals like *nja* can be interpreted in functional terms as the annual renewal of the state and the assertion of solidarity of its inhabitants. Yet such events give insight into cosmological concepts, into the way the protagonists perceive and construct their world. In the *nja* masquerade, the Bamum universe is put on display, and it is a tamed, highly organized universe in which each being assumes its proper place in the hierarchy. The animals of the wilderness have been domesticated and integrated into the realm of beings all dominated by the gigantic leader mask, by the king himself. The masquerade thus becomes a performed metaphor for Bamum view of the world, Bamum dominance, wealth, social structure, and history.

In the final analysis, the role of the elephant, its ivory, and tail hairs in the Grassfields peoples' material discourse has evolved from broader conceptualizations of the world in which animals in general and the elephant in particular assume symbolic significance. The concrete reality of the elephant's strength and destructive powers and of the highly valued materials it provided made it one of the catalysts in the symbolic systems of thought of the Grassfields peoples. Its evocation of the powers of the wild and its economic value when subdued make it an apt metaphor of economic and political power. Deeply embedded in the Grassfields peoples' systems of thought, the elephant has thus proven a resilient metaphor, despite its extinction at the beginning of this century.

NOTES

1. There are no common designations for related units, with the exception of "Bamileke," an ethnic label which the colonials assigned populations in the southern part of the region, because they are closely tied and have created a multitude of chiefdoms resembling each other in political structure (Littlewood 1954:87).
2. Some of the political units are matrilineal, such as the kingdom of

Kom, while others, located at crossroads, integrated both patrilineages and matrilineages. The patrilineal chiefdom of Weh in the north of the Grassfields has harbored many migrants from neighboring matrilineal political units and thus both forms of descent can be found in its boundaries. Among the many patrilineal polities are large states, such as Bamum and Bafut.

3. The term *fon* (also found in variations such as *fo* and *foyn*) has been translated as "leader," "chief," or "king," depending on different authors' preferences. In this paper, I am using the term "king" for rulers of centralized, large polities, whereas "chief" denotes rulers of smaller, but not necessarily differently organized political units.

4. A good example is Bamum and the rise to political power of King Njoya at the turn of this century. His rule was endangered by political rivals, until he was aided by his alliances with the Fulbe ruler of Banyo and with the Germans.

5. This situation varies according to regions in the Cameroon Grassfields. In Bamum, for instance, the royal masquerades which included animal masks, have not been performed in their prescribed forms since the 1920s. In smaller places, such as Weh on the northern periphery, most masks were sold in the 1950s and masquerades rarely take place. In some areas, however, such as Kom or Bafut, the changes have not been as radical as elsewhere.

6. Ruel made similar observations among the Banyang, who live to the south of the Grassfields in the Cross River area (1969:49-59).

7. There are many historical narratives about the secession of political units, in which the renegade act is played out in the constitutive idiom of rights over animals. When the small hamlet of Zua in the northern parts of the Grassfields seceded from the village chiefdom of Weh, the new leader appropriated the leopard due the chief of Weh. This was, in effect, the official declaration of independent status. Rights over particular animals thus enact the prerogatives of leadership (Geary 1976:83-86).

8. Marion Johnson (1978) has traced this trade in her essay on the struggle for the ivory originating in the Cameroon and has shown that the direction of the trade changed during the 19th century. At the beginning of the 19th century, ivory reached the coast in considerable quantities and was then diverted by Hausa traders to major markets on the Niger and Benue, only to be re-directed once more to the coast when the Germans had appropriated Cameroon.

9. During the so-called Congo Conference of Berlin in 1884-85, Africa was partitioned among the European powers and Cameroon officially placed under German rule. The Germans remained in Cameroon until 1916, when they left as a result of the First World War. The colony was then divided into two parts under British and French colonial rule.

10. Elephant tails were sold by Hausa traders who supposedly fashioned necklaces out of them, to trade with populations around Ibi in what is now Nigeria. The Hausa would buy a tail for a thousand cowries in Bamum or the Tikar region and sell it for twenty to twenty-five thousand cowries in the areas around Ibi, making a remarkable profit.

11. The Bamum King Njoya also commissioned the Babanki-Tungo chief to carve a royal bed for him, which is now in the collection of the Bamum Palace Museum in Foumban. In return for Fontshue Ase's services, Njoya gave him several wives (Geary 1983:127-58; Emonts 1922:171-72).

12. Tita means "father" and is a title of honor bestowed on important men.

13. Harter (1986:186-92) gives the history of the carvers in Babanki-Tungo and Big-Babanki and analyzes their works. Yuefainyi is spelled "Aseh Yufanyi," and Fontshue Ase appears as "Phonchu Aseh" in his text. I am using Harter's dating of their reigns. Fontshue Ase was none other than the famous artist chief whom missionary Emonts introduced to the German readership in 1922 (Emonts 1922:168-74).

14. The beaded gourd shown in Figure 11-10 is part of the Field Museum of Natural History's large Cameroon collection acquired from J.F.K. Umlauff in Hamburg. The original German catalogue accompanying the photographs of the objects is still in the museum. In many instances it specifies the chiefdoms in which the objects were *collected* by specialists working for Umlauff. These men had basic training in collection techniques and were aware of the fact that museums needed information on the origin of the collections. Of course the chiefdom where pieces were

documented as being collected is not necessarily where they were *made*. A very similar calabash, collected in Bamum, belongs to the collection of the Museum für Völkerkunde in Dresden (Arnold 1980:35, pl. 18).

15. The example seen in Figure 11-19, from the Linden-Museum in Stuttgart, was collected in Bafoussam in 1905 and was not exhibited until after undergoing extensive restoration several years ago. Indeed, most of the known beaded elephant stools of this type come from an area that extends roughly from Bagam in the north, to Bangangte in the south, Bafu-Fondong in the east, and Bafoussam in the west.

16. The stool pictured in Figure 11-18 was collected by Captain Hans Glauning and came to the Museum für Völkerkunde in Berlin with Glauning's estate after his death in 1908 (Archives of the Museum für Völkerkunde Berlin, File no. E 2068/08). A museum worker compiled an "emergency" list of objects, which might explain the questionable provenance given to this stool in the Berlin catalogues. Supposedly Glauning collected it in Banso (kingdom of Nso), albeit there is a question mark (Krieger 1969:14, no. III C23814; see also Northern 1984:107). In the original list of the estate, Banso is spelled "Bansso" which may be a misreading of Banssa. It is indeed much more likely that Glauning (1905) collected the stool in Banssa during a military expedition in 1905. He also acquired another, very similar stool in Baham, 15 miles south of Banssa (Krieger 1969:13, no. III C20341). The piece compares favorably with an elephant caryatid which Harter photographed in the Bamileke chiefdom of Balum, a neighbor of Banssa, and attributed to the hand of Mintan, a carver who worked for almost fifty years for the chiefs of Balum and whose carvings may well have been traded to other chiefs in the region (Harter 1986:255).

17. I thank Ronald Engard for the information on the exact origin of the society.

18. Rarely have photographers missed the chance to present these masks in lavish picture books. See for example Huet (1978:ills. 90-98) and Etienne-Nugue (1982:figs. 120,121). An elephant masquerader also graced a Cameroon Airlines poster in the 1970s.

19. Various spellings appear in the literature, not only because writers have chosen different transcriptions, but also because there exist local variations of the terms in the more than ninety Bamileke chiefdoms.

20. All over the Grassfields, the week traditionally comprised eight days, including six workdays, one day of rest from farmwork (the day the societies met), and a market day. Although many now obey a seven-day week, women farmers follow the traditional calendar.

21. These are part of many European and American collections.

22. In many languages of the northwestern part of the Grassfields, *nkum*, *kum*, or closely related terms with singular and plural prefixes are the most widely used designations for the mask persona. In Weh, for example, *kumm nutshu'ume* designates a mask persona with a carved mask as headpiece, while *kumm ntenju* indicates that the mask persona wears a feather headdress only. The term for the single wooden mask is *kummetou* (the head of the *kumm*).

23. These terms and their variations are also widely used in the area (see for example Koloss 1977:51-54). In Weh, the terms are *kamm* and *ngow* respectively.

24. In Oku, the final mask of lineage masquerades would be a buffalo crest (Koloss 1977:51).

25. The name indicates that he probably based it on examples from Bafut, although he did not say so when I questioned him about this point. He stated that the name "came from the Coast."

26. The system of acquiring societies either within or from outside Weh has been described by Geary (1979).

27. In 1984, the masquerade had not performed for two years because the owner had been accused of witchcraft and was "locked" in his house, which meant that he was shunned by the community and not permitted to participate in any social gatherings, least of all bring out his masks.

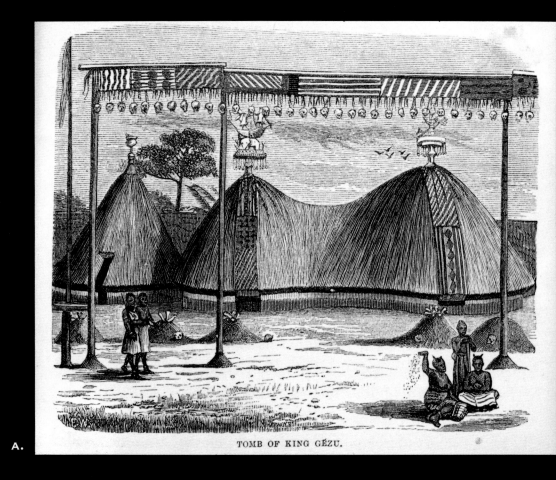

TOMB OF KING GÉZU.

A.

A. The tomb of Gézu [Guezo]. From Skertchly 1874:437.

B. Palace wall of King Behanzin, Abomey, Dahomey. Photograph, Guy Mols.

C. Elephant figure from the Republic of Benin (Fon peoples). 19th Century. Silver. Height 12 inches, length 23 5/8 inches. The Metropolitan Museum of Art, Lent anonymously, L.1980.76.2.

D,E. Altars (*asen*) from the Republic of Benin (Fon peoples): Left, height 115 cm; Right, height 128 cm. Musée Barbier-Mueller. Photographs, P.A. Ferazzin.

B.

AMONG THE FON PEOPLES OF BENIN (formerly Dahomey), the elephant is most closely associated with two 19th-century kings, Guezo (1818-1858) and his son Glele (1858-1889). Elephants appear quite often on memorial staffs (*asen*) commissioned to honor deceased relatives, each functioning as "a visual praise poem that links the living to the dead" (Bay 1985:9). *Asen* images derive special meaning from oral literature. An *asen* dedicated to Guezo by Glele evoked two aphorisms: *If the elephant defecates in a basket, it takes very little for it to be filled* and *The animals pass without leaving a trace, only the elephant leaves traces* (Mercier 1952:38). Both celebrate the sheer size of the elephant, and by extension the king it represents.

The silver elephant is linked with royal ancestral veneration and may be a memorial to a dead king (Blier 1988:134). Relief images of elephants are found on the palaces of Glele (Blier 1991:46) and King Behanzin (left). King Guezo's tomb (above) was topped by an elaborate elephant roof finial, described in some detail by Skertchly (1874:437-438):

> … a square disc of silver with a raised border, and a string of silver hearts dangling from its lower edge. Above this an elephant, standing in the middle of a number of silver trees like laurels, had overthrown a soldier. On the back of the elephant was a ship, with mast and three soldiers two of whom rivaled the mast in altitude, while the third, much smaller held a cannon on his lap, on top of the mast. The allegory is that as soldiers who go out to shoot elephants are often killed by them, so the enemies of Dahomey who look with envious eyes upon the kingdom must be destroyed.

TWELVE

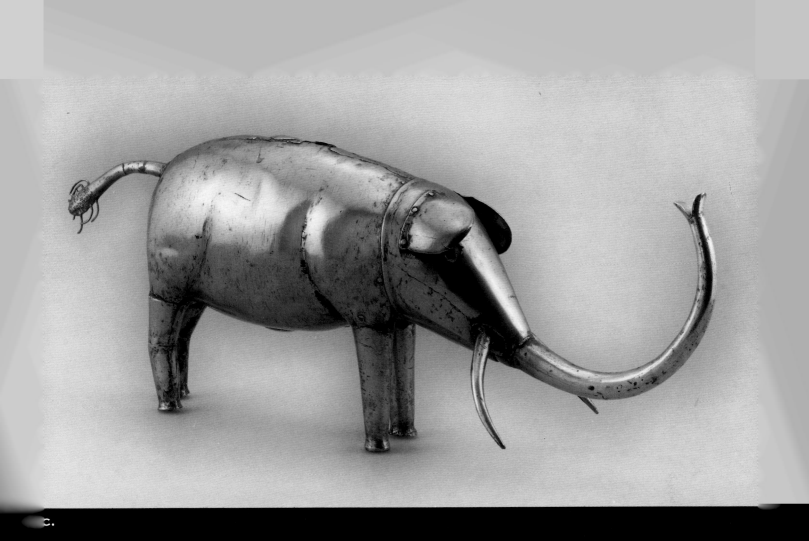

ELEPHANTS, IVORY, AND ART

DUALA OBJECTS OF PERSUASION

ROSALINDE G. WILCOX

The Duala are a riverine people who live in and around the port city of Douala,[1] Cameroon, and the region of the Wouri estuary. The low-lying terrain along the coast and in the estuary is characterized by mangrove swamps and a crisscrossing of rivers and creeks that extend into the interior. The Duala economy, spiritual beliefs, and material culture reflect this environment. Much of Duala expressive culture centers on the maritime arts, which culminate in dugout racing, *pembisan*. Of the animals populating the Duala artistic vocabulary, it is not the elephant and its confreres, but rather sea and swamp creatures, such as serpents, sea birds, and water fowl, that dominate. Nevertheless, the elephant plays an important role in Duala verbal arts and its appearance in material culture is not insignificant (Fig. 12-1).

Although elephants are gone from the forests around Douala today, European trading accounts indicate that two hundred years ago they were present in great numbers. It is certain that the elephant's economic importance to the Duala increased in the course of the ivory trade, even as the animals themselves disappeared from the coast. For centuries the Duala trading network brought them into contact with African and European peoples. Gradually it placed them at the nexus of a trade that changed their relationship with the elephant and influenced their arts. Duala material culture is an aggregate of both indigenous and foreign realities; the latter broadened the

spectrum of subjects and ultimately reinforced the image of the elephant in Duala art.

Even when small, the elephant is lord of the bush[2]

For the Duala as for surrounding groups, the elephant's size and strength translate into a metaphor for authority. The elephant is associated with potency and greatness, qualities frequently assigned to the leopard by Duala neighbors.[3] Both animals were represented by closed associations[4] which proliferated along the coast in the nineteenth century. The Leopard Society, Ekpe, operated mostly in the territory adjacent to Duala trading areas; the Duala themselves had an Elephant Society, Njou, which is no longer extant (Ittmann 1976:435).

Duala folktales and proverbs like the one cited above describe the special role of the elephant. Many proverbs about Elephant are lessons in power and bring into focus admirable leadership qualities — for example responsibility: *The elephant never tires of carrying his tusks*[5]; wisdom and diplomacy: *The elephant does not listen to those who talk behind him*[6]; and

12-1 (OPPOSITE). Detail of a carved canoe prow ornament, *tange*, collected in 1884 and now in the Staatliches Museum für Völkerkunde, Munich. See full prow ornament in Figure 12-10b.

12-2. Decorated stools are associated with chieftaincy and leadership. Known in English as chief's 'palaver' stools, and in Duala as *bekoko* (*ekoko,* s.), they are carved from a single block of wood, open at the sides and elaborately ornamented, front and back. The elephant motif is a metaphor for power; it may also may refer to the Duala Elephant Society, Njou. The elephant is surrounded by "mythical creatures" (Museum accession notes). Wood. Length 50.17 cm. No. III C 43774, Museum für Völkerkunde, Berlin.

interdependency and community support: *One cannot cut up an elephant with one hand.*[7]

Similar associations between elephant and authority are suggested visually. Elephants appear, for example, on some of the carved wooden stools that are emblems of chiefly status[8] (Figs. 12-2, 12-3[9]). Other genres of Duala-carved wooden objects bearing elephant iconography include canoe prow ornaments, racing dugout replicas,[10] and masking forms such as horizontal headpieces (see below). Much of what we recognize as Duala art is based on our knowledge of artifacts collected by missionaries, traders, and government officials in and around Douala from the late nineteenth century until just before the outbreak of World War II. Many changes took place during that time. By the nineteenth century, European paints and images of weapons and luxury goods had been introduced into the Duala artistic repertoire. Christianity

became the dominant religion of the coastal and forest regions, and as missionaries influenced indigenous art production, Duala material culture was transformed. Some of the artifacts created under missionary influence were modifications of the traditional Duala stool. Others were entirely new forms based on European furniture types, such as the table produced at the Basel Missionary Society Mangamba station (Fig. 12-4), some fifty kilometers from Douala. When literacy became widespread, figurative imagery was frequently replaced by letters, names, and words.

It is not the elephant who wants for ivory[11]

Ivory as a commodity was profoundly important in shaping Duala life from the eighteenth century onward. Europeans singled out one feature of the elephant, the tusks, and in unparalleled greed, coveted them almost to extinction. For centuries their insatiable demand for ivory, their willingness to pay any price, their efforts to control ivory commerce, and finally their love of elephant hunting as a sport had to have exercised an impact on the Duala beyond the economic rewards of the ivory trade.

Seventeenth-century trading accounts indicate the existence of an ivory and slave trade in the estuary,[12] but it was not until the eighteenth century that the Duala began to

operate as middlemen in the trade between the Europeans anchored in vessels off-shore and the hinterland groups. The vigorous competition to establish trade relations with Europeans brought about changes in the Duala social and political structure,[13] ultimately empowering two major lineages, Bell (Bonanjo) and Akwa (Bonembela), and later several smaller lineages.[14] Bell and Akwa lineage heads were known then as kings, while lesser figures were known as chiefs.

By the mid-eighteenth century the Duala had taken advantage of their position as trade intermediaries, monopolizing the access between the interior peoples and Europeans, and thereby establishing themselves as the paramount traders of coastal Cameroon. Records of the Dutch Middelburgh Commercial Company indicate that ivory was the preferred export trade item (Austen 1974:13), which the Duala supplied in increasing amounts. Records do not indicate whether the Duala themselves did the killing, and if they did, in what numbers. One may assume that at the beginning of the ivory trade, they hunted elephants in the coastal forests surrounding what is now Douala. Shortly after annexing the area in the late nineteenth century, the German colonial government banned Duala elephant hunting, much to the chagrin of local leaders.

Well before the German ban on Duala hunting, however, the rapid acceleration of European demand for ivory had forced the Duala to maintain suppliers indigenous to the

12-3 (RIGHT). Chief Felix Ewande's stool shows his coat of arms flanked by two elephants. Today stools remain an important part of chiefly regalia, and a chief receives his stool during his installation ceremony. Elephant imagery may have become more popular since Cameroon independence. The elephant is no longer part of the Duala economy or ecology, but its reemergence as a symbol of authority may be associated with the power of the elephant as expressed in the verbal arts, which has generated its popularity as a visual image. Photograph, Rosalinde G. Wilcox, Douala, May 1989.

elephant's forest habitat. The Kundu, who hunted the elephant until the early twentieth century, were one of several groups obtaining ivory for the Douala depot. Among the Kundu and other coastal forest peoples, the severed tail of a slain elephant proved the hunter's deed and became his victory trophy. Hunters also wove the hairs of the elephant's tail into good luck arm bands (Ittmann 1939:158). The tusks were particularly valuable, and ivory armbands were worn by esteemed men and their wives (p. 159). Ivory trumpets, known as signal horns, were also used in this region, often in connection with closed associations. Such instruments were communal property, according to Ittmann, and could be used only by appropriate persons.

The indigenous use of ivory has always been minor in contrast to the amount shipped to European markets. From

12-4 (RIGHT). Table with carved elephant motifs made at the Basel Mission Mangamba station. Missionaries would have proposed the European shape, but the motifs appear more African than European, with elephants, geometric patterns, and birds (other side). Wood. Height 60 cm. No. III 23015, Basel Mission collection, Basel. Photograph, Rosalinde G. Wilcox.

12-5. Insignia for German Kamerun combining the imperial eagle and the African elephant. From Hücking and Launer (1986:back cover).

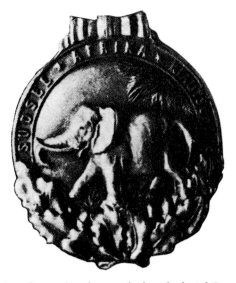

12-6. Elephant depicted on the army badge of colonial German troops. From Tantum and Hoffschmidt (1968:178).

1700 to 1750 the Dutch traded iron bars, copper basins, salt, beads, bells, cloths, guns, and powder (Austen 1974:20) for more than 56,000 lb. (25,200 kg) of ivory (Austen and Derrick Ms.). This figure represents only the recorded amount of ivory traded to the Middleburgh Commercial Company and does not include unrecorded amounts of ivory taken out of Cameroon during those years. The ivory obtained by the Duala during the early part of that century was most likely the forest-zone variety sent to the coast from the interior (Austen 1974:15). Later in the century it was replaced by white savannah ivory from the Grassfields to the north.[15]

The English supplanted the Dutch in the mid-eighteenth century as the major traders in the region (Austen and Derrick Ms.). During the nineteenth century ivory continued to be an important trade item. The ivory acquired in Cameroon was described as a very superior quality:

> The ivory is generally speaking very large, as well of an excellent species; and so inexhaustible is the supply here, that sixty tons are known to have been procured in one season by English vessels and Portuguese from the islands. (Bold 1819:87-88)

While the English remained active in the Wouri estuary, they were joined by traders from other European countries. In 1884, Germany declared the Wouri estuary and surrounding coastline the Cameroon Protectorate. By this time, Douala was no longer the exclusive ivory depot on the coast. Hausa controlled the long-distance ivory trade, negotiating the tusks from the Grassfields to the large markets along the Niger and Benue rivers and at Calabar. The Germans intervened and, at the beginning of this century, successfully recaptured the trade by diverting the Hausa northern ivory route to the Cameroon coast. By forcefully establishing direct trade relations between the southern ivory markets and the coast, the Germans also eliminated all middlemen from the ivory trade, including the

Duala (Johnson 1978:542-46). The German takeover of the ivory trade produced some interesting results. German exports destined for Africa, reflecting the latest German scientific technology, included celluloid armrings to be "worn by the natives as ivory substitutes."[16]

The importance Europeans attached to the elephant was manifest in the visual references they incorporated into their own power emblems, such as ships, flags, and uniforms. Many images of seventeenth-century ships reveal elephants carved on the sterns.[17] Nineteenth-century European images of the elephant appear not only on ships, but on symbols of community identity, such as flags, banners, and coats of arms, for example the insignia for German Kamerun (Fig. 12-5). On the 1914 German Army badge for its colonial troops (Fig. 12-6), the elephant represents all German colonies. The animal assumed connotations of wealth, authority and conquest, both to the Duala and the Europeans, and converged in icons that were equated with power.

The elephant tusk is more valuable than the elephant[18]

The concept of ivory as an object of trade is clearly expressed in the Duala proverb above, recorded by a Basel missionary. Given that the Duala were middlemen in the ivory trade, the literal interpretation is obvious; but according to missionary Hecklinger, this proverb extended metaphorically to other trading aspects of Duala culture. To the Duala, it also applied to the practice of bride price. The missionary's informants explained: A Duala high chief takes a wife from the Bakoko tribe, a neighboring people, and pays 1,000 Mark in goods for her. She then gives birth to a daughter. With her marriage, 5,000 Mark in goods must be paid in bride price, since she is the daughter of a Duala high chief, i.e., the wife is the elephant, her daughter's bride price are the tusks (Hecklinger 1920/21:127).

King Bell and King Akwa were "great holders of ivory," according to one English merchant (Bold 1819:89). Never-

12-7A, B (TWO VIEWS). The elephant and the elephant hunter. Wood, paint. Length 71.12cm. Kam. 109. Bernisches Historisches Museum, Bern. Photographs, Rosalinde G. Wilcox.

theless, except for ivory earplugs[19] and bracelets worn by persons of rank as chiefly insignia or prestige objects, ivory was rarely used either ritually or for personal adornment. It seems ivory was worth more to the Duala as a commodity than as a display of local social status. Duala leaders capitalized on the value Europeans placed on ivory and used it to promote and strengthen their position with the colonial administration. A letter dated 26 January 1903, written on behalf of King Manga Ndumbe Bell, tells of two gifts being shipped to the Kaiser as a gesture of friendship and good will, and in gratitude for an audience and a photograph. The first gift was a carved wooden stool, in general shape and style probably like the one seen in Figure 12-5. In the event that the Kaiser was unimpressed by the stool, the second gift was intended to be more convincing:

> Although the stool does not possess special artistic value, because the request from the so-named paramount chief carries the highest feelings, permit me, with hindsight, to request from your majesty the emperor, [his] benevolent acceptance as a gift, two elephant tusks from Manga Bell's personal property. (ZSP/RKA 4102:72)

The stated purpose of his letter was to thank the Kaiser, but King Bell also hoped to address troubling changes in German colonial policy that threatened many Duala liberties, including hunting rights. Formerly, the German government and German commercial ventures had operated from coastal locations. Now they intended to take an active role in the interior. New German restrictions included an injunction that the Duala were not "to hunt…elephants and hippopotami, with rifles or other hunting weapons" within a large area (Rüger 1968, II:197). In July 1902, King Bell petitioned the German Foreign Office to restore local hunting rights, citing loss of personal income without which he would no longer be in the position to employ and sustain his people (p. 199). Relenting after pressure from the Foreign Office, the governor of Cameroon, a man named Puttkamer, reinstated King Bell's hunting license in April 1903 (p. 200).

The German prohibition, and the Duala opposition to it, may account in part for the persistence of elephant hunting imagery in Duala expressive culture. Proverbs allude to the significance of elephant hunting, which is considered especially dangerous because the animal is so powerful. The hunter who kills an elephant is stronger than his prey (Chief Richard

Din Same, pers. com. 1988), and a braggart is apt to be challenged with the words, *Go kill an elephant or a hippo.*[20] According to Helmlinger, "to kill either an elephant or a hippo is to have good luck and future success" (1972:266). After slaying the animal, however, a hunter should remain humble: *I killed an elephant, but it is not true that I carried it home on my shoulders.*[21] Hunting imagery appears in the plastic arts as well, frequently on the canoe prow ornaments known as *tanges* (*tange,* s.) (Fig. 12-7).

Dugout canoes have played an important role in Duala economic history – first in fishing, then as transportation for trading expeditions to and from the interior. Dugouts are also used in activities and ritual ceremonies involving the ancestors and water spirits, *miengu* (*jengu,* s.), which inhabit the waterways of the estuary. Now as in the past, various dugout types are associated with individual and community status. The most dramatic events are dugout racing competitions, *pembisan* (Fig. 12-8). For these, painted dugouts called *myolo ma pen* (*bolo ba pen,* s.) are specially commissioned and ornamented with carved prow decorations. Late nineteenth- and early twentieth-century racing canoe replicas are rich in visual information about Duala culture (Fig. 12-9).[22]

12-8. Youth Day Dugout Races. Photograph, Rosalinde G. Wilcox, Limbe, April 1989.

Many actual canoe prow ornaments from that era are extant as well. One now in Munich[23] and another in Berlin are among the most interesting, both excellent examples of power-laden imagery (Figs. 12-10a, 12-10b and 12-11). *Tange* motifs were selected by the patrons, based on the image they desired to project about themselves and their lineage or community. Since the elephant was a status emblem for European and Duala alike, its appearance on the prow ornament is not surprising. According to a Duala friend, "The elephant is at home on the *tange* because the elephant is a Duala animal by virtue of its power as well as its connection with the ivory trade" (Valere Epee, pers. com. 1989). Its choice also suggests that the elephant's energy has been harnessed for personal achievement. The animals inhabiting Duala physical and spiritual domains are powerful instruments in the hands of ritual specialists, who can control the movements of such creatures. The elephant image on the replica (Fig. 12-9) may also publicize the preternatural capabilities at the disposal of

12-9 (ABOVE). Miniature canoe replicas such as this offer detailed information about Duala culture in the late 19th and early 20th century. Here the entire crew and the owner (seated under the umbrella) are painted with white faces. In some dugouts, paddlers are white, ritual specialists black; other examples depict all figures in black. Duala colleagues suggested that replicas depicting white men at work for Africans were a form of social protest against colonialism. The origins of such replicas are unclear; European tourists have collected them since at least the mid-19th century, and German colonial administrators may have encouraged their production. Today the Duala themselves also collect replicas as souvenirs of racing events they have attended. Wood, paint. No. III C 44044, Museum für Völkerkunde, Berlin.

its owner. Since leadership qualities are bound up in *tange* imagery, the selection of the elephant provokes proverbial associations of wisdom and power.[24]

Both the Munich and Berlin *tanges* depict elephant hunters. The image on the Berlin *tange* may represent not the actual killing of elephants, however, but rather the figurative con-

12-10 A, B (TWO VIEWS). The carved canoe prow ornament, *tange*, is one of the most spectacular achievements of Duala art. A log is carved lengthwise and a transverse section added. The ornament carved in an intricate openwork tableau is painted and attached to the canoe prow. This *tange* was collected in Douala in 1884 by Max Buchner, one of the envoys sent by Bismarck to claim Cameroon as a German protectorate. Buchner rescued it from the burning house of Chief Lock Priso, which had been set afire during the German shelling of Douala. The *tange* was his "main booty" (Buchner 1914: 194), which he claimed for the museum in Munich. Wood, paint. Length 145.10 cm. No. 7087, Staatliches Museum für Völkerkunde, Munich.

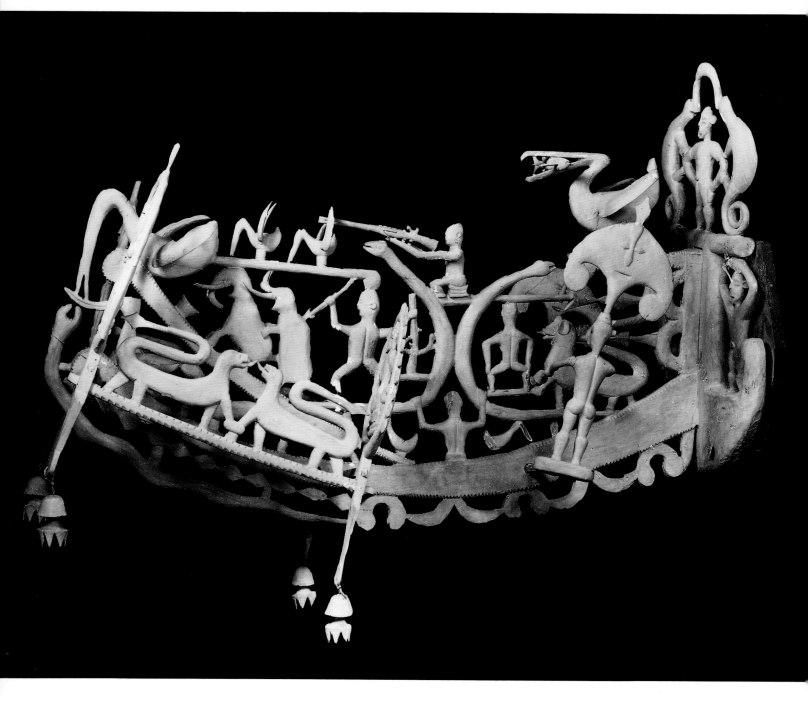

12-11. This canoe prow ornament was collected in Akwa town, Douala in 1897. Wood, white pigment. Length 146 cm. No. III C 7029, Museum für Völkerkunde, Berlin.

tainment of the Bell lineage by its competitors.[25] King Bell was a major player in the ivory trade, receiving for a time favored status from the Germans. At one time the elephant may have been his family symbol, hence the lineage name, Bonanjo (*bona* - family, *njo* - elephant).[26] What makes this speculation so tantalizing is the provenience – unknown to my informant – of the Berlin *tange*. According to Berlin accession notes, the carving was obtained in the *quartier* of Douala that belongs to the Akwa lineage,[27] whose enmity with the Bells during the trading era is well documented.

Another typical nineteenth-century motif evident on the Munich *tange* is that of the animal tamer or hero,[28] who

lightly touches or "tames" the elephant. In both the Munich and Berlin *tanges*, the message is quite clear. The humans represented on the objects (which by extension represent their owners) have control over the lord of the bush, either by killing an elephant, or by taming it. The source for such controlling power, however, does not originate from sheer untutored courage, but rather from acquired spiritual strength. In the Munich *tange,* the hunter and tamer have either been ritually prepared, or they actually represent ritual experts. All wear ivory bracelets, an indication of special status. As on other *tanges* from this period, the hunter wears a distinctive headdress similar to those documented in nineteenth-century field photographs as worn by Duala men and boys engaged in ritual activity. The tamer holds in his left hand a carved dance wand, probably used for rituals. All the figures are painted in the white, red, black triad associated with the water spirit cult,

Jengu (Chief Felix Ewande, pers. com. 1989). The Berlin hunter may also have been ritually prepared. The entire *tange* is painted white, the color the Duala use to paint the body when communicating with spirits and ancestors.

Another aspect of the hunter depictions reinforces the implied importance of the spiritual dimension. In each case the hunter holds a European rifle in his right hand, but actually slays the animal with an African weapon, the spear, held in his left hand. This suggests that although the hunter has effective European arms at his disposal, his primary source of authority and ritual hunting power is Duala. His European weapons represent threats more of the mortal variety.

Every 'thing' that can be named exists in reality, and a person may assume its shape[29]

The Duala believe that people may alter their appearance by changing into any object that has a name, including animate and inanimate objects, human and superhuman beings, and elephants. The concept of transformation is fundamental in Duala cosmology, and may have flourished under the aegis of closed associations (*losango*, pl., *isango*, s.). Today the masking tradition is no longer common among the Duala. In former times, however, *isango* members performed in masquerade costumes. The carved and painted horizontal headdress seen in Figure 12-12[30] is treated in a typically Duala fashion and may have been associated with the now defunct Duala Elephant Society, Njou. Ridyard, who collected the mask in 1896, gave its provenience as Duala.

There is a mystery, however. According to Liverpool museum accession notes, the mask was obtained not in Douala but at the "bottom of Cameroon Mountain," an area inhabited by the Bakweri people, who were at times within the Duala trading network and at others contiguous to it. Elephants are important to the Bakweri, who believe that a man may have an elephant spirit double. Those with special knowledge and power can transform themselves into their spirit doubles (Daniel Lyonga Matutue, pers. com. 1988). Such men belong to Njoku Male, an association whose masqueraders perform enclosed in raffia body costumes and simulate the movement of elephants (Fig. 12-13).[31] Perhaps the mask in question was traded into Bakweri territory.

But there is another dimension to the mystery. In 1898, Basel Missionary Keller collected a large number of sculptures from the Duala slave village at Susa, approximately twenty kilometers from Douala. The population of that village, and others like it, was comprised of diverse coastal forest and Grassfields peoples.[32] Slave populations were permitted to maintain their own closed associations and related paraphernalia. At Susa, Keller collected a carved wooden, unpainted elephant headdress (Fig. 12-14), similar in configuration to the Liverpool Museum piece. The mask was from Aboland, according to Keller's notes. Two unrelated Abo groups, an eastern and a western one, live in the region.[33] The Duala

12-12. Late 19th-century elephant headdress, atypical of Duala headdresses but decorated in a characteristic Duala style, with paints arranged cloisonné-like on the surface along the elephant's trunk and behind the ears. Collected by A. Ridyard for the West African Department of Ethnography, Liverpool Museums. Wood, paint. Length 75.25 cm. No. 14.9.1896.1, National Museums & Galleries on Merseyside, Liverpool.

12-13 (LEFT). Bakweri dancers from the Njoku Male association. Holding sticks to simulate elephants' tusks, the performers raise and lower their body coverings, imitating the movements of the animal. From Ardener (1959:32).

12-14 (BELOW). Elephant headdress from a Duala slave village in "Aboland," collected in 1898 by Basel missionary Keller. It is very similar to the Duala headdress seen in Figure 12-14. Wood, white pigment. Length 56.5 cm. No. 591, Basel Mission Collection, Basel.

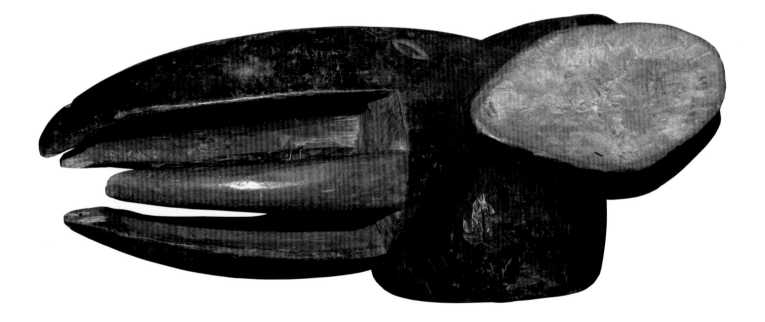

generally regarded the Abo as a group having slave status. The western Abo traded with the Duala and made objects for Duala consumption such as stools and iron implements. They were not always friendly with them, however, and whether they or the eastern Abo produced the masks is a question that remains unanswered.

The painted and unpainted elephant headdresses raise issues of patronage. Did the Duala commission non-Duala groups as their craftsmen? Since they had an Elephant Society, and also believed (then as now) in transformation, they may have produced or commissioned the Liverpool mask. On the other hand, it is possible that they added the elephant to their masking repertoire based on the strength of their neighbor's beliefs.

Over the centuries, Duala society and culture have undergone vast changes. While Duala material culture may no longer be produced in the manner and quantity it was in former times, this does not signal the desiccation of Duala culture. On the contrary, the resiliency of the Duala rests in their language and verbal arts. It is in this discourse that the elephant is still alive, still regarded as a creature of great strength. Today, as in the past, the Duala create a visual statement of power by incorporating elephant imagery into their stylistic vocabulary. The combined effect is that when the Duala refer to Elephant, past and present coalesce. As my friend Manga Doualla-Bell said: *The power of belief is the power of the word.*

NOTES

This research was supported by a UCLA Edward A. Dickinson Art History Travel Grant and an International Research Exchanges Board (IREX) Fellowship. I would like to thank Herbert M. Cole and Ralph A. Austen for their helpful suggestions after reading early drafts of this manuscript.

1. Duala refers to the people and the language of the same name. The spelling Douala refers to the city. Out of an urban population of approximately 1,000,000, the Duala number about 20-30,000.

2. *To njou a salo nde ne, a nde sango eyidi* (Chief Felix Ewande, pers. com. 7/12/89).

3. In terms of leadership and wisdom, the leopard is not as esteemed as the elephant in Duala proverbs. The leopard generates fear, while the elephant inspires respect.

4. The use of "closed association" is deliberate, in reaction to offense taken by my Duala colleagues to the term "secret society."

5. *Njou e si membele mbango mao* (Moume Etia 1984:71).

6. *Njou e si masenga pe mambuse* (Moume Etia 1984:105).

7. *Dia diwo a si maba njou* (Hecklinger 1920/21:50).

8. Although stool motifs from the late 19th and early 20th centuries ranged from geometric to animal, it seems that felines were rare, and elephants even rarer. I do not presume to have seen all the Duala stools held in public and private collections, but in the more than one hundred stools I have seen, only five depicted the elephant.

9. This is one of at least two contemporary stools embellished with elephant motifs. The stool of Chief Richard Din Same of Bonassama is also carved with an elephant.

10. Sometimes these have been referred to in the literature as models; the Duala I spoke with, however, prefer the term 'replica', since the term 'model' suggests a preliminary design model, whereas these forms actually replicate, not a specific canoe, but a genre.

11. *Njou e si m'embele m'bango* (Dika Akwa 1955:14-15).

12. The Wouri estuary is first mentioned in the Portuguese navigational expeditions of c. 1472. The early European contacts during the sixteenth century seem to have been limited, revealing little about Duala people. See Ardener (1956) and Austen (1974) for discussions about the Duala prior to the seventeenth century.

13. These changes are recorded in Duala oral and European written accounts. I am indebted to Ralph Austen for his generosity in sharing his unpublished chapters of a forthcoming Duala history he and Jonathan Derrick are writing. For published material about Duala precolonial and colonial history, please refer to the works of Austen (1974, 1977, 1983), Derrick (1980), and Ardener (1956, 1959).

14. Today Duala social and political structure follows the same organization of families based on lineages. The city of Douala is partitioned into residential units or *quartiers*. Each quarter is under the leadership of a Duala chief, who is responsible to his lineage head.

15. Marion Johnson (1978) has written an excellent comprehensive account of the Cameroon ivory trade which discusses the northern and southern ivory routes.

16. Linden Museum collection accession notes, 11693: Collection Gustav Umlauf Hamburg Exchange, January 1, 1939.

17. See for example the carved and gilded elephant prominently displayed on the stern of the seventeenth-century Dutch ship, the *Witte Olifant* (the *White Elephant*), seen in a painting *The Dutch Fleet Under Sail*, by Willem van de Velde, the Elder, 1672 (Keyes et al. 1990:156), and the carved elephants among the mythological animals and saints on the model of the Danish ship *Sophia Amalia*, 1649 (Hansen 1968:39).

18. *M'bango ma njou mu buki njou malongo*, (Hecklinger 1920/21:127).

19. The Linden Museum collection in Stuttgart includes several ivory earplugs with incised designs. Apparently the earplugs also functioned as hollow containers, and two of them still hold tobacco. Adolf Deihl collection, 1909.

20. *Bwa njou na ngubu*, (Ittmann 1976:435).

21. *Mba nde na bo njou, nde e titi mbale na na wan mo o mboa o makata*, (Dika Akwa 1955:38-39).

22. Two particularly fine examples of racing dugout replicas are located in the United States. One is in the National Museum of African Art, Smithsonian Institution; see "Duala Ceremonial Racing Canoe Model," museum notes by Lydia Puccinelli. The other is in the Field Museum of Natural History, Chicago; see Tamara Northern (1984).

23. I am grateful to Dr. Maria Kecskési, Staatliches Museum für Völkerkunde, Munich, for her interest and helpful comments.

24. Of thirty-three documented *tanges*, six of these include elephant representations.

25. This is the interpretation of Valere Epee, who is a member of the Bell lineage.

26. Valere Epee, pers. com. 1/27/89. The uncertainty, however, arises with the diacritics necessary in written Duala to distinguish the tonalities of the spoken language. The word "Bonanjo" was first recorded before the use of diacritics which would have solved this problem. The Duala word *njo* is pronounced in different ways, one is *njou* (elephant), a second is *njo* (leopard). There is a third pronunciation whose meaning is lost.

27. Museum notes list the provenience as "Akwastadt."

28. Douglas Fraser (1972:263) discussed a similar image, the "Animal Master," in connection with motifs found in Benin and Yoruba art as having non-African parallels in the Ancient Near East and Egypt. Duala *tanges* produced during the late nineteenth-century also contain male images holding serpents or other animals on either side of their heads. The central figure of the Berlin *tange* transverse section (Fig. 12-11) is one example. Although the source of the heroic figure in the *tanges* is unknown, it may have been inspired by the exploits of a popular Duala culture hero, *Djeki*, that are recounted in the oral narratives *Djeki la Njambe*. The *Djeki* cycles are commonly found among Cameroon coastal peoples. See Johannes Ittmann (1952).

29. This is not a proverb, but an idea communicated to me in French by Manga Doualla-Bell, 5/31/89 [translation mine].

30. Although Ittman identified the Njou Society (1976:435), it has not been found among the Duala today, and no information is available about either the use of this particular mask or of the organization that sponsored it.

31. For a more elaborate description of the Bakweri Njoku Male, see Ardener (1959).

32. The Duala kept slaves to work on the plantations located close to Douala which supplied them with agricultural produce and palm products.

33. The Abo have received virtually no scholarly attention, and the problem of distinguishing between the two groups is too complex to be included here.

A.

ELEPHANTS ARE "WORN" IN MANY WAYS: as ivory ornaments, wooden masks, or clothing with elephant imagery. The animal has been embroidered, appliquéd, resist-dyed, stamped, and commercially printed on numerous textiles throughout Africa. Local interpretations range from simple appreciation of a pleasing design to profound respect for a politically explicit symbol. Such images are clearly not restricted to male use; women also wear cloth elephants. Elephants appear on non-clothing textiles as well – flags, wall hangings, and even cloth calendars advertising the products of a textile mill.

B.

C.

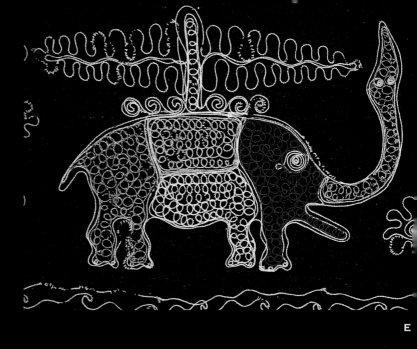

E

A. Wax-resist Batik of elephant rider by Nike Olaniyi, Yoruba peoples, Nigeria. Cotton cloth and imported and natural dyes. Length 227 cm. Collection of Simon Ottenberg.

B. Ghanaian textile stamp, *adinkra*, in the shape of an elephant (Asante people). Gourd with thread, cotton cloth, and vegetable fiber. Length 12 cm. FMCH X82.303. Gift of Mrs. Elizabeth Lloyd Davis.

C. Elderly Fante woman, Anomabu, Ghana. Photograph, Doran H. Ross 1977.

D. Wax-resist calendar, Abidjan, Côte d'Ivoire, 1988. Cotton and indigo dye. Height 114 cm. Private collection.

E. Detail of elephant and palm tree from embroidered Cloth of the Great (*akunitan*), Fante peoples, Ghana. Wool and rayon. Length of elephant, 42 cm. FMCH X82.736.

F. Detail from painted cloth, Senufo peoples, Fakaha Village, Côte d'Ivoire. Cotton and pigment. Height 60 cm. Collection of Joanne Eicher.

G. Woman's cotton wrapper from South Africa. Width 151 cm. FMCH X91.238. Museum purchase.

D.
F.

G

THIRTEEN

THE TEETH OF THE NYIM

THE ELEPHANT AND IVORY IN KUBA ART

DAVID A. BINKLEY

The Kuba form a kingdom comprising more than seventeen different ethnic groups who reside in south-central Zaire.[1] Although their origins and languages differ, they are in many respects culturally alike. The Kuba share similar titleholding traditions and all pay tribute to the paramount ruler (*nyim*), who is Bushoong and traces his dynasty to the seventeenth century.[2]

Among the Kuba, images of the elephant are surprisingly rare as compared with the arts of other African peoples with traditions of kingship. When they do occur, they are invariably associated with leadership and rarely occur in other contexts. The elephant and its ivory tusks are associated principally with the *nyim* and his representation. This is all the more remarkable since with the exception of the *Mukenga* mask, elephant images are almost entirely absent from the rich symbolic vocabulary of titleholding, in which eagle feathers, leopard pelts, and those of other forest creatures figure more prominently than the elephant and its ivory.[3]

A Kuba proverb links the elephant with the *nyim*:

An animal, even if it is large, does not surpass the elephant.
A man, even if he has authority, does not surpass the king.[4]

This proverb, which clearly associates the elephant with chieftaincy, is also a metaphor for titleholding; for no matter how important an individual may be in his own community, he never surpasses the paramount ruler.

While the connection between elephants and the *nyim* is very old, the strength of the linkage seems to be rooted in the enormous wealth and power that accrued to the Kuba paramount chieftaincy in the nineteenth century as a result of the Kuba control of the ivory trade.

THE KUBA AND THE IVORY TRADE

Local trade between the Kuba and peoples living to the north may have existed as early as the seventeenth century.[5] Several strains of evidence suggest that long distance trade

13-1 (OPPOSITE). Mbop Mabiinc maMbeky, king (*nyim*) of Kuba peoples (r. 1939-1969), flanked by royal drums for a 1947 photograph. Since the days of the ivory trade, the *nyim* have dressed elaborately when receiving foreign visitors. Their costumes are made of copper, brass, cowrie shells, beads, leopard skin, and eagle and parrot feathers. Photograph, Eliot Elisofon, National Museum of African Art, Eliot Elisofon Photographic Archives, Smithsonian Institution.

13-2. A one-franc postage stamp issued in 1894 reflects the importance of ivory to the Congo State.

began or became somewhat more pronounced in the first quarter of the seventeenth century during the reign of the paramount ruler and culture hero Shyaam aMbul aNgoong, who is depicted in Kuba oral history as a trader.[6] Long-distance trade was certainly not extensive, however, because ivory could easily be obtained from areas closer to the coast (Vansina 1978:187-91).[7] Jan Vansina characterizes Kuba trade at this time as "a slender tendril at the end of the network of routes feeding the Atlantic trade" (p. 189).[8]

Increased demand for ivory in the nineteenth century resulted in substantial increases in the quantities exported and the prices realized on the international market.[9] Competition for a share of the lucrative trade was fierce. The rising cost of ivory in the mid-nineteenth century and its increasing scarcity near the coast made the equatorial forest in the area of the Kasai and Sankuru Rivers a focal point for traders hoping to capitalize on the enormous profits to be made from the ivory trade. Traders were forced to extend their networks further inland as elephant herds in the great equatorial forests of central Africa were decimated in areas near the Atlantic coast.[10] This left the Kuba region with some of the last remaining elephant herds in central Africa at a point when ivory was in highest demand on the world market.[11]

By the nineteenth century the Kuba were important middlemen in the burgeoning ivory trade (Vansina 1978:191-96). Situated at the southern edge of the equatorial forest, they controlled trade routes leading to the forested region in the north and trading centers to the south and southeast. They exploited trade relationships with southern Mongo peoples to the north, imported ivory from the Ndengese (also to the north) and exported ivory and other products to traders such as the Lulua, Pende, and others to the south (Vansina 1962b: 204-5; 1964:23). Vansina notes that "by 1900 the unchallenged Kuba state had become the hub of trade routes leading to Angola, to Shaba and to the lands east of the Sankuru and north of the Lokenye"(1983:97).[12]

The latter half of the nineteenth century brought numerous European explorers in search of ivory and other products. In 1885 the Congo State (L'État Indépendant du Congo) was formed under the control of King Leopold II of Belgium who "seized so-called 'vacant' land not directly occupied by Africans" (Jewsiewicki 1983:96). In 1890, the State, declaring itself "owner of all natural products of the forest," quickly developed a concessionary system which "gave over to the [trading] companies for a pre-determined period of time exclusive development rights. These included the sole right to purchase products from Africans, who were obliged to furnish them solely to the concessionary company" (pp. 97-98).[13] Exports of rubber and ivory – its two major products – almost doubled during this period (p. 99), and the importance of the latter is reflected in a postage stamp of that period (Fig. 13-1).[14]

In the late 1880s trading stations were set up at the borders of the Kuba kingdom and in 1910 a post was established at the Kuba capital of Nsheng (Vansina 1960:269-70; 1971: 159). The Congo State, followed by the government of the Belgian Congo, effectively ended Kuba control of the ivory trade.[15] Soon traders were entering Kuba country directly to trade in ivory and other products.[16] Although ivory and the wealth it brought to those who controlled its trade was enormous, it was also short-lived. As Robert Harms points out (1981:43),

> the ivory trade, like the Atlantic slave trade, was essentially an extractive type of enterprise: it neither stimulated the growth of subsidiary industries nor encouraged greater productivity on the part of common people. Certain classes of Africans gained short-term benefits from the sale of tusks, but because elephants could be killed at a much faster rate than tusks could be grown, it was only a matter of time before this resource became scarce. It did not provide a foundation for long-term prosperity or a basis for self-sustaining economic growth.

By the time the Congo State gave way to the Belgian colonial administration, "the best quality rubber and ivory resources had been extracted" (Jewsiewicki 1983:113).

During the nineteenth century, the strength of the Kuba confederacy made it impossible for those with competing interests to enter the area without detection by royal authorities living in the center of the kingdom. Early travel accounts suggest that severe punishment was administered to those who allowed foreigners to enter the kingdom. William H. Sheppard, the first Westerner to visit Nsheng, recorded the visible fear on the face of any Kuba when he inquired about the road to the capital.[17] He was told that anyone showing "a stranger the road will be beheaded" (1893:183).[18] The Bushoong, who held military supremacy over the Kuba area, were able to take advantage of this situation. They not only controlled trade within the kingdom, but effectively blocked the Chokwe,

Ovimbundu, and other trading interests from direct access to elephant herds north of the kingdom as well.

The Bushoong imported raw materials to their capital and used them to fabricate finished products (Vansina 1978:194). These locally produced prestige goods were consumed by the Kuba elite classes and were also traded for imported luxury items. In this way, masks, other woodcarvings, belts, hats, knives, and decorated textiles were traded for pottery, salt, camwood, ivory, cowries, copper, and slaves (Vansina 1962b: 204-5; 1964:19-23; 1978:183-96). The wealth brought into the kingdom at this time filtered down to lower classes as well. Regional and long-distance trade helped to foster the development of craft industries, which were already experiencing a renaissance due to the proliferation of titletaking and the resultant demand for prestige goods.[19]

But the principal beneficiaries of the ivory trade in the Kuba region were the ivory traders and the eagle feather chiefs (*kum aphoong*), especially the Kuba paramount ruler, the *nyim*. By collecting tribute and controlling the ivory trade, the *nyim* and other high court officials grew wealthy.[20] As the price of ivory increased, external trade, rather than tribute, became the principal means for the central authority to gain wealth.

Although the wealth brought by the ivory trade undoubtedly encouraged the display of ivory, the association between the *nyim* and ivory tusks may be much older. Until long-distance trade reached the Kuba region, the display of ivory signified the importance of the *nyim* as owner of all lands and products under his control. This is implicit in the tribute given to the ruler after a successful hunt.

TRIBUTE, TUSKS, AND IVORY REGALIA

The collection of tribute was one of the traditional means by which the *nyim* exercised control over subject villages in his chiefdom. In this, both the meat of the elephant and its ivory played a significant role. The *nyim* collected an annual tax of dried agricultural and hunted products levied from village to village; in addition, he held proprietary rights to certain parts of animals killed in areas under his control. Animals deemed "noble" and thus subject to the proprietary rights of the *nyim*—at least in some parts of Kubaland—included the civet cat, leopard, eagle, buffalo, hippopotamus, warthog, and elephant. "Anyone killing or finding a 'noble' animal was to send either the whole or a prescribed portion of it to the king through hierarchical channels" (Vansina 1978:143). In Bushoong areas, the only noble animals were leopards and elephants, which special, titled officials were in charge of collecting.[21] One official was the *nyim ancok,* meaning "king of the elephants." His specific duties included collection of the *nyim's* ivory harvest from lands under his control (Vansina 1978:141, 342 n. 42).

The portions of the elephant required by the *nyim* were "one tusk, the tail hair, and nine blocks of meat" (Vansina 1978:143; see also Sheppard 1917:132-33). The other tusk went to the head of the chiefdom who may have been also a village headman. Although the *nyim* controlled the harvest and trade of elephants in his own chiefdom, he had to balance his right as paramount ruler and the right of other eagle feather chiefs at the head of tributary chiefdoms. The annual tribute paid by these chiefdoms showed allegiance to the paramount ruler but also respect to their individual claims to authority in their own regions and villages.[22] If we count early reports as accurate, however, it appears that the display of ivory tusks was unique to the person of the king.[23]

The use of tusks as an emblem of royalty can be dated to at least the mid-seventeenth century. Hungarian ethnographer Emil Torday was told that the ivory tusk he collected for the British Museum was set in place by the paramount ruler and culture hero, Shaam aMbul aNgoong (Torday and Joyce 1910:73; 1925:120).

Reports from the late nineteenth and early twentieth centuries mention the display of ivory at the royal court and along the route of the paramount ruler's passage through Kuba villages. The royal exhibition of tusks, together with other symbols of title, were noted by William Sheppard (1917: 106-7), describing his first visit to the *nyim* at the royal capital in 1892:

> The king's servants ran and spread leopard skins along the ground leading to his majesty. I approached with some timidity. The king arose from his throne of ivory, stretched forth his hand and greeted me....The king's great chair, or throne, was made of carved tusks of ivory, and his feet rested upon lion skins.

Hilton-Simpson, who accompanied Emil Torday on his visit to the Kuba capital in 1908, described the regally garbed ruler as "leaning his back upon an elephant's tusk planted point downwards in the ground" (1911:202).

These accounts suggest that both Sheppard and Hilton-Simpson saw the same royal backrest (*ndaang amyoong*) recently described by Joseph Cornet (1982:301). When in use, that backrest, constructed from three ivory tusks decorated with beads and shells, was planted in the earth with points downward. The last known example of its kind was buried with Mbop Mabiinc maMbeky, the *nyim* who died in 1969.

Ivory tusks were also employed in the construction of the king's palanquin. According to Conway Wharton (1927: 44-45), it was "fashioned of antelope hides laced upon a rectangular boxlike frame some six feet long by four feet wide and two deep.... Against one end of the interior reclines a back-rest fashioned by lashing four ivory tusks together." This palanquin was most likely the same one Emil Torday described the *nyim* as using on the day of his installation, when he "perambulates the village, the people fighting for the honor of carrying him" (1925:178).

Ivory tusks were placed in the ground as testimony to royal passage in Kuba villages (Fig. 13-2). Sheppard, describing his

1892 visit (1917:103), noted that at one village on the road leading to the Kuba capital:

[I was] attracted by a large elephant tusk inverted and driven firmly into the ground at the entrance of the village court house, a big shed. The king's son informed me that his father had visited the town and had sat near that spot and the villagers had planted the ivory there in honor and memory of his visit.

Hilton-Simpson (1911:190) reported seeing an elephant tusk "planted point downwards" under a covered shelter. When he inquired about the tusk, he was told:

… it was formerly the custom when the great king paid a state visit to the villages to plant an elephant's tusk in such a manner that he could lean back upon it when sitting upon his throne; the tusks so placed were never removed, but were left sticking in the ground as a souvenir to the villagers of the visit of their king.

Conway Wharton (1927:45), in his travels in the Kuba area, mentioned the same phenomenon:

… here and there about the kingdom, one may still see great tusks of ivory planted point downward in the soil. These are usually so old and weathered that they scarcely resemble ivory any longer. Each of these is mute evidence that a Bakuba king has at some time deigned to hold court at this spot. Seated on a slave or a mat, he has had the tusks so placed as to afford a rest for his back….When he broke up his court the tusk was invariably left buried in the ground as a monument to mark the spot where the king had held court.

When planted in the ground, the tusk may have served as an emblem not only of the *nyim*'s royal authority, but also of his fertility. In central Africa, elephants are regarded as highly fertile creatures. The Valley Bisa of Zambia, for example, consider the elephant the "mother of all animals" (Marks 1976:93). The Kuba paramount ruler is thought to be a nature spirit (*ngesh*) and therefore intimately associated with the fecundity of the earth, controlling fertility of the fields and the forest and its animals. Numerous rituals, prohibitions, and charms surround the *nyim* in order to protect his person as well as the fertility of the soil (Vansina 1958:733-42; 1964: 98-103; 1978:200). Thus we may deduce that when an ivory tusk was planted firmly in the ground, it alluded to the life-giving blessing the *nyim* bestowed upon the community.

Ivory tusks were also displayed after a king's death as a reminder of his power and wealth.[24] Hermann Norden (c. 1925:258) described visiting the grave of *nyim* Kot aPe, who had died in 1916:

The dead king is buried in the centre of the room where he used to sleep. The room is empty except for one thing. At the foot of the grave I saw a huge elephant tusk, richly carved, and to it was fastened the Lukengo's sword. There was no guard, but that carved ivory which is worth a king's ransom is safe as though an army stood by.

In the nineteenth century the display of ivory, which had long symbolized the *nyim*'s ownership of the land, took on new meaning. Now it represented his control of the ivory trade, of which he was the principal beneficiary. This notion was visually expressed when the *nyim* gave an ivory tusk to a colonial trading officer in return for his gifts (Sheppard 1893:183). Foreign visitors were also treated to a conspicuous display of riches in the *nyim*'s elaborate costume, which incorporated copper, brass, cowrie shell, beads, leopard skin, and eagle and parrot feathers – as it does to this day (Fig. 13-3). Many of these materials are also traditionally displayed by eagle feather chiefs in other chiefdoms, but not in the same quantity as that displayed by the *nyim*.

Together, ivory tribute and the ivory trade so swelled the king's storehouses that by the end of that century they were believed to contain thousands of ivory tusks and other valuable possessions.[25] Missionary Samuel P. Verner declared that the remaining elephant herds in the region should be spared because there were "large stores of old ivory still uncollected, which forms a legitimate article of trade" (1903: 469). Hermann Norden, after visiting the grave of a deceased ruler, speculated on the "untold riches" that must have been buried with the deceased (c. 1925:258). Conway Wharton, an American missionary, describing the Kuba capital village of Nsheng, mentioned "vast stores of ivory said to be there" (1927:17).

With the lavish display of ivory and other prestige materials, and gifts of ivory to visiting colonial agents, the *nyim* acted out a collective fantasy of wealth and prosperity as if it would never end.

ELEPHANT HUNTING: PERILS AND PRESTIGE

While ivory display has been well documented, less is known about Kuba elephant hunting. The principal hunters of ivory in the Kuba region were the Cwa people and the Ndengese and Nkucu to the north. Describing the Cwa, or "Batouas" [sic] in the Kuba area, Louis Wolf noted (1888:40):

They are exclusively hunters and do not cultivate the land. They dry animal meat and offer it in exchange for corn, manioc, and other grains, also for weapons and other essential objects to the Bakoubas [sic] and to the Baloubas [sic], at a neutral site, in the middle of the forest, that serves as a market…. I also found the Batouas

13-3. Decorated ivory tusks were planted in the ground when the *nyim* passed through a Kuba village. This one was collected by Emil Torday in 1909. Photograph #1909.5-13.12, courtesy of the Trustees of the British Museum.

at the court of the Bakouba king, where they were serving as cup-bearers at the king's table.[26]

(Author's translation)

Torday also observed "pygmies who have a permanent arrangement with some chief, according to which they keep him regularly supplied with meat and honey, while he provides them with flour, beans, salt and iron" (1925:58).[27] He considered the Cwa the greatest of all hunters. His awe of their forest knowledge is evident in a passage describing his experiences on an elephant hunt with a Cwa guide (pp. 59-60):

We kept to the path for about half an hour, when my guide suddenly turned off to the left. We had now entered a pygmy path: there was no visible track and we seemed to be absolutely surrounded by the impenetrable undergrowth, except for a path, now in front, now to the right or left, which enabled one to see about a yard's distance....Now and then I looked back, but the path seemed to close up behind me so that I could never have found my way back by myself. It struck me that the pygmy's uncanny path was nothing more than the usual native thoroughfare, only more so.

Cwa living in the central Zaire basin worked singly or in groups utilizing several different methods, all of which were dangerous.[28] Elephant hunting was precarious. As Harms points out, "most Pygmy hunters killed fewer than six elephants in

13-4. Ngongo hunting charm from an enclosure in the center of a Kuba village, where rituals were performed before and after a successful hunt. Misumba, March 5, 1908. Photograph, M.W. Hilton-Simpson from Hilton-Simpson's *Journal of the Congo Expedition.* #27021. Courtesy of The Royal Anthropological Institute.

13-5. A Bushoong hunting charm consisting of a wooden trough cradled by two small trees. Water from this trough would be sprinkled on the hunter's feet in hopes of blinding animals to his approach. Photograph, David A. Binkley, 1981.

their lifetimes" (1981:41). After a successful group hunt, the group leader took the ivory which he shared with local land chiefs, while the others shared the meat (pp. 41-43).

Although the Cwa were the principal hunters of the region, the Kuba also hunted elephant. Because of its danger, elephant hunting required special skills and involved ritual observances. In the late nineteenth century, the Kuba had an elephant hunter's association which concerned itself primarily with rituals of protection and success in hunting. The society, called Itwiimy,[29] was similar to an organization among the Ndengese who lived in the equatorial forest to the north of the Kuba (Vansina 1978:194,354 n. 87). Its development and purpose may have pertained more to the control of the ivory trade rather than the actual hunting of elephants. Itwiimy, like the men's initiation society, was suppressed by the colonial government.[30] Ultimately, the hunting society was closely tied to central authority in the personage of eagle feathered chiefs and the *nyim* who controlled the harvesting of ivory in their respective territories.

Hilton-Simpson describes an elephant killed near the Ngongo town of Misumba in a trap made with a large harpoon and a log weight (1911:101).[31] Torday and Joyce describe elephant traps which include barbed wire, *"piques barbelées"* (1910:142). Apart from these brief descriptions, little is known about actual Kuba elephant hunting techniques. It is known that the Kuba used village hunting charms to help insure the success of the hunt (Torday and Joyce 1910; Hilton-Simpson 1911; Vansina 1971). An Ngongo charm photographed by Torday and Hilton-Simpson consisted of a wooden figurine with a large head which was kept in a small enclosure situated in the center of the village (Fig. 13-4). Rituals performed here included sacrifices both preceding the hunt and at the conclusion of successful hunts.[32]

Such charms are evidently still in use. In 1981, I documented a non-figurative hunting charm called *ituma* in a northern Bushoong village (Fig. 13-5).[33] Located on the central thoroughfare of the village, it consisted of two small trees with a wooden trough supported in the branches between the two trees. Water taken from this trough would be sprinkled on the feet of hunters before they set out to hunt large animals. I was told that it was specifically associated with hunting elephants. In 1989, an elderly Pyaang informant described the *ituma* as being associated with an elephant hunters' society. Before the hunt, sexual abstinence and food prescriptions were especially critical. Food consumed by hunters could only be prepared by members of the society. The power attributed to the *ituma* included the power to blind elephants to the approach of hunters. Thus, after a successful attack, a wounded and violent elephant would be less of a threat to the hunter. The hunting charm also had the power to kill an elephant and make it continue to walk erect until it would fall where the hunters wished it to fall. The individual in charge of maintaining the *ituma* possessed the ability to divine where the elephant had fallen.[34] The charm was also believed to protect the community from lightning.

Although elephant hunting has lost its economic and nutritional importance to the Kuba and their neighbors, it is still an activity shrouded in ritual, and one that brings honor and prestige to successful hunters. Certain elements of regalia are still worn by hunters living in the northern Kuba region. Figure 13-6 shows a Bushoong village headman (*kubol*) wearing a hat, necklace, arm band with attached animal horn and a pouch suspended from a belt.[35] These items are part of the ritual paraphernalia employed by elephant hunters.

The successful hunter is recognized in Southern Mongo culture as well. There is a society of elephant hunters found to the north of the Kuba area among Southern Mongo peoples. The society is called Ilumba and is responsible for protecting elephant hunters and increasing their chances for success through the manufacture and use of certain talismans. Members of the society who have killed an elephant have the right to wear a special necklace consisting of engraved pendant nuts suspended from a length of cord – one for each animal killed.[36] From time to time one can still see men wearing necklaces of this kind in Nkucu and Shoowa villages near the Sankuru River. The pendants, called *lodjika* in Shoowa villages, are worn by individuals who have killed an elephant (Fig. 13-7). This emblem of successful hunting can be displayed by both the hunter and his family members, including wives and children (Cornet 1980). Figure 13-8 shows a pendant worn by the wife of a successful hunter.

Another testament to the former importance of elephant hunting can be seen in northern Kuba villages near the Sankuru River. There, one can still see on occasion ivory tusks being employed as pestles in food preparation (Fig. 13-9). Such pestles, worn from years of use (Fig. 13-10), speak to the clear relationship between success in hunting and the display of status-imbued objects during the late nineteenth and twentieth centuries.

13-6. A Bushoong village headman, dressed in the ritual paraphernalia of an elephant hunter, wears a small hat, a necklace, an arm band with attached animal horn, and a pouch suspended from a belt. Photograph, David A. Binkley, 1981.

13-7. Elephant hunter's necklace of engraved palm nut and brass, such as could be worn by a hunter or any member of his family. The necklace has one seed for each elephant killed. IMNZ collection, 75.287.83, Nkundu, Oshwe zone. Photograph, David A. Binkley.

13-8. A Booli (Nkucu) woman wears a pendant necklace signifying that her husband killed two elephants. Between Kasai and Lokenye Rivers. Collection of Marc Leo Felix. Photograph, A. da Cruz.

ELEPHANTS, MASKS, AND TITLEHOLDING

Outside the realm of royal display, the use of ivory is limited among the Kuba. Among the prestige items utilizing ivory are ivory-handled flywhisks which in the nineteenth and early twentieth centuries were carried by Kuba elites on ceremonial occasions (Fig. 13-11). Several Kuba masked dancers also carry flywhisks as emblems of status during funeral dances.[37]

There is only one context in which elephant imagery appears with any frequency: during activities of the men's initiation society found among Bushoong, Shoowa, Ngeende, Ngongo, and other Kuba-affiliated villages in the northern half of the kingdom. This form of men's initiation is distinct from that found in the Southern Kuba area (see Binkley 1987a,b).[38] The principal masks associated with this society are a grouping of three male masks, *Mukenga*, *Ishena malu*, and *Bongo*, the most important of which is the elephant mask, *Mukenga* (Figs. 13-12, 13-13).[39] *Mukenga* is characterized by a conical projection that extends upward and over the front of the mask to form an elephant's trunk. The association with the elephant is made explicit by the attachment of two tusks made of fiber, cloth, beads and shells near the base of the trunk.

While other society masks perform during initiation rituals of new members into the society as well as at funeral rituals for society members, *Mukenga*'s appearance is relegated to funeral dances for deceased members who belong to certain aristocratic clans. The relationship between *Mukenga* and titleholding is apparent in the lavish use of costly and labor intensive materials – beads and shells – which visibly distinguish *Mukenga* from other masks employing painted decoration. The accumulation of cowrie shells, beads, copper, spotted cat fur, and bird feathers are important symbols of titleholding and of wealth in the Kuba region. *Mukenga* is the most lavishly adorned example of this aesthetic. The sides, back, and trunk of the mask are covered with extensive cowrie and beaded decoration. In the finest examples, cowrie shells are especially selected for their uniformity of size and whiteness before being attached to the raffia cloth that covers the mask. Several colors of beads are employed to sew intricate patterned decoration on the sides, back and trunk of the mask. These patterns may display several Kuba design motifs, including the interlace design of leadership known as *imbol* (Cornet 1982:160,168).

13-9. A Shoowa woman prepares food with an ivory pestle that recalls the relationship between success in hunting and the display of status objects. Photograph, David A. Binkley, 1981.

13-10. An ivory pestle from the Kuba region, showing wear from years of use. Length 60 cm. FMCH x90.373.

Several other details of the mask relate directly to title-holding. A flat rectangular panel forms the face of *Mukenga*. This panel is often covered with spotted cat fur, but other materials may also be employed before the eyes, eyebrows, nose and mouth are attached. Some early examples, probably dating from before 1880, utilize elephant skin as a foundation for the attachment of facial details (Vansina, pers. com. 1989; Maesen 1960:pl. 22; Neyt 1981). Copper and beaded strips are then applied to form and decorate the facial features.

The trunk projecting from the top of the *Mukenga* mask is comparable to similar projections found on headdresses worn by Kuba, Ndengese, Nkucu titleholders, at dances and other occasions requiring display of one's achieved title (Figs. 13-14, 13-15).[40] Identical headdresses are also displayed on corpses as one of the principal elements of funerary attire. Suspended from the end of the elephant trunk is a tuft of red parrot feathers, an insignia of titleholding in the Kuba region as among Luba and Luba-Kasai peoples living to the south.[41]

During masquerade, *Mukenga* personifies an important titleholder dancing to honor the deceased (Figs. 13-16a,b).

13-11. Ivory-handled flywhisks, Kuba peoples. Ivory, hair, skin, twine, shell, encrustation. Height of largest, 58 cm. Private collection.

The *Mukenga* costume, like the mask itself, evokes not only titleholding and wealth, but death as well. The cowrie shells attached to raffia cloth strips (*mabiim*) are among the most visible objects of wealth displayed at funerals. They are placed on the ankles and arms of corpses and are included in the inventory of burial goods. The association with death is also made apparent by the masker's vest, leggings, gloves, and footwear. These are identical in appearance to the funerary attire of titleholders as they are presented for several days before burial (Binkley 1987a).

The elaboration of funerary dress displayed before burial is also seen to the north of the Kuba among the Ndengese. After the death of a senior titleholder, a mannequin-like figure is dressed in the funerary attire of the deceased (Fig. 13-17).[42] The individual who will succeed the titleholder in office is confined in a room with the costumed effigy for a period

13-12 (ABOVE). A Kuba elephant mask called *Mukenga* is danced for elite funeral ceremonies and sometimes used as part of the funerary attire. Western Kasai Province, Mweka Zone, Zaire. Beads, cowrie shells, feathers, hair, fiber, skin, metal, 5.1 x 7.6 x 7.6 cm, Laura T. Magnuson Fund income, 1982.1504. Ex-Hautelet Collection, The Art Institute of Chicago.

13-13. A *Mukenga* mask assembled from wood, raffia, textile, beads, cowries, leather, and copper. Height 53.34 cm. FMCH x65.5401. Gift of the Wellcome Trust.

13-14. This prestige hat (*kalyeem*), worn by a Northern Kete man, proclaims his status as a titleholder. The ivory trade brought wealth to the Kuba region, enlarging the class of titleholders who earned the right to wear such hats. Photograph, David A. Binkley, 1982.

13-15. Prestige hat (*kalyeem*). Beads, shells, fiber. Height 27 cm. J. Hautelet Collection.

of time. Rituals performed during this period of seclusion are centered on the transference of power. The appearance of Kuba style masks and costume details in areas to the north of the Kuba heartland clearly indicate that these elements of regalia moved along the same trade routes that brought ivory from the north to the Kuba region in the nineteenth century and possibly earlier.

CONCLUSION

For the Kuba, the elephant was one of a number of animals designated as "noble" whose products formed a part of tribute given over to the central authority. This corresponds to the rich symbolic vocabulary developed by the Kuba relating title-

holding to various forest birds and animals. Ivory tusks, being a supreme symbol of royalty, were restricted to the display surrounding the immediate family and person of the *nyim*, who was at once paramount chief of the Bushoong and paramount ruler of all the Kuba.

When the long-distance ivory trade finally reached the great equatorial forest, the Kuba, situated at its southern borders, were able to control access to some of the last remaining elephant herds in Central Africa. Trade in ivory brought wealth to the kingdom and established the Kuba as a regional power in the nineteenth century. As profits of the trade increased, so did the fortunes of the *nyim*. During this period, ivory was primarily thought of as a commodity rather than as a raw material for the production of luxury items to be consumed

13-16A,B. A *Mukenga* dancer performing at a funeral. On such occasions the masquerader personifies an important titleholder dancing to honor the deceased. Bushoong village. Photographs, David A. Binkley, December 1991.

at home or abroad.[43] Kuba dominance of the ivory trade lasted only until the turn of the twentieth century, when colonial intervention put an end to it.

Many nineteenth-century accounts of Central African cultures, including descriptions of Kuba culture, were made by explorers who were financed in part by the trade in ivory (Jewsiewicki 1983:96). The Portuguese ivory trader António da Silva Porto reached a Kuba market in 1880. Hermann Von Wissmann reached another market in 1881, and Dr. Louis Wolf met the Kuba paramount ruler's son at a border village in 1884 (Shaloff 1970:33; Torday 1925:79; Vansina 1978: 78-79). Upon his return to Europe, Dr. Wolf's glowing reports of seemingly inexhaustible ivory resources, published in the *Proceedings of the Royal Geographical Society* and the *Bulletin de la Société Royal Belge de Géographie* (1888:41-42), must have been a powerful incentive to anyone wishing to exploit the rich ivory stores remaining in the Kasai region.[44] Ethnographic research in the Kasai region as elsewhere in sub-Saharan Africa was also initially fueled by economic interests. Emil Torday, the first ethnographer to study the Kuba, was for a period of time in the employ of the Congo State and later one of the concessionary companies (Compagnie du Kasai) organized by Leopold II to exploit and manage the State's resources of rubber and ivory.[45] Without the strong economic incentive in the Kasai region, brought about by the trade in ivory and other products, the historical and ethnographic baseline for Kuba studies would certainly not be as complete as it is today.

Like the kingdom of Kongo during the fifteenth and sixteenth centuries, and the Mangbetu in the nineteenth century, the Kuba kingdom sparked the imagination of Europeans looking for a mirror image of the royal traditions they knew — an elite centralized government, the grandeur of divine kingship, and highly evolved artistic traditions in the service of a courtly life. The image of the Kuba ruler leaning back on tusks of ivory with leopard skins at his feet and surrounded by his adoring subjects added immensely to the creation of the Kuba myth. This myth was in part built on the Western demand for ivory and the Kuba control of that ivory in the nineteenth century.

13-17. Funeral effigy with *Mukenga* mask. After the death of a senior titleholder, an effigy is dressed in the funerary attire of the deceased. The person who will succeed him in office is confined in a room with the effigy while transference of power rituals are performed. Ndengese area, ca.1955. Photograph, M. Cremers. Courtesy of Jean Willy Mestach.

NOTES

1. Portions of this paper relate to research undertaken among a number of Kuba-related groups in the Republic of Zaire during 1981-82 and in 1989. The 1981-82 research was made possible by grants from IIE – Fulbright-Hays, Samuel H. Kress Foundation and the Wenner-Gren Foundation for Anthropological Research. I would like to thank Pat Darish, John Mack and Jan Vansina for commenting on a draft of this paper. I would also like to thank The Art Institute of Chicago, National Museum of African Art, Eliot Elisofon Photographic Archives, Smithsonian Institution, The Royal Anthropological Institute, the Trustees of the British Museum, Marc Leo Felix and Jean Willy Mestach for their permission to reproduce photographs from their collections.

2. The Bushoong have been politically dominant since the 17th century. The *nyim* is chosen from the Bushoong *matoon* clan. See Vansina (1954, 1964, 1978) for detailed information on Kuba kingship and history. Kuba terms are given in the Bushoong language unless otherwise indicated.

3. Cornet (1982:220) also notes the lack of ivory utilized by the Kuba for ornamentation.

4. Vansina (1964:103), who recorded this Kuba proverb, renders it in French as: *L' animal, même s'il est grand, ne dépasse pas l'éléphant; l'homme, même s'il exerce une autorité, ne dépasse pas l'homme des Matoon (le roi).*

5. A war is mentioned in Kuba oral traditions "against the populations north of the Sankuru, where traders bought camwood and ivory in the area of the Lokenye [River]" (Vansina 1978:63).

6. See list of Kuba rulers in Vansina (1978:245-47).

7. The export of ivory by the Kuba prior to the 18th century is uncertain. Trade during this period may have also included raffia cloth. See Vansina (1978:191, 352 n.77).

8. See Vansina (1962a:379; 1978:191) for Kuba imports and exports at this time.

9. Ivory exports increased fifty times between the years 1832 and 1859 alone. See Curtin et al. (1978:370-71) and Harms (1981:39-40) for price increases at this time.

10. Many of the long-distance trading networks were an elaboration of earlier local and regional networks interlocking in various patterns to create a long chain from local markets in the interior to the coast. Central African trading systems to the Atlantic coast are described in Curtin et al. (1978:420), Miller (1983:154) and Vansina (1978:188, 190; 1983:90,101).

11. In the second half of the 19th century the Chokwe, the Ovimbundu, and on a smaller scale, the Imbangala were among the most successful traders (Miller 1983:153-57; Vansina 1962a:382-86; Curtin et al. 1978:429-33). Phyllis Martin describes some of these groups as "mobile bands of hunters and gatherers who trapped elephants, foraged wild rubber and processed gathered wax" (1983:3). This led to what has been described as a "'moving traders' frontier. The richest area for great herds of elephants and for their valuable large tusks was always further into the interior, beyond the region where the hunters had already taken their first harvest" (Curtin et al. 1978:398).

The Chokwe, in particular, aggressively moved into south-central Zaire in search of the remaining elephant herds. Their hunting and trading were competing with Ovimbundu and Imbangala traders south of the Kuba area by 1860 (Vansina 1962a:385). Although these traders and others had been buying ivory at centers like Mai Munene to the south of Kuba country, they were unable to broach the Kuba area and trade directly with Ndengese, Nkucu and other Southern Mongo groups living in the equatorial forest to the north.

By the 1880s Atlantic coast traders had crossed the Kasai and Kunene Rivers and met their east-coast counterparts in the Zambezi Basin (Martin 1983:3).

12. Vansina (1960:269) also notes that "from 1857 onward the name …[Kuba]…was known in Loanda, and other trade-routes led to Katanga, to Stanley Pool, and eastwards well into the Songye country."

13. See Jewsiewicki's map (1983:97) of the concessionary system. See also Curtin et al. (1978:476-77). Vansina (1969) discusses the impact of the Compagnie du Kasai on the Kuba.

14. Jewsiewicki (1983:99) notes that by 1900 rubber and ivory made up 95% of exports with rubber accounting for at least 84% of the total.

15. Slade (1962:176) notes that "[e]ven before 1890 State officials were paid commission on the ivory which they brought and thus became the rivals of the European traders. . . ." See also Johnston (1908:416).

16. See Vansina (1969) for a discussion of competing commercial interests in the Kuba area at this time. See also Vansina (1978:354, n.91) and Verner (1903:359-63).

17. American Presbyterian missionary William Sheppard, the first Westerner to enter the Kuba region and visit its capital, did so by following several ivory traders traveling to the Kuba capital of Nsheng (Sheppard 1917:87-104; Shaloff 1970:33-34).

18. According to Torday (1925:79), Dr. Wolf's visit in 1884 at a Kuba market was "expiated by the sacrifice of a certain number of slaves." See also Vansina (1969:11).

19. Other factors related to increase in production during the "Age of Kings" are discussed in Vansina (1978:172-96).

20. Vansina (1969:10) notes how commerce reinforced the position of the nyim; he controlled one half of all ivory in the Kuba region and collected taxes imposed on traders at all markets. See also Vansina (1978:141,195).

21. Chiefs in other areas of Central Africa also held such rites. "Mboshi and Tio chiefs...got the ground tusk; Likuba chiefs got both tusks, leaving the hunters with only the meat" (Harms 1981:41). Compare with Marks (1976:61-62).

22. In the Ngongo area, the right tusk was reserved for the chief and the left tusk went to the hunter who first wounded the elephant or into whose trap the elephant had fallen (Torday and Joyce 1910:142).

23. The display of brass was also a royal prerogative. An oral tradition mentions that a nyim fought a war with the chief of Bokila because he wore a necklace made of brass (Vansina 1964:108 and 1978:191).

24. Ivory was also displayed on the grave of other members of the royal clan. Sheppard (1893:186) visited the grave of the king's mother in 1895 and described it as situated "in a grove of palms. It was planted with tusks of ivory and surrounded by a great many other graves."

25. Vansina (1978:185) comments that "[e]ven in 1953 the Kuba still believed that the king was fabulously rich." Compare this view with descriptions of the royal storehouses of the Maloango at Buali which were believed to be full of ivory (Martin 1970:142,145).

26. The original reads: "[Ils] sont exclusivement chasseurs et ne cultivent pas la terre. Ils sèchent la viande des animaux et la donnent en échange pour du blé, du manioc et autres céréales, même pour des armes et autres objets nécessaires aux Bakoubas et aux Baloubas, à un endroit neutre, au centre de la forêt, qui sert de marché.... Je trouvai aussi des Batouas à la cour du roi Bakouba, où ils servaient d'échansons à la table du roi."

27. Hilton-Simpson described "Batwa [sic] who hunt for the chief" of the Kuba-affiliated group the Ngongo at the capital village of Misumba (1911:96). This is similar to the arrangement described by Robert Harms (1981:41-42) for pygmies living in the central Zaire basin. "Along the Sanza each Pygmy family was a client of a chief of an agricultural village. He supplied them with protection and settled their marriage payments and debts in return for meat and ivory."

28. Vansina (1978:91) states that Cwa residing in the Kuba region favor hunting individually.

29. The Edmiston Kuba dictionary (1932:537) notes the word ituimi is both a fetish and a fetish song for hunting elephants.

30. Vansina (1978:194) notes that by the 1950s, Itwiimy "had taken on the character of a classical religious movement." It would be interesting to study the relationship between Itwiimy and the men's initiation society (nkaan or babende) whose duties included maintaining order and solving disputes at regional market places in Kuba territory (See Vansina 1962b:196).

31. See discussion of professional hunter's guilds and techniques of elephant hunting among the Bisa of Zambia in Marks (1976:61-64; 80-83). See also Harms (1981:41-43).

32. Torday and Joyce (1910:118,120-21) gives the name of this charm as tembo. Vansina (1971:162-165) gives the name as tambo among the Ngongo, taam among the Bushoong and tambwe among the Songye. See Torday and Joyce (1910) and Vansina (1971) for more detailed description of the rituals surrounding this charm.

33. I collected the name ituma for this charm. Vansina (pers. com. 1989) notes that it may be ituum meaning 'the war' or itwim. In 1989, I collected the name itumba from an Ngongo informant for a charm carried by elephant hunters. The charm was believed to blind elephants from seeing the hunters pursuing them.

34. I also collected a song for the ituma in 1989 which describes this characteristic. "You shot an elephant near Iyeeka [village]. It will die near Lumia river. Come on people our brothers/friends have killed an elephant."

35. Cornet (1980:242-43) describes several types of talisman carried by Southern Mongo hunters in the zone of Oshwe to the north of the Kuba. See also Delanghe:1982.

36. The palm nut is called ilika (pl., belika). The necklace and nut or nuts are called okoli belika. The palm nut is from the enteke palm tree, which grows near water sources and is carved by a specialist (botuli elika). See Cornet (1980) for detailed information.

37. Masks carrying flywhisks include the female mask Ngady mwaash and the male masks Bwoom, Ishena Malu, and Mukenga. My fieldwork experience suggests that while flywhisks are still carried by Kuba elites and masked dancers, the handles are carved from wood with metal decoration.

38. See Harroy (1907:178-81), Torday and Joyce (1910:87-89), Torday (1925), and Vansina (1954:32-33) for discussion of the Northern Kuba initiation society.

39. The Ngongo and other Northern Kuba term for this mask is Mukenga, while the Bushoong name is Mukyeeng.

40. See Biebuyck and Van den Abbeele (1984:pls.22,27). See also Torday and Joyce (1910:164) and Cornet (1976:12-13; 1982:215-16).

41. Among the Lulua and Luba-Kasai, parrot feathers are the insignia of the supreme chief. Among Southern Mongo peoples to the north of the Sankuru the eagle feather is the highest insignia. Only in Kuba country do the two insignia appear at the same time (Vansina 1964:135 n.33).

42. Photo by Mr. Cremers, Ndengese area, circa 1955. I want to thank Jean Willy Mestach for allowing me to reproduce this photograph from his personal archive.

43. The trade in ivory spurred Kuba artistic traditions including wood carving. European interest in Kuba arts also influenced the manufacture of objects such as decorated boxes, cups and masks. However, these interests did not influence the manufacture of luxury objects made from ivory as they did among other central African peoples such as the Mangbetu. See Schildkrout and Keim (1990:249-53).

44. "The Kasai, the Sankuru and the Lomami (rivers) form a lovely path of water that leads to the heart of Africa by traversing previously unknown regions and where ivory as much fossilized as living is found in such quantities that it is no longer necessary to think of determining the moment when it will be depleted" (Wolf 1888:41-42, Author's translation).

45. Mack (1991:11-12) notes that "[by] 1906, when [Torday] resigned from the Compagnie du Kasai, he was already being consulted as an established authority on Congolese ethnography." See also Shaloff (1970:139 n.7).

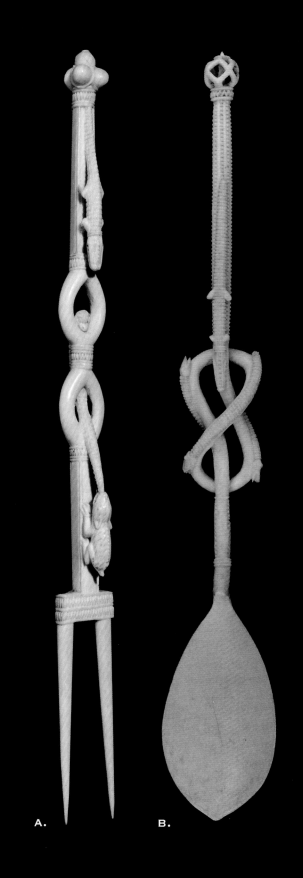

A.

B.

C.

A. Fork, Temne-Bullom peoples, Sierra Leone. Length 24.5 cm. The Trustees of the British Museum (Inv. no 7845).

B. Spoon, Temne-Bullom peoples, Sierra Leone. Length 24 cm. The Trustees of the British Museum (Inv. no. 1856.6-23.163).

C. Saltcellar, Temne-Bullom peoples, Sierra Leone. Height 30.5 cm. The Trustees of the British Museum (Inv. no 1981.AF.35.1).

D. Oliphant, Temne-Bullom peoples, Sierra Leone. Height 63.5 cm. The Paul and Ruth Tishman Collection of African Art, the Walt Disney Company. Photograph, Richard Todd.

ALL THE CARVINGS on these two pages were produced for Portuguese patrons by the Temne/Bullom peoples in what is now Sierra Leone. The saltcellar (opposite) is topped by an image of the Madonna and the Christ child. The three nude male figures on its lid have been interpreted as Shadrach, Meshach, and Abednego, who were thrown into a fiery furnace by the king of Babylon, but saved from death by an angel. On the base (far left) is an image of Daniel in the lion's den. The arms of Portugal appear three times (Curnow 1983:391-393; Bassani and Fagg 1988:72-75). On the ivory hunting horn, in addition to the stag hunting scenes there are heraldic devices identifying the rulers of both Spain (King Ferdinand of Castile and Aragon) and Portugal (King Emanuel I). The fork and spoon, probably by the same artist, were based on 16th-century European metal prototypes (Bassani and Fagg 1988:106-109,131). See also pp. 33-35.

D.

FOURTEEN

THE STAMPEDING OF ELEPHANTS

ELEPHANT IMPRINTS ON LEGA THOUGHT

ELISABETH CAMERON

Bwami, the stampeding of elephants;
The place where it has passed cannot be forgotten.[1]

Though they are physically almost gone now, elephants still move through Lega consciousness, leaving their indelible mark on everyday life. They are kept alive principally through Bwami, a Lega voluntary association that provides moral, artistic, political, and economic structure. Bwami members are visualized as elephants (*nzogu*), and they claim the exclusive use of objects made of ivory and other elephant products (Biebuyck 1976:343). This chapter examines Lega conceptions of elephant as expressed in oral and sculptural traditions, particularly those relating to the Bwami society.

The Lega live in eastern Zaire in the dense central African tropical rainforest. Their economy is based on agriculture, hunting, fishing, and animal husbandry. Great herds of elephants and other large game animals were plentiful before the turn of the last century and in the early part of this one. David Livingstone, as he traveled in this area between 1865 and 1873, commented repeatedly in his journal on the large number of elephants (Waller 1874, I: 206, 208, 259; II: 23). Elephants were snared or trapped by Lega hunters (Delhaise

1909:122-23; Biebuyck 1973:27-28), who then distributed the meat and sold the tail, ivory, skin, bones, and other remaining parts (Biebuyck 1973:111). Livingstone gives a rare description of a Lega elephant trap (Waller 1874, II:38):

> We passed several huge traps for elephants: they are constructed thus – a log of heavy wood, about 20 feet long, has a hole at one end for a climbing plant to pass through and suspend it, at the lower end a mortice is cut out of the side, and a wooden lance about 2 inches broad by 1½ thick, and about 4 feet long, is inserted firmly in the mortice; a latch down on the ground, when

14-1. Hat worn by a member of the Bwami Society of the Lega people of Zaire. Bwami members wear their hats (also called *bwami*) at all times. The particular hat embellishements reveal the wearer's status within Bwami. This hat, with its attached elephant tail, signifies that the wearer is a member of *lutumbo lwa kindi*, the highest level of the society (Biebuyck and Abbeele 1984:84). Height 55 cm. Private collection.

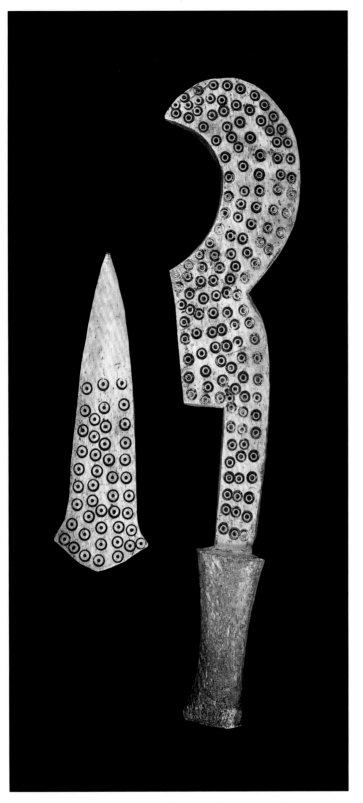

14-2. A variety of ivory utensils are used in many different Bwami ceremonies. The "skinning of the elephant" is accomplished with ivory spoons and knives, and masked dancers are fed with spoons. Such utensils emphasize continuity through references to hunting, feeding, and growth (Biebuyck 1973:117,226; 1986:17,59,116,190). Lega people. Left, 20 cm. FMCH x378.597; right, 15 cm. FMCH x378.587.

touched by the animal's foot, lets the beam run down on to his body, and the great weight of the wood drives in the lance and kills the animal. I saw one lance which had accidently fallen, and it had gone into the stiff clay soil two feet.

The hunters were familiar with elephant's habits and had great respect for its power. Although never directly involved, the Lega area was impacted by the Arab ivory and slave trade which peaked in the late nineteenth century. Due to more efficient hunting techniques and the international demand for ivory, elephants became so scarce that today very few remain in this area.

THE BWAMI SOCIETY

The central organizing principle of Lega life is Bwami: almost all Lega men are members, at least at the lowest grade. The association comprises five or six ranks, with variations in names and sequence occurring from area to area. Biebuyck lists six, starting with *bwami* at the entry level and continuing upwards through *bombwa, bubake, ngandu,* and *yananio,* to the highest level, *kindi. Yananio* and *kindi* are each further sub-divided into three levels (1973:72).[2] There is also a women's version of Bwami with fewer grades, but its significance for women or for the larger community is difficult to know because so little research has been done.[3]

A young Lega man's introduction to Bwami is through an initiation (which includes circumcision) into the lowest grade, or *bwami.* First, he must obtain tutors who coach his performance of the initiation rituals and who teach him the appropriate proverbs and their meanings. The fearlessness and strength he must demonstrate on the threshold of initiation rigors are stated in the following proverb: *The one without fear, banana tree, the tough one, is waiting for the stampeding of the elephant* (Biebuyck 1973:127). The initiate must respect his tutor as well as all those senior to him in rank; he must listen to them and obey them because they are more powerful and knowledgeable than he is. This is understood in the proverb, *The stampeding of buffaloes does not equal that of elephants* (Biebuyck 1986:116). As a mark of his new status, the Lega man is allowed to wear a hat identifying him as a Bwami member; its particular construction distinguishes his rank in the association (Fig. 14-1).

If a young man is ambitious, however, he isn't content to stay at the lowest level. He wants the added prestige, influence, and financial benefit associated with membership in higher Bwami levels. Then he begins to marshal his forces, talking to different members of his lineage to gain their financial and moral support. He also seeks the help of members of the higher grade, who will act as his sponsors and tutors.

The final decision of who is allowed to undergo the progressive initiations depends on a number of factors, including "character, kinship support, wealth, initiation, [and] moral

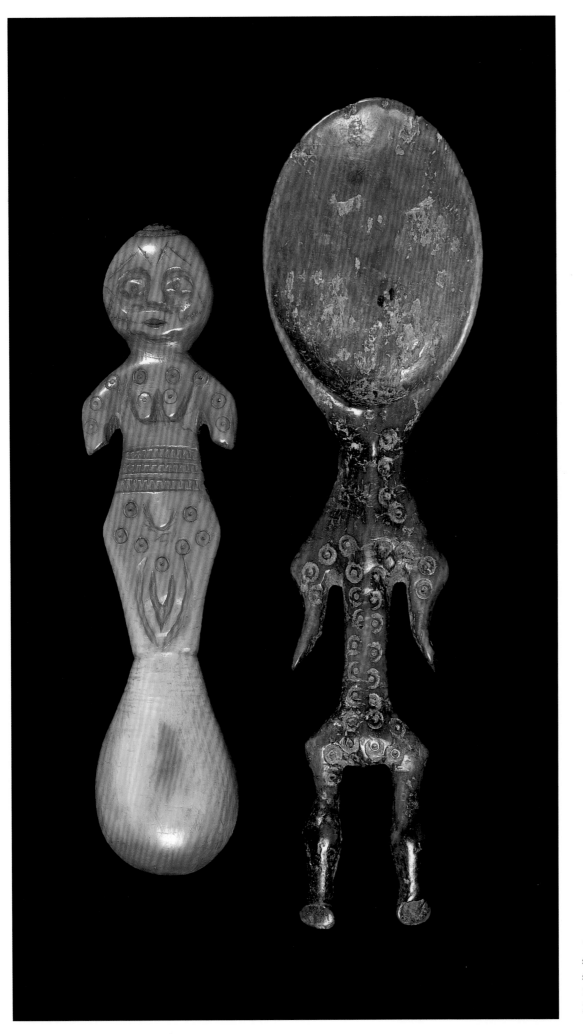

14-3. Occasionally ivory spoons take anthropomorphic shapes. Lega people, Zaire. Left, 17 cm. FMCH X67.830A; right, 22.2 cm. FMCH X378.106.

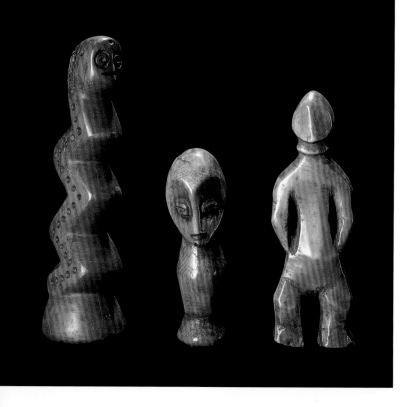

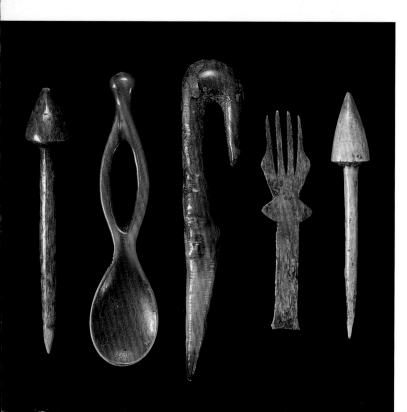

perfection" (Biebuyck 1973:66), the latter being the most important. Economic factors are also significant because the candidate must supply quantities of goods and food to distribute during his initiation ceremonies; the amounts required are proportionately greater with each increase in rank.

In addition to material distributions, initiation involves the transferral of esoteric knowledge through the didactic use of oral traditions and special artifacts which are often linked. Objects used in this way range from found objects – seed pods, twigs, etc. – to sculptures and masks made of wood, ivory,[4] and bone (Kjersmeier 1937:34). Typically, these items belong to a given grade. They are contained in a basket which is entrusted to the newest initiate, who keeps them on behalf of the other members (Biebuyck 1973:95,151). Certain artworks are individually owned but must be passed on within the owner's lineage when he moves to a higher level. If there is no one within the lineage who can receive the object, it is held by a member of another lineage until someone from the owner's lineage achieves the appropriate rank.

Bwami initiation objects are not intended for shrine display; rather they are designed to be handled in rituals (Biebuyck 1986:3), manipulated by Bwami tutors, and used in conjunction with oral traditions to impart esoteric knowledge to the candidate. Biebuyck has referred to them as mnemonic devices (1976:338). De Kun characterizes Lega art as a closed circle in which sayings describe sculptures and objects represent oral traditions (1966:78). This is much like the connection, or "visual-verbal nexus," noted by Herbert Cole and Doran Ross for the Akan of Ghana: "the ... sculptural representations of symbols, objects, or scenes which are directly related to proverbs or other traditional sayings" (1977:9). Thus through a combination of visual and verbal art, Bwami initiates are taught new moral principles.

The most prestigious way to enter and advance in Bwami is through one's own efforts; but a number of other avenues are available. The most common is when a father invites his son to join. A father's grief at not having a son to follow him in Bwami is recorded in the proverb, *The parasol tree which I had designated for the shield becomes a small tree to be trampled by an elephant* (Biebuyck 1973:193). Occasionally, a clan member is asked to enter a specific grade to replace a relative who died

14-4 THROUGH 14-11. Ivory and elephant-bone utensils used in Bwami society ritual. Lega people, Zaire.

14-4 (LEFT, TOP). Height of largest, 16 cm. Private collection.
14-5 (LEFT, MIDDLE). Height of largest, 9 cm. Private collection.
14-6 (LEFT, BOTTOM). Height of largest, 15 cm. Private collection.
14-7 (RIGHT, TOP). Height of largest, 19 cm. Private collection.
14-8 (RIGHT, MIDDLE). Height of largest, 15 cm. Private collection.
14-9 (RIGHT, BOTTOM). Height of largest, 10 cm. Gift of Helen and Dr. Robert Kuhn.
14-10 (FAR RIGHT, TOP). Height of largest, 17 cm. Private collection.
14-11 (FAR RIGHT, BOTTOM). Height of largest, 27 cm. Private collection.

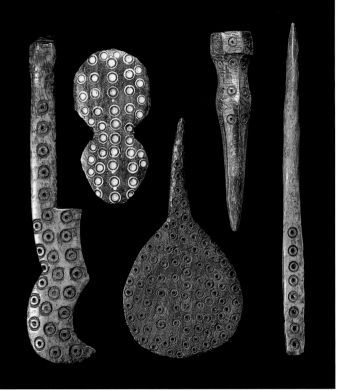

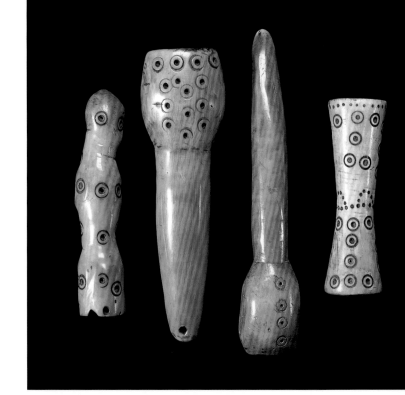

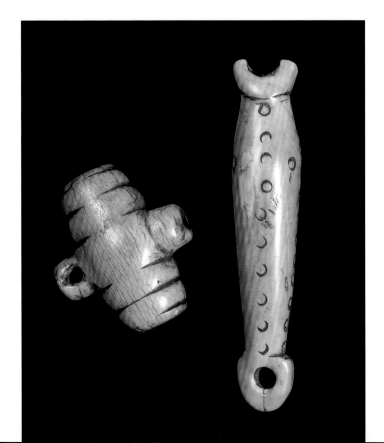

before or during initiation. In case of illness, an oracle may determine that the person will return to health when he joins or advances a grade in Bwami. Finally, anyone who breaks specific Bwami rules is initiated into the level of Bwami that is able to control the results of his transgression (Biebuyck 1973:85-86).

As a man is able and motivated, he moves up the grades until as a much older man he reaches the highest level, known in most areas as *lutumbo lwa kindi*, or simply *kindi*. *Kindi* is usually open to men of all clans and lineages (Biebuyck 1972:12-13). To reach it is a Lega man's highest achievement and goal in life, for *kindi* is considered "the promise of glory, immunity, [and] perpetuity" (Biebuyck 1973:175). A successful move to the top is fairly rare, however, due to the expense and difficulty; only one or two men in each village achieve that peak. While all Bwami initiates are loosely identified with the elephant, *kindi* members are especially connected to the animal. *Kindi* initiates refer to themselves as Banamulua, or People of the Elephant Herd (Biebuyck 1973:162,206); Bananzogu, or Children of the Elephant (Biebuyck 1986:101); and Bakinsamba, or People of the Elephant Tail (Biebuyck 1986:101). A hat topped with an elephant tail identifies the wearer as a member of *kindi* (Fig. 14-1) (Biebuyck and Abbeele 1984:84). *Kindi* initiates are perceived by the Lega to have specific elephantine qualities: power, destructive ability, restraint, retentive memory, hospitality,[5] and the ability to live peacefully in a group as seen in the socialized nature of the herd (Biebuyck 1986:40,101; 1973:128). The Lega also note elephant's keen sense of smell (Biebuyck 1986:40). A proverb alludes to the authority of *kindi*: *The place where elephant stampeded cannot be forgotten, the place where Nzogu passed the trace cannot be obliterated* (Biebuyck 1986:116). Thus *kindi*, through social, political, and moral teachings, make their daily impression upon Lega life.

In the rites of *kindi*, concepts of Elephant are dramatically enacted through pantomime. In one ceremony, for example, male and female Bwami members sit on the roof of a house waving banana leaves in imitation of elephant trunks (Biebuyck 1986:101). The initiation house itself is also thought of as an elephant. Initiation into the highest level of *kindi* (*lutumbo lwa kindi*) ends with the ceremony called "skinning of the elephant," *ibago lwa nzogu* (Biebuyck 1973:117). Bwami members "skin" the initiation house/elephant by recklessly removing the roof and other parts of the house with small ivory utensils (Fig. 14-2)(Biebuyck 1986:17,59,116,190), leaving its frame or skeleton. The ivory spoons, *kalukili* or *kakili* (Fig. 14-3), seem to emphasize continuity (Biebuyck 1973:226), perhaps through reference to feeding and growth.

The house-skinning ceremony, mirroring the actual skinning of an elephant, also parallels the ritual distribution of food which is required of a candidate in the course of his initiation process (Biebuyck 1986:190). As with most Bwami rites, the ceremony carries both a positive message and a warning, as do associated proverbs. Some allude to the joyous food distribution that will take place during the iniation process,

and to the Bwami members who will come from surrounding villages for the occasion:

There is joy, as when an elephant is cut up, because there are many goods.

When he hears about the young fields with new shoots, the elephant does not know to flee.[6]

One saying addresses *baki*, those who are not initiated into *kindi*: *Baki, miserable ones, come and see the herd of kindi* (Biebuyck 1986:116).

On the negative side, careless handling of the ivory knives and spoons recalls the proverb: *The banamulua skinned the elephant in a confused manner*, referring to the necessity of leadership and presumably stressing the community's need for *kindi* (Biebuyck 1986:190). In the same vein, a ceremony, *ndinde*, refers to this carelessness as a warning against taking what is not one's due, an action that would result in tension within the community.

THE OWNERS OF IVORY

Except for the ivory spoons, which are used at all levels of Bwami, objects made of ivory are reserved for the top rank.[7] *Kindi* members call themselves *nenemulamba*, or owners of ivory (Biebuyck 1986:40), and claim for themselves the use of ivory, elephant bone, and other elephant parts in sculpture and dress (Figs. 14-4 to 14-11). One of the objects used in *kindi* is the mask *lukungu*, literally "skull," which may be of ivory (Fig. 14-12), bone (Fig. 14-13), or elephant hide (Fig. 14-14). Each initiate of *lutumbo lwa kindi* possesses one such mask (Biebuyck 1976:344) which is never worn on the face, but rather carried in the hand, displayed on the ground, or hung from a fence — depending on the specific *kindi* ceremony.

In addition to individual masks, *kindi* members also share collective ownership of a large ivory figure (Fig. 14-15) which must be present at important ceremonies such as the initiation of new members (Biebuyck 1986:62). The figure's custodian is a descendant of the man who originally introduced *kindi* to the community, and the lineage of ownership is carefully recorded in oral traditions (p. 55).[8]

Certain *kindi* ivory figurines are associated with or serve as their visual counterparts of specific aphorisms (Biebuyck 1973:218). When a figurine is removed from the context of that particular saying, its unique meaning is impossible to reconstruct. For example, a many-headed figure named Sakimatwematwe directly refers to the saying, *Mr. Many Heads has seen an elephant on the other side of the large river.* This proverb speaks to the *kindi* qualities of wisdom and knowledge (Biebuyck 1972:17; 1973:220,221, pl. 74). A double figurine (Fig. 14-17) can carry either positive or negative messages. When a piece is called Kakinga, it carries a negative message: *The little maiden used to be beautiful and good; adultery is the reason that she perished*

14-12 THROUGH 14-14. Masks known as *lukungu* ("skull") and used by members of the highest grade of the Bwami society, *kindi,* which claims exclusive use of all parts of the elephant, including the ivory, bone, hide, and tail. Each *kindi* member owns such a mask which he carries in his hand, displays on the ground, or hangs from a fence during ceremonies. At the owner's death, the mask is placed on his grave, then stored until the next member of the lineage reaches *lutumbo lwa kindi* (see Biebuyck 1953:1078-79; 1954:111-13; 1973:211-13; 1976: 344). Lega people, Maniema, Zaire.

14-12 (TOP). Elephant-ivory mask. Height 22.2 cm. Section of Ethnography. Royal Museum of Central Africa, Tervuren, Belgium.

14-13 (MIDDLE). Elephant-bone mask. Height 26.5 cm. Section of Ethnography. Royal Museum of Central Africa, Tervuren, Belgium.

14-14 (BOTTOM). Elephant-hide mask. Height 22.7 cm. Section of Ethnography. Royal Museum of Central Africa, Tervuren, Belgium.

14-15. Ivory figurine used in Bwami initiation activities. Ivory anthropomorphic sculptures, such as this one, are not ancestor figures, but are didactic tools used in instructing Bwami initiates. They come in many different forms, including the head and neck, as here, and the full figure. Height 13 cm. Lega people, Zaire. U and W Horstmann Collection, Zug, Switzerland.

(Biebuyck 1973:77). It can also refer, however, to the positive link between initiate and wife, or initiate and tutor (Biebuyck 1981:122).

Certain other objects can be associated with many different sayings, all of which are didactic, teaching Lega moral code to the candidate and anyone else within earshot (Mulyumba 1973:5). Many ivory and wood *kindi* figures are formed with no distinguishing features so as to avoid their direct correlation with a specific proverb; being indistinct in shape and meaning, they can be used in a variety of contexts. Biebuyck has argued that such Lega figures in themselves cannot be interpreted because of the practice of using the same objects with different sayings. Thus, "form is not necessarily a sign; form alone does not necessarily convey meaning" (Biebuyck 1973:146).[9]

An object, through use, gains a patina, and in the Lega view, a well-patinated figure or mask acquires a power or heaviness (*masengo*) of its own along with its patina (Biebuyck 1976:

338). Treatment for illness may include drinking water in which an ivory object has been soaked or ingesting scrapings from an ivory figure in order to partake of the power of the object and promote healing (Biebuyck 1986:27). The owners carefully oil the surfaces of the figurines in the same fashion and with the same materials that they use to oil their own bodies (Biebuyck 1973:179).

He who dies does not come back, On ivory, mushrooms do not grow.[10]

When a Bwami member dies, specific initiation objects that he owned, such as the *lukungu* mask discussed above, are displayed on the grave before being passed to the new owners. When the next member of the owner's lineage reaches *kindi*, he will be given the mask (Biebuyck 1953:1078-79; 1954:111-13; 1973:211-13). Thus, *kindi* masks and sculptures are passed down for many generations, and the history of each piece is carefully remembered. With objects that specifically represent *kindi*, such as the ivory figures and the *lukungu* mask, the genealogy is especially strong. The proverb '*on ivory, mushrooms do not grow*' metaphorically compares ivory to a man's skeleton, a permanent durable memory (Biebuyck 1973:174). The reference to the mask as a skull, the association of ivory with human remains, and the connection of the mask and the grave all stress the idea of continuity already seen in the ivory spoons and knives. The latter, however, are merely subtle references to feeding and growth; they are not passed down and do not have genealogies. The ivory masks and figures, on the other hand, directly connect the past and the present, creating an unbroken chain of ancestors (Biebuyck 1973:104-05; 1976:339; Brain 1980:178).

In spite of its focus on continuation of the clan and on ancestors, Bwami is not, strictly speaking, an ancestor cult, according to Biebuyck (1954:113): "It must be made clear that they don't form part of the ancestor cult, which was formerly directed toward the human skull itself . . . the social significance of the masks is by far more important than their ritual meaning. They are mainly social symbols, marks of recognition and concrete means for teaching." In this way of thinking, the very existence of Bwami, and its age, as well as the unbroken line of high-level Bwami members, serve to legitimize current political and social structures, rather than offer supernatural help.

Nevertheless it is impossible not to see some connection between Bwami and the Lega belief in ancestors. When individuals die, the Lega say that they live as disembodied ancestors in a situation which reflects the status and relationships the individual had when alive.[11] The ancestor is able to communicate with the living through apparitions and mediums, and to affect the lives of those on earth in both positive and negative ways; therefore, a good relationship with the ancestors is an important consideration in Lega life and institutions.

14-16. Ivory figurines in the shape of elephants, used in the Bwami society. The elephant, left, with its trunk in the air (as if to pick wild mangoes) was said to be used to accompany songs about the foolish behavior of those intoxicated, who are likened to the elephant when it has eaten mangoes. With its foot raised, the figure topples over easily, like a drunkard. Left, height 8.6 cm. Right, length 11.4 cm. Lega people, Zaire. Collection of Marc Felix, Brussels.

In order to facilitate this communication as well as to appease the ancestors, official ancestor cults exist on both a domestic and a public level. Although Bwami is not one of the official cults, the only dead able to return to, communicate with, and affect the living are those who in life had Bwami rank – i.e. were circumcised or married. Ceremonies to honor specific ancestors use Bwami ceremonies, songs, and sayings that reflect the Bwami rank of the deceased. Bwami exists in the worlds of the living and the dead, acting as a bridge between them. Thus, Bwami is important in both realms, and is essential to the cult of the ancestors.

BWAMI AND CHIEFTAINCY

Authority, whether it be *kindi* or a hereditary chief, is often compared to the elephant. A song setting forth some of the attributes of rulership makes the linkage explicit:

> *The chief is like an elephant.*
> *He is large like him,*
> *But, like him, he must protect all his children,*
> *The good and the bad.*
> *See the elephant!*
> *He does not hunt all the villainous parasites*
> *that he has on his side.*[12]

The extraordinary nature of rulership is further suggested in the proverb: *The pregnancy of Elephant is not like that of any other animal.*[13] The meaning of this saying is particularly rich if applied to Bwami.

Although the situation differs from area to area, Bwami functions in a majority of Lega villages, to provide government without political centralization by providing a series of checks and balances within Bwami's hierarchical tiers (Biebuyck 1973:93). Evidence of the beginning of a hereditary chieftaincy – or perhaps of its remnants – is seen in the eastern Lega area, where only members of particular clans are permitted to reach the highest levels of Bwami (Vansina 1990:181). Among the Sile, a Lega subgroup, Bwami certifies the royal clan, gives it political power, and bestows it with sacred dignity (Mulyumba 1978:28).

The exact origins of Bwami are uncertain, but it is clear that it evolved under the influence of immigrations to the Lega area. As different people moved in, they brought with them many of their own traditions but seemed to have adopted and modified Bwami to serve their own needs and traditions. Some contend that Bwami was introduced in order to stop internal fighting (Yogolelo 1975:23). In some groups, the term *mwami* (a singular form) was the name of the sacral king, suggesting that *bwami* (its plural form) means kings (Bishikwabo 1979: 14). Among the Lega, Bwami became the culture's central principle, forming a loose organization with as little tension between villages as possible. The highest level of Bwami, whether called *kindi* or *ngandu*, replaced the individual king or ruler. As a man approached the high levels, he had to draw from a wider area and among more clans and lineages to obtain the support and resources needed for a successful initiation. This broad support was important, not only during the initiation, but also as the *kindi* member carried out his administrative duties – much like a chief! In some areas, only members of specific clans or lineages were able to obtain *kindi*, reflecting a step towards (or perhaps, if the *bwami* were originally kings, away from) centralization.

The Lega area was isolated from the nineteenth-century ivory and slave trade (Biebuyck 1976:343; de Kun 1966:73). The Arab traders knew about the large amounts of ivory in the

14-17A,B (TWO VIEWS). Ivory double figures show both how the initiate is supposed to act and how he is not supposed to act. The two figures can refer to the essential ideal link between the initiate and his wife, or an initiate and his tutor. It can also refer to individuals who cause division within the community (Biebuyck 1981:122-23). 13 cm. Lega people, Zaire. Collection of Clayre and Jay Haft.

area, but the Lega and their neighbors were able to defend themselves against Arab raids. David Livingstone's people were afraid of the area "lest the Manyuema [another name for the people of that region[14]] should kill them. Here was the barrier to traders going north, for the very people among whom we now are murdered anyone carrying a tusk" (Waller 1874, II:24-25). He also noted "the Balegga will be let alone because they can fight" (p. 67). Many of the surrounding peoples were impacted by the slave trade, resulting in what has been called the Maniema-Arab culture (Felix 1989:22-25). As the traders struggled to obtain access to the Lega area, villages were attacked and the raiders stole all the ivory they could find, which included, unfortunately, many ivory artifacts (Biebuyck 1976:343). The Lega themselves made no differentiation between ivory and elephant bone (de Kun 1966:83; Biebuyck 1973:pl. 57). This lends strong support for the argument that

the Lega did not participate in the ivory trade. If ivory had become a commodity through trade the Lega would have been tempted to sell it and use elephant bone in its place. The resulting scarcity of ivory would then have made it more valuable than bone. But this did not happen. For the Lega, ivory and bone are interchangeable. In 1910, the Belgian colonial government attempted to control the ivory supply by regulating ivory and making it *de facto* illegal for the Lega to own it (Biebuyck 1976:334).

A further examination of elephant metaphors and the use of other elephant products – bone, hide, ivory – among the Lega and their neighbors, as well as the objects used to identify the highest ranked in Bwami will help us further understand the history of the Lega and the development of their unique and flexible system of government, enacted on the model of the elephant, as expressed in Bwami.

NOTES

1. Proverb cited in Biebuyck (1973:127). Daniel Biebuyck is the primary scholar of the Lega people. This study is similar in method to Biebuyck's paper (1979) on animals in Lega art in which, unfortunately, he does not deal with elephant. Of necessity, Biebuyck's writings are a primary source for this article, but as many other sources as possible have been used in order to emphasize the diversity of the Lega people.

2. Different scholars have given different versions of the names of the grades, reflecting the diversity of the Bwami organizations within the Lega area. Delhaise lists "the profane" or uninitiated as the first level, then proceeds to *bwami*, *bonbwa*, *punza*, *gandu*, *ianani*, and *kindi* (1909:xv). Mulyumba notes that among the Sile, a Lega subgroup, the highest grade is *ngandu* (1978:23-25).

3. Women join Bwami in conjunction with their husbands, but must not obtain a higher level than he holds. Spouses must advance together in pursuing the highest grades. The names of the grades echo male levels. Slightly different lists of the women's grades are also given by Biebuyck (1973:85) and Delhaise (1909:xvi). According to Biebuyck the grades are *bombwa*, *bulonda*, and *bunyamwa*, but according to Delhaise they are *bubake*, *bonbwa*, and *bulonda*. As with the men's Bwami, differences in names simply reflect that the two Europeans gathered the names in different Lega villages.

4. There has been a debate within the literature concerning ivory and wood figures and masks. Wingert (1947) and Segy (1951:1041) stated that wood had only been used recently as ivory became harder to obtain. Kjersmeier (1937) wrote that ivory was used because of its abundance, but de Kun (1966:75) pointed out that surrounding groups didn't carve ivory, although it was just as abundant. De Kun hypothesized that the hierarchical development of Bwami produced the differentiation in

materials. He also points out that wood objects do not last in a hot, wet environment, while ivory does, therefore more ivory has survived.

5. Biebuyck cites the Lega proverb *Elephants do not shake off the little bloodsucker* to stress this idea of hospitality (1973:128).

6. Biebuyck (1973:192,199).

7. It is associated with *ngandu* in the areas where that is the peak of Bwami (de Kun 1966:75; Mulyumba 1978:28; Biebuyck 1953:1078).

8. The figure's guardian can choose not to have an ivory mask (Biebuyck 1954:111), as the mask and figure fill many of the same symbolic roles.

9. One scholar, Sandra Klopper (1985), has debated this idea, using Victor Turner's theory that symbols that are seemingly different on one level may in fact be related on other levels (Turner 1967:100). As a result, Klopper states (1985:69): "One can also try to interpret sculptures for which the meanings of associated aphorisms are either unclear or unknown. For although the aphorisms and ritual contexts of carvings undoubtedly emphasize or highlight certain aspects of meaning...the generic if not the specific meaning of an image will always be accessible."

10. Biebuyck (1973:174).

11. This discussion is based on Mulyumba (1968).

12. Cited in Delhaise (1909:268), in French; my translation. Caution must be used with Delhaise's records, as well as those of other Belgian officials, because they often understood an important man to be a chief and forced villages which were loosely bound together by associations or clans to form coherent "tribes" for the ease of Belgian administration.

13. Biebuyck (1986:116) interprets this proverb as referring to "the master of the land."

14. The current orthography for this region and its people is Maniema.

A.

B.

C.

WOMEN RIDING ELEPHANTS, masks
that can squirt water through their hollow trunks
and a variety of stools with elephant supports all
suggest that the animal plays a significant role in the
culture of the Luba peoples of Zaire. The research
of Maes (1924) and Burton (1961) indicates that
there was an "elephant society" among at least
some of the Luba, but details are not clear. The
potential complexity of elephant imagery among
the Luba is evoked by the sculpture, at right, of
a woman with her hands on a wall from which
seem to emerge two identical fugures standing on
elephants. Luba origin myths mention twins but
elephants do not appear with them in the recorded
versions. Perhaps the carving is the sculptor's own
aggrandizement of the powers of these twins. Such
sculptures remind us how much more we have to
learn about the role of the elephant in much of
the expressive culture of Africa.

A. Elephant sculpture. Wood. Height 47 cm. Nieder-
sächsisches Landesmuseum Hannover.

B. Elephant stool. Wood. Height 29 cm. Section of
Ethnography, Royal Museum of Central Africa, 1980
Tervuren (Belgium), 60.39.82.

C. Elephant stool. Wood. Height 31 cm. Linden-Museum
Stuttgart, 26707.

D. Figural scene. Wood, pigment. Height 19.2 cm.
Collection of Paolo Sprovieri.

D.

FIFTEEN

IVORY FROM ZARIBA COUNTRY TO THE LAND OF ZINJ

SIDNEY LITTLEFIELD KASFIR

I n East Africa, elephant ivory has been coveted for millennia, both as a source of wealth through its export and as an opulent material for personal adornment and ritual or ceremonial objects. Historical references to its export along the coast are usually said to appear first in the *Periplus of the Erythraean Sea* (ca. A.D.130-40) and Ptolemy's *Geography* (ca. A.D.150); but if allowances are made for geographic vagueness, Biblical texts furnish a much earlier date, linking the trade in ivory to the Red Sea fleet of Hiram and Solomon (ca. 950-60 B.C.).[1]

Inland, however, there is little or no documentation of ivory use until the period of European exploration that was triggered by the search for the source of the Nile in the nineteenth century. From the thorn-fenced *zaribas*[2] deep in the hinterland, to the Great Rift Valley of Kenya and Tanzania, powerful kings, nomadic cattle keepers, and big game hunters coexisted with the largest elephants in the world. Among all these peoples, ivory has played diverse roles. But since ivory use has substantially declined in recent decades, we can only get a glimpse, from a melange of travelers' journals, colonial documents and early ethnographies, of what its importance might have been. This essay surveys the documentation of the

elephant and its ivory across that broad spectrum of East Africa, noting the impact of the nineteenth-century slave-and-ivory trade on newly emergent political roles and aesthetic systems.[3]

IVORY IN THE LAND OF ZINJ

Along the East African coast, the export of elephant ivory, along with ebony, gave rise to ancient trading settlements. Biblical references to King Solomon's ships which traded with Ophir (Abyssinia) make mention of gold, ivory, apes, and peacocks (I Kings 10:22). Similarly the old trading routes from Egypt, Arabia, and Persia spread down the coast as far as Sofala in Mozambique (Stigand 1913:2-3). The coast was then known in Arabic as the land of Zinj (Zenj, Zanj), or as Zanjibar, "land of the Blacks." Masudi, a Muslim writing in the early tenth century, recorded that "from the country of Zenj come tusks of 150 mann each," which are sent to India and China.[4] By the thirteenth century, the cities along the

15-1 (OPPOSITE). Turkana elder with ivory lip plug. Photograph, Herbert M. Cole, 1973.

15-2. Swahili chair, *kiti cha enzi* ("grandee's chair"), with ivory inlay. Chairs like this, probably inspired by an Egyptian model, were in use in Swahili courts by the early 17th c. (Allen 1989:54-63). Wood, ivory, string. Height 123 cm. FMCH X89.367. Gift of Steve and Linda Nelson.

seaboard imported cloth, beads, porcelain, and other luxury goods in exchange for ivory, tortoise shell, copper and gold (Davidson 1966:94). This trade was in the hands of Hadhrami, and later, Omani Arabs who constituted the merchant class. Their settlement and intermarriage with African women eventually gave rise to a Swahili-speaking town culture which, primarily through these women, retained its essential African character but was transformed in its public manifestations (such as architecture, dress, and religion) to that of an Arabized, Muslim society.[5]

Considering that the Swahili coastal towns of Kilwa, Mombasa, Pate, and Lamu were the major shipping points for all this ivory, and that there was a highly developed artisan tradition within Swahili society, it would be reasonable to expect a highly elaborated use of ivory in jewelry, furniture decoration, and ceremonial objects. Yet with the exception of the ivory inlay used in Swahili chairs (Fig. 15-2), this seems not to have been so. The preferred materials for personal ornament in the Swahili towns were (and continue to be) gold and silver.

Nonetheless there was one important ivory artifact which did have great significance. This was the *siwa*, a large ceremonial side-blown horn carved from ivory or wood, and in one case, cast in brass. *Siwas* have been known on the East African coast at least since 1498, when Vasco da Gama arrived in Malindi and was met by the king attended by musicians with flutes and "two trumpets of ivory, richly carved and the size of a man, which were blown through a hole in the side and made sweet music" (Allen 1976:38). The explorer brought one back to Europe with him as a gift for the Portuguese king. The *siwas* were distinctly African, and in the governance of the Swahili coast, came to symbolize political legitimacy. Thus when an Arab or Persian installed himself as a Swahili ruler, he found it expedient to adopt elements of African regalia such as the *siwa* (Allen 1976:40).

In non-royal Swahili communities, any person of sufficient wealth and political standing could dress elaborately and have the *siwa* played at initiations, marriages or funerals; and at a more egalitarian level, the owners of *siwa* would sometimes hire them out to other families or communities in order to confer *baraka* (good fortune) on the recipients (Allen 1976:40). The advent of royal rule, however, brought restrictions on its use. When the Vumba conquered the Shirazi towns south of them in the seventeenth century, they prohibited the use of the *siwa* and the wearing of certain status symbols. In essence, the person who held the *siwa* ruled the town (Nurse and Spear 1985:93). So powerful a symbol of authority was the *siwa* that by destroying or transferring it, one destroyed or transferred political legitimacy. In Kilwa, an unsuccessful claimant to the throne actually seized the *siwa* and threw it into the sea, saying that by doing so he would destroy the sultanate forever (Allen 1976:40). By contrast, the Vumba *siwa* (Fig. 15-3)[6] was a gift from Pate, a northern Swahili kingdom in the Lamu Archipelago, symbolizing Vumba's status as a client of the more powerful state (Nurse and Spear 1985:93).

IVORY IN THE HINTERLAND

The Lado Enclave

By the end of the nineteenth century, the bulk of the East African ivory came from in and around a huge tract of land colloquially known as the Lado,[7] that region south of the Bahr-el-Ghazal River and north of Lake Albert in what is now the West Nile region of Uganda, northeastern Zaïre, and Equatoria province of the Sudan. By 1899, this tract had largely passed from Egyptian to British control (Stigand 1913:183, 1923 passim). The very core of elephant country, this land was home to numerous small groups – farmers such as the Alur and Madi, and cattle owners like the Latuka who used and traded ivory.

In and around the Lado Enclave, ivory was both the symbol of political power and the most valuable economic resource. There and in the nearby Zande, Buganda, and Bunyoro kingdoms discussed below, the ivory trade went hand in hand

with the slave trade, both being exchanged for weaponry and luxury goods.[8] While slave-and-ivory traffic was dominated by Arab merchants in Zanzibar and Khartoum, Europeans were involved in the ivory sector. Throughout the Nile-Congo divide, the economic interests of the European mercantile class and the Arab ivory-and-slave traders both converged and conflicted with those of the indigenous people.[9]

In the White Nile/Bahr-el-Ghazal commerce, a secondary slave trade developed as a result of the ivory trade, and increased over time to supply the northern markets. The thorn-fenced *zaribas*, built by Arab traders as places to stockpile ivory, were set down along navigable watercourses in places where elephants were the most abundant and were then visited annually by the traders who owned them.[10] But these enclosures later became the starting point for expeditions of Danagla, armed mercenaries employed by the same Arab traders to capture slaves (and sometimes ivory) by force, and in this way gained their notoriety in England as places that supplied slaves to the Eastern and North African traffic.[11]

For the indigenous people, it was wealth in ivory (or ivory and slaves) which made possible the acquisition of European and Arab material goods (as well as the Arabic language). In this sense, ivory was responsible for two very different types of artifacts in the East African interior: the old and highly valued ivory ornaments worn by pastoralists and sedentary

15-3. The ivory *siwa* of Pate town, made between 1695 and 1700, now in the Lamu Museum in Kenya, is 2.15 meters long and made from two elephant tusks in three interlocking sections. Interlacing guilloche motifs such as seen in openwork and relief on this *siwa* were common in the Swahili coral and wood carving from the 14th, 15th, and 16th centuries (Allen 1976:38-41). The few extant ivory *siwas* are among the finest achievements in African art of this genre. Photograph, Tom Wilson, 1981.

people alike, and the new, foreign artifacts (most importantly, glass beads, brass wire, and cloth) introduced by the ivory-trading caravans. The changes had to do with the way Africans saw themselves vis-à-vis the expanding world of foreigners, and involved clothing and adornment as well as political change.

In Equatoria and the Bahr-el-Ghazal, southern provinces of the Egyptian Sudan where the trade developed surprisingly late, Europeans were eye-witness to dramatic changes occurring with the influx of European goods and guns exchanged for ivory and slaves. A Welsh ivory trader named Petherick was the first to open up the Bahr-el-Ghazal; reports of his success brought competing Arab merchants who by 1866 had opened a trade route to the south as far as the Azande (Evans-Pritchard 1971:294-95). During this same period, several European explorers penetrated the region either by traveling up the Nile from Khartoum or making their way northward from Lake Albert. Schweinfurth, Junker, Casati, and Emin

Pasha all recorded their experiences and brought a meticulously detailed attention to their writings about life and customs, including personal adornment.[12]

Emin Pasha (Edward Schnitzer), German-born medical doctor, botanist, and linguist, was for a time governor of Equatoria province; his letters and journals for the years from 1877 to 1887 were edited and annotated in a volume by Schweinfurth, Ratzel, Felkin, and Hartlaub (1889). Emin's description of a trading *zariba* in Bunyoro captures the market ambience that prevailed (1889:116-17):

> People stream thither from all directions; some as sellers laden with goods or driving before them cattle intended for sale; others as buyers, noisily bargaining with strings of cowries in their hands, or goods for purposes of exchange; the light-brown Wahúma herdsman, with his handsome clear-cut profile and his costume of skins, brings for sale fresh butter neatly wrapped in banana leaves; the deep-black Wichwézi pariah, decked in many-colored tatters, hung all over with amulets and other curious ornaments, is begging, and extolling his art- he is the gipsy of the country; light-colored Muscat Arabs, proudly conscious of their colour and superiority, with their hooked dagger . . . stuck in the girdle . . . Wagánda, draped in neat tan-coloured bark cloth, have brought for barter the handsome soft mats of Ugánda, together with bark cloths and thick copper wire; . . . the fair-skinned inhabitants of the hill-country to the south have cattle exposed for sale, and the tall Wákidi warriors, with their towering hair and iron gorgets, look on at the busy scene with indifference. They do not need dress materials, *and what they want of iron, copper, glass beads, &c., Kabréga [king of Bunyoro] gives them in abundance, in return for the ivory they bring him* [emphasis added].

Here as on the coast, tusks were valued not only as raw material but as symbols of authority. In 1879, when Emin Pasha wanted to move the government station upriver from Lado to what came to be called Wadelai, the Alur chief of that name sent his foster-brother Gimoro with an elephant tusk and 300 followers (Stigand 1923:109). The tusk in this case was a symbol of Chief Wadelai's authority. It may also have suggested his willingness to trade in ivory, a substance which was already known to have a high export value to the Arab traders. We know, for example, that the chief of the Pandoro, living west of the Alur, armed his people with rifles which he received in exchange for ivory prior to his capture by the Belgians in 1912.

The Europeans were quick to see the economic advantages of controlling this wealth. Emin Pasha reported that profits accruing to Equatoria Province were almost entirely from ivory. Indeed, in 1887, when the Welsh-American journalist Henry Stanley and a column of 465 soldiers, carriers, and followers set out to rescue Emin Pasha and his beleaguered garrison at Wadelai, the ivory waiting there, reputed to be

worth 60,000 pounds sterling, was meant to compensate for a considerable part of the expense of the expedition.[13] Despite the fact that all ivory had been declared by General Gordon to be government property, it was nonetheless traded far beyond the official Egyptian sphere of interest, southward into Buganda and Bunyoro (Moorehead 1960:169).

Not all elephant ivory was traded or kept as tusks. Great quantities of it were used for personal ornament, as is clear from Emin Pasha's journals (Schweinfurth et al. 1889). In November 1879 he noted the use of ivory rings among the Alur in Wadelai district (pp. 143-44). Emin noted other groups using ivory for personal adornment, from the Latuka elephant hunters east of Gondokoro to the agricultural Madi on the Nile at Bora (pp. 13,229,234). In addition to wearing their own ivory ornaments, it appears that Madi (and Barambo) artisans also supplied ivory and other kinds of necklaces to their Zande neighbors (Giorgetti 1957:181; Evans-Pritchard 1971:99-100).

Zande and Mangbetu Ivory [14]

The Azande, living partly within and partly to the west of the Lado Enclave, amassed great wealth in ivory and used it to establish trade and expand their political hegemony. It also enabled them to sustain one of their most important ritual systems, the poison oracle (*benge*), which required a type of plant located outside of Zande country to the south. Junker (1890, I:437) claimed that the Zande king Gbudwe traded ivory in exchange for the poison with the Baka chief Ansea.

In the days before colonization, Zande men were primarily hunters and only women cultivated crops (Evans-Pritchard 1971:71-72). Whenever a herd of elephants was sighted, great numbers of huntsmen and drivers were gathered together by signals on huge drums for the chance to obtain "many hundred-weights of ivory, and perchance ten times the weight of meat" (Schweinfurth 1874, I:438-41). Typically, the elephants were lured into a field by means of hunt medicine, then surrounded by fires and trapped until they expired (Lagae 1926:148-49; Schweinfurth 1874, I:438).

Later this method of killing elephants was forbidden by the British, and the Azande learned to spear them instead. They sat in trees and plunged a heavily weighted poisoned spear into the elephant's back. In addition, the chiefs of the ruling clan, known as Avongara, had rifles that their wives carried for them on elephant hunts (Brock 1918:256-57). In this new method, the hunting medicine continued to be essential, but now enabled the hunter to shoot straight. Bullets that had killed an elephant became greatly prized as gun medicine (Anderson 1911:258). The chief had a right to all the ivory as well as his choice of the meat, which was then preserved and eaten throughout the dry season.[15]

It is not easy to separate the material culture of the Azande from that of their southern neighbors the Mangbetu, despite their political differences.[16] So thoroughly interwoven are issues of art production and patronage in this area that Schildkrout and Keim (1990), in the first major exhibition-

15-4 (ABOVE). Mangbetu woman dancing with an ivory side-blown trumpet. Photograph, Angela Fisher, early 1980s.

15-5 (RIGHT). Inland as well as on the coast, the elephant tusk was an important emblem of regalia. This side-blown ivory trumpet with raised mouthpiece, carved head, and beads for eyes may be either Mangbetu or Azande. Height 61.5 cm. FMCH X87.58.

publication of artifacts from Zande and Mangbetu country, advocated a regional rather than ethnic approach to questions of origin. According to Evans-Pritchard, the Azande freely borrowed styles, techniques, and customs from wherever they conquered or traded (1971:93-106). This included objects made from ivory as well as pottery, clothing, weapons, and woodcarving.

One ivory artifact used by both cultures was the elephant tusk trumpet (Figs. 15-4, 15-5). Emin Pasha, while governor of Equatoria Province (an area that included both eastern

Zandeland and Mangbetu country), noted its use by a Zande ruler in 1882: "Wando was accompanied by three of his fourteen sons, all wearing the handsome hide-dress of the Zande, and tall straw hats decorated with parrots' feathers. The indispensable trumpeters accompanied them, carrying gigantic horns and trumpets made out of elephants' tusks and decorated by leopard-skins" (Schweinfurth et al. 1889:374). A year later, Emin wrote of his visit to Mangbetu ("Monbuttu") and his entry into the village of Jondi "accompanied by the deafening sound of huge horns carved out of elephant tusks" (p. 190). Whether the horns of the Azande were carved by Mangbetu smiths and imported into Zandeland or were indigenous, they were associated with the power of the ruler in both Mangbetu and Zande courts and are one of several types of shared artifact common to both cultures.

Another Zande object with Mangbetu associations was the carved bowharp (*kundi*), sometimes with an ivory neck and finial. While these are often said to be a Mangbetu influence,

313

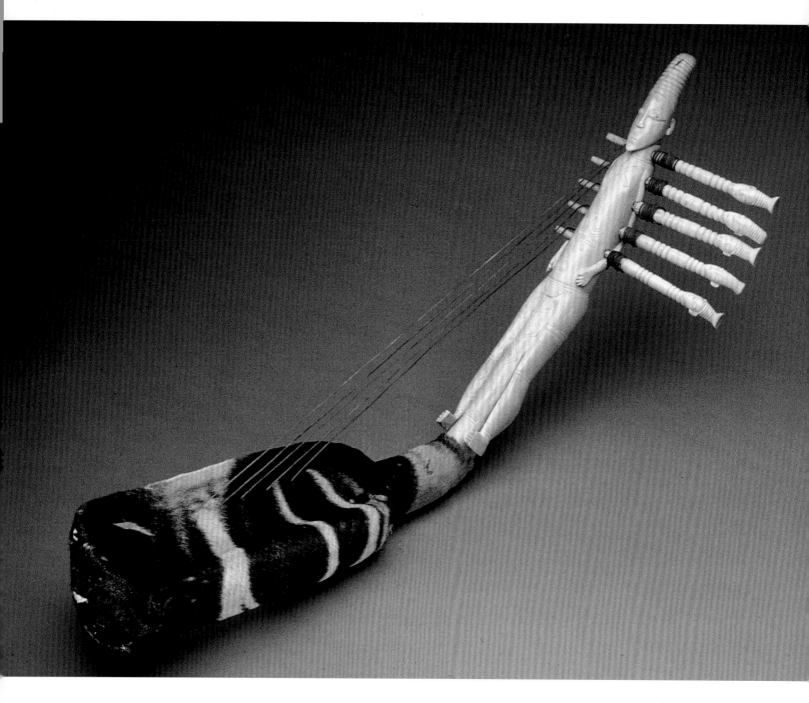

15-6. Mangbetu bowharp with an ivory finial. Ivory, okapi hide with fur. Length 68 cm. Lang, coll. Medje, 1914. American Museum of Natural History 90.1/2230.

Schweinfurth asserted that the Mangbetu had no mandolins (bowharps) or other stringed instruments (1874, II:117). Casati (1891, I:195), on the other hand, remarked that *both* Azande and Mangbetu had the same stringed instrument of the mandolin type. What is indisputable is that some of the supposedly Zande bowharps depict the artificially elongated Mangbetu head and disc coiffure (Fig. 15-6). Since the Azande did not adopt this Mangbetu practice, it seems clear that the *subject* of these carvings is Mangbetu, whether or not the workmanship is Azande. Other Zande bowharps depict heads with the chequered cicatrice patterns on forehead, cheeks, and temples, and the elaborately braided hair characteristic of the Azande. Evans-Pritchard posited a dual explanation for Mangbetu heads on Zande harps: some were Mangbetu imports and others were Zande copies of Mangbetu prototypes (1971:96-97). The tendency to see the Mangbetu as the donor culture and the Azande as recipients is due partly to

the "Mangbetu myth" of cultural superiority (Schildkrout and Keim 1990:29,34) and partly to real Zande enthusiasm for cultural appropriation (Mack 1990:217-18).

A third category of shared Zande-Mangbetu usage was that of the personal ornament. People in both cultures wore elaborate hats and hairstyles in which long hairpins of ivory or bone (Figs. 15-7, 15-8) were attached. Of the Mangbetu, Emin Pasha wrote: "Headdresses and straw hats are kept in place with ivory hairpins. They are neatly made with square, round or crescent-shaped heads which are sometimes decorated with burnt-in dotted patterns" (Schweinfurth et al. 1889: 211). Czekanowski, who visited the Azande in 1907-8, wrote that their hairpins were the same as the Mangbetu ones, and

15-7. Ivory hairpins used by Mangbetu and Azande people. Length of longest hairpin, 39.4 cm. Left to right, FMCH X67.728, X67.767, X65.10036, X67.759.

15-8. A Mangbetu woman, wife of the chief of Medie village, poses in the hairstyle of an earlier era, to illustrate ivory hairpins. Eliot Elisofon Photographic Archives, Smithsonian Institution, 1970.

were fashioned from iron, brass, ivory, and bone, enabling "both men and women [to] achieve hairstyles that are works of art" (1924, VI,2:33). Early travelers' descriptions of Zande royalty do not mention the pin though they often remark on headgear or elaborate long tresses. Junker noted that younger Zande princes wore elaborate hair arrangements "often decked with cowrie shells, glass beads, little copper plates and other trinkets" (1891:287-88). The adoption of ivory and bone hairpins would have seemed very natural in these circumstances, whether or not they originated with the Mangbetu.

The Zande-Mangbetu also used ivory bracelets (Fig. 15-9, 15-10), and necklaces (Fig. 15-12). According to Schweinfurth,

"imitation lion fangs made of ivory worn over the breast" were very abundant among the Azande (1874, I:4). From the reports of others, however, it appears they may have adopted ivory necklaces quite late, from assimilated neighboring cultures. This is suggested by two European accounts of the appearance of a Zande chief in late 1879-80. Romolo Gessi Pasha, governor of Bahr-el-Ghazal from 1878 to 1880, describing his encounter with Zande chief Ndoruma (Mdarama) in 1879, mentioned a presentation of forty tusks, but no personal ivory ornament (Evans-Pritchard 1962:99-100).

A year later in 1880, Junker met the same Zande chief wearing a costume composed of both European and Arab elements, assembled expressly for the occasion (1891:101). But

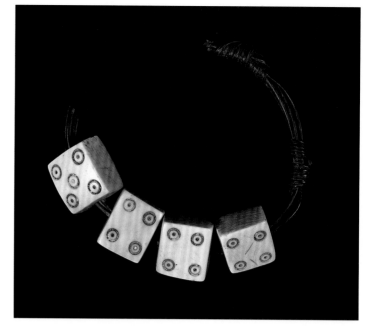

15-9 (ABOVE). Ivory bracelet of the type traded into the Azande area of northern Zaire, probably of Darfur origin. FMCH X67-2084. Photograph, Richard Todd.

15-10 (RIGHT). Mangbetu elephant hair and ivory bracelet, collected in the late 19th or early 20th century. Newark Museum.

his ordinary dress was still the short wrapped barkcloth known as *rokko* and he still affected the Zande hairstyle. Junker further stated that Zande chiefs of this early contact period wore *no* personal ornament at all.

This was either an overstatement or a custom in flux. Junker, who made no secret of his disapproval, compared the simplicity of the older kings' dress and manners to the "foppish" dress and ornamentation of the younger generation (1891:287-88). Among the elaborate artifacts of the princes were objects made of ivory:

> The most costly and highly prized is an ivory ornament falling low down on the breast, and consisting of thirty or forty cylinders from 1½" to 2½" long, strung according to size, and terminating in a point downwards. They represent the teeth of predatory animals, especially lions, which are very difficult to procure.... These ivory ornaments involve an amazing display of skill and belong to a classical period of native art – now [late nineteenth century] possessed only by a privileged few.

Zande expansion eastward brought them into the Nilotic cultural sphere where elaborate hairstyles and personal adornment were and still are the norm. Given their propensity for absorbing artifacts and ideas from outside the culture, it would not be surprising to find that some of these came from within the Lado.[17]

Ivory and Elephant Hunting in the Buganda and Bunyoro Kingdoms

South and east of the Lado, on the northern shore of Lake Victoria, in the highly stratified kingdom of Buganda (one of the few East African kingdoms with a detailed record of material culture), elephant hunting was a specialized occupation reserved for members of the Reedbuck Clan occupying the Mabira Forest in Kyagwe (Roscoe 1911:168). From earliest times they had hunted elephant; after the establishment of the monarchy, according to Roscoe, they became hunters to the king (*kabaka*) and paid him tribute in ivory. Immediately following his installation, the king would jump over an ivory tusk in a ritual effort to increase the elephant population (p. 168). When an elephant was killed, the hunters drew the nerve from the tusk and buried it at a safe distance, for it was thought to hold the spirit of the elephant and evil would befall anyone who stepped over it. Prior to a hunt, clan members would place their spears in a shrine overnight and would make offerings of beer and sacrifice a goat to the god of hunting (p. 168).

It was not only the tusks that were signifiers of power for the Baganda, for the metaphoric strength of the animal might be seen to lie elsewhere. The *hearts* of elephants (along with those of lions, leopards, crocodiles and buffaloes) were frequently an ingredient in power emblems (*mayembe*) made of horn, wood, or clay and filled with substances to make the owner brave or strong (Schweinfurth et al. 1889:279).

Like elephant hunting, ivory-working was a specialized occupation.[18] The ivory carver (*moga*) had existed as a specialist prior to the arrival of Arab traders in the country, mainly because of the demand for ivory ornaments. While ivory trading prior to the late nineteenth century was probably on a small scale, it was enough to encourage the king to keep hunters and to exchange the tusks procured in this way for wives or cattle. The recipients frequently had the tusks made into bracelets (*magemu*) for women and children. Of these, the

15-11. Songye tooth-shaped necklace. Photograph, Angela Fisher, early 1980s.

favored type was about three inches in thickness. It had at one side a thick lip, worn uppermost, and tapered to a fine edge at the bottom side. It was also jointed and had four holes, two at the top and two at the bottom so that it could be tied in place on the arm. The ivory carver first soaked the ivory in water until it was soft enough to cut. He used a double-handled saw with a thin iron blade to cut pieces from the tusk. After this a short adze was used to shape the bracelet and to cut away the inside to the right thickness. The final carving was done with a knife, then polished with an abrasive leaf. Another type was a very thin ring of ivory, perhaps an eighth of an inch thick and half an inch wide. Mair, in her inventory of the traditional Ganda household (1934:107-8), included the occasional ivory bracelet along with cow-hair bracelets covered with brass wire and beads, though by the time of her writing the former were rarely seen.

15-12. "Ivory" necklace actually made of hippopotamus teeth, probably from northern Zaire. Hippos and warthogs provided alternative sources of "ivory" for personal adornment. FMCH X67.881.

15-13. Young Shilluk man from Sudan, with ivory bracelets and facial marks characteristic of his age and status. In 1968, at the time of this photo, elephants had not been seen locally for some time. But neighboring Nuba people still had an elephant priest whose job was to protect crops from marauding elephants. His services were sometimes engaged by the Shilluk. Photograph by James Faris, first published in Faris, *Nuba Personal Art*, London and Toronto, 1972.

Like their Zande counterparts, district chiefs in Buganda made money on ivory. Most of the chiefs had their own huntsmen who captured elephants and paid their masters in ivory for hunting on their lands (Roscoe 1911:251). Traditionally, ivory had been used as ornament and as a currency, but its acquisition was limited by royal proscription (pp. 268-69). After the kingdom was opened to Arab trade in the nineteenth century, a great demand for ivory was established. In Buganda neither ivory nor slaves were taken into the marketplace but both were sold privately.[19]

Prior to the cowrie shell currency introduced in the eighteenth century reign of Semakokiro,[20] a blue bead (*nsinda*) had been used, and before that, a small ivory disc known as *sanga*.[21] The ivory workers made these for the king, though he had no monopoly on their manufacture. Any skilled worker could produce them, but since most ivory carvers were in the king's service and the king owned most of the ivory, the discs were *de facto* an item of limited manufacture (Roscoe 1911:412-13).

South of the Lado and west of Buganda in the heart of elephant country lay the kingdom of Bunyoro. In his journal for 1883, Emin Pasha recorded the rivalry between Mutesa (Mtésa), the king of Buganda and Kabarega (Kabréga), the ruler of Bunyoro. Representing Kabarega as his vassal, Mutesa for many years had refused to let Arab traders from the coast into Bunyoro. Instead he acted as middleman, sending gifts of cloth, copper, brass and glass beads to Kabarega and receiving in return ivory and slaves. It was not until about 1878 that two traders, "the Arab called Said-ibn-Seifi and the Fundi, Hassan, a freedman, managed to reach the capital of Unyoro from Karagwa and reaped a good harvest of ivory" (Schweinfurth et al. 1889:115). Emin Pasha went on to describe how profitable (if dangerous) the ivory trade was:

It is the practice in Unyóro, as well as in Uganda, for every trader on his arrival to present about half of his goods, especially powder, lead shot, and guns, to the ruler, who in turn places at his disposal a house and garden . . . and . . . at his departure makes him a present of ivory, the value of which usually amounts to five times that of the original present. . . . The king . . . pays nothing for the ivory, since it is supplied by his faithful subjects.

Not only did Mutesa use the ivory trade for his own political ends, he further enhanced his economic gains by circumventing the caravan traders altogether whenever possible. This was accomplished by sending his own representatives to Zanzibar where they exchanged their ivory directly for guns and ammunition (Schweinfurth et al. 1889:116).

Ivory in the Nilotic Sudan: The Shilluk, Nuer, and Dinka

North of the Lado Enclave toward the Bahr-el-Ghazal region in the southern Sudan are groups of pastoralists who, like their southern neighbors, have made extensive use of ivory as a material for personal ornament. Because studies of East African pastoralists have very rarely focused on their visual arts,[22] however, historical information is fragmentary, drawn from reports of government officials, missionaries, explorers, occasional ethnologists, and more recently, professional photographers.

The first clue to the importance of ivory as adornment among the Shilluk comes in Westermann's wordlists (1912: 107), which include five different terms for ivory rings. In dressing for a dance, the most common adornments for men were thick, heavy bracelets and armlets made of twisted tree-bark, shells, iron, brass, and ivory (Fig. 15-13). Women and girls wore armlets too, but not ones made of ivory (Westermann 1912:xxvi). Dempsey illustrates a Shilluk man wearing a pair of ivory back-scratchers – a favorite and obviously useful adornment (1955:opp. 52).

Elephant tusks were ritually symbolic and were kept in the shrine house of Nyakang, the deified ancestor of the Shilluk (Seligman and Seligman 1932:78). Ivory bracelets had to be worn by certain title-holders at the installation of a Shilluk king, or *reth* (Howell and Thomson 1946:38), along with necklaces of ostrich-eggshell discs (Seligman and Seligman 1932:78). In 1943, for example, this was provided by the tusks of elephants that had invaded Shilluk country from Malakal in 1938 (Howell and Thomson 1946:38). But normally elephants were very rare in the Shilluk area, so ivory had to be obtained through trade.

Among the Nuer, ivory was similarly valued as both ornament and symbol. Nuerland lacks iron, stone, and trees suitable for carving; there was therefore a preponderance of ornaments made from ivory and leather. Evans-Pritchard related that the Nuer, particularly those of the Zeraf River, had a reputation for their courage and skill in hunting elephants which they would surround in a large party and then spear (1940:74,86).

Nuer men who were soon to be married wore a set of three ivory armlets: a large one above the elbow, a smaller one on the other arm in the same position, and a third and smaller one

on the upper arm above the largest one (Huffman 1931:6). The enormous importance the Nuer attached to owning ivory bracelets was evidenced in the distribution of tusks after a successful hunt, according to rules much like those governing bridewealth cattle. "The central portion must be given to the *gwan buthni* of the lineage, this portion being sufficient to make one large bangle; of the remainder a portion must go . . . to the father's side, and a portion . . . to the mother's or maternal uncle's side. . . . There are strong ritual sanctions for observing the correct rules" (Howell 1954:189).

If these rules of distribution were violated, according to Nuer belief, the spirit of the dead elephant would bring misfortune upon the guilty parties. Most important of all, the Nuer see a mystical link between themselves and elephants, which means that their killing is dangerous not only in the physical sense but also spiritually. It is symbolically analogous to homicide and requires the performance of a compensatory ritual in which the first spearer must let some of his own blood (Howell 1954).

The Dinka, occupying an arc south and west of the Nuer in the Nile floodplain, share an appreciation of ivory armlets as well as finger rings, pendants, and earrings (Fig. 15-14), often incised with the circle and dot pattern seen on ivory carving from Zaïre (Segy 1953). One such type, *afiok,* is worn on the wrist by girls ready for marriage (Fisher 1984:57). Bracelets figure prominently in a number of Dinka myths, usually as a metaphor for the female principle.[23] They are also appropriate to expressions of divinity: Lienhardt (1961:49) described a wandering black billy-goat, revered by the Dinka as sacred, which wore a large bundle of finger-rings and bangles attached by a cord to its neck.

But the most visually distinctive forms are circle-and-dot ivory pendants in the shape of an inverted cow's horn, suspended from the back of the glass bead necklaces (Fig. 15-14), which men give to their wives as marriage gifts (Fisher 1984: 57). For the Dinka, like other Nilotic-speaking cattle keepers, cows are not only a measure of economic wealth, but of beauty, strength, divine favor, and spiritual wellbeing. Here one finds the substance of the most powerful animal of the Wild – elephant ivory – as a carved and decorated symbolic substitution for that of a more sacred domestic one – the cow – which has direct associations with divinity.

Ivory in the Great Rift Valley and the Montane Forests

Directly west and south of Lake Turkana (formerly Lake Rudolf) near the Uganda border live the Turkana herders, spatially and culturally intermediate between the Karamojong of northeast Uganda and the Samburu and Rendille of northern Kenya. To the east of the Turkana, in the dry floor and wetter uplands of the Great Rift Valley, pastoralists such as the Samburu tend their herds and coexist with elephants.[24] To the south, elephants, now greatly reduced in numbers, share the grasslands with cattle-keeping Maasai pastoralists, scattered groups

of hunters such as the Okiek, and farmers like the Chagga and the Kikuyu.

In terms of their personal art, the Turkana are best known for an elaborate chignon hairstyle decorated with ochre, ostrich feathers and curved wire, first described by Ludwig von Höhnel (1894) and persisting up to the present time. Their use of ivory, on the other hand, seems to be a twentieth century adoption. Von Höhnel's detailed description of a century ago made no mention of ivory ornaments at all but claimed that nearly all jewelry was of iron or brass, including iron neck clasps and chains, brass rods in the lower lip and oval brass plaques in the septum (1894, II:230-34). But by the late 1920s, men were wearing a hook-shaped piece of ivory in the pierced lower lip, while women had adopted a plaited wire with a bead hanging from its lower end (Emley 1927:183). At the time of Cole's visit (1974:20), men still were wearing ivory or metal ornaments in their pierced lower lips (Fig. 15-1). Despite their relative lack of contact with other cultures, fashions of ornament do change among pastoralists, and are often heavily dependent on materials which originate outside the area and are acquired through trade.

Among the Samburu (Lokop, Lo'eborkeneji) of the Loroki plateau, ivory has a specialized use. Here it is worn in the form of ring-shaped plugs in the ears of warriors, *Imurran* (Fig. 15-16). Today these ear plugs are becoming scarcer because of the decline in the Kenyan elephant population, and a number of warriors substitute white plastic for the ivory. Formerly warriors carved their own — an exceptional activity in a culture where the women do most of the carving.[25]

The choice of ivory works on several levels: first, as a metaphor for the Wild, an appropriate symbol for the young *Imurrani*, who spends long periods of time in the forest away from the family settlements and who sees himself as free from the constraints of marriage, community, and the ownership of cattle. Secondly, ivory forms one part of the black-white-red aesthetic triad so common in East African pastoralist body arts. The black in this case is the natural color of the skin, while red is the ochre from the Abedare mountains mixed with mutton fat to make a cosmetic paste called *ol-karia*, which is smoothed over the lower face, neck, and chest. Finally, ivory is also part of the black-white dyad which is particular to the Samburu because it is a metaphoric representation of themselves, the "people of the black and white cattle." Women and older Samburu men do not properly wear ivory, though the women and often the "younger older" men (so-called junior elders) wear elaborate beadwork. Ivory appears to be associated exclusively with the warrior age grade.

The Maa-speaking Samburu share many habits of dress, especially hairstyles, with the Maasai who were their neighbors (and by Samburu accounts their kinsmen) before being driven south from Laikipia in the nineteenth century. But ivory ornaments are very scarce among the hundreds of modern published photographs of the Maasai.[26]

15-14 (OPPOSITE). Dinka woman wearing ivory bracelets and an ivory pendant of inverted cow's horn. Photograph, Angela Fisher.

15-15 (ABOVE). Dinka earrings, finger rings, and armlets made of ivory. Photograph, Angela Fisher.

Unlike the Turkana, however, at the turn of the century the Maasai *did* wear ivory ornaments such as ivory ear-stretchers and snuff bottles (Fig. 15-17, 15-18), even though these seem to have all but disappeared from their inventory. The explorer Joseph Thomson mentions ivory ear stretchers (ear plugs) worn by young Maasai warriors, and also illustrates an ivory snuff bottle worn around the neck (1887:248-49). Bottles, like earplugs, are increasingly made of plastic today. In 1905, Hollis described an ivory arm ring (*ol-masangus*) cut from an elephant tusk or buffalo horn and worn by elders with many children and cattle (p. 284). This same type is still seen occasionally on Samburu men. Another ivory artifact common to both cultures is the gourd-shaped pendant found tied around sheep's necks.[27] In Samburuland these pendants are associated with well-being and fertility, and are often worn by babies and small children as well as by animals (Kirati

15-16. Ear plugs are still worn but plastic is replacing ivory and the two are nearly indistinguishable. This Samburu man wears matching ear plugs – one of ivory (seen here), the other of plastic. Mtwapa, 1991. Photograph, Sidney Kasfir.

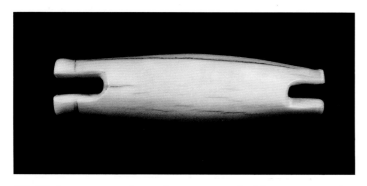

15-17. Ivory ear stretcher such as once worn by Maasai warriors; this one, however, is of Meru provenance. Length 8.9 cm. Collection of the Newark Museum, Purchase 1927, J. Ackerman Coles Bequest Fund, Delia J. Akeley Collection.

Lenaronkoito, pers. com. April 1991; Michael Rainy, pers. com. February 1991).

As potentially significant as any personal ivory ornaments were the bone and ivory decorative and ritual objects which some Maasai and Samburu say that they used prior to the twentieth century. Until very recently, few examples of these objects were publicly known, but a representative collection has now been donated to the National Museums of Kenya.[28] Included are ceremonial weapons, notably *rungu* (clubs/throwing sticks) – some of solid ivory, others tipped with an "eye" of obsidian (Fig. 15-20) which is reported to hold sacred powders (Gillies Turle, pers. com. March 1991). Among the Samburu, these ivory clubs reputedly were used by the *lai'isi*, a class of ritual specialists, to point with while pronouncing a curse upon an individual (Kingore Lenaronkoito, pers. com. April 1991). On other occasions, they were used for bestowing ritual blessings. But such clubs are very rarely seen in Samburu today and it is only men and women over the age of seventy who remember their use.[29]

Recent fieldwork by Roderic Blackburn (pers. com. November 1991) in connection with some of these artifacts has suggested a history of usage of ivory and bone ritual and decorative objects among nineteenth-century and early twentieth-century Maasai.[30] Elderly Maasai informants related that objects of bone and ivory were carved for them by "Dorobo" (Il Torrobo), who supplied many of the ritual and utilitarian artifacts of Maasai and Samburu culture – from cosmetic red ochre to shields used in warfare.

The Okiek, or in earlier accounts, Dorobo/Ndorobo, are a hunting and gathering people who live in close interrelationship with various pastoralist and agriculturalist communities in Kenya, and to a much lesser extent in Tanzania.[31] There are detailed descriptions of "Ndorobo" elephant hunters in Theodore Roosevelt's account of his East African safari in which, with their help as trackers on the slopes of Mt. Kenya, he shot an elephant for the Smithsonian collection and another for the University of California. Roosevelt described the hunter-gatherers of Mt. Kenya (possibly the group who would be called Digiri today) as wearing "the usual paint and grease and ornaments" but made no mention of their having ivory decorations, despite their known skill at elephant hunting and as artisans.[32]

Von Höhnel, who had hunted elephant on the slopes of Mt. Kenya twenty years before Roosevelt, described the local "Dorobo" as bee-keepers and ivory hunters: "The so-called Masai ivory is really supplied by them, as the Masai themselves never go hunting" (1894, II:261). From these accounts one might conclude that those who hunted and killed elephants, such as the Okiek, were not necessarily those who wore its ivory. For them, it might have been only a "mode of production."

One possible reason for this is supplied by Merker in his study of Tanganyika Maasai (1910:251-52). In [then] Tanganyika, the Dorobo were said to be forced by the Maasai to hand over elephant tusks, hippopotamus teeth (as in Fig. 15-12) and rhinoceros horns for a small compensation. The Maasai are said to have bought *kwa nguvu* ("with force," a coastal Swahili trading term) – there was no question of barter trade.

On the other hand, in recent fieldwork on the western Mau Escarpment in Kenya, Kratz learned that Okiek groups there did in fact wear ivory bangles, used and still use ivory tobacco containers and, like Maasai and Samburu, even have ivory decorations for domestic animals (pers. com. June 1991). One may conclude not that any of these accounts is necessarily wrong, but that they are all very fragmentary and represent pictures of different groups of Okiek (and other Dorobo) over considerable time and space. These stories could easily be used to illustrate the dialogic (or sometimes dialectic) nature of ethnographic truth. Perhaps equally, they reveal the ways in which these same "truths" are ideologically constructed.[33]

For example, Maasai dominance (or purity) and Okiek subordination (or pollution) are staple themes. A creation myth recorded by Hollis includes an "Ndorobo," an elephant, and a serpent, in a prelude to the familiar theme of cattle descending from the sky as a gift of God (1905:266-69). The story establishes that both "Ndorobo" and elephants figure prominently as quasi-human Others in the Maasai imagination (as they also do in Samburu).[34] Hollis later wrote, "they [Maasai] eat neither birds, nor fish, nor flesh of wild animals ... if they kill elephants, they only take the tusks, which they exchange for cattle" (p. 319). The Maasai are thus represented as not only fearlessly aggressive toward others but also as very selective in their diet, hence "pure."[35]

Such accounts with their assumptions of Okiek or Dorobo inferiority point to a need to reappraise the position of the Okiek as artists vis-à-vis the Maasai as patrons, just as the recognition of the exaggerated "Mangbetu myth" has caused Schildkrout, Keim, and Mack to reappraise the position of the Zande artist vis-à-vis the Mangbetu. Because the fact of Okiek elephant hunting is so prominent in these stories, and because we know that Okiek provided so many artifacts used by the Maasai (Blackburn 1974:146), there is every reason to investigate further the possible Okiek (especially Saleta and Digiri) origins of Maasai ivory ornaments as well as ritual implements.

Like the Dorobo, the Chagga agriculturalists inhabiting the lower slopes of Mt. Kilimanjaro, in Tanzania, were elephant hunters. The Smithsonian Expedition of 1890 noted that the "natives take them in huge pitfalls or shoot them with poisoned arrows" (Abbott 1892:395). Abbott saw tracks in the snow at 16,000 feet. Elephants frequent the montane forest, just as they do on Mt. Kenya, and ascend the mountain to the central ridge. Yet the inventory of objects collected by the expedition contains no ivory. The sole item of interest listed is a set of armlets made from the toenails of the elephant (p. 405). Nonetheless, some of the ivory armlets in German collections carry a Chagga attribution (e.g., Böhning et al. 1972:34). From this one must conclude that ivory was worn by some sectors of Chagga society.

15-18. Ivory snuff bottles from Kenya – one Luo (left), one Maasai (right), – probably worn around the neck. Like the ear stretchers, ivory bottles have largely disappeared, but their use was noted in early accounts. Left, length 14.6 cm, FMCH X65.10888; right, diameter 4.5 cm, FMCH X 84-630.

The ivory ornaments of the Akamba, while also restricted in their use, are much better documented. A seminal essay on Kamba ivory armlets (*ngotho*) by Jackson establishes that these were an important status emblem for Kamba elephant hunters (1977:52-65 ff). These hunters were crucial to the Kamba traders dominating the hinterland ivory trade before 1850, prior to Arab control. Later, as the ivory commerce widened in scope and competition, these elephant hunters coalesced into associations which took unto themselves some of the attributes usually associated with Maasai and other warriors. That is, they went on raiding parties and developed an elaborate system of body arts, including cosmetics, hair designs, ear-piercing and ornamentation (pp. 52-53). The ivory armlets, in this system, occupied a special rank and also involved as a corollary the development of an ivory aesthetic: an appreciation of its suppleness during carving, its ability to gleam when rubbed with oils or to glow in a more understated fashion when brushed (p. 54). As the nineteenth century progressed, *ngotho* gradually began to appear as elements of notable dress among Kamba

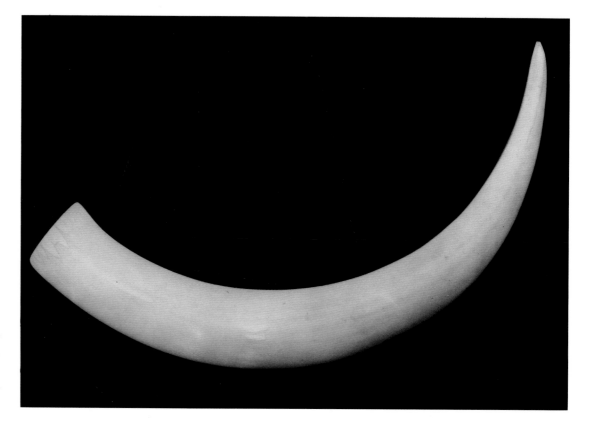

15-19. Hippopotamus-ivory pendant made by Hehe people of Tanzania. See also Fig. 5-12. Length 22.8 cm. Ernst Anspach collection.

ivory traders and were widespread by the late 1860s. They underwent further social transformation over the next thirty years as wars and famines, coupled with the loss of control of the ivory trade, forced the Akamba into new coalitions (pp. 62-63). When two individuals committed themselves to a mutual obligation, they exchanged *ngotho* before witnesses. When whole villages joined a coalition, they had an ivory armlet carved as a presentation gift (p. 64). It is difficult to know how far beyond Ukambani (the Kamba homeland) these armlets were circulated, but given the wide-ranging travels of the Kamba ivory traders, it is safe to say that they were seen and admired by many neighboring cultures.

At the turn of the century, the agricultural Kikuyu dressed much like the Maasai, their neighbors, but due to heavy missionary influence and British settlement in the Kikuyu highlands they long ago gave up all forms of precolonial dress except in specially arranged performance contexts. Even by 1950, Joy Adamson had difficulty finding any Kikuyu willing to pose for portraits in traditional ornaments (1967:65). Yet elephants were ubiquitous in Kikuyuland, and ivory readily available. One early source on the Kikuyu illustrates a solid ivory ear plug known as *muti wa gutu* and an ivory ring (*ngozo*) worn on the upper arm (Routledge and Routledge 1910:pls. xiv, xxvii); the latter can still be seen on occasion. The fact that the terms for the ivory arm ring are cognate in Kikamba (*ngotho*) and Kikuyu (*ngozo*) suggest a shared history.

These and fine iron chains made by Kamba and Kikuyu blacksmiths were highly valued as jewelry, predating the glass trade beads which were brought by Arab traders to be bartered for slaves and ivory. Since the early colonial period, beads have continued to be imported into Kenya by the Indian firm of Lalji and Sons on Biashara Street in Nairobi. Their main customers are Maasai women from the nearby Ngong Hills but the beads also find their way upcountry by a variety of routes. Without the export of ivory, the import of trade beads into East Africa might never have taken hold.

CONCLUSION:
THE PRICE OF CHANGE

The ivory-and-slave trade brought not only new styles of adornment and ideas of self, but also political and economic instability; and in its wake, the influx of mercenaries. At first, all the Arab traders wanted was the permission of the Azande to pass through their country with caravans of ivory and slaves from Mangbetu and Abarambo country. The Zande kings were powerful and therefore their subjects were safe from enslavement and pillaging. Furthermore, their kingdoms were far from the Nile and Bahr-el-Ghazal rivers where the trade was centered. But since the "leaders of the trading companies were brigands and their followers a rapacious rabble," the good terms for Zande leaders couldn't last long (Evans-Pritchard 1971:290). What is worse, the plunderers hired by the Arabs were later taken over by the British for more or less the same purpose.[36]

Von Höhnel, who accompanied the Austrian aristocrat Count Teleki in the exploration of Lake Rudolf (now Lake Turkana) in northern Kenya, reported that many of the exploring expeditions augmented their food supplies by purchasing and selling ivory. He also complained of the

15-20. Throwing sticks (*rungu*) from Kenya, made of ivory and tipped with obsidian, reportedly carved by Okiek (Dorobo) artisans for Maasai use. Gillies Turle Collection. Photograph, Peter Beard.

effect of the caravans on trade. The Nyemps (Njemps) south of Lake Baringo would have nothing to do with glass beads but would only accept "stuffs" [cloth] in payment for grain and cattle in payment for ivory: "They are spoiled by constant and long visits from caravans, so are exacting about what they want" (1894, II:5).

According to von Höhnel, the Rendille east of Lake Rudolph engaged in ivory trading in exchange for wool cloth and the Marle on the north shore of Lake Stefanie traded with the Reshiat, exchanging cattle, woolen material and beads for ivory. In addition to trading, there was also the matter of *hongo*, or tribute, which had to be paid to groups through whose country the expeditions and caravans passed. This was often demanded in ivory. The Akamba, who like the Okiek were well known as elephant hunters, often made trips to the coast to sell ivory which they got either by hunting or as tribute from "half-starved home-returning caravans" (pp. 185,187, 307-8). It seems clear that not only Arab traders and European hunters were involved in the ivory trade, but a great many indigenous cultures as well. Furthermore, some of the best

known ivory traders, such as the Maasai, did not hunt elephant at all but were middlemen in this trade.

While the pastoralists and the coastal Swahili elite have continued to wear precolonial forms of ornament in Eastern Africa, among the pastoralists, European glass trade beads (and lately plastic as well) have largely supplanted the older forms of jewelry made from iron, brass and ivory. Although decorations made from these glass beads are looked upon as "traditional" by many writers, they date back only to the late nineteenth century for most people. The Maasai speak of 1902, the year of completion of the Uganda Railway and with it an influx of trade, as "the year many beads fell into the land" (Klumpp pers. com. January 1991; see also Klumpp 1987). This eclipsing of ivory and metal with readily available glass beads is further reinforced by the scarcity of ivory in recent years due to the decimation of the elephant herds by professional poachers. In a sense, we are experiencing the last phase of a long process initiated by the earliest trading caravans. Not only Arab traders but also colonial governments and African rulers profited from the ivory trade.

But for the Africans, the profit was costly. While the trade did enrich chiefs and titleholders, and allowed considerable territorial expansion through the importation of firearms, it also contained within itself the inevitable transformation of an earlier lifestyle in which ivory was appreciated for its beauty but also recognized as a metaphor for the linked destinies of elephant and hunter.

Arguably, the most far-reaching effect of the ivory trade in the great Nile-Congo Divide was the fragmenting and redistribution of local styles of ornament over a much broader region. The establishment of the old ivory and slave-trading *zaribas* broke down previous barriers between different ethnic and language groups, while culturally heterogeneous outposts formed in their locales (Stigand 1923:25). Like early missionary stations elsewhere in Africa, the *zaribas* were multicultural communities, small microcosms of foreign dress, manners and customs, and places where imported goods could be obtained in exchange for ivory. They thus became locales from which brass wire, trade beads and cloth, to name only three

commodities of many, diffused into local communities. And recalling Emin Pasha's description of Kaberaga's *zariba*, they were important meeting places for the cultures whose members came to trade. This had its effect on styles of ornament and may partly account for the widespread similarity of ivory armlets in this region. A distribution study of East African arm and leg rings shows the prevalence of ivory in the Lado and eastward to Lake Turkana, while coiled iron or brass predominate in the grasslands of the Great Rift Valley (Huntingford 1961:284-85).

The flourishing ivory trade went hand in hand with the slave trade in East Africa and the same dealers, whether from Zanzibar or Khartoum, trafficked in human lives and the lives of elephants. In a terrible caricature of Nuer belief, the mystical connection between the two species became instead an expedient commercial arrangement. Recent ivory poaching in East Africa is a disturbing echo of those times, a reminder that scarcity incites greed and that power and profit are still to be had by the exploitation of the elephant.

NOTES

1. Prior to Solomon's time, elephant ivory probably came from Syria, but by the mid-ninth century B.C., Syrian elephants were apparently extinct (*Interpreter's Dictionary of the Bible* 1962, II:774-75). In any case, ivory coming from Syria would not have arrived by ship. Solomon's fleet is said to be "of Tarshish," a quasi-mythical locale which has never been identified satisfactorily by scholars.

2. Literally, *zariba (zeriba)* refers to the thorn-fenced enclosure and by extension the settlement within the enclosure. The entire Lado Enclave was known colloquially to Europeans in the late 19th century as "zariba country."

3. This essay was originally written in 1989 in a substantially different form. I am grateful to editor Henrietta Cosentino, who guided me through subsequent revisions. I would also like to thank Rosalinde Wilcox for locating several sources I had overlooked.

4. Stigand (1913:7). Stigand comments that the Indian *maund* was equal to 80 pounds so the figure cannot be accurate (1913:7, n. 2).

5. Contemporary scholarship on Swahili history and culture (e.g., Nurse and Spear 1985:passim) points out that the influence of Arabized Muslims is exaggerated in many accounts and argues that there is in fact a strong indigenous base for what emerged as coastal Swahili culture. Carol Eastman distinguishes between the *waungwana* (Swahili gentlemen's) world, based in Arab elite culture, and the much more African world of the *wanawake*, the Swahili women (Eastman 1988:3).

6. Evidence from the Swahili manuscript known as the Pate Chronicle confirms that the *siwa* was made between 1695 and 1700 in a deliberately archaicizing design (Allen 1976:41).

7. The Lado, so named after the town of Ladó, one of its administrative centers, was essentially coterminous with Equatoria Province of the Egyptian Sudan, but the term is used somewhat more broadly in this essay to include present-day northeastern Zaïre, western Uganda, and southern Sudan. Its string of fortified garrisons along the Nile – Ladó, Dufilé, Gondokóro, Wádelai – are famous in East African history as

places to which Emin Pasha, then governor of Equatoria Province, retreated with his loyal Egyptian troops during the Mahdist uprising and after the subsequent fall of Khartoum to the Mahdi in January 1885.

8. Edward Alpers argues in this volume that slaves and ivory were not traded together as often as is usually thought and in particular, the porterage of ivory to the coast was not always done by slaves. While this is undoubtedly the case for many parts of the continent and periods of the slave trade, there is abundant firsthand evidence that the caravans originating in Zanzibar and later Khartoum during the last half of the 19th century (the region and period upon which this essay is focused), traded both slaves and ivory. See Schweinfurth (1874), Junker (1890-92), Casati (1891), (1894) and Emin Pasha (in Schweinfurth et al. 1889). For early descriptions of trading caravans see Sheriff (1987:187 passim). Schildkrout and Keim (1990), and Vansina (1990:27, 30-31, 34, 87) describe the effect of this trade on the Zande and Mangbetu.

9. In addition to the peoples detailed in this essay, these included the Alur, Pandoro, Madi, Abarambo, Latuka, Bari, Acholi, Kakwa, Lugbara, and Baka (Stigand 1923:27).

10. They usually bore the name of the Arab trader to whom they belonged and are so designated on maps of the time (Wauters 1890:12).

11. Wauters (1890:13); see also Emin Pasha's letter written from Wadelai to Dr. R.W. Felkin, 22 July 1886 (Schweinfurth et al. 1889: 503-5). These slaves were needed as domestics, fieldhands, and concubines in the *zaribas* themselves, which were often large trading outposts the size of towns. Slaves were also given out as payment to middlemen in order to reduce overheads, and finally they were used as direct payments for ivory (Holt and Daly 1988:69-72).

12. Schweinfurth, explorer and naturalist, set the format and tone for a series of explorer-monographs of the Lado region (1874). Dr. Wilhelm Junker, a Moscow-born German who traveled widely in the Lado between 1875 and 1883, published his experiences in 1890-92. Captain Gaetano Casati, an Italian who spent a decade there in the 1880s, had a volume published in 1891. The diaries of Emin Pasha, medical doctor, botanist and speaker of a dozen languages, appeared in Schweinfurth et al. (1889). Three of these early ethnographers were scientists whose discipline served them well despite their European prejudices.

13. "Stanley wrote: 'When I was in Cairo Dr. Junker told me that Emin Bey [Emin Pasha] has in his possession about seventy tons of ivory. At eight shillings a pound this would be worth more than £60,000 [pounds sterling]. Not only would this cover all the expenses of our expedition, but would make it a financial success.'" (Wauters 1890: 144). See also Stanley's own account (1890, II:14).

14. Schildkrout and Keim's major publication on Mangbetu and Zande art appeared in 1990, a year after the initial draft of this essay was submitted. I am grateful to Enid Schildkrout for her willingness to share the then-unpublished text of chapter 12, "Reflections on Mangbetu Art," in November 1989. While reading both texts has greatly enriched my own understanding, it did not require me to change any of the main points of the initial draft, largely because we were working from the same nineteenth century sources. The long gestation period for the present volume requires an apology to these authors, lest they conclude that their work was merely cannibalized for this essay.

15. Given the importance of the elephant in Zande culture, it is fitting that they should express the idea of causation with an elephant hunting metaphor. For example, they say of witchcraft that it is the "second spear" (*umbaga*). This refers to the traditional division of meat between the first and second spearer in an elephant kill. Thus if a man is killed by an elephant during the hunt, the Azande will say that the elephant was the "first spear" and witchcraft the "second spear," which together killed him (Evans-Pritchard 1937:73-74).

16. Schweinfurth, on seeing the relative grandeur of the Mangbetu court, assumed that the Mangbetu kingdom was larger, more permanent, and more powerful than was actually the case. For a full description of the Mangbetu myth and Schweinfurth's part in its creation, see Schildkrout and Keim (1990:29,34). The consolidated Mangbetu kingdom lasted only two generations (Vansina 1990:83) and by the late nineteenth century, the Azande had become militarily more powerful (Schildkrout and Keim 1990:241).

17. As mentioned earlier, Giorgetti (1957:181) argues that necklaces of ivory, as well as those of dogs' and leopard's teeth, were of Barambo-Madi workmanship, and Evans-Pritchard (1971:99-100) mentions necklaces made of human fibula, called *nguma,* also made by the Madi. Mack points out that many of the early writers on the Azande only penetrated the eastern edges of their territory, Junker being an important exception (1990:218-19). And some of the best documented collections, such as that made by Lang for the American Museum of Natural History during their Congo Expedition of 1909-1915, date from a time long after the radical changes in Zande and Mangbetu culture had begun to take place.

18. The following description comes from Roscoe (1911:412-13), based on fieldwork during 25 years of missionary experience in Buganda.

19. At the time of Suna's reign (early nineteenth century) an ivory tusk weighing 62 pounds was sold for 1000 cowrie shells, while a female slave cost 10,000 cowries (Roscoe 1911:456).

20. Semakokiro was the 27th Kabaka (king) of Buganda. Since Mutesa, the 30th Kabaka, was in power when Europeans such as Speke (1861) and Stanley (1875) visited Buganda, one might guess that the ivory disc currency was in use in the 1700s.

21. One ivory disc was valued at 100 cowries (Roscoe 1911:457).

22. Exceptions are the two brief but important essays on northern Kenya body arts by Cole (1974, 1979) in which ivory is mentioned as a part of Turkana and Samburu adornment. The only major study of Maasai adornment (Klumpp 1987) deals exclusively with beadwork. Huntingford's (1961) distribution study of arm and leg rings in East Africa deals with metal, stone and grass as well as ivory, and is essentially quantitative.

23. Four examples are recounted by Lienhardt (1961:171,176,187,201).

24. Despite the inhospitable vegetation in the drier valley floors, their thick skins enable elephants to break through the thornbush and with their trunks they can uproot succulent plants for water (Brown 1965:165).

25. As among the Turkana, lowland Samburu women use an adze and drill to carve milk vessels from wood. Samburu data, unless noted otherwise, is taken from my 1987 and 1991 field notebooks.

26. Ricciardi (1971), Ole Saitoti and Beckwith (1980), Fisher (1984), Amin et al. (1987), Thesiger (1987).

27. According to Donna Klumpp, among Maasai the pendant symbolically replaces the missing testicle of a castrated sheep (pers. com. January 1991).

28. The age and provenance of these pieces is currently under review by the Museum. Though they have not yet been authenticated satisfactorily and are the object of some disagreement among scholars, they represent a potentially major contribution to the known corpus of East African ivory artifacts and therefore are included here.

29. The collection also includes small zoomorphic ivory figures similar in size to the natural ovoid shapes of ivory and bone which are to be found in the contents of a diviner's gourd. See Turle (1992).

30. The testimony of Maasai elders collected by Blackburn refers frequently to Saleta and Digiri groups. Opinion differs on whether these groups were once Okiek. Blackburn prefers to refer to them more generally as Dorobo while Kratz (1988:48, fig. 2.2) includes them as Okiek.

31. The Okiek are more often known in anthropological writings and government reports as Ndorobo, Eldorobo, Wandorobo, and so forth. Dorobo is the Anglicized KiSwahili derivative of the Maa term Il Torrobo, meaning essentially "people without cattle." The Kalenjin-speaking Okiek are the largest and most widely distributed of the "Dorobo" hunting-gathering groups in East Africa. The issue of whether the Okiek are autochthones or simply Maasai, etc., who have lost their cattle and turned to hunting through necessity has been long debated in the ethnographic literature. For modern reviews of the problem see Blackburn (1976), Kenny (1981), and Kratz (1981, 1988). I am grateful to Corinne Kratz (pers. com. June 1991) and Roderic Blackburn (pers. com. November 1991) for guiding me through the thicket of Okiek ethnicity. The nomenclature used here is an uneasy compromise whose aim is to make intelligible the older literature in terms of recent ethnographies of the Okiek and other hunter-gatherers in East Africa.

32. Roosevelt (1910:202,246,292-98,302-7,418-23). Roosevelt described elephant hunters on Mt. Kenya near Nyeri (p. 293) as "Kikuyu [speaking] 'Ndorobo'." He also identified as "Ndorobo" the Okiek of the Mau Escarpment (pp. 418-21). Both are illustrated in his book and neither are wearing ivory.

33. The Maasai-Okiek relationship has long been represented in ethnographic writing as one of Maasai cultural superiority – an attitude not necessarily shared by the Okiek (Kratz 1988:61). Various aspects of this "Maasai myth" are discussed in Dorothy Hammond and Alta Jablow, The Myth of Africa (1977), Galaty (1979, 1982), Kenny (1981), Kratz (1988).

34. See Fratkin (1974) for Samburu elephant symbolism. Samburu *Imurran* also entertain each other with "Torrobo" stories, usually at the expense of the subject.

35. Muriuki (1976:131) and Jacobs (1979:48) have shown how exaggerated accounts of Maasai ferociousness furthered the aims of British imperialists and Arab and African traders alike. Ideas of Maasai superiority are further bolstered by stories which stress the Maasai as a cultural model to be imitated, as in Merker (1910).

36. The Khartoum merchants recruited Nubians from Dongola, known as Danagla, as armed guards to accompany the caravans. When the Egyptian and later the British Government took over the ivory trade they enlisted the Danagla as irregular soldiers.

A.

B.

WILSON MWANGI, a Kikuyu gourd carver in his early thirties, works out of Kariokor market in Nairobi, Kenya, practicing the art learned from the reknowned Kamba artist Peter Nzuki. The image is first incised on the surface of the gourd, then darkened with a mixture of charcoal and oil. Gourds traditionally served utilitarian functions. Mwangi's gourds, however, are primarily created to adorn the homes of expatriates, tourists, and middle-class Kenyans. Design motifs include village views, road accidents, baobab trees, and beer drinking scenes. His elephants recur in three basic compositions: a zigzag line of elephants descending Mt. Kenya; a receding line of elephants approaching the viewer; and two elephants facing each other. Mwangi's elephants are commercially viable; they seem to hold no major symbolic importance for him (Donna Clump and Cory Kratz, pers. com.).

C.

...pengraved gourd. Kenya, 1991. Diam-
... cm. FMCH x91.579. Museum purchase.

... view of Figure A.

...pengraved half-gourd with leather strap.
... 1991. Height 29 cm. FMCH x91.578.
... purchase.

...pengraved half-gourd with leather strap.
... 1985. Length 24.5 cm. Collection of
...olfe III.

D.

ተወልደ መኃኤል ጌናን ቀታኒሰ ‑ እኅዋ

SIXTEEN

UNDER THE GUN

ELEPHANTS IN ETHIOPIAN PAINTING

GIRMA FISSEHA

In Ethiopia, the elephant has long played a considerable role in the lives, lore, and arts of a diverse population. The high esteem accorded the elephant is evident in a title of honor given the Ethiopian Emperor: *Gan hoy*. The term, meaning "majesty," can be traced to a Kushitic root, *gan*, which translates in Amharic as *zohon*, or "elephant" (cf. Caqout 1957: 211f; Cerulli 1938:198). While the elephant and its ivory have been represented in many ways throughout Ethiopian history, the most notable elephant depictions in recent times appear within the distinctively Ethiopian genre of painting, with its admixture of Byzantine, Roman, Arabian, and Judaic elements. Such paintings were traditionally done in tempera on a ground of stretched cloth or skin. After sketching outlines in charcoal, the painter would fill in colors with a homemade mixture of ground mineral and organic substances and egg white or yolk. More recently, artists have begun using European tube colors, and are replacing tempera with oils.

Until a century ago, Ethiopian painters did not concern themselves with profane subjects such as hunting, which were in fact forbidden. Rather, they devoted themselves to religious themes; their patrons were wealthy Ethiopians of the ruling class. It was only following Ethiopia's victory in the war against Italy that this tradition changed. As a result of the diplomatic recognition accorded to Ethiopia in 1896, foreigners flooded into the country and began commissioning secular paintings from local artists.

The examples that reached Europe in the hands of the diplomats are singular products of the time. The works were generally undated, unsigned, and without note of the place of origin, since the painters were working "illegally." Nevertheless, the early paintings can be roughly dated based upon the subject, if it is historical, together with the initial entry in museum registers and the biographies of donors. Collecting was concentrated in two periods: the first from 1896 until 1913; the second, following World War I, from 1920 to 1935, when the Italian-Ethiopian war and then the Second World War put an end to diplomatic relations and the possibility of collecting.

The elephant makes a remarkable showing in the paintings of this era. It appears in many contexts: mythological, biblical, and historical (Figs. 16-2 to 16-4, 16-15). Most often, however, the elephant is depicted in scenes of the hunt (Figs. 16-1, 16-5 to 16-11, 16-13, 16-14), one of the favorite subjects of Ethiopian painting.

16-1 (OPPOSITE). Hunting Scene, by an unknown painter (19th century). At the top of the painting, a nobleman rides to the hunt with his companions, under the protection of a saint, whose wings arch over them. In the scene below, six hunters are seen shooting an elephant, or perhaps a family of elephants, all at the same time. Two solitary trees, one leafless, lend poignancy to an otherwise barren landscape. Collection of Joseph Knopfelmacher, New York.

16-3 (RIGHT). Noah's Ark, by Wondemu Haile Maryam. The artist depicts the events of the flood: the animals saved on Noah's Ark, and those lost in the flood. Left, against a background of Ethiopian round houses, goats, antelopes, and snakes wait in pairs as Noah and his family bring animals onto the ark. Right, the ark floats in the flood waters as those outside beg for help, are threatened by crocodiles, and drown. At the horizon are crosses of sunken churches and a dove with a new branch, signaling the end of the flood. Canvas 89.5 x 186 cm. Collection of Linden G. Leavitt, Los Angeles.

16-2 (LEFT). The Battle of Magdala (c. 1930), by Balatschaw Yimer. When the British captured the mountain fortress of Magdala on April 13, 1868, they used elephants imported from India to transport supplies. *They carried English cannon,* says the text. From Magdala mountain, Ethiopian soldiers pelt their attackers with stones; the inscription reads, *That is a stone.* Abyssinians have their faces to the viewer, but colonial troops (reported to have numbered over 30,000) are portrayed in profile: traditionally, those considered evil are depicted with a single eye. The foot of the mountain is littered with dead English soldiers and the detritus of war. Canvas 135 x 85 cm. Museum für Völkerkunde der Universität Zürich, Inv.-Nr. 12207 (Collection of Frau von Schröter).

16-4. Animal Society, by an unknown painter. Under leadership of the lion, the animal society meets. At the round table, the elephant sits to the right of the lion. Rays of the Holy Spirit float over the animals. At front, the king of the monkeys reads from the Gospel of John about peaceful coexistence. In the foreground is a defeated and repudiated devil. Parchment 70 x 100 cm. Collection of Linden G. Leavitt, Los Angeles.

THE PRESTIGE OF THE HUNT

The high social prestige of successful hunters and warriors is linked to the danger involved in their occupations. Ethiopians, independent of their religious or cultural identity, idealized hunters and warriors who had to face death – to kill or be killed (Haberland 1957:331). No other men, despite financial or social success, could achieve comparable prestige. For the hunter or warrior, success was so important that he hardly dared return home empty-handed for fear of losing face. His status was revealed by the awards he received and by the songs and narratives that celebrated him within a festive context.

Several objects were symbols of a successful hunter. Perhaps most significant were gold earrings (Figs. 16-7, 16-9), which only a killer of elephants and other big animals (lion, buffalo, leopard, python, rhinoceros) could wear. Other objects included ivory or metal bracelets, a phallic forehead decoration, ornate hairstyles highlighted with earth colors, and head ornaments of feathers.

Awards and trophies (in Amharic, *mirga* "records" of hunting triumph) were distributed according to a value-scale. Five elephants were needed to accrue a second earring. In the case of ivory bracelets, two bracelets corresponded

16-5 (LEFT). Hunting Scenes, by Balatschaw Yimer (before 1927). In the upper left, where two hunters try to free their comrade, the text reads: *A comrade of the hunters was embraced by a snake.* To the right, as a coward flees an attacking animal, leaving a dead comrade, the text reads: *He was killed by the leopard.* Lower level: *After they have killed the elephant, they sing.* To the right, a lion hunter shoots at an oversized lion and a second hunter lies trampled (See Norden 1930:26). Canvas 133 x 34 cm. Museum für Völkerkunde der Universität Zürich, Inv.-Nr. (Collection of Charles-Henri Steiner 1927-29).

to a killed elephant, rhinoceros, giraffe, buffalo or lion. One bracelet was awarded for a leopard, two boars, or four other wild animals. Slaughtered animals were valued according to a set scale: an elephant equaled forty people, one lion counted the same as twenty-five people, a giraffe corresponded to twenty, a buffalo to ten, and a leopard to five people. Whoever killed an enemy in a duel received two bracelets of ivory, as for a killed game animal. If a hunter killed ten elephants, he was allowed to decorate his horse with a red band on the breast strap, and his wife received the right to wear a red silk belt (Fig. 16-6), which symbolically transferred his success to her (Merab 1921:192f; Bruce 1791:557f). As recently as 1930, a man had to have proved himself a successful hunter before his wedding. Women would receive their first ivory jewelry (for example a wide bracelet or necklace) as a wedding gift. Afterwards, a wife would receive additional jewelry for each animal killed by her husband. The husband's hunting success could thus be determined by the amount of jewelry the wife had.

After a successful hunt, it was customary that the hero, accompanied by music and drums, led a procession across the market so that everyone could take part in the joyous occasion, and he could celebrate his deed (Plowden 1868: 215f; Raffray 1876:366f; Montandon 1913:316f). In the old kingdom of Kaffa, the hunter rode to the king's court in order to present the ivory trophies in the aura of victory to the ruler and to receive the desired accolades. When the heroic Abato was received at Menelik's court in Guebi after a successful hunting expedition, he entered the court of honor under a volley of guns, accompanied by his men who carried the spoils – elephant tusks – two by two before the ruler. Menelik congratulated Abato, whose title was *Like Mekuas,*[1] on his success while his hunting companions and the onlookers broke into triumphant song (Vanderheym 1896:134-37).

Singing and storytelling accompanied the celebration of a successful hunter. Playful or dangerous occurrences during the hunt were reenacted in songs and dance, thus publicizing a hero's deeds (Escherich 1921:78-80). Public enthusiasm impelled the hunter to exaggerate his hunting success, to praise himself immensely and to defame his "enemy." The women of a camp would celebrate an elephant's death with song (Plowden 1868:215-16). The entire camp would join in for the refrain, *addo ouochebai* ("on my gold earring"); the songs could be heard as long as the camp and the celebration lasted (Merab 1921:193). Throughout the festivities, the "hero" of the day wore his victory awards.

ELEPHANT HUNTING

In Ethiopia, elephants were hunted sometimes for ivory and sometimes for meat. Islamic (Moslem) and Christian Ethiopians would not eat elephant meat as they considered the animal unclean; they killed elephants only for the ivory and as proof of their courage (Figs. 16-1, 16-6). Southerners such as the Shangalla, however, who followed the older nature- and ancestor-based religions, considered elephant meat a delicacy, which they ate raw or roasted in huge quantities after a successful hunt. For this, the Amhara considered them barbarians (Fig. 16-11).

Elephant hunting customs thus varied from region to region. Weapons included those customary from ancient times – the knife (used for cutting the animal's tendons), spear, saber, and bow and arrow – and the rifle, introduced in the late nineteenth century, which soon became the most widely used and effective device (Fig. 16-9).[2]

Traps were also utilized. One type was made of well-camouflaged holes which were filled with pointed spears.

16-6. St. George and Hunting Scenes, by an unknown painter. Above, St. George on his horse spears the dragon. Below, a lion is hunted with spear and rifles; two hunters wait behind a rock for the elephant; yellow headbands proclaim their valor. A hunter wearing a wide hunter's belt kneels in the foreground. Canvas 76 x 149 cm. Istituto Italo-Africano, Roma. Photograph: Rudolf Bauer, Staatliches Museum für Völkerkunde München.

16-7. Hunting Scenes, by an unknown painter (1935). Danger is the theme here. In the upper scene a lion tears apart the face of a hunter while his comrades try to save him; another hunter is jumped by a leopard. In the middle scene, a slain buffalo still holds a hunter in his mouth as another cuts off its tail; a rhinoceros is being hunted. Below, an elephant having trampled two hunters is being attacked with guns and knives; a hunter struggles with a snake. Canvas 88 x 98 cm. Staatliches Museum für Völkerkunde München. Inv.-Nr. 86-306518.

The animal who fell on the spears would be badly wounded and die. A second type of trap was a snare which the elephant would brush and trigger in passing, causing a lance to snap and pierce its back. The waiting hunters, camouflaged nearby, would then spear and kill the wounded elephant.

Regional hunting customs in the specific area and the wealth of the hunter determined the kind of arms used. For example, the Christian Amhara (as in the northern part of the country in general) preferred the hunting rifle and the saber, while in the southern part of Ethiopia people such as the Shangalla hunted almost exclusively with bow and arrow (Fig. 16-11). After a successful hunt the hunters would first cut off the elephant's tail and then triumphantly pose with the dead animal (Fig. 16-13). Especially courageous hunters would try to cut the tail off of the living elephant.

Hunters worked both alone and in groups. By one method, about ten men would sneak up on a herd and single out a suitable young animal with a comparatively small girth, which they would bind with cords and tie down. The full-grown animals, coming to its defense, would then be shot. This type of hunt, which could easily turn into a massacre of the entire herd, did not occur until after the introduction of firearms, but it happened frequently thereafter (Fig. 16-10) (Zervos 1935:103).

Somali hunters were known to conduct a group elephant-kill by following the elephants on horseback. They would usually separate an animal from the herd in order to throw

spears at it and push it along until it was tired. One of the hunters would then carefully sneak up on it and cut the tendons on the back legs so that the elephant would fall and be unable to get up. This method of killing was relatively free from danger.

Among the Oromo, entire herds were entrapped by the clever use of fire and then killed, less for their meat than for their ivory. Another method was to drive the elephants into a marshy area where, due to their weight, they could not get out. After three days, when the elephants were exhausted, they were easy to kill. Oromo hunters also hunted solo. An individual hunter sneaked up on an elephant from an ambush position, armed with only two spears. The spear edges were specially made: not actually pointed, since the soft iron used would only have bent on the elephant hide, but rather slightly rounded and razor sharp. At an opportune moment the hunter would pierce a spear into the animal's side and then hide himself again. The angry, wounded elephant would try to find the hunter but was usually unsuccessful. The well-hidden hunter would wait for another opportunity and pierce the second spear into the elephant's side, which often led to its death. Sometimes, the elephant was faster than the hunter, so that the unlucky man was badly wounded or even stomped to death (Fig. 16-8) (Paulitschke 1983:232-33).

In the old kingdom of Kaffa, in southern Ethiopia, only occasional hunts were conducted for a variety of reasons.

16-8. Hunting scenes by an unknown painter (before 1927). This picture, with six distinct scenes of preferred big game hunting, illustrates the dangers of the hunt: wounded and dead hunters lie trampled on the ground! The hunters, mostly dressed in khaki uniform, wear colorfully decorated leather cartridge belts accommodating 20-50 cartridges. They take aim with one eye closed – all but the lion hunter, depicted as especially fearless. Inscriptions read, top level: *Elephant hunters. After the hunters have killed the elephant, they chop off the tusks with an axe.* Middle level: *Rhinoceros hunters. Buffalo hunters.* Bottom level: *Lion hunters. Giraffe hunters.* Canvas 84 x 58 cm. Museum für Völkerkunde der Universität Zürich, Inv.-Nr. 16853 (Collection of Charles-Henri Steiner 1927-29).

Only smaller animals such as antelopes were slaughtered for their meat. The prestigious big game hunt included the killing of elephants, lions, buffalo, and leopards (Figs. 16-8, 16-12). The greatest incentive for the hunt was ivory, which could be used as annual tribute to the ruler. Most of it was not processed in the province of Kaffa, but was sold to outside areas, especially to Europe. After 1897, when Kaffa became a province in the empire of Ethiopia, half of the ivory captured in Kaffa had to be given to the Ethiopian emperor in Addis Ababa (Fig. 16-15).

The Jidenitsch (Yidani) and Batscha (Baca) people, who were traditionally hunters, had their own methods. A hunter, having smeared himself completely with the animal's droppings to disguise his own scent, would sneak up to his

16-9. Hunting Scenes, by Hailu Woldayes. Fanciful episodes of a traditional hunt. Some men are armed with customary local weapons such as spears, swords, and shields, but the majority already own European rifles. Gold earrings identify several of the hunters as especially successful marksmen. Inscriptions clarify the scene. Upper left, an elephant is killed by an *elephant hunter* as *rhinoceros hunters* try to save a comrade. A *giraffe* eats leaves from a tree. Center, a *courageous man* spears a *lion* that has swallowed a hunter. Right, a *rhinoceros hunter* fires at a rhinoceros and a hunter shoots a *buffalo*. Lower left, a *buffalo hunter* sits on his prey as three swimmers hunt *crocodile* and *hippopotamus*. Canvas 118 x 78 cm. Museum für Völkerkunde der Universität Zürich, Inv.-Nr. 14208.

16-10 (OPPOSITE, TOP). Hunting Scene, by an unknown painter (c. 1935). The hunters in this picture carry French grass-rifles, customary equipment of the Ethiopian infantry of the time. The introduction of such rifles changed hunting methods and gave hunters far more power over their prey, as suggested by the badly bleeding animals in this picture. Canvas 90 x 25 cm. Istituto Italo-Africano, Roma. Photograph: Rudolf Bauer, Staatliches Museum für Völkerkunde München.

prey as it was resting at night and kill it with a stab of the lance to the side. A similar method was used to hunt a hippopotamus (*Altvölker Süd Äthiopiens* 1959:416). Professional hunters hunted naked so that they would make the least possible noise when they sneaked up on the animals (Bruce 1791:58).

Elephant and big game hunting was considered dangerous not only physically, but also spiritually, because it was believed that some animals were possessed by demons or spirits (*quollye*) which could in turn possess hunters (Griaule 1963:833-35). There are two types of possession spirits: bush and animal. Bush spirits follow and persecute the hunter, but do not stay in him when he leaves the bush. He can appease them with the blood sacrifice of killed animals. The spirits of dead animals are bound to the personality of the hunter, and remain in him until his death. When the hunter feels sick, he believes the spirits caused the sickness. He tries to satisfy them so that he can regain his health. If the hunter dies, he may bequeath his possession to his favorite son or daughter, if the spirit (*zar*) has already accustomed itself to village life and no longer wishes to return to the bush.

IVORY

As the hunting of elephants led to the acquisition and sale of ivory, the ivory business was regulated by decree. A permit was needed to hunt for an elephant, and all ivory had to be turned in to the government. The possibility of buying the ivory back at market value did exist, however, and it was legally possible to take hunting trophies out of the country (Rein 1920:353).

Since the hunt for elephants was considered especially lucrative because of the tusks, it soon evolved that half of the captured tusks were to be turned over to the ruler. Emperor Menelik II issued a proclamation concerning elephant hunting in 1887 (Ethiopian dating) (see below). Haile Selassie issued a decree in 1930 which, in addition to elephants, regulated the hunting of giraffes, pelicans, and other animals for a period of five years.

In 1944, a new hunting decree was issued as the Ethiopian government was preparing for an increase in tourism. Hunting and photographing game as well as exporting hunting trophies was allowed only if a grant was filled out by the Minister of Agriculture. This minister also regulated the decisions about protected animals, hunting weapons, fees, and limitations (Rikkli 1947:206-7).

Some ivory remained within Ethiopia and was used in a variety of ways. For example, a necklace of ivory, a large

EXCERPTS FROM THE DECREE OF MENELIK II

All hunters who live on the border will not undertake a hunt alone, but rather in groups.

Before a hunter proceeds to his specified hunting site he must procure confirmation/permission for the hunt in Addis Ababa.

After the hunters have killed an elephant, they will turn in one tusk per animal to the government representative for the respective area. They may keep the other one.

The dead elephants must have a tusk weight of at least 17 kg, the killing of elephants with a lower tusk weight is not allowed. If a hunter kills an elephant with a tusk weight under 17 kg, he is no longer recognized as a hunter.

If a hunter wishes to sell his tusk, he will deliver it to the customs officer of the government. The ivory price will be set according to the current market value at the time of sale.

The buyer or trader will pay attention that all official certifications for the tusks in question are at hand. They will not buy any tusks without certification.

❄ **1887** ❄

16-11 (ABOVE). Hunting Scenes, by Tesfaye Taye (c. 1970). An inscription above reads: *How, in the past, the hunters have hunted lions, giraffe, leopards, buffalo, and jackals in difficult (hilly) country and how the Shangalla hunted, cooked, and ate large snakes.* Shangalla hunters in loincloths, far right, hunt with bows and arrows and then cook their game. Other scenes depict Amhara, in long pants and shirts, armed with guns. 1st row: lion, giraffe, leopard and buffalo hunts. 2nd row: far left, successful elephant hunters celebrate, one seated triumphant on the dead animal; a rhinoceros hunter is gored; next to an unhappy leopard hunter, a jackal hunt has begun. Below, a hunter rests in his tent with his bodyguards as hunters bring ivory into camp. The elephant hunt, middle, is not without injuries. Lower right, a Shangalla is gobbled by a crocodile. The hilly landscape and Shangalla hunting scenes suggest a location in Gimira. Canvas 81 x 131 cm. Collection of Baron von Fölkersamb, Tutzing.

16-12 (OPPOSITE, TOP). Ethiopian Animal World, by an anonymous painter (c. 1927). This gives an overview of the animals native to Ethiopia, but since the painter was not personally acquainted with all types, some of his portrayals require the help of the accompanying transcriptions, e.g., the *bear* (3rd row), which has an improbably long tail. 1st row: *elephant, rhinoceros, buffalo, snake.* 2nd row: *giraffe, leopard, hunting leopard, cliff springer, zebra, tortoise, kudu, hare (?), lion.* 3rd row: *fox, hyena, oryx-antelope, gazelle, bear, pig, wild boar.* Next to the couple in the 4th row, text reads: *These animals are eaten by the Shangalla.* Further inscriptions identify two species of *gazelle,* a *bush-antelope,* several more obscure animals, and, in the lake, *hippopotamus, crocodile.* Canvas 163 x 85 cm. Übersee Museum Bremen, Inv.-Nr. 14823.

16-13 (OPPOSITE, BOTTOM). Hunting Scenes, by Balatschaw Yimer. 1st level: *Elephant hunters* fire at elephants as a hunter is trampled by a bleeding animal; two *buffalo hunters* follow and an animal falls on a hunter. 2nd level: A successful elephant hunt. Text reads: *After the killing of an elephant they sing.* One hunter has cut off the elephant's tail, a coveted trophy. In the next scene hunters are en route to camp. The text reads: *After killing elephants, they remove the tusks and leave.* It takes two men to carry a single tusk. At *the camp of the hunters,* right, a man prepares bowls of coffee as the transport mules graze. 3rd level: with saber and gun, two hunters attack a lion that has trampled their companion, whose eyes are still open. The hunters' hair, standing on end, signifies that they have been in the wilderness a long time. Also, rhinoceroses attack other *rhinoceroses;* hunters lie dead; four *giraffe hunters* fire at an animal standing in the trees. Canvas 136 x 88 cm. Übersee Museum Bremen, Inv.-Nr. 14834. (Melchers Collection).

shield of elephant skin, and an ivory trumpet belonged to the regalia of the chiefs of the Ut people. Ivory gifts to Ethiopian royalty were not uncommon (Fig. 16-15). The ivory trumpet was one of the insignias of Bodi chiefs as well (*Altvölker Süd Äthiopiens* 1959:245). Among the Bodi, small girls wore a pubic apron dotted with pieces of ivory strung on a cotton cord. Jimma women used ivory hair pins, which in other areas were retained for men, and jagged (notched) bracelets made out of the skin of elephant soles.

Most ivory, however, was exported. Next to coffee and civet perfume,[3] ivory was one of the main trade products of the province Kaffa. Ivory was transported by long mule caravans from isolated areas in the interior to the coast and other trading areas (Figs. 16-13, 16-14). Each tusk was individually wrapped in leather and the caravans often took three to four months, stopping at stations along the way from Ethiopia to the Sudan. The mule caravans were used into the 1950s. The Ethiopian term for this type of transport is *Sirara Negade*. Some of the tusks went to China and India, but most were exported to Europe. Until the introduction and acceptance of the "Species Protection Agreement," the demand for ivory was immense in Europe, especially in the German jewelry industry. This led to the slaughter of elephant herds, because the sale of ivory meant fast money and prestige for the hunter.

Elephant hunting in Ethiopia has changed through time. Once widely engaged in by numerous groups in many regions, the elephant hunt is a rarity today. The slaughter of elephants has made the animal scarce in the Ethiopian landscape. Years of civil war and drought have driven wildlife to neighboring countries. Laws have made hunting licenses unaffordable, and few men are now willing to leave work or home to venture into the bush for six or seven months. Men are no longer expected to win a hunting trophy before marriage. Nevertheless, elephant hunting remains a popular theme for painters in Ethiopia who portray their people heroically confronting larger and stronger creatures – elephants.

NOTES

All photographs for this article were done by Rudolf Bauer and S. Autrum-Mulzer, Staatliches Museum für Völkerkunde, Munich.

Thanks are due to Beverly Freelander, who did the initial translations from the German, and to Ursula Coleman, for translating the conclusion. Editorial help from Mary Kay Kendall, Kristin Lang, and in particular, R. Mark Livengood, is also much appreciated.

1. *Like Mekuas* was a dual title meaning roughly "ceremonial-master." The *Like Mekuas* dressed like the king in order to mislead enemies.
2. Now, however, hunting with rifles is illegal.
3. A secretion out of the gland of a male civet cat served as a perfume base.

16-14 (OPPOSITE, TOP). Daily and Hunting Scenes on Lake Tana, by Kengeta Dschambara Hailu (c. 1979). Lake Tana, top, is suggested by the strong blue background, and in its vicinity are a church, a field being plowed, hunters with a *slain antelope*, and two men transporting ivory tusks by mule. Inscriptions explain the hunting scenes that follow. 1st row: A *hyena* jumps a *mule*, a *lion* attacks an *ox*, a coward climbs a tree. 2nd row: Two hunters shoot at *bush antelopes*, a *leopard* awaits two *antelopes*, two hunters stand at right. 3rd row: Two *rhinoceroses*, two *mountain nyalas*, two *giraffes*, two hunters. 4th row: Hunters stalk two *buffalo* and *elephants*. Canvas 112 x 82 cm. Staatliches Museum für Völkerkunde München, Inv.-Nr. 80-301214.

16-15 (OPPOSITE, BOTTOM). King Solomon Receives the Queen of Sheba, by Wandemu Wandé (c. 1970). The inscription reads: *Queen of Sheba and King Solomon*. The queen comes with her court before Solomon and presents him with jewelry and elephant tusks set in gold. The red turban-like headpiece of the king's bodyguard identifies him as a Moslem; this is anachronistic, however, since Islam did not exist in Solomon's time. The gifts spread out at the king's feet include tusks, wine carafes, baskets, cups, a shield, and a buffalo-skin water container – articles that were plentiful in Addis Ababa tourist shops at the time of the painting. Canvas 128 x 85 cm. Collection of Walther Kraft.

A. Maskettes from Zaire (Pende people) ranging in height from 5.5 cm to 6.35 cm. Top, left: Private collection; Top, right: Collection of Helen and Dr. Robert Kuhn; Bottom: Private collection.

IVORY FINGER RINGS and ear ornaments are not as common as one might first guess. The former may occasionally be found in scattered parts of Africa but are best known from the Dinka, Nuer and related peoples of Southern Sudan. Ivory ear ornaments have a wider range but still are largely East African in origin. Lip plugs in ivory range from the Turkana of Kenya down to the Makonde of Mozambique. Necklaces and pendants have an even broader distribution with splendid figurative examples coming from several parts of Zaire and Angola. For some pendants, adornment is a secondary function to their primary roles as whistles, snuff containers, or charms.

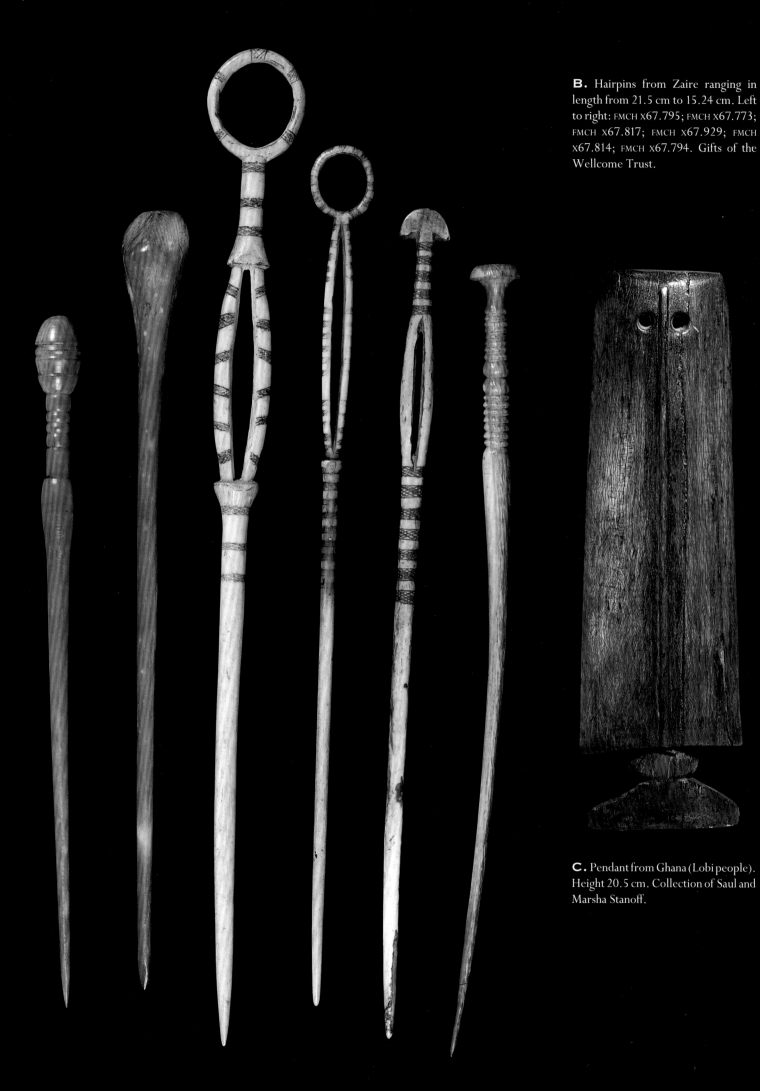

B. Hairpins from Zaire ranging in length from 21.5 cm to 15.24 cm. Left to right: FMCH X67.795; FMCH X67.773; FMCH X67.817; FMCH X67.929; FMCH X67.814; FMCH X67.794. Gifts of the Wellcome Trust.

C. Pendant from Ghana (Lobi people). Height 20.5 cm. Collection of Saul and Marsha Stanoff.

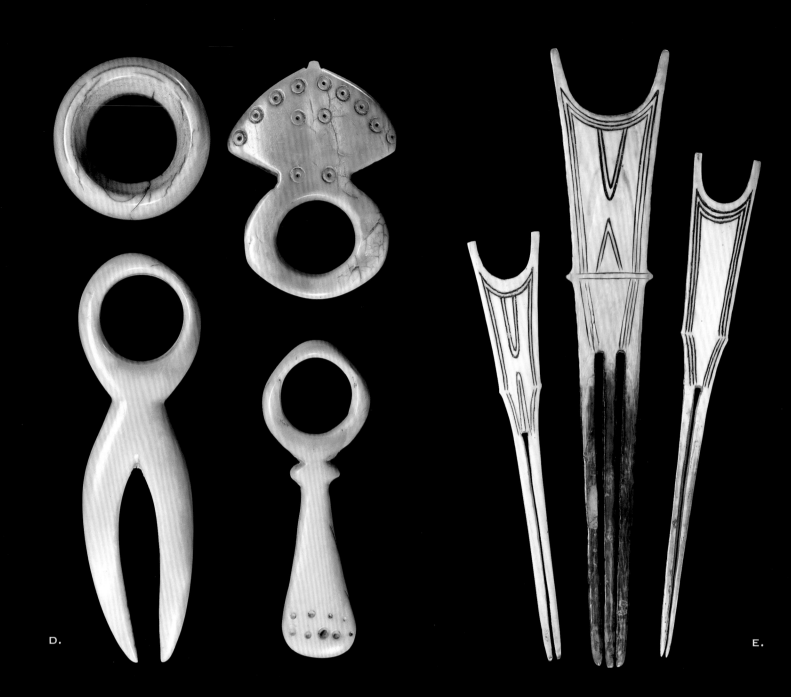

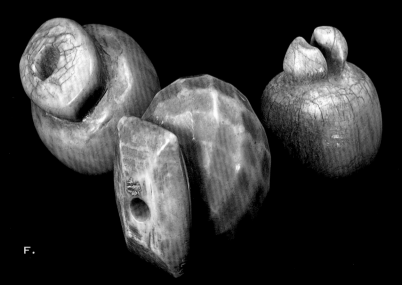

D. Rings from Sudan (Dinka people). Clockwise, from upper left: Diameter 3.9 cm. FMCH X81.1; 5.7 cm. FMCH X81.4; 8 cm. FMCH X81.5; 10.2 cm. FMCH X81.3. Museum purchases.

E. Hairpins from Zaire ranging in length from 14.5 cm to 18 cm. Left to right: FMCH X67.820; FMCH X67.801; FMCH X67.800. Gifts of the Wellcome Trust.

F. Beads from Zaire. Diameter 4 cm. FMCH X67.838a-c. Gifts of the Wellcome Trust.

G. Hairpins from Zaire: Left, 13.3 cm. FMCH X67.937; Right, 17.5 cm. FMCH X67.936. Gifts of the Wellcome Trust.

H. Hairpins from Zaire. Longest is 19 cm. Left to right: FMCH X67.765; FMCH X67.738; FMCH X67.749; FMCH X67.811. Gifts of the Wellcome Trust.

I. Left to right: Button from Namibia (Ovahimba people), width 8 cm. Lip plug from Mozambique (Makonde people), width 6 cm. "Cow bell" from Kenya, length 11.5 cm. U. & W. Horstmann Collection, Zug, Switzerland.

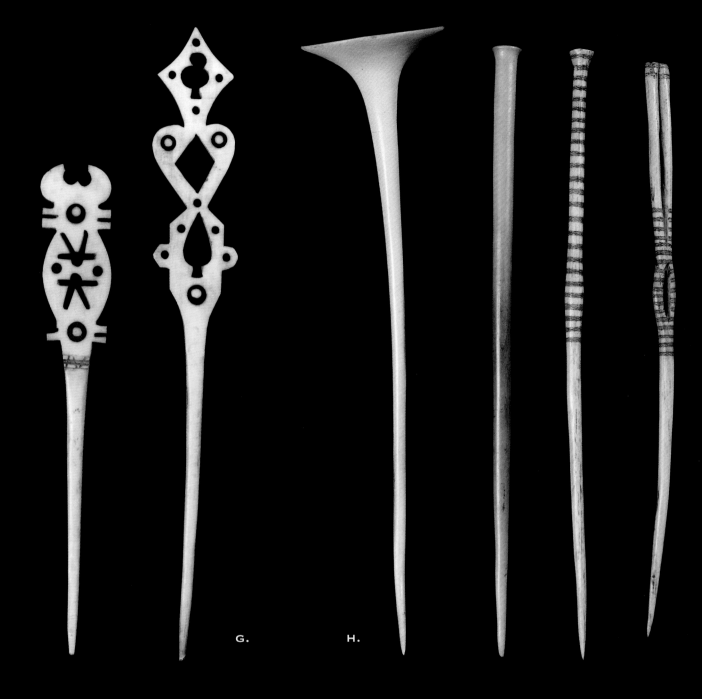

G.   H.

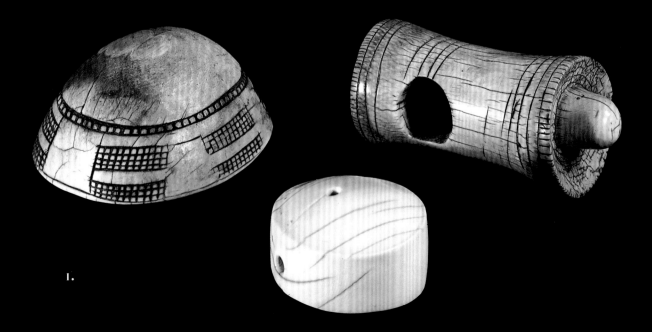

I.

One of the original Nuer... was called Loh. Loh's wife gave birth to a monstrous girl-child with long teeth. She was named Nyalou. Her appetite was enormous and increased with the growth of her body, so that when she was still quite young, the food of man was insufficient to satisfy her hunger. Every day she would go into the forest and fill her belly with grass and the branches of trees, with roots and heglig nuts, and every day she grew larger and larger. At last she swelled to such proportions that she could no longer squeeze herself through the door of her home. She called her people together and said to them, "The time has come for me to leave

you. I must go to the forest and live there, for there only can I find sufficient food to feed me." Then she took her sleeping skins and attached them to her ears and straight-away they became part of her body. "I am now different to you," she said, "and my descendants will live in the forest apart from mankind. Men will want to kill me because of my huge teeth and because my flesh is fat and sweet...." She went off to the forest with her child, and has remained there ever since.

(Howell 1945:96-97)

—————→►◄—————

The history of Miono and Mandera [in eastern Tanzania] *begins with twelve hunters from Manyoni* [in western Tanzania].... *The purpose of their expedition was to hunt elephant.*

(Kambi 1972)

—————→►◄—————

The elephant roams in herds throughout the country [modern Tanzania], affecting the low grounds where stagnating water produces a plentiful vegetation: with every human being his foe and thousands living by his destruction, the animal is far from becoming scarce;... The elephant hunt is with the African a solemn and serious undertaking. He fortifies himself with periapts and prophylactics given by the mganga [traditional doctor], who also trains him to the use of his weapon... Zanzibar is the principal mart for perhaps the finest and largest ivory in the world... It is perhaps the only legitimate article of traffic for which caravans now visit the interior.

(Burton 1859:374,441)

—————→►◄—————

Curiously symbolizing profligate luxury as well as purity, ivory has for uncounted millennia been procured from vast distances and masterfully carved into objects of rare beauty. Since elephant tusks are its chief source, and since Man is the elephant's only serious predator, ivory is at the root of the African elephant's threatened extinction....

(Adams 1989)

SEVENTEEN

THE IVORY TRADE IN AFRICA

AN HISTORICAL OVERVIEW

EDWARD A. ALPERS

By its very size the African elephant inspires awe and respect. A symbol of power and wisdom in African lore, the elephant also represents a dangerous threat posed by all elements of the bush to the civilized life embodied in human society. Anyone who has witnessed the destruction wrought to a village farm by a browsing elephant knows how vividly these elements can come together in everyday life. Given their relative distribution, population density, and preferred environments, however, humans and elephants might well have coexisted peaceably for much longer than they have were it not for the external market for the ivory of elephants. I do not claim that Africans would not have independently discovered some luxury value in ivory for themselves – this they certainly did. Rather, I argue that the relentless hunting out of the elephant, which has proceeded apace in fits and starts since the early nineteenth century and which now threatens the African elephant with extinction, can only be understood in the broader context of the exploitation of Africa's natural resources – including most especially its peoples – primarily by economic and social forces external to the continent.

Initially, however, this was not the case. The history of the ivory trade in Africa is quite ancient, and its earliest source of demand came from the most advanced African – indeed, world – society of its epoch: Egypt. In fact, one of the initial motivating factors for Egyptian expansion south into Nubia was the desire of successive dynasties to control the natural wealth of interior Africa, including ivory (Sheriff 1971:248, 256). By the time of the Sixth Dynasty (2420-2258 B.C.), during the reign of Pharaoh Merenre, a series of explorations beyond the known borders of Nubia was undertaken by Harkhuf, the monarch or governor of Elephantine.[1] From an inscription in Harkhuf's tomb at Aswan, we know that on his third expedition he followed the western oasis route to the country of Yam, to the south of the Second Cataract, perhaps in Darfur, and returned "... *with 300 asses laden with incense, ebony, heknu [a kind of oil?], panthers [two words indecipher-able], ivory, throw sticks [?] and every good product"* (Emery 1965: 131; Breasted 1906:154,336).

The Eighteenth Dynasty, which marks the beginning of the New Kingdom, was another important period of exploration that reveals the importance of ivory in the luxury economy

17-1 (OPPOSITE). *... 'Men will want to kill me because of my huge teeth and because my flesh is fat and sweet...' She went off to the forest with her child, and has remained there ever since.* Photograph, Terry G. Murphy. Animals, Animals.

17-2. This ivory neckrest, which accompanied Tutankhamun into the afterworld (ca. 1325 B.C.), is among the quantities of carved ivory objects and inlaid ivory tomb furniture found in Egyptian royal graves. The Griffith Institute Ashmolean Museum, Oxford.

of ancient Egypt. During the reign of Queen Hatshepsut (1504-1490 B.C.), a fleet of five ships was dispatched down the Red Sea to the land of Punt, primarily in search of incense. Among the many gifts with which the fleet returned, according to a depiction in the temple at Dayr al Bahri, at Thebes, was ivory; and ivory was counted among the tribute to Thutmose III (1490-1468 B.C.) from Wawat (First Cataract) and Kush (Zayed 1981:147; Emery 1965:184). Once again, ivory appears as tribute from Kush to Ramses II (Nineteenth Dynasty, 1298-1234 B.C.) in a scene from the temple at Beit el Wali (Emery 1965:201).

Egyptian royal graves have yielded, not surprisingly, significant quantities of carved ivory objects and inlaid ivory tomb furniture: small discs that were used as a game from the tomb of Djer, the third king of the First Dynasty, around 3200 B.C.; four intricately carved dolls with unusual facial expressions from the pyramid of Senusret I at Lisht (Twelfth Dynasty, ca. 2000-1929 B.C.); and, perhaps most notably, the exquisite ivory headrest (Fig. 17-2) that accompanied Tutankhamun into the afterworld (Eighteenth Dynasty, ca. 1334-1325 B.C.) (Williamson 1938:127-28 and Gilbert 1976:162-63, pl. 29).

The Egyptian evidence makes it quite clear that ivory was a major product of the central and eastern Sudanic regions from very remote times. We cannot know how deeply this demand needed to penetrate into the heart of the continent, nor what impact the Egyptian demand may have had on the elephant population of those regions that supplied successive dynasties. We do know, however, that elephants disappeared from the eastern Sahara after 2750 B.C. and around 2000 B.C. in the central Sahara (Monod 1963:184). But this earliest epoch was surely to find its echoes in succeeding eras, as evidenced in the Meroitic temple site from Musawwarat, Nubia (Figs. 17-3, 17-4), where there may have been an elephant cult.[2]

The demand for African ivory experienced a second period of enormous growth during the heyday of the Roman empire,

17-3 (TOP), **17-4** (BOTTOM). Musawwarat, Nubia, site of a Meroitic temple circa A.D. 0-200, may have been the center of an elephant cult. Iconographic references to the animal include a restored stone statue of Elephant and an elephant decoration at the base of the temple column. Photographs, Merrick Posnansky.

as wealthy Romans began to use it for all sorts of things, great and small, domestic and public. Among the latter, Caesar rode in a chariot of ivory and an ivory stable was constructed for the imperial horse (Williamson 1938:42; Sheriff 1971: 561). The principal sources of ivory for the Roman empire were the far interior of the Upper Nile (probably beyond the catchment area that was necessary for the trade of ancient Egypt) and East Africa, which became an integral part of the international system of trade from this period. North Africa was also involved in supplying Rome with ivory. Until the seventh century, when the animals finally disappeared from that region, North Africa maintained a dwindling population of elephants, due mainly to their use first as war machines by both the Carthaginians and the Romans, and then as performing animals in public spectacles in late Roman and early Byzantine times (Cutler 1985:23-24,30; Spinage 1973:281).

The principal source of ivory for Rome was certainly Aksum, through its port of Adulis, in what is today Eritrea in northeast Africa. According to Anfray, "Whenever the authors of antiquity talk of Adulis, Aksum or Ethiopia (East Africa), they always give prominence to elephants and their ivory" (1981:377). Both Pliny (first century) and *The Periplus of the Erythraean Sea* (a Greco-Egyptian commercial guide dating probably to the first century, but perhaps somewhat later), cite ivory as the chief export from Adulis and refer to Aksum as the great collecting point for it. Koloé, according to the latter source, served as an intermediate ivory market some three days inland from Adulis (Anfray 1981:363,369). Evidence from Byzantium also confirms that ivory from Aksum was a major item of trade well into the reign of Justinian, in the mid-sixth century A.D. (Cutler 1985:23), when large herds of elephants were still observed near the Eritrean coast. Internal corroboration of the importance of elephants and ivory in the Aksumite realm comes from the discovery of a tusk in the ruins at Adulis and fragments of a terracotta elephant figurine in the walls of the castle at Dongour, the finest remaining example of Aksumite architecture.

The collapse of the Roman empire deprived northeast and east Africa of their leading ivory market, but it was gradually replaced by India and, more remotely, China. Until about the sixth century, India remained fairly self-sufficient with respect to its need for ivory, but by the beginning of that century the Indian demand for ivory bridal ornaments, which had to be destroyed at the death of either marriage partner, began to outstrip local supplies. By the tenth century, India and China were firmly established as the major markets for ivory from eastern Africa, including the Horn, and they remained so into the nineteenth century (and for China, even the twentieth century). But as Abdul Sheriff points out, this shift in market did not signal a change in character, for "it diversified the market for its ivory, but did not divert its economy from reliance on the exchange of a few raw materials for manufactured luxuries" (1971:566).

From the tenth century until the sudden arrival of the Portuguese in the Indian Ocean at the very end of the fifteenth century, all Arabic sources emphasize the importance of ivory from eastern Africa, stretching from the Somali coast to as far south as Sofala, beyond the mouth of the Zambezi river in modern Mozambique. Chinese sources from the period reiterate this theme for the Somali coast during the same period (Ricks 1970; Chittick 1977:192). Finally, the abundance in coastal sites of imported wares from the Indian Ocean world bears further witness to the international trading network in which eastern Africa was situated. All of the coastal communities about which these sources speak were ultimately grounded in a local economy of production, of course, but to the extent that each was dependent upon trading overseas, ivory was at the center of that relationship.

Like the situation at Adulis in the Roman period, eastern African exports depended on a system of supply in which demand at the coast percolated inland through an increasingly complex network of exchange linking hunters, agro-pastoralists, and coastal traders. The earliest evidence of ivory working and coastal trade in the interior comes from Schroda, in the Shashi/Limpopo region of South Africa, which dates to the ninth century (Huffman 1988:673). Two important interior sites yield abundant evidence of ivory trading and ivory working dating to the fourteenth and fifteenth centuries: Ingombe Ilede, on the north bank of the middle Zambezi in what is today Zambia, and Mapungubwe, in the Limpopo Valley in what is now South Africa (Fagan 1965). According to Peter Thorbahn's provocative thesis (1979), sources of ivory from the coastal hinterland — that is, up to 300 km inland — would already have been exhausted by the fifteenth century. Therefore, in order to supply adequate supplies of ivory for export, a well-developed system of interlocking networks must necessarily have been established. While Thorbahn's argument may prove difficult to verify empirically, it makes good sense of what we know about the way in which trading networks developed historically in eastern Africa, and what we know about the distribution of elephants in the nineteenth century. Certainly, the evidence from Ingombe Ilede and Mapungubwe demonstrates beyond question that the demand for ivory had stimulated a profound response among peoples of the far interior before 1500. Thus, while elephants certainly did not become extinct in the coastal hinterland of eastern Africa, where they may still be found even today, there is some reason to believe that the Indian Ocean ivory trade of the first half of the present millennium had a significant impact on the elephant population of the region.

Northeast Africa also experienced a resurgence in the ivory trade at this time due to the consolidation of Christian Abyssinia under the Solomonid dynasty and, in particular, to the vigorous imperial expansion of Amde-Siyon (1314-1344), which brought new ivory-producing lands in the far interior under state control (Tamrat 1984:438). This trade fed into the larger Indian Ocean network, as it had in earlier eras.

This same period witnessed a renewed demand for African ivory from Europe, on a scale unprecedented since Roman times. In the three hundred years before the mid-tenth century, very little ivory carving was done in Europe, due to a combination of the fall of the Roman empire, the Persian conquest of southern Arabia, and the over-exploitation of the North African elephant (Cutler 1985:30; Horton 1987:86). But by about A.D. 960, at the latest, a great many magnificent carvings from African ivory were being regularly executed by artists in both the Islamic and Christian Mediterranean worlds. Subsequently, from the twelfth century, the Crusades further invigorated the European demand for African ivory. Given the absence of North African sources of ivory and the emerging international system of ivory trade in the Indian Ocean, there is no doubting that the major source for this renaissance in European ivory carving was eastern Africa.

At the same time, however, there is some evidence that the demand for ivory had also reached down into Central and West Africa well before 1500. The earliest evidence that ivory was being exchanged with the forest regions of West Africa comes from the major savannah commercial center of Jenne (ca. 800), in what is now Burkina Faso, which is reinforced by findings at Begho, in northern Ghana, from the period ca. 965-1125 (Niane 1984:118; Andah and Anquandah 1988: 496,499). But the major development of the ivory trade, which always remained secondary to that of gold in western Africa, dates to the domination of the empire of Mali, and is particularly documented for the fourteenth century (Mauny 1961:264-65; Levtzion 1977:369; Niane 1984:620).

THE IVORY TRADE IN THE MODERN PERIOD

The Portuguese circumnavigation of Africa marked the beginning of a new orientation for the trade of Africa, and it had two dimensions. First, while both the Mediterranean and Indian Ocean worlds continued to provide important regional markets for Africa, European expansion opened up the entire littoral of western Africa to overseas trade in a way that significantly impacted the character, volume, and flow of trade within the subcontinent. Second, the inexorable development of a Euro-American capitalist world system progressively heightened the extractive quality of Africa's overseas trade – particularly with respect to the removal of labor and (during the colonial period) minerals and primary agricultural products from Africa – without the corollary development of productive forces, especially industrialization, on the continent itself.

While the ivory trade needs to be situated squarely in this broader context, we need also to appreciate that it stands somewhat apart from these trends because of its essential character as a purely luxury item of trade and because the overseas market for African ivory remains to this day truly international, and has never been entirely dominated by Euro-American capital. On the first count, in the debate about the origins and dynamics of underdevelopment in Africa, one cannot argue for the ivory trade from Africa that it in any way fueled the productive capacity of the West, as one surely can for the overseas slave trade or for the exploitation of minerals and agricultural staples. This was a luxury trade, pure and simple, with no significant infrastructural impact on the development of international capitalism, at least until the late nineteenth century (see Shayt, Chapter 18). On the other hand, one can argue that the enormous growth of the ivory trade in Africa itself deeply affected those communities which were tightly linked to the trade. Similarly, there can be little doubt that the hunting out of elephants in large areas of the continent has had a significant environmental impact, with ramifications for human society. That is not to diminish the impending tragedy that humans have visited upon elephants in Africa, but instead to remind us that we must not ignore the human dimensions of this unhappy history. On the second count, the Asian market for African ivory remained strong, if not in fact dominant, throughout the heyday of the Euro-American ivory trade, and is today without question the driving force in the world market for ivory. With this introduction to the modern period in mind, let us turn to the history of the trade over the past five hundred years.

When they first edged their way along the West African coastline and downward to the mouth of the Congo River (in 1483), eventually rounding the Cape of Good Hope into the Indian ocean (in 1498), the Portuguese were not specifically seeking ivory. However, they soon took advantage of the opportunity presented by the still abundant herds along the coast. By the beginning of the sixteenth century, a regular commerce in ivory was established from the Upper Guinea coast by way of the Cape Verde islands (Figs. 17-6, 17-7). Some of this ivory was obtained through African middlemen at coastal settlements, while south of the Gambia River it was possible to penetrate inland along various waterways to trade for ivory and other products. It was not until the Dutch and English established themselves in Sierra Leone in the seventeenth century, however, that ivory was intensively exploited. By the 1660s, when competition between the Dutch and the English for trade along the Upper Guinea coast had become fierce, it is clear that thousands of elephants were being slaughtered annually to provide the volume of tusks that were being purchased for export. So active was this trade that it led one Portuguese observer to proclaim that "there are, therefore, more elephants in Guinea than there are cattle in the whole of Europe!" (Rodney 1970:154-55). But there was also a price to be paid in the depletion of elephant herds near the coast before the mid-seventeenth century (Rodney 1970:155; Curtin 1975:224). Consequently, ivory exports declined throughout the eighteenth century, although in Sierra Leone their value exceeded that of slaves until the middle of that century (Hopkins 1973:88).

Even though the techniques of elephant hunting in the Upper Guinea coast area did not change significantly during

17-5. One of the largest tusks ever taken out of Africa, weighing about 228 lb. and measuring nearly 12 feet in length, according to the markings in Gujerati. It was purchased circa 1908 by E.D. Moore, author of *Scourge of Africa*. The Ernst D. Moore Collection. Archive Center. National Museum of American History. Smithsonian Collection. Neg. 89-20440.

these centuries, they were clearly sufficient to respond to the new demand for ivory that was stimulated by the Europeans. Typically, elephant hunters with poison-tipped spears would await their prey from perches above likely feeding grounds. Once they had wounded the animal, they would need to track it to its death before its tusks could be removed, returned to camp, and carried back to a central collecting point for transportation to the coast, where it would finally be exchanged for export. Elephant hunting was generally dangerous and required considerable skill, organization, and ritual protection; and escalating demand could only be met by significant intensification of traditional procedures. At the end of the eighteenth century, however, Africans began to use firearms for elephant hunting; they employed the long Dane gun loaded with a small iron rod (Rodney 1970:156).

During this period, West Central Africa experienced a history of ivory exploitation similar to that of the Upper Guinea coast. The Portuguese established a close relationship with the kingdom of Kongo from the late fifteenth century, and by the early decades of the following century, ivory was among the regular items of commerce. By the 1570s, it was one of the most important items of trade between the Kongo and the Tio of the middle Congo River (Harms 1981:39). In the early seventeenth century, the Dutch were exporting considerable quantities of ivory from Loango (Fig. 17-8); and by the middle of the century the Vili, who inhabited the coastal hinterland and specialized in hunting elephants, were hunting as far east as the middle Congo (Martin 1972:41). But the ivory

trade slacked off during the eighteenth century, when slaves constituted the principal item of European exportation from West Central Africa.

The pattern that obtained in West and West Central Africa – of initial slow growth in the sixteenth century, accelerated activity in the seventeenth century, and then decline in the eighteenth century – finds no precise parallel in eastern Africa. There, as we have already seen, the Portuguese encountered an already vigorous Indian Ocean trading system that had for many years supported a significant trade in ivory. Portuguese accounts from the ports of what is today Mozambique speak unambiguously of a major trade in ivory as far south as Delagoa Bay. Unlike the situation on the other side of the continent, the ivory export trade was never successfully captured by the Portuguese, who simply taxed the Indian merchants handling the trade in the ports that were under Portuguese control. English traders were also active along the coast of southeastern Africa in the late seventeenth century. By the later eighteenth century, the steady demand for ivory in this part of the continent had led to the creation of a vast procurement network in that part of the continent (Smith 1970).

This was certainly not the case in the northern reaches of Portuguese influence, where throughout the eighteenth century the ivory trade flourished in the hands of Yao traders from east of the Lake Nyasa region and Indian trading houses at Mozambique Island. However fragile the data, there is no question that large quantities of ivory were exported to India during the century, though the impact on the elephant popula-

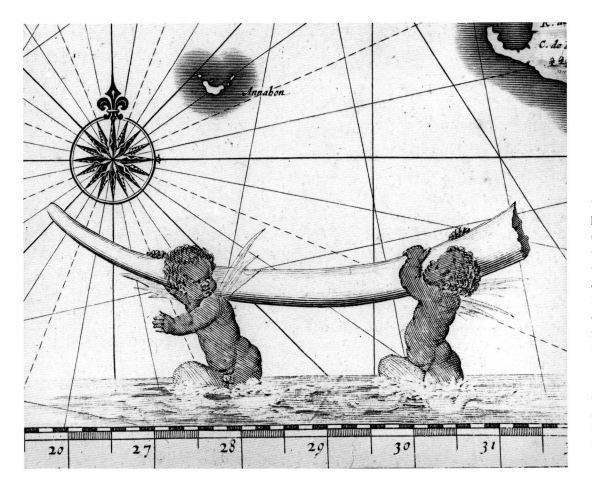

17-6 (TOP), **17-7** (BOTTOM). While a regular ivory commerce had developed in the 16th century along the Guinea coast, it was only in the 17th century, when the Dutch and English established themselves in Sierra Leone, that ivory began to be extensively exploited. Early maps of the region reveal the European agenda: Above left, 17th-century Dutch map of *Guinea*, by W.J. Blaeu, Amsterdam, 1663 (see Blaeu's *Grand Atlas*, vol. 10). Below, detail from an 18th-century Dutch map of *Guinea Propria...*, by Homan Heirs, 1743.

tion of East Central Africa can only be guessed. At the end of the eighteenth century, however, the supply of ivory to India from Mozambique collapsed under the burden of Portuguese taxation. It is indicative of the commitment of the Yao to the ivory trade that they readily transferred their coastal outlets away from those ports under Portuguese control to those under the suzerainty of the Omani rulers of Zanzibar in what is today southern Tanzania. East Central Africa is also a region in which the complementary relationship of the ivory and slave trades can be unambiguously identified. But if it is clear that during the later eighteenth century traffic in both of these commodities was very active at Mozambique Island, we cannot so confidently assert the image of slave porters bearing ivory tusks down to the coast from the interior that became a common feature of European anti-slave trade propaganda in the nineteenth century (Alpers 1975).

Although the evidence is thinner for the coasts of modern Tanzania, Kenya, and southern Somalia during these centuries, it is sufficient to establish that trade in ivory was an important – perhaps the dominant – item in the region's export trade (Alpers 1975; Ylvisaker 1982:221-22,224). What little we know about the trade of Ethiopia and the Sudan during this period suggests that there was not much activity in the former region, probably due to considerable political unrest on the plateau, and no more than a modest traffic from the latter (Abir 1970:122-23).

THE 19TH CENTURY: SURGING DEMANDS FOR IVORY

The general decline in the ivory trade that occurred across the continent at the end of the eighteenth century was entirely transformed over the next quarter century by a dramatic rise in the prevailing European price for ivory, which increased some tenfold between the 1780s and the 1830s (Curtin 1975: 224 and Supplement:111, Table A15.14). Added to the steady demand for East African ivory in India, the new demand reflected in this price rise precipitated a drive to obtain ivory. This led both to the decimation of remaining elephant herds nearer the coast, and to the opening up of new hunting grounds in the far interior that were now economically worth exploiting despite the higher costs of transportation from the interior to the coast. Moreover, the new European demand continued to grow throughout the century as industrialization and the maturation of Euro-American capitalism created a new mass market for items such as piano keys, billiard balls, and combs that were manufactured out of African elephant ivory. For all intents and purposes, ivory became the plastic of the era. Thus began a century of intensive hunting of elephants for the international ivory trade that was unprecedented in the history of the continent until the most recent decades of the present century.

The African response to this new demand was characterized by several phenomena. First, as the century wore on, greater numbers of elephant hunters adopted firearms as their principle weapon of choice, although traditional methods, such as traps and poisoned arrows – which prevailed among such prominent elephant hunters and ivory traders as the Kamba of eastern Kenya – were never entirely abandoned. Second, ever greater numbers of men were undoubtedly drawn into elephant hunting as a quasi-professional undertaking, a development which had inevitable social and economic consequences that affected concepts of social significance and the availability of male labor for agriculture and other domestic tasks. Specifically, the absence of men and the access to foreign trade goods in those societies which participated significantly in elephant hunting and the ivory trade made possible the acquisition of substantial amounts of domestic slave labor (Alpers 1969; Cummings 1975:200; Harms 1981:30). Third, the organizational implications of devoting large numbers of men to elephant hunting and the caravaning of ivory (and other products, of course) generally reinforced the concentration of economic and political power in the hands of prominent individuals, of whom some had traditional claims to authority and others had none (Alpers 1969; 1974:236-40; Miller 1970).

It merits comment here that the popular notion of an intimate connection between the slave trade and the ivory trade, which was featured prominently in the influential writings of such European explorers as David Livingstone, was not so pronounced historically as is often portrayed, for example in the common image of slave porters bearing ivory tusks down to the coast from the interior (Beachey 1967:276). Ivory porterage was a prestigious undertaking (Roberts 1970: 61), and came to represent for many young men something of a rite of passage (as well as being economically advantageous) that can be compared to labor migration in the present century. The intertwining of ivory porterage and slaving that has been recorded for the Yao and some of the Arab-Swahili caravans in the later nineteenth century was not, I think, typical of the ivory trade in general, but represented a late development that reflected the increasing pressure of intensified profit taking on the eve of European colonial conquest. This aberration is also reflected in the use of slave retainers as caravan labor for the ivory trade in West Central Africa (Miller 1983: 153) and in the escalating cycle of violence that joined the ivory and slave trades in the southern Sudan (Gray 1961:33,46-66) and the eastern marches of the West Central African savannah (Reefe 1983:197,204) during this half century.

The principal ivory trading market in West Africa during the nineteenth century had shifted from the Upper Guinea coast to Cameroon, which had sustained a prominent ivory trade from the seventeenth century (Austen 1983:3), and where fierce competition over control of the trade now pitted Europeans on the coast against Hausa traders from northern Nigeria operating through Adamawa who transported ivory by camel caravan across the Sahara to the ports of North Africa for export to Europe. In the early decades of the century, the Saharan trade was minimal, but by the middle of the century

17-8. This ivory tusk was probably produced for French traders by Vili people of Loango, 1859-60. Since the 17th century, ivory had been a regular item of commerce in the area, and the Vili, elephant hunters inhabiting the coastal hinterland, were highly involved in this trade. By 18th and 19th centuries, slaves had become another important item of export. Chained slaves (2nd level from bottom) and ivory bearers (5th level) are depicted on the tusk seen here. Other vignettes of life include a sailor woodworking, coconuts being picked, a trader selling gin, a European lighting a cigar, fishermen with their catch, processions of dignitaries, banquet preparations, and so forth. Height 113 cm. Walters Art Gallery 71.586.

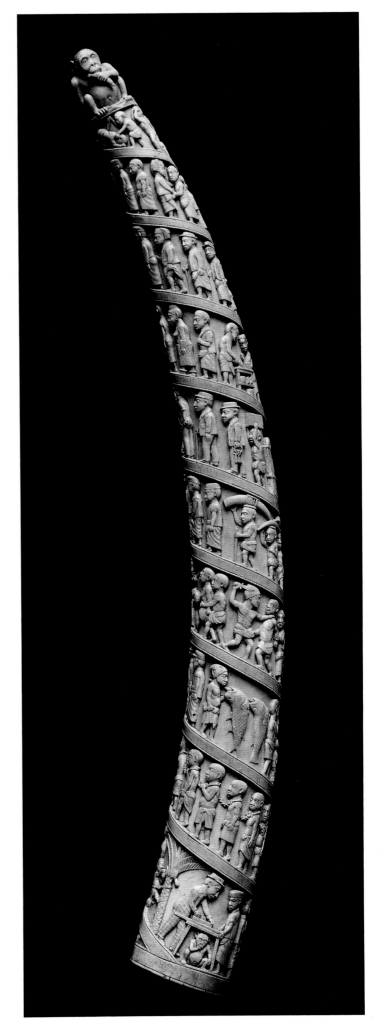

it had become quite significant (Newbury 1966:238-39). The struggle over control of the Cameroon trade continued right to the end of the nineteenth and into the early years of the twentieth century, by which time European professional hunters armed with modern firearms were now an important factor in the trade. By the beginning of World War I, though the Saharan trade outlet had dwindled and new hunting grounds had been opened in the interior, the trade had declined to a shadow of its nineteenth century heyday (Johnson 1978).

West Central Africa also witnessed a significant increase in the ivory trade in the second half of the nineteenth century, following the abolition of the official Portuguese monopoly of the export trade in 1836 and the winding down of the trans-Atlantic slave trade after 1850. Utilizing the same trade routes that had brought countless slaves to the coast for export in earlier decades, the apparently insatiable European demand for ivory now caused vast areas of the far interior of the Congo basin to be opened up to elephant hunting. An extensive and complex network penetrated the entire region and brought many tons of ivory to the coast annually. As Vansina notes, what has been called "the Great Congo Commerce" was by 1880 "fundamentally a trade in which ivory was exchanged for goods imported from Europe" (Harms 1981; Miller 1970; Vansina 1973:248).

Although Southern Africa remained no more than a secondary source of ivory, the demand for ivory nevertheless caused European hunters to press ever farther into the interior in search of elephants. As a result of their aggressive activity, and in combination with that of African elephant hunters throughout the region, by the end of the century the elephant population south of the Zambezi River was virtually decimated (Spinage 1973:283; Smith 1983:242; Beach 1983:253,273).

Abdul Sheriff's meticulous study (1987) of the commercial economy of Zanzibar during the first three-quarters of the nineteenth century provides vivid testimony to the magnitude of the ivory trade in East Africa during this period. While the Asian trade remained very important throughout the century, there is no question that it was the new Euro-American demand that really stimulated the growth of the ivory trade in East Africa, as elsewhere on the continent. Not only did the ivory trade rise in absolute terms at Zanzibar, which was the central collection point for the trade of the East African interior, but

17-9. By the late 19th century, the demand from Zanzibar spurred a vast network of supply routes far into the interior, as far west as the Congo basin.... "An ivory poacher's caravan fording a stream in the Belgian Congo with their illicit ivory. These tusks were puchased by the author on their arrival in British territory." So reads the caption to this photograph in E.D. Moore's *Ivory: Scourge of Africa* (1931:opp. 180).

its importance to the British market also rose in relation to other regions of the continent. For example, whereas in the first two decades of the century some seventy percent of the ivory imported into the United Kingdom came from West Africa, by 1840 only thirty-five percent was provided from that source. The East African trade also was boosted by the re-export of its ivory through Bombay to England (Sheriff 1987: 87-90). As the century wore on and Zanzibar emerged as a major Indian Ocean commercial entrepôt, American, French, and German trading houses established there also added to the demand for ivory from East Africa. By 1891, Zanzibar provided some seventy-five percent of the world's supply of ivory (Beachey 1967:289). As was the case in West Central Africa, the demand that emanated from Zanzibar spurred the development of a vast network of supply routes that extended far into the interior of the continent, reaching as far west as the Congo basin (Fig. 17-9), as far north as the upper Nile and

the marches of the Ethiopian highlands, and as far south as the northern tributaries of the Zambezi River.

The last area to be considered during this period is the southern Sudan, which was penetrated by Arab merchants operating out of Khartoum after it was founded in 1822. The opening up of this vast area was intimately linked to Egyptian expansion into the Sudan and much of the exploitation of both ivory and slaves that took place to the southwest of Khartoum occurred under the guise of Egyptian administration. The Nile became a major outlet for ivory during this period, at least until the Mahdist revolution in the 1880s prevented normal commerce (Gray 1961; Beachey 1967:278-81; Keim 1983). But by that time, it appears, a combination of the extreme exploitation of ivory that had already occurred and competition from elephant hunters seeking to supply both the Cameroon and Zanzibar markets had begun to affect supplies from this area (Spinage 1973:285).

Any attempt to calculate the actual volume of ivory that was exported from Africa during even the second half of the nineteenth century is bound to be misleading. What is indisputable is that the trade reached a magnitude and the killing of elephants assumed proportions that were certainly unprecedented. Elephants were hunted out from many areas and decimated in others, although at least some areas remained

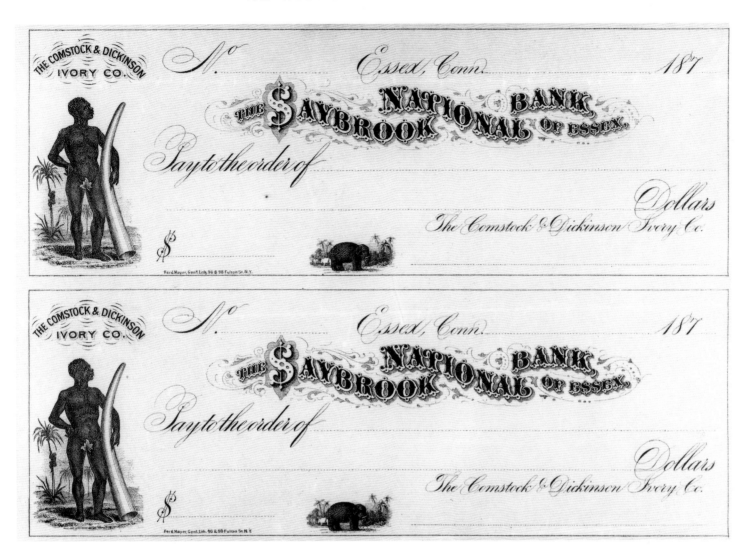

relatively unscathed. But because the object of this hunting was to procure ivory and the best and largest tusks were obtained from mature animals, the elephant populations that remained at the beginning of the twentieth century were young, despite evidence of indiscriminate killing in some areas of the continent in the late nineteenth century.

The establishment of colonial rule throughout the continent brought with it a level of security from the most volatile conditions of the nineteenth century that had been fueled by the partial integration of Africa into the expanding world capitalist system (Figs. 17-10 through 17-13), as well as a wide range of restrictions on Africans that were designed to move them into the wage labor economy. Thus, on the one hand, Africans were able to establish farms in areas that were previously too dangerous for cultivation, in the process reclaiming lands that might have been available to elephants, while, on the other hand, they were forbidden to possess firearms and to hunt. Colonial regimes created game reserves that both protected elephants and other wildlife from uncontrolled hunting and, contrarily, created the conditions for elephants to destroy the habitat as a consequence of overgrazing. Meanwhile, big game hunting became something that Europeans and Americans did "on safari" in Africa, while Africans provided the labor that sustained this fledgling industry.[3]

17-10. The commercial importance of the elephant and its ivory is reflected in checks from the Saybrook National Bank of Essex, Connecticut, circa the 1870s, personalized for the Comstock & Dickinson Ivory Co, a local firm. P-RCR, Archives Center, National Museum of American History, Smithsonian Institution, 91-6780.

By the 1920s reports began to appear that indicated an increase in the elephant populations of East Africa, and these were repeated with somewhat greater insistence over the next twenty years. Elsewhere, although there was some migration of elephant populations from one sanctuary to another, elephants virtually disappeared from West Africa and were losing ground in West Central Africa. Thus, East Africa emerged as the principal preserve for the African elephant population, while at the same time the ivory trade began to experience a slight revival in its fortunes. There was a steady rise in ivory exports from the mid-1930s to the early 1960s, as well as the gradual replacement of Zanzibar by Mombasa, Kenya, (Fig. 17-13) as the principal African, and indeed world, market for ivory (Spinage 1973:286-87; Beachey 1967:289).

Since the 1970s, there has been a marked increase in knowledge about African elephants and matching concern for their survival. Aerial surveys and international cooperation

17-11. Ivory sale at a warehouse at the London Docks, sometime in the 1890s. The Bettman Archive/BBC Hulton.

17-12. Ivory from the interior being weighed on the Kenya-Tanzania Coast. Eliot Elisofon Photographic Archives. National Museum of African Art, Smithsonian Institution.

17-13. Street scene in Mombasa, British East Africa, ca. 1915. Tusks are stenciled with port and trader destinations. In the first half of the 20th century, Momabasa gradually replaced Zanzibar as the main African and world market for ivory. Smithsonian Institution. Neg. 90-14113.

17-14. Twenty-franc note from the Banque du Congo Belge, 1917-1937. An elephant's head can be seen in the watermark, lower right corner. National Numismatic Collection, Smithsonian Institution.

have made possible the approximation of a reasonable continental census of elephants, which were estimated at about 1.3 million or more in 1979 (Douglas-Hamilton 1980:51) and just slightly under 1.2 million in 1980. Concomitantly, rising ivory prices during this period, fueled primarily by demand from the Far East (Burton 1976:138-39; Parker and Martin 1982:236-37 and 1983; Anon. 1981:20-21) rendered the ivory trade especially attractive to young African nations that were faced with declining world commodity prices and vulnerable national economies that they had inherited from the colonial era. At a different level, given the enormous profits that could be made, equivalent to well over a year's wages from one tusk of ivory (Anon. 1980:23), poaching of elephants was a temptation to African men who were either unable to obtain jobs for wages or who sought greater return for their labor than they could find through agriculture or employment. Furthermore, political unrest in much of the continent where elephants still flourished and the consequent ready availability of modern weapons of destruction made elephant hunting, however risky from a legal perspective, no longer a specialized skill. Civil wars and automatic rifles have made victims of many in Africa, including elephants, while military forces and police have been implicated elsewhere in elephant poaching and ivory trading (Douglas-Hamilton 1987:13-20). By 1980 it was possible for Iain Douglas-Hamilton to state, "…we can quite confidently assert that the volume of ivory exports has increased with the price, and is now back to pre-1914 levels in the prime elephant ranges of Africa" (1980:86).

During the 1980s, growing efforts focused on closing down the illegal ivory trade from Africa and thereby on the poaching of elephants. Wildlife preservation advocates, acting through their governments and the Convention on International Trade in Endangered Species (CITES), have

endeavored to get both importing and exporting countries to endorse the declaration of the African elephant as an endangered species, or at least to ban the ivory trade. Zaire banned all ivory exports in 1980, as did the Sudan in 1983, though importing nations were not always cooperative and much smuggling through false labeling occurred (Douglas-Hamilton 1987:23). By the mid-1980s, however, steadily rising prices together with active poaching and smuggling continued to wreak havoc with the rapidly dwindling elephant populations of East Africa (Montgomery 1988). Between 1979 and 1987, for example, the Tanzanian population plummeted from something over 300,000 to about 85,000 (Gup 1989:69), while an authoritative estimate of the continental population in 1989 suggests a figure of about 625,000 (Poole and Thomsen 1989:188), half of what it was a decade before.

In May 1989, prompted by considerable international pressure and seeking to avoid negative publicity that might affect its important tourist trade, Kenya called for a complete international ban on the buying and selling of ivory, a position also subscribed to by neighboring Tanzania (Battiata 1989). In a flamboyant and much publicized gesture that made the front pages of many international newspapers, President Moi of Kenya torched a pile of about twelve tons of ivory in July 1989 (Fig. 17-15). Nevertheless, there was no unanimity on the need to ban the ivory trade. Both Botswana and Zimbabwe, which have developed excellent programs of herd management and which view the ivory trade as an important source of hard currency to fund wildlife protection, opposed the ban on the grounds that it would hurt them and was, in any case, unenforceable (Bartholet 1989). Finally, in October 1989 at Lausanne, Switzerland, the seventy-six parties to CITES voted to place the African elephant on the list of endangered species

17-15. In July 1989, to publicize his country's ban on the buying and selling of ivory, Kenyan president Daniel arap Moi set fire to a twelve-ton pile of ivory. This flamboyant gesture captured international attention. Wide World Photos.

and thereby invoked a worldwide ban on all trade in ivory. The vote was only achieved, however, by the inclusion of a critical rider favored by the eleven nations opposed to the ban, who threatened to withdraw from CITES if it were not included in the final agreement. That rider states, "well-managed elephant populations may be removed from the endangered list, which would permit controlled trading in ivory and other byproducts" (Wallace 1989).

Given the unstable nature of international agreements, it seems to me that the future of the African elephant remains problematic, the 1989 CITES agreement notwithstanding. For most Africans the future of the elephant is arguably the least of their daily concerns and until the rest of the world pays as much attention to the people of Africa as it has to its wildlife, there will be no good reason for them to think and behave otherwise.

NOTES

I would like to thank Christine Choi Ahmed for research assistance and for reading an early draft of this essay.

1. The elephant hieroglyph as part of the ideogram for "Elephantine" is found in a tomb painting of Sarenput II, commander of the frontier garrison of the southern lands during Amenemhet II's reign (see Gardner 1957: 461; Helme 1894:155; Bianchi 1991:70, fig. 2).
2. A good reference to elephants and the elephant cult can be found in Adams (1977:320-21). See also Hintze (1979); Shinnie (1967); and Wenig (1973:493 n.).
3. For a wicked sketch of the safari industry, see Sinclair (1967).

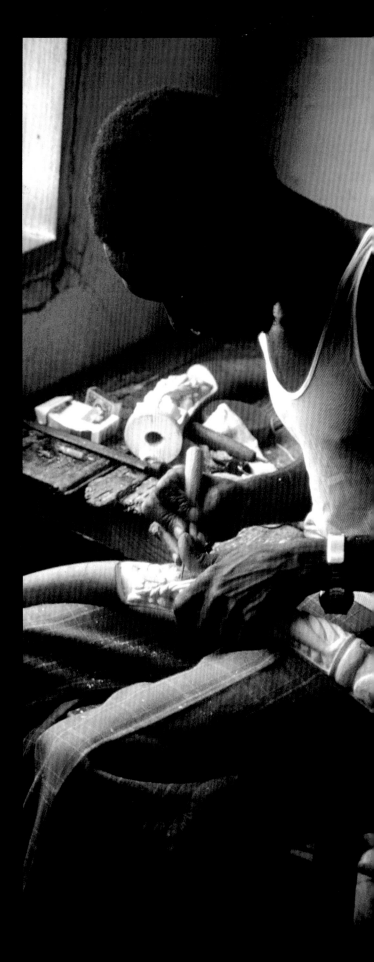

RY WORKSHOP, photographed
1980 in Monrovia, Liberia, was run
go man named Seku Dama and his
s, Kramo Omar Traoure and Dama
ha's nephews, the master carvers,
bracelets, combs, letter openers,
, and assorted sculptures. From the
and pieces, they produced rings,
iniature elephants. A large tusk took
weeks to carve. In 1980, the most
was a bust of a Fulani woman, sel-
.

rkshops such as this have virtually
since the 1989 passage of a ban on
ial trade in ivory by the Convention
onal Trade in Endangered Species
e ban was extended in 1992. Docu-
d photographs, Thomas Seligman

CATALOGUE OF GOODS

SOLD BY
JULIUS PRATT & CO.
86 CHAMBERS ST.

NEW YORK.

THE MATERIAL CULTURE OF IVORY OUTSIDE AFRICA

DAVID H. SHAYT

Scholarly interest in ivory use outside Africa has focused almost exclusively on its application as a medium of expression for sculptors and carvers.[1] But the lure of aesthetic traditions has diverted attention from the historic industrial applications of ivory. Ironically, the first era of modern published works on the ivory arts coincided with the period of ivory's greatest diffusion throughout the world, roughly from 1850 to 1930 – that is, from the rise of heavy industrialization to the arrival of a mature synthetics industry.[2]

This paper uses the end products of the African ivory trade – the statuary, knife handles, piano keys, billiard balls – to look at how an "ivory entitlement" gradually obliterated the vital relationship once perceived between an animal and its various parts (Kunz 1916:166). Factory records and museum collections of machine-cut ivory exist in volume.[3] Topical periodicals such as *Piano Trade Magazine*, *Billiards Digest*, *Blade Magazine*, and *Knives Illustrated* are also critical sources of industry data for factory-made ivory goods. One consequence of studying such evidence is a realization of how design and production decisions facing industrial engineers and their ivory workers differed from those faced by free-hand carvers.

The contrast that emerges between traditionally crafted ivory works in Africa and those of the ivory-working centers of Europe, North America, and Asia juxtaposes not only cultural perceptions of the natural world but the relationships between a source of raw materials and its finished products.[4] To under-stand ivory's dichotomous use outside Africa, the extraordinary nature of the material itself offers an important clue.

THE APPEAL OF IVORY

Even the untrained eye may readily appreciate the creamy, light-diffusing beauty and silky coolness of finished elephant ivory. For Europeans and Asians, its resemblance to skin is perhaps its greatest subliminal attribute[5] – one that found limitless associations in the Victorian world, where whiteness of skin was an absolute measure of class and status. Other white workable substances found in nature (bone, shell, marble, alabaster, white jade) lack one or more of ivory's principal attributes – size, purity, availability, or micro-workability.

Indeed, ivory of the elephant responds to cutting tools and polishing wheels like no other material, natural or manufac-tured. It accepts deep relief work and filigree without excessive weakening, and it ages gracefully, developing a mellow, amber patina if kept in darkness. Over time, prolonged shifts in surrounding temperature and humidity do cause it to fracture as the porous material expands and contracts (LaFontaine and Wood 1982).

18-1 (OPPOSITE). Cover of ivory goods catalog, mid-19th century, American. Pratt-Read Corporation Records (320), Archives Center, National Museum of American History, Smithsonian Institution.

18-2. Egyptian war elephant tile inlay from 12th century. Elephant ivory. Double-lipped trunk and dipped back show elephant to be African. Height 7.1 cm. Walters Art Gallery, Cat. 71.563.

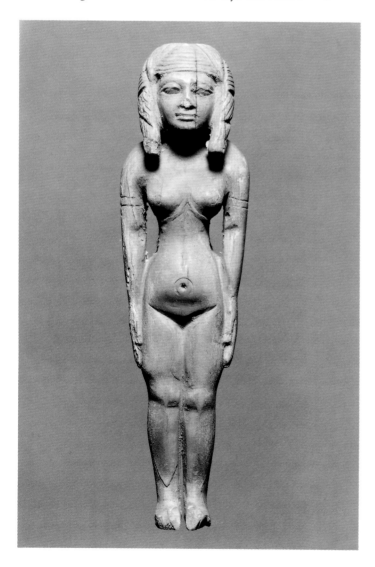

18-3. Egyptian figurine ("Concubine") from the 18th dynasty (c. 1650 B.C.). Elephant (?) ivory. Height 11.8 cm. Walters Art Gallery, Cat. 71.505.

Animals other than elephants grow lesser forms of ivory for more modest uses, chiefly grubbing for food and chewing (Espinoza and Mann 1991). The ivory tusks of the wart hog and the hippopotamus also have made the passage through folk art to industrialized product (umbrella and beer stein handles, dice, jewelry, walking stick knobs). Marine animals (the walrus, sperm whale, killer whale, and narwhal) have yielded ivory that again has been utilized initially by indigenous groups but subsequently worked by distant others into the trappings of urban consumer cultures (Holtzapffel 1846: 137-40). The scrimshawing of marine ivory by American whalers of the nineteenth century probably mirrors the early uses of elephant ivory in proclaiming the courage and skill required to slay a great beast with simple hand weapons (Flayderman 1972:29).

The tusks of the mammoth, ancestor to the modern elephant, attracted prehistoric ivory artists during the Pleistocene Epoch some 20,000 years ago, and their survival in permafrost soils was heavily exploited outside Africa during the nineteenth century (Kunz 1916:345-48). Today, fossil mammoth ivory (odontolite) continues to to be mined in the polar regions of Asia and North America, but largely as a legal, guilt-free alternative to elephant ivory. Its bluish brown hues and rock-like, frequently cracked condition render it mechanically less desirable than the "live" ivory of the elephant (Newman 1991).

The ivory nuts that grow on certain species of palm trees in tropical regions of the western hemisphere have been among the most commercially active of the lesser ivory sources, second only to elephant ivory (Kunz 1916:278-89). The tagua nut, surprisingly similar in hardness and appearance to elephant ivory, was machine-worked in the United States into baby rattles, dice, dog whistles, and sewing thimbles during the nineteenth century, and became a customary material for clothes buttons and earrings in America and Europe of the 1920s and 1930s (Barfod 1989). Today vegetable ivory is experiencing a revival of interest in the fashion industry with elephant ivory's banishment.[6] Wider uses of vegetable ivory are restricted by the golf ball size of tagua nuts and their hollow cores.

As a workable material, however, elephant ivory is unrivaled. For craftsmen and mechanics, its physical advantages have placed it in a class of its own since the fourth millennium B.C. (Holtzapffel 1846:chap. 8). The fine crosshatched microstructure of the grain, so apparent in the swirling surface finishes achieved, allows the ivory to be cut in almost any direction without severe splintering. While harder than most woods, ivory does not dull cutting tools as quickly, due in part to the gelatinous lubricant found in the network of tiny vas-

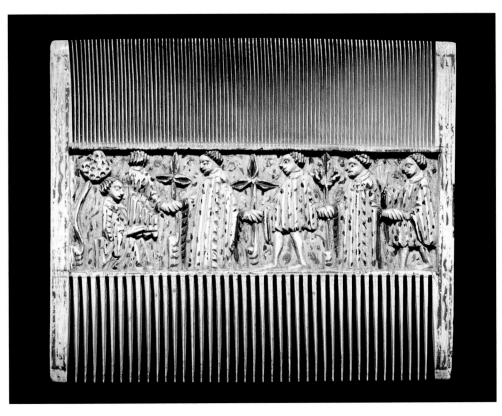

18-4. North Italian double comb from 15th century. Polychromed and gilded elephant ivory. Height 11.5 cm. Walters Art Gallery, Cat. 71.215.

cular tubes interlacing the material and that gives ivory its characteristic shine. A single black pinhole down the center of the solid portion of the tusk serves as a nerve canal, but also provides tool orientation once the coarse dark bark of the tusk has been removed.

The only principal physical limitations of the material typically have been its size (a maximum working diameter of four to five inches) and the deep pulp cavity in the upper third of the tusk, a hollow region that restricts the use of the ivory around it to shallow carving. But the long intricate history of ivory-working has shown how marginal such limitations can be when the remaining ivory is so versatile and visually striking. Were it not for the sad circumstances of its acquisition (Landy 1989), the ivory of the elephant would be among the choicest of materials.

A Prestige Material of the Ancient World

Beyond sub-Saharan Africa, the romance with elephant ivory as an artistic medium for spiritual expression and the mark of privilege began more than six thousand years ago. A now-extinct elephant subspecies that roamed North Africa and the Near East supplied ivory to Egyptian, Phoenician, and Assyrian carvers who worked it into an assortment of wares, both utilitarian and ceremonial (Cutler 1985:23-25). Their work ranged from ivory beads, amulets, and combs to headrests, small statuary (Fig. 18-3), relief panels, and room furnishings (Canby 1985).

While much of Egypt's early work derived from animal bone and the teeth of the hippopotamus, elephant ivory had emerged by the fourth millennium B.C. for work unsuited to the lesser configurations of hippo teeth and the lower social status

of bone. Bone's very porous structure and ready deterioration restricted its use, while hippo teeth, encased in a thick armor-like enamel, were difficult to penetrate with the available cutting tools (Holtzapffel 1846:139-40; Canby 1985:33-38).

The mastery of detail evident in the archaeological ivory recovered from sites of these early periods is an important indicator of what was to become of this medium when subjected to the more sophisticated ivory-working technologies of later eras. Almost from the outset, the excellent cross-sectional strength of elephant ivory (Fig. 18-2) and its ability to receive colored pigments were employed in statuettes, body ornamentation, and hair combs with needle-like teeth (Fig. 18-4). Centers of ivory working developed in Dilmun (modern Bahrain), Abu Matar in Palestine, and across Anatolia (modern Turkey). Ivory stylistic traditions ebbed and flowed as tastes shifted toward greater anatomical detailing or shallow relief, depending on the state of the craft's development within the shops, and the supply of ivory. Royal expeditions to the Sudan and elsewhere in Africa sought ivory, either from traders or directly from elephants.

Ivory reigned as a mark of wealth and regional authority, and as a means to capture in portable forms the images of scenes and figures important to the cultures. The Minoan, Etruscan, Greek, and Roman civilizations inherited appetites for ivory from the Near Eastern cultures, together with the means to locate and work it (Buitron and Oliver 1985).

The elephant's domineering stature in African cultures as a beast of supreme size, strength, and longevity (Ezra 1984: 16,21) is mirrored by perceptions of the animal and its ivory in ancient Greece and Rome (Scullard 1974). As mobile armor which could and did decimate enemy troops and fortifications,

18-5. Japanese netsuke depicting "Masayuki" boy acrobat, 19th century. Elephant ivory. Height c. 4. cm. Walters Art Gallery, Cat. 71.894.

18-6. Swiss animal miniature ("Lion of Lucerne"), from c. 1900. Elephant ivory. Height 11 cm. National Museum of American History, Smithsonian Institution, Cat. 380634. Photograph, Eric Long. SI Negative 90-10953/12.

trained war elephants acted out on foreign soils the martial traits for which they were most revered in Africa. For centuries (roughly 400 B.C. to A.D. 100) the acquisition and possession of elephants and their ivory appear to have been imperial prerogatives in Ptolemaic Egypt, Macedonia, and Greece, but especially in Rome. Ownership of elephants represented both mastery of a formidable animal and the potential to vanquish a lesser-equipped human foe.

Elephant ivory seems to have taken on associated totemistic powers, with tusks carried aloft in triumphal processions and sanctified in temple ceremonies. Ivory's employment in the statuary of deities and the insignia of high political office reinforced this cross-cultural endurance of a material's close association with its animal origins.

To the high civilizations of the Aegean and Northeastern Mediterranean may be credited the advancement of ivory-carving beyond the purely pictographic to a fully narrative form. By the second century B.C., ivory working had emerged from its wood-carving roots as an honored professional specialty with its own internal standards of workmanship, training programs, and exclusionary employment policies.

The development of iron saws, gouges, files, rifflers, and hand drills enabled carvers to begin working their material to its greatest expressive potential, and develop a more sophisticated understanding of the material's properties. During this long period, while ivory was gradually absorbed into cultures farther and farther removed from those of Africa (Randall 1985:116-51), ivory-working skills were honed empirically. Craftsmen learned to distinguish the varying attributes of hard and soft ivory, determine the optimal portions of the

tusk, prepare ivory blocks prior to their carving, and assemble multiple pieces of ivory to create large composite works.

Ivory's popularity with the Aegean and Mediterranean aristocracy may obscure the fact that no comparable material existed then, as it does today, for the creation of exceedingly precise artwork in miniature. The Mediterranean world's acquisition of ivory from Africa as a medium for works of both art and utility had many reflections in the applications found for ivory in African cultures of the period (Barnett 1982). The volume differed, as did any awareness of the extent of the supply. But there remains a certain seamlessness to the pattern of ivory usage between the ancient cultures of Europe and those of Africa, both perceiving ivory as a special substance reserved for highly decorative, political, or spiritual uses.

In the Byzantine world, ivory was used increasingly to dramatize Christian images and symbols. From the dawn of Byzantium (fourth century A.D.), to the nineteenth century, no single subject seems to have been quite so exploited through the medium of elephant ivory as the corpus of Christ. Every conceivable phase of the persecution, crucifixion, deposition, lamentation, and resurrection is modeled in the kind of narrative depth and anatomical richness that only ivory could have provided. Ivory permitted miniaturization, thanks to a physical portability and density of artistic expression that eluded marble, ivory's principal rival in stone. Thus it answered an important need for the personalization of Christian liturgy in places beyond the shrines, temples, and churches that contained the stationary life-size figures rendered in stone. Ivory-sheathed boxes, for example, served as Byzantine reliquaries to contain sacred objects for private devotional use (Cutler 1984). Even the outright Christianization of the elephant is arguable, with the animal's image and unworked tusks finding places of honor in early European cathedrals (Bedini 1981; Guarducci 1978-80).

Byzantine carving techniques reached a zenith in works that used the swirling grain structure of ivory to accentuate the muscular definition of the human form. Carvers employed subtle devices such as foreshortening and undercutting to manipulate the depth of field of relief images that appear to rise out of flat slabs of ivory, the very limitations of the tusk giving birth to new modes of artistic expression.

The durability of the finished carving and the realism of the figural forms served as incentives for patrons to buy and further encourage carvers to stretch sculptural techniques and technologies. Such market responses would facilitate the great flow of Gothic, Baroque, and Victorian ivory carvings unleashed by the political and religious upheavals that were to occur in Europe in the coming centuries, as ivory grew into a medium of popular expression, and eventually, mass consumption.

The Most Sumptuous Ivories

Gazing in upon the Asian ivory-carving sweat shops and packed ivory showrooms of Hong Kong and New York City in the early 1980s, there is a tendency to feel as if this has been the elephant's darkest hour, where young carvers with little power saws and dental drills create repetitious works of dubious artistry embodying all that may have seemed deplorable about both the ivory trade and modern commercialism.[7] But how familiar would these scenes and possibly these ruminations be to the visitor entering one of the ivory-carving ateliers in eighteenth-century Dieppe, France, or nineteenth-century Nuremberg, Germany, where bench workers turned out religious figurines, fans, animal miniatures (Fig. 18-6), and storybook triptychs — all to join the profusion of goods in metal, stone, leather, and cloth intended entirely for the visiting foreigner (Johnston 1985:281-86; Percival 1920:157, 161,201-9)?

While the long tradition of Japanese netsuke ivory-carving (Fig. 18-5) occupies a historic niche in the internal art world of Japan (Jonas 1928), the technological *tours de force* produced for the export market by Asian carvers in the twentieth century display levels of mechanical intricacy that seem unreachable. The concentric balls within balls, the tusks rendered entirely in openwork, the sailing vessels, the lacy fans — such work has pushed ivory to its greatest physical extremes largely for the amazement of the foreigner (Deane 1990).

European carvers of the fourteenth through the nineteenth centuries fashioned ivory work with more specific topical agendas in mind, predominantly of a religious nature. Several dozen museums throughout the world today own achievements in early European ivory art recognized by scholars as authentic expressions of their cultures, despite the motivations of a foreign market. In similar fashion, the Afro-Portuguese ivory art forms of the sixteenth century carved exclusively

18-7. German neo-Baroque tankard, 1850-70. Elephant ivory. Height 30 cm. National Museum of American History, Smithsonian Institution, Cat. 380643. Photograph, Dane Penland. SI Negative 89-21420.

for European export have become the subject of scholarly scrutiny in recent years (Bassani and Fagg 1988).

Unlike our perception of the work that issued from Asian ivory mills, renowned for industrial efficiency, the finest Renaissance and Baroque chests, tankards (Fig. 18-7), panels, and statuettes emerged from celebrated ivory- and bone-carving communities and family dynasties in Europe. Names such as Quellinus, Lenckhardt, and Moreau-Vauthier evoke tremendous admiration today for their individual achievements in ivory (Randall and Theuerkauff 1985:242-72).

The flow of raw ivory to these shops became both an incentive for and a consequence of the intensity of European interest in colonizing Africa. Together with spices, gemstones, minerals, and hides, unworked ivory was one of the more conspicuous prizes available to Portugal, Germany, Belgium,

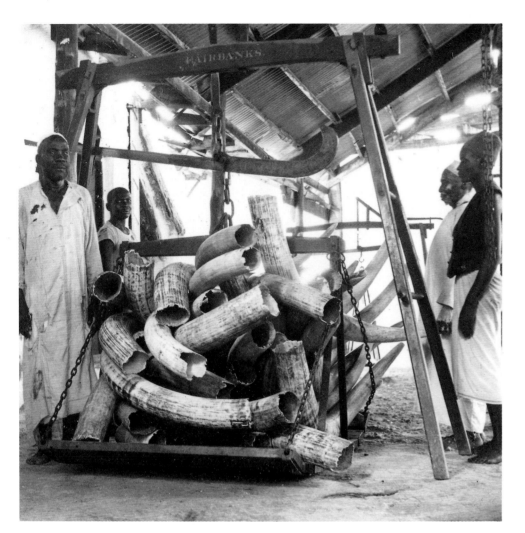

18-8 (LEFT). Tusk-weighing station in Zanzibar, 1910. Scale crossbeam reads "FAIRBANKS," premier American manufacturer of weighing instruments. Ernst D. Moore Collection (321), Archives Center, National Museum of American History, Smithsonian Institution. SI Negative 89-16792.

18-9 (OPPOSITE). Trade catalog photograph. Studio image in the ivory product catalog of Heinrich Adolf Meyer, Hamburg, Germany, c. 1890, juxtaposing one of the firm's record-length tusks with an African laborer, a more accurate depiction than that in Figure 18-19. From Plate 12, Geschäfts-Album, Otto Gerdau Collection (363), Archives Center, National Museum of American History, Smithsonian Institution. SI Negative 89-16406.

Spain, France, and England (Fig. 18-8), with their establishment of permanent political and economic zones of control in Africa during the eighteenth and nineteenth centuries.

Certainly less visible were the actual methods employed to acquire the ivory, the toll in human and animal life being the most insidious aspect of the harvest. Inadvertently, the mystery and risk surrounding ivory's acquisition, including occasional periods of short supply, lent to ivory yet another alluring dimension.

With the more pedestrian non-African ivory commodities even further removed from the material's African roots, the continuity of the ivory trade took on greater public importance, while the association of the elephant with the ivory (and native African peoples with the elephant, Fig. 18-9) in advertising served to validate ivory products that were not simply decorative or religious in nature. The uses of ivory outside Africa ultimately involved a substantial element of contrived exoticism. As Cutler has observed, "No other artistic medium has been appreciated by laymen and women as much for the material of which it is composed as for the messages it carries" (1985:54).

Scientific Ivory

The perception of ivory as a material exclusively in the service of the artist began to broaden in the late Middle Ages with the establishment of scientific disciplines and a realization that the best ivory made an excellent ground for the scribing and dying of lines used in instruments of measurement and navigation. No hardwood, the other standard material for such applications, provided quite the level of sharp contrast and wear resistance to be found in ivory. Whether for the pocket sundials of Nuremberg in the sixteenth century (Gouk 1988), the sectors and sextants of the British Navy in the seventeenth century, the French mathematician's slide rule of the eighteenth century, or the American carpenter's folding rule of the nineteenth century (Stanley 1984), ivory quickly became a material of choice (Fig. 18-10). Both the reading of engraved lines and the dovetailing of working parts were facilitated by the tight but porous structure of ivory, which receives dyes and pigments extremely well. Ivory intended for such uses typically was sun-bleached to retard yellowing and set into wood or metal fittings within the instrument once graduations and numerals had been engraved by hand or by machine.

Like earlier art ivories, precision instruments and hand tools with ivory scales, knobs, or other fixtures continue to be highly prized by European and North American collectors. Like their counterparts in the fine arts, the scientific ivory enthusiasts, whether hobbyists or scholars, have tended to disassociate themselves from Africa and the unsavory elephant

issues while honoring the stark exactitude of ivory in one of its most pragmatic roles.[8]

Ivory to Handle

Another of ivory's legendary attributes is its feel in the human hand. Unlike bone or animal skin, which degrade with constant heavy rubbing, ivory generally retains its overall form and finish even under constant usage.[9] This dual quality of handling endurance and beauty was recognized by the ivory comb makers of ancient Egypt and Phoenicia (Mumcuoglu and Zias 1989), but was fully tapped in the cutlery and hand implement industries of Great Britain in the nineteenth and twentieth centuries.

The ease with which ivory handles fit both metal tooling and the human hand is demonstrated in the host of professions that favored ivory-handled implements: dentistry (Fig. 18-11), surgery, hair cutlery, the culinary arts, and others that also valued ivory's sanitary aspects. At the dressing table, hand-mirror makers incorporated the entire usable width of the largest of elephant tusks (Fig. 18-12), while brush makers used the shell-like sections of tusk around the pulp cavity as a natural concave grip area for men's brushes, allowing the inserted bristles on the opposite side to spread radially. In the salon, ivory handles performed handsomely on British teapots, capitalizing on the material's poor ability to conduct heat.

Ivory import statistics for British knife and table cutlery handles in the late-nineteenth century occasionally exceeded those for all other ivory uses (Kunz 1916:413). Sheffield was home to the world's most prolific knife maker, the C.B. Rodgers Co., Ltd., whose vast basement ivory vault held ranks of tusks sorted by type and grade, together with antler, horn, and bone, and ivory from the narwhal, wart hog, walrus, and hippo (Voyles 1986).

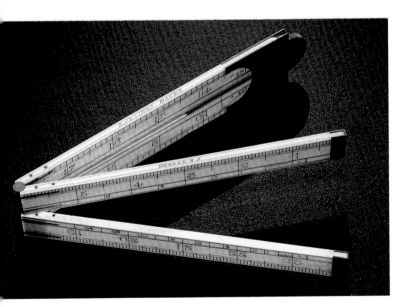

18-10. American folding rule from 19th century (S. Jaggers, Newark, N.J.). Elephant ivory. 61 cm. National Museum of American History, Smithsonian Institution, Cat. 236088.6. Photograph, Eric Long. SI Negative 90-10949.

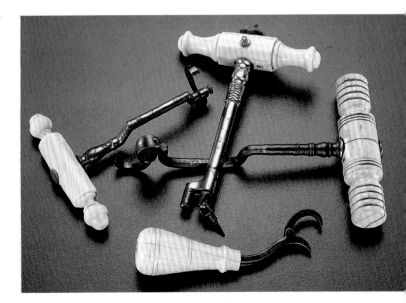

18-11. Dentist's tooth-extraction keys from 18th- and 19th-century Europe. Elephant ivory handles, c. 8 cm. National Museum of American History, Smithsonian Institution. Photograph, Eric Long. SI Negative 90-10948.

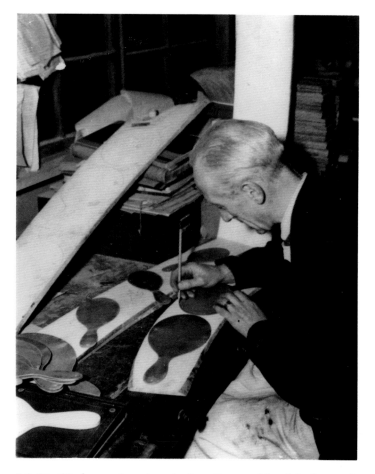

18-12. Worker tracing mirror back outlines on slabs of elephant tusk at Puddlefoot, Bowers and Simonett, London, 1946. Prints and Pictures Dept., Free Library of Philadelphia. SI Negative 90-8337.

Whether pinned to the haft of a jack knife or slipped onto the tang of a delicate grapefruit knife, Rodgers ivory symbolized an era whose most signal material achievements combined machine production with the uses of the most noble materials. If cast iron was the symbolic material of the new industrial age, machined ivory may be regarded as a material of the new democratic order. In its many mass-produced, identical forms, ivory had become available to the masses, not just the anointed few (Plimmer and Plimmer 1951). To the engineer, the elephant was thoroughly abstracted from the ivory, now with a self-sufficient economic life of its own, much like stone or timber (Owen 1856).

The ivory-handled knife has remained one of the most enduring and sought-after applications of ivory outside Africa. Up to the day of the landmark 1989 ban on ivory imports, when all elephant ivory made its historic entry into the world of forbidden raw materials, custom knife makers in the United States and elsewhere were proudly fashioning African elephant ivory into some of the most elegant handle forms seen outside the Baroque and Art Nouveau periods (Burdette 1989; Shackleford 1989).

Musical Ivory

Western musical-instrument crafts have been especially receptive to ivory usage, both as a decorative treatment and as a primary structural element. The production of Scottish bagpipes traditionally has required the use of lathe-turned ivory as pipe connections and finials. Flutes have experienced several material transformations, from wood, silver, and glass to rubber, steel, and ivory. Those few made entirely of ivory have been especially subject to cracking, given their thin walls and the large surface areas exposed to light and moisture (Kühnel 1971).

The stringed instruments, especially the violin and the guitar, have held ivory bridges, posts, frets, picks, bows, and inlay. Within the family of horns, the oliphant or ceremonial tusk trumpet of the ancient Islamic world stands with its traditional African counterparts as one of the most assertive transformations of an entire elephant tusk (ibid.).

It is the piano key, however, that stands as the most visible symbol of ivory's service to musical history and to the production of ivory goods beyond the world of the carvers. Here was a product that permitted ivory to perform several of its most useful roles, as a touchable, resilient, high-contrast material capable of being cut to a thin veneer without loss of structural integrity. "Tickling the ivories" implies more than playing a lively piano tune. Ivory's smooth but slightly tacky texture and rate of moisture absorbency, as well as its whiteness, were important reasons for its early selection as a replacement for the various hardwoods that had been used as keyboard material for clavichords, harpsichords, and early pianos (Sachs 1940:339).

While the keys of pipe organs are still cut from the bones of cows, elephant ivory achieved permanence on piano keyboards from the mid-eighteenth century to the late 1950s. Its slight tackiness and ability to absorb perspiration are well known to concert pianists. But color contrast with the black sharps or raised keys was one of the most important reasons for this choice of materials in a world that knew nothing of plastics. Although tortoise shell, mother-of-pearl, and various colored woods were attempted, the simple blacks and whites of ebony wood and ivory prevailed overwhelmingly. Some seventeenth- and eighteenth-century keyboard instruments reversed the roles, with ivory sharps and ebony naturals, before settling into the familiar pattern of white keys interspersed with raised blacks.

As the instrument grew in dynamic range, keyboards doubled in length, from four octaves (forty-four keys) to the eight-octave standard of today. Corresponding advances in the production and assembly of keys necessarily were matched by heightened interests in the quality and quantity of tusks available, with the less grainy ivory in the tusk's center being preferred. Ivory's mastery of the keyboard in America quietly ended in 1988 with a short resolution passed by the Council of the Piano Technicians Guild opposing "the use of new ivory in the manufacture and restoration of pianos."

A simple geometric form requiring none of the freehand artistry of the ivory carvers, the three-piece ivory piano key became one of the dominant machine products issuing from

18-13. Off-loading tusks at piano key factory, Comstock-Cheney Company, Ivoryton, Conn., 1890. Pratt-Read Corporation Records (320), Archives Center, National Museum of American History, Smithsonian Institution. SI Negative 90-9208.

the ivory factories of Germany, England, and the United States. The Connecticut ivory-working mills that sprang up in the towns of Deep River and Ivoryton began machine-sawing ivory combs in the 1790s, and the ivory heads, tails, and faces of piano keys by the 1850s (Roth 1981:138-41), the telltale seam crossing each key proclaiming the keyboards to be finished with carefully matched elephant ivory.

The collective reliance of such piano makers as Steinway, Chickering, and Sohmer on the piano key factories of the lower Connecticut River Valley vaulted Americans into the first rank of world ivory product producers and consumers by the mid-nineteenth century. Between 1860 and 1958, the Pratt-Read Company and the Comstock-Cheney Company used intricate systems of ivory acquisition, transport, processing, and finishing to keep up with the burgeoning national demand for pianos, the fine wood cabinetry of the piano and the tone of the strings matched by gleaming, beckoning ivory. The communities themselves grew into model forms of the American company town, instilling into generations of ivory workers a special pride in the uniqueness of their products. Today, street names, city park signage, and barber shop conversation keep alive the memory of that special trade for which Ivoryton, Connecticut was established.

For many decades, American buyers employed by Arnold, Cheney, and Co. were permanently stationed in Zanzibar to purchase tusks directly from Arab and African traders for shipment to ivory storerooms in New York, and thence to Connecticut (Fig. 18-13). To the end of the American trade, acquisition remained a passive act, dependent upon the fortunes of independent hunters, local people, or whomever returned from the African interior bearing ivory. No American ivory-working firms appear to have engaged in elephant hunts. The lack of regulation and control over ivory sources is one of the trade's most insidious legacies (Moore 1931).

Once at the factory, the tusks were graded by size (Fig. 18-14) and quality and rough-sawn into sections (Fig. 18-15) from which the keys would be cut, always along the grain. The better keys came from around the axis of the tusk where the grain was tighter and less subject to yellowing. One tusk of good size and with no significant defects could yield as many as fifty-five sets of piano keys, each set containing as many as fifty-two separate keys (Conniff 1987).

The working of the tusk on "junking" and "grailing" machines, the sun-bleaching of the cut keys to a uniform whiteness, and the application of the ivory slips to the sugar

18-14. A festive scene at Pratt, Read & Co. published in *Piano Trade Magazine,* Feb. 1947. Headlined: "Biggest Shipment of African Ivory Since the War!" The caption below reported the weight of this tusk to be 92 lb., 8 oz. (41.6 kg), destined for grand piano keys; the largest tusk in the shipment (not shown) weighed 139 lb. (62.6 kg). Pratt-Read Corporation Records (320), Archives Center, National Museum of American History, Smithsonian Institution. SI Negative 89-1771.

18-15. "Junking" a tusk into blocks for piano key tails on a specialized bandsaw at Pratt, Read & Co., Deep River, Conn., c. 1920. Ernst D. Moore Collection (321), Archives Center, National Museum of American History, Smithsonian Institution. SI Negative 89-20427.

pine keyboards involved some of the most skillful knowledge of materials and precision machine work developed in the nineteenth century. Payroll and other records of Pratt-Read and Comstock-Cheney indicate the highly specialized nature of the work in the ivory-processing shops — some occupations being held by master craftsmen with careers lasting in excess of fifty years.[10]

Ivory keys also appeared as standard equipment on American electrical apparatus of the nineteenth century. Telegraph transmitters (Fig. 18-17) and telephone receivers with ivory pads and buttons made use of ivory's power as an insulator of electrical current.

The remoteness of the telegraph and the piano from the realities of African life and culture is one of the more poignant aspects of ivory's passage into distant lands and hands. Unlike the art ivories of Europe and Asia, and the knife handles of Great Britain, the piano has no obvious claim to indigenous African precedent. The keyboard material was entirely a

18-16. Business decal used by Pratt, Read & Co, Inc., Ivoryton, Conn., 1950s. Width, 6 cm. Author's collection.

18-17. Harmonic Telegraph Transmitter. American, 1874. Elephant ivory keys. Width 47 cm. National Museum of American History, Smithsonian Institution, Cat. 219294. Photograph, Eric Long. SI Negative 90-10941.

function of the machine, the little veneers of ivory skin exquisite expressions of mechanical rationalism.

This total reconfiguration of the African elephant tusk required overt public reminders of the material's authentic origins. This was achieved principally by appropriating the art motif of a bull elephant or his tusks in everything from factory weathervanes and stained glass windows to company logos and stone sculpture on civic buildings (Figs. 18-16, 18-18). As further validation, the engraving of a male African native appears regularly in the classic pose of a black Hercules at ease, supporting an upright tusk (Figs. 18-1, 18-19).

Pratt, Read & Co., the last of the American ivory piano key makers, stopped their ivory cutting in the 1950s, gradually replacing their stockpile of the natural material with molded plastic. Company records indicate this to be a decision related more to costs of key production at a time of falling piano sales, than any enforcement of elephant conservation measures.[11] The black sharps, formerly crafted from another costly

18-18. Relief sculpture ("Foreign Trade"). Carl Schmitz, 1937. Limestone. 3.7 m x 2.2 m. Southwest entrance, Federal Trade Commission Building, Washington, D.C. Photograph, Eric Long, 1990. SI Negative 90-10132/28A.

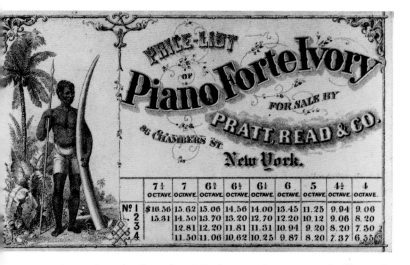

18-19. Price list from the 1860s for piano key ivory, ranked by grade (clear to grainy) and octave (keyboard width). Courtesy of Pratt Read Corp. SI Negative 91-7698.

Zanzibar import — ebony wood — joined the naturals as products of a mushrooming synthetics industry soon to engender its own forms of outrage and debate over the use of materials that were not "the real thing."

Ivory for Sport

The traditional rough treatment administered to some small ivory goods contrasts with the hands-off museum quality of the more widely known ivory carvings and ivory's linkage with Western elite classes. The most vivid illustrations of this are found in the sporting uses made of ivory, chiefly in the nineteenth century. Children's spinning tops, puzzles, and some marbles were often of ivory, vegetable or elephant. For adults, ivory chessmen, backgammon pieces, dominoes, and dice made use of the material's exceptional marking and edge-holding characteristics. But one particular sport gave ivory its most athletic and physically taxing role.

If any finished product may be regarded as an ultimate expression of the material substance from which it derives, the ivory billiard ball is a classic example. All properties for which ivory traditionally has been known — touch, appearance, surface finish, internal stability, density, resistance to wear, elasticity, and privileged social status — come into play. Billiard balls produced an unmistakable ivory "click" on impact with one another, an atmospheric effect that the makers of synthetic billiard balls would find very difficult to imitate.

A variety of multicolored hardwood billiard balls were precursors to the ivory ball (Hendricks 1977:20), precision machinery coupled with a vast body of arcane material science facilitating its ascension (Marchmay 1921), and synthetic materials insuring its passing (Friedel 1983:34-36). Ivory-turning ball lathes in France and England began producing balls early in the nineteenth century. Unlike piano keys, which could emerge at a rate of over 2,000 per tusk, only four or five billiard balls of sufficient size and symmetry could be won from the choicest of tusks (Figs. 18-20, 18-21).

The importance attached to the uniform roll, carom (ricochet), and general liveliness of ivory balls on the billiard table required that the ivory grain run true around the center of the ball, a result achieved by using the tusk's black nerve canal

18-20 (OPPOSITE, TOP). This scene, photographed about the same time as Figure 18-21, shows the other side of the equation: a mountain of raw ivory awaiting export from Zanzibar, surmounted by buyers and laborers. Pratt-Read Corporation Records (320), Archives Center, National Museum of American History, Smithsonian Institution, SI Negative 89-4243.

18-21 (OPPOSITE, BOTTOM). James Burroughes recumbent amidst rough-turned ivory billiard balls netted and warehoused for seasoning. With a yield of 5 balls per tusk, this mountain of 20 thousand balls required a herd of 2,000 elephants. From frontispiece, Billiards Simplified, Burroughes and Watts, London, 1889. Courtesy of Victor Stein. SI Negative 89-15405.

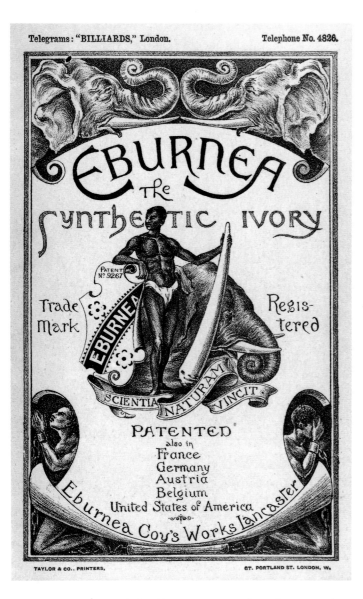

Telegrams: "BILLIARDS," London.   Telephone No. 4826.

EBURNEA
THE
SYNTHETIC IVORY

PATENT Nº 9267

Trade Mark   Registered

EBURNEA

SCIENTIA NATURAM VINCIT

PATENTED
also in
France
Germany
Austria
Belgium
United States of America

Eburnea Coy's Works Lancaster

TAYLOR & CO., PRINTERS.   GT. PORTLAND ST. LONDON, W.

18-22. Cover for trade booklet, George Wright and Co., London, 1890, promoting substitute ivory "eburnea" billiard balls, after the Latin (*ebur*) for ivory. Beleagured elephants and slaves symbolize ivory's negatives, contrasting with freed-African trademark. The Latin banner reads: "Science Conquers Nature." Warshaw Collection of Business Americana (60), "Ivory" box, Archives Center, National Museum of American History, Smithsonian Institution. SI Negative 90-2.

as the centerline. The two black pinholes that remained on opposite sides of the ball were evidence of the ball's internal balance. Many months of seasoning were required after the balls had been rough-turned (Fig. 18-20) and before they were finished to final diameters, a period during which the balls would shrink while drying (Kunz 1916:241-49). The immaculate finishes, close tolerances, and care demanded of ivory balls in the rulebooks of billiards regulating authorities reduced the elephant to a silent collaborator in an activity that certainly could not otherwise have attained such levels of performance in the pre-synthetics age.

A few blocks of shops in lower Manhattan, a small section of London, and neighborhoods in Antwerp, Belgium, and Hamburg, Germany, emerged as the centers of the billiard ball trade, turning out sets of dyed and etched balls for pocket

billiards, snooker, and specialty billiard sports requiring varying diameters and numbers of balls.

Billiard parlors and pool halls worldwide depend today on composite balls introduced late in the last century. Built up from a series of natural and synthetic materials, none of them ivory, the balls initially were products of a perceived ivory shortage in the 1860s. Manufacturers had called upon inventors and chemists to create a new material equally responsive on the billiard table, but perhaps not as difficult to work or maintain as ivory (Friedel 1983:29-34). Nevertheless, the sport of "artistic billiards," pursued mainly in continental Europe, has retained a solid preference for ivory balls, the trick shots, jumps, reverse spins, and other gymnastics requiring the responses that only ivory seemingly is capable of executing.[12]

In supporting roles are the ivory rings, washers, and inlay that have been integral parts of cue sticks in the billiard sports. These too have been functional as well as decorative elements, adding critical amounts of weight, sweat-absorbing grip area, and impact resistance to an article of sports equipment that has achieved an extremely high standard of artistic and technical mastery.

IVORY'S REPLACEMENTS: SUBSTITUTION BY IMITATION

The ivory fear of the 1980s, based on reports of the alarming reductions in African elephant populations, was not without precedent. Ivory scares also occurred in the 1860s and 1890s in the United States, based upon low elephant counts (along the African coastlines, before the interior had been effectively penetrated). That news had an instrumental effect in establishing an American (and later European) plastics industry. Billiard ball makers and other ivory-using industries warned that supplies of ivory were running low and sending costs ever higher at a time of mushrooming consumer demand. The alarms they sounded launched a quest for a "new" ivory.

The period from the 1860s well into the twentieth century was marked by a search for natural and synthetic ivory replacements (Fig. 18-22), the latter inspiring an uninhibited experimentation with chemical and physical formulae, as shown in the United States patents issued for "ivory-like substances." But none could fully replicate ivory's special attributes. Although the patents received for ivory-like compounds initially were spurred by the perceived billiard ball shortage, other uses quickly materialized. The critical point at which ivory substitutes graduated from pretender and hopeful imitation to unabashed replacement occupies a vast gray area in the culture of materials science.

Celluloid, produced beginning in the 1860s, began as an ivory look-alike, but its tendency to explode on impact when molded into billiard balls, given the nature of its chief ingredient (nitrocellulose), encouraged its developers to seek other markets. While celluloid did supplant ivory as a new and therefore desirable material for cosmetic boxes, combs, and knife handles (grained initially with ivory-like figuring), celluloid's greatest successes occurred in the shirt-collar and motion-picture industries.[13] Later developments (Bakelite, polycarbons, phenolic resins) proved more successful in displacing ivory from the billiard table and concert hall. Here again, as in most cases, the costs associated with acquiring tusks and managing their special production requirements appear to have been the primary incentives, rather than a direct awareness of the elephant's plight.

Ivory's departure from the functional worlds of instrumentation, musicology, and athletic sports returned it to the realm of the fine arts, where it now came under the knowledgeable eye of the highly mechanized business community. As ivory retreated into the aesthetic traditions from which it had emerged, it fell into the hands of industrialized carvers, producing one of the ivory trade's final ironies: the very forms of ivory artwork that once had celebrated the elephant's prowess now were in danger of bringing about the animal's doom.

The broad compass of ivory's historic roles suggests how blurred the distinctions can become between art, industry, and depravity. The incremental upset of native African views of the elephant as an embodiment of supreme strength and authority, as ivory markets grew in depth and breadth overseas, is not easily disentangled from the colonial mercantilism that has redirected so much of African life. And yet, as a material of vital interest to both worlds, ivory's transition from hand-crafted arts to factory-made machine product describes an important and revealing continuum of common usage.

Many of ivory's functions outside Africa mirrored its traditional uses within Africa as body ornamentation and a mark of authority. Other uses have tapped ivory's undeniable physical endowments in a host of precision machine products for which no equivalent alternative material existed. In all cultures, the fidelity of ivory workers to their material, regardless of who receives the work, has been the most salient theme.

How different the outcome might have been if the patience, intelligence, and high skills required to work ivory into its countless forms could have extended to the other end of the trade! By waiting and collecting tusks only from elephants that had died of old age, the ivory would have been allowed to grow to its most luxurious extent, and, like mammoth tusks today, remain unsullied by associations with the extinction of an animal species.

NOTES

The author wishes to acknowledge the invaluable assistance of Craig Orr, Edith DeForest, and John Fleckner.

1. Ivory's special appearance and workability have attracted many centuries of the world's finest artists, and in their wake a community of art historians who have established a substantial body of scholarship — sifting, debating, and consecrating many schools and eras of ivory art (see bibliography in St. Clair and McLachlan 1989:123-32).

2. Early works include Holtzapffel (1846), Maskell (1905), Kunz (1916), and Williamson (1938), whose visual richness and depth of research continue to make them important fine art resources. More recently, the dense works of Philippovich (1982), Randall (1985), and Vickers et al. (1987) have updated our visual appreciation of ivory's artistic legacy, principally in Europe. Some of the world's most noteworthy collections of ivory art are housed at the Metropolitan Museum of Art in New York City, the Walters Art Gallery in Baltimore, the Victoria and Albert Museum in London, the Royal Museum of Art and History in Brussels, the National Archaeological Museum in Madrid, the Louvre in Paris, and the Bavarian National Museum in Munich. Additional repositories are listed in Vickers et al. (1987:346).

3. The National Museum of American History at the Smithsonian Institution holds a diverse quantity of industrial ivory and an important body of archival and photographic materials relating to the American acquisition of tusks and the production of ivory piano keys (Archives Center Collections 320, 321, 363, 457). Selections from these collections have appeared in the museum's exhibit: "Elephant Ivory: The Tarnished Treasure" (August 1992-January 1993).

4. That this enigmatic material loved by artists and industry has also been an agent of sweeping change for an animal species and indigenous peoples is a conundrum beyond the scope of this paper. Moore (1931), Alpers (1975), and Sheriff (1987) address issues pertaining to the latter.

5. This association of ivory with skin tone is mentioned in the Old Testament's *Song of Solomon* (5:14): "...his belly is as bright as ivory...." Soap, shampoo, toothpaste, and other modern personal-care products continue to employ the metaphor of "ivory" as an ultimate standard of cleanliness and brightness.

6. See "The Look of Ivory Without the Guilt" in *Newsweek* magazine, 9 October, 1989, p. 83 (no author cited).

7. The latter-day ivory industries of the Far East have not yet shared in the degree of scholarly attention given to the earlier work of Europe. Yet similar craft traditions are visible, as well as a broad evolution of ivory-cutting technologies.

8. Recent auction sales records indicate that ivory-finished instruments and hand tools continue to be blue-chip collectibles within such groups as the Early American Industries Association (U.S.A.) and the Tools and Trades History Society (U.K.).

9. Some detailing on carved Christian images has been known to disappear beneath sufficient devotional touching and kissing.

10. One of the most thorough, illustrated accounts of ivory piano key manufacture appears in three consecutive issues of *Piano Trade Magazine*: February, March, and April of 1925 (no author cited).

11. Pratt-Read launched its conversion to plastic keys with considerable fanfare, citing greater production economies and improved product maintenance, among other reasons.

12. The continued reliance on ivory balls by artistic billiardists was described to the author by Michael Shamos, chief archivist of the Billiard Archive, Pittsburgh (Bryne 1988), stating that in 1991 the Conservatoire Internationale de Billard Artistique (CIBA) ceased requiring the use of ivory balls.

13. Patent and production records of the pioneering celluloid-based billiard ball factory in the United States reside in the Albany Billiard Ball Company Records (11), Archives Center, National Museum of American History, Smithsonian Institution.

A.

A. Caddy suite, made by Edward Cornock, London, 1730. Scene depicts the great country house, Stowe, seat of the Dukes of Buckingham and Chandos. Ivory, metal, wood, pigment. Width 28.7 cm. FMCH x87.1018. Gift of the Francis E. Fowler, Jr. Foundation.

B. Billiard ball. Ivory. Diameter 6 cm. Collection of Ernie Wolfe III.

C. Glove stretcher. Ivory. Length 22 cm. Bowers Museum of Cultural Art.

Letter opener advertising the Pontiac Buggy Co., Western Amesbury Line, Pontiac, Michigan. Ivory, pigment. Length 15 cm. Bowers Museum of Cultural Art.

Fan. Ivory, cloth, metal? Length 21 cm. Bowers Museum of Cultural Art.

Memo book. Ivory, metal. Length 7 cm. Bowers Museum of Cultural Art.

Mahjong tiles. Ivory, pigment. Length 3 cm. Collection of Mr. and Mrs. Gilbert Rice.

Razor. Ivory. Metal. Length 14 cm. Bowers Museum of Cultural Art.

Shoe horn. Ivory. Length 21.5 cm. Bowers Museum of Cultural Art.

ARTISTS AND INDUSTRIES in Europe and the United States have fashioned ivory into a dazzling array of object types ranging from profound religious sculpture and other fine arts to forms as mundane as buttons and shoe horns. Ivory was frequently the material of choice for playing pieces used in games such as chess, dominoes, mahsjong, billiards, and dice. Among more eccentric items are glove stretchers and jagging wheels for crimping pies. Some Western machine-made ivory products were used by Africans as models for hand-crafted tourist souvenirs such as letter openers and napkin rings.

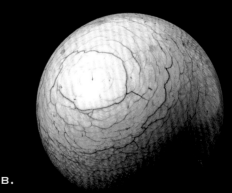

B.

BUILDERS OF **BEST**
39273
MEDIUM GRADE VEHICLES ON EARTH

C.

EPILOGUE

THE FUTURE OF ELEPHANTS, REAL AND IMAGINED

DORAN H. ROSS

The elephant *is* an endangered species. Between 1979 and 1989, the African elephant population dropped from 1.3 million to about 600,000. *In other words, there were less than half as many elephants after a period of only ten years.* In Kenya alone, the numbers dropped from 130,000 in 1973 to an estimated 16,000 by 1989 (Poole 1992:29). Illegal poaching and an illegal international trade in ivory were clearly the root causes for this population crash.[1]

The fact that we have reproduced so many beautiful ivory carvings in this volume may seem to be at odds with our expressed concerns over the current endangered status of the elephant. But the contradiction is more apparent than real. The decimation of elephant populations that has occurred since the second half of the nineteenth century is not the result of indigenous ("traditional") ivory use in Africa. To put this in perspective, it is important to recognize three broad categories of ivory use: *(1) ivory worked by Africans for their own use; (2) ivory worked by Africans for export; (3) raw ivory exported for foreign arts and industries.*

Although there is as yet no way to measure it,[2] indigenous ivory use never threatened the African elephant as a species. After ancient Egyptian times, ivory had a higher value outside the African continent than inside, as Edward Alpers points out in Chapter 17. Within most African societies, there were inherent limitations on supply and demand: it was generally reserved for the elite; it was used for a relatively limited number of object types; and it was hand-crafted, not mass-produced. In addition, its durability lessened the need for frequent replacement and encouraged its value as an heirloom. Thus elephant populations were never compromised by indigenous consumption of ivory. By contrast, ivory for export – both carved and raw – has posed a serious threat to the elephant species.

Ivories Worked by Africans for Export

In this volume, African-made ivories for export have deliberately been slighted, since in subject and function these objects reflect the tastes of their foreign consumers more than those of their producers. Although consideration of such ivories has been confined to the Afro-Portuguese ivories (Interleaf XIII) of the fifteenth and sixteenth centuries, and the Loango ivories (Interleaf VII) of the nineteenth century, it should be noted that tourist ivories from the twentieth century are considerably more numerous than either of the aforementioned. As many parts of Africa opened up for tourism, the demand for souvenirs provided a new market for Africa artists. While brass castings and woodcarvings were popular, works in ivory had a special attraction. Tourists tended to view ivory as a unique and especially "authentic" part of Africa (since it was an actual

19-1 (OPPOSITE). "Painting of a Greedy Man" by Romanus Nkwonta a.k.a. Cas Creation, 1991, Onitsha, Nigeria. The message here translates as: *All the riches of this world can never satisfy.* The hunter has killed a bush cow, an antelope, a warthog, and of course an elephant. Still this is not enough for him, so he bends down to capture the cricket. 28 x 33 cm. Private collection.

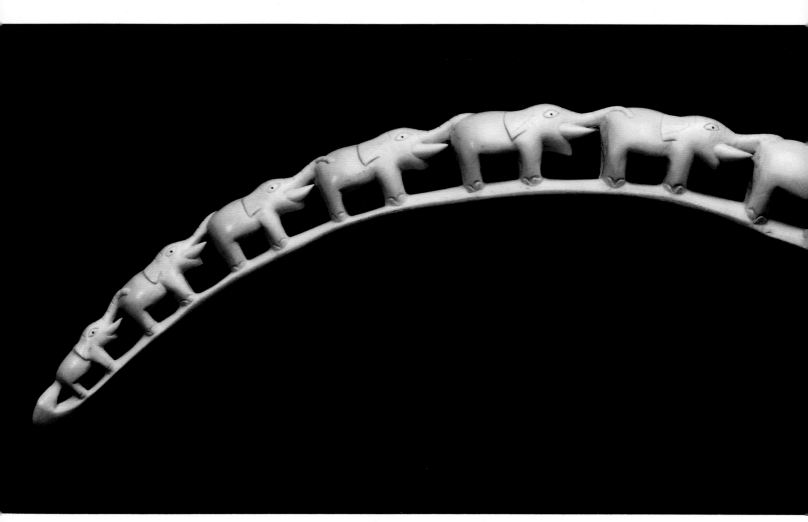

19-2 (ABOVE). "Elephant Bridge" featuring a procession of pachyderms from Zaire (Nandi peoples). Length 98 cm. FMCH X392.5. Museum purchase.

19-3. A display of ivory souvenirs — bracelets, figures, carved tusks, and knick-knacks from a tourist art market in Dakar, Senegal. Photograph, Raymond A. Silverman, 1982.

part of the elephant), with the added allure of luxury. For the same reason, they also acquired elephant-foot umbrella stands and stools (Fig. 19-5). Small ivory carvings had even greater appeal since they were easily portable and generally affordable. Ivory rings, bracelets, and necklaces were widely available in most major cities until recently.

While the form and style of ivory jewelry often echoed traditional African practices, the profusion of ivory knick-knacks created for the tourist market was entirely alien to African sensibilities (Fig. 19-3). Bare-breasted African "princesses" and "madonnas" became exceedingly popular genres. As if to emphasize that the material was elephant ivory, the figure was often relegated to the bottom of the tusk, with the tip left unworked. Antelopes, crocodiles, and of course elephants carved in ivory also attracted a broad spectrum of buyers. Especially popular were "Elephant bridges" featuring a carved procession of pachyderms, trunk to tail, that span a whole tusk (Fig. 19-2). More functional, but perhaps equally superfluous, were ivory bookends, letter openers, and napkin rings.

Curbing the Export of Raw Ivory

The amount of ivory carved for tourist consumption is still insignificant, however, when compared to the amount of ivory exported in raw form. To cite a single example, Zimbabwe prior to the trade embargoes had one of the largest ivory-carving industries in Africa and worked approximately fifteen metric tons in 1983 (Martin 1991:26). This compares with 475

19-4. African ivory burn. Nairobi, Kenya. Photograph, Peter Beard, Visions, 1992.

metric tons of raw ivory imported into Japan, mostly for local consumption, the same year (Milliken 1985:15). Other statistics could be cited, all showing that considerably more ivory was worked and consumed by Asian, European, and American industries and markets than by African ones. The external demand for raw ivory, though greatly diminished, is still a threat to the African elephant.

To control what was largely an illegal trade based on poaching, a number of consuming nations unilaterally passed laws such as the United States' African Elephant Conservation Act of 1988 (Fig. 19-7). The listing (effective January 18, 1990) of the African elephant as an "endangered species" in the Convention on International Trade in Endangered Species (CITES) further strengthened international efforts. In addition to legislative action, a strong media campaign (Fig. 19-6) has made the wearing or using of ivory and other products — elephant skin for cowboy boots, for example — unfashionable if not outright offensive.

The Kenyan government set fire to twelve tons of ivory on July 18, 1989, and again in early 1992 (Figs. 19-4, 19-15). That act of burning has become a widely publicized symbolic icon for international efforts to destroy the market in ivory. According to Richard Leakey (1991:22), Director, Kenya Wildlife Service:

We could hardly say to people in affluent countries, "Don't buy ivory," while we were still selling ivory.

19-5. Stool made from African elephant foot. Height 40 cm. Private collection.

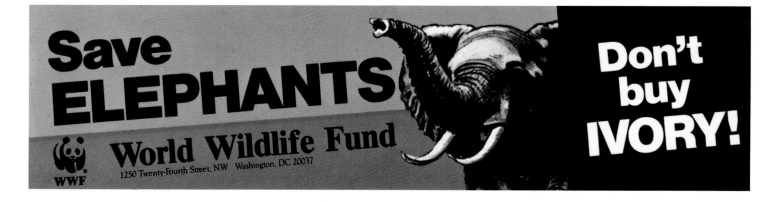

19-6. Bumper sticker distributed by the World Wildlife Fund.

19-7. *A Primer to Endangered Species Law*, compiled by Kim Saito and published by the Smithsonian Institution, Office of the Registrar, 1992 (Washington, D.C.). The text of the African Elephant Conservation Act, as summarized in the *Primer*, appears on the opposite page.

We felt such a double standard would be inappropriate. So we burned our ivory, and the world noticed. A few months later the CITES ban on the ivory trade was passed.

The message was not only *No!* to the ivory trade, but also *No!* to the consumption of ivory in any context.

Although the various national and international prohibitions on the ivory trade have been in place for only about four years (as of October, 1992), it is clear that they are having a profound effect on protecting the elephant. The ivory workshops of India, China, and Japan have reduced production to a trickle (Perlez 1990; Vigne 1991). Likewise, the tourist ivory industries of Zimbabwe and other African countries have been virtually shut down (Martin 1991). The price of ivory has fallen dramatically because the demand is at record lows. The effects are also seen in the wildlife parks of Kenya and Tanzania, where evidence of poaching has nearly disappeared (Leakey 1991:20). Although there are scattered exceptions, the ivory trade bans are clearly working.

Trophy-taking as a Symbol

Ivory taken as a trophy of the hunt is worth considering because of its symbolic importance, even though it accounts for a very small share of ivory taken from Africa and does not fall into the three categories listed earlier.[3] Today the words "sport," "game," and "trophy" seem dramatically inappropriate in describing the killing of elephants. Yet during the first half of this century, such notables as the Prince of Wales, Teddy Roosevelt, Winston Churchill, and Ernest Hemingway went on East African safaris for "sport." The newspapers and their readers followed the exploits of these hunters with admiration. Their "trophies" included stuffed wall-mounted heads of big-tuskers, large ivory tusks mounted vertically to frame doorways, elephant foot umbrella stands and stools and photographs of themselves with their prizes (Fig. 19-9).

These personal trophies had institutional counterparts in stuffed specimens of complete elephants, such as the "family" of animals clustered at the American Museum of Natural History, New York City, or the monumental bull in the rotunda of the National Museum of Natural History, Washington D.C. (Fig. 19-10). These museum specimens are not only trophies,

THE AFRICAN ELEPHANT CONSERVATION ACT

Agency: U.S. Fish and Wildlife Service of the Department of the Interior

Permit applications and inquiries: U.S. Fish and Wildlife Service, Office of Management Authority, 4401 N. Fairfax Drive, Room 432, Arlington, Virginia 22203, 703-358-2104

In an effort to assist in the conservation and protection of the African elephant populations, the United States passed the African Elephant Conservation Act in 1988. This Act works in conjunction with the CITES Ivory Control System to protect the African elephant and eliminate any trade in illegal ivory. Currently the African elephant is listed in Appendix I of CITES and as such any import or export of African elephants, including their products (ivory, skins, etc.) for commercial purposes is prohibited. Any import or export for other than commercial purposes must be accompanied by valid CITES documents.

PROHIBITIONS

The African Elephant Conservation Act specifically forbids:

Import of raw African elephant ivory from any country other than an ivory producing country (any African country within which is located any part of the range of a population of African elephants);

All exports from the U.S. of *raw ivory* from African elephants;

Import of raw or worked ivory from African elephants that was exported from an ivory producing country in violation of that country's laws or of the CITES Ivory Control System;

Import of worked ivory from any country unless that country has certified that such ivory was derived from legal sources;

Import of raw or worked ivory from a country for which a moratorium is in effect. The Secretary of the Interior makes a determination, according to criteria set out in the Act, whether an ivory importing country meets certain standards.

EXEMPTIONS

Most non-commercial ivory imports are prohibited. Any allowed import or export of African elephants, including their parts must be accompanied by CITES documents.

Antique articles may be imported under a CITES Pre-Convention Certificate issued by the exporting country. The Pre-Convention Certificate must contain the following information:

(a) specimen acquired on or before February 4, 1977;
(b) bona fide antique
(c) proof that the article is not less than 100 years old on the date of export
(d) composed in whole or in part of African elephant ivory; and
(e) has not been repaired or modified with any ivory on or after February 4, 1977.

Sport-Hunted Trophies — Allows import of a sport-hunted trophy legally hunted in certain African countries by the individual who actually took the trophy.

Reprinted from "A Primer to Endangered Species Law," pages 25 and 26, compiled by Kim Saito and published by the Smithsonian Institution, Office of the Registrar, 1992 (Washington, D.C.).

19-8. "The 'Ma Robert' and Elephant in Shallows, Shire River, Lower Zambesi." Thomas Baines.
65 x 44 cm. Dated April 6, 1859. Royal Geographic Society, London.

19-9. "The governor's game-bag: Sir Hesketh Bell poses with his trophies in Uganda, 1908." Y3011D.
Hesketh Bell Collection, Plate 26. Royal Commonwealth Society.

19-10. Fénykövi elephant in the rotunda of the National Museum of Natural History. Shot near the Cuito River in Angola on November 13, 1955, the two-ton skin, 1800-pound skull, 192-pound tusks (96 each), and leg bones were given to the museum by J.J. Fénykövi and installed in 1959. Smithsonian Institution.

but also serve important didactic functions within the educational programs of their respective institutions.

The concept of the trophy, while not entirely absent from some African cultures, is alien to most Africans. Perez Olindo, former Director of Wildlife and Parks in Kenya, eloquently states his position on trophy hunting (1991:63-64):

> … the developed world taught Africans how to become efficient killers, using modern weapons. They taught Africans to kill wild animals for pleasure or, as it is called, sport. Africans have learned to kill and take away only trophies, leaving the rest to the animal's biomass to go to waste. This kind of behavior is not typically African. Most older Africans would be horrified by it.

Ironically, sport-hunting of elephants is still legally allowed with expensive licenses in several African countries even after implementation of the various international bans or restrictions of the ivory trade. Sport-hunted trophies are also exempted under the U.S. African Elephant Conservation Act of 1988 and can legally be imported into the United States by the individual who actually killed the animal.

Wildlife Preserves

Hunters and poachers are not the only threat to the future of the African elephant. Loss of habitat due to agricultural expansion, increased urbanization, and desertification all seriously jeopardize elephant populations. Their confinement to game reserves and national parks is a strategy designed in theory to protect the herds and the ecology that sustains them. Ironically, however, it can have the opposite result. Within the reserve, the herds tend to multiply too fast; in their restricted search for food they destroy their own habitat, finally facing famine. Nevertheless, such parks are essential to the management of elephant populations.

Wildlife parks are also necessary to the promotion of tourism. Growing numbers of tourists on photographic safaris travel to east and southern Africa specifically for the wildlife. Tourism has become the number one industry of several countries and elephants are a major part of the attraction (Fig. 19-11). According to Leakey (1991:20):

> Kenya … depends heavily upon its number one industry, tourism. Wildlife — centered on the elephant — is the foundation of our tourist industry. Some months before I was appointed I likened the slaughter of elephants to

19-11. Photographic safari, Amboseli Game Reserve, Kenya. Photograph, Don McClelland, January, 1987.

an act of deliberate economic sabotage. I queried in the press whether we would tolerate saboteurs who burned down our coffee plantations and tea estates in the way that we apparently tolerate those who were destroying our elephants.

To be fair, this is not necessarily an opinion held by everyone. David Western, in a well-reasoned assessment of the CITES trade ban acknowledged (1992:22-23):

In a survey of Taita district adjacent to Tsavo National Park in Kenya, John Waithaka found that 90 percent of all Kenyan farmers see elephants as nothing but three-ton bulldozers ploughing up their crops and crushing people. They want them all removed.

Western goes on to emphasize that any elephant management equation must include the needs of the people who live with and near the animals.

Impact of CITES on the Image of the Elephant

So where does all this leave the elephant as a cultural entity in African society? Since the focus of this volume is on the elephant and its ivory in African culture, we have to raise the question of the impact of the CITES ban on indigenous patterns of use and representation.

The trade ban has had a negligible effect on the African use of ivory as adornment, since this was already in severe decline. European style jewelry in gold, silver, glass, and plastic has largely supplanted ivory in much of Africa. The story is a bit different, however, for ivory objects that are more fully integrated in the ritual and ceremonial life of Africa. Ivory is still an integral part of the expressive culture of Africa. Ivory trumpets

are widely employed in royal courts (Fig. 19-12), and other forms persist as well. Although many are heirloom pieces, there is still some demand for the creation of new regalia from ivory. Procedures for supplying ivory for indigenous use have not been developed in most countries. Nevertheless, there is little question that ivory can be a sustainable resource, as long as it is taken from elephants that died of natural causes (Pilgram and Western 1984). The real problem will be that of controlling the trade, if trade is allowed at all.

It is tempting to draw a parallel between the elephant as an endangered species and the cultural traditions using the elephant for inspiration, which are often seen as endangered. But the parallel is false. Although the elephant may be endangered, the art it inspires is very much alive. It is true that certain modes of using and representing the elephant no longer exist; however, new forms of expression employing the elephant regularly evolve out of the human imagination. New contexts extend the limits of the "traditional." Masquerades once played in a village context may nowadays appear in annual "cultural festivals" presented at regional venues. The children's *Dodo* masquerades of the Mossi peoples of Ouagadougou, Burkina Faso, for example, once constituted a Moslem Ramadan entertainment featuring bovine masks. Now they have evolved into staged competitions held in the city auditorium featuring groups wearing a wide array of animal masks, including elephants (Fig. 19-13a,b) made from materials scrounged from a variety of sources (Hinckley 1986:74).

The image of the elephant is alive and well in the expressive cultures of Africa, even though the same cannot necessarily be said of the elephant itself. Yet its image in art does not require

19-12 (ABOVE). Unidentified southern Ghanaian chief with entourage, including trumpeter. Photograph, Willis Bell, c. 1970.

19-13A,B (BELOW). Baby elephant costume from the children's *Dodo* masquerade, Ouagadougou, Burkina Faso. Photograph, Priscilla Baird Hinckley, 1983.

19-14. Three children in elephant masks at the 1992 ivory burn. Nairobi, Kenya. Photograph, Peter Beard, Visions, 1992.

19-15 (OPPOSITE). Nairobi, Kenya, 1992. Photograph, Peter Beard, Visions.

the living, breathing elephant, any more than unicorn stories require an actual unicorn. The elephant has long been part of the mythology of Africa and that mythology will undoubtedly perpetuate the existence of the animal in the minds and arts of Africans.

Still, the image of the elephant may be affected by the endangered status of the actual creature. Increasingly, the media blitz portrays the pachyderm as a fragile victim; perhaps its symbolic role in African culture will change accordingly.

The grade school skit that accompanied the 1992 ivory burn in Kenya featured cloth masks (Fig. 19-14) that represented the elephant as both vulnerable and lovable — traits more in keeping with Western images such as Dumbo and Babar than with that of a three-ton bulldozer. We cannot predict the future, but most evidence suggests that the intelligence and imagination of the human species will encourage both the elephant and its image to evolve further. At least one hopes that is the case.

Notes

1. For detailed discussions of the ivory poaching problem and of the CITES ban on the ivory trade please see various articles published during the past ten years in *Pachyderm*, *Swara*, and *Wildlife Conservation,* and *Elephant*, the Publication of the Elephant Interest Group.
2. In contrast, there are statistics available for quantifying the amount of ivory consumed abroad.
3. An exception would be some of the massive late-19th century ivory hunts of southern Africa, in which the amount of ivory left after trophy-taking was so great that it got shipped to the coast for export.

THE GREAT "KILIMNJARO TUSKS," THE LARGEST PAIR OF ELEPHANT'S TEETH
OF WHICH THERE IS ANY AUTHENTIC RECORD, AS THEY STOOD OUTSIDE THE
CARVED TEAKWOOD DOORWAY OF THE AUTHOR'S HOUSE IN ZANZIBAR.

As captioned in *Ivory: Scourge of Africa* by E.D. Moore, 1931.

REFERENCES CITED

Abbott, W.R.

1892 "Ethnological Collections in the U.S. National Museum from Kilima-Njaro, East Africa." In *Report of the U.S. National Museum, Smithsonian Institution*, 381-428. Washington, D.C.

Abimbola, Wande

1976 *Ifa: An Exposition of Ifa Literary Corpus*. Ibadan: Oxford University Press.

1977 *Ifa Divination*. New York: Nok.

Abiodun, R.A.

1975 "Ifa Art Objects: An Interpretation Based on Oral Tradition." In *Yoruba Oral Tradition*, ed. Wande Abimbola, 421-69. Ile-Ife: University of Ife.

1983 "Identity and the Artistic Process in the Yoruba Aesthetic Concept of Iwa." *Journal of Cultures and Ideas* 1 (1):13-30.

1989 "The Kingdom of Owo." In *Yoruba: Nine Centuries of African Art and Thought*, ed. H.J. Drewal, J. Pemberton III, and R.A. Abiodun. New York: Center for African Art.

Abiodun, R.A., H.J. Drewal, and J. Pemberton III

1991 *Yoruba Art and Aesthetics*. Zürich: Rietberg Museum.

Abir, Mordechai

1970 "Southern Ethiopia." In *Pre-Colonial African Trade*, ed. Richard Gray and David Birmingham. London: Oxford University Press.

Abraham, R.C.

1958 *Dictionary of Modern Yoruba*. London: University of London Press.

1962 *Dictionary of the Hausa Language*. London: Hodder and Stoughton.

Adams, Marie Jeanne

1963 "The Distribution and Significance of Composite Animal-Headed Masks." M.A. thesis, Columbia University.

Adams, Robert McCormick

1989 "Smithsonian Horizons." *Smithsonian* 19 (12):14.

Adamson, Joy

1967 *The Peoples of Kenya*. New York: Harcourt, Brace, and World.

Adepegba, C.

1986 "Animals in the Art of Ife." *African Notes* 10 (1):50-58.

Afigbo, A.E.

1981 *Ropes of Sand: Studies in Igbo History and Culture*. Ibadan: University Press.

Akpata, A.

1937 "Benin: Notes on Altars and Bronze Heads." *Ethnologia Cranmorensis* 1:5-10.

Allen, James de Vere

1976 "The *Siwas* of Pate and Lamu: Two Antique Side-blown Horns from the Swahili Coast." *Art and Archaeology Research Papers* 9:38-47.

Alpers, Edward A.

1969 "Trade, State and Society Among the Yao in the Nineteenth Century." *Journal of African History* 10 (3):405-20.

1974 "The Nineteenth Century: Prelude to Colonialism." In *Zamani*, ed. B.A. Ogot. Nairobi: East African Publishing House.

1975 *Ivory and Slaves in East Central Africa*. Berkeley: University of California Press.

Altvölker Süd-Äthiopiens

1959 Vol. 1. Stuttgart: Kohlhammer.

Amin, Mohamed et al.

1987 *The Last of the Maasai*. London: Bodley Head.

Andah, B.W., and J. Anquanda

1988 "The Guinean Belt: The Peoples Between Mount Cameroon and the Ivory Coast." In *General History of Africa*, Vol. 3, ed. M. Elfasi. Berkeley: University of Calfornia Press.

Anderson, Martha G., and Christine Mullen Kreamer

1989 *Wild Spirits, Strong Medicine: African Art and the Wilderness*. New York: The Center for African Art.

Anderson, R.G.

1911 "Some Tribal Customs in Their Relation to Medicine and Morals of the Nyam-Nyam and Gour People Inhabiting the Eastern Bahr-El-Ghazal." In *Fourth Report of Wellcome Tropical Research Laboratories*, vol. B, 239-77. London: Bailliere, Tindall & Cox.

Andersson, C.J.

1861 *The Okovango River: A Narrative of Travel, Exploration, and Adventure*. New York: Harper & Brothers.

Andrews, Peter

1988 "Hominoidea." In *Encyclopedia of Human Evolution and Prehistory*, ed. Ian Tattersall, Eric Delson, and John A. Van Couvering, 248-55. New York: Garland Press.

Anfray, F.

1981 "The Civilization of Aksum from the First to the Seventh Century." In *General History of Africa*, Vol. 2, ed. G. Mokhtar. Berkeley: University of California Press.

Aniakor, Chike

1978 "The Igbo Ijele Mask." *African Arts* 11 (4):42-47,95.

Anonymous

1980 "Has the Elephant a Place in Modern Africa?" *African Wildlife* 34 (4): 23-25.

1989 "Carrying the Torch for Elephants." *Los Angeles Times* (July 19).

Arbelbide, Cyprien

1974 *Les Baoules d'après leurs dictons et proverbes*. Poitiers: CEDA.

Ardener, Edwin

1956 "Coastal Bantu of the Cameroons." In *Ethnographic Survey of Africa, Western Africa, Part II*, ed. Daryll Forde. London: International African Institute.

1959 "Bakweri Elephant Dance." *Nigeria* 60:30-38.

Areje, Raphael

1985 *Yoruba Proverbs*. Ibadan: Daystar Press.

Arnold, Bernd

1980 *Kamerun: Die höfische Kunst des Graslandes*. Die Schatzkammer 33. Dresden: Prisma-Verlag.

A self-contained Curriculum Resource Unit for K-12, entitled *Elephant: The Animal and Its Ivory in African Culture* (Quick, et al. 1992), was developed by the education department of the Fowler Museum of Cultural History, in conjunction with the Museum's exhibition. This teaching resource is available from the Museum for $20.00.

Arnoldi, Mary Jo

1983   "Puppet Theatre in the Segu Region in Mali." Ph.D. diss., Indiana University.

1986   "Puppet Theatre: Form and Ideology in Bamana Performances." *Empirical Study of the Arts* 4 (2):131-50.

1988a   "Performance, Style and the Assertion of Identity in Malian Puppet Drama." *Journal of Folklore Research* 25 (1-2):87-100.

1988b   "Playing the Puppets: Innovation and Rivalry in Bamana Youth Theatre in Mali." *TDR, The Drama Review* 32 (2):65-82.

1989   "Puppet Masquerade and the Construction of Identity in Youth Drama in Mali." In *Proceedings of the May 1988 Conference and Workshop on African Material Culture*, ed. Mary Jo Arnoldi et al. New York: The Joint Committee on African Studies - ACLS/SSRC.

Ms.   "Power and Play in Mande Theatre."

Augé, Marc et al.

1989   *Corps sculptés, corps parés, corps masqués: Chefs d'oeuvre de la Côte d'Ivoire.* Paris: L'Association Française de l'Action Artistique.

Austen, Ralph A.

1974   "Dutch Trading Voyages to Cameroon, 1721-1759." *Annales de la Faculté des Lettres et Sciences Humaines* 6:5-27.

1977   "Duala vs. Germans in Cameroon: Economic Dimensions of Political Conflict." *Revue Française d'histoire d'Outre-mer* 64 (237):477-88.

1983   "The Metamorphoses of Middlemen: The Duala, Europeans, and the Cameroon Hinterland, ca. 1800 - ca. 1960." *International Journal of African Historical Studies* 16 (1):1-25.

Austen, Ralph A., and Jonathan Derrick

n.d.   "Duala." Unpublished manuscript.

Babalola, S.A.

1966   *The Content and Form of Yoruba Ijala.* Oxford: Oxford University Press.

Barber, K.

1991   *I Could Speak until Tomorrow: Oriki, Women, and the Past in a Yoruba Town.* Washington, D.C.: Smithsonian Institution Press.

Barfod, Anders

1989   "The Rise and Fall of Vegetable Ivory." *Principes* 33 (4):181-90.

Barnes, Sandra

1989   *Africa's Ogun.* Bloomington: Indiana University Press.

Barnett, Richard D.

1982   *Ancient Ivories in the Middle East and Adjacent Countries.* Jerusalem: Institute of Archaeology, Hebrew University.

Bartholet, Jeffrey, and Phil Williams

1989   "A Tussle Over Tusks." *Newsweek* (July 24):25.

Basden, George T.

1921   *Among the Ibos of Nigeria.* London: Seeley, Service & Co., Ltd.

Bassani, Ezio

1984   "A Newly Discovered Afro-Portuguese Ivory." *African Arts* 17 (4):60-63,95.

Bassani, Ezio, and William B. Fagg

1988   *Africa and the Renaissance: Art in Ivory.* New York: Center for African Art.

Bassing, Allen

1973   "Grave Monuments of the Dakakari," *African Arts* 6 (4):36-39.

Battiata, Mary

1989   "Kenya Calls for Ban on Ivory Trade." *The Washington Post* (May 12).

Bay, Edna

1985   *Asen: Iron Altars of the Fon Peoples of Benin.* Atlanta: Emory University.

Beach, D.N.

1983   "The Zimbabwe Plateau and its Peoples." In *History of Central Africa,* Vol. 1, ed. David Birmingham and Phyillis M. Martin. London: Longman.

Beachey, R.W.

1967   "The East African Ivory Trade in the Nineteenth Century." *Journal of African History* 8 (2):269-90.

Bedaux, Roger, and Jan Smits

1992   "A Seventeenth Century Ivory Figure in the Rijksmuseum Voor Volkerkunde in Leiden." *African Arts* 25 (1):76-77,100.

Bedini, Silvio

1981   "The Papal Pachyderms." *Proceedings of the American Philosophical Society* 125 (2):75-90.

Ben-Amos, Paula

1976   "Men and Animals in Benin Art." *Man* 2 (2):243-52.

1980   *The Art of Benin.* New York: Thames and Hudson.

1983   "Who is the Man in the Bowler Hat? Emblems of Identity in Benin Court Art." Baessler-Archiv, N.F.31:161-83.

1984   "Royal Art and Ideology in Eighteenth Century Benin." *Iowa Studies in African Art* 1:67-86.

Bentor, Eli

1988   "Life as an Artistic Process: Igbo Ikenga and Ofo." *African Arts* 21 (2):66-71,94.

Berns, Marla, and Arnold Rubin

forthcoming   *Sculpture of the Benue River Valley.* Los Angeles: UCLA Fowler Museum of Cultural History.

Biebuyck, Daniel

1953   "Some Remarks on Segy's Warega Ivories." *Zaïre* 7 (10):1076-82.

1954   "Function of a Lega Mask." *International Archives of Ethnography* VXLVII (1):108-20.

1972   "The Kindi Aristocrats and Their Art among the Lega." In *African Art and Leadership*, ed. D. Fraser and H. Cole, 7-20. Madison: University of Wisconsin Press.

1973   *Lega Culture: Art, Initiation, and Moral Philosophy among a Central African People.* Berkeley: University of California Press.

1976   "The Decline of Lega Sculptural Art." In *Ethnic and Tourist Arts: Cultural Expressions from the Fourth World*, ed. Nelson H. Graburn, 334-39. Berkeley: University of California Press.

1979   "The Frog and Other Animals in Lega Art and Initiation." *Africa-Tervuren* XXV (3):76-84.

1981   "Plurifrontal Figurines in Lega Art in Zaire." In *The Shape of the Past: Studies in Honor of Franklin D. Murphy*, ed. Giorgio Buccellati and Charles Speroni, 115-25. Los Angeles: Institute of Archaeology and Office of the Chancellor, University of California, Los Angeles.

1986   *The Arts of Zaire. Volume II: Eastern Zaire: The Ritual and Artistic Context of Voluntary Associations.* Berkeley: University of California Press.

Biebuyck, Daniel, and N. Van den Abbeele

1984   *The Power of Headdresses: A Cross-Cultural Study of Forms and Functions.* Ghent: Snoeck-Ducaju en Zoon and Brussels: Tendi S.A.

Bikoi, B., and E. Soundjak

1978   *Les contes du Cameroun.* Yaounde: CEPER.

Binger, L.G.

1892   *Du Niger au golfe de guinée par les pays de kong et le mossi (1887-1889).* Paris: Hachette et cie.

Binkley, David A.

1987a   "Avatar of Power: Southern Masquerade Figures in a Funerary Context." *Africa* 57 (1):75-97.

1987b   "A View from the Forest: The Power of Southern Kuba Initiation Masks." Ph.D. diss., Indiana University.

Bird, Charles, Mamadou Koita, and Bourama Soumaouro

1974   *The Songs of Seydou Camara.* 2 vols. Bloomington: African Studies Center, Indiana University.

Bishikwabo, Chubaka

1979   "Notes sur l'origine de l'institution du 'bwami' et fondements du pouvoir politique au Kivu Oriental." *Les Cahiers du CEDAF*, Series 1, no. 8.

Blackburn, Roderic

1971   "Honey in Okiek Personality, Culture and Society." Ph.D. diss., Michigan State University.

1976   "Okiek History." In *Kenya Before 1900*, ed. B.A. Ogot. Nairobi: East African Publishing House.

Blackmun, Barbara

1983   "Reading a Royal Altar Tusk." In *The Art of Power, the Power of Art: Studies in Benin Iconography*, ed. Paula Ben-Amos and Arnold Rubin. Los Angeles: Museum of Cultural History, UCLA. Monograph Series 19.

1984a   "The Iconography of Carved Altar Tusks from Benin, Nigeria." Ph.D. diss., University of California, Los Angeles.

1984b   Art as Statecraft: A King's Justification in Ivory. Geneva: Musee Barbier-Mueller.

1987   "Royal and Non-Royal Benin: Distinctions in Igbesanmwan Ivory Carving." *Iowa Studies in African Art* 2:81-115.

1988   "From Trader to Priest in Two Hundred Years: Transformation of a Foreign Figure on Benin Ivories." *Art Journal* (Summer):128-38.

1990   "Oba's Portraits in Benin." *African Arts* 23 (3):61-69, 102-4.

1991a   "Who Commissioned the Queen Mother Tusks? A Problem in the Chronology of Benin Ivories." *African Arts* 24 (2):54-65, 90-92.

1991b   "The Face of the Leopard: Its Significance in Benin Court Art." *Bulletin*, Allen Memorial Art Museum, Oberlin College XLIV (2):24-35.

Blackmun, Barbara, and Matthew Schoffeleers

1972   "Masks of Malawi," *African Arts*, Summer: 36-41, 69, 88.

Blake, J.W., ed.

1942   *Europeans in West Africa, 1450-1560*. London: The Hakluyt Society.

Blier, Suzanne

1991   "King Glele of Danhomé, Part Two: Dynasty and Destiny," *African Arts* 24 (1): 44-55.

1988   "Melville J. Herskovits and the Arts of Ancient Dahomy," *Res: Anthropology and Art* 16: 124-42.

Boesch, Chr., and H. Boesch

1989   "Hunting Behavior in Wild Chimpanzees in the Tai National Park." *American Journal of Physical Anthropology* 78:547-74.

Bold, Edward

1819 [1823]   *The Merchant's and Mariner's African Guide; Containing an Accurate Description of the Coast, Bays, Harbours*. Salem: Cushing & Appleton.

Bouchart, François, and Nadine Beautheac

1988   *Atelier Aujourd'hui: Koffi Mouroufié*. Paris: Centre Georges Pompidou, Musée National d'Art Moderne.

Bouchaud, J.

1952   *La côte du Cameroun dans l'histoire et la cartographie*. Memoires de l'institut francais d'Afrique Noire. Centre Cameroun. No. 5.

Böhning, Walter et al.

1972   *Ostafrika-Geräte, Waffen, Schmuck*. Heidelberg: Völkerkundenmuseum.

Bradbury, R.E.

1957-67   "BS Series: Benin Scheme Field Notes." University of Birmingham, England: Special Collections Library.

1973   *Benin Studies*. London: Oxford University Press.

Brain, Robert

1980   *Art and Society in Africa*. New York: Longman.

Brain, Robert, and Adam Pollock

1971   *Bangwa Funerary Sculpture*. London: Duckworth, and Toronto: University of Toronto Press.

Breasted, J.H.

1906   *Ancient Records of Egypt*. Vol. 1. Chicago: University of Chicago Press.

Brock, Major R.G.C.

1918   "Some Notes on the Zande Tribe as Found in the Meridi District (Bahr El Ghazal Province)." *Sudan Notes and Records* 1:249-62.

Brooks, Alison S.

1988   "Paleolithic." In *Encyclopedia of Human Evolution and Prehistory*, ed. Ian Tattersall, Eric Delson, and John A. Van Couvering, 415-19. New York: Garland Press.

Brown, Leslie

1965   *Africa: A Natural History*. London: Hamish Hamilton.

Bruce, M. James

1791   *Voyage en Nubie et en Abyssinie, entrepris pour découvrir les sources du Nil,*

pendant les années 1768, 1769, 1770, 1771, 1773, Vol. 8, tran. M. Castera. Paris.

Buchner, Max

1887   *Kamerun. Skizzen und Betrachtungen*. Leipzig: Verlag von Duncker & Humblot.

1914   *Aurora colonialis*. Munich: Verlagsanstalt Piloty & Leohle.

Buitron, Diana, and Andrew Oliver

1985   "Greek, Etruscan, and Roman Ivories." In *Masterpieces of Ivory*, ed. Richard H. Randall, Jr. New York: Hudson Hills Press.

Burdette, Nathan

1989   "Ivory-Handle Knives: On The Endangered List?" *Blade Magazine* 16 (6):58.

Burton, John

1976   "The Ivory Connection." *New Scientist* 70 (996):138-39.

Burton, Sir Richard F.

1859   "The Lake Regions of Central Equatorial Africa, ..." *Journal of the Royal Geographical Society* 29:1-464.

1961   *The Lake Regions of Central Africa: A Picture of Exploration*, Vol. II. New York: Horizon Press.

Burton, William F. P.

1961   *Luba Religion and Magic in Custom and Belief*. Tervuren: Musée Royal de l'Afrique Centrale.

Buss, I.O.

1990   *Elephant Life: Fifteen Years of High Population Density*. Ames, Iowa: Iowa State University Press.

Byrne, Robert

1988   "The Amazing Michael Shamos: Billiard Archivist." *Billiards Digest* (April): 30-35.

Caillié, René

1968   *Travels Through Central Africa to Timbuctoo in the Years 1824-1828*. 2 vols. London: Cass. Original Edition 1830.

Canby, Jeanny Vorys

1985   "Ancient Egypt and the Near East." In *Masterpieces of Ivory*, ed. Richard H. Randall, Jr. New York: Hudson Hills Press.

Canu, Gaston

1975   *Contes du Sahel*. Paris: Conseil international de la langue francaise.

Caqout, A.

1957   "La royauté sacrale en Éthiopie." In *Annales d'Ethiopie* 10, publiées par la Section d'Archéologie du Gouvernement Impérial d'Éthiopie X. Paris: C. Klincksieck.

Cardinall, A.W.

1931   *Tales Told in Togoland*. Oxford: Oxford University Press.

Carrington, R.

1958   *Elephants: A Short Account of Their Natural History, Evolution and Influence on Mankind*. London: Chatto and Windus.

Carroll, Robert L.

1988   *Vertebrate Paleontology and Evolution*. New York: W.H. Freeman & Co.

Carter, William G.

1971   "The Ntahera Horn Ensemble of the Dwaben Court: An Ashanti Surrogating Medium." M.A. thesis, University of California, Los Angeles.

1984   "Asante Music in Old and New Juaben: A Comparative Study." Ph.D. diss., University of California, Los Angeles.

Casati, Gaetano

1891   *Ten Years in Equatoria and the Return with Emin Pasha*. Vol. I. London: F. Warne and Co.

Cashion, Gerald Anthony

1984   "Hunters of the Mande: A Behavioral Code and Worldview Derived from the Study of their Folklore." Ph.D. diss., Indiana University.

Celenko, Theodore

1983   *A Treasury of African Art from the Harrison Eiteljorg Collection*. Bloomington: Indiana University Press.

Cerulli, Enrico
1938   *Studi etiopici: La Lingua e la storia dei Sidamo.* Vol. 2. Rome: Instituto per l'Oriente.

Chittick, Neville H.
1977   "The East Coast, Madagascar and the Indian Ocean." In *The Cambridge History of Africa,* Vol. 3, ed. Roland Oliver. Cambridge: Cambridge University Press.

Christaller, Johann Gottlieb
1879   *A Collection of Three Thousand and Six Hundred Tshi Proverbs.* Basel: Basel German Evangelical Missionary Society.
1990   *Three Thousand Six Hundred Ghanaian Proverbs (from the Asante and Fante Language).* Studies in African Literature, Vol. 2, tran. Kofi Ron Lange. Lewiston: The Edwin Mellen Press.

Cissé, Youssouf
1964   "Notes sur les sociétés de chasseurs malinke." *Journal de la Société des Africanistes* 34 (2):175-226.

Clark, J. Desmond
1970   *The Prehistory of Africa.* Southampton: Thames and Hudson.

Clutton-Brock, Juliet, ed.
1989   *The Walking Larder: Pattern of domestication, pastoralism, and predation.* One World Archaeology Series, Volume 2. London: Unwin Hyman.

Cole, Herbert M.
1972   "Igbo Art and Authority." In *African Art and Leadership,* ed. D. F. Fraser and H. M. Cole. Madison: University of Wisconsin Press.
1974   "Vital Arts of Northern Kenya." *African Arts* 7 (2):12-23+.
1979   "Living Art Among the Samburu." In *The Fabrics of Culture,* ed. Justine Cordwell and Ronald Schwarz. The Hague: Mouton.
1982   *Mbari: Art and Life among the Owerri Igbo.* Bloomington: Indiana University Press.
1985   (ed.) *I am Not Myself: The Art of African Masquerade.* Los Angeles: UCLA Museum of Cultural History. Monograph Series 26.

Cole, Herbert M., and Chike C. Aniakor
1984   *Igbo Arts: Community and Cosmos.* Los Angeles: UCLA Museum of Cultural History.

Cole, Herbert M., and Doran H. Ross
1977   *The Arts of Ghana.* Los Angeles: UCLA Museum of Cultural History.

Colyer, F., and A.E.W. Miles
1957   "Injury to and Rate of Growth of an Elephant Tusk." *Journal of Mammalogy* 38:243-47.

Conniff, Richard
1987   "When the Music in Our Parlors Brought Death to Darkest Africa." *Audubon* 89 (4):77-92.

Coppens, Yves, Vincent J. Maglio, Cary T. Madden, and Maurice Beden
1978   "Proboscidea." In *Evolution of African Mammals,* ed. Vincent J. Maglio and H.B.S. Cooke, 336-67. Cambridge, Mass.: Harvard University Press.

Cornet, Joseph
1975   *Art from Zaire: 100 Masterworks from the National Collection.* New York: The African-American Institute.
1976   "À propos des statues Ndengese." *Arts d'Afrique Noire,* 17:6-16.
1980   "La société des chasseurs d'éléphants chez les Ipanga." *Annales Aequatoria* 1 (1), Mbandaka, Zaire.
1982   *Art royal kuba.* Milan: Edizioni Sipiel.

Cosentino, Donald
1982   *Defiant Maids and Stubborn Farmers.* Cambridge: Cambridge University Press.

Crow, Hugh
1830   *Memoirs of the late Captain Hugh Crow of Liverpool.* London: Longman, Rees, Orme, Brown, and Green.

Crooks, J.J.
1923   *Records Relating to the Gold Coast Settlements from 1750 to 1874.* Dublin: Brown and Nolan, Ltd.

Cummings, Robert J.
1975   "Aspects of Human Porterage with Special Reference to the Akamba of Kenya: Towards an Economic History, 1820-1920." Ph.D. diss., University of California, Los Angeles.

Curnow, K.
1983   "The Afro-Portuguese Ivories: Classification and Stylistic Analysis of a Hybrid Art Form." Ph.D. diss., Indiana University.

Curtin, Philip
1975   *Economic Change in Precolonial Africa.* Madison: University of Wisconsin Press.

Curtin, Phillip et al.
1978   *African History.* Boston: Little, Brown and Company.

Cutler, Anthony
1984   "On Byzantine Boxes." *Journal of The Walters Art Gallery* 42/43:32-47.
1985   *The Craft of Ivory. Sources, Techniques and Uses in the Mediterranean World: A.D. 200-1400.* Washington, D.C.: Dumbarton Oaks.

Cuvier, G.
1849   *Anatomie comparée recueil des planches de myologie.* Paris: C. Laurillard and Mercier.

Czekanowski, Jan
1924   *Forschungen im Nil-Kongo Zwischengebiet,* Vol. 6, pt. 2. Leipzig: Klinkhardt and Biermann.

Daaku, Kwame Yeboa
1970   *Trade and Politics on the Gold Coast 1600-1700: A Study of the African Reaction to European Trade.* Oxford: Oxford University Press.

Dapper, Olfert
1668   *Umstandliche und Eigentliche Beshreibung von Afrika.* Amsterdam.

Darbois, Dominique
1962   *African Dance.* Prague: Artia.

Dark, Philip
1960   *Benin Art.* London: P. Hamlyn.
1962   *The Art of Benin.* Chicago: Chicago Natural History Museum.
1969   *Some Prominent Bini People.* Benin City.
1973   *Introduction to Benin Art and Technology.* Oxford: Clarendon Press.
1975   "Benin Bronze Heads, Styles and Chronology." In *African Images,* ed. D. McCall and Edna Bay, 25-103. New York: Africana Publishing Company for the African Studies Center, Boston University.
1982   *An Illustrated Catalogue of Benin Art.* Boston: G.K. Hall.

Dark, Philip, and W. Forman and B. Forman
1951   "Tribal Sculpture and the Festival of Britain." *Man* (June):73-76.

Darwin, C.
1859   *The Origin of Species and the Descent of Man.* Toronto: Random House.

Davidson, Basil
1966   *Africa: History of a Continent.* London: Weidenfeld and Nicolson.

Davis, L.B. and Reeves, B.O.K., eds.
1990   *Hunters of the Recent Past.* One World Archaeology Series, Vol. 15. London: Unwin Hyman.

Deane, Daniela
1990   "The End of the Ivory Trade." *Newsweek* (July 16):35.

Delafosse, Maurice
1912   *Haut-Sénégal-Niger.* 3 vols. Paris: E. Larose.

Delanghe, Achille
1982   "Les Balumba ou chasseurs d'éléphants de la zone d'Oshwe." *Mai-Ndombe II* 75:105-115. Bandundu, Zaire.

Delhaise, Le Commandant
1909   *Les Warega.* Brussels: Albert de Wit.

Dempsey, James
1955   *Mission on the Nile.* London: Burns & Oates.

Denton, George H., and Thomas J. Hughes, eds.
1981   *The Last Great Ice Sheets.* New York: Wiley.

Deraniyagala, P.E.P.

1955   *Some Extinct Elephants, Their Relatives and the Two Living Species.* Colombo, Sri Lanka: Ceylon National Administration.

Dercourt, Jean et al.

1986   "Geological Evolution of the Tethys Belt from the Atlantic to the Pamirs since the Lias." *Tectonophysics* 123:213-41.

Derrick, Jonathan

1980   "Germanophone Elite of Douala Under the French Mandate." *Journal of African History* 21 (2):255-67.

Diamond, Jared

1984   "Historic Extinctions: A Rosetta Stone for Understanding Prehistoric Extinctions." In *Quaternary Extinctions*, ed. Paul S. Martin and Richard G. Klein, 824-66. Tucson: University of Arizona Press.

Dieterlen, Genevieve, and Youssouf Cissé

1972   *Les Fondements de la société d'initiation du Komo.* Paris: Mouton.

Dika Akwa, Guillaume Betotede Bonambele

1955   *Bible de la sagesse Bantoue.* Collection CENTRACCAM, Serie A. Paris: Centre Artistique et Culturel Camerounais.

Dillon, Richard

1973   "Ideology, Process, and Change in Pre-Colonial Meta' Political Organization (United Republic of Cameroon)." Ph.D. diss., University of Pennsylvania.

Dinesen, Isak

1937   *Out of Africa.* New York: Random House.

Dorst, Jean, and Pierre Dandelot

1970   *A Field Guide to the Larger Mammals of Africa.* London: Collins.

Dosso, Sindou

1988   *Rapport de mission ellectuée dans le département de Mankono du 21 au 27 juillet 1988.* Abidjan: Musée National.

Douglas, Mary

1975   *Implicit meanings.* London and Boston: Routledge & Kegan Paul.

1990   "The Pangolin Revisited: A New approach to Animal Symbolism." In *Signifying Animals: Human Meaning in the Natural World.* One World Archaeology, ed. Roy G. Willis, Vol. 16. London: Unwin Hyman.

Douglas-Hamilton, Iain

1980   "African Elephant Ivory Trade Study: Final Report (Excerpts)." *Elephant* 1 (4):69-99.

1987   "African Elephants: Population Trends and Their Causes." *Oryx* 21 (1): 11-24.

Douglas-Hamilton, Iain, and O. Douglas-Hamilton.

1975   *Among the Elephants.* New York: Viking Press.

Drewal, H.J.

1977a   "Art and the Perception of Women in Yoruba Culture." *Cahiers d'Études Africaines*, 68, 17 (4):545-67.

1977b   *Traditional Art of the Nigerian Peoples.* Washington, D.C.: Museum of African Art.

1978   (ed.) Special issue on "The Arts of Egungun among Yoruba Peoples." *African Arts* 11 (3).

1980   *African Artistry: Technique and Aesthetics in Yoruba Sculpture.* Atlanta: High Museum of Art.

1988   *Shapes of the Mind: African Art from Long Island Collections.* Hempstead: Hofstra University Museums.

1989a   "Ife: Origins of Art and Civilization" and "Art and Ethos of the Ijebu." In *Yoruba: Nine Centuries of African Art and Thought*, 44-75, 116-45. New York: Center for African Art.

1989b   "Meaning in Osugbo Art among the Ijebu Yoruba: A Reappraisal." In *Man Does Not Go Naked: Textilien und Handwerk aus Afrikanishen und Anderen Landern*, ed. B. Engelbrecht and B. Gardi, 151-74. Basel: Basler Beitrage zür Ethnologie.

Forthcoming   *The Joss Collection of African Art.* Los Angeles: Fowler Museum of Cultural History, UCLA.

Drewal, H.J., and M.T. Drewal

1983   *Gelede: Art and Female Power Among the Yoruba.* Bloomington: Indiana University Press.

Drewal, H.J., J. Pemberton III, and R. Abiodun

1989   *Yoruba: Nine Centuries of African Art and Thought.* New York: Center for African Art.

Drewal, M.T.

1977   "Projections from the Top in Yoruba Art." *African Arts* 11 (1):43-49, 91-92.

1992   *Yoruba Ritual: Performers, Play, Agency.* Bloomington: Indiana University Press.

Drewal, M.T., and H.J. Drewal

1983   "An Ifa Diviner's Shrine in Ijebuland." *African Arts* 16 (2):60-67,99-100.

1987   "Composing Time and Space in Yoruba Art." *Word and Image* 3 (3): 225-51.

Duprey, Pierre

1962   *Histoire des ivoiriens: naissance des ivoiriens.* Abidjan: Imprimerie de la Côte d'Ivoire.

Dupuis, Joseph

1824 [1966]   *Journal of a Residence in Ashante.* London: Frank Cass.

Eastman, Carol M.

1988   "Women, Slaves, and Foreigners: African Cultural Influences and Group Processes in the Formation of Northern Swahili Coastal Society." *International Journal of African Historical Studies* 21 (1):1-20.

Edicef

1978   *Contes et récits du Tchad.* Paris: Conseil International de la Langue Française.

Edmiston, Althea Brown

1932   *Grammar and Dictionary of the Bushonga or Bukuba Language as spoken by the Bushonga or Bukuba Tribe who Dwell in the Upper Kasai District, Belgian Congo, Central Africa.* Luebo: American Presbyterian Congo Mission.

Edmond-Blanc, François

1954   *Le grand livre de la faune africaine et de sa chasse.* 2 vols. Zürich and Geneva.

Egharevba, Jacob

1957   *Bini Titles.* 2nd ed. Benin City: Kopin-Dogba Press.

1968   *A Short History of Benin.* Ibadan: Ibadan University Press.

Egudu, Romanus N., and Donatus Nwoga

1971   *Igbo Traditional Verse.* London: Heineman.

Eisenberg, J.F.

1980   "Ecology and Behavior of the Asian Elephant." *Elephant* 1:36-56.

Eisenberg, J.F. et al.

1971   "Reproductive Behavior of the Asiatic Elephant (*Elephas maximus maximus* L.)." *Behavior* 38:193-225.

Eltringham, S.K.

1982   *Elephants.* Poole, Dorset, England: Blanford Press.

1992   "Longevity and Mortality." In *Elephants*, ed. J. Shoshani. Emmaus, Penn.: Rodale Press.

Emery, Walter B.

1965   *Egypt in Nubia.* London: Hutchinson.

Emley, E.D.

1927   "The Turkana of Kolosia District." *Journal of the Royal Anthropological Institute* 57:157-201.

Emonts, Johannes

1922   *Ins Steppen und Bergland Innerkameruns.* Aachen: Xaverius-Verlag.

Engard, Ronald K.

1986   "Bringing the Outside In: Commensality and Incorporation in Bafut Myth, Ritual, Art, and Social Organization." Ph.D. diss., Indiana University.

Escherich, Georg

1921   *Im Lande des Negus.* Vol. 2. Berlin: G. Stilke.

Espinoza, Edgard, and Mary-Jacque Mann

1991   *Identification Guide for Ivory and Ivory Substitutes.* Washington D.C.: World Wildlife Fund.

Etienne-Nugue, Jocelyne

1982   *Crafts and the Arts of Living in the Cameroon.* Baton Rouge: Louisiana State University Press.

1985   *Artisanats traditionels: Côte d'Ivoire.* Paris: Harmattan/Institut Culturel Africain.

Evans-Pritchard, E.E.

1937   *Witchcraft, Oracles and Magic Among the Azande.* Oxford: Clarendon Press.

1940   *The Nuer.* Oxford: Clarendon Press.

1962   "Zande Kings and Princes." In *Essays in Social Anthropology.* London: Faber & Faber.

1971   *The Azande.* Oxford: Clarendon Press.

Ewusi, Francis Stanley

1971   "Cape Coast Asafo Symbols." B.A. Thesis. Kumasi: College of Art, University of Science and Technology.

Exposition Universelle de 1900

1900   *Les colonies françaises Sénégal-Soudan.* Paris: Augustin Challamel.

Eyo, Ekpo, and Frank Willett

1980   *Treasures of Ancient Nigeria.* Detroit: Founders Society, Detroit Institute of Arts.

Ezra, Kate

1983   "Figure Sculpture of the Bamana of Mali." Ph.D. diss., Northwestern University.

1984   *African Ivories.* New York: Metropolitan Museum of Art.

1986   *A Human Ideal in African Art: Bamana Figurative Sculpture.* Washington, D.C.: Smithsonian Institution Press.

Fagan, Brian M.

1965   *Southern Africa During the Iron Age.* New York: F.A. Praeger.

Fagg, W.B.

n.d.   Photo Archive. Los Angeles: Fowler Museum of Cultural History, UCLA.

1963   Nigerian Images. London: Lund Humphries.

1970   *Divine Kingship in Africa.* London: British Museum.

1981   "Hunting Horn" entry (cat. 30) in *For Spirits and Kings: African Art from the Tishman Collection,* ed. Susan Vogel. New York: The Metropolitan Museum of Art.

Faulkner, Laurel Birch

1988   "Basketry Masks of the Chewa," *African Arts* 21 (3):28-31, 86.

Faris, James C.

1972   *Nuba Personal Art.* Toronto: University of Toronto Press.

Flayderman, E. Norman

1972   *Scrimshaw and Scrimshanders.* New Milford, Conn.: N. Flayderman.

Felix, Marc

1989   *Maniema: An Essay on the Distribution of the Symbols and Myths as Depicted in the Masks of Greater Maniema.* Munich: Berlage Fred John.

Finnegan, Ruth

1970   *Oral Literature in Africa.* Oxford: Oxford University Press.

Fischer, Eberhard, and Hans Himmelheber

1975   *Das Gold in der Kunst Westafrikas.* Zürich: Museum Rietberg.

1984   *The Arts of the Dan in West Africa.* Zurich: Museum Rietberg.

1985   *Die Kunst der Guro.* Zurich: Museum Rietberg.

Fischer, Eberhard, and Lorenz Homberger

1986   *Masks in Guro Culture, Ivory Coast.* New York: Center for African Art.

Fischer, M.S.

1989   "Hyracoids, The Sister-Group of Perissodactyls." In *The Evolution of Perissodactyls,* ed. D.R. Prothero and R.M. Schoch, 37-56. New York: Oxford University Press.

Fischer, M.S., and U. Trautmann

1987   "Fetuses of African Elephants (*Loxodonta africana*) in Photographs." *Elephant* 2 (3):40-45.

Fisher, Angela

1984   *Africa Adorned.* New York: Abrams.

Fisher, D.C.

1987   "Mastodont Procurement by Paleoindians of the Great Lakes Region: Hunting or Scavenging?" In *Evolution of Human Hunting,* ed. M.H. Nitecki and D.V. Nitecki, 309-421. New York: Plenum Press.

Foa, Edouard

1900   *De l'Océan Indien à l'Océan Atlantique: La traversée de l'Afrique du Zambèze au Congo français.* Paris: Librairie Plon.

Fraser, Douglas

1972   "The Fish-legged Figure in Benin and Yoruba Art." In *African Art and Leadership,* ed. D. Fraser and H. Cole, 261-74. Madison: University of Wisconsin Press.

1975   "The Tsoede Bronzes and Owo Yoruba Art." *African Arts* 8 (2):30-35,91.

1981   "Pair of Armlets" entry (cat. 128) in *For Spirits and Kings,* ed. Susan Vogel. New York: Metropolitan Museum of Art.

Fraser, Douglas F., and Herbert M. Cole, eds.

1972   *African Art and Leadership.* Madison: University of Wisconsin Press.

Fratkin, Elliot

1974   "Why Elephant is an Old Woman: Animal Symbolism in Samburu." Seminar Paper, no. 63. University of Nairobi: Institute of African Studies.

Freedberg, David

1989   *The Power of Images: Studies in the History and Theory of Response.* Chicago: The University of Chicago Press.

Friedel, Robert

1983   *Pioneer Plastics.* Madison: University of Wisconsin Press.

1988   *A Material World.* Washington, D.C.: Smithsonian Institution.

Frobenius, Leo

1897   *Der Kameruner Schiffsschnabel und seine Motive.* Abhandlungender Kaiserlichen Leopoldinisch-Carolinischen Deutschen Akademie der Naturforscher. Vol. 70, No. 1.

Galaty, John G.

1979   "Pollution and Anti-praxis: The Issue of Maasai Inequality." *American Ethnologist* 6:803-16.

1982   "Being 'Maasai', Being 'People of Cattle': Ethnic Shifters in East Africa." *American Ethnologist* 9:1-20.

Gangambi, Muyaga

1974   *Les Masques Pende de Gatundo,* Série II, Vol. 22. Bandundu: Ceeba Publications.

Garrard, Timothy F.

1980   *Akan Weights and the Gold Trade.* London: Longmans.

Gary, Romain

1958   *The Roots of Heaven.* Trans. Jonathan Griffin. New York: Simon and Schuster.

Geary, Christraud M.

1976   *We: Die Genese eines Häuptlingtums im Grasland von Kamerun.* Studien zur Kulturkunde 36. Wiesbaden: Steiner.

1979   "Traditional Societies and Associations in We (North West Province, Cameroon)." *Paideuma* 25:53-72.

1982   "Casting the 'Red Iron': Bamum Bronzes." In *The Art of Metal in Africa,* ed. Marie-Thérèse Brincard. New York: The African-American Institute.

1983   *Things of the Palace: A Catalogue of the Bamum Palace Museum in Foumban (Cameroon).* Studien zur Kulturkunde 60. Wiesbaden: Steiner.

1988   "Art and Political Process in the Kingdoms of Bali-Nyonga and Bamum (Cameroon Grassfields)." *Canadian Journal of African Studies* 22 (1):11-41.

1989   "Slit Gongs in the Cameroon Grassfields: Sights and Sounds of Beauty and Power." In *Sounding Forms: African Musical Instruments,* ed. Marie-Thérèse Brincard. New York: The American Federation of the Arts.

1990   "Photographie als kunsthistorische Quelle. Das *nja*-Fest der Bamum (Kamerun) im späten 19. und 20. Jahnhundert." In *Der Sinn des Schönen. Ästhetik, Soziologie und Geschichte der afrikansichen Kunst,* ed. Miklós Szalay, 113-177. Munich: Trickster Verlag.

Gebauer, Paul

1968   *A Guide to Cameroon Art from the Collection of Paul and Clara Gebauer.* Portland, Oregon: Portland Art Museum.

1979   *Art of Cameroon.* Portland, Oreg.: Portland Art Museum.

Germann, Paul

1910 "Das plastisch-figurliche Kunstgewerbe im Grasland von Kamerun." *Jahrbuch des Städtischen Museums für Völkerkunde zu Leipzig* 4:1-35.

Gilbert, Katherine Stoddard, Joan K. Holt, and Sara Hudson, eds.

1976 *Treasures of Tutankhamun.* New York: Ballentine Books.

Giorgetti, Filiberto

1957 "Il Cannibalismo dei Niam Niam." *Africa* 27:178-86.

Glauning, Hans

1905 "Bericht des Hauptmanns Glauning, Leiters der Station Bamenda, über seine Expedition nach Bali, Bameta und dem Südbezirk." In *Deutsches Kolonialblatt*, 667-72.

Glaze, Anita J.

1981 *Art and Death in a Senufo Village.* Bloomington: Indiana University Press.

Goodman, N.

1972 *Problems and projects.* New York: Bobbs Merrill.

Gordon, J.A.

1966 "Elephants Do Think." *African Wildlife* 20:75-79.

Gouk, Penelope

1988 *The Ivory Sundials of Nuremberg, 1500-1700.* Cambridge: Whipple Museum.

Goutman, A.

1978 *Il était une fois ... Félix Houphouet-Boigny.* Paris: Afrique Biblio-Club.

Gray, Richard

1961 *A History of the Southern Sudan, 1839-1889.* London: Oxford University Press.

Griaule, Marcel

1938 [1963] *Masques Dogons.* Paris: Institut d'Ethnologie, Musée de l'Homme. Université de Paris. Travaux et Mémoires de l'Institut d'Ethnologie.]

Guarducci, M.

1978-80 "Artichi Elefanti in Vaticano." *Atti della Pontifica Accademia Romana di Archeologia Rendiconti* 51/52:47,fig. 2.

Guenneguez, André, and Afo Guenneguez

1988 *Centenaire de la Côte d'Ivoire 1887/1888 - 1988 en cartes postales.* Abidjan: Art et Edition.

Gup, Ted

1989 "Trail of Shame." *Time* (October 16):66-73.

Haberland, Eike

1957 "Verdienstfeste in Äthiopien." *Paideuma* 6:326-41.

Hall, H.U.

1922 "Great Benin Royal Altar." *The Museum Journal*, University of Pennsylvania Museum 13 (2):104-67.

Hammond, Marie, and Alta Jablow

1977 *The Myth of Africa.* New York: Library of Social Science.

Hanks, J.

1979 *The Struggle for Survival: The Elephant Problem.* New York: Mayflower Books.

Hansen, Hans Jurgen, ed.

1920-21 [1965] "Dualasprichworter Ein Beitrag zum Verstandis des Afrikaners." In *Zeitschrift für Eingenbornen-Sprachen* 11:35-70,125-60,306-15. Kraus Ltd.

1968 *Art and the Seafarer. A Historical Survey of the Arts and Crafts of Sailors and Shipwrights.* Trans. James Moore and Inge Moore. London: Faber and Faber.

Harley, George W.

1941 *Notes on the Poro in Liberia.* Cambridge: Papers of the Peabody Museum of American Archaeology and Ethnology, Harvard University.

Harms, Robert W.

1981 *River of Wealth, River of Sorrow: The Central Zaire Basin in the Era of the Slave and Ivory Trade, 1500-1891.* New Haven: Yale University Press.

Harris, J.M., and G.T. Jefferson, eds.

1985 *Rancho La Brea: Treasures of the Tar Pits.* Los Angeles: Los Angeles County Museum of Natural History, George C. Page Museum of La Brea Discoveries. Science Series No. 31.

Harrison, R.

1847 "On the Anatomy of the Elephant." *Proceedings of the Royal Irish Academy* 3 (61):385-98.

Harroy, Ferdinand

1907 "Les Bakuba." *Bulletin de la société belge de géographie* 21:171-92,234-55.

Harter, Pierre

1986 *Arts anciens du Cameroun.* Arnouville-les Gonesse, France: Arts d'Afrique Noire.

Hatley, Thomas, and Jon Kappelman

1980 "Bears, Pigs, and Plio-Pleistocene Hominids: A Case for the Exploitation of Below-Ground Resources." *Human Ecology* 8:371-87.

Hecklinger, Philipp

1920/21 [1965] "Dualasprichworter Ein Beitrag zum Verstandnis des Afrikaners." *Zeitschrift für Eingenbornen-Sprachen.* Kraus Ltd., 11:35-70,125-60, 306-15.

Helmlinger, Paul

1972 *Dictionnaire duala-français.* Paris: Editions Klincksieck.

Hemingway, Ernest

1935 *The Green Hills of Africa.* New York: Scribner.

Henderson, Richard N.

1972 *The King in Every Man: Evolutionary Trends in Onitsha Ibo Society and Culture.* New Haven: Yale University Press.

Henderson, Richard N., and I. Umunna

1988 "Leadership Symbolism in Onitsha Igbo Crowns and Ijele." *African Arts* 21 (2):28-37,94-96.

Hendricks, William

1977 *History of Billiards.* Roxana, Ill.: William Hendricks.

Herskovits, Frances S., and Melville J. Herskovits

1958 *Dahomean Narrative.* Evanston, Ill.: Northwestern University Press.

Hess, D.L., A.M. Schmidt, and M.J. Schmidt

1983 "Reproductive Cycle of the Asian Elephant (*Elephas maximus*) in Captivity." *Biology of Reproduction* 28:767-73.

Hill, K.

1982 "Hunting and Human Evolution." *Journal of Human Evolution* 11:567-73.

Hilton-Simpson, M.N.

1911 *Land and Peoples of the Kasai.* London: Constable and Company Limited.

Himmelheber, Hans

1951 *Aura Poku, Mythen, Tiergeschicten und Sagen (der Baule).* Eisenach: E. Roth.

1972 "Gold-Plated Objects of Baule Notables." In *African Art and Leadership*, ed. Douglas Fraser and Herbert M. Cole. Madison: The University of Wisconsin Press.

Hinckley, Patricia Baird

1986 "The Dodo Masquerade of Burkina Faso," *African Arts* 19 (2):74-77,91.

Hintze, Ursula

1979 "The Graffiti from the Great Enclosure at Musawwarat es-Sofra." In *Meroitica* 5: *Africa in Antiquity, The Arts of Ancient Nubia and the Sudan*, ed. Fritz Hintze. Berlin: Akademie-Verlag.

Hodder, Ian

1989 *The Meaning of Things: Material Culture and Symbolic Expression.* One World Archaeology, Volume 6. London: Unwin Hyman.

Holas, Bohumil

1966 *Arts de la Côte d'Ivoire.* Paris: Presses Universitaires de France.

1968 *Craft and Culture in the Ivory Coast.* Abidjan: Centre des Sciences Humaines.

1969a *Animaux dans l'art ivoirien.* Paris: Librairie Orientaliste Paul Geuthner S.A.

1969b   *Arts de la Côte d'Ivoire: Trésors du Musée d'Abidjan.* Vevey: Musée des Beaux Arts.

1969c   *Arts traditionnels de la Côte d'Ivoire.* Abidjan: CEDA.

1969d   *Masques ivoriens.* Abidjan: CEDA.

n.d.   *Masques de Côte d'Ivoire.* Abidjan: Société Générale de Banques de Côte d'Ivoire.

Hollis, A.C.

1905   *The Masai: Their Language and Folklore.* Oxford: Clarendon Press.

Holt, P.M., and M.W. Daly

1988   *The History of the Sudan, From the Coming of Islam to the Present-Day.* 4th ed. London: Longman.

Holtzapffel, Charles

1846   *Turning and Mechanical Manipulation.* Vol. 1. London: Holtzapffel & Co.

Hopkins, A.G.

1973   *An Economic History of West Africa.* London: Longman.

Horton, David R.

1984   "Red Kangaroos: The Last of the Australian Megafauna." In *Quaternary Extinctions*, ed. Paul S. Martin and Richard G. Klein, 639-80. Tucson: University of Arizona Press.

Horton, Mark

1987   "The Swahili Corridor." *Scientific American* 257 (3):86-93.

Horton, Robin

1965   *Kalabari Sculpture.* Lagos: Department of Antiquities.

Howard, A.L.

1979   "'Motty' – Birth of an African/Asian Elephant at Chester Zoo." *Elephant* 1 (3):36-4l.

Howell, F. Clark

1978   "Hominidae." In *Evolution of African Mammals*, ed. Vincent J. Maglio and H.B.S. Cooke, 154-248. Cambridge, Mass.: Harvard University Press.

Howell, P.P.

1945   "A Note on Elephants and Elephant Hunting Among the Nuer." *Sudan Notes and Records* 26:95-103.

1954   *A Manual of Nuer Law.* London: Oxford University Press.

Howell, P.P., and W.P.G. Thomson

1946   "The Death of a Reth of the Shilluk and the Installation of His Successor." *Sudan Notes and Records* 27:4-85.

Höhnel, Ludwig von

1894   *Discovery of Lakes Rudolf and Stefanie.* 2 vols. Trans. Nancy Bell. London: Longmans, Green.

Huet, Michel

1978   *The Dance, Art, and Ritual of Africa.* New York: Pantheon.

Huffman, Ray

1931   *Nuer Customs and Folklore.* London: Published for the International Institute of African Languages and Cultures by Oxford University Press.

Hunn, Judith

1985   "Cameroon Grasslands." In *I am Not Myself: The Art of African Masquerade*, ed. Herbert M. Cole. Los Angeles: Museum of Cultural History, UCLA. Monograph Series 26.

Huntingford, G.W.B.

1961   "The Distribution of Certain Culture Elements in East Africa." *Journal of the Royal Anthropological Institute* 91 (2):251-95.

Hutter, Franz

1902   *Wanderungen und Forschungen im Nord-Hinterland von Kamerun.* Braunschweig: F. Vieweg und Sohn.

1907   "Bamum." *Globus* 91:1-47.

Hücking, Renate, and Ekkehard Launer

1986   *Aus Menschen Neger Machen.* Hamburg: Galgenberg.

Ingold, T.

1988   *What is an Animal?* One World Archaeology, Vol. 1. London: Unwin Hyman.

Isaac, Barbara

1987   "Throwing and Human Evolution." *African Archaeological Review* 5:3-17.

Isaac, Glyn Lleyn, and D. Crader

1981   "To What Extent were Early Humans Carnivores? An Archaeological Perspective." In *Omnivorous Primates: Gathering and Hunting in Human Evolution,* ed. R.S.O. Harding and G. Teleki, 37-103. New York: Columbia University Press.

Ittmann, Johannes

1939   "Die Tierwelt des Kameruner Waldlandes in magischen Gebrauche." *Evangelische Missions-Magazin*, 151-59.

1952   "Verschlingemarchen aus dem Vorderen Kamerun." *Afrika und Ubersee* 36 (1-2):17-30; 36 (3):115-35; 36 (4):173-89.

1976   *Worterbuch der Duala-Sprache.* Berlin: Verlag von Deitrich Reimer.

Jackson, Kenell A., Jr.

1977   "Ngotho (The Ivory Armlet): An Emblem of Upper-Tier Status Among the 19th Century Akamba of Kenya ca. 1830-1880." *Kenya Historical Review* 5 (1):35-69.

Jackson, Michael

1990   "The Man Who Could Turn Into an Elephant: Shape-Shifting Among the Kuranko of Sierra Leone." In *Personhood and Agency: The Experience of Self and Other in African Cultures*, ed. Michael Jackson and Ivan Karp. Uppsala Studies in Cultural Anthropology: Uppsala, Sweden.

Jacob, Alain

1974   *Bronzes de l'Afrique noire.* Paris: Musée de l' Homme.

Jacobs, Alan H.

1979   "Maasai Inter-Tribal Relations: Belligerent Herdsmen or Peaceable Pastoralists?" In *Warfare Among East African Herders*, ed. Katsuyoshi Fukui and David Turton. Suita, Osaka, Japan: National Museum of Ethnology.

Jeannin, Albert

1947   *L'Éléphant d'Afrique.* Paris: Payot.

Jewsiewicki, Bogumil

1983   "Rural Society and the Belgian Colonial Economy." In *History of Central Africa*, Vol. 2, ed. David Birmingham and Phyllis M. Martin, 95-125. London: Longman.

Johnson, Marion

1978   "By Ship or By Camel: The Struggle for the Cameroons Ivory Trade in the Nineteenth Century." *Journal of African History* 19 (4):539-49.

Johnston, Harry A.

1908   *George Grenfell and the Congo.* 2 vols. London: Hutchinson & Co.

Johnston, William R.

1985   "Later Ivories." In *Masterpieces of Ivory,* ed. Richard H. Randall. New York: Hudson Hills Press.

Jonas, Frank M.

1928   *Netsuke.* Rutland, Vt.: Charles E. Tuttle.

Jones, G.I.

1984   *The Art of Eastern Nigeria.* Cambridge: Cambridge University Press.

Junker, Wilhelm

1890-92   *Travels in Africa during the Years 1875-1878*, Vol. 1; *1879-1883,* Vol. 2; *1882-1886,* Vol. 3. Trans. A.H. Keane. London: Chapman and Hall, Ltd.

Kasfir, Sidney

forthcoming   "The Idoma and their Lands." In *Sculpture of the Benue River Valley,* ed. Berns, Marla, and Arnold Rubin. Los Angeles: Fowler Museum of Cultural History.

Kecskési, Maria

1987   *African Masterpieces and Selected Works from Munich: The Staatliches Museum für Völkerkunde.* New York: Center for African Art.

Keim, Curtis A.

1983   "Long-Distance Trade and the Mangbetu." *Journal of African History* 24 (1):1-22.

Kenny, Michael G.

1981   "A Mirror in the Forest: the Dorobo Hunter-Gatherers as an Image of the Other." *Africa* 51 (1):477-95.

Kerchache, Jacques, Jean-Louis Paudrat, and Lucien Stéphan
1988   *Africain.* Paris: Édition Citadelles.

Keyes, George S. et al.
1990   *Mirror of Empire. Dutch Marine Art of the Seventeenth Century.* Cambridge: The Minneapolis Institute of Arts and Cambridge University Press.

Kirtley, Michael, and Aubine Kirtley
1982   "The Ivory Coast – African Success Story." *National Geographic* 162 (1).

Kjersmeier, Carl
1937 [1967]   *Centres de style de la sculpture nègre africaine. Volume III: Congo Belge.* New York: Hacker Art Books.

Klein, Richard G.
1983   "The Stone Age Prehistory of Southern Africa." *Annual Reviews in Anthropology* 12:25-48.

Klein, Robert G.
1984   "Mammalian Extinctions and Stone Age People in Africa." In *Quaternary Extinctions,* ed. Paul S. Martin and Richard G. Klein, 553-73. Tucson: University of Arizona Press.

Klopper, Sandra
1985   "Speculations on Lega Figurines." *African Arts* 19 (1):64-69.

Klumpp, Donna Rey
1987   "Maasai Art and Society: Age and Sex, Time and Space, Cash and Cattle (Kenya)." Ph.D. diss., Columbia University.

Knappert, Jan
1971   *Myths and Legends of the Congo.* London: Heinemann.

Koloss, Hans-Joachim
1977   Kamerun-Könige, Masken, Feste. *Ethnologische Forschungen im Grasland der Nordwest-Provinz von Kamerun.* Stuttgart: s.n.

Kratz, Corinne Ann
1981   "Are the Okiek Really Maasai? or Kipsigis? or Kikuyu?" *Cahiers d'Etudes Africaines* 79, 20 (3):355-68.
1988   "Emotional Power and Significant Movement: Womanly Transformation in Okiek Initiation." Ph.D. diss., University of Texas (Austin).

Kreutzer, Lynne A.
1988   "Megafaunal Butchering at Lubbock Lake, Texas: A Taphonomic Re-analysis." *Quaternary Research* 30:221-31.

Krieger, Kurt
1969   *Westafrikanische Plastik III.* Berlin: Museum für Völkerkunde Berlin.

Krieger, Kurt, and Gerdt Kutscher
1960   *Westafrikanische Masken.* Berlin: Museum für Völkerkunde Berlin.

Kriger, Colleen
1988   "Robes of the Sokoto Caliphate," *African Arts* 21 (3):28-31.

Kuchta, Ronald A.
1973   *Antelopes and Elephants, Hornbills and Hyenas: Animals in African Art.* Santa Barbara, Ca.: The Santa Barbara Museum of Art.

Kun, M. de
1966   "L'Art Lega." *Africa-Tervuren* XII (3-4).

Kuhn, S.L.
1989   "Projectile Weapons and Investment in Food Procurement Technology in the Eurasian Middle Paleolithic [abstract]." *American Journal of Physical Anthropology* 78:256.

Kunz, George F.
1916   *Ivory and the Elephant in Art, in Archaeology, and in Science.* New York: Doubleday.

Kühnel, Ernst
1971   *Die Islamischen Elfenbeinskupturen.* Berlin: Duetscher Verl. f. Kunstwissenschaft.

Kuper, Hilda
1973   "Costume and Cosmology: The Animal Symbolism of The Ncweala." *Man* 8 (4):613-30.

Kyerematen, A.A.Y.
1961   *Regalia for an Ashanti Durbar.* Accra: Kwame Nkrumah University of Science and Technology.
1964   *Panoply of Ghana.* London: Longmans.
1969-70   *Kingship and Ceremony in Ashanti: Dedicated to the memory of Otumfuo Sir Osei Agyeman Prempeh II, Asantehene.* Kumasi: UST Press.
1977   *Durbar: In Honour of His Royal Highness the Prince of Wales.* Program printed in Dwaberem, Manhyia, Kumasi, (21 March).

Labouret, Henri
1934   *Les manding et leur langue.* Paris: Larose.

Lafontaine, Raymond H., and Patricia A. Wood
1982   "The Stabilization of Ivory Against Relative Humidity Fluctuations." *Studies in Conservation* 27:109-17.

Lagae, C.R.
1926   *Les Azande ou Niam-Niam: L'organisat zande, croyances, religieuses et magiques, coûtumes familiales.* Séries Bibliothèque-Congo, Vol. 18. Brussels: Vroman and Co.

Laitman, Jeffery T.
1984   "The Anatomy of Human Speech." *Natural History* 93:20-27.

Landolphe, J.F.
1823   *Mémoires du capitaine Landolphe, contenant l'histoire de ses voyages,* 2 vols., ed. J.S. Quesne. Paris: A. Bertrand.

Landy, Susan L.
1989   "CITES: Banning the Ivory Trade – An Attempt to Save the African Elephant from Extinction." *International Law Journal* 5 (1):111-22.

Lange, Kofi Ron, tran.
1990   *Three Thousand Six Hundred Ghanian Proverbs (From the Asante and Fante Language).* Lewiston, N.Y.: Edwin Mellen Press.

Laursen, L., and M. Bekoff
1978   "Loxodonta africana." *Mammalian Species* 92:1-8.

Law, Robin
1973   "Traditional History." In *Sources of Yoruba History,* ed. S. O. Biobaku, 25-40. Oxford: Clarendon Press.
1983   "Trade and Politics Behind the Slave Coast: The Lagoon Traffic and the Rise of Lagos." *Journal of African History* 24:327-33.
1986   "Early European Sources Relating to the Kingdom of Ijebu (1500-1700): A Critical Survey." *History in Africa* 13:245-60.

Laws, R.M.
1966   "Age Criteria for the African Elephant *(Loxodonta a. africana).*" *East African Wildlife Journal* 4:1-37.
1970   "Biology of African Elephants." *Sci. Progr. Oxf.* 1 (58):251-62.
1978   "Déja vu." *Swara* 1 (3):126-28.

Laws, R.M., et al.
1975   *Elephants and their Habitats: The Ecology of Elephants in North Bunyoro, Uganda.* Oxford: Clarendon Press.

Leakey, Richard
1991   "Introduction." In *Elephants: the Deciding Decade,* ed. Ronald Orenstein. Toronto: Key Porter Books, Ltd.
1992   "A Wildlife Director's Historical Perspective." In *Elephants,* ed. J. Shoshani. Emmaus, Penn.: Rodale Press.

Lecoq, Raymond
1953   *Les Bamileke.* Paris: Présence Africaine.

Lévi-Strauss, Claude
1963   *Totemism.* Boston: Beacon Press (London: Merlin Press, 1964).
1969   *The Raw and the Cooked.* New York: Harper and Row.

Levtzion, Nehemia
1977   "The Western Maghrib and Sudan." In *The Cambridge History of Africa,* Vol. 3, ed. Roland Oliver. Cambridge: Cambridge University Press.

Levtzion, Nehemiah, and J.F.P. Hopkins, eds.
1981   *Corpus of Early Arabic Sources for West African History.* Cambridge.

References Cited

Lewis-Williams, J. David

1988 *The World of Man and the World of Spirit: An Interpretation of the Linton Rock Paintings*. Margaret Shaw Lecture 2. Cape Town: The South African Museum.

1983a *The Rock Art of Southern Africa*. Cambridge: Cambridge University Press.

1983b (ed.) *New Approaches to Southern African Rock Art*. The South African Archaeological Society, Goodwin Series, Vol. 4. Cape Town.

1981 *Believing and Seeing: Symbolic Meaning in Southern San Rock Paintings*. New York: Academic Press Inc.

Lhote, Henri

1973 *The Search for the Tassili Frescoes*. London: Hutchinson.

Lienhardt, Godfrey

1961 *Divinity and Experience: The Religion of the Dinka*. Oxford: Clarendon Press.

Ligers, Z.

1960 "La chasse à l'éléphant chez les Bozo." *Journal de la Société des Africanistes* 30:95-99.

Little, Kenneth

1967 *The Mende of Sierra Leone*. London: Routledge and K. Paul.

Littlewood, Margaret

1954 "The Bamileke of the French Cameroons." In *Peoples of the Central Cameroons*. Ethnographic Survey of Africa IX. London: International African Institute.

Livingstone, David

1865 [1971] *Narrative of an Expedition to the Zambesi and its Tributaries; and of the Discovery of the Lakes Shirwa and Nyassa 1858-1864*. London: John Murray, Albemarle Street. Johnson Reprint Corporation, N.Y. as part of *Landmarks in Anthropology*, Gen. ed., Weston La Barre.)

Long, Chaille C.

1871 *Central Africa: Naked Truths of Naked People. An Account of Expeditions to the Lake Victoria Nyanza and the Makraka Niam-Niam West of the Bahr el-Abiad (White Nile)*. New York: Harper & Brothers.

Lovejoy, C. Owen

1981 "The Origin of Man." *Science* 211:341-50.

Luschan, Felix von

1919 *Die Altertumer von Benin*. Berlin: Vereinigung Wissneschaft Licher Verlager.

Macdonald, David

1984 *The Encyclopedia of Mammals*. New York: Facts on File.

Macfie, D.F.

1916 "A Case of Triplets in an Elephant." *Journal of the National History Society of Siam* 1:53.

Mack, John

1990 "Art, Culture and Tribute Among the Azande." In *African Reflections: Art from Northeastern Zaire*, ed. Enid Schildkrout and Curtis A. Keim. Seattle: University of Washington Press.

1991 *Emil Torday and the Art of the Congo 1900-1909*. Seattle: University of Washington Press.

Maes, Joseph

1924 *Aniota-Kifwebe: Les masques des populations du Congo belge et le matériel des rites de circoncision*. Anvers: Editions de Sikkel.

Maesen, Albert

1960 *Umbangu: art du Congo au Musée Royal du Congo belge*. Brussels.

Mage, Abdon Eugene

1868 *Voyage dans le Soudan occidental (Sénégambie, Niger), 1863-1866*. Paris.

Maggs, T.M. O'C., and J. Sealy

1983 "Elephants in Boxes." In *New Approaches to Southern African Rock Art*, ed. J. D. Lewis-Williams. Goodwin Series 4. Cape Town: The South African Archaeological Society

Maglio, Vincent J.

1973 "Origin and Evolution of the Elephantidae." *Transactions of the American Philosophical Society* 63 (3:)11-49.

Mair, Lucy P.

1934 *An African People in the Twentieth Century*. London: G. Routledge and Sons.

Marchmay, T.A.

1921 "Making Billiard Balls from Ivory." *Scientific American Monthly* 3 (4): 316-18.

Marees, Pieter de

1602 [1987] *Description and Historical Account of the Gold Kingdom of Guinea (1602)*. Trans. Albert van Dantzig and Adam Jones. New York: Oxford University Press.

Marks, Stuart A.

1976 *Large Mammals and a Brave People: Subsistence Hunters in Zambia*. Seattle: University of Washington Press.

Marshall, Lawrence

1985 "Geochronology and Land-Mammal Biochronology of the Transamerican Faunal Exchange." In *The Great American Biotic Interchange*, ed. Francis G. Stehli and S. David Webb, 49-85. New York: Plenum Press.

Marshall Lorna

1981 "Foreword." In *Believing and Seeing: Symbolic Meaning in Southern San Rock Paintings*, J. David Lewis-Williams. New York: Academic Press Inc.

Martin, Esmond Bradley

1985 "Malawi's Ivory Carving Industry,' *Pachyderm: Newsletter of the African Elephant and Rhino Specialist Group* (July): 6-11.

1986 "The Ivory Carving Industry of Zambia," *Pachyderm: Newsletter of the African Elephant and Rhino Specialist Group* (December):12-18.

1991 "The Effects of the International Ivory Bans on Zimbabwe's Ivory Industry," *Swara* November/December 14 (6):26-28.

Martin, Paul S.

1984 "Prehistoric Overkill: The Global Model." In *Quaternary Extinctions*, ed. Paul S. Martin and Richard G. Klein. Tucson: University of Arizona Press.

Martin, Paul S., and Richard G. Klein, eds.

1984 *Quaternary Extinctions*. Tucson: University of Arizona Press.

Martin, Phyllis

1970 "The Trade of Loango in the Seventeenth and Eighteenth Centuries." In *Pre-colonial African Trade: Essays on Trade in Central and Eastern Africa before 1900*, ed. Richard Gray and D. Bermin. London: Oxford University Press.

1972 *The External Trade of the Loango Coast 1576-1870*. Oxford: Clarendon Press.

1983 "The Violence of Empire." In *History of Central Africa*, Vol. 2, ed. David Birmingham and Phyllis M. Martin, 1-26. London: Longman.

Marzke, Mary W., and Myra S. Shackley

1986 "Hominid Hand Use in the Pliocene and Pleistocene: Evidence from Experimental Archaeology and Comparative Morphology." *Journal of Human Evolution* 15:439-60.

Maskell, Alfred

1905 *Ivories*. London: Methuen & Co.

Maud, Chez, and René Garcia

1987 "Les Ijo, Oturkpo & Nkporo," *Arts d'Afrique Noire* (autumn):34-37.

Maugham, R.C.F.

1906 *Portuguese East Africa: The History, Scenery, & Great Game of Manica and Sofala*. New York: E.P. Dutton.

Mauny, Raymond

1961 *Tableau géographique de l'Ouest africain au moyen age d'après les sources écrites, la tradition et l'archéologie*. Dakar: IFAN.

1954 *Gravure, peinture et inscriptions rupestres de l'ouest africain*. Intitiations Africaines XI Dakar: Institut Français d'Afrique Noire.

McCaskie, T.C.

1983 "Accumulation, Wealth and Belief in Asante History." *Africa* 53 (1): 25-43.

McLeod, M.D.

1971 "Goldweights in Asante." *African Arts* 5 (1):8-15.

1981 *Asante*. London: British Museum.

McLeod, Malcolm

1976 "Verbal Elements in African Art." *Quaderni Poro 1*. Milan.

McNaughton, Patrick R.

1979　*Secret Sculptures of Komo: Art and Power in Bamana (Bambara) Initiation Societies.* Philadelphia: Institute for the Study of Human Issues.

1991　"Is There History in Horizontal Masks? A Preliminary Response to the Dilemma of Form," *African Arts* 24 (2):40-53, 88-90.

Meester, J., and H.W. Setzer, eds.

1971　*The Mammals of Africa: An Identification Manual.* Washington, D.C.: Smithsonian Institution Press.

Merab, Docteur

1921　*Impressions d'Éthiopie (L'Abyssinie sous Mènèlik II).* 3 vols. Paris: H. Libert.

Mercier, Paul

1952　*Les ase du musée d'Abomey.* Catalogues VII. Dakar: Institut Français d'Afrique Noire.

Merker, Meritz

1910　*Die Masai.* Berlin: D. Reimer.

Meyerowitz, Eva

1940　"Four Pre-Portuguese Bronze Castings from Benin." *Man* 40 (September):129-32,155-78

1951　*The Sacred State of the Akan.* London: Faber and Faber.

Midgely, Mary

1988　"Beasts, Brutes and Monsters." *What is an Animal?* ed. T. Ingold, pp. 35-46. *One World Archaeology*, Vol. 1. London: Unwin Hyman.

Miller, Joseph C.

1970　"Cokwe trade and conquest in the nineteenth century." In *Pre-Colonial African Trade*, ed. Richard Gray and David Birmingham. London.

1983　"The paradoxes of impoverishment in the Atlantic zone." In *History of Central Africa*, Vol. 1, ed. David Birmingham and Phyllis M. Martin, 118-59. London: Workman.

Milliken, Tom

1985　"Recent Developments in the Japanese Ivory Trade and the Implementation of Cites in Japan." In *Pachyderm: Newsletter of the African Elephant and Rhino Specialist Group* (July):15-16.

Mmanwu Festival '88

1988　*Anambra State Mmanwu Festival Program.* Enugu: Ministry of Information, Social Development, Youth, Sports and Culture.

Mmanwu Festival '90

1990　"Masquerade as as Entertainer." *1990 Mmanwu Festival Program.* Enugu: Ministry of Information, Social Development, Youth, Sports and Culture.

Mongory, Jonathan

1980　"An African Carnival: The "Do-Do" of Ouagadougou," *Balafon*, October (49):13-17. Abidjan: Air Afrique.

Monod, Theodore

1963　"Late Tertiary and Pleistocene Sahara." In *African Ecology and Human Evolution*, ed. F. Clark Howell and François Bourliere. Chicago: Aldine Co.

Montandon, George

1913　*Au Pays Gimirrha (1909-1911).* Paris: A. Challamel.

Montgomery, Sy

1988　"A Crisis in East Africa." *Los Angeles Times* (April 4).

Moore, Deima, and F.G. Guggisberg

1909　*We Two in West Africa.* London: Heinemann.

Moore, Ernst D.

1931　*Ivory: Scourge of Africa.* New York: Harper & Brothers.

Moorehead, Alan

1960　*The White Nile.* London: H. Hamilton.

Morrison-Scott, T.C.S.

1947　"A Revision of our Knowledge of African Elephants' Teeth with Notes on Forest and 'Pygmy' Elephants." *Proceedings of the Zoological Society of London* 117:505-27.

Morton-Williams, P.

1960　"The Yoruba Ogboni Cult in Oyo." *Africa* 30:362-74.

Moss, Cynthia

1988　*Elephant Memories.* New York: William Morrow.

1990　"The Young Ones." *BBC Wildlife* 8 (11):738-44.

Moume Etia, Leopold

1984　*Mbasa. Proverbes Duala.* Langues et Litteratures Nationales 15. Douala: College Libermann.

Mulyumba wa Mamba, Itongwa

1973　"Les proverbes, un langage didactique dans les sociétés africaines traditionnelles. Le cas des Balega-Bashíle." *Les Cahiers du CEDAF*, Series 4, no. 8.

1978　"Aperçu sur la structure politique des Balega-Basile." *Les Cahiers du CEDAF*, Series 1, no. 1.

Mulyumba, Barnabé

1968　"La croyance religieuse des Lega traditionnels." *Etudes congolaises* 11 (3): 1-14; 11 (4):3-19.

Mumcuoglu, Kostas Y., and Joseph Zias

1989　"How the Ancients De-Loused Themselves." *Biblical Archaeology Review* 15 (6):66-69.

Munamuhega, Ndambi

1975　*Les masques pende de Ngudi.* Série II, Vol. 23. Bandundu: Ceeba Publications.

Muriuki, G.

1976　"The Kikuyu in the Pre-Colonial Period." In *Kenya Before 1900*, ed. B.A. Ogot. Nairobi: East African Publishing House.

Murray, N.

1976　*The Love of Elephants.* London: Octopus Books.

Nassau, R.H.

1912　*Where Animals Talk: Tales from West Africa.* Boston: Richard G. Badger.

Neaher, Nancy Christine

1976　*Bronzes of Southern Nigeria and Igbo Metalsmithing Traditions.* Unpublished dissertation, Stanford University.

Newbury, C.W.

1966　"North African and Western Sudan Trade in the Nineteenth Century: a Re-evaluation." *Journal of African History* 7 (2):233-46.

Newman, Barry

1991　"Mammoths May Be Extinct, but They Save the Elephants." *Wall Street Journal* (July 16):Al,A10.

Neyt, François

1973　"Les motifs décoratifs des itumba leele: étude ethnomorphologique," *Revue des archéologues et historiens d'art de Louvain,* Louvain-la-Neuve: 189-206.

1981　*Traditional Arts and History of Zaire.* Brussels: Société d'Arts Primitifs et Institut Supérieur d'Archéologie et d'Histoire de l'Art.

Niane, D.T.

1984　"Mali and the Second Mandingo Expansion." In *General History of Africa*, Vol. 4, ed. D.T. Niane. Berkeley: University of California Press.

Niangoran-Bouah, Georges

1987　*The Akan World of Gold Weights: The Weights and Society.* Paris: Les Nouvelles Editions Africaines - M.L.B.

Nicklin, Keith

1982　"Kuyu Sculpture at the Powell-Cotton Museum," *African Arts* 17 (1): 55-59, 88.

1982　"The Cross River Bronzes." In *The Art of Metal in Africa*, ed. Marie-Térèse Brincard. New York: African American Institute.

Nkamgang, S.M.

1970　*Les contes and légendes du bamileke.* Yaounde: Édition de l'Auteur.

Norden, Hermann

c.1925　*Fresh Tracks in the Belgian Congo.* Boston: Small, Maynard & Company.

1930　*Durch Abessinien und Eryträa.* Berlin: Scherl.

Northern, Tamara

1975 *The Sign of the Leopard: Beaded Art of Cameroon*. Storrs, Conn.: The William Benton Museum of Art, University of Connecticut.

1984 *The Art of Cameroon*. Washington, D.C.: Smithsonian Institution.

Nott, J.F.

1886 *Wild Animals Photographed and Described*. London: Low, Marston, Searle, and Rivington.

Novacek, M.J., and A.R. Wyss

1986 "Higher-Level Relationships of the Recent Eutherian Orders: Morphological Evidence." *Cladistics* 2:257-87.

Nunley, John

forthcoming *Jolly Masquerades of Sierra Leone: Colonization and Creolization*. Los Angeles: Fowler Museum of Cultural History.

Nurse, Derek, and Thomas Spear

1985 *The Swahili: Reconstructing the History and Language of an African Society, 800-1500*. Philadelphia: University of Pennsylvania Press.

Nyendael, David van

1705 [1967] "A Description of the Rio Formosa, or the River of Benin." In *A New and Accurate Description of the Coast of Guinea*, ed. W. Bosman. London: Cass.

Nzekwu, Onuora

1963 "Ivory Ornaments." *Nigeria Magazine* 77:105-16.

Olatunji, Olatunde

1982 *Adebayo Faleti: A Study of His Poems, 1954-1964*. Ibadan: Heinemann Educational Books.

1984 *Features of Yoruba Oral Poetry*. Ibadan: University Press.

Ole Saitoti, Tepilit, and Carol Beckwith

1980 *Maasai*. New York: Abrams.

Olindo, Perez

1991 "An African Perspective." In *Elephants: the Deciding Decade*, ed. Ronald Orenstein. Toronto: Key Porter Books, Ltd.

Olivier, R.C.D.

1978 "Present Status of the Asian Elephant (*Elephas maximus*)." *Elephant* 1 (2):15-17.

Omijeh, Matthew

1975 "Some Notes on the Significance of Orhue (Native White Chalk) in Bini Symbolism." *The Nigerian Field* (December):184-91.

Onwuejeogwu, M. Angulu

1981 *An Igbo Civilization: Nri Kingdom and Hegemony*. London: Ethnographica.

Osborn, H.F.

1936 *Proboscidea*, Vol. 1. New York: The American Museum of Natural History.

1942 *Proboscidea*, Vol. 2. New York: The American Museum of Natural History.

Orenstein, Ronald, ed.

1991 *Elephants: the Deciding Decade*. Toronto: Key Porter Books, Ltd.

Owen, Richard

1856 "The Ivory and Teeth of Commerce." *Journal of the Society of Arts* 5 (213): 65-72.

Pager, Harald

1975 *Stone Age Myth and Magic*, Graz: Akademische Druck-u. Verlagsanstalt.

Park, Mungo

1983 *Travels into the Interior of Africa*. London: Eland.

Parker, I., and M. Amin

1983 *Ivory Crisis*. London: Chatto and Windus.

Parker, I.S.C., and Esmond Bradley Martin

1982 "How Many Elephants are Killed for the Ivory Trade?" *Oryx* 16 (3):235-39.

1983 "Further Insight into the International Ivory Trade." *Oryx* 17 (4):194-200.

Partridge, E.

1963 *Origins: A Short Etymological Dictionary of Modern English*. New York: Macmillan.

Pasha, Emin [Eduard Schnitzer]

1889 *Emin Pasha in Central Africa* [letters and journals], ed. Georg Schweinfurth et al. New York: Dodd.

Patten, R.A.

1940 "'Jessie' Joins Her Ancestors." *Parks and Recreation* 23 (5):200-202.

Paulitschke, Phillip

1893 *Ethnographie Nordost-Afrikas. Die materielle Kultur der Danakil, Galla und Somal*. Berlin: D. Reiner.

Payne, K.

1989 "Elephant Talk." *National Geographic* 176 (2):264-77.

Payne, K.B. et al.

1986 "Infrasonic Calls of the Asian Elephant (*Elephas maximus*)." *Behavioral Ecology and Sociobiology* 18:297-301.

Paz, Octavio

1970 *Claude Lévi-Strauss: An Introduction*. Ithaca, N.Y.: Cornell University Press.

Percival, MacIver

1920 *The Fan Book*. London: T. Fisher Unwin, Ltd.

Pereira, Duarte Pacheco

1505 [1937] *Esmeraldo de Situ Orbis*. Trans. and ed. G. Kimble. London: The Hakluyt Society.

Perlez, Jane

1990 "Ban on Ivory Trading is Reported to Force Cutbacks at Factories," *New York Times*, May 22.

Perrois, Françoise

1985 *Ancestral Art of Gabon: From the Collections of the Barbier-Mueller Museum*. Geneva: The Museum.

Person, Yves

1968 *Samori, une révolution dyula*. 3 vols. Dakar: IFAN.

Petherick, Mr. and Mrs.

1869 *Travels in Central Africa*. London: Tinsley Brothers.

Petri von Hartenfels, G.C.

c.1723 *Elephantographia curiosa, Editio altera auctior et emendator, cui accessit ejusdem auctoris oratio panegyrica de Elephantis, nec non Justi Lipsii epistola de endoem argumento erudite conscripta*. Lipsiae et Erfordiae. Typis Joh. Mich. Funckii.

Philippovich, Eugen Von

1982 *Elfenbein*. Munich: Klinkhardt & Biermann.

Picton, John

1989 "Ekpeya Masks and Masking." *African Arts* 21 (2):46-53,94.

Pillai, N.G.

1941 "On the Height and Age of an Elephant." *Journal of Bombay Natural History Society* 42:927-28.

Plimmer, Charlotte, and Denis Plimmer

1951 "White Treasure from the Dark Continent." *Saturday Evening Post* (November 24):32-33,73-74.

Plowden, Walter Chichele

1868 *Travels in Abyssinia and the Galla Country with an Account of a Mission to Ras Ali in 1848*, ed. Trevor Chichele Plowden. London: Longmans, Green and Co.

Polet, Jean, and B. Saison

1981 "Enceintes fortifiées de la séguié." *Recherches, Pédagogie et Culture* 55: 52-55.

Poole, Joyce H.

1992 "Kenya's Elephants – A Very Different Story to Tell." *Swara*, Jan./Feb. 15 (1):29-31.

Poole, J.H., and C.J. Moss
1981   "Musth in the African Desert (*Loxodonta africana*)." *Nature* 292 (5826): 830-31.

Poole, J.H. et al.
1988   "The Social Contexts of Some Very Low Frequency Calls of African Elephants." *Behavioral Ecology and Sociobiology* 22:385-92.

Poole, J.H., and Jorgen B. Thomsen
1989   "Elephants are not Beetles: Implications of the Ivory Trade for the Survival of the African Elephant." *Oryx* 23 (4):188-98.

Poynor, Robin
1976   "Edo Influence on the Arts of Owo." *African Arts* 9 (4):40-45,90-91.
1978   "The Ancestral Arts of Owo, Nigeria." Ph.D diss., Indiana University.

Preston, George Nelson
1972   "Twifo-Heman and the Akan Leadership Complex." Ph.D. diss., Columbia University.

Prost, R.P. André
1953   *Les langues mandé-sud du groupe mana-busa*. Dakar: IFAN, mémoire no. 26.

Quarcoo, A.K.
1975   *Leadership Art*. Legon: Institute of African Studies.

Quarcoopome, Nii
n.d.   *British Colonial Medals and the Transformation of Ghanaian Society in the 19th and 20th Century*. Unpublished manuscript.

Rachewiltz, Boris de
1960   *Africkanische Kunst*. Zurich: Artemis Verlag.

Racine, R.N.
1980   "Behavior Associated with Feeding in Captive African and Asian Elephants." *Elephant* 1:57-71.

Raffray, Achille
1876   *Abyssinie (Ouvrage enrichi d'une arte spéciale et de gravures sur bois dessinés par L. Breton, d'après des aquarelles et des croquis de l'auteur)*. Paris: E. Plon.

Randall, Richard H., Jr., ed.
1985   *Masterpieces of Ivory*. New York: Hudson Hills Press.

Randall, Richard H., Jr., and Christian Theuerkauff
1985   "Renaissance and Baroque Ivories." In *Masterpieces of Ivory*, ed. Richard H. Randall, Jr. New York: Hudson Hills Press.

Rattray, Robert Sutherland
1916 [1969]   *Ashanti Proverbs: the Primitive Ethics of a Savage People*. Oxford: Oxford University Press.
1923 [1969]   *Ashanti*. Oxford: Oxford University Press.
1927 [1959]   *Religion and Art in Ashanti*. Oxford: Oxford University Press.
1929   *Ashanti Law and Constitution*. Oxford: Oxford University Press.
1930   *Akan-Ashanti Folk Tales*. Oxford: Clarendon Press.

Ravenhill, Philip L.
1976   *The Social Organization of the Wan: A Patrilineal People of Ivory Coast*. Ann Arbor: University Microfilms.
1980   *Baule Statuary Art: Meaning and Modernization*. Working Papers in the Traditional Arts, No. 5. Philadelphia: ISHI.
1984   "The Do Traditions of Northwestern Ivory Coast." Paper read at the Annual Meeting of the African Studies Association, Los Angeles.
1986   "Horizontal Helmet Masks of Central Ivory Coast: The Historical Implications." Paper read at the Seventh Triennial Symposium on African Art, Los Angeles.
1988   "The Do Masquerade of the Wan: Comparative Identities of Spirit Powers." Paper read at the Annual Meeting of the African Studies Association, Denver.
1989   "An African Triptych: On the Interpretation of Three Parts and the Whole." *Art Journal* 47 (2)88-94.

Redmond, I.M., and J. Shoshani
1987   "Mount Elgon's Elephants are in Peril." *Elephant* 2 (3):46-66.

Reefe, Thomas Q.
1983   "The Societies of the Eastern Savanna." In *History of Central Africa*, Vol. 1, ed. David Birmigham and Phyllis M. Martin. London: Longman.

Rein, Georg Kurt
1919-20   *Abessinien. Eine Landeskunde nach Reisin und Studien in den Jahren 1907-1913*. 3 vols. Berlin: D. Reimer.

Ricciardi, Mirella
1971   *Vanishing Africa*. London: Collins.

Ricks, Thomas M.
1970   "Persian Gulf Seafaring and East Africa: Ninth-Twelfth Centuries." *African Historical Studies* 3 (2):339-57.

Rikli, Martin
1947   *Seltsames Abessinien*. Zürich: Interverlag.

Roberts, Andrew D.
1970   "Nyamwezi Trade." In *Pre-Colonial African Trade*, ed. Richard Gray and David Birmingham. London: Oxford University Press.

Roberts, Arthur
1951   *The Mammals of South Africa*. Cape Town: Central News Agency, for Trustees of "The Mammals of South Africa" Book Fund.

Rodney, Walter
1970   *A History of the Upper Guinea Coast 1545-1800*. Oxford: Clarendon Press.

Romer, A.S.
1966   *Vertebrate Paleontology*. 3rd Edition. Chicago: University of Chicago Press.

Roosevelt, Theodore
1910   *African Game Trails*. New York: Scribner's.

Roscoe, John
1911   *The Baganda: An Account of Their Native Customs and Beliefs*. London: MacMillan.

Ross, Doran H.
1977   "The Iconography of Asante Sword Ornaments." *African Arts* 8 (1):16-25,90-91.
1979   "Fighting with Art: Appliqued Flags of the Fante Asafo." Los Angeles: UCLA Museum of Cultural History Pamphlet Series, I,5.
1980   "Cement Lions and Cloth Elephants: Popular Arts of the Fante Asafo." In *Five Thousand Years of Popular Culture: Popular Culture before Printing*, ed. Fred E. H. Schroeder. Bowling Green, Oh.: Bowling Green University Press.
1982a   "The Heraldic Lion in Akan Art: A Study of Motif Assimilation in Southern Ghana." *Metropolitan Museum Journal* 16:165-80.
1982b   "The Verbal Art of Akan Linguist Staffs." *African Arts* 16 (1):56-67,95.
1984   "The Art of Osei Bonsu." *African Arts* 17 (2):28-40,90.

Roth, Henry Ling
1903   *Great Benin, Its Customs, Art, and Horrors*. Halifax: F. King & Sons.

Roth, Matthew
1981   *Connecticut: An Inventory of Historic Engineering and Industrial Sites*. Washington, D.C.: Society for Industrial Archaeology.

Routledge, W. Scoresby, and Katherine Routledge
1910   *With a Prehistoric People: the Akikuyu of British East Africa*. London: E. Arnold.

Rowland, B.
1970   *The Art and Architecture of India: Buddhist / Hindu / Jain*. Baltimore: Penguin Books.

Rubin, Arnold
forthcoming   "Jukun Art in its Cultural and Historical Context." In Berns, Marla, and Arnold Rubin, *Sculpture of the Benue River Valley* (forthcoming).

Rudin, Harry R.
1938 [1968]   *Cameroons, 1884-1914: A Case Study in Modern Imperialism*. New Haven: Yale University Press.

Ruel, Malcolm

1969   *Leopards and Leaders: Constitutional Politics Among a Cross River People.* London: Tavistock Publications.

Ruiters, D.R.

c. 1602[1905-07]   "A Description of Guinea." In *His Pilgrimes,* ed. S. Purchas, Vol. 6, 353-59. Glasgow: J. MacLehose.

Rüger, Adolf

1968   "Die Duala und de Kolonialmacht 1884-1914. Eine Studie uber die historischen Ursprunge des afrikanischen Antikolonialismus." In *Kamerun unter deutscher Kolonialherrschaft,* ed. Helmuth Stoecker, 181-259. Berlin: VEB Deutscher Verlag der Wissenschaften.

Ryder, A.F.C.

1969   *Benin and the Europeans.* Harlow, England: Longmans.

Sachs, Curt

1940   *The History of Musical Instruments.* New York: W.W. Norton.

Saito, Kim

1992   *A Primer to Endangered Species Law: Obtaining Federal Permits for Specimens Protected by Endangered Species Laws.* Washington D.C: Smithsonian Institution.

Salverte-Marmier, Philippe de, and M. A. de Salverte-Marmier

1962-64   "Les étapes de peuplement d'avant 1730." *1930 Etude Régionale de Bouaké,* Tome I:11-58. Abidjan: Ministère du Plan.

Sanderson, Ivan T.

1962   *The Dynasty of Abu: A History and Natural History of the Elephants and Their Relatives Past and Present.* New York: Alfred A. Knopf.

Sandrock, Leutnant

1902   *Bericht des stellvertretenden Stationschef von Banyo, Leutnant der Deutschen Schutztruppe für Kamerun Sandrock, über den Handel der Eingeborenen mit Landesprodukten.* National Archives Yaoundé, FA112:8-10.

Sassoon, Hamo

1975   *The Siwas of Lamu: Two Historic Trumpets in Brass and Ivory.* Nairobi: The Lamu Society.

Savage, Donald E., and Dale E. Russell

1983   *Mammalian Paleofaunas of the World.* London: Addison-Wesley Publishing Co.

Savage, Robert J.G., and M.R. Long

1986   *Mammal Evolution: An Illustrated Guide.* Oxford: Facts on File Publications.

Savary, Claude

1980   *Cameroun: Arts et cultures des peuples de l'Ouest.* Geneva: Musée d'Ethnographie Genève.

Schechner, Richard, and Willa Appel, eds.

1990   *By Means of Performance: Intercultural Studies of Theatre and Ritual.* Cambridge: Cambridge University Press.

Schildkrout, Enid, and Curtis A. Keim, eds.

1990   *African Reflections: Art from Northeastern Zaire.* Seattle: University of Washington Press.

Schwab, George

1947   *Tribes of the Liberian Hinterland.* Ed. with additional material by George W. Harley. Peabody Museum Papers, Vol. 31. Cambridge, Mass: The Peabody Museum of Archaeology and Ethnology.

Schweinfurth, Georg et al, eds.

1889   *Emin Pasha in Central Africa* [letters and journals]. New York: Dodd.

Schweinfurth, Georg

1874   *The Heart of Africa. Three Years' Travels and Adventures in the Unexplored Region of Central Africa from 1868 to 1871.* 2 vols. New York: Harper and Brothers.

1875   *Artes Africanae.* London: S. Low, Marston, Low, and Searle.

Scullard, Howard H.

1974   *The Elephant in the Greek and Roman World.* Ithaca, N.Y.: MacMillan Co.

Segy, Ladislas

1951   "Warega Ivories." *Zaïre* (December).

1953   "Circle-dot Symbolic Sign on African Ivory Carvings." *Zaïre* 7:35-54.

1976   *Masks of Black Africa.* New York: Dover Publications.

Seligman, C.G., and Brenda Z. Seligman

1932   *Pagan Tribes of the Nilotic Sudan.* London: G. Routledge and Sons, Ltd.

Seliquer, Capitaine

1943   "À propos d'éléphants." *Notes Africaines* (17):9.

Shackleford, Steve

1989   "Out of Africa: Ivory Prices Soar." *Blade Magazine* 16 (1):36-41,70-73.

Shaloff, Stanley

1970   *Reform in Leopold's Congo.* Richmond, Va.: John Knox Press.

Shanklin, Eugenia

1982   "Dancing History Lessons: A Catalogue of Jujus." Unpublished paper.

1990a   "The Odyssey of the Afo-a-Kom." *African Arts* 23 (4):62-69.

1990b   "The Track of the Python: A West African Origin Story." In *Signifying Animals,* ed. Roy Willis. London: Unwin Hyman.

Shaw, C.A., and J.P. Quinn

1986   "Rancho La Brea: A Look at Coastal Southern California's Past." *California Geology* 39 (6):123-33.

Shaw, Thurstan

1970   Igbo-Ukwu: An Account of Archaeological Discoveries in Eastern Nigeria. Evanston, Ill.: Northwestern University Press.

1978   *Nigeria: Its Archaeology and Early History.* London: Thames and Hudson.

Sheppard, William

1893   "Into the Heart of Africa." *Southern Workman* 22:182-87.

1917   *Presbyterian Pioneers in Congo.* Richmond, Va.: Presbyterian Committee of Publication.

Sheriff, Abdul M.H.

1971   "The Rise of a Commercial Empire: An Aspect of the Economic History of Zanzibar, 1770-1873." Ph.D. diss., School of Oriental and African Studies, University of London.

1987   *Slaves, Spices and Ivory in Zanzibar.* London: James Curry.

Shinnie, P.L.

1967   *Meroe: A Civilization of the Sudan.* New York: Frederick A. Praeger Pubs.

Shoshani, J.

1986   "Mammalian Phylogeny: Comparison of Morphological and Molecular Results." *Molecular Biology and Evolution* 3:222-42.

1991   "Elephant Migration." In *Fantastic Journeys: The Marvels of Animal Migration,* ed. R.R. Baker, 194-99. London: Merehurst.

1992   (ed.) *Elephants.* Emmaus, Penn.: Rodale Press.

Shoshani, J., and J.F. Eisenberg

1982   "*Elephas maximus.*" *Mammalian Species* 182:1-8.

Shoshani, J., C. Gans, F. Hensen-Smith, and C.S. Zajac

1990   "Elephant Trunk Musculature." Unpublished Manuscript.

Shoshani, J. et al.

1982   "On the Dissection of a Female Asian Elephant (*Elephas maximus maximus* Linnaeus, 1758) and Data from Other Elephants." *Elephant* 2 (1):3-93.

Shoshani, J., J.C. Hillman, and J.M. Walcek

1987   "'Ahmed', the Logo of the Elephant Interest Group: Encounters in Marsabit and Notes on his Model and Skeleton." *Elephant* 2 (3):7-32.

Shoshani, S.L., J. Shoshani, and F. Dahlinger, Jr.

1986   "Jumbo: Origin of the Word and History of the Elephant." *Elephant* 2 (2):86-122.

Sieber, Roy

1961   *Sculpture of Northern Nigeria.* New York: Museum of Primitive Art.

1972   *African Textiles and Decorative Arts.* New York: The Museum of Modern Art.

1980   *African Furniture & Household Objects.* New York: The American Federation of Arts.

Sikes, S.K.

1971   *The Natural History of the African Elephant.* London: Weidenfeld and Nicolson.

Silverman, Raymond

1986a "The Arts of Tano." Paper presented at the Seventh Triennial Symposium on African Art, Los Angeles.

1986b "Dress for Success: Adorning the Gods of the Akan." Paper presented at the African Studies Associaton Meeting, Madison, Wis.

Simpson, G.G.

1942 "Proboscidean Dental Histology." In *Proboscidea*, ed. H.F. Osborn, 1607-8. New York: American Museum Press.

Simpson, G.G., and Carlos de Paula Couto

1957 "The Mastodonts of Brazil." *Bulletin of the American Museum of Natural History* 112:125-89.

Sinclair, John

1967 *Twilight of the Wild*. Johannesburg: Hugh Keartland.

Siroto, Leon

1977 "Njom: The Magical Bridge of the Beti and Bulu of Southern Cameroon." *African Arts* 10 (2):38-51,90,91.

Sklertchly, J. Alfred

1875 *Dahomey as it is: being a narrative of eigth months' residence in that country...* London: Chapman and Hall.

Slade, Ruth

1962 *King Leopold's Congo*. London: Oxford University Press.

Smith, Alan

1970 "Delagoa Bay and the Trade of South-eastern Africa." In *Pre-Colonial African Trade*, ed. Richard Gray and David Birmingham. London: Oxford University Press.

1983 "The Indian Ocean Zone." In *History of Central Africa*, ed. David Birmingham and Phyllis M. Martin. London: Longman.

Smith, R.L.

1974 *Ecology and Field Biology*. 2nd Edition. New York: Harper & Row.

Smith, R.S.

1969 *Kingdoms of the Yoruba*. London: Methuen.

Smith, Edwin William, and Andrew Murray Dale

1968 *The Ila-Speaking Peoples*, Vol. 1. New Hyde Park: University Books.

Sofer, Olga

1988 "Late Paleolithic." In *Encyclopedia of Human Evolution and Prehistory*, ed. Ian Tattersall, Eric Delson, and John A. Van Couvering, 304-12. New York: Garland Press.

Spinage, C.A.

1973 "A Review of Ivory Exploitation and Elephant Population Trends in Africa." *East African Wildlife Journal* 11:281-89.

Spuhler, J.N.

1988 "Evolution of Mitochondrial DNA in Monkeys, Apes, and Humans." *American Journal of Physical Anthropology* 31:15-18.

St. Clair, Archer, and Elizabeth Parker McLachlan, eds.

1989 *The Carver's Art: Medieval Sculpture in Ivory, Bone, and Horn*. New Brunswick, N.J.: Rutgers University Press.

Stammers, M.K.

1983 *Ships' Figureheads*. Shire Album 109. Aylesbury, Bucks, UK: Shire Publications, Ltd.

Stanley, Henry M.

1872 *Thirty Years Adventures and Discoveries of Dr. David Livingstone and the Herald-Stanley Expedition*. Philadelphia: Hubbard Bros.

1878 *Through the Dark Continent*. New York: Harper & Brothers.

1885 *The Congo and the Founding of its Free State: A Story of Work and Exploration*. Volume II. New York: Harper and Brothers.

1890 *In Darkest Africa or, the Quest, Rescue and Retreat of Emin, Governor of Equatoria*. 2 vols. New York: Scribner's.

Stanley, Philip E.

1984 *Boxwood and Ivory: Stanley Traditional Rules, 1855-1975*. Westborough, Mass.: Stanley Publishing Co.

Steiner, Christopher

1986 "Interpreting African Masks: The Harley Collection at the Peabody Museum," *Symbols* (September):13-18. Cambridge: The Peabody Museum of Archaeology and Ethnology.

Stevens, Walter K.

1989 "Huge Conservation Effort Aims to Save Vanishing Architect of the Savannah." *New York Times* (February 28): C1,C15.

Stigand, Chauncy Hugh

1913 [1966] *The Land of Zinj*. London: Cass.

1923 *Equatoria: the Lado Enclave*. London: Constable.

Stock, C.

1956 *Rancho La Brea: A Record of Pleistocene Life in California*. Los Angeles: Los Angeles County Museum of Natural History, George C. Page Museum of La Brea Discoveries. Science Series No. 20.

Stringer, Chris B.

1988 "Homo Sapiens." In *Encyclopedia of Human Evolution and Prehistory*, ed. Ian Tattersall, Eric Delson, and John A. Van Couvering, 267-74. New York: Garland Press.

Styles-McLeod, Catherine

1986 "Houseboat on the Seine: A Cosmopolitan Mooring at Neuilly." *Architectural Digest* (April):152-57.

Sukumar, R.

1989 *The Asian Elephant: Ecology and Management*. Cambridge: Cambridge University Press.

Sutherland, D.A.

1954 *State Emblems of the Gold Coast*. Cape Coast: Government Printer.

Swann, Alfred J.

1969 *Fighting the Slave-Hunters in Central Africa*. London: Frank Cass and Company Ltd.

Tamrat, Tadesse

1984 "The Horn of Africa: the Solomonids in Ethiopia and the States of the Horn of Africa." In *General History of Africa*, Vol. 4, ed. D.T. Niane. Berkeley: University of California Press.

Tantum, W.H. IV, and E.J. Hoffschmidt, eds.

1968 *German Army, Navy Uniforms and Insignia 1871-1918*. Old Greenwich, Conn.: W.E., Inc.

Tardits, Claude

1980 *Le royaume bamoum*. Paris: A. Colin.

Tassy, Pascal

1986 *Nouveaux Elephantoidea (Mammalia) dans le Miocäne du Kenya*. Paris: Editions de CNRS (Cahiers de Paleontologie, Travaux de Paleontologie est-africaine).

Tassy, P., and J. Shoshani

1988 "The Tethytheria: Elephants and Their Relatives." In *The Phylogeny and Classification of the Tetrapods*, Vol. 2, ed. M.J. Benton, 282-315. London: The Systematic Association, the Linnean Society, and the Paleontological Association of London.

Tattersall, Ian, Eric Delson, and John A. Van Couvering, eds.

1988 *Encyclopedia of Human Evolution and Prehistory*. New York: Garland Press.

Thesiger, Wilfred

1987 *The Visions of a Nomad*. London: Collins.

Thomas, T.

1960 "Les itombwa, objects divinatoires sculptés conservés au Musée Royal du Congo Belge." *Congo-Tervuren*, 6 (3):78-83.

Thomas, David Hurst

1988 "Paleoindian." In *Encyclopedia of Human Evolution and Prehistory*, ed. Ian Tattersall, Eric Delson, and John A. Van Couvering, 412-15. New York: Garland Press.

Thompson, Robert Farris

1989 "Body and Voice: Kongo Figurative Musical Instruments." In *Sounding Forms*, ed. Marie-Thérèse Brincard. New York: The American Federation of Arts.

Thomson, Joseph

1887 [1968]   *Through Masai Land.* London: Cass.

Thorbahn, Peter F.

1979   "The Precolonial Ivory Trade of East Africa: Reconstruction of a Human-Elephant Ecosystem." Ph.D. diss., University of Massachusetts (Amherst).

Thorbecke, Franz

1914   *Im Hochland von Mittel-Kamerun; pt. 1: Die Reise, Eindrücke und Beobachtungen.* Hamburg: L. Friedrichsen.

Tisdale, S.

1989   "A Reporter at Large: The Only Harmless Great Thing." *The New Yorker* (January 23):38-40,42,46-48,77-82,84-89.

Torday, Emil

1925   *On the Trail of the Bushongo.* Philadelphia: J.B. Lippincott.

Torday, Emil, and T.A. Joyce

1910   Notes éthnographiques sur les peuples communément appelés Bakuba, ainsi que sur les peuplades apparentées: Les Bushongo, MRAC, Brussels.

Travélé, Moussa

1923 [1977]   *Proverbes et contes bambara.* Paris: P. Geuthner.

Turle, Gillies

1992   *The Art of the Maasai.* New York: Alfred A. Knopf.

Turnbull, Colin M.

1962   *The Forest People: A Study of the Pygmies of the Congo.* New York: Simon and Schuster.

Turner, Victor

1967   *The Forest of Symbols: Aspects of Ndembu Ritual.* Ithaca, N.Y.: Cornell University Press.

Tutuola, Amos

1953   *The Palm Wine Drinkard.* New York: Grove Press.

Umlauff, J.F.G.

1914   *Kamerun Sammlung 1914.* Catalogues no. 222, 223 and typewritten list of objects. Chicago: Archives and Library of the Field Museum of Natural History.

Vacquié, P.

1950   "Les éléphants du cercle de Nioro (Soudan)." *Notes Africaines* 47:98-99.

Valentin, Peter

1972   "Plastiken der Kundu (Kamerun) im Basler Missionsmuseum." *Ethnologische Zeitschrift Zürich* 2:35-51.

Vanderheym, J.G.

1896   *Une expédition avec le negous Mènèlik. Vingt mois en Abyssinie.* Paris: Hachette.

Vansina, Jan

1954   Les tribus ba-kuba et les peupla des apparentées, MRAC, Ethnographic monograph, 1, Tervuren.

1958   "Les croyances religieuses des Kuba." *Zaïre* 12:725-58.

1960   "Recording the Oral History of the Bakuba." *Journal of African History* 1:45-54,257-270.

1962a   "Long-distance Trade-routes in Central Africa." *Journal of African History* III (3):375-90.

1962b   "Trade and Markets among the Kuba." In *Markets in Africa*, ed. Paul Bohannan and G. Dalton, 190-210. Evanston, Ill.: Northwestern University Press.

1964   Le royaume kuba, MRAC, Ser. in 8, 49, Tervuren.

1969   "Du royaume kuba au territoire des Bakuba." *Etudes congolaises* 12:3-54.

1971   "Les mouvements religieux kuba (Kasai) l'époque coloniale." *Etudes d'Histoire Africaine* 2:157-89.

1973   *The Tio Kingdom of the Middle Congo, 1880-1892.* London: Oxford University Press.

1976   "Religious Movements in Central Africa." *Comparative Studies in Society and History* 18:458-75.

1978   *The Children of Woot: A History of the Kuba Peoples.* Madison: University of Wisconsin Press.

1983   "The Peoples of the Forest." In *History of Central Africa*, Vol. 1, ed. David Birmingham and Phyllis M. Martin, 75-117. London: Longman.

1990   "Reconstructing the Past." In *African Reflections: Art from Northeastern Zaire*, ed. Enid Schildkrout and Curtis A. Keim. Seattle.

1990   *Paths through a Rainforest.* Madison: University of Wisconsin.

Verner, Samuel P.

1903   *Pioneering in Central Africa.* Richmond, Va.: Presbyterian Committee of Publication.

Vézia, R.

1957   "À propos d'un éléphant de la région de Nioro-du-Sahel." *Notes Africaines* 73:26-27.

Vickers, Michael, et. al.

1987   *Ivory: An International History and Illustrated Survey.* New York: Harry N. Abrams.

Visonà, Monica Blackmun

1985   *Art and Authority among the Akye of the Ivory Coast.* Ann Arbor: University Microfilms.

Vogel, Susan

1974   *Gods of Fortune: The Cult of the Hand in Nigeria.* New York: Museum of Primitive Art.

1977   *Baule Art as the Expression of a World View.* Ann Arbor: University Microfilms.

1979   "Art and Politics: A Staff from the Court of Benin, West Africa." *Metropolitan Museum of Art Journal* 13:87-100.

1980   *Beauty in the Eyes of the Baule: Aesthetics and Cultural Values.* Working Papers in the Traditional Arts, No. 6. Philadelphia: ISHI.

1988   (ed.) *Art/Artifact.* New York: Center for African Art.

Volavka, Zdenka

1981   "Fly-Whisk Handle" entry (cat. 122) in *For Spirits and Kings: African Art from the Paul and Ruth Tishman Collection*, ed. Susan Vogel. New York: Metropolitan Museum of Art.

Volman, T.P.

1984   "Early Prehistory of Southern Africa." In *Southern African Prehistory and Paleoenvironments*, ed. Richard G. Klein, 169-220. Rotterdam: A.A. Balkema.

Voyles, J. Bruce

1986   "The Sun Never Sets." *Blade Magazine* 13 (6):23-4,55-6.

Vrba, Elisabeth S.

1985   "Ecological and Adaptive Changes Associated with Early Hominid Evolution." In *Ancestors: The Hard Evidence,* ed. Eric Delson, 63-71. New York: Alan R. Liss.

Wallace, Ellen

1989   "World Vote Bans Ivory Trade." *The Christian Science Monitor* (October 19).

Waller, H., ed.

1874 [1970]   *The Last Journals of David Livingstone in Central Africa from 1865 to his Death continued by a Narrative of his last Moments and Suffering Obtained from his faithful servants Chuma and Susi.* 2 vols. Westport, Conn.: Greenwood Press.

1875   *Livingstone's Last Journals.* New York: Harper & Brothers.

Wallis, J.P.R., ed.

1956   *The Zambezi Expedition of David Livingstone 1858-1863. Volume One, Journals.* Central African Archives, Oppenheimer Series, No. 9. London: Chatto and Windus Limited.

Warnier, Jean-Pierre

1985   *Échanges, développement et hierarchies dans le Bamenda pré-colonial (Cameroun).* Studien zur Kulturkunde 76. Stuttgart: Steiner verlag Wiesbaden.

Wauters, A.J.

1890   *Stanley's Emin Pasha Expedition.* Philadelphia: Lippincott.

Webb, S. David

1985   "Late Cenozoic Mammal Dispersals Between the Americas." In *The Great American Biotic Interchange*, ed. Francis G. Stehli and S. David Webb, 357-86. New York: Plenum Press.

Weinberger, Bernhard Wolf

1948   *An Introduction to the History of Dentistry*, Vol. 1. St. Louis: C.V. Mosby & Co.

Welsh, James

1903   "A Voyage to Benin … set foorth by Master Bird and Master Newton Marchants of London, with a shippe called the Richard of Arundell and a Pinesse; Written by James Welsh, who was chiefe Master of said Voyage, begunne in the yeere 1588." In *The Principal Navigations, Voyages, Traffiques, and Discoveries of the English Nation*, Vol. 4, ed. R. Hakluyt. Glasgow: J. MacLehose and Sons.

Westermann, Diedrich

1912   *The Shilluk People: Their Language and Folklore*. Philadelphia: The Board of Foreign Missions of the United Presbyterian Church of North America.

Western, David

1986   "An African Odyssey to Save the Elephant." *Discover* 7 (10):56-70.

1991   "When the Forest Falls Silent." In *Elephants: The Deciding Decade*, ed. R. Orenstein, 83-95. Toronto: Key Porter Books.

1992   "Taking Stock of the Ivory Ban," *Swara*, Jan/Feb., 15 (1): 21-23.

Weston, Bonnie E.

1984   "Northeastern Region/Ogbodo Enyi." In *Igbo Arts: Community and Cosmos*, ed. Herbert M. Cole and Chike C. Aniakor, 153-59. Los Angeles: UCLA Museum of Cultural History.

Wharton, Conway T.

1927   *The Leopard Hunts Alone*. New York: Fleming H. Revell Company.

Whitehouse, A.A.

1904   "An Igbo Festival." *Journal of the African Society* 4 (3):134-35.

Wilkie, David S.

1989   "Impact of Roadside Agriculture on Subsistence Hunting in the Ituri Forest of Northeastern Zaire." *American Journal of Physical Anthropology* 78:485-94.

Wilks, Ivor

1975   *Asante in the Nineteenth Century: The Structure and Evolution of a Political Order*. London: Cambridge University Press

1979   "The Golden Stool and the Elephant Tail: An Essay on Wealth in Asante." *Research in Economic Anthropology* 2:1-36.

Willcox, A.R.

1984   *The Rock Art of Africa*. New York: Holmes & Meier Publishers.

Willett, Frank

1967   *Ife in the History of Western Sculpture*. London: Thames and Hudson.

1971   *African Art: An Introduction*. New York: Praeger Publishers.

1973   "The Benin Museum Collection." *African Arts* 6 (4):8-17.

1980   *Treasures of Ancient Nigeria*. New York: Alfred A. Knopf, Inc.

1988   "The Source and Significance of the Snake Winged Bird in Southwestern Nigeria." *Art Journal* (Summer):121-27.

Willett, Frank, and S.J. Fleming

1976   "A Catalogue of Important Nigerian Copper-Alloy Castings Dated by Thermoluminescence." *Archaeometry* 18 (2):135-46.

Williams, Denis

1974   *Icon and Image*. New York: New York University Press.

Williams, J.H.

1950   *Elephant Bill*. New York: Doubleday.

Williamson, George C.

1938   *The Book of Ivory*. London: Frederick Muller Ltd.

Willis, Roy G.

1990   *Signifying Animals: Human meaning in the natural world*. One World Archaeology, Vol. 16. London: Unwin Hyman.

Wilson, Monica

1951   *Good Company: A Study of Nyakyusa Age-Villages*. Boston: Beacon Press.

Winch, Julian

1971   "Religious Attitudes of the Mende Towards Land." *Africana Research Bulletin* 2 (1).

Winfrey, Laurie Platt

1980   *The Unforgettable Elephant*. New York: Walker and Co.

Wing, C.D., and I.O. Buss

1970   "Elephants and Forests." *Wildlife Monographs* 19.

Wingert, Paul

1947   "Congo Art." *Transactions, New York Academy of Sciences*, Series 2, Vol. 10: 320-37.

Wolf, Ludwig

1888   "Explorations sur le Kassai supérieur et le Sankourou." *Bulletin de la Société Royale Belge de Géographie* 12:26-43.

Ylvisaker, Marguerite

1982   "The Ivory Trade in the Lamu Area, 1600-1875." *Paideuma* 28:221-31.

Yochelson, Ellis L.

1985   *The National Museum of Natural History: 75 Years in the Natural History Building*, ed. Mary Jarrett. Washington D.C.: Smithsonian Institution.

Yogolelo, Tambwe ya Kasimba

1975   "Introduction à l'histoire des Lega. Problèmes et méthodes." *Les Cahiers du CEDAF*, no. 5.

Zahan, Dominique

1960   *Sociétés d'initiation bambara: le n'domo, le kore*. Paris: Mouton.

1963   *La dialectique du verbe chez les bambara*. Paris: Mouton.

1974   *The Bambara*. Leiden: E.J. Brill.

Zayed, A.H.

1981   "Egypt's Relations with the Rest of Africa." In *General History of Africa*, Vol. 2, ed. G. Mokhtar. Berkeley: University of California Press.

[ZSP/RKA] Zentrales Staatsarchiv Potsdam

Auswartiges Amt. Kolonial Abteilung. Reichs Kolonialamt 10.01. Geschenke an Hauptlinge in Kamerun. Band I, 4102:17,72.

Zervos, Adrien

1935   *L'empoire d'Éthiopie. Le miroir de l'Éthiopie moderne (1906-1935)*. Addis Ababa.

Zintgraff, Eugen

1895   *Nord-Kamerun: Schilderung der im Auftrage des Auswärtigen Amtes zur Erschliessung des nördlichen Hinterlandes von Kamerum während der Jahre 1886-1892 unternommenen Reisen*. Berlin: Paetel.

CONTRIBUTORS

EDWARD A. ALPERS, Professor of History and Dean of Honors and Undergraduate Programs at UCLA, has written extensively on the economic, social, and cultural history of eastern Africa. He is currently Vice President and President-elect of the African Studies Association.

MARY JO ARNOLDI, Associate Curator in the Department of Anthropology at the National Museum of Natural History, Smithsonian Institution, is an art historian by training. She has a special interest in the performance arts of Mali, where she continues to do research.

DAVID A. BINKLEY has concerned himself for nearly two decades with the art of the Kuba people. He is Assistant Professor of Art History at the University of Missouri in Kansas City, and Associate Curator at the Nelson-Atkins Museum of Art.

BARBARA WINSTON BLACKMUN is Professor of Art History at San Diego Mesa College. She has also taught as adjunct faculty in Art History at the University of California, San Diego and at UCLA, and is a Benin consultant for the Field Museum of Natural History in Chicago. She is preparing a book on the chronology and iconography of Benin ivories.

ELISABETH CAMERON, a doctoral candidate in art history at UCLA, has studied and written frequently about the arts of Zaire, where she spent her childhood. She is currently conducting dissertation research in Zambia.

HERBERT M. COLE, African art historian and photographer, has conducted over three years of fieldwork in Southeastern Nigeria, Ghana, and Kenya. His most recent publication is *Icons: Ideals and Power in the Art of Africa*, which accompanied an exhibition of the same name at the National Museum of African Art (Smithsonian Institution). He teaches at the University of California, Santa Barbara.

DONALD J. COSENTINO, Associate Professor of African folklore at UCLA, is co-editor of *African Arts* magazine and author of *Defiant Maids and Stubborn Farmers*, a study of Mende oral narrative performing traditions.

HENRY JOHN DREWAL has conducted research and published widely on the arts of Yoruba-speaking and related peoples in West Africa and Brazil. He is presently Evjue-Bascom Professor of Art History at the University of Wisconsin-Madison.

KATE EZRA, Associate Curator Department of the Arts of Africa, Oceania and the Americas at the Metropolitan Museum of Art in New York City, did fieldwork on Bamana sculpture in 1978 and 1985. She has curated several exhibitions and has written on the art of Mali and Benin, Nigeria.

GIRMA FISSEHA, Founder and Curator of the Ethiopian Department in the Staatliches Museum für Völkerkunde, Munich, is an expert in Ethiopian art and culture. Before coming to Munich, he worked for fifteen years at Addis Ababa University's Ethnological Museum, of which he was a co-founder.

CHRISTRAUD M. GEARY is Curator of the Eliot Elisofon Photographic Archives at the National Museum of African Art, Smithsonian Institution, Washington, D.C. A specialist in the arts of Cameroon and in photography in Africa, she received her doctorate in anthropology from Frankfurt University.

SIDNEY LITTLEFIELD KASFIR teaches the history and theory of African art at Emory University. She has conducted research on Idoma masking and sacred kingship in Nigeria, and on Samburu blacksmiths and non-canonical arts in Kenya.

PHILIP L. RAVENHILL, Chief Curator at the National Museum of African Art, Smithsonian Institution, has conducted fieldwork in Côte d'Ivoire for two decades. He is founder and former Director of the West African Museums Program.

DORAN H. ROSS has been Deputy Director and Curator of African Collections at the Fowler Museum of Cultural History since 1981. He is a specialist in the arts of the Akan and co-author with Herbert M. Cole of *The Arts of Ghana*, published by the Museum in 1977. He has also been co-editor of *African Arts* since 1988.

JEHESKEL (HEZY) SHOSHANI is founder of the international Elephant Interest Group and editor since 1977 of its publication, *Elephant*. A natural scientist, Hezy specializes in mammalian and proboscidean evolution and conservation, interests born of his early experience as a shepherd (in an Israeli kibbutz) and zookeeper (in Israel and Britain), and field observations in Africa and Asia.

DAVID H. SHAYT is a specialist in occupational history with the Division of Community Life at the National Museum of American History, Smithsonian Institution.

JOHN VAN COUVERING is a geologist at the American Museum of Natural History in New York City, with a long term interest in the dating of fossil beds in Africa. He heads the Micropaleontology Press.

ROSALINDE WILCOX, a doctoral candidate in art history at UCLA, recently carried out a year of fieldwork in coastal Cameroon and is writing her dissertation on the maritime arts of the Duala people.

PUBLICATION PRESENTATION

DESIGN AND PRODUCTION
Daniel R. Brauer & Anthony A.G. Kluck

EDITING
Henrietta B. Cosentino

EDITORIAL ASSISTANCE
Mark Livengood   Judith Herschman

PHOTOGRAPHY
Denis J. Nervig

*Editing and design were accomplished on Macintosh computers
using Aldus PageMaker 4.2, Adobe Illustrator 3.01,
and Adobe Perpetua, Copperplate,
and Woodtype Ornament font software.*

The following photography is the work of Denis J. Nervig:

Cover: Front and back.
Pages X, XVI, XXII.
Chapter 1: Figures 3,5,6,13,14,15,17,18,21,22,24,25,26,28,31,35,37,38,40,42B,
45,50,51,53,54,55,60,63,64.
Interleaf I:Figure A.
Interleaf II:Figure B.
Interleaf III:Figures A,B,C,D.
Chapter 4: Figure 9.
Interleaf IV:Figures A,B,C,D,E.
Chapter 5: Figures 1,9.
Chapter 6: Figures 1,2,4,5,9,10,11,24.
Interleaf VI:Figures A,D,E.
Chapter 7: Figures 7,8,10,13A,13B,14A,14B,14C,14D,16,22.
Interleaf VII:Figures A,B,C,D,E,F,G.
Chapter 8: Figure 17.
Interleaf VIII:Figures A,B,C,D,E.
Chapter 9: Figures 1,6,10,11,13,14A,14B,21.
Interleaf IX:Figures A,B,C,D,E,G.
Interleaf X:Figures A,B,E.
Chapter 11: Figures 10A,10B,13,17A,17B,20,27,28,31,32,35,36.
Interleaf XII:Figures A,D,G.
Chapter 13: Figures 10,11,13.
Chapter 14: Figures 1,2,3,4,5,6,7,8,9,10,11,15,16,17A,17B.
Interleaf XIV:Figures C,D.
Chapter 15: Figures 2,7,9,10,12,17,18.
Interleaf XV:Figures A,B,C,D.
Interleaf XVI:Figures A,B,C,D,E,F,G,H,I.
Chapter 17: Figure 8.
Interleaf XVIII:Figures A,B,C.
Chapter 19: Figures 2,5.
Page 424: Inset.

The following graphics are the work of Anthony A.G. Kluck:

All elephant rock art icons used throughout the publication.
Map of Africa, page XXIII.
Chapter 2: Figure 5.
Chapter 3: Figures 2,4,6.

FOWLER MUSEUM OF CULTURAL HISTORY

Pages 416-17: Botswana, 1990. Frans Lanting, Minden Pictures.

Pages 418-19: Near Hoamib Floodplain, Namibia, 1985. Gavin Thompson, Anthony Bannister Photo Library.

Pages 420-21: Botswana, 1990. Frans Lanting, Minden Pictures.

Pages 422-23: Botswana. Frans Lanting, Minden Pictures.

Page 424: Saltcellar, Temne-Bullom peoples, Sierra Leone, Height 24.3 cm. Museum für Volkerkunde, Vienna, 118.609a,b.

African elephant skin. Zig Leszczynski, Animals, Animals.